Producing and Directing
the Short Film and Video

Producing and Directing the Short Film and Video

THIRD EDITION

David K. Irving and Peter W. Rea

ELSEVIER

AMSTERDAM • BOSTON • HEIDELBERG • LONDON
NEW YORK • OXFORD • PARIS • SAN DIEGO
SAN FRANCISCO • SINGAPORE • SYDNEY • TOKYO
Focal Press is an imprint of Elseviser

Acquisitions Editor: Elinor Actipis
Project Manager: Dawnmarie Simpson
Developmental Editor: Becky Golden-Harrell
Assistant Editor: Robin Weston
Marketing Manager: Christine Degon Veroulis
Cover Design: Alisa Andreola
Interior Design: Julio Esperas

Focal Press is an imprint of Elsevier
30 Corporate Drive, Suite 400, Burlington, MA 01803, USA
Linacre House, Jordan Hill, Oxford OX2 8DP, UK

Library of Congress Cataloging-in-Publication Data
Rea, Peter W.
　　Producing and directing the short film and video / Peter W. Rea, David K. Irving.– 3rd ed.
　　　　p. cm.
　　Includes bibliographical references and index.
　　ISBN-13: 978-0-240-80735-5　　ISBN-10: 0-240-80735-9 (pbk. : alk. paper)
　1.　Short films–Production and direction.
　2.　Video recordings–Production and direction.　I. Irving, David K.　II. Title.
PN1995.9.P7R375 2006
791.4302'32–dc22

2005029830

British Library Cataloguing-in-Publication Data
A catalogue record for this book is available from the British Library.

ISBN-13: 978-0-240-80735-5
ISBN-10: 0-240-80735-9

For information on all Focal Press publications
visit our website at www.books.elsevier.com

07　08　09　10　10　9　8　7　6　5　4　3　2

Printed in the United States of America

Contents

Online Companion Site (http://www.focalpress.com/companions) for *Producing and Directing the Short Film and Video, Third Edition*

Contents

Associations
Distributors
Film and Video Festivals
Grants and Financing Sources
Internet Sites
Traditional Film and Video Post Production

FORMS to download, save, and print:
Script Breakdown Sheet
Header and Stripboard
Call Sheet
Short Budget Top Sheet
Release Form
Location Contract
Short Budget-2
Short Budget-3
Short Budget-4
Short Budget-5
Animation Budget
Video Postproduction Budget

Preface: Third Edition

Many key aspects of film and television production are constant. Telling a story visually is juxtaposing one image with another and then next to another, the sum of which makes a narrative, documentary, animation or experimental piece. However one captures the image, manipulates it editorially, or projects it for an audience, the basic steps of visual storytelling have been the same for the hundred years since film was invented.

But technology is an integral part of film and television production. Cameras, lenses, lights, editing machines, and even film stocks have evolved with the demands of this popular medium. Most of the technological changes have occurred gradually. But whereas evolution is gradual change, revolution is quick change, and we are currently in a technological revolution.

With the introduction of digital technology, the nature of the industry has changed. Digital computer images and digital tape have blurred the lines between film and video, film and television production, film and television projection. It is only the last, projection, that marks a difference between film and tape. Cost and quality are the two factors that keep the lines between film and video projection clearly delineated, but even that will change shortly with the advent of digital projection systems and satellite delivery.

Very few of these changes affect the text in this book, as the responsibilities of a producer and a director are directly tied to their hearts and minds, not their toys. No matter what the tools, art is created out of the heart. Technological advances can aid the process, but not sidestep any of the steps.

But we would be remiss if we did not make the young film- and videomaker aware of these new technologies and how they can be employed to achieve excellence. A tremendous amount of useful techno-logical information now exists on the Web that can be of great use to the beginning film- and videomaker. We include some in this book, but the book has its own Web page that includes these and more updated URLs. Our Web site also contains all the forms in this book plus many more. You may access our Web site at **www.focalpress.com/companions**.

Besides updating the book to address new technologies, we have been fortunate to receive comments and suggestions from many of our readers since the book was originally published. We are happy to make changes to better explain a concept or illustrate a point. This edition boasts the addition of an animated film with the supporting materials for those interested in this time-honored film technique.

EFFICIO COGNOSIO (LEARN BY DOING)

There is no substitute for experience. In this book, we want to emphasize the importance of the School of Hard Knocks. Whether you are in a film or video program or making a project on your own, this is an excellent time to be studying film- and videomaking. Profound changes are taking place in the communications field. The Academy of Motion Picture Arts and Sciences announced that in 1992, 72 percent of first-time directors had graduated from film school. In 1980, the figure was 34 percent. The Academy announced that in the year 2000, the number jumped to 90 percent.

There is no better way to learn how to make a film or video than by actually doing it. Books and manuals can serve as a guide. Other films and videos can act as inspiration, and talking about and critiquing films and videos can trigger ideas. However, the two best teachers are failure and success. Experiencing the process of putting a project together, building work muscles, and understanding the craft and discipline of the process are ultimately the best ways to develop your skills.

THE POWER OF THE MEDIA

Finally, your short film or video has the potential to influence a great many people. Both media have gained great exposure in the past 20 years, and their potential is growing rapidly. All indications are that by the year 2010, products from the communications industry will be the United States' chief export commodity.

Coupled with the wide distribution of these media is the issue of the power of their content to influence. We are now grappling with crucial problems, from overpopulation to racial discrimination, from management of the Earth's resources to the management of human resources. Film and video already have a powerful voice in the dialogue about these challenges. Our hope is that in expressing yourself through film and video, you will consider the world in which it will be viewed and will use your talents wisely.

Acknowledgments

FIRST EDITION

We would like to thank the following people who assisted us in the writing of this book—in particular, the faculty, staff, and students at New York University, Tisch School of the Arts, Undergraduate Film and Television: Arnold Baskin, John Canemaker, Pat Cooper, Carlos DeJesus, Tom Drysdale, Carol Dysinger, Dan Gaydos, Fritz Gerald, Chat Gunter, Ron Kalish, Julia Keydel, Marketa Kimbrall, Dan Kleinman, Lou La Volpe, Rosanne Limoncelli, Ian Maitland, Barbara Malmet, Rick McKinney, Lynne McVeigh, Lamar Sanders, Julie Sloane, George Stoney, Nick Tanis, Darryl Wilson, Brane Zivkovic, and especially Steven Sills. Also, New York University Professor Richard Schechner, who saw an early version of *Producing and Directing the Short Film and Video*.

We would also like to thank Mitchell Block, John Butman, Steve Hanks, the law firm of Rudolf & Beer, Doug Underdahl, Nancy Walzog, and a special thanks to Carol Chambers for her continued support throughout the writing process and Steve West for his editing skills.

We would also like to thank Ken Bowser, Hamilton Fish, Jr., David Gurfinkel, Tova Neeman, Priscilla Pointer, and Robert Wise, for inspiration and encouragement.

For the editorial and production skills they provided to Focal Press, we would especially like to thank Mary Ellen Oliver, Marilyn Rash, and Judith Riotto, who made the process of assembling these final pages a rewarding one.

SECOND EDITION

Special thanks to Mitchell Block, John Butman, John Canemaker, Michael Carmine, Gary Donatelli, Fritz Gerald, Fred Ginzberg, Chat Gunther, Milly Itzack, Suzie Korda, Dow McKeever, Stevin Michals, Marsha Moore, Mo Ogrodnik, Sam Pollard, Paul Thompson, Mike Thornburgh, Mika Salmi, Simon Lund, and Lamar Sanders.

Also, special thanks to Terri Jadick for her patience and support and Maura Kelly for her production skills.

THIRD EDITION

Special thanks to Norman Bebell, Mitchell Block, John Canemaker, Michael Carmine, Michelle Coe, Fritz Gerald, Joe Hobeck, Marsha Moore McKeever, Jamaal Parham, David Russell, David Spector, and Debra Zimmerman. Special thanks to Lou LaVolpe. We are also indebted to Etgar Keret for allowing us to reprint his short story. Adding a fourth film would not have been possible without the contributions made by filmmaker extraordinaire Tatia Rosenthal and the dean of the Savannah School of the Arts, Peter Weishar.

Introduction

The idea of being in a darkened screening room and watching your film or video touch an audience is exciting. There is deep satisfaction in communicating on this basic level. The fantasy of creating something that has an emotional impact on others is what motivates many people to go into picture-making in the first place. There is, also, the artistic satisfaction.

Why make a short film or video? The market for "shorts" is limited. It occupies a very small niche in media sales, and rarely do shorts recoup their investments, let alone make money. For these reasons, the creation of a short work is usually motivated by considerations other than profit.

Most short works are created to give film- and videomakers an opportunity to express themselves and to display their talents. The key advantage to making a short is learning the process, honing the craft. It is a way of getting experience on a project of manageable scale. If the work turns out well, shorts can be entered into festivals. The producer and director can parlay awards and the fame of winning competitions into meetings, agents, and (ideally) employment.

How do you go about making a successful short film or video? Picture-making is a complex and demanding activity, even for the experienced. A myriad of problems inevitably arises involving script, crew, budget, casting, lighting, and so on. Each project has its own unique set of challenges. For example, one film might need a difficult location such as Grand Central Station; another might call for a school gymnasium. One script might require a talented young boy who must also be meek and scrawny; another might need a homeless person. One project might run out of money before postproduction; another budget might not allow for crucial special effects. Even before starting production, you must understand sophisticated technical crafts; resource management; political and social interaction; and personal, financial, and professional responsibility.

The process of producing a film or video, be it a half-hour or a five-minute piece, has been refined over the years and developed into an art. As you will discover, there is a straightforward logic behind these steps—a logic governed by the management of time, talent, resources. Each step is informed by pragmatism and common sense:

- Script development: Your script must be well crafted before preproduction can begin.
- Preproduction: The production must be efficiently organized before the camera can roll.
- Production: The project must be shot before it can be edited.
- Postproduction: The project must be edited before it can be distributed.
- Distribution: A film or videotape that is not distributed serves as an exercise.

This is only a broad outline of what must happen during the production of a short work. It describes the general flow of activity, but it does not address what these steps mean or when and how they must be performed. Translating an idea into a film or video involves the execution of thousands of details over a long period of time. In fact, the success of any film or video project relies as much on management as it does on storytelling. Knowing where to put the camera to capture the right dramatic moment of a scene requires as much skill as marshaling the necessary people, equipment, and supplies to the location in the first place. One can't happen without the other.

This book is organized according to the general logic of how a short work is assembled. Each of the preceding stages is fleshed out in detail with concrete examples. Our goal is to impart to the beginner a fundamental understanding of what is required to organize and execute the production of a successful short picture. Bear in mind, though, that no two shows are alike and that there are no rules. This book is a guide, not a formula.

Each chapter presents a clear picture of what the producer and director do at any given time during the production. Unfortunately, in many beginning productions, the director and producer are the same person. Having to tackle two very different and complex responsibilities at the same time puts undue and unnecessary pressure on the novice. We discourage it.

CRAFT VERSUS ART

Moving pictures are arguably the greatest art form of the 20th century. After all, the medium combines elements of literature, art, theater, photography, dance, and music, but is in itself a unique form. For the sake of all beginning film- and videomakers who read this book, we take the pressure off by refusing to emphasize the creation of art. Instead, we stress the craft of storytelling, and telling a story well is not an easy task. Telling a short story well is even more difficult.

For us, it is difficult to think of film- and videomaking as an "art"-making endeavor. Orson Welles probably did not intend to make art when he conceived and produced *Citizen Kane*. Instead, he probably set out to make the best film he could from a particular script. The result was a well-crafted film, which was later deemed to be one of the finest feature films ever made and ultimately came to be considered "art." This label has more to do with the consensus of a critical audience long after the fact than it does with the intention of the filmmaker. Our advice to you is to set out to shoot the best short story you can, and let the audience decide whether it is art.

Let's not give Welles all the credit for the success of *Citizen Kane*. Filmmaking is a collaborative enterprise in which many creative people lend their expertise to the director's vision. Too many ingredients affect the outcome of a film to allow any one person to take credit for its success. Welles himself said that "making a film is like painting a picture with an army."

Above all, to make a successful short film or video, the entire creative team must share a passion for the material and the process. If there is no passion, the process will be no more than going through the motions of manufacturing a product. Lack of passion shows on the screen.

FOUR SHORT FILMS

In this book's chapters, we try to illustrate that the potential of realizing magic on the screen is directly proportional to the quality of management in the production stages. In fact, any artistic success can be achieved only through the well-planned and well-executed management of time, talent, and resources. To help you understand this critical relationship between organization and creative success, we use examples throughout the book from what we consider to be four successful shorts: two narratives, an animated film, and one documentary.

The case studies are *Truman*, a 12-minute color narrative film written and directed by Howard McCain; *Mirror Mirror*, a 17-minute documentary film produced and directed by Jan Krawitz; *The Lunch Date*, a 12-minute black-and-white narrative film written and directed by Adam Davidson; and *Crazy Glue*, a 5-minute animated short produced and directed by Tatia Rosenthal. Each of these films has won competitions, and one, *The Lunch Date*, won an Academy Award. The three narratives were made as student films: *Truman* and *Crazy Glue* at New York University and *The Lunch Date* at Columbia University. *Mirror Mirror* was made by a documentary filmmaker who teaches at Stanford University. *Truman* is distributed by Direct Cinema Inc., *Mirror Mirror* is distributed by Woman Make Movies, *Crazy Glue* is self distributed by Ms. Rosenthal and *The Lunch Date* is distributed by The Lantz Office. More detail information about these distributors is included in this Introduction and in Appendix B. The scripts for the three narrative films and the transcript of *Mirror Mirror* are reprinted in Appendix C.

Why did we choose these films? They are excellent examples of well-produced and well-directed short films. As stories, they are appropriate for the short form. We chose two narratives that are similar in length but differ in storytelling styles, subject matter, and production organization. *Crazy Glue* is a new addition to this book and affords us the opportunity to share with you experiences and techniques required of this demanding form of film expression. *Mirror Mirror* was included because the documentary is an important short form. Many young film- and videomakers explore the documentary as a means of self-expression. Although *Mirror Mirror* is different in nature and structure from most traditional documentaries, the form offered Jan Krawitz a unique arena in which to explore her views. The rules of production planning for the short form can be applied to any live-action (not animated) subject matter, whether it is narrative, documentary, experimental, industrial, or corporate in nature.

As teachers, we find it difficult to talk generically about production without using examples from specific films and videos. Many basic concepts and terms are alien to the beginner, and relating them to an actual production creates a common reference and a strong context. Throughout each chapter, we quote from the filmmakers' personal narratives about that part of the production process. Citing their films, which you can see and whose scripts you can read, offers concrete evidence of the range of procedures and challenges encountered in producing and directing a short film or video.

Contact information to rent or purchase a DVD copy of the short films:

TRUMAN
Howard McCain
Direct Cinema Ltd.
P.O. Box 10003
Santa Monica, CA 90410
Tel: (310) 636-8200/(800) 525-0000
Fax: (310) 636-8228
Area of specialty: Outstanding short films (live action and animated), documentaries, specialized features
Contact: Mitchell Block
www.directcinemalimited.com

THE LUNCH DATE
Adam Davidson
The Lantz Office
200 West 57th Street
Suite 503
New York, NY 10019
Tel: (212) 586-0200

CRAZY GLUE
Tatia Rosenthal
Tel: (917) 613-2667
rosenthal@yahoo.com

MIRROR, MIRROR
Jan Krawitz
Women Make Movies
462 Broadway
Suite 500
New York, NY 10013
Tel: (212) 925-0606
Fax: (212) 925-2052
Area of specialty: Films and videos by women about women
Contact: Talar Attarian (x300) to obtain distribution guideline
www.wmm.com
email: info@wmm.com

FILM AND VIDEO

Advances in audio and video technologies, especially the digital tape and editing revolution, have blurred the line between film and video. Although film stocks continue to improve, and most feature films still originate and are projected on 35mm film, the video image is coming closer and closer to approximating the "film look." This is all thanks to HD and 24p and sophisticated NLE systems. Digital imaging has taken over the finishing tasks that were once the proprietary realm of the laboratory.

Independent filmmakers have access to a wide range sophisticated equipment. The options are substantial: DV, Mini DV, DVCAM, DVCPRO, and 24p to name a few. With the advent of HDV (HD in DV format), what was once the domain of the rich can now be placed in the hands of the beginner.

Video is playing an ever-expanding role in media production, not only in the professional world, but also in film and television training programs across the country. Most film departments use video to train students because of the financial burden of shooting film. Those who shoot film, edit on video. Compression allows the storage of hours of material on a computer's hard drive. The drives keep getting bigger and less expensive.

No one knows where the convergence of telephone, cable, television, and computer technologies will lead the industry. The shift from film has been slow but steady. The obstacles that stand in the way of a complete digital takeover (as in editing) are:

- quality of the image
- standarization of digital projection
- business model to pay for shift to digital projectors
- foolproof encryption (is this possible?)
- copyright protection

The process of producing and directing a short project is very similar whether it is shot on film or video. Basic production sequences can be applied. Grammar and aesthetic principles for both media are interchangeable. Industry and technologies are merging; similar opportunities can be found in both media.

ANIMATION

Animation has become a very large and significant segment of filmmaking. With the advent of digital media, the definition of animation has expanded to include large portions of the visual effects and commercial production industries.

Animation is not a separate genre. You will find animation utilized in many genres: commercials, children's programs, feature films, short narratives, experimental films, video art, TV sitcoms, and animated features.

Animation has been a part of our visual and popular culture since the turn of the century, mostly in the form of cartoons. Hanna-Barbera, Disney, Fleischer, and Chuck Jones are names that represent a rich and dense creative body of work.

Most animation projects are short. The production principles are similar to those for live-action film and video, except that instead of actors, an animator employs characters and/or designs that are created from scratch. Drawing on paper, molding clay, or generating images on a computer are among the numerous techniques that bring animated characters, graphics, and special effects to the screen. The work of creating an animated film is time-consuming and requires great patience.

Creating an animated film involves creating an entire world from scratch. Anything that can be manipulated in space can be animated. Animation characters range from stick figures and paper cutouts to three-dimensional clay figures and elaborate Disney-style cel animation

The styles of individual artists can be as varied as their imaginations. Norman MacLaren, John and Faith Hubley, and Frank and Caroline Mouris are animators who developed their unique non-Disney styles with great success. Clay animation, perfected by Will Vinton and others, has been incorporated into mainstream entertainment. Year after year animated features, a popular form of entertainment that is accessible to all ages, are traditionally the highest-grossing films. Some of the most original and visually dynamic films of all time were animated.

We are now experiencing technological revolutions in this field. Computer techniques and the enhancement of existing images are creating a branch of animation that will be available to everyone. The use of home computers for applications such as morphing and image manipulation will allow more of us to storyboard, animate, and tell stories in a visual manner unlike anything we know today.

Computer Generated Images (CGI)

CGI or just CG has become the most popular form of animation and visual effects in film and video production. Usually, the term CG refers to 3D computer animation and modeling. It is called "3D" because three-dimensional virtual models of all the characters and models are constructed within the computer. CGI has proven to be an effective method of producing almost anything a filmmaker can imagine. Hollywood films from *The Incredibles* to *The Matrix* trilogy have relied on CG to astound audiences with effects and believable animation that were not achievable without the computer.

TIMELINE

Producing and Directing the Short Film and Video explores both the producer's and the director's points of view. It is imperative that each know what the other is doing at all times. We have divided most chapters into two parts, reflecting the management, or "producing," skills and the storytelling, or "directing," skills required to create a successful short film or video. This organization is designed to give the novice a detailed understanding of and respect for the processes of both producing and directing, one step at a time, from idea to final print. It can also serve as a practical guide to help navigate through creative and managerial straits.

Students and beginners often find themselves taking on the role of the producer and director. This problem exists for many reasons. Primarily, it is because the director, in most cases, financially supports the project and either can't find someone willing to do the job or is unable to trust someone the manage her money properly. This burden of having to direct and produce can have a deleterious impact on either important function.

The Producer

The most misunderstood and mysterious role in the filmmaking process is that of the producer. We've been asked hundreds of times, "What does a producer actually do?" That his role is a mystery to most laypeople is not altogether surprising. The producer's position in the film and television industry is amorphous and has varying definitions. In addition, the producer never has the same job description from one project to another, and on many kinds of films and videos, it is common to see more than one producing credit.

In this book, we use the term *producer* to describe the driving force in the making of a short. We also use *producer* to describe the person who engineers all the elements necessary for the creative and business aspects of production. One of the main elements—if not the most important—is the money. The producer is responsible for raising it, budgeting it, and ultimately accounting for it to the investors. His role might be limited to the practical planning of a show, or it might include artistic collaboration. The producer might also be the director of the piece. However, if one person tackles both jobs, he must keep an eye on the "big picture." The producer's challenge is to maintain the delicate balance between script and budget.

A movie begins with an adaptation from an existing short story, a script, an original idea, a true story, or simply an image that has dramatic and visual potential. The imagination and belief that such an idea or story can be transformed into a motion picture or tape are what begin the process. What is not widely understood is that the producer can be, and often is, the creative instigator of most short film and video projects. The producer frequently is the one who has the original inspiration that launches the whole project and then sails it home, with himself as the captain. In a general sense, we could say that without the producer, the picture would not be made. The Academy of Motion Picture Arts and Sciences gives the Best Picture Award to the producer of a film. This is the industry's acknowledgment that the producer is the person who is responsible for putting the pieces together, the person who creates the whole.

The Director

Because of the images of several contemporary superstar directors, including Spike Lee, Martin Scorsese, and Martha Coolidge, the role of the film director has taken on a romanticized image: The director shouts "Action," and the whole set swings into motion; the director chats with actors between takes and enjoys posh dinners after the day's wrap.

In reality, the director's work is never done. Because her job is to supply the creative vision for a one-of-a-kind and essentially handmade product, the choice and effect of thousands of decisions fall to her. Solving all creative problems on and off the set is the director's final responsibility, from how much light to what color blouse, from which location to how long a scream. The director alone has the "vision" of the whole film in her head, and she alone is obligated to make the sum of all her decisions throughout the process add up to its fulfillment. The director's goal is to deliver a finished film or video ready for an audience.

Although the producer strives to support the director's work and the director is the authority figure on the shoot, the director answers to the producer. However, the producer complements the director's work. When her decisions affect the budget or the schedule, the director consults the producer. The responsibilities of the producer and director often overlap. Ideally, the director and producer should be able to work well together and understand the script in the same way. Picture-making is, after all, a creative collaboration.

The director must be demanding but not dictatorial. She must do her best to draw out each cast and crew member by making him or her feel involved. The director is an active observer. She directs the actors by being part coach, part audience, and part performer. She will stand on her head if necessary to elicit a good performance. The director should have unlimited patience and be methodical, organized, articulate, and succinct. She should be broadly educated in the arts and have a working knowledge of the duties and responsibilities of each member of the team.

The director needs six things to execute a successful short: a good script, a talented cast, a devoted crew, adequate funds, good health, and luck (a major variable in any artist's work).

The Digital Producer

Films and videos have been successfully made for years without the aid of a computer. The film and television industry has, however, embraced the computer as a valuable and effective tool. Computer applications are now used at each stage of the film- and videomaking process from script to screen.

Computers can seem to be more trouble than they are worth, especially when the hard disk fails, software freezes, and precious files are lost. Maintaining them involves some frustrations, but on the whole, if used effectively, computers can save time and effort by helping to accomplish tedious jobs more quickly, leaving more time and flexibility for the creative work. And because time is money, it is easy to understand why the computer has found its way into the manufacturing of film and videos.

However, the computer is just another tool, a facilitator. This book outlines all the necessary steps for completing a short film or video project with or without this tool. These are some of the ways in which the computer has been utilized.

Preproduction

Stand-alone scriptwriting software (see the examples listed in the Bibliography) was originally designed to do one thing: write scripts. Most will handle feature film, sitcom, and stage play as well as other formats. These programs have progressed considerably, not only as writing tools but as inventive applications that can, for example, develop your dramatic ideas (Dramatic Pro from Screenplay Systems). As a screenwriting program, most format your script in real time, autocorrect typos, have import and export capability, create electronic index cards, and include templates from many TV shows. One in particular, Movie Magic from Screenplay Systems, is set up to interact with scheduling and budgeting software.

As with scriptwriting software, there are a number of storyboarding software programs that are integrated, stand-alone, or add-on-type programs. Storyboard Quick and Storyboarder have built in predrawn characters (through clip art), locations, and props. With a click of the mouse you can move predrawn characters around within a full-color scene, move props, or bring in graphics and photos through PICT files from other graphic stations. Storyboard Quick can also import scripts from the Final Draft screenwriting program.

For more extensive storyboards, there are pieces of software such as Virtus Walkthrough (created by the Virtus Corporation) that allow you to create virtual environments for storyboards. This computer-based visualization program lets the user draw a structure (set or room), and the software develops a three-dimensional color drawing that allows the user to walk around within the environment.

Production management applications offer easy-to-use scheduling and breakdown software that provide a depth of features for the film and video producer, production manager, or assistant director. A program such as Movie Magic Scheduling (from Screenplay Systems) can break down your script into dozens of predefined or custom categories (for props, vehicles, stunts, costumes, audio, lighting, and talent). You can sort and print a variety of reports and lists such as shooting days, shooting schedules, shot lists, breakdown sheets, calls sheets, cast lists, prop and costumes lists, and general production forms. You can even bring storyboard images into your breakdown sheets and create schedules that are linked directly to your script.

Over the years popular spreadsheet programs have been utilized to prepare budgets for both large and small productions. These programs allow users to break down and define every phase of production and the associated cost. Because every item of the production process is listed on the budget form, it acts like a checklist ensuring that no budget consideration, however small, is neglected. The better programs are designed for the feature film industry, but are easily adapted for the short form. Movie Magic Budgeting (from Screenplay Systems) is flexible, easy to use, and offers libraries of databases for rates, crews, and talent charges and subgroups for handling multiple versions of a budget.

With the use of a laptop and a digital camera, location scouts can take digital stills from the various areas outlined in the script and dump those images directly into the script or storyboard program on their computer. Production designers are using simple CAD (computer-aided design and drafting) programs to design and lay out sets before construction.

Production

For continuity and tape logging, there are programs such as Production Magic's Shot Logger™ that combine effectively designed software with the palm-sized Apple Newton. The Executive Producer™ from Imagine Products and AutoLog™ from Pipeline Digital are more in-depth software applications for use on desktop computers or laptops. AVID's own software is called Media Log. These computerized videotape logging systems help organize the production, save time in the editing process, and catalogue tapes for future use. They allow you to read and log timecode information directly from the field recorder into your laptop computer. This type of software will allow you to walk away from a day's shoot with a completed EDL (edit decision list) paper edit of your best takes.

There are also programs that let you design lighting plots for both studio and field production.

Postproduction

The area most affected by the rise of computers in the production process is in postproduction. Computer-based nonlinear systems (examples are discussed in Chapter 16) have taken over in all aspects of media production. Such systems have brought broadcast-quality editing systems to film- and videomakers at affordable prices. In the area of audio, DAWs (digital audio workstations) have made an indelible impact on the manufacturing of sound tracks for film and video. Multitrack audio mixing, sweetening, and editing are now done on the personal computer.

CHAPTER BREAKDOWNS

Chapters 1 and 2 cover the development preliminaries that need to be dealt with prior to the preproduction phase of any project. Each chapter in Parts I and III, covering the preproduction and distribution processes, begins with the producer's responsibilities. The production and postproduction chapters in Parts II and III begin with the director's duties. The typical timeline graphic that follows this introduction summarizes the activities of the producer and director during the process of making a short work. Although it is difficult to determine the specific amount of time needed for each phase, the following breakdown may provide some insight.

- Financing might be immediately available or might take years to obtain.
- Scripts can come from many sources and may be ready to shoot or could take years to get into shape.
- Preproduction usually requires two to eight weeks.
- Production usually takes somewhere between a day and two weeks.
- Postproduction details take anywhere from two to ten weeks.
- Distribution can take as long as several months.

The Filmmakers Speak

Culled from hours of interviews, relevant quotes from the four short filmmakers have been inserted to support the specific topic of each chapter. We hope that these pearls of wisdom will personalize their experience in producing and directing the short films we use as case studies in our book. All four have gone on to do wonderful things with their careers. Check them out on imdb.com.

Adam (Davidson)
The writer and director of *Lunch Date* (live action narrative)
Adam Davidson made *Lunch Date* as a graduate student at Columbia University School of the Arts

Jan (Krawitz)
The director of *Mirror Mirror* (documentary)
Jan made *Mirror Mirror* as a professor at Stanford University

Howard (McCain)
The writer and director of *Truman* (live action narrative)
Howard made *Truman* as a student at NYU, Tisch School of the Arts, graduate Film and Television

Tatia (Rosenthal)
The writer and Director of *Crazy Glue* (animated narrative)
Tatia made *Crazy Glue* as a student at NYU, Tisch School of the Arts, undergraduate Film and Television

Timeline

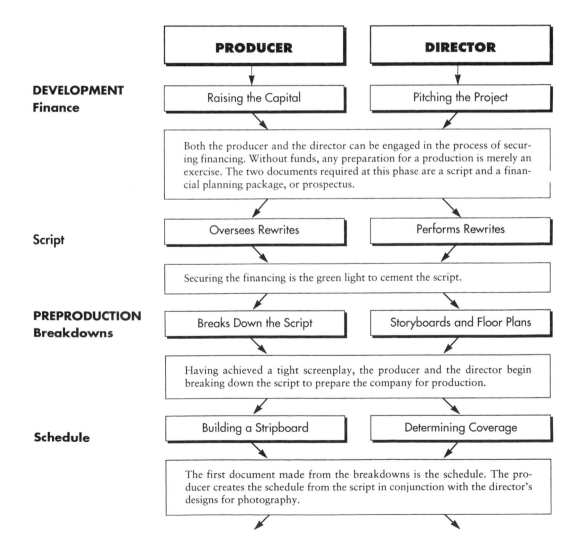

PRODUCER	DIRECTOR

DEVELOPMENT
Finance

Raising the Capital	Pitching the Project

Both the producer and the director can be engaged in the process of securing financing. Without funds, any preparation for a production is merely an exercise. The two documents required at this phase are a script and a financial planning package, or prospectus.

Script

Oversees Rewrites	Performs Rewrites

Securing the financing is the green light to cement the script.

PREPRODUCTION
Breakdowns

Breaks Down the Script	Storyboards and Floor Plans

Having achieved a tight screenplay, the producer and the director begin breaking down the script to prepare the company for production.

Schedule

Building a Stripboard	Determining Coverage

The first document made from the breakdowns is the schedule. The producer creates the schedule from the script in conjunction with the director's designs for photography.

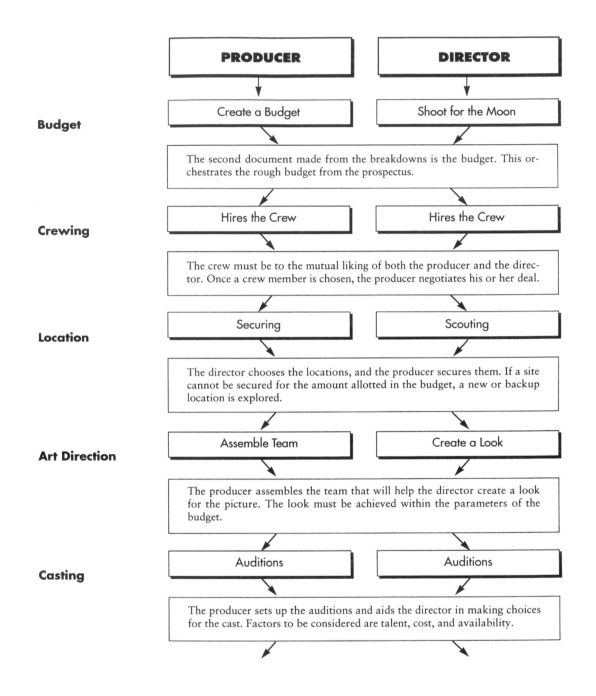

Budget

PRODUCER — Create a Budget

DIRECTOR — Shoot for the Moon

The second document made from the breakdowns is the budget. This orchestrates the rough budget from the prospectus.

Crewing

Hires the Crew | Hires the Crew

The crew must be to the mutual liking of both the producer and the director. Once a crew member is chosen, the producer negotiates his or her deal.

Location

Securing | Scouting

The director chooses the locations, and the producer secures them. If a site cannot be secured for the amount allotted in the budget, a new or backup location is explored.

Art Direction

Assemble Team | Create a Look

The producer assembles the team that will help the director create a look for the picture. The look must be achieved within the parameters of the budget.

Casting

Auditions | Auditions

The producer sets up the auditions and aids the director in making choices for the cast. Factors to be considered are talent, cost, and availability.

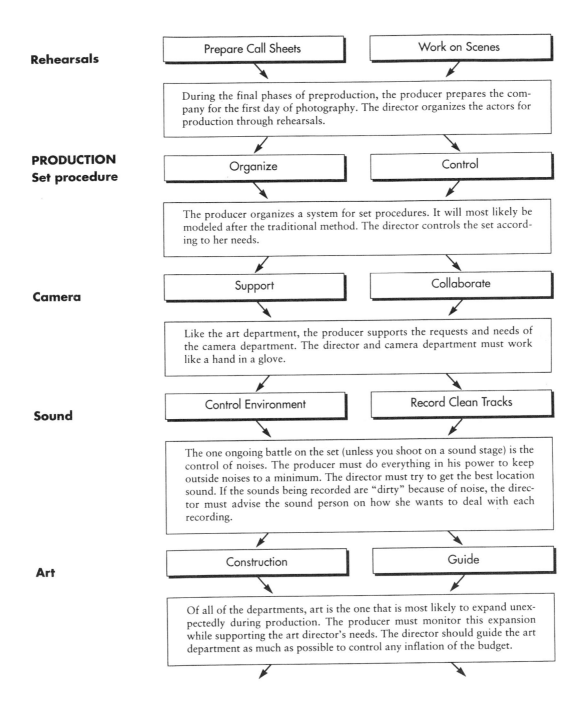

Rehearsals

| Prepare Call Sheets | Work on Scenes |

During the final phases of preproduction, the producer prepares the company for the first day of photography. The director organizes the actors for production through rehearsals.

PRODUCTION
Set procedure

| Organize | Control |

The producer organizes a system for set procedures. It will most likely be modeled after the traditional method. The director controls the set according to her needs.

Camera

| Support | Collaborate |

Like the art department, the producer supports the requests and needs of the camera department. The director and camera department must work like a hand in a glove.

Sound

| Control Environment | Record Clean Tracks |

The one ongoing battle on the set (unless you shoot on a sound stage) is the control of noises. The producer must do everything in his power to keep outside noises to a minimum. The director must try to get the best location sound. If the sounds being recorded are "dirty" because of noise, the director must advise the sound person on how she wants to deal with each recording.

Art

| Construction | Guide |

Of all of the departments, art is the one that is most likely to expand unexpectedly during production. The producer must monitor this expansion while supporting the art director's needs. The director should guide the art department as much as possible to control any inflation of the budget.

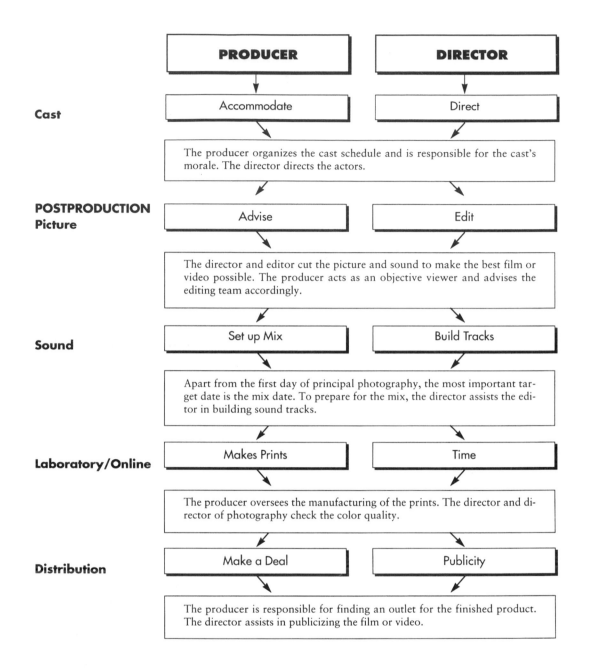

Cast

PRODUCER → Accommodate

DIRECTOR → Direct

The producer organizes the cast schedule and is responsible for the cast's morale. The director directs the actors.

POSTPRODUCTION
Picture

Advise

Edit

The director and editor cut the picture and sound to make the best film or video possible. The producer acts as an objective viewer and advises the editing team accordingly.

Sound

Set up Mix

Build Tracks

Apart from the first day of principal photography, the most important target date is the mix date. To prepare for the mix, the director assists the editor in building sound tracks.

Laboratory/Online

Makes Prints

Time

The producer oversees the manufacturing of the prints. The director and director of photography check the color quality.

Distribution

Make a Deal

Publicity

The producer is responsible for finding an outlet for the finished product. The director assists in publicizing the film or video.

chapter one

Finance

We basically put a lot of things on credit cards—my credit cards.

Adam

PRODUCER
Raising the Capital

If there is one role with which the producer is traditionally associated, it is the role of fund-raiser. The producer finds the money to fund the film or video. This role is paramount because money is the lifeblood of any project. In fact, without adequate financing, there is no project. However simple the production demands might seem, it is impossible to produce something for nothing. Even if you are a one-person crew shooting videotape, you still need to purchase tape stock and rent a camera and editing equipment to complete the project.

Most beginners get turned on by romantic notions and the tantalizing creative possibilities of the visual media, but they soon find out that much of their time and energy are focused on raising funds. Independent film- and videomakers spend much of their time filling out grant applications, writing to investors, and organizing fund-raisers. Howard McCain, Tatia Rosenthal, Adam Davidson, and Jan Krawitz struggled to secure financing for their projects. For Jan, it was a process that lasted years.

I wrote a lot of grants over the years, and I finally got the first grant in the spring of '87. Initial money came from the Paul Robeson Fund for Film and Video. I only had two grants when I began shooting, and the subsequent three came during postproduction. I think that's significant, because I find it's always a little easier to get funding once you have something to show from the project.

Jan

BASIC FUND-RAISING PROBLEMS

You can expect to encounter two basic problems in funding your projects. The first is the potential of either a sizable return on an investment or no return at all. Overwhelming odds support the latter. Suffice it to say that the market for short films is financially anemic. (This problem is discussed at length in Chapter 19, "Distribution.")

The second problem you will face is lack of experience. How do you persuade an investor to finance a first-time producer or director, someone who has yet to complete a project or, at best, has only a minimal track record? To look at it another way, would you hire a contractor who had never built a house?

All novices confront these two major obstacles as they start out to create their first films. The problem of inexperience is no less real or daunting than the problem of a limited market, but the producer and director definitely have more control over it. Although it might seem like a catch-22—the "Can't get a job without experience, can't get experience without a job" syndrome—there are specific ways to overcome this seemingly insurmountable obstacle. Each year, many young film- and videomakers with little experience but with lots of ingenuity, energy, and verve are able to persuade investors to believe in their talent and trust them to manage their dollars responsibly.

There is no secret formula for raising money successfully. In the pursuit of funding, you are almost guaranteed to come up against tremendous odds and constant rejection. Many potential investors will say no before one says yes. Some may even say yes at first and then change their minds. To sustain excitement

1

for your beloved project after weeks, months, and sometimes years of effort demands a strong belief in yourself, the utmost patience and perseverance, and an unbridled passion for the medium and your message.

How Much Money Will You Need?

Although short narrative films vary in cost, the average student film costs approximately $750 per minute. Therefore, a 10-minute film will cost around $7,500, and a 30-minute film will cost about $22,500, if you go back to print. Many projects are shot on film and then finished on digital tape.

> *We were doing* Lunch Date *cheaper than you would generally do a student film. Generally, I would estimate $1,000 a minute. This project was definitely budgeted for less. Adam didn't have a lot of money, and he didn't want to spend a lot of money. I think originally he wanted to spend $5,000 because it was going to be a fun project to do. He had a little extra money, and he wanted to make this film. It ended up costing more because in postproduction he wanted to spend that money. He wanted to get a good sound editor and get good music and do a good mix. But he always had the option to not do that, to just finish it cheaply, do his own sound editing and mix.*
>
> Garth Stein (producer of *The Lunch Date*)

The figures are less for video productions. For documentaries, the decision whether to shoot on film or video greatly affects the price. Professional shoots, especially those using several unions, can be very expensive. (For more on these topics, see Chapter 5, "Budget.")

> *Total funding for* Mirror Mirror *was $12,000, and the final budget through release prints and a one-inch, but not including festival entry fees, was $14,300. The film stock, processing, location travel expenses, and the cinematographer's salary were the major production expenses. A lot of money went to research and acquisition of the archival footage. And all the postproduction costs, sound mix and all of that, probably ate up $4,000 or $5,000. Easy.*
>
> Jan

FUNDING OPTIONS

Both students and independent film- and videomakers can employ similar methods for raising funds.

However, some opportunities available to students are not open to independents and vice versa. For example, some students can take advantage of their university's tax-exempt status without having to create a not-for-profit business entity. In addition, students work in a supportive environment with resources such as equipment and a sizable pool of free and willing labor. Independents must put their production teams together from scratch. On the other hand, student film- and videomakers are almost completely shut out of the grant world.

There are no rules when it comes to finding money. If you win the lottery, use it to finance your project. Putting the lottery windfall aside, here are seven possible sources of money for short films and videos.

Private Investors

This group includes any individuals who are interested in investing in your project. Private investors might be friends, family members, or associates—even complete strangers. Some people might invest because they want to see you succeed even though they understand they might not see a return on their investment. Others might be looking for a tax shelter, and still others might be shrewd businesspeople who believe in the investment opportunities and market potential of your project.

> *As a recent alumnae, I was eligible to apply for the $100,000 Richard Vague Award from the Kanbar Film Department at New York University. Based on the work I did on* Crazy Glue, *I received the award to expand my short claymation film into a feature. It was an amazing, amazing gift. I plan to use that money to make the first five minutes of the film.*
>
> Tatia

Corporate Sponsorship

Private and public corporations sometimes fund films and videos; for example, Mobil and Sony have traditionally backed public television shows. The public relations people at these corporations will guide you through the application process for various proposals. Contact as many companies as you can. To avoid wasting your time, research the types of projects each company has funded in the past (see www.focalpress.com/companions).

Public Foundation Grants

Some public foundations financed by federal, state, and local governments offer grants and other forms of financial aid to film- and videomakers. The National Endowment for the Arts (NEA), the National Endowment for the Humanities (NEH), and the American Film Institute (AFI) are three examples.

I started with $5,000, and then when I was in the editing stage, I received three more grants of $3,000, $2,000, and $2,000—three grants totaling $7,000. That was my total outside funding.

Jan

It might be easier to secure financing from your home state, city, or town, rather than from national organizations. By tailoring your short project to a particular local issue (especially for documentaries), you have a greater chance of finding financial backing.

Private Foundation Grants

There are hundreds of private foundations in the United States, but only a few support film and video projects. Finding the ones that might be interested in your particular project requires exploration. Most major public libraries have information to assist you. Examples of sources of media fellowships are the Jerome Foundation and the Rockefeller Foundation.

Bank Loans

Banks will loan almost anyone money if the borrower provides sufficient collateral. Taking out a loan against a car, a boat, or a house can provide adequate funding for a short film or video project. The money is not a gift or an investment, and it will have to be paid back with interest.

Personal Savings

If the cost of a short work is not exorbitant, your personal savings might be sufficient. Saving money gradually in an account earmarked for your project might take less time than you think. Although a financial adviser might try to convince you that your savings are for the future or for hard times, investing in yourself is also protecting your future.

I took money from my savings, I sold my motorcycle, and I borrowed money from my parents. I raised enough to get me through the first stage, which was shooting and developing the rushes.

Adam

In-Kind Services and Donations

Anything that is given or donated is called *in-kind*. In-kind donations are the equivalent of hard cash. If 70 percent of your total costs are raised as currency and the remainder comes in the form of goods or services, it still equals 100 percent of your budget. Examples of in-kind donations are food from a local restaurant, deferred laboratory fees, reduced car or van rental, and a free location.

These donations are usually given in exchange for a screen credit and for the goodwill. One possible way to acquire in-kind donations is to shoot your project in your hometown. This might prompt newspaper articles with a "hometown boy/girl makes good" slant, inspiring favorable public relations with businesses that could translate into money or in-kind donations.

There is also a practice in the business called *product placement*. This is when a producer convinces a manufacturer to donate goods to the production in exchange for featuring its product in a film or video. For example, Ford might loan cars to a production for use both on and off camera with the agreement that Ford cars and trucks be used prominently in the film. Should the producer interest a clothing manufacturer, a similar arrangement might work for costuming.

Other in-kind opportunities exist for independent media artists. Here are some examples:

- Low-cost or free access to production or postproduction equipment and facilities
- Financial support for artists facing work-related personal emergencies
- Information on or assistance with taxes, record keeping, accounting, or financial management
- Free legal advice or referrals

THE PROSPECTUS

To attract private or corporate support, the producer should create a proposal called a *prospectus*. The prospectus should excite potential investors by communicating on paper a strong sense of the project in a professional manner. The information gathered for the prospectus can easily be rewritten to fulfill a grant application or tailored to the needs of a specific investor.

The prospectus should contain at least the following elements:

- Cover letter
- Title page
- One-liner
- Synopsis of story
- History of project
- Research
- Top sheet of budget
- Production schedule
- Cast list
- Brief résumés of creative team
- Description of market for project
- Financial statement
- Means of transferring funds

Cover Letter. Use the cover letter to introduce the project to the investor. It can be targeted to all potential investors or slanted to a specific individual. The impression you make with this letter sets the tone for everything that follows. Be clear about what you want. Are you asking for many small investments or donations? What is the total amount of capital you are trying to raise?

The key to a good cover letter when soliciting funds is to tailor each letter to the specific investor/contributor. As the market for short films and videos is limited, an investment will rarely see a return, so the investor must be putting up funds for some other reason. What does the investor want? What is in his or her best interest?

A wonderful enticement to invest is as a tax deduction. If an investor is in a tax bracket such that he or she has the option of contributing money to your project through a not-for-profit fiscal sponsor, then the investor gains something, a tax write-off, as does the film- or videomaker, production capital.

Here is an example of a cover letter geared toward an investor who wants to both support the filmmaker and be eligible for a tax deduction.

Dear Investor,
This letter will serve as an introduction to my short film titled "Everyman." Planned for around 15 minutes, this 16-mm film is a comedy about a romance between a bum and a princess. Through a series of comical events, we discover that the bum was once a prince and the princess is a phony. But love triumphs, and the film ends on a very happy note.
"Everyman" is my thesis film here at Citizen University, and I am seeking funds with which to make the film. The university provides each thesis student with equipment and postproduction facilities. The remainder of the budget, approximately $12,000, is raised by the individual filmmaker—me.
Therefore, I humbly seek your support to make this film a reality. Each dollar contributed to the project is eligible for a tax deduction through the university's Film Production Fund. Simply make out a check to Citizen's University, and specify in the "transferal of funds" document enclosed in this prospectus that you would like the funds to go to my project, "Everyman."
I am a dedicated filmmaker with a 3.76 GPA. I have made four very short films, a documentary on dog walkers, and an animated short shot on 35-mm film. As you can see by the letters of support from my professors, my chances to complete this project successfully are extremely high.
I hope you will take this opportunity to help a budding artist.

Sincerely,

Title Page. A good title conveys the essence of the project. Keep it short; a short title has more punch. Include artwork on the title page that catches the eye and makes an immediate impression. The right image can capture the feel and tone of your piece. Any artwork here or anywhere else in the prospectus must look professional.

One-Liner. A one-liner is a brief pitch of your project. (See Figures 1.1 to 1.4.)

Synopsis of Story. (See Appendix C.) The synopsis should be a brief narrative of the story's action. Move the story or plot forward with minimal details. The synopsis is difficult to write because you must capture the flavor of the piece and tell the story at the same time.

History of Project. Briefly describe how the project evolved. Elaborate on the subject matter and what inspires you to want to make this film or video. This section of the prospectus is especially applicable if the idea comes from another medium (stage play, short story, etc.).

Research. Research is imperative for a documentary project. Potential investors will need to understand the materials on which your story is based. Is this a true story of a living person? Is it based on a real event? Has the story been done before? What slant will the director

Figure 1.1 Scene from *Truman*. An eleven-year-old boy confronts his imaginary fears while attempting to climb a rope during gym class.

Figure 1.2 Scene from *The Lunch Date*. A well-to-do woman's unusual encounter with a homeless man while waiting at a train station to return to the suburbs.

take? Have the rights to tell this story been secured?

Top Sheet of Budget. (See Figure 5.1.) The top sheet summarizes the budget. This summary should represent the broad categories; it is not a detailed or itemized breakdown. Too much information might prompt an investor to question why you need $400 for a special wig. You don't want to end up justifying

this and every cost of the project. Investors need to trust that you are the expert. It is your business, not theirs. Only after you have prepared an accurate budget for the script can you begin to finance the project realistically. However, you might have begun to raise money long before this by approaching investors with an early draft of the script or a "treatment" and a projected estimate of production costs. Experienced producers and production

Figure 1.3 Scene from *Mirror Mirror*. A documentary featuring women speaking about how they and others perceive their own bodies, intercut with historical footage of how the media emphasize women's bodies.

Figure 1.4 Scene from *Crazy Glue*. An animated clay puppet short tells the story of one innovative attempt to patch up a disintegrating marriage—through the use of crazy glue!

managers have the skill to examine a script and estimate the cost of the project. If you have been involved in other productions of similar size and scope, you might get a sense of how much money you need before you actually work out the budget.

At the prospectus stage, the budget is likely to be an overall guesstimate. Later, it will be modified to include input from all department heads, including the director. At the prospectus stage, the director can help the producer by confirming that the bottom-line figure in the budget adequately covers her needs.

You might be able to complete the project for less than your projection, but ask for more than you anticipate needing. Who knows? You might get it and you might need it. (See Chapter 5, "Budget," for more information.)

Production Schedule. Give the approximate dates when the production will begin and end should financing become available.

Cast List. Draw up a list of the prominent cast members, and give a succinct résumé of their credits. The quality and ability (and in some cases recognizability) of the cast are part of the insurance that investors require to feel confident that their money is being spent wisely. Casting is essentially the domain of the director. Her or his input into this list is imperative.

Brief Résumés of Creative Team. Present the pool of talent associated with the production at the time the prospectus is written. The personnel can be introduced in simple paragraphs or in complete résumés.

Writing a résumé is an art in itself. A résumé can be anywhere from a single paragraph to a full page in length. Try to find a balance between giving too much information and too little. Clearly identify each person's strengths, relevant experiences, and job description. A résumé for a producer that indicates that he or she can write, direct, produce, shoot, and act might overwhelm investors.

Having said that, we remind you that there are no rules. Although not all potential investors will know how to judge the subtleties of a varied background, an eclectic résumé might indeed catch an investor's eye. Work experiences as a camp counselor, location scout, or editor of a student film all point to leadership skills.

Description of Market for Project. Devise a distribution plan to include in the prospectus. (See Chapter 19, "Distribution," for further details.)

Financial Statement. In the financial statement, you should estimate the income you expect to receive, based on your distribution plan. In addition, explain your business identity. If you can offer investors any sort of tax break, you will have a greater chance of attracting financing. Tax breaks are allowed sometimes if your company is set up as a not-for-profit entity. Consult an entertainment attorney.

Means of Transferring Funds. At the end of the prospectus, include a letter addressed to the company from the investor, committing the investor to a specific figure. The letter should show how money can be transferred to the production account.

Presentation Is Everything

The prospectus can be peppered with graphics that support the project's concept and lend excitement to the presentation. People respond to visuals. If you can create images that connect potential investors to the idea of your piece, it will enhance their appreciation of the supporting data.

A well-written prospectus makes a professional impression. When writing the prospectus, use easy-to-understand and grammatically precise language. Stick with simple declarative sentences and clear, unpretentious words. Arrange your thoughts logically, avoid jargon, and make the ideas flow.

Don't give potential investors an obvious reason to turn down your proposal. "No" is the easiest decision to make because nothing is risked by making it. In fact, most people look for reasons to say no. Imagine yourself on the other side of the table. Would you support someone whose business plan wasn't thought out carefully or who didn't take the time to proofread his or her work? Would you trust this person with your money?

The prospectus forces the filmmaker to think objectively about the project as a whole. The challenge becomes how to communicate an idea's potential to a complete stranger who might not be interested in the project. Beginners think that enthusiasm is enough to sell an idea. This energy can be contagious, but it must also be followed by hard information about the exact nature of the project, the talent, and the investment structure.

The prospectus is an important tool for galvanizing interest without having to pitch verbally to hundreds of people. It also identifies the sincerely interested parties whose concerns can then be addressed specifically and personally. Some producers are naturally facile and relaxed communicators. You might be one. Even if you have an innate ability to sell in person, the written presentation must be well designed. Good interpersonal skills will come in time. The by-product of a thoroughly prepared prospectus is twofold:

- First, it trains you to think logically and sequentially about your idea so that when you do have the opportunity to speak face-to-face with potential investors, you will be well prepared.
- Second, it is an important step in the preproduction process. Now you have your first budget!

I started writing proposals. The first one was to the American Film Institute, which resulted in a rejection. I actually applied to them three years in a row and got rejected three years in a row for a historical legacy idea. But when I started refining the idea, I abandoned the whole thing, and the reason was because I felt this was too hard to do on film. It was really more like a slide show because it was all inanimate, and it worried me that I would have to rely on still material and a disembodied voice.

Jan

SPENDING THE MONEY RESPONSIBLY

As a producer, you have the responsibility of handling and managing the money after it has been raised. You will need to create some type of corporate identity to receive funds. This might involve something as simple as setting up a bank account into which checks can be deposited, or it can be as complex as choosing a corporate structure. Consult an entertainment attorney for details.

The business and legal skills required to handle money responsibly are based on the needs of the production. Throughout the production process, the producer supervises the allocation of cash, or the *cash flow*, through the production pipeline. This ensures that he or she will be able to deliver a thorough financial statement to the investors at the end of production.

DIRECTOR
Pitching the Project

Next to the film's concept, the director and her abilities are the key element that the producer touts when raising funds. If the director has a track record or other career support, such as an award for a previous work or glowing reviews, investors will treat the venture more favorably. The director must infect investors with her enthusiasm for the project. Investors often know very little about how to read a script or how to respond to production problems. What they do understand is good storytelling ability. The director who can "pitch" her film or video idea well is more apt to impress investors with her vision than someone who becomes tongue-tied or is shy. Verbal agility is crucial at the moment of "closing."

Whether you like it or not, you are now into sales. Smart investors look at the bottom line, but they are greatly influenced by the presenter. Everyone appreciates a performer and an entrepreneur. Keep in mind, however, that there is a fine line between razzle-dazzle and being obnoxious. The former is a turn-on, the latter a turnoff. Learn to observe, by the reaction of those to whom you are pitching, which approaches seem to work and which don't. There is nothing like asking for money; it trains the producer and director to deal with a naturally uncomfortable situation gracefully. Through the process of defining your project and shaping your pitch, you will learn how best to sell your idea.

> *I get really unhappy when I hear of people, not just students but independent filmmakers, who pitch an idea, start developing a particular idea, because they feel like that's what's "fundable" these days. I think the thing people fail to understand is that originality is what gets attention, not derivative filmmaking.*
>
> Jan

In the verbal and the written pitch, present a tone that grabs the target investor's attention. Use active and colorful words. Some people have a talent for this type of promotional presentation. A director's raw enthusiasm, coupled with a clear interpretation of the material, makes an effective presentation. In a verbal presentation, be enthusiastic, but speak clearly and slowly. When pitching material with a partner, know when to be silent and when to assist. If you seem like a cohesive team, your target will be impressed.

GENERAL FUND-RAISING SUGGESTIONS

Be Positive and Be Patient

Project supreme confidence in the picture and in your ability to execute it successfully. People are investing not only in the picture, but in you. In addition, you must be able to sustain a positive attitude over the long haul. If you are the kind of person who requires short-term rewards, this business is not for you. Perseverance and patience are the watchwords. Looking for money requires a dogged determination. You'll need the energy of the hare but the patience of the tortoise.

> *I thought I'd really like to make a film and figured I could probably raise enough money somehow to shoot it. I didn't think it would be very expensive. It basically came down to the fact that I was just dying to get near a camera and shoot something. What was the worst that could happen? I'd lose some money.*
>
> Adam

Act Professionally

Professionalism is a theme that we stress in all aspects of the production process, and it is also vital when you approach potential investors. You will be respected if you appear to be organized, efficient, well prepared, and articulate. You might see yourself in the role of the artist, but fund-raising is a business proposition.

You are asking people to trust you with their money. If you can give the impression of knowing what you are doing, you will most likely get your foot in the door. Once in, assuming that there are quality and substance in your project idea, a coherent presentation will be critical to your success.

Be sure to allocate enough time to raise the money you need. It won't happen overnight. If you are planning to shoot in several months and have not yet begun fund-raising, you'd better hope that you win the lottery.

Be Informed

Do your homework. When looking for funding sources, knowing what information to seek is as important as knowing where to find it and what to do with it. The goal is to know how things work and how to work them to your advantage. Read as much as you can. Surf the Net. The Internet has become a potent and valuable tool for research (see the Bibliography for a list of Web sites). Examine the budgets of pictures of a similar length.

Be dogged in the pursuit of the facts. Examine all sides of a problem; there could be more than one solution. Go to conferences. Talk to professionals and amateurs who have been successful at fund-raising, particularly with genres similar to yours. Become adept at asking the right questions. Don't be shy. Believe it or not, people like to share their knowledge with beginners as long as it doesn't cost them anything. With this information in hand, evaluate the potential investor pool.

The key is to consider everything. Focus your energies on multiple strategies. Don't pin your hopes on getting that one investor or grant. If it doesn't work out, you will be left stranded. Learn to keep many balls in the air, and learn to live with rejection. It may take 100 no's before you finally hear one yes.

FUND-RAISING TIP

Financing can be secured in two tiers. First, there's the money you need to get the project shot and "in the can." This money is raised on a script and a pitch. When the principal photography has been completed, you will require "finishing" or postproduction money. This second phase of fund-raising can be done while the project is being edited. Use the footage to show potential investors just how fabulous the picture will eventually be. As opposed to the first funds, which were raised on the ephemeral qualities of a pitch and a prayer, having footage to show makes a more solid presentation.

SOURCES FOR STUDENTS

What help is available to students? The following brief list summarizes resources you should explore.

Other Students. Other students are invaluable resources of solid advice and information. Who better to ask about fund-raising strategies than fellow students who are in the same position? Surprisingly, many students overlook their peers as a resource. It is up to you to brainstorm with others who are seeking production support.

Internships. If your film or television program is located in a media center such as New York, Los Angeles, Chicago, or San Francisco, it behooves you to take advantage of internship opportunities to learn about not only the raising, but also the management, of money.

Facilities. Students at media programs have access to free equipment. They also have the use of production and postproduction facilities, such as stages, locations, editing rooms, mixing facilities, and screening rooms.

Learning Opportunities. Keep your eyes open for ways to develop yourself. Listen to guest speakers from the industry. Take courses in a business school. Tackle writing, acting, and public speaking classes. In a pitch meeting, the topic of conversation could easily switch from your project to current events to acting techniques to writing styles. Students with varied interests and a broad background will be best equipped to converse on a number of topics and will make a favorable impression. Your ultimate goal is to know both how to communicate and what to communicate.

FUND-RAISING STRATEGIES

Find creative ways to earn money. Entrepreneurial students capitalize on their skills by creating a product to sell. Hard cash is made each week by those who know how to bake, garden, arrange flowers, do accounting, type, troubleshoot computers, and videotape weddings.

Generate interest and create energy around your project. Set up fund-raisers, have parties, and hold screenings of your unfinished work. Use the newspapers. Create publicity by sending a press packet to newspapers and magazines.

You need not look only for big-dollar investments. Make a list of everyone you know and everyone your parents, relatives, and friends know, and ask them for a modest amount (from $15 up). They will be surprised when you ask for a small amount and will gladly donate a few dollars to the cause. If 25 friends each give $25, you'll collect $625! This is enough to buy and process three rolls of 16-mm film or 60 rolls of tape stock.

I'm in debt, but I got lucky in several ways. I was no longer paying for film school because I had become a graduate assistant. My parents didn't pay for my undergraduate education, so they were ready to pay for graduate school. Since I didn't have to pay for tuition, the money went into production. My high school friends who had done well financially helped me. So between my friends, my parents, and student loans, I paid for the film.

Howard

KEY POINTS

- Allow ample time to generate the funds you will need to shoot the entire picture.
- Present your project and yourself in a professional manner. Use a prospectus—a professional business plan with which investors are familiar.
- Research your targets for funds. If you know as much about them as they do, they will be impressed.
- Generate enough enthusiasm to pitch the project and sustain yourself for the year or two it might take to make your film or video.

chapter two

Script

The whole preproduction process is about writing the script.

Howard

This chapter introduces you to some necessary guidelines for writing a short film or video script. It does not, however, explore in depth the nuts and bolts of writing technique. We recommend that you consult books written specifically about screenwriting for the short form. You'll find suggestions in the Bibliography.

The guidelines in this chapter are not absolutes. Violating some of these principles should not keep you from moving ahead if you feel strongly about the idea. You will be living with this project for quite a while, so it is important that you feel passionate about the material and its message. Remember, though, that film and video are art forms that communicate via visual images. If the script cannot visually convey a message, it might not engage an audience.

PRODUCER

Overseeing Rewrites

The first step in producing a short film or video is securing a script. There are many ways you can do this. You can write one yourself, develop an original idea with a writer or director, adapt a script from another genre (a play or short story), or find a script that is already written. However you go about this— and we cannot emphasize this point too strongly— without a well-crafted script, you cannot have a good film or video.

Producing a documentary script involves a different process than generating a narrative text. The specific nature of a documentary script is addressed later in this chapter.

The script is your guide through production. From it you know the story, the characters, the approximate budget, the locations, the final length, and your target audience. With a script, you can finance the production and attract the creative team that will transform the script into a final product. The first and most important member of that team is the director. Because her job is to bring a personal vision to the material, she either rewrites the script herself or supervises the rewrite until the script best suits a production based on her design.

Writing a good short script is difficult. The most common mistake novices make is trying to explore complicated or grandiose ideas that are more suited for the feature film format. They want to say it all in 10 minutes. The short film idea doesn't have the time to explore more than one topic. It needs to be focused and specific. Simple is best. The four examples provided in this book are good scripts because they are simple stories told well. (See Appendix C for the complete scripts.)

SCRIPT DEVELOPMENT

The producer supervises the development of an idea until a director is brought on board to complete the rewrites and prepare the script for production. What starts out as a simple notion might go through many evolutions before it is ready to go before the cameras.

The goal is to end up with the best script possible from your original idea. Be prepared to work and rework the material.

The elements that the short form can contain are limited. Before embarking on production, see and study as many shorts as possible to get a feel for the form and what can be accomplished in its time frame. (Shorts that are available for rental are listed in Appendix B, and their distributors appear in our Web site.)

The length for shorts varies from 2 minutes (*Bambi Meets Godzilla,* United States, 1969) to 34 minutes (*The Red Balloon,* France, 1956). The subject matter is limited only by imagination.

> *Probably the biggest influence—besides all the films I'd ever seen in my life—was looking at student films, what was working and what wasn't. One thing that I thought wasn't working was that the stories went all over the place and that there was an emphasis on the technical rather than substance.*
>
> Adam

It is important to know what has come before. You don't want to latch onto an idea that has already been made.

> *I think that I had seen a couple of films on eating disorders, and I had a feeling that I knew what was out there. I did seek out one film on beauty pageants, which was pretty irrelevant to this subject matter. But I do think that's important. I didn't want to make a film like this if there was a film that had just come out a year earlier. I did enough of a search to convince myself that there was really not one that took this particular perspective.*
>
> Jan

Many of the great film- and videomakers were influenced by existing material. Orson Welles saw and studied John Ford's famous western *Stagecoach* more than 50 times while preparing to shoot *Citizen Kane.*

> *I made a list of the films that really affected me as a child. One of them was* An Occurrence at Owl Creek Bridge *(which most people have seen). Then, of course, so did* The Red Balloon. *In film school, I saw many other films, such as Truffaut's* Les Miston

> (The Brats). *This film didn't influence me in a conscious way but filled me up emotionally. It was so melancholy and beautiful that it made me want to run out and make films, even though I ended up making a film like* Truman.
>
> Howard

WHAT IS A SCRIPT?

Think of your script as a blueprint for the final film or tape. It depicts the moment-to-moment progression of events by indicating what the audience will see and hear. Unlike a novel or a poem, the script is an unfinished work; it is only a part of the media-making process. It has no inherent literary value other than as a guide from which a film or video is wrought.

A script is to filmmaking as a blueprint is to shipbuilding or as a score is to a symphony performance. Imagine the ensuing difficulties of a shipbuilder who begins construction on a boat with only a few sketches to work from, or the cacophony of a full orchestra trying to play a concert from a sketchy musical score. Just as the drawings tell the shipbuilder exactly where to place the mast and the notes on the score tell the musicians what and when and how loudly to play, so a script dictates how each member of the production team is to go about fulfilling his or her job.

WHAT DOES A SCRIPT LOOK LIKE?

The script of *The Lunch Date* in Appendix C is presented in Writers Guild of America (WGA) standard screenplay format. This format is an industry convention that has a direct relationship to how the script is photographed. (See Chapter 3, "Breakdowns," for more about screenplay format.) Writing a script in proper format has become simplified with the availability of software systems. Some of the current scriptwriting programs are Final Draft, Scriptware, Movie Magic, and Script Thing (more in the Bibliography). Most can format your script as you type it. They can be found where computer programs are sold, and some companies will send you a free demo disk.

However, a story doesn't have to be presented originally in screenplay format to make dramatic sense. You can work from an outline or from a simple scene description. This is called a *treatment.* It is the bare bones of a story told in narrative prose rather than in descriptions of individual scenes. A treatment reads like a short story and can be as straightforward as the way the case studies are described later in this chapter. However, it is imperative that the idea eventually conform to the standard script format.

A common format for documentary scriptwriting is a two-column page: one side lists the visuals, and the other side lists the audio. The reader will get an idea of the show by imagining these two elements together. Documentarians learn to be especially responsive to their material. By the time the documentary gels, the story might have changed, taking a direction very different from the original outline. For example, in Errol Morris's Academy Award–winning documentary *The Thin Blue Line*, his original intent was to interview inmates on death row in Texas. In the course of conducting the interviews, he met and interviewed a man who was to become the sole subject of his film. Believing the man on death row to be innocent, Morris took his case to the film audience. The argument was so compelling the man was retried and eventually freed from prison. This example demonstrates not only the adjustments documentary film- and videomakers undergo in the discovery process of their topic, but also the power of cinema to make a change, to affect the world.

During the interview with my first subject, I asked way too many questions. After shooting 800 feet on that single interview, I reduced the number of questions from eight to four and really simplified the content. Because, despite a "test" interview, I had overestimated how much information I could cover in a 400-foot (11-minute) roll of film.

Jan

WHERE DO SCRIPTS COME FROM?

Scripts are developed from whatever might inspire you to express and communicate something in visual and dramatic terms. All of the following sources can serve as the basis for a dramatic or documentary project:

Ideas	Dreams
Images	Real events
Characters	Fantasies
Concepts	Memories
Historical events	Real-life experiences
Places	Social issues
Adaptations from	News stories
short stories	Magazine articles

You might be inspired by a single event that occurred on a bus or train, an interaction between two people that strikes you as funny or poignant, an uncle who told you wonderful stories as a child, or a favorite teacher who was a memorable character. You might have a compelling need to express something about the social conditions in your neighborhood. The best scripts are written from the heart. They are based on subjects about which the writer knows on a first-hand basis.

Truman *focuses on conquering feelings of inadequacy in public. Most of us can empathize with Truman's transcendental moment when his perception of himself in the world undergoes a major shift, a spurt of personal growth.*

During the summer, I kept notebooks full of different ideas, random stuff. I kept drawing the picture of a little boy hanging from a rope. That image propelled me forward. I can't remember why. I also wanted to make a film that if I were an eight-year-old boy, would amuse me. The sort of film teachers would roll out on rainy days in fifth grade. I wanted it to be fun to make. I wanted to enjoy it.

Howard

The woman in *The Lunch Date* also has a personal revelation. She and a homeless man share an unusual moment together, and then she escapes back to the suburbs. (See Figure 2.1.) This moment probably does not have the same impact on her life as the events in *Truman* do on the boy because she is older. We see her, however, experience the unexpected, which then affords her the ability to know the homeless in a new way. Both characters are changed in some way by the events of their stories.

I remember that several years before, I had heard a story similar to the one I used in the film, which was a story about a person misidentifying something of someone else's as belonging to themselves. And I thought this was a pretty human mistake that anybody could make and that I had probably made somewhere along the line—assuming something about somebody else. So I played with the idea of setting this story in New York and having the two most opposite people I could think of meet.

Adam

Figure 2.1 Two hungry diners, from *The Lunch Date*.

Crazy Glue is an animated clay puppet short adapted from a story by Israeli author Etgar Keret. This claymation (see Glossary) film tells the story of one innovative attempt to patch up a disintegrating marriage—through the use of Crazy Glue!

While *Truman, The Lunch Date,* and even *Mirror Mirror* are original ideas developed into screenplays, *Crazy Glue* is an adaptation. Writer Etgar Keret is one of the leading voices in Israeli literature and cinema. In the last 10 years he has published three books of short stories and novellas, two comics books, two feature screenplays, and numerous teleplays. His stories have been published in 15 different languages and have gained both critical acclaim and success with the public. His book *Missing Kissinger* was named one of the 50 most important books written in Hebrew.

As a going away gift when I left Israel I received a short book by Etgar Keret the writer with whom I now work. I finished it on the plane. It was about 50 short stories of his. I thought every single one of them should have been a short film. In fact, I think since they do lend themselves so well, more than a hundred of his stories were adapted to short films at this point. I adapted quite a few of them through many different classes at NYU, and when it came time to have my senior thesis project made, that story Crazy Glue *was just so beautiful. I thought it was the most beautiful short story I ever read. It also had a lot of magical realist sensibilities to it. I thought it was very appropriate for stop motion animation.*

Tatia

The film *Mirror Mirror* focuses on the topic of how women perceive their bodies. The filmmaker had a specific theme to explore and set about devising a situation that would allow women to express their innermost thoughts. (See Figure 2.2.)

I believe that this self-deprecation and striving for an unattainable body type is a generalized experience among a lot of women. All you have to do is eavesdrop in department store dressing rooms or women's locker rooms to hear the laments that women have about their bodies.

Jan

ADAPTATION

The beginning film- and videomaker may look for ideas for a short project from preexisting material. In our list of where scripts come from we site short stories, real-life experiences, news stories, historical events, real events, and magazine articles.

The history of motion pictures has been dominated by adaptations, mostly from novels. At the height of the studio period in the 1930s, Hollywood was turning out more than 600 films a year. To supply this pipeline of production, studios looked to material that had already proven itself in the marketplace. Novels served this purpose. Although the studios in the United States produce nowhere near that amount of films a year now, roughly half are adapted from another medium, usually from a novel or play.

Figure 2.2 A masked woman surrounded by mannequins, from *Mirror Mirror.*

The Academy of Motion Picture Arts and Sciences honors the craft of adaptation; a separate Oscar is given to best adaptation in addition to best original screenplay. Yet there are few books devoted to adaptation and only a handful that reserve a substantial section for the craft. Most how-to writing manuals focus on creating original stories. Although all the important lessons about dramatic writing apply, the ability to transpose a well-written short story (or even a real-life incident) into a film script requires a specific discipline. This part of the chapter will introduce you to some important guidelines if you are considering some form of adaptation.

Why Adapt?

One obvious reason to adapt is because you have already found a story that has inspired you to produce it as a motion picture. A short story comes with built-in characters, plot, setting, and a theme or central idea. You may have been moved by the words on the page; now you want to transfer those feelings to the screen.

There may a short story that you always loved that you thought had dramatic or visual potential. It could have been written years ago and by someone not well known. It doesn't have to be an example of classic literature (for these stories may be out of your price range as well). Some successful adaptations have come from mediocre books or stories. What they did offer was a strong plot. There is a well-worn axiom that the best books make the worst movies (not always true). This has something to do with the expectations that come with adapting a classic. We have all experienced the reaction of "it wasn't as good as the book."

Another reason to adapt is that original ideas may be harder to come by. Developing an idea from scratch, alone or with a writer, may be more challenging than working with already established material. But don't think that adapting a preexisting work is any easier. (This also goes for true stories that we will address at the end of this section.) Literature is another medium with its own set of rules. Capturing the spirit of the work but placing it in another package can be equally if not more challenging than developing an original idea for the screen. In this section, we will discuss some strategies to help you discover if the story you are considering is an appropriate candidate for a successful adaptation.

Rights

If you have found a story, comic book, magazine article, or video game that you want to adapt, the first step would be to find out if the underlying rights to the material are available. This step is a very important, and it is one that many beginning filmmakers fail to take. (Refer to another part of the chapter for specifics.) If the rights are available, you can take the next steps. If they are not, you will have saved yourself from a lot of effort for nothing (unless your were using the process as an exercise).

However, we suggest another step before approaching the author or the author's agent. Spend some time thoroughly scrutinizing the story's potential for the screen. Come up with ideas on how to adapt the work. If you are lucky to be able to contact the author personally, having a well thought out plan may be a key selling point in receiving the author's permission. If you are not offering a lot of money, you will have demonstrated that you have done your homework. You have nothing to lose and everything to gain. This step also should solidify your belief in the dramatic and visual potential of your story.

What Is the Story About?

This next step involves picking apart the story to discover the relationship between the characters, plot, and theme. Read the story over two or three times so it is firmly in your head.

Ask these questions:

- What do you feel after you have read the story? Why does the story move you?
- Whose story is it? Do you identify with the main character?
- What actually happens? Do you identify with the plot?
- Is there a relationship between the main character and the plot?
- Does the plot tell us something about the main character?
- What does it say about the human condition? Do you identify with the theme?
- How much of the story is developed through internal thoughts and feelings?
- Are you able to tell what happens in the story in one sentence?

Find Your Plot and Characters

To find the plot (what actually happens), strip the story of its dialogue and internal monologues (what the characters are thinking and feeling). This will reveal the dramatic through line of your story. Once you have eliminated what you can't see or hear, what do you have? Do you have a plot? Does this action reveal something about the main character? Is there a beginning, middle, and end?

The well-to-do women in *The Lunch Date*, the boy in *Truman*, and the wife in *Crazy Glue* are defined by what they do and say. Their actions represent their internal life. Among the three films, only *Truman*

attempts to get inside the head of the main character. Truman's fears are illustrated by his colorful, dramatic and funny fantasies. We know Truman is scared, but these fantasies bring us closer to what he is experiencing.

In Tatia Rosenthlal's story *Crazy Glue*, a frustrated wife takes a creative approach to livening up her sexual connection with her husband who has been playing around with another woman. She glues herself to the ceiling. This is the action that defines the story and the main character. However, there is a subtle difference between the structure of the story and the film. The short story is told through the husband's point of view. Tatia shifted the focus and presented the action through the wife's point of view in the film. It is now her story.

Crazy Glue
by
Etgar Keret

She said, "Don't touch that."

"What is it?" I asked.

"It's glue," she said. "Special glue. The best kind."

"What did you buy it for?"

"Because I need it," she said. "A lot of things around here need gluing."

"Nothing around here needs gluing," I said. "I wish I understood why you buy all this stuff."

"For the same reason I married you," she murmured. "To help pass the time."

I didn't want to fight, so I kept quiet, and so did she.

"Is it any good, this glue?" I asked. She showed me the picture on the box, with this guy hanging upside-down from the ceiling.

"No glue can really make a person stick like that," I said. "They just took the picture upside-down. They must have put a lamp on the floor." I took the box from her and peered at it. "And there, look at the window. They didn't even bother to hang the blinds the other way. They're upside-down, if he's really standing on the ceiling. Look," I said again, pointing to the window. She didn't look.

"It's eight already," I said. "I've got to run." I picked up my briefcase and kissed her on the cheek. "I'll be back pretty late. I'm working—"

"Overtime," she said. "Yes, I know."

I called Abby from the office.

"I can't make it today," I said. "I've got to get home early."

"Why?" Abby asked. "Something happen?"

"No . . . I mean, maybe. I think she suspects something."

There was a long silence. I could hear Abby's breathing on the other end.

"I don't see why you stay with her," she whispered. "You never do anything together. You don't even fight. I'll never understand it." There was a pause, and then she repeated, "I wish I understood." She was crying.

"I'm sorry. I'm sorry, Abby. Listen, someone just came in," I lied. "I've got to hang up. I'll come over tomorrow. I promise. We'll talk about everything then."

I got home early. I said "Hi" as I walked in, but there was no reply. I went through all the rooms in the house. She wasn't in any of them. On the kitchen table I found the tube of glue, completely empty. I tried to move one of the chairs, to sit down. It didn't budge. I tried again. Not an inch. She'd glued it to the floor. The fridge wouldn't open. She'd glued it shut. I didn't understand what was happening, what would make her do such a thing. I didn't know where she was. I went into the living-room to call her mother's. I couldn't lift the receiver; she'd glued that too. I kicked the table and almost broke my toe. It didn't even budge.

And then I heard her laughing. It was coming from somewhere above me. I looked up, and there she was, standing barefoot on the living room ceiling.

I stared openmouthed. When I found my voice I could only ask, "What the hell . . . are you out of your mind?"

She didn't answer, just smiled. Her smile seemed so natural, with her hanging upside-down like that, as if her lips were just stretching on their own by the sheer force of gravity.

"Don't worry, I'll get you down," I said, hurrying to the shelf and grabbing the largest books. I made a tower of encyclopedia volumes and clambered on top of the pile.

"This may hurt a little," I said, trying to keep my balance. She went on smiling. I pulled as hard as I could, but nothing happened. Carefully, I climbed down.

"Don't worry," I said. "I'll get the neighbors or something. I'll go next door and call for help."

"Fine," she laughed. "I'm not going anywhere."

I laughed too. She was so pretty, and so incongruous, hanging upside-down from the ceiling that way. With her long hair dangling downwards, and her breasts molded like two perfect teardrops under her white T-shirt. So pretty. I climbed back up onto the pile of books and kissed her. I felt her tongue on mine. The books tumbled out from under my feet, but I stayed floating in midair, hanging just from her lips.

Translated by Miriam Shlesinger

Your story may include several characters, but no leading contender for the main one. In the Raymond Carver story *Are These Actual Miles?*, a man in desperate financial straits spends a day in his house while his wife is out trying to sell their car and his kids are with their grandparents. Nothing actually happens inside his home. The man sits around and drinks and mulls over how he and his family got into the fix they are in. The action or plot of the story (selling the car) takes place somewhere else, and his and our only contact with its progress is through the telephone. The bulk of the story, however, is internal and communicated through the man's thoughts and feelings while he waits for his wife to come back. Although, as written, it the husband's story because the world is seen through his eyes, the wife is the only active character.

Make the Internal External

The Carver story underscores one of the ways literature differs from films in its ability to explore internal conflict. In literature, whole stories can take place inside a character's head. The challenge to writing for the screen has always been to make the internal external. For an excellent example of how it was successfully achieved in a feature, review Scorsese's *Age of Innocence*, an adaptation of the Edith Wharton book. The challenge was to explore the sexual and emotional attraction of two people forbidden to reveal their feelings by the strict laws of New York City society in the 1870s. Pages of internal thoughts must somehow be translated into physical action. Scorsese did an admirable job of visually and aurally dramatizing the internal lives of these characters.

What Do You Do Now?

You have dissected your story completely. The question to ask now is: Do you have a story that will translate to the screen? This wonderful literary property you have fell in love with may or may not be able to fulfill the dramatic requirements of a film story. Now comes the specific craft of adaptation. How creative you have to be will be based on the story itself. Tatia Rosenthal had to do very little. In Carver's story, I suspect a great deal would have to be done.

Some General Guidelines

These are some general guidelines to follow as you or your writer tackle the adaptation of you story:

- Don't cut and paste.
- Be willing to reinvent.
- Make it your story, not the author's.
- Be true to the essence or spirit of the story.
- Keep it simple.
- Be aware of the economy of time, place, and action.

Short stories can be episodic and take place over decades. There may be many characters with many goals. Keep the action focused in time (a short as possible), in place (as few locations as possible), and in action (one plot line). *Truman* and *The Lunch Date* take place over an hour at best, *Crazy Glue* over two days. In each of these stories, there is one main character with one goal in one to two locations.

The goal is too create an organic piece, not one that has been constructed piecemeal from another medium. Probably the biggest hurdle to overcome is the feeling that you are obligated to the author of the story (or in case of a true story, the facts) to retain as much as possible of the structure and dialogue of the story. This is a normal reaction, but one that will not result in the best adaptation.

Film and literature are separate media. They shouldn't have to compete with one another. Neither film nor theater can surpass the power of literature to explore the internal life of the characters, but what a film can offer that a book cannot are powerful images (as well as a creative use of sounds). The idea that a picture is worth a thousand words rings true. The camera has the ability to see into the soul of the character and read her true intentions. With film dialogue, what is not said, the subtext, is often far more meaningful than the words themselves.

You are out to make the best motion picture possible and one that will hopefully retain all the emotions of the story but presented in a different package. Achieving this is the goal of adaptation. The enormity of the task will depend entirely on the nature of the story you have chosen. The lesson from this section— look for material with active characters.

TRUE STORIES AND EVENTS

Follow the lessons of literary adaptation if you have the rights to a true story or something that happened to you, a friend, or a member of your family that you thought would be the foundation of a screenplay.

Don't be seduced by the notion of "this is really what happened." I once heard a phrase that has stuck with me for 30 years: Facts are the enemy of truth. The artist needs to manipulate the facts to satisfy the dramatic need of the story. Use the event as a springboard to develop a character. Just like Howard McCain used the rope ladder to express an event that could have happened to anyone of us and to explore a child's fear, look inside the event that you would like to express in a film. What does it mean to you? What truth does it reveal about life and what do you have to do to manipulate the event to make that truth self-evident?

HOW ARE SCRIPTS DEVELOPED?

Write down the events that you observe in your quest for a good idea or story in a notebook or diary. Moments in life happen at breakneck speed. You might think at the time that you will remember them when you go home at night, but chances are you will have forgotten some significant detail that struck you as funny or compelling. You should always be on the lookout for interesting material. Good ideas beget good ideas. The events you write down will stimulate your imagination further.

Workshops

A constructive way to deal with this accumulation of ideas and material is to "workshop them" with interested people. Invent a scenario or outline of the story, and present it to someone you trust or someone who might be a part of your creative team. The logical choice is someone who is already interested in writing or directing this short piece. Develop scenarios that most efficiently communicate what is happening and to whom.

There was a phase in the middle of writing the script where I went off and tried to make it a little bit of a self-reflecting piece where the husband was going to go to work, and at work he's a three-dimensional animated character. So he goes to work, goes to the computer, and his job is to move inside a computer. It was quite amusing, but technically it would have made the script much much harder to produce. I ended up taking all of that out and going back to the original story as it was. The only one reference I left in there was when the woman is having an argument with her husband. She is doodling inside of a cookbook, and what she has done is made a flipbook inside the cookbook. That was the little leftover of that idea.

Tatia

Ideas that are spoken out loud have a different impact than those that are read. They can either sound better than you thought or fall flat. Not only can you test an idea or concept on an ad hoc audience, but, more important, these verbalized ideas will be stimulating. A thought or image conjures up different impressions in each person's mind. If one of these ideas becomes the core of your final script, these brainstorming sessions will serve as a bond and the start of a long and fruitful collaboration that will hopefully continue throughout the entire process.

During the workshop phase of development, it might be necessary to develop many ideas before you discover one that is not only one you feel most keenly about but that also suits the short form.

I had a couple of people to whom I would read my drafts, fellow students who knew what I was going for and what I had to deal with. These story sessions became the most important thing I did the whole year. That's where I got excited about the work. It was a great think tank.

Howard

Working with a Writer

Some producers can write, and some can't. If writing is not your strength, develop your script with a writer who can effectively put your ideas on paper. You might become a cowriter or act in a supervisory role. Most producers follow the latter path unless they are confident writers themselves. The give-and-take between two creative individuals can energize the process, resulting in a union in which the sum is greater than the parts.

During the process of developing and producing a project, producers work with many different kinds of creative people. No two egos are alike. Learning how to maximize people's varied talents is essential to becoming a good producer. The writer is the first of these individuals.

Any agreement with a writer to develop an idea, whether it is the writer's idea or yours, should be for-

malized on paper in a deal memo (see our Web site). Once a director is brought on board, it will then be the responsibility of the producer to supervise the collaboration between the director and the writer (if the director is not going to personally rewrite the script herself or himself).

Filmmaking today encourages the writer/director auteur and it is a bit of a shame because when you have the same person write and direct, you miss one generation of imagination. I think adapting from a book is having that one extra generation of imagination in both writer and person. I think it becomes more profound and valuable.

Tatia

LEGALITIES

Rights and Adaptations (Preexisting Material)

For the privilege to profit from the commercial sale or rental of your short film or video, rights to original material must be purchased. This gives you complete control of the story in that medium. For a well-known story, commercial rights can be expensive, if not prohibitive, for a producer on a limited budget.

It is essential for you to obtain permission to use existing material or even to dramatize someone's biography unless he or she is within the public domain as public figures (e.g., Madonna, Elizabeth Taylor). If you read about some extraordinary man in the newspaper, get permission to write about him. You'll also need permission from the author of the article if she has exclusive information about the subject.

If you find a short story you like, make a legally binding arrangement with its author for the right to use it as the basis for your film. Contact the author's representative, perhaps an agent or an attorney, through the publisher. If the author is deceased, an agent or lawyer will represent the estate. If you have a personal relationship with the author, you might want to bypass the publisher, agent, or attorney and appeal directly to the author. This approach might also be worth trying in the case of well-known authors whose representatives categorically reject any request from unknown producers.

In any case, make no assumptions. You make think that a story is out of your reach, but you'll never know unless you ask. Nothing ventured, nothing gained. This philosophy applies to all aspects of film- and videomaking.

The work might be in the public domain (see Glossary) and free to use if it has been 50 years since the author's death. A book is in the public domain when its copyright protection has expired. Examples are stories by Aesop, Dickens, or from the Bible. If you have any doubt as to what is or isn't in the public domain, write to the copyright office: Reference and Bibliography Section, LM-451 Copyright Office, Library of Congress, Washington, DC 20559.

> *Securing rights was a concern. With "Crazy Glue," Etgar Keret had an agreement with his publishers who owned the rights for his stories at the time that he can just grant students the right to use the material. It becomes an issue when money exchanges hands. I just had to ask his permission and I could do it. Maybe I should have had it in writing, but as soon as you know somebody—you know if you can trust—the reality they are presenting—he is a very trustworthy person.*
>
> Tatia

Noncommercial/Festival Rights

Film students and beginners exhibit their work primarily at festivals, museums, or conferences. A basic use of a short work is as a springboard to future employment. It might be possible to strike a deal with the author's representative for noncommercial, or festival, rights. These are easier to attain than commercial rights. They're also cheaper—sometimes even free. Prizes at festivals are not considered profit.

Original Material

On the opposite end of the spectrum is an original story written directly for the screen. The producer has already discovered a screenplay that he wants to produce. If you decide to go this route, you should purchase the rights to the material from its author, even if only for a dollar. A simple letter of agreement (see our Web site) between you and the author will make the process legal. This letter is your protection against future disputes concerning ownership or division of any profits.

Copyright

Be sure to obtain a copyright from the Library of Congress for any original material in treatment, outline, or screenplay form. A copyright certifies that the material existed on a certain date. If someone presents the same project later, you have grounds for a claim of copyright infringement. Register only the first draft unless the story changes dramatically from one draft to another.

A documentary producer must secure the rights to tell the story of a particular subject. Rights are not necessary when dealing with historical or public figures, however. Private subjects must sign a release (see our Web site) providing the producer with all rights necessary. If you have any question about the process of securing rights to a nonpublic figure or subject, consult an entertainment lawyer.

EXPANDING THE CREATIVE TEAM: THE DIRECTOR

When the screenplay is well into development, the producer brings in the next important member of the creative team: the director. The producer seeks an individual who is aware of the material's dramatic potential and shares or complements the producer's vision. A director frees the producer to focus on fund-raising and preproduction. The director will shepherd the script through the final stages of development, supervising the rewrites or completing them herself.

HOW DO SCRIPTS AFFECT BUDGETS?

To begin fund-raising, the producer needs to have an accurate budget that reflects the complete cost of producing the script. Changes in the script that affect the budget must be examined at this stage. Suppose, for example, the writer describes a character's interaction with another in a crowded restaurant. The extras become one of the many items that must be delivered to the set on the day when the particular scene is to be shot. The producer looks at the script and says to himself, "Where do I get the 50 extras? Won't it require extra makeup personnel? Where am I going to get the costumes? Where am I going to hold them? How much food will be required? How much will it add to the budget?"

Aware of budget constraints and responsible for the schedule, the producer might ask that a more manageable and less expensive solution be found. If the story is not compromised, an outdoor table, which is a smaller, well lit, and a less expensive production item, could replace a crowded restaurant. The producer should request this substitution during preproduction, rather than on the day before the scene is to be shot.

Sometimes, compromises cannot be made without adversely affecting the project. In *The Lunch Date*, for example, one location could not be compromised. Grand Central Station is a very expensive location, but it had to be secured for two days of shooting. The film would not have had the same impact if it had been shot in the train station at Stamford, Connecticut.

DIRECTOR
Supervising or Performing Rewrites

The director puts her personal stamp on all projects through the creative decisions she makes along the way, such as the choice of cast, crew, locations, and visual style. She provides the creative glue that holds the project together. However, the foundation on which all else is built is the script. A director who writes, rewrites, or supervises the rewrite contributes her focused and personalized vision to the project. In so doing, she should ensure that the final draft is the best it can be. After all, any story worth telling is worth telling well.

DIRECTOR AS STORYTELLER

A script represents the events and dramatic moments of the story, which must be translated into visual images. The director must evaluate whether the story is being told properly. Is the present draft the best realization of the central theme or concept behind the story? If the script needs work, the director must apply her own storytelling skills to reshape the screenplay.

The work to be done might vary from a slight "polish" (minor dialogue changes) to a complete rewrite (restructuring the story). If the script is in relatively good shape, the director need only prepare it to be photographed by creating a *shooting script*. This process requires numbering the scenes to reflect the locations. Each scene is given a number to make the breakdown of the screenplay precise. When this stage has been completed, the real work of preproduction can begin—that is, the stripboard, budget, and schedule.

Elements other than story content and structure can influence the development of the screenplay. The director might be inspired by a location or a particular actor. While scouting locations, she might come upon a unique setting that inspires a rewrite of a particular scene or even the whole story. After hearing a strong performer read a part, the director might decide to shape the character to better fit the talents of that actor.

It's always, I think, about discovering the story. You write it on paper. You rewrite it. Then you start shooting it. You shoot a lot. You start editing the film together and then—where's the story? So you've got to find it all over again. You start editing things out, changing things around slightly.

Adam

WORKING WITH THE WRITER

If the producer has developed the script with a writer, several important decisions are made at this point. If the writer has been paid to turn in several versions of the script, the producer has the right to terminate the relationship and bring on the director to take on the responsibilities of rewriting the script. However, if all parties are pleased with the progress of the script, the writer will now work with the director to complete whatever work has yet to be done. It makes sense to keep a writer whose work has been good, but a writer can become creatively dry and be unable to further enhance a project. Also, the director and the writer may not be able to see eye to eye on how to solve the creative challenges of the script. At this point, the director can either take over the writing responsibilities or request that another writer be brought on.

Up to this point, the writer has supplied the creative direction for the project. His vision, coupled with the producer's, has governed the direction of the screenplay. With a director on board, it will be her vision that guides the project. Depending on how much work has to be done (from polish to complete rewrite), the progress made will depend on the creative relationship between the writer and the director. The success of this collaboration is key, and it is the producer's job ultimately to see that the project is best served by this union.

It is our experience that most students want to write their own scripts. They feel that it is not "their story" if they don't. However, the failure of many student projects is most often the result of script, not directorial, problems. There are writers, there are directors, and there are some who can do both. Recognizing where your talent lies is a part of the learning experience. Developing a relationship with a writer in a film school setting will more accurately mirror what will happen in the professional world, where directors usually don't write their own scripts but must work with sometimes many writers on a single project.

BASIC GUIDELINES FOR THE SHORT FORM

How do you evaluate a script? There are limits to what can be accomplished in the short form. Because most beginners are not familiar with its format, let's examine these common attributes and furnish a critical point of view. The following are general guidelines; there will always be exceptions.

The screenwriting process is about research, discovery, and crystallization. Watching your story develop is an exciting experience. The final result should feel as if each scene is in the right place.

Achieving this feeling, however, comes from patience and hard work. You will soon understand the age-old rule: Writing is rewriting. Subscribe to it. Only be satisfied with the best you can do.

Short films or videos can be developed from many different kinds of ideas. Some stories stretch the boundaries of the 30-minute format. Let's examine what *Truman, Mirror Mirror, The Lunch Date, Crazy Glue,* and a few classic shorts have in common. This will give you a greater understanding of the dramatic parameters of the short form.

Length

Is there an ideal length for a short? The best length is the one that satisfies your particular story. Work from this point. If you are concerned about the ideal length for distribution markets, submit your proposal or script to several distributors for feedback. If you have already found a market for your picture, the ideal length might be predetermined.

Anxious to impress people with their talent, beginning film- and videomakers often want to say too much with their short film or video project. They tend to compress feature-length ideas into 10-minute pictures. Resist this temptation.

The Central Theme

The central theme is what the story is all about. It is the raison d'être, the cement that holds the story together. In *Truman,* the theme is conquering a fear. *The Lunch Date* is about letting go of one's prejudice. *Crazy Glue* is an intimate story about a lonely wife's attempt to draw back her philandering husband. *Mirror Mirror* centers on how women see themselves juxtaposed with society's mirror. The universal qualities of these ideas and emotions allow the audience to relate to the material on a more profound level than just the plot. It represents the reason why you want to make the film or video in the first place: to say something about the human condition. All the scenes in your film or video should be subordinate to the main theme. If a scene doesn't support your theme, eliminate it.

Conflict

A basic element common to all visual drama is the need for a specific and identifiable conflict. Conflict creates tension. Tension engages the viewer's emotions until the conflict is resolved and the tension relieved at the end of the piece.

What is conflict, and how is it created? Conflict is realized through characters. Most narrative stories begin by establishing a problem, dilemma, or goal. Someone wants something or is unhappy or unfulfilled in some way. The process of working out this issue defines the drama. Obstacles to solving the problem intensify the conflict. The necessity of overcoming obstacles to resolve the conflict places a greater value on the lesson learned.

What I knew from the script was the basic structure of the events that would happen. The important things to me were that the woman would get bumped, lose her wallet, miss her train, and that she'd enter this restaurant. She'd sit down, get up to get a fork, and come back, and the guy would be there. And they would share a salad, and he would get up and get coffee, and come back, and ta da. I had to figure out how I was going to reveal her mistake. That was the framework that I had. Then the lines, the bits of action, and the small details would come out of that.

Adam

The Basic Conflicts

Different kinds of conflict are possible in a story, regardless of whether it's fictional or nonfictional:

Individual versus self (internal)
Individual versus individual (personal)
Individual versus society (social environment)
Individual versus nature (physical environment)

Each one of these conflicts, alone or in combination, draws our attention to the plight of the main character, or protagonist, when confronted by personal or another individual's demons, or the forces of society, or nature. The director creates a deep emotional connection between the audience and the protagonist by clearly identifying the protagonist's dilemma.

Truman employs three levels of conflict: individual versus society, individual versus individual, and individual versus self. The class represents society and is punished because of Truman's weakness. By overcoming his fear and climbing the rope, Truman is accepted to the bosom of the group. The film also deals with the conflict of individual versus individual, with the coach as the antagonist. He tries to humiliate Truman into climbing the rope, thereby forcing the boy to make his final decision.

These two levels are, however, extensions of the primary conflict that is at the heart of the story: Truman's internal conflict with himself. His need to climb up the rope (and his fear of doing so) is the reason the story exists. As an audience, we strongly identify with that need and are emotionally involved in finding out if Truman can overcome his fear and climb the rope. Once he does, the conflict is resolved, the tension is diffused, and the story ends.

The protagonist in *The Lunch Date* faces two levels of conflict: internal and personal. Her goal is to eat her salad. The obstacles are the homeless man (personal) and her prejudices (internal). This is the basis for conflict. How she deals with this unexpected situation creates a tension that will be resolved only when the woman either gets her salad or does not. The tension created by this expectation impels us to watch. We are eager to learn how she will handle this unique situation. Will she overcome her aversion to the homeless man? The transition from outrage to mutual respect is a satisfying leap for the character and the audience.

Crazy Glue shows a lonely wife's attempt to draw back her philandering husband through the use of common household glue. This individual versus individual story has a universal appeal.

Crazy Glue is a universal story. It was written in Israel. Setting it in New York helped to establish the distance between the husband in his Manhattan office and the wife who stays at home watching daytime TV.

Tatia

The conflict in *Mirror Mirror* is one of individual versus nature, society, and self. The goal is for the women to accept their physical appearances. Tension arises from the fact that their looks are at odds with society's standards of beauty. It is intensified by the emphasis and importance our culture places on how a woman's body looks.

In each of these stories, the filmmaker sets up an expectation by establishing a conflict. We are engaged by the main character's need to overcome the conflict and deal with the problem, and we will only be satisfied when the conflict is resolved. If the characters could get what they wanted easily, there would be no story.

Equally important, the basic conflict existed even before the story began. Truman was scared to climb the rope ladder, and the woman of *The Lunch Date* had her social prejudices well before the film began. The story setting presents a situation to reveal conflict that already exists. There is no time to develop conflict in a short piece, so conflict should be inevitable.

The Dramatic Arc

Every story should have a beginning, a middle, and an end—but, as Jean-Luc Godard once said, not necessarily in that order. In *Truman, Crazy Glue*, and *The Lunch Date*, each main character has a goal (the rope, the husband, the salad), and each has an obstacle (fear, the other woman, and the homeless man). Most narrative stories can be reduced to this basic formula of goal/obstacle/resolution, creating this progression:

Beginning (setup)
Middle (development)
End (resolution)

This formula creates the natural arc of all narrative and nonnarrative drama. All stories follow this progression. The problem is introduced, developed, and then resolved. When the resolution has been achieved, the story is over.

> *My whole script hinges upon the fantasy sequences. They are small and contained in the final film, but they are very important in showing who the main character is. What role they play in the film constantly changed. Originally, they were the entire film. But as the story developed, they became shorter and their importance changed. They became more an element of surprise and gave clues showing what Truman was feeling. But this weeding out and connecting occurred over 13 drafts; eventually, however, the fantasies found their proper place in the story.*
>
> Howard

The story should have some twists and turns along the way (obstacles) to add tension to its development. Either the characters or situations cause the events of a story. In the case of *Truman,* each time Truman attempts to climb the rope ladder, his fantasies distract him from achieving his goal. *The Lunch Date* has several unexpected twists along the way. First, the homeless man allows the woman to share his salad; then, he buys coffee for her; and finally, she discovers that it wasn't her salad after all. In *Crazy Glue,* the use of the key prop, a tube of glue, introduced in the first scene, become the "bond" that reunites the married couple. Each of these events defies the dramatic expectation of the story setup. They give each story its originality.

The director can map these emotional beats out on a graph so that no matter what scene is being shot, she can understand the dynamics of each moment and its relationship to the whole. This map allows the director to communicate with the creative team out of sequence. For example, knowing what transpires in scene 4 will inform her work with an actor in scene 3. If the actor plays scene 3 too forcefully, he may have nowhere to go emotionally for the climax in scene 4.

Most of these principles hold true for the documentary form. A documentary also needs a dramatic arc by which it can tell a true story.

One Major Character

Both *Truman* and *The Lunch Date* are approximately 11 minutes long. *Crazy Glue* is half that length. This is time to focus on only one main character. A dilemma is introduced, expanded, and resolved for Truman, the wife in *Crazy Glue,* and the woman in *The Lunch Date.* It's true that the gym coach, the husband, and the homeless man go through some sort of change, but only in direct relationship to the main character. We don't care for them in the same way as for the main characters. They are the antagonists (see Glossary). They force the conflict by serving as obstacles to the protagonist's goal. Although there can be other characters, our emotions focus on one person's story in each film.

When expanded to 30 minutes, it is possible for a short film or video to deal fully with two characters, although their destinies should be interlocked in some way. An excellent example of a two-character piece is an award-winning short film titled *Minors,* written and directed by Alan Kingsberg (1984, New York University). It is the story of a teenage girl who needs a subject for her science project and a minor league pitcher struggling to make it to the majors. The story brings these two people together. The girl, who is a baseball fanatic, convinces the pitcher that if she can teach him to throw a curve ball, he will be called up to play in the majors. She puts the pitcher through a training program, and he eventually develops a terrific curve ball. He is called up to the majors, but she is left without a project. He helps her present their pitching experiment as the science project, and it is a success. She passes her science class, and he pitches for the Yankees.

Even though there are two main characters in *Minors,* their goals intersect. Each wants something different, but the success of one is directly tied to the success of the other. The pitcher makes it to the majors because of the student, and she completes her science project because of him.

Follow Through

Your main character must be capable of following through with the primary action or story purpose of the film. The conflict cannot be sustained if the character is not relentless in the pursuit of his or her goal.

Truman does not give up in his attempts to climb the rope ladder. Neither does the woman give up in her pursuit of "her salad" in *The Lunch Date.* Aristotle established this dramatic principle in his *Poetics* 2,000 years ago. It is this ability to follow through that keeps the audience engaged and the story alive.

Likewise, the antagonist must be a suitable adversary, up to the challenge of the main character. The coach is also relentless in his attempts to make Truman climb the rope ladder before he will let the class have some fun. If he let Truman off the hook too easily, there would be no conflict and no story (or it would be much shorter). "Unity of opposites" is a common term in dramatic writing. The major characters must be at least evenly matched for conflict to exist. If the antagonist is even stronger than the protagonist is, the audience will question whether the main character will succeed, and when he or she does, the victory will be that much more satisfying.

One Primary Event

Crazy Glue, Truman, and *The Lunch Date* are stories told in a contained time period. By experiencing the illusion of real time, the audience is brought into the immediacy of the drama. The director's challenge then becomes to show what is outstanding about this bit of time.

A short film ideally focuses on a single event around which the action of the story revolves: in *Crazy Glue,* prying his wife off the ceiling; in *Truman,* climbing the rope; in *The Lunch Date,* sharing a salad. The event in *Mirror Mirror* is the coming together of many women to express their feelings about their bodies. The single event is an important element in the success of each film. In a short of less than 30 minutes, it is difficult to balance any more.

By focusing on the playing out of just one event, the director can fully explore the event's dramatic potential. This simplicity of purpose frees her to give depth to the piece. The audience comes away satisfied because their expectations have been fulfilled.

> *The short films I think really work all deal with single incidents. That's what I've concluded. Even the ones that are longer than 10 minutes, or apparently more complicated, are really all about a specific moment in time.*
>
> Howard

It's not always necessary to work within a confined time period to create a successful story. *Le Poulet (The Chicken),* a 15-minute Academy Award–winning short film written and directed by Claude Berri (B&W, 1963), takes place over a period of days. *Le Poulet* is the story of a young French boy who

becomes so fond of a rooster that his parents bought for Sunday dinner that he secretly decides to convince them that it's a hen. He steals an egg from the refrigerator and places it under the rooster. This ploy works until one morning when the rooster wakes the father up with its crow. Frightened that his parents are now going to kill the bird, the boy pleads for its life. The parents, surprised and touched by the boy's attachment, decide to let him keep the bird as a pet.

The story focuses on a single conflict that arises out of the main character's goal to keep the rooster as a pet. That conflict takes place over a week, not hours. The film is told in small vignettes that underscore the young boy's dilemma and how he attempts to resolve it.

> *Things don't necessarily always influence you in a conscious way but sometimes excite you to do more. I had seen a lot of films, and even more in film school. I had seen* Le Poulet, *about a boy who falls in love with a chicken. (It's in the New York Public Library.) It has 38 scenes in nine minutes yet is not choppy at all. The boy tries to keep the chicken alive when everyone wants to eat it. Great stuff.*
>
> Howard

Dramatic Expectations

Question the dramatic expectations of the material. Do they exceed the short form? In 6 to 30 minutes, can you expect us to believe that your character could arrive at a major life decision? Will Truman climb the rope ladder? Will the wife fight for her husband? Will the woman be able to eat her salad? These are attainable goals within 12 minutes. Could we expect the woman to change her attitude toward the homeless in 12 minutes of screen time? Certainly not. In fact, as she leaves the cafeteria, she completely ignores a homeless man asking for spare change, and as she enters the train, she collapses in relief. That is not to say that change can't happen, but it must be small in scope. We must believe it could happen in the short "screen time" we have with these characters.

> *I was amazed at how hard it is to have a cohesive story come across and be moving, or even clear. I think I was so terrified by my live action film experiences in the early years of film school that I went into animation in order to hone my storytelling skills in a more contained environment.*
>
> Tatia

Minimum Back Story

What is back story? It is the historical information, or exposition, about the characters that is necessary to understand their motivation during the course of the story. In a short, back story must be communicated quickly and efficiently. A feature film has 30 to 40 minutes of setup time, but a short has only a few minutes. Your story and character might need to be simplified if you are unable to set up your character succinctly.

Truman is immediately presented as a young boy with a fear of climbing up a rope. We do not need to know any more about his history to relate to his present situation. The character of the woman in *The Lunch Date* is well defined by her wardrobe and demeanor. She is a wealthy woman headed back to the suburbs. Her reaction to the street people in Grand Central Station sets up an expectation about how she will react to the man who has "stolen" her lunch. A lonely wife in *Crazy Glue* fighting to revive her marriage is something to which we can all relate. There is no need to know any more about these characters to understand the rest of the films.

Internal Motives, External Action

Communicating internal problems is one of the challenges of writing for the screen. This is a visual medium. Dramatic events must be manifested visually and audibly. Truman, the wife in *Crazy Glue*, and the woman from *The Lunch Date* expose their internal conflicts through their actions. Truman's outrageous fantasies are external representations of his fear. The wife in *Crazy Glue* sticks by her marriage, literally. In *The Lunch Date*, the woman's prejudice is revealed when she tries to avoid dining with a homeless man. These stories throw their characters into unexpected situations. We *see* who they are by the way they *act*.

No Talking Heads

If your story contains a lot of dialogue and very little action or dramatic movement, it might be better as a radio drama or a play. Films and videos are usually about action. The rule most often quoted is "Show, don't tell." *Truman* and *Crazy Glue* have very little dialogue; *The Lunch Date* has little meaningful dialogue. The motives of the characters are exposed through their actions.

The dialogue that exists supports the action, defines the characters, and enhances our appreciation of the images. Viewers should be able to watch a film with the sound off and still understand the story. If you are interested in adapting a play, you will need to "open up" the drama by devising actions and movement to replace many of the words and to create a visual component that doesn't exist on the stage.

Rewriting

The axiom "Writing is rewriting" is true. Stories go through evolutionary stages. They are like puzzles, worked at until all the pieces fit together. The goal is to find the right balance among the elements. Each draft reveals something that was hidden in the previous version.

Professionals know that creating a well-crafted script takes time, patience, and devotion. The key is to get it right before walking on the set. Don't hope to work out script problems during the heat of production. During preproduction, you have the time. Take it.

> *I counted 13 drafts altogether, but I don't think that is a lot of drafts for a 10-minute film. Part of it is due to the fact that the short film form is not necessarily a very natural writing form; it's sort of a sonnet. It's very tough. Thirteen drafts is pretty much the average. Looking back through my files, it's clear that in each draft the story became shorter and clearer and also moved closer to becoming a shooting script.*
>
> Howard

Readings

Once the script is close to being finalized, the director should conduct readings to audition the material. It is one thing to write a line on paper, but quite another to hear it read aloud or see it performed by an actor under a director's guidance. What the director and actor want to discover is whether the lines ring true. How do the words flow off the tongue? Are there too many words or too few? Is the space between the words (pauses) more poignant than the words themselves?

As a writer and director, it is difficult for you to analyze what comes off the page, because you know too much. You have all this back story swimming in your brain and expect that we know the characters as well as you do. You know how to read between the lines. We don't. You must be able to take a step back and be critical about what each scene tells us, not what you hope it tells us.

Images before Words

The unspoken rule about visual storytelling is that if you can show it, don't say it. A director is aware that on the screen, the actor's face itself becomes part of the dialogue. A well-placed closeup could serve better than a word or phrase; an image usually speaks louder than any word. Use the words to enhance, not replace, an image.

> *That's what's so great about* The Lunch Date. *I think that's why it is so successful. There's so much that the audience has to assume because nothing is spoken, and you make false assumptions. I think it's really brilliant in that way.*
>
> Jan

Scripts are usually overwritten because writers feel the need to put it all in. It is the director's job to trim the "fat" (unnecessary words or actions). In *The Lunch Date*, the original screenplay called for the woman to be accosted by a homeless person on her way to the train after the salad incident. She was to tell the man, "Get a job!" The scene was shot because it was in the script, but it is not in the final film. In the film, the woman is approached by a homeless man on her way to the train, but she completely ignores him. Why? This physical slight seemed to the director far more potent a gesture than the words "Get a job!" Addressing the man acknowledges that he exists; ignoring him treats him as if he doesn't exist.

> *I was determined to try to make this sequence work somehow. When I did that one shot of her coming into the train station, of returning after discovering her bags, I only covered it in one shot. So every take, there she was saying, "Get a job!" or "Get lost!" or whatever. So I took part of the dolly shot from her earlier entrance, before she bumps into the guy, and I cut the two together. There is a slight jump, but now what she was doing was just giving him the silent treatment. And I think it worked.*
>
> Adam

STORY QUESTIONS

While you analyze your idea, story, or script, here are some questions to keep in mind:

Whose story is it? Is it clear?

Who is the main character and what does he or she want? (For a short work, it's best to focus on no more than one character's story.)

Is the main character's goal achievable (and believable) within the time frame?

Is the main character capable of following through with seeking her or his goal?

What is the conflict? What obstacles are preventing the main character from getting what he or she wants?

What are the stakes? How important is it for the character to get what she or he wants? What does it mean to the character?

How is exposition cleverly woven into each scene? (For example, the woman in *The Lunch Date* carefully cleans the fork and wipes the table before eating.)

What are the audience's expectations? Why should they care?

What do you want to say with this story? What is the theme?

What is your motivation to make this particular piece? Are there other ideas that excite you as well?

SCENE ANALYSIS

How does each scene:

Advance the story and expand our awareness of the characters and the conflict?

Follow from the previous scene?

Lead to the next scene (the importance of transitions)?

Advance the arc of the character(s)—what do we know that we didn't before?

Feel rhythmically?

Change the relationship between the characters?

Give information to characters?

Give information to the audience?

Resolve the dramatic need of the main character?

THE SHOOTING SCRIPT

Having supervised the rewrite or having rewritten the screenplay herself, the director must now develop the shooting script, which is a visual plan for the project. This draft is written in the standard format of the Writers Guild of America (WGA) and has markings and numbers that communicate the director's vision to the producer and the camera and art departments. Up to this point, it has not been important for the script to reflect shots or visual references. The emphasis has been on structure, character, and dialogue.

The first step is to number each scene, enabling the production team to identify each scene by its numbered code. The director then previsualizes the script—that is, she creates a shooting plan for each scene. The plan should reflect how the director will "cover" each scene in the project. The term *coverage* refers to the amount and type of shots the director will need to tell the story adequately in each scene. Developing a shot plan requires that the director break down the script and create floor plans, storyboards, or both. (See Chapter 3, "Breakdowns," for more information.)

The director then marks the script with her shot plan. It will include abbreviations such as *CU* (closeup, a very tight shot on an object or a character's face), *LS* (long shot, in which the camera takes in a lot of visual information), *2S* (two-shot, in which two characters are in the frame at the same time), and *OTS* (over-the-shoulder shot, which is like a two-shot except that the camera favors the face of one of the two characters).

The shooting script gives the producer information from which to construct an accurate schedule. The rest of the production team obtains from the shooting script a point of view from which to design the project.

ANIMATION

Live action usually starts with a script, then a breakdown, which is often followed by storyboarding. An animator will often start with concept sketches and a short treatment followed by an elaborate storyboarding process. Live action boards often block out the basic shots in a scene. Animation boards frequently show every "beat" of the scene. There can be a new beat with every change in emotion or significant character movement. For animation, specific production notes often accompany the boards. Animators often use the boards and sketches as guides to build a rough animation known as an animatic. The animatic can have crude details and unrefined movement. It is meant to resolve issues of blocking, composition, and, most important, timing. Since CG character modeling and setup take such a long time, studios often produce

the animatic while primary modeling is still under way.

DOCUMENTARIES

Because the development and execution of a documentary (nonfictional narrative) might take months or even years, be sure to choose subject matter about which you feel strongly and have a great desire to learn more. You might need to do extensive research to determine whether the subject matter warrants making a short film or video. You might have to view films or videos on the same or similar subjects, research newspaper and magazine articles, or conduct preinterviews.

> *A crucial question I always ask myself before setting out to make any film is, is this subject eminently "filmable" and uniquely appropriate to be treated in film? While I'm making a film, I try to foreground that issue to ensure that I am exploiting (in a good way) the unique properties of film—the interface of sound and image, and an opportunity to frame things differently from how one normally processes the world.*
>
> Jan

The subject matter should contain inherent dramatic value that engages the viewer in the same way a narrative story does, but with real, not imagined, events. This could be an examination of an individual's or a group's struggle to overcome adversities.

> *I thought I was interested in this whole notion of the "ideal" and how women in our culture are tyrannized by the belief that there exists an ideal body type and that it is ultimately unattainable. I wanted to present the ideal as something not fixed in stone, but as a representation of something separate and different from all of us. I was interested in the vagaries of the ideal. So I began to read a lot of books about concepts of beauty during different decades, trying to identify the prescriptions for this ideal type. I read about how the White Rock girl, who adorned bottles of White Rock, was redesigned every decade so that her dimensions would reflect the changing concepts of the perfect physical type.*
>
> Jan

From research notes, an outline for the documentary can be created. This outline serves as the genesis of a script during preproduction. From the outline, a series of questions are prepared for each interview. The combination of on-camera interviews, stock footage, and cinema verité (in some cases, staged events) constitutes the visual components of the piece.

It is acceptable to write out the script in its entirety. This includes creating the answers you anticipate recording. By writing out the script, you can prepare questions that will help your subject respond according to your design. This gives the director a target during the interviews. The questions might be answered very differently than you expected, but together with the subject, you can explore fully the issues at hand.

> *A lot of documentarists, and particularly women, have moved into fiction films after 5 or 10 years. They say, I got tired of sitting around waiting for people to say what I wanted them to say. I always find that so interesting because for me, that's why I will stay in documentary—because you never know what people are going to say, and I really like the unpredictability of it.*
>
> Jan

Depending on the subject, the questions you compose can be easy, or provocative. If the subject is forthcoming with the information required, the questions can be probing but cordial. If the subject needs to be drawn out, a more provocative approach might be required.

> *I asked my 13 subjects the same set of four questions, changing the composition for each question. I knew that I would intercut their responses, relying on a jump-cut technique. One question was, "Describe your body from head to foot, discussing different parts as you go." Some women would start with their hair, and were very diligent about hitting every body part, and some people would start with their neck and jump to their knees, and that was okay. If they did that, I didn't ask them to talk about their breasts, waist, or hips.*
>
> *It was quite revealing to observe what they chose to talk about or ignore. Some parts were complimented, and some parts were totally derided. A second question was, "If you could redesign your body to conform to the concept of your ideal, what would it look like?" I didn't realize it at the time, but the two questions are essentially the same. Because while they were redesigning, they might say, "I really hate my shoulders," for example, and that was an answer to the earlier question.*
>
> Jan

The final script for a documentary can be fully developed only in postproduction. With all of the visual and audio materials in hand, the director begins to grasp the shape that the film or video will eventually take. The audio portion of the show will be the voices from the on- and off-camera interviews, the track of the verité footage, any audiotape recorded, and possibly a narration. The assemblage of these audio elements, especially the narration (if applicable), becomes the final script.

KEY POINTS

- Without a good script, you cannot have a good final product.
- Proper format has a direct bearing on the production breakdowns.
- Good scripts are not written, they are rewritten.
- Understand the short form. As the feature is to the epic poem, the short is to the haiku.

part one

Preproduction

I spent a lot of hours in Grand Central, almost an entire day, getting a sense of the building. That was when I first noticed how the light streams through the windows.

Adam

You have an idea, an outline, a treatment, or a rough draft of a script that you like and are determined to shoot. You are eager to begin production and get out into the field. Assuming that you have secured the appropriate funds, you are now ready to start preproduction. During this phase, you will ready virtually every aspect for the filming process. Decisions made during this time are the most important of the whole production, for they are the foundation on which everything else is built. The producer and director share many of these responsibilities. The next eight chapters indicate the specific responsibilities of each. These responsibilities are outlined in Figures I.1 and I.2.

PREPARE THOROUGHLY FOR THE SHOOT DATE

One of the major goals of preproduction is to try to anticipate anything and everything that can go wrong during a shoot. This gives you time to react sensibly to things that could not have been anticipated and are entirely beyond your control (and invariably occur, such as acts of God). These things happen because all film shoots are ruled by Murphy's law: Anything that can go wrong inevitably will. When you plan a production, work with assumption, and always plan for the worst-case scenario.

Preproduction is also the time to research and develop your idea, to build in all the elements instrumental to the foundation of your project, to design what it should look like, and to explore all of the variables needed to create a successful production. Most vitally, preproduction is the time to make sure the script is the very best it can be. Never lose sight of the fact that this is cost-effective time. All the effort you expend on preparation now will pay off during production. During preproduction, you have an abundance of something you won't have when you start shooting—time. When actually shooting, spending time is spending money. Settling on an efficient game plan and solving potential production problems during preproduction will save precious dollars later.

You can't do too much preproduction work. The more thoroughly a project is planned, the smoother the production will be. For some reason, this is a difficult concept for many novices to understand. They often return from their first major shoot dejected, having experienced just how ill prepared they really were. They realize too late that many mistakes or disasters during production could have been averted if they had been more organized before they started to shoot. All the talent in the world won't help if your schedule isn't realistic, the meals aren't served on time, you lose the use of your location, or you don't have enough stock on hand. These are only a few of the contingencies that require forethought.

31

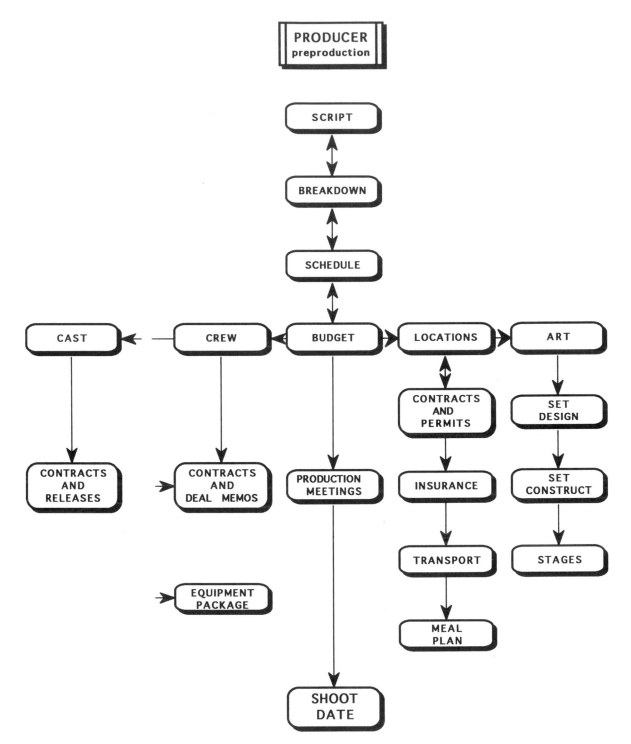

Figure 1.1 Producer's preproduction responsibilities.

WITHOUT A GOOD SCRIPT, YOU CANNOT MAKE A GOOD FILM

Even after getting a good script as discussed in Chapter 2, there is no guarantee of producing a good film. However, a poorly thought out script has little chance of yielding a successful finished product. It is true that many serendipitous events can occur during shooting and editing that will add evocative imagery, inspired characters, and atmospheric locations to your project. The script will come to full-color

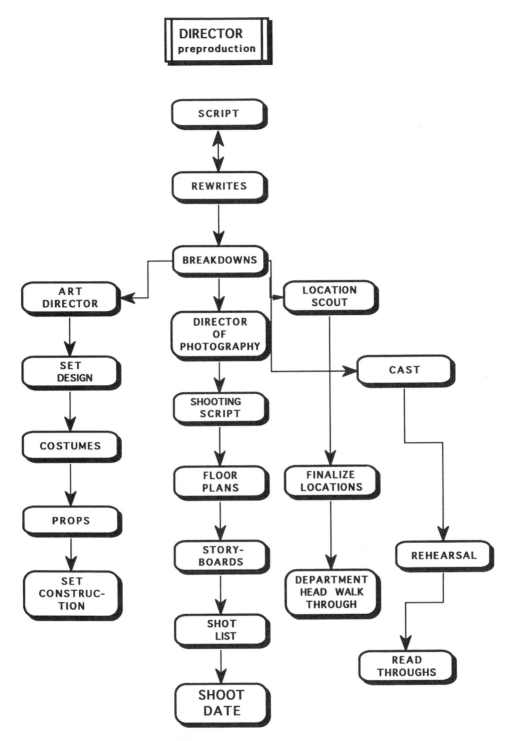

Figure 1.2 Director's preproduction responsibilities.

life, but the progression of events—your story—will not change.

To ensure that you have the best script possible, be prepared to rewrite many times before production begins. You would be ill advised to go out into the field with a story that doesn't live up to its full potential.

The investment of time, money, talent, and effort will be wasted unless the original blueprint is solid.

Don't expect to solve lingering script problems magically during production. Unexpected surprises in action or dialogue will add measurably to the texture of a scene, but don't count on them. Rewriting the script on the set is usually too demanding for beginning film- and videomakers. The pressures of filming the original script will keep you more than occupied.

PREPRODUCTION GUIDELINES

Intangible managerial skills are as important as technical know-how in preparing successfully for production. The following are some general guidelines to help with the intangibles of preproduction. It all starts with confidence and a positive attitude.

Keep a Positive Attitude. Lack of experience makes it difficult for beginning film- and videomakers to assess their day-to-day preproduction progress. You might sometimes doubt that so many tasks could possibly be accomplished by the shoot date; perhaps you have one part still uncast, there is no sound recordist, and the key location has not yet been secured. Don't panic. A positive attitude is as important as efficiency and organization. Professionals understand that things can come together at the last moment. The producer situates himself or herself at the middle of all of the activity and keeps the production team focused. A producer must inspire confidence that all of the elements will come together in time, no matter what the obstacles.

Allow Enough Time for Preproduction. How long should it take to prepare a short script for production? This is a difficult question because much depends on the experience of the creative team and the complexity of the script. A story set in one room with two characters is easier to preproduce than one demanding 10 different and unique locations. However, any short project can seem overwhelming to the first-time film- or videomaker.

Aside from the time spent securing the financing, a workable formula is to allow one week of preproduction for each day of principal photography. It might take less time or more, based on script complexity and the director's experience. In the end, you will do it in the time that is available.

Set a Production Schedule. Use your shoot date as the final target. Create deadlines for securing cast, crew, and locations, and strive to follow them.

Delegate Responsibility. Preproduction responsibilities fall on many shoulders. The producer must assign tasks to the whole creative team (art director, director, director of photography) and then keep track of each person's progress.

Hold Regular Production Meetings. Don't rely on ad hoc gatherings to keep everyone informed. Events happen too fast and plans change too often for everyone to be kept abreast via casual chats. Schedule regular production meetings, and stick to them. Keep in constant touch with the key creative staff. Don't work in a linear fashion. The production team needs to work on many things at the same time.

Never Assume Anything. Double- and triple-check everything. If the producer assumes that the location manager has checked the electric supply of an apartment location, chances are only 50–50 that he or she did. Do you want to take that chance?

Break Some Rules. This book is meant as a guide to a complex process. Picture-making is built on ingenuity, creativity, improvisation, and instinct. The entrepreneurial spirit is alive in the film and video business. Often, it is the breaking of a rule that leads to an exciting opportunity.

Remember That All Things Change. The process of preproduction is an evolution. The script, schedule, and budget will go through many changes before they are finalized, sometimes right up to the shooting date. The essential caveat is that once shooting begins, changes cease and you must concentrate on fulfilling the script, schedule, and budget.

Stay Healthy. Putting together all of the ingredients needed to create a film or video can be exciting but stressful, especially if you're doing this for the first time. The daily stress makes demands on the body. You want to be healthy when you are in production. This means taking care of yourself during preproduction and staying at your peak. You cannot slow down production because of a cold or postpone it because of the flu.

Breakdowns

We would have a nightly meeting for an hour. We would go over the schedule, which matched the lined script, which matched the storyboard, which matched the breakdowns.

Howard

PRODUCER
Breaking Down the Script

Before a shooting schedule can be devised, the producer examines the script from all practical angles. Up to now, the emphasis has been on making the structure and the dialogue of the story work. Although it might be dramatically effective for the main characters to have an intimate conversation in a park during a rainstorm on a bridge at night, from a practical point of view it might be difficult to accomplish. The producer must think about the difficulty of obtaining permission to shoot in the park and the problems of making rain, lighting a bridge at night, and recording dialogue with the sounds of rain and traffic in the background.

The producer is trained to see the logistical repercussions of every aspect of the script. A scene in Grand Central Station (such as the one in *The Lunch Date*) might be stylistically or thematically correct, but what impact will this location have on the schedule and the budget? To evaluate the feasibility of this scene in the context of the whole picture, the producer must first extract, or break down, all relevant production information from the script. The combined breakdowns of all of the scenes give the producer an overview of the practical challenges of the project.

A producer can't begin to raise money for the project until he has an idea of how much it is going to cost. He can't know how much the project will cost unless he knows what equipment the film or video

requires and how long it will take to shoot it. Finally, the producer can't begin to create a schedule until the script is broken down to reveal all production information.

In essence, the producer cannot begin preproduction until the script has been completed. Although the script might change, the producer works at the breakdowns and incorporates the changes as they arise. To assist the producer, the director prepares her shot list, which will provide information for the schedule.

> **STUDENTS** If the producer and director are the same person (which we discourage with extreme prejudice), often the budget will dictate the aesthetics. Money will define how ambitious the idea can be.

PRODUCTION BOOK

Organization is the key to a successful production. To stay organized, the producer needs easy access to the production information that he will gather during preproduction. An effective way of doing this is to buy a large loose-leaf binder and a set of tabbed dividers so that each section can be easily identified. The first document in this book should be the script. In addition, you will eventually include a crew list, schedule, breakdown pages, props and furnishings list, cast list, budget, transportation and meal plans, insurance package, and all permits, clearances, and releases.

PROPER SCRIPT FORMAT

Before you can begin breaking down the script, it must be in proper screenplay format, which refers to how to set up the script information on a page. Professional scripts are written in a standard format to enable the production manager to evaluate the production value of each page correctly and translate it into the schedule and budget.

There are many computer software programs on the market (examples are given in the Bibliography) that automatically conform your screenplay to proper screenplay format. One of these, Movie Magic, offers companion scheduling and budgeting software so that script changes are reflected in the schedule and budget.

The format size relates to the size of the type (12-point Courier), the spacing between dialogue and action (two lines), the width of the margins, and the length of the page. (See the sample script page in Appendix C.) The standard settings are as follows:

- Left margin: $1\frac{1}{2}$ inches
- Right margin: $1\frac{1}{2}$ inches
- Tab for left dialogue margin: $2\frac{1}{2}$ inches
- Tab for right dialogue margin: $2\frac{1}{2}$ inches
- Tab for speaker's name: $4\frac{1}{2}$ inches

These elements should be capitalized in the script:

- All camera instructions (use sparingly until writing the shooting script draft)
- All sounds, including music ("The log SNAPS")
- All characters the first time they appear.
- Every word in the header ("INT. GRAND CENTRAL STATION"—DAY)
- The speaker's name, above each line of dialogue

A properly formatted screen page should equal approximately one minute of screen time. For this formula to work, the script must be typed to include a specific amount of information on each page. If you have crammed too many words of description or dialogue on one page, a 10-page script might, in fact, turn out to be a 15-minute project. Conversely, a loosely typed script will also give you an inaccurate assessment of the length of the project. Time equals money, and an accurate estimation of time is imperative for you to know how to schedule and budget a project.

Keep in mind that this "one page equals one minute" rule is only a guess. A five-page dialogue scene might run up to six or seven minutes in length, whereas five pages of action, say a chase sequence, will

most likely play quicker on the screen. This rule is merely an average of the action and dialogue elements in the script.

BREAKING DOWN THE SCRIPT

Following are the first steps in organizing a production:

1. BREAKDOWNS
   - Prepare breakdown sheets.
   - Line the script.
   - Prepare strips for the stripboard.

2. SCHEDULE
   - Place strips on the stripboard.

3. BUDGET
   - Price each line item.

These steps are discussed in more detail in this chapter.

Step 1: Breakdowns

Prepare Breakdown Sheets

Breaking down the script requires that all the production elements that affect the schedule and the budget (cast, locations, props, wardrobe, etc.) be lifted from the script and placed in their respective categories on breakdown sheets (Figure 3.1). Each scene from the script is given its own breakdown sheet. The breakdown sheets inform the budgeting process because they single out the production requirements of each scene that will likely cost money (see step 3).

Once the relevant production information has been separated from the script, the producer need not refer back to it unless changes are made in casting, locations, or props. Dialogue changes do not affect the breakdowns unless they alter the length of a scene.

The breakdown sheets are color coded to indicate day/exterior, night/exterior, day/interior, and night/interior scenes. If the project takes place outside during the day, you need only use day/exterior-colored breakdown sheets. The color code is a helpful scheduling tool.

The first step in the process of breaking down a script is to number the first scene (if it isn't numbered already) and draw a line in black pencil across the page at the scene's end. This visually isolates the scene you are about to break down (see Figure 3.2).

SCRIPT
BREAKDOWN SHEET

_____
(DATE)

CODE – BREAKDOWN SHEET
Day Ext – Yellow
Night Ext – Green
Day Int – White
Night Int – Blue

_____
production company

_____
scene no.

_____
description

_____
production title/no.

_____
scene name

_____
breakdown page no.

_____
int/ext

_____
day/night

_____
page count

CAST RED	STUNTS ORANGE	EXTRAS GREEN
	EXTRAS/SILENT BITS YELLOW	
SPECIAL EFFECTS BLUE	PROPS VIOLET	VEHICLES/ANIMALS PINK
WARDROBE CIRCLE	MAKE-UP/HAIR ASTERISK	SOUND EFFECTS/MUSIC BROWN
SPECIAL EQUIPMENT Box	PRODUCTION NOTES	

Figure 3.1 Script breakdown sheet. Visit the companion Web site at www.focalpress.com/companions to download and print a copy of this form.

6. INT. GRAND CENTRAL—DAY 6
The woman walks quickly through the station and then stops. She left her bags in the luncheonette! She runs back toward the luncheonette.
   7. INT. LUNCHEONETTE BOOTH—DAY 7
<u>She arrives</u> at the booth and the bags are gone. Only <u>two empty cups of coffee</u> and a plate remain. She begins to pace the floor nervously. She paces back and forth. In the next booth we see her shopping bags and HER SALAD uneaten. The woman discovers her bags and the salad. She sits down and laughs to herself. Realizing the time, she grabs her bags and runs out of the luncheonette laughing.
   8. INT. GRAND CENTRAL—DAY 8
<u>The woman</u> runs quickly through the crowds to her platform. She passes a <u>BLACK BEGGAR</u> on crutches.

BEGGAR

   Spare some change. Please, please ma'am. I'm starving.
She ignores him and continues through the crowd.
   9. INT. GRAND CENTRAL PLATFORM—DAY 9
The woman runs down the platform to the train.
10. INT. TRAIN—DAY 10
<u>The woman</u> runs into the train.
11. INT. TRAIN PLATFORM—DAY 11
The train rolls down the tracks into darkness.
FADE OUT

Breakdown Sheet Header

Before adding the important information, fill in the following items at the top of the breakdown sheet:

- *Date.* The date that you are preparing the breakdown page is important when revisions are made.
- *Title of script.* Breakdown page number. This will most likely correspond to the script page, but not always.
- *Name of production company.* Give your production unit an identity. This can come in handy when identifying yourself on the phone, on letterheads, on cards, and, most important, on the production bank account.
- *Scene number.*
- *Scene location.*
- *Interior or exterior* (indoors or outdoors).

- *Description.* This should be a brief and concise description, or "one-liner," of what happens in the scene. The description plays an important part in quickly and efficiently identifying the scene.
- *Day or night.* You can also indicate dawn or dusk if appropriate.
- *Page count.* Proper page count is an important factor in scheduling. Pages are broken down into eight sections, with one-eighth approximately equal to one inch. If a scene is smaller than one inch, it is still considered to be one-eighth of a page. Use a ruler and mark the page horizontally into inches. This will serve as a guide. Put the total page count, in eighths (for example, a scene might be 3⅜ pages), at the end of the scene on the right side, and circle it. This will indicate the page count for that particular scene. (See Figure 3.2.)

Lining the Script

Now that you have filled in the breakdown sheet header, the next step is to mark up the rest of the scene and transpose the relevant information to the breakdown page. You will need the following:

- Several pencils and a pen
- Transparent ruler
- Colored pencils or crayons
- Three-hole punch
- Blank breakdown sheets (use the sample breakdown sheet in Figure 3.1 as a model, or design your own)

The colored pencils are used to "line" the script, which is printed on white pages. This color coding of the script enables the reader to identify specific breakdowns at a glance.

Begin with the first scene in the script. As you line, or mark, each sequence in the script, transpose the information onto a corresponding breakdown page. Don't mark the whole script and then go back to fill in the breakdown pages. You might change the configuration of scene numbers. For example, what the writer has indicated as scene 4 you might actually mark to be a continuation of scene 3.

Make sure to underline, not highlight, the script. The important elements will not show through if you photocopy the script. Use colored pencils to make the following distinctions:

6	INT. GRAND CENTRAL - DAY	6

The woman walks quickly through the station and then stops. She left her bags in the luncheonette! She runs back toward the luncheonette. ⅛

7.	INT. LUNCHEONETTE BOOTH - DAY	7

<u>She arrives </u>at the booth and the bags are gone. Only <u>two empty cups of coffee </u>and a plate remains. She begins to pace the floor nervously.

She paces back and forth. In the next booth we see her shopping bags and HER SALAD uneaten.

The woman discovers her bags and the salad. She sits down and laughs to herself.

Realizing the time, she grabs her bags and runs out of the luncheonette laughing. ⅜

8.	INT. GRAND CENTRAL - DAY	8

<u>The woman </u>runs quickly through the crowds to her platform. She passes a <u>BLACK </u>BEGGAR on crutches.

> BEGGAR
> Spare some change. Please,
> please ma'am. I'm starving.

She ignores him and continues through the crowd. ⅜

9.	INT. GRAND CENTRAL PLATFORM - DAY	9

The woman runs down the platform to the train. ½

10	INT. TRAIN - DAY	10

<u>The woman </u>runs into the train ⅛

11	INT. TRAIN PLATFORM- DAY	11

The train rolls down the tracks into darkness. ⅛

FADE OUT

Figure 3.2 A script page from *The Lunch Date* that has been broken down.

Cast (red). This refers to anyone with at least one word of dialogue. The name of each speaking character should be underlined the first time he or she appears in the scene and once on each succeeding page of the same scene. The first time a character appears in the script, his or her name should be typed in capital letters.

Extras and Silent Bits (yellow). This refers to a "silent bit" of action (no dialogue), performed by an extra, that has an effect on the plot. For example, the homeless man who wanders around Grand Central Station in *The Lunch Date* interacts with the main character and is a physical presence in the film, yet he has no specific dialogue.

Extras and Atmosphere (green). Extras fill out the frame and create atmosphere around which the central action takes place. Extras are used in crowd scenes and background activity. The choice of extras is important in setting the right tone for each scene. Note that working with extras might require additional crew. Holding extras for many days can become expensive. If possible, schedule crowd scenes together.

Stunts (orange). Any physically hazardous activity that a character performs, such as a fistfight or a fall, is a stunt. These should ideally be performed by a trained stuntperson. If you have many stunts in your project, it is wise to hire a stunt coordinator.

Wardrobe (circled). Any reference to specific wardrobe to be worn by anyone should be circled in the script. If the script indicates that food or blood must stain costumes, have doubles for these wardrobe items.

Makeup and Hair (indicated by an asterisk, *). This highlights any situation requiring special makeup or hair in the course of a scene or for the run of the show. Examples are wigs, facial hair, bruises, or special aging requirements. Projects set in different time periods have special hair requirements that have to be researched for accuracy. This should be noted on the breakdown page.

Props (violet). Any object indicated in the script that is handled by a character in the course of a scene, such as a knife or gun, a key, or a glass, is considered a prop. It is imperative to have backups for disposable props, such as breakaway glass and food. Props (lamps, pictures, knickknacks) should not be confused with set dressing, which is a fixed item on the set that is not handled by the characters in the course of a scene.

Special Effects (blue). This can refer to explosions and fireworks, but it also relates to any physical or mechanical activity that must happen on screen. Examples include a special lighting effect, blood packs, and firearms. When a scene calls for special effects, ample time should be allocated for setup and rehearsal, and a special effects person should discharge the special effects.

Special Equipment (boxed in ink). Using a pen, draw a box around any activity in the script that requires special equipment to execute a scene, such as a dolly, crane, zoom, or Steadicam. Special equipment needs might be specifically indicated or implicit in the way the action is described ("We move through the train station" or "Truman's moving POV up the rope ladder").

Vehicles (light pink). This refers to "picture cars" (vehicles used by the actors in the course of the scene) as well as vehicles used as background for atmosphere.

Animals (dark pink). This flags the need for an animal to perform an action in a scene. A special trainer, or wrangler, is usually necessary because waiting for animals to perform specific stunts can be time-consuming and frustrating. The wrangler will train the animal to perform the specific task before the shooting so the scene will go smoothly.

Sound Effects and Music (brown). This refers to sound or music that must be prerecorded and played back on the set during production. This could refer to music that the actors will mouth, or lip-sync, or to particular sounds that you want an actor to respond to on the set, such as a door slamming or a gunshot.

Production Notes. This space on the breakdown sheet is provided for additional thoughts or questions about production issues reflected in the script but not covered in the preceding categories. It could contain questions for the director as to how she plans to cover the scene. Your job as producer is to evaluate the exact production needs of a scene in order to create a realistic schedule and budget. Leave no stone unturned. If you are unclear about something or have a question, write it down.

At the end of this process, you will have a lined and color-coded script and a set of completed breakdown pages.

Prepare Strips for the Stripboard

After you have marked each scene and transferred the information to a corresponding breakdown sheet, you are ready to begin preparing a stripboard. A portion of the information you have culled from each scene can now be transposed to a production strip—a thin, 15-inch-long strip of cardboard. One strip represents each sequence in the script (Figure 3.4). Each strip should contain the following information about the particular scene:

- Breakdown page number
- Day or night
- Interior or exterior
- Location or studio
- Scene number
- Number of pages
- Where the scene takes place

Header	Stripboard													
Breakdown Page #														
Day or Night														
Exterior or Interior														
Location or Studio														
Scene														
Number of Pages														
Title: Director: Producer: Assistant Director: Production Manager:														
Character Artist No.														
1														
2														
3														
4														
5														
6														
7														
8														
9														
10														
11														
12														
13														
14														
15														
16														
17														
18														
Stunts 19														
Sound Effects 20														
Music 21														
Extras 22														
Special Effects 23														

Figure 3.3 Header and stripboard. Visit the companion Web site at www.focalpress.com/companions to download and print a copy of this form.

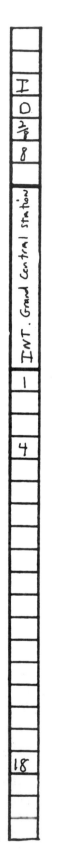

Figure 3.4 A strip.

- Who is in the scene
- What happens in the scene
- Special effects/stunts
- Extras/atmosphere
- Animals and vehicles
- Any special requirement unique to the script

Create the header first—the header serves as a key to the strips. All of the characters, extras, animals, and so on are given a corresponding code number, which serves as shorthand so all of the information will fit on each individual strip.

Step 2: Schedule

Place Strips on the Stripboard

A production stripboard is the producer's shorthand, or "show-at-a glance" (see Figure 3.3). When lined up on a stripboard, each strip becomes a building block of the production schedule. A stripboard is a series of cardboard panels into which strips can be inserted and removed with ease. From these strips, grouping scenes together can create shooting days.

The schedule is determined by arranging the strips in the order that makes the most "production sense"— that is, that requires the least amount of time to shoot. The next chapter discusses in detail all of the variables that you must consider when creating the schedule for your project.

Color-Coding

Color-coding the strips allows you to see your project in groups of shots with a common designation. It gives the department heads an immediate visual reference of how the shoot will unfold. Indicate day or night, interior or exterior, location or studio, and anything out of the ordinary by a colored strip. At once you can see the passage of days into nights, moving from interiors to exteriors, stunts, "magic hour" shots, and major special effects, all of which have an impact on the schedule.

The production board is laid out with any color combination the producer chooses. A typical use of color is as follows:

- All day exterior scenes on powder-blue strips
- All day interior scenes on white strips
- All night exterior scenes on blue strips
- All night interior scenes on yellow strips

- All "magic hour" (see Glossary) scenes on purple strips
- All special effects and stunt shots on red strips

Step 3: Budget

Price Each Line Item

From the breakdown pages, the producer can accumulate vital information from which to make an accurate budget. Every item that will cost money should be pulled from the breakdown pages and assigned an estimated price. This includes props, costumes, locations, special effects, special makeup, picture vehicles, and animals.

These lists will become important when you prepare the preliminary budget. You won't have to refer to the script again unless it goes through changes during the rewriting process. If there are changes, everything, including the breakdown pages, the strips on the stripboard, and the budget, will need to be adjusted to reflect these changes.

DIRECTOR
Storyboards and Floor Plans

Guided by the breakdown sheets, the department heads prepare for the day when a scene will be shot. The director adds to the breakdowns any information that is not reflected in the script, such as complicated camera movements, special lighting requests, and the number of extras needed.

Understanding, memorizing, absorbing, and living the script are all part of the director's homework. You should have a specific vision for the script and firm ideas about how you want to realize that vision. At the same time, however, you should remain flexible.

Everything—locations, storyboards, rehearsals, even walking down the street and hearing a piece of music—is a springboard for your writing. You become a conduit for all these ideas. The whole process is about focusing those ideas into 10 pages, keeping the good ones, and removing the bad ones. I remember going over the shot that introduces the main character, Truman. The shot follows the rope down the noose and then rack-focuses on Truman. Originally, it was not like that. Initially, we saw the rope, the noose, and then cut to Truman. The DP suggested the change, and it made the introduction work. Everything is for the script.

Howard

Why does the director have to be so prepared? Organization in preproduction leads to flexibility on the set. In the heat of production, changes, additions, alterations, and compromises are made. Perhaps a location falls through, requiring the company to move to the backup location. A cast member leaves the production, or the sun won't cooperate. Only a director who knows her material cold will be able to guide the production through troubled waters and come out the other side with a well-told story.

Flexibility also means the ability to alter the plan to accommodate the creativity of the moment if an actor or crew member has a good idea. A well-prepared director should be open to the creative ideas of her crew as long as they fit within her overall interpretation of the script.

I had done my homework and done my time line. I was always very conscious of where my energies should be going at what time. I was allocating my time in terms of getting things done as they were supposed to be. It all goes back to being a production assistant on the feature, where I really saw that if you didn't have your act together you were going to sink and you were going to be pretty miserable while it happened.

Howard

DEVELOPING A SHOOTING PLAN

The director is the storyteller: She tells the story through the placement of the camera and the actors. Every creative decision flows from her vision of the script. The director defines this vision by developing a profound understanding of the script and a clear sense of its theme or central idea. It is from that point that she begins to break down each scene to discover how it will serve that central idea. There are many decisions to be made as to what the camera and actors will reveal at any given moment.

The director is responsible for every element in front of the camera. She must be clear as to why each element, each character, each speech, each detail is in the film or video. Every element should have a function and make an impression that will affect the telling of the story. A story takes place in time and space, and the director defines that time and space. In addition, she determines the pace at which the story is told.

The director's preparation for principal photography centers on breaking the script down into shots. This shooting plan, or shot list, is an important factor in finalizing the shooting schedule.

Know the Theme

It is not enough merely to know the story line; the director must also understand the central theme—what the story is really all about. The theme represents your desire to communicate something specific about the human condition. It may be one of the reasons that attracted you to the story in the first place.

The message of *Truman* is the importance of confronting one's fears early in life. This message is embodied in the coach's last line, "Today it was only a rope, but when it's your big turn in life...." By climbing the rope ladder, the boy gained a small victory that one hopes will give him confidence to face challenges in the future. Your theme and how you present it will influence all your creative decisions for the project, such as cast, crew, and locations.

Know What Each Character Wants in the Story

The director needs to understand each character's objective during the course of the story or during the time that character appears in the story. The nature of that objective can be conscious or unconscious. The woman in *The Lunch Date* wants to eat her salad and get back to the suburbs, but the homeless man's motivation is less clear. Why does he not only allow the woman to share his salad, but also buy her coffee? In reacting to the unusual turn of events, the man decides to treat the woman to an experience she will most likely never have again. Unlike the woman, his objective is ambiguous and more unconscious in nature.

Truman's objective is to climb the rope ladder; the coach forces him to. The kids support Truman because if he climbs, the coach will let them play kickball. At first, it seems that the coach is just being mean, but later he reveals that his motivation is to teach Truman a life lesson. By gaining a clear understanding of each character's objective in the story, the director can make sure that each scene, and each dramatic beat within each scene, reflects that objective.

Develop a History of the Main Characters

To gain a deeper understanding of each character's objectives, it is important to know not only what the characters say and do in the script, but also what they might have said and done before and even after the story ends. This is called the character's back story. It can be as detailed (in-depth life history from birth) as it needs to be to help the actor really "know" the character he or she is playing. By creating this history, the director can help the actors shape their parts during rehearsals and in production.

For example, is the character an eccentric? What elements in the script bring out this quality, and how is the eccentricity revealed? How can a director use the camera to illustrate this trait? The director of *The Lunch Date* fleshed out the well-to-do woman's character by filming her compulsively cleaning her fork and the table.

In the theater, the director and actors of a play are given a tremendous amount of rehearsal time to explore the script and the characters that inhabit the story. In a film or video, the director might have very little or even no rehearsal time. To get an actor up to speed and "in character" requires that the director know the character intimately. She needs to develop a verbal skill for communicating her ideas about the character quickly to the actor.

However, we encourage that beginning film- and videomakers rehearse as much as possible. This will allow them time to develop a rapport with the actors, explore creative ways to interpret the material, fine-tune the script, and work with the actors to develop their roles. The rehearsal period is an opportunity to tap the creativity of the actor without the pressure of having to perform on the set.

Break Down Each Scene into Dramatic Beats

The director controls what the audience should be seeing and hearing at all times within the shot. Storytelling is all about understanding how each dramatic moment or beat connects to the next. A beat is a moment of change, a shift in the narrative flow. The primary beats of a story are its beginning, middle, and end. Within these major beats are the scenes, and within each scene are smaller beats that represents the subtler dramatic shifts from moment to moment.

Beats are motivated by the characters' objectives. When the action or objective changes, so do the beats. They are the internal signposts that guide us along the emotional road that the story or scene is following.

In analyzing and breaking down each scene in the script, the director must determine the following:

INT. LUNCHEONETTE BOOTH—DAY

The woman sits down across from the homeless man in the booth.

                    WOMAN
            That's my salad.

            HOMELESS BLACK MAN
            Get out of here.

                    WOMAN
            That's my salad.

(This is the end of beat 1. We wait for her next move.)
(Woman: Stake her claim)
She reaches for the plate. He pulls it back.

            HOMELESS BLACK MAN
                Hey!

(Beat 2. There is a pause.)
(Woman: Checking him out)
The woman watches him chomping away at the bits of lettuce. He ignores her. Moments pass.

(Beat 3. We wonder, "What will she do?")
(Woman: Test the water)
She reaches over with her fork and swipes a piece of food off the plate. She looks to the man to see if he objects. He continues eating. She takes another bite. Then another. And another.

Still, the man does not respond. Suddenly he stands and walks down the aisle.

(Beat 4. Left alone, she continues to eat.)
(Turning point)
She continues munching away at what remains. He returns with two cups of coffee with saucers. He places the cup on the table and sits.

(Beat 5. She finishes.) (Man: Makes a peace offering)
He offers her sugar.

                    WOMAN
            No, thank you.

He offers her a packet of Sweet & Low from his coat. She accepts.

                    WOMAN
                Thank you.

(Beat 6. The scene has reached its climax.)
(Woman: To accept his offering)
Checking her watch, she stands with her purse and leaves. He watches her exit, somewhat disappointed.

(Beat 7. The scene winds down on a sad note.)

- What are the beats?
- How will they be built?
- How will they be staged?
- What is the pace of each beat?
- How will the characters move from one beat to the next?
- How do all the beats together make up the scene?

Every scene has one major objective, and the characters define that objective. In this scene from *The Lunch Date*, the woman's objective is to eat her salad. She thinks that the homeless man has taken hers, and since she has no more money (having lost her wallet), she can't buy another. The obstacle to her objective is the homeless man; this causes the conflict. We have broken down the scene into the beats that chart the progression the character is making toward or away from her goal.

Each beat in this scene is a moment when the direction of the story could shift; instead of letting her share his salad, the man could simply refuse. At each beat, each character reassesses the situation and then decides to act or not. All beats, however, are not created equal. Certainly, an important beat in the scene is beat 4 when the man walks away. This is arguably the turning point of the scene. Turning points are the major beats on which the action of the scene hinges. If he doesn't allow her to share, the scene will most likely end here. In this regard, the most dramatic turning point is the climax, when he brings her some coffee and they have their "lunch date."

Within the primary objectives or actions of the scene are smaller but equally important ones that motivate the actor's intentions, beat by beat. Her overall intention is to eat her salad, but faced with how the man responds to her objective, she must shift gears and try different means to achieve her goal.

The woman's first attempt to retrieve her salad is verbal. Rebuffed by this, she reaches out for the salad, only to be snubbed again. This is beat 1. Her action with this beat is to stake her claim. Moments pass as she considers the situation. This is beat 2, to check him out. At beat 3, her action is to test the water. This results in her quickly reaching out to snatch a piece of salad. She stops for a reaction, and when there is none, she takes another bite and then another. Without responding, the man suddenly stands and walks away. This is beat 4, the turning point. By his action, he has tacitly allowed her to share his salad with him. When he returns with her coffee, his action is to make a peace offering, which is beat 5. Beat 6, the climax, is when she accepts the coffee and sugar. Her action is to accept his peace offering. The tension between the characters shifts to camaraderie. There is a deflation of energy in the scene upon her exit as he watches her, somewhat disappointed. This is beat 7.

These directions are conjectures on our part, but they seem to work with the action of the scene. You may come up with others that would work equally well. The bottom line is, will they help the actor? During rehearsals, the actor and director discover and shape each of these beats. Shaping the beats together is also called phrasing a scene.

Another example of an important beat in your story is the introduction of the main character. What is the character doing when we first see him or her? The introduction of Truman is a good example. All eyes are focused on Truman, the last to climb up the rope ladder. Introducing or revealing a character can be an exciting visual moment. The character can suddenly appear on a cut, you can cut to an empty frame and have the character step out of the darkness into the light, or the character can be revealed at the end of a long pan. The character's behavior and the way it is photographed will give the audience a world of information. Take full advantage of this golden opportunity.

Determine a Visual Style for the Story

Now that you understand the important moments or beats of each scene, you need to develop an appropriate way to capture those moments on film or tape. An excellent way to begin this process is to pore over paintings, photographs, and even magazine advertisements to look for images that express a visual style similar to the one you want to capture. (See Chapter 8, "Art Direction," for ideas on how to define a look.) One key image could serve as a visual motif for the entire project. Sharing your visual ideas with the director of photography will begin the collaborative relationship that will ultimately and ideally lead to a mutual approach. In preparing for *The Lunch Date*, the director shared his love of Alfred Stieglitz's photographs as an inspiration for style.

You can begin to think visually when you understand the story, the characters, and the theme. What is the nature or genre of your script? Are there conventions that should be followed or broken?

The style in which a horror film is shot is very different from the style for a comedy. Horror films are usually dark and moody, and the camera work is often shaky or canted. Comedies are generally brightly lit, and the camera is often static or fluid, allowing the actors to perform their comedic action without camera distractions. Or you can think about playing against the expectation of the genre.

The director places and lights the objects and people in the frame in such a way as to create a dramatic tension. The overall visual plan for a sequence, or mise-en-scène, requires that the director decide whether the camera will be static or moving and whether the shots will be long or short. The beauty of the art of film- and videomaking is that the director's style, combined with the nature of the script, will always make for a unique approach to the text.

> There's no such thing as a compelling subject; there's only a compelling filmmaker. You can give the greatest subject in the world to a mediocre filmmaker and they'll make it boring and nonfilmic.
>
> Jan

Settle on Pacing and Tone

Rhythm and pace drive the audience to the emotional response that a scene demands. This is one of the director's primary responsibilities. A well-written script has a built-in style and pace. The author clearly presents the time and space of the story. The director merely translates the written word into pictures. This is why it is said that obtaining a good script is half the director's battle. Does the script indicate that the pace of a scene should be slow or fast, frantic or constrained?

The rehearsal period is an opportune time to develop the pace of the story. The director is able to explore performance and staging options and make whatever adjustments are needed to represent the best that the script has to offer.

Create Floor Plans and Storyboards

With a thorough understanding of the script, the characters, and the visual style for the show, the director can be specific about the shots she plans to use to tell the story.

At this point, the director can work out the kind of coverage she will want for each scene. Coverage refers to how many and what kinds of shots are needed to tell the story through each scene. To record a scene, you might use a series of rapidly edited images or a single long choreographed shot. To facilitate this process, it is recommended that the director work with floor plans and storyboards.

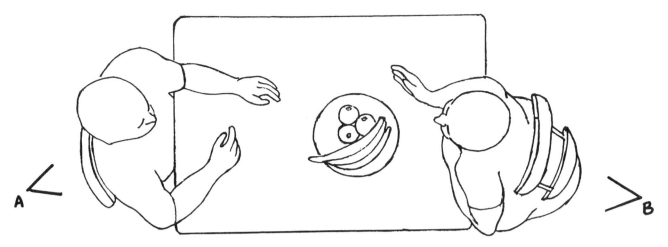

Figure 3.7 Floor plan. The camera angle on the left is a mirror of the angle on the right.

> *I prioritized, after I made the shot list, which were our most important shots. There were always a few little shots, or a few other angles at the end of each day, that I would have liked to have covered, but I never got the opportunity.*
>
> Adam

Floor Plans

A floor plan is a ceiling viewpoint of the space in which you will be shooting your scene. On it show the character's movements and the camera angles necessary to cover the scene properly. The camera angles are indicated by small "V"s, and the direction they are pointing (with indicated camera moves) allow the director and all department heads to know where the camera will be positioned (see Figures 3.5 to 3.7). Furniture pieces, walls, and set dressing can be indicated and shifted to allow the director to visualize her best angles.

A floor plan will help you consolidate your intentions for blocking and indicate how to use the fewest and most effective camera angles. This diagram, growing out of the blocking developed during rehearsals and adjusted by the realities of the location, can help in working out editing ideas in advance and can enable the director of photography (DP) to devise a complementary lighting plan. The art department will know from the floor plans which part of the set or location will be in the frame and which part will be out of the frame. The location department will see from the floor plans where the cars and trucks can be parked so that they will not appear in any of the shots.

From this floor plan, the director can prioritize her shot list, leaving extra shots, sometimes called beauty or "gravy shots," until the end. If she goes over sched-

ule, she can sacrifice a gravy shot, but she will still have the meat of the scene in the can.

> *At this point, we brought out our little overhead maps of the gym, which was basically just a basketball court with lines drawn on it. We started laying out camera positions, determining who would be seen and what would be needed in each shot, and then we tried to group the shots in terms of efficiency: you know, those facing the same direction, so you're using the same lighting setup or the same number of kids in the shot.*
>
> Howard

Storyboards

Storyboarding is one of the ways in which directors prepare for a production. The detailed use of storyboards, or continuity sketches as they were originally called, began at Walt Disney Studios as early as 1927, in the creation of animated films. This technique consists of making a series of sketches in which every basic scene and every camera setup within the scene are illustrated like a black-and-white comic book. Storyboards give the director and all department heads a visual record of the film before it is shot (Figure 3.8).

> *The class at NYU where I made the film is a yearlong class. The first six months I was very, very, very lax. I only did storyboards, which were very helpful. John Canemaker, my teacher, was giving the course. He is a major advocate of storyboarding. He thinks it is one of the most important tools in the animated short.*
>
> Tatia

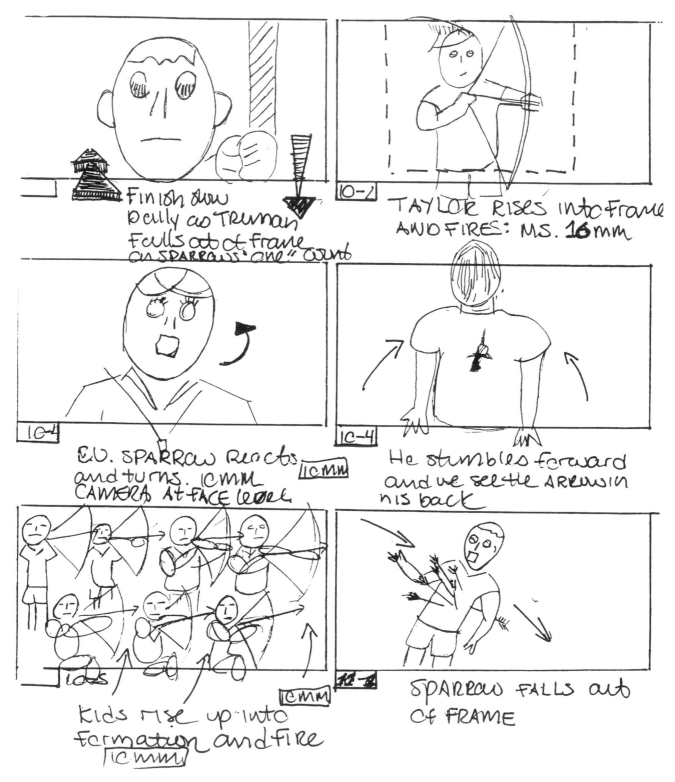

Finish slow belly as Truman falls out of frame on sparrows "one" count

10-2 TAYLOR RISES INTO FRAME AND FIRES: MS. 16mm

10-4 E.U. SPARROW Reacts and turns. 16MM CAMERA AT FACE level.

10-4 He stumbles forward and we see the ARROW in his back

10-5 kids rise up into formation and fire 16mm

10-6 SPARROW FALLS out of FRAME

Figure 3.8 Storyboards from *Truman*.

Having a storyboard is not essential for a dialogue sequence of two people in a room, but it is critical for an action sequence. If the director cannot draw, a storyboard artist can flesh out her visual ideas. Without the benefit of a storyboard artist, the director can use computer software programs that are now available such as StoryBoard Quick or Story-Board Artist, both created by PowerProduction Software (www. powerproduction.com).

I had a pretty complete shot list. As the script was getting closer and closer to a final draft, I started to storyboard. The storyboard really just mirrored the shot list, but again, it also informed the shots and changed the shots slightly. You begin to realize you don't quite need as many shots as you thought.

Howard

Make a Shot List

The list of the shots required for a particular sequence is termed a shot list. The shots indicated on the storyboards and floor plans are prioritized so that a shooting schedule can be ascertained from this list. The assistant director and production manager need to know the number of shots planned in order to schedule each day correctly. Once the storyboards, floor plans, or shot list all have been approved, the director can turn to principal photography confident that she has an effective shooting plan.

I did a combination of storyboarding and floor plans, but mainly I relied on a floor plan. In terms of storyboarding, I knew I wanted to have a closeup of her hands getting the ticket, and the stuff with the wallet falling out, and her entrance. I designed it to have the camera here for this shot, here for that shot, here for that one there. We numbered the shots and then made a shot list.

Adam

A shot list is not a list of setups. The term *setup* refers to every time you move the camera. A shot list details every shot. From one camera position, you might change lenses and therefore have two or more shots from one setup. Your choices when making a shot list range the entire width and breadth of camera language. Here is a partial list of elements you can explore before you decide what shots you will employ in your piece. For a more detailed exploration of visual grammar, please refer to Chapter 12, "Camera."

- ECU—extreme closeup (eyes and nose)
- CU—closeup (complete face)
- MS—medium shot (torso)
- WS—wide shot (full body)
- LS—long shot (full body in landscape)
- XLS—extreme long shot (small body in vista)

The following is a sample of the order in which the scenes of *The Lunch Date* could have been shot:

Monday

1. Scotty gets on train
2. Train leaves, Scotty in frame
3. Train leaves, nobody in frame
4. CU Shot of Scotty after train missed
5. Medium shot Scotty straightening up

Lunch

6. Master of accident action

6A. Post train master

7. Super dolly of entire action

8. Dolly on face

9. Dolly on purse

10. Tight 2-shot collision

11. After all pickup, Bernard hands Scotty last stuff, she rushes off

12. Medium shot Bernard pickup

13. CU Bernard pickup

14. Medium shot pickup

15. CU Shot pickup

Tuesday

1. Scotty enters, dolly
2. Scotty enters, again, dolly
3. Scotty enters, last time, dolly
4. Scotty takes out ticket
5. Panhandler approaches—wide
6. Panhandler talks—2-shot
7. Ladies room sign
8. Ladies room door
9. Scotty decides not to go in

WORKSHOP IDEAS ON VIDEO

Whether you are shooting on film or video, it is recommended that you workshop your visual ideas on video before you finalize your shot list. You don't need to do this with your actors. This is not for performance, but for the camera. It is better to try out shots in the comfort of preproduction.

In the world of animation much of the work is shot like a test on video so one can actually see the film as it unfolds in the computer or on the animation stand.

I shot Crazy Glue *with no video assist. People use lunchboxes to see how their animation is going. They don't take the next frame unless they know it works well with the animation. We didn't have that, so I didn't use that. You shoot it on a lunchbox first. You test your animation as you go along. For stop motion we didn't have a lunch box. Today there are solutions that are computer based for such things, but at that time there was no computer software that would do the same thing. The lunchbox was a device hooked up to a video camera—a little hard drive that takes one frame at a time and it's hooked up to a TV monitor and plays it reel time for you. Then it looks at the next frame that you are about to film but you haven't committed to yet and plays that with the sequence you already have committed to film, and you get to chose if it's a good idea or not to have the frame exactly there.*

Tatia

THE FINAL WORD

It is not easy to transfer the script onto storyboards or floor plan sketches. Both aesthetic and practical factors must be considered. The director must ask, "How can I best cover this scene?" and, at the same time, "Do I have the resources to realize my vision for the camera choices I have made?" Aesthetic and practical considerations are often so inextricably bound together that the director makes decisions about shots in a discretionary manner. The final word rests with the director. It is part of her job.

KEY POINTS

- Breakdowns are the link between the script and the budget.
- The shot list, storyboards, and floor plans inform the schedule.
- The director breaks down the script beat by beat.
- Be familiar with visual language.

chapter four

Schedule

I remember thinking there were four major components to building the shooting schedule. One was location restraints. Two was actor availability. Three was scene order. Four was the individual shots within the scenes, particularly with regard to how difficult they were as camera movements or how tough they were going to be for the actors.

Howard

PRODUCER

Building a Stripboard

Once the producer has dissected the script and stripped it of the essential production elements, he can create a shooting schedule. The schedule is the primary road map of the production and an essential factor in discovering how much the picture will actually cost. This chapter focuses on the variables that you will need to consider when making your schedule.

The shooting, or production, schedule shows the order in which scenes are to be shot during production. Films and videos are rarely shot in continuity—that is, in the exact order in which they appear in the script. Shooting out of continuity is a common practice in the industry because production considerations usually make it impossible to follow the script's chronology when shooting. The shooting schedule is designed so that scenes are grouped together in an order that allows for the most efficient use of time, personnel, and resources.

Production efficiency is paramount to getting the most from each dollar; there is a direct link between the number of days required to shoot the project and the budget. We will focus on budget in the next chapter, but it is important here to understand the logic of how these steps relate to one another. Don't tackle a detailed budget before you have made a schedule.

If you have correctly broken down the script into breakdown sheets and have transferred the key information onto production strips, you are ready to create a schedule. The scene strips are the tools, and the stripboard is the mechanism on which the order

of the scenes can be easily manipulated. The stripboard serves as a visual representation or overview of the production schedule. The beauty of this time-tested system is the ease in which strips can be maneuvered in and out of the board (whether manually or by computer) and the ability to access the entire schedule at a glance (Figure 4.1).

Don't think that this first pass at a schedule will be the final one. You are creating what might be considered a first draft. It is a launching point, not something written in stone. This initial schedule will go through many transformations during the preproduction period. Many factors influence the ideal shooting order of scenes for any particular project, and these invariably change as the shoot date approaches.

GENERAL GUIDELINES

Consider the following general guidelines as you arrange the strips on the stripboard—that is, as you put the scenes in the order in which they are to be shot. Remember, with color-coded strips, the schedule can be laid out and grouped by color, which will afford the department heads an overview of the schedule at a glance. For example, group all shots from one location, all shots featuring an expensive player, all night exteriors, or all crowd scenes.

Fixed Dates

You might encounter situations beyond your control involving actors or locations that will set fixed

THURSDAY MARCH 23, 1989

TIME	SHOT	CAMERA DESCRIPTION	TALENT	NOTES
8:00-9:00	4-3	TRUMAN POV ROPE OVERHEAD TO CEILING		HAND HELD: = 1 POSITION FOR 2 -1
	CHANGE ROPES			
	2-1	DOLLY: WS TRUMAN AND CLASS THRU NOOSE	TRUMAN/ CLASS	RACK: MATCH = 1-3 LINE UP CONTINUITY TAYLOR HOLDS KICKBALL
9:00-10:30	**PUSH IN CAMERA/LIGHTS FOR KID'S LINE UP**			
	1-3	WS KID'S LINE UP: MASTER SHOT	CLASS	NOTE LINE-UP ORDER FOR CONTINUITY II
				TALOR HAS BALL AT END OF SHOT
10:30-12:00	**PUSH IN CAMERA/LIGHTS FOR TRUMAN/SPARROW 2 SHOT**			
	2-3	MS SPARROW GRABS TRUMAN/THEY TALK	ENTIRE CAST	LOTS O'COVERAGE: THIS IS MASTER SHOT
12:00-1:00	**CLASS LUNCH: 1/2 HOUR**			
	3-3	MS 2-SHOT TAYLOR/SPARROW: NO KICKBALL	TAYLOR/ SPARROW	TAKES KICKBALL
	3-2	CU SPARROW: TAKES KICKBALL	SPARROW	CONTINUITY W/3-3
1:00-1:30	**CREW LUNCH**			
1:30-2:30	**MOVE LIGHTS/CAMERA FOR SHOT = 3-4: TAYLOR IN LINE-UP**			
	3-4	MCU TAYLOR WANTS KICKBALL	TAYLOR/ CLASS	KICKBALL
	3-4A	MCU AMY DISAPPOINTED RE: KICKBALL	AMY/ CLASS	ADDITION
2:30-4:30	**MOVE CAMERA/LIGHTS FOR DOLLY SHOTS = 3-1, 3-5**			
	3-1	DOLLY/MS TRUMAN WALKS THE LINE	TRUMAN/ CLASS	
	3-5	DOLLY/CU SPARROW GLARING TO WS	ENTIRE CAST	SAMETRACK POSITION 3-1
4:30-5:30	3-6	WS CLASS GLARES AT TRUMAN	CLASS/ SPARROW	NO TRUMAN
	RELEASE CLASS			
	2-4	OTS SPARROW: TRUMAN'S REVERSAL	TRUMAN/ SPARR	FOLLOW 2-3 MASTER SHOT CONTINUITY
	TURN AROUND LIGHTS/CAMERA FOR SPARROW REVERSAL			
	2-2	OTS TRUMAN: SPARROW'S REVERSAL	TRUMAN/ SPARR	FOLLOW 2-3 AND 2-4 CONTINUITY
6:00-6:30	**CREW DINNER**			

Figure 4.1 Schedule for one day from *Truman*.

parameters before you've even begun to formulate a schedule. Perhaps an actor has a prior commitment to start another project on a specific date before or after your picture begins, or perhaps a particular location is only available on specific dates or during certain hours. The crew of *The Lunch Date* was not permitted to shoot in Grand Central Station during rush hours. This restriction limited shooting time to four hours in the middle of the day.

It can be difficult to work with fixed parameters such as these. Normally, you would prefer the schedule to be totally flexible. However, if there are givens, you must adhere to them. A note pinned to the strip-board will remind everyone of fixed dates as the strips are shuffled.

Scotty was just starting a play, so she was in rehearsals and had to be out every day by five. That wasn't a problem at Grand Central because we had to be out of there by two. The last day at the restaurant we got her out in time as well. Scotty was basically in every shot. I had Clebert come down just one of the shooting days because he was just in the one scene there. I tried to stick as close as possible to continuity, where things like locations became important.

For example, as I mentioned before, we were only allowed to shoot on the train platforms when the supervisor came down. So suddenly in the middle of the day, we would have to stop and go to the platform. That was day one. On the second day, the supervisor didn't show up. So we went down on the platform and started shooting and then got kicked out. . . . They just didn't want us near the platform because of the danger of the electrical rails.

Adam

Locations

Group all of your locations. The goal is to complete photography of all the scenes in any given location before going on to the next one. In the industry, this is referred to as *shooting out* a location. It doesn't make sense to travel back and forth to a location, because every move the production company makes takes time and must be factored into the schedule. This was not an issue in the case of *Truman, Crazy Glue,* and *Mirror Mirror* because each film took place in one location. However, in *The Lunch Date*, it made sense to shoot out the cafeteria before moving to Grand Central Station or vice versa.

Organizing and executing a quick and efficient move of the entire production company, a *company move,* is an art unto itself. A skilled location manager can save a production time and money. Making a

move once or twice in a day is not uncommon, but adequate time must be allocated in your schedule for such moves. A move is considered to be a company move if it is across the street, across the city, or across the county. For example, if you were to schedule two company moves across town in a day, it might take two hours to break down all the equipment, or *wrap out* of the location, and move it across town. Two moves would take up four hours, or a third of a 12-hour day.

One of the stipulations they gave me for shooting in Grand Central Station was that they'd only let me shoot in between rush hours. I could only shoot from about ten to two each day. So we had a schedule of where we would be at what times.

Adam

If your story requires multiple locations, it is advisable to locate them as close as possible to one another. This will reduce travel time. Proximity should be factored into your creative choice of locations. This permits the establishment of a home base close to all of the locations that will serve as a production center.

If the script requires shooting at a distant location, travel days must be factored into the schedule. (See Chapter 7, "Location," for variables to consider when making this decision.)

Cast

Along with locations, the availability of actors is a major factor that influences the formation of the schedule. There are many variables you should consider when scheduling cast members. If you are working with members of the Screen Actors Guild (SAG), you must honor SAG contract rules and regulations regarding the length of a workday, travel time, meal guarantees, and turnaround time. Actors usually work a 10-hour day. The crew needs setup time at the beginning of the day and wrap-out time at the end of the day. Therefore, if an actor's schedule is pushed, so are the hours of the crew.

When planning the schedule, make the most economical use of your talent. Actors work for a daily, a weekly, or a picture rate. If there are fewer than 10 days between shooting for an actor, he or she becomes eligible for a weekly rate; that is, if an actor works as a day player and then is called back to work four days later, the actor's contract is adjusted to a weekly player salary. You can hire an actor on a daily rate and then upgrade him or her to a weekly player, but it doesn't work the other way around. The actor on a weekly rate gets paid by the week, so that if the picture schedule carries the actor over even one day, he or she must receive the full week's rate.

Picture actors are paid a flat rate for the whole project and are available for the entire schedule, so their availability is not a factor. However, it doesn't make sense to pay an actor for two weeks if you only need her for the first and last day. It would be best to adjust the schedule and move the actor's scenes to the beginning or end of the schedule to "shoot out" the actor. It can benefit the production to do this, even if it means going into overtime with the crew to keep the actor from having to return to the set for another day. If, however, the actor's salary is less than the cost of the overtime, it would be wiser to wrap and return to the location the next day.

> *We knew that we could only get the kids at certain hours each day. We promised the parents that we would be working from eight to six every day, with an hour off for lunch. We really had to maintain that schedule with all the kids, so then that went for the rest of the crew, too.*
>
> Howard

STUDENTS Actors who work for free or whose salaries are deferred under an agreement with SAG might have full- or part-time jobs that limit their availability to your production. You might need to adapt your schedule to these constraints.

Exteriors

It is recommended that you begin the shoot with any exterior scenes. This general industry rule should be adhered to if possible. If you complete all the exterior scenes first, then when the company moves indoors, bad weather can no longer force you to change the planned schedule. If, on the other hand, you shoot all the interiors first, when the production moves outdoors, you will be at the mercy of the weather.

In this case, it would be advisable to keep at least one interior location or *cover set* available to move to in case of bad weather. Without a cover set, the production company has to shut down until the weather improves. A delay like this can be expensive as well as disruptive to your carefully organized schedule.

Night Shooting

It's best to consolidate all the night exteriors of each location. (Most night interiors can be shot during the day by blacking out the windows.) There are two schools of thought on how to schedule night exteriors. You can either shift the entire schedule over to nights and, instead of shooting from 6 a.m. to 6 p.m., shoot from 6 p.m. to 6 a.m., or you can organize the schedule to work on *splits*, meaning noon to midnight. This requires the company to shoot sunlight or exterior/day scenes the first half of the day and devote the second half of the shooting day to exterior/night shots. The nature of the material might dictate only one of these alternatives.

When scheduling night shooting, you must remember that the actors require 12 hours (per the SAG contract) between the end of one day and the beginning of the next. This period is referred to as *turnaround time*. This regulation means that you can't end a day shoot and immediately begin a night one and vice versa. Weekends are often used to make the transition from a day schedule to a night schedule or vice versa. Otherwise, the required turnaround time must be absorbed into the daily schedule.

SCHEDULING Be aware that night shoots are hard on the body, even if the crew requests a night routine. Don't expect the crew to work as efficiently at night as they would during the day. Reduce your expectations of how many scenes you'd like to accomplish in an hour, and factor this into the schedule.

Night exterior shoots are expensive and logistically challenging. Arranging for the amount of equipment needed to illuminate a night exterior is complicated. The smaller the shot, the better your chances to accomplish the scene.

Continuity of Sequences

Although you might not be able to shoot the entire project in its order in the script, it is recommended that you shoot sequences in continuity as much as possible. This allows the actors and the director to work through the dramatic arc of a scene naturally. It would be awkward and emotionally difficult to start the day's work with the end of an argument and then end with the beginning.

However, in filming interior scenes, try to complete as many shots as you can from each lighting setup. This is done by "shooting out" one side of the room before turning around and shooting with a new lighting setup. This might interfere with the continuity of the sequence, but it is standard procedure. It is also common sense. Having to keep changing lighting setups between each shot wastes time and energy.

Child Actors

There are strict rules governing the use of child actors. Generally, they can't work as many hours as adults can, and their parents or a teacher or social worker must be present during shooting if the child is missing school to be in the picture. Consult the SAG guidelines and child labor laws for more details.

A child's short attention span and limited energy can also be a major factor in shooting a scene. It might take longer to shoot a scene with a child, especially if the child is not a professional actor. Factor this into the schedule.

> *I remember one of our first ideas was to shoot in script order to make it easier for the kids. It's such a short script, I figured we could have the luxury to do that. I was afraid that if the kids got disoriented, they would get bored, confused, and tired. We did decide to do all the fantasy scenes on the first day. We thought that was a good way to get the kids really involved in the process. They got to do three costume changes, dress up as Robin Hood, wear the Civil War costumes, do the little fire engine thing. . . . We believed that if the first day seemed exciting and appealing, we could hold their interest and make the whole shoot seem like an adventure.*
>
> *It also worked out well for the costume person who had to come up from New York to fit the kids and iron all the costumes; she had to leave after two days to go back to New York for another job, so that was a good piece of planning.*
>
> Howard

Time of Year

The time of year when you are planning your production is an important consideration when scheduling exteriors. The amount of available daylight varies from summer to winter, the winter months having less available daylight, particularly in the north. To catch as much available light as possible for exteriors in winter, begin each day early.

Weather

The biggest variable in a production that features outdoor locations is the weather. Weather conditions such as extreme heat, cold, snow, rain, and strong winds always have an impact on exterior photography, slowing down the company's usual pace. Cold weather will naturally slow down the movement of people and equipment, and even more so at night. Extreme cold can affect the camera's mechanism, shorten the life of a battery, and damage sensitive video equipment. You can shoot in a moderate rain, but not at a normal pace.

Research natural weather conditions (rain, snow, hurricanes, tornadoes, etc.) for the time of year that you plan to shoot. The weather bureau puts out breakdowns for annual precipitation, and farmer's almanacs are amazingly accurate when it comes to weather prediction. As you get closer to your shoot date, see Weather.com (the Internet site for the Weather Channel) for up to seven-day forecasts. You should keep a permanent bookmark at this site. In addition, check the date when daylight saving time begins and ends.

There are three types of weather situations for which you should be prepared:

Light. Light rain, light snow, light fog, and so on are weather conditions that should not affect your shoot. Light rain stops and starts, and it is invisible to the camera lens as long as it is not back-lit. Light snow melts quickly. Keep the equipment and actors dry and continue shooting.

Medium. It rarely rains all day. Show up at your location and wait. It might stop.

Heavy. It is impossible to shoot in heavy weather, such as a storm. This is a good opportunity to move to a *cover set* (see Glossary).

Special Effects, Stunts, and Animals

Whenever the script requires a special effect, even something as simple as an active fireplace, special preparation and execution time must be added to the schedule. This guideline also applies to stunts and the use of animals. As a general rule, it always takes three to four times longer to prepare and shoot anything that is considered out of the ordinary. Special effects, stunts, and animals' parts should all be rehearsed long before the shoot. This preparation will give you a chance to meet the production schedule.

Crowd Sequences

It is advisable to consolidate crowd sequences. The organization, feeding, and wardrobing of large crowds of extras (also referred to as *background*) is a logistical challenge and a large expense. Additional personnel must often be hired to support the assistant directors, the costumers, and the hair and makeup artists. Police might even be required for traffic control. Proper communication often involves the use of bullhorns and walkie-talkies. Always schedule more time than you think you'll need when working with crowds.

Special Equipment

You might need to rent additional equipment for a specific sequence, such as a Steadicam, or dolly. Steadicams require the hiring of an operator in addition to the rig. Scenes requiring any special equipment should be consolidated to save money.

Turnaround, Setup Time, and Swing Crews

Transportation to and from the set, prelighting, set dressing, and construction are all factors that you should take into consideration when setting up the stripboard. For example, it can be frustrating if the production department settles on a schedule only to discover later that it will not coincide with the construction timetable. In this case, the art director should inform the production manager of the amount of time required to get the sets ready so that art department turnaround time becomes part of the equation.

Money can easily solve this sort of problem by allowing you to hire additional construction personnel. If money is tight, however, it will be back to the drawing board for the production staff to rearrange the schedule to accommodate this new information.

Much time can be saved if the production can afford to have a swing crew of electricians prerig the lights at an interior location. While the primary crew sleeps, the B team can set up the lights and "rough in" the lighting plan dictated by the director of photography. Then, when the A team arrives on the set, they merely tweak the lights, and the cameras can roll.

Novice producers usually have problems estimating how long it will take to move and set up grip and electrical equipment. Consult with as many experienced people as possible when scheduling your project. An experienced director of photography, gaffer, or key grip can be of enormous help in this area.

Animation

Animation requires its own set of scheduling parameters. Preproduction considerations include screenplay, storyboarding, creating the sound track, animatics, and then a rough animation. Production issues include lip-synch, textures, and lighting. Postproduction is all about rendering and compositing.

One takes the storyboards and makes a story real with the sound track. So you record both actors, you would read for your own use for animating later the sound track frame by frame, so you know exactly which syllable, which letter is sitting on which point in time, frame by frame. Alongside with that you would have a story reel. So you make a video of all your storyboards set to their corresponding time on the sound track, and you just watch your film without motion but just with the images of the storyboard and see if it makes sense. I do believe I did that a long time ago. After that you have your sound track broken down to frames. You decide exactly how long each shot would be. I think when I came to shoot Crazy Glue, *it was nearly edited in camera. I would just pick up the 16-mm Bolex, put it down, animate the shot, move it to the next cut and shoot from there, which is not how it's usually done, but that's how* Crazy Glue *was 80 percent done. Just shot in order.*

Tatia

In animation, a first recording of the dialogue is done for timing as the artist must match their creations with the actor's voice. This is referred to as a predub and is executed in a standard automatic dialogue replacement (ADR) facility. When the animation is completed, the actors may be brought back to rematch their voices.

Other Considerations

Examine your script for any special circumstances unique to your project that will have an impact on the schedule. Each script poses its own particular set of problems. Keep an eye out for any unusual scheduling challenges.

BEGINNING THE SCHEDULE

Must you keep all of these factors in mind at all times when creating a schedule? The answer is no. The right schedule for your project evolves over time. Begin with a rough draft that takes into account the major considerations, and then gradually factor in the issues that are relevant to your particular project. Each script has a unique set of organizational challenges. Don't expect to solve all of them in the first pass. The shooting schedule might not be finalized until the week or even the day before actual shooting begins.

In fact, it is not uncommon for the schedule to continue to change during principal photography. A lost location, a sick actor, or an unexpected weather condition could force the production unit to shift around scenes and even shooting days. Beginners might have to keep adjusting their schedules because they have overestimated how much they can shoot in a day.

CREATING THE SCHEDULE

Don't start scheduling actual shooting days until you have grouped all of the scenes in a logic that is governed by the 14 important guidelines just described. This will enable you to conceptualize the "big picture" before deciding how to structure each shooting day. Follow these general priorities for scheduling:

- Start with any fixed dates of which you are aware. These will become the anchors around which you must work.
- Group your locations together, but try to place the exteriors first.
- Factor in the actors' schedules.
- Factor in the day and night schedule if appropriate. Remember that 12 hours of turnaround time is required between days and nights. Use the weekend to make this transition.
- Identify any other special adjustments your project demands, such as special effects or crowd sequences.

Begin to form the strips into days to get a rough idea of how long it is going to take to shoot the picture. Start off with an easy day if you can. Don't schedule the climactic love scene before the actors have had a chance to work together.

Everything went smoothly for me, I thought, in terms of getting what I wanted in the shots, feeling they were working okay—until we got to the restaurant and I did the shot of her entrance. I just couldn't get it to work. I wanted to cover it all in one shot, but it felt like it was taking forever.

This was the first shot of the day. I began to panic. I felt that the time I was spending on the shot was eating into my already tight schedule. I was getting bogged down, and it threatened to put me behind, but I didn't want to settle for anything that wasn't right. It started off as a two-minute shot, so little by little, I eliminated business. Scotty started by asking for the salad, picking out the salad, speaking with the cook, etc. My problem was that I was looking at the scene in real time, not film time, which is death. Also, in a long take, one time the actors may work well, but the dolly is off. Another time the dolly hits the marks perfectly, but the focus puller misses his mark. We did eight takes, and during that time, the shot dropped from 2 minutes to 30 seconds.

Adam

MAKING THE DAY

How is a *day* defined? How do you know how many pages a day your unit will be able to complete? The phrase *make the day* is an industry term that refers to successfully completing photography on the scenes scheduled for a particular day. The production unit should get off to a good start by making the first couple of days and keeping on schedule. Remember that many members of the cast and crew might not have worked together before. Considering all the variables, going over schedule is easy to do. Successfully completing the first few days provides a psychological lift that bonds the unit and gives everyone confidence to complete the rest of the shoot.

Most feature films complete an average of between two and three script pages a day. Many low-budget features and television movies, on the other hand, average from five to ten pages a day. Student projects usually come in at around two pages a day. Remember that these are averages. The industry is governed by what it can afford. Television budgets are small, so the tight schedules reflect that fact.

If your budget will allow, set your sights on averaging two pages a day. This does not mean that you always end up with exactly two pages completed each day. There might be days when you can accomplish only two-eighths of a page of difficult action (Figure 4.2). There might also be days when you will be able to make five to ten pages. This is usually the case with dialogue scenes. Dialogue tends to take less time to shoot because it involves fewer lighting setups. Once the lights are in place, you can achieve a variety of shots quickly and efficiently.

13 INT GYM - DAY   13
    LONG: TRUMAN stands alone in the gym.

    CLOSE: His face burns. There is nothing he can say and no one to say it to.

    LONG: TRUMAN stands alone again.

    CLOSE: He bites his lip and starts to take a small step forward and then, in midstep, stops. Another pause, shorter than the last, as if is about to step in front of a speeding train. Then he wheels quickly around and is off like a shot, running for the rope.

    The CAMERA DOLLYS with him, as he speeds across the gym.

    HIS P.O.V.: as rushes headlong at the rope.

    THE CAMERA DOLLYS back with him as he leaps up and grabs hold of the rope. He swings back and forth once and then begins to climb upwards.

    CLOSE: TRUMAN struggles upwards.

    HIGH ANGLE: TRUMAN is nothing but an ant at the bottom.

                                                                CUT TO:

14 INT GYM - DAY   14
    INT. SAME - MOMENTS LATER.

    The gymnasium door opens and in steps TAYLOR. He picks up a sweatshirt, left lying near the door and then looks up. A smile breaks over his face.

                                                                CUT TO:

    15 - INT. SAME - SECONDS LATER   15

    HIGH ANGLE: TRUMAN struggles upwards.

                                                                CUT TO:

16 INT. SAME - MOMENTS LATER.   16
    The CAMERA TRACKS down the faces of entire gym class. They stand huddled near the door, staring silently upwards.

    LONG: TRUMAN nearing the top.

    CLOSE: He pulls himself up into FRAME and suddenly the tremendous NOISE of CHEERING fills the air.

    The CLASS is going wild. From down the hall comes sound MR. SPARROW approaching, barking angrily.

Figure 4.2 Shooting script from *Truman*.

At NYU, though it is probably true of any place, the first thing that occurred after settling on an idea was choosing a shooting date. The shooting date is so important because it gives you something definite, a tangible thing from which to work. From there I could create a timeline, a calendar which told me by November I should have a draft, by December I should be casting, by January I should have the locations lined up. Without that, you can lose your way and postpone endlessly.

I often saw students who were not set with their dates who'd write and write, and at the end of the semester they'd say, "I need to shoot now." They left themselves three weeks for preproduction and, consequently, were doing preproduction while shooting.

I think choosing a date and sticking to it is very important because it forces you to create a funnel where everything is marching toward that moment in time. It keeps you structured, keeps you organized, and really makes you focus in on something. It keeps you from letting anything slip.

Howard

Keep the Day under 12 Hours!

The two-page daily average should be accomplished in less than 12 hours. It is not wise to schedule longer days than this. A tired company works less effectively than one that's well rested. Too many long days will force the law of diminishing returns. The crew's performance as crew members execute difficult lighting setups and complicated camera moves diminishes as the day drags on.

Student productions start out with the best intentions of working within the 12-hour limit, but something usually happens during the shoot that slows down the day. An inexperienced crew will take longer than expected to execute lighting and camera setups. As a result, the director will need to simplify her shot list to make the day.

SHOOTING DURING PREPRODUCTION

It is sometimes necessary to be in production during preproduction. If an actor needs to appear on television during a scene, the video portion of the show must be recorded in advance of the shooting day. If you are shooting a scene that requires playback of an original song, the song must be recorded before the shoot. Playback, which is music piped onto the set for the actors and musicians to lip-sync to and mime, eliminates the need for a live recording. With a live recording, mistakes might slow down the production. With playback, the director knows that the song will be perfect each time.

Animation Lip-Sync

Lip-syncing is the process of making a character's mouth move so it looks like it is speaking. In Computer Graphics (CG) the animator will create multiple versions of a character's head with the mouth positioned in different phonemes. A phoneme is the shape a mouth makes when it is forming different sounds (e.g., a circular shape for an "oh" or closed lips for an "em"). Usually the animator will make expressions as well (happy, sad, etc.). The animator will then load the sound track into the 3D software and match the phonemes to the sound along the timeline. The software will use a process known a morphing or blend shape to make the transition smooth between phonemes.

So I recorded the voices during preproduction so I could lay out my storyboards and get a proper timing for the shoot.

Tatia

LOCKING THE SCHEDULE

The director dictates the pace of the film. The production schedule might be greatly influenced by the budget—that is, how many days you can afford. If money is not a major consideration, the number of scenes you can comfortably schedule in a day is influenced by the speed of the director and the director of photography. You might be lucky enough to work with a director who can knock off 30 setups in a day. It is important, in any case, that the director be closely involved in finalizing the schedule. She is responsible, after all, for shooting it.

All department heads should be consulted before you lock down the board, especially the director, the director of photography, the location manager, the assistant director, and the art director. It is customary for all the department heads to meet before the shoot to go over each day of the schedule. This is the final opportunity they have to recommend any changes.

It was a three-day shoot. There were things to organize, such as actors' schedules, when we could get in, how we would shoot the sequence. We knew that Grand Central would only give us the four hours a day, so we would need two days. And then a third day in the restaurant.

Adam

The director is the key person at this meeting because she is the one who is responsible for shooting the schedule. The assistant director is the second most important person because he is responsible for keeping everyone on schedule. The director must be confident that she can make each day. Any reservations she has should be addressed at this meeting. Once the schedule is finalized, it is published and distributed to the cast and crew as the working shooting schedule.

CALL SHEET

The call sheet is the distillation of the schedule. This single sheet of paper is handed to all cast and crew members the night before each day of shooting

CALL SHEET

Producer:

Date:

Director:

Title:

Set	Scenes	Cast	D/N	Pages	Location

Cast & Day Players	Part of	Makeup	Set-Call	Pick-up Time

Atmosphere & Extras	Set Call	Crew	Set Call

Advantage Schedule or Changes	Cover Set or Weather Alternative

Figure 4.3 Call sheet. Visit the companion Web site at www.focalpress.com/companions to download and print a copy of this form.

(Figure 4.3). If the shoot is only a few days, a call sheet might reflect the entire shooting period. The call sheet is a distillation of all pertinent information regarding the next shooting day, including call time, location, actors' call times, special equipment, crew call time, and scene shot list.

The director supplies the shot list segment of the call sheet. All the other information on the sheet is culled from the stripboard or production schedule and breakdown sheets. The shot list is the list of scenes to be recorded during the next day's production period. It is customary for the director to review the call sheet just before it is printed for distribution. Should the director want to change the order of the scenes to be shot, she has this last opportunity to do so.

If the order is to be changed, the director should do it before the day of the shoot. If it is changed on the day of the shoot, there is no time to change the calls for actors, the crew, and the equipment.

Each day, a schedule for the following day was printed up and distributed before we wrapped. It started out with a wakeup time, then loading vehicles, call time on the set, lunchtime, wrap, and finally home. We handed out one of those to every crew member. Additionally, any revisions we realized we had to make were included in that schedule. Every night after we went home, the director of photography, the assistant director, and the production manager (those being the key people) would go over the next day's schedule. We would talk about what we had initially intended to do and whether that was what we were still going to do. Could we foresee any new problems we hadn't anticipated? That's how we set up the schedule on a daily basis.

Howard

The director might want to change a shot list for several reasons:

- An actor will play a scene better at a certain time of the day.
- A scene needs to be completed from the previous day.
- A light or sound problem might influence the schedule.

SCHEDULING DOCUMENTARIES

Unlike the narrative form, documentaries are scheduled on a piecemeal basis. The scheduling of shoots is based on the availability of the subject or an event. For the most part, a documentary can be scheduled on weekends or on a day-to-day basis.

Some aspects of scheduling a documentary can be easy: Book the subject and the equipment for a particular day, and then shoot. Plan a full shooting day so as not to waste the equipment rental. If you own your own equipment (which many documentarians do), the scheduling is even easier. In contrast, if your subject is tied to specific dates and times of day, then it behooves you to be there by his or her side. This might require a more rigorous schedule than a narrative shoot.

I had to work around the schedules of my subjects. They were busy during weekdays, so I filmed them exclusively on weeknights and weekends. I tried not to schedule more than three interviews a day for our sake. Obviously, it didn't matter to them as they came in one at a time. I usually took about two hours with each person. They arrived, I explained the process to them, and I tried to make them comfortable while we adjusted the lights, and so on. I didn't want to feel rushed or to adopt an assembly-line approach.

Jan

STUDENT SCHEDULING TIPS

Break up the Shooting Schedule. It may be advisable to schedule your first production, if possible, not consecutively but over several weekends or smaller periods of time. This will enable you to gauge how well you are able to "make" the planned schedule and if not, make the necessary adjustments for the next sequence. It also will enable you to see your rushes before the next shoot date. If you are not happy with what you are getting either from the performances or from the camera and sound, it will allow you the time to make adjustments. For beginning filmmakers, this can sometimes prevent the crew from making the same mistakes throughout the entire shoot.

The downside of planning this way is that it makes it difficult to create momentum with your crew. It may take a couple of days for the production unit to gain a rhythm and feel comfortable with one another. Student productions may, in fact, have little choice in this matter. If actors are not being paid and have day jobs during the week, then weekends may be the only time available to them to work.

Schedule Reshoots Ahead of Time. Assume that you will need to reshoot some of your project either because it didn't come out the way you expected or because you weren't able to get it the first time around due to unexpected problems or an unrealistic schedule. Warn everyone that reshooting might be required to ensure that your crew and actors will be available. Make sure to determine the schedules of cast and crew members after the shoot. Finally, schedule reshoots far enough in advance that you are able to view all the rushes before you return to production.

In all my films, I've never had the possibility to go back to any of the subjects because they've been location shoots all over the country. I am used to working that way. The whole notion of pickups in documentary has been completely moot for me in my work. We have never done it. The only kind of subsequent material would be stills or archival footage, but no more live shooting after the shooting period. Period.

Jan

Make Use of Available Resources. Review the schedule with your production instructor or other experienced personnel as many times as possible during this process. Most students and beginners start off with unrealistic expectations of what they can achieve in a day. They are usually too ambitious. This enthusiasm must be constantly tempered with doses of realism, common sense, and experience.

Consolidate Locations. Your schedule, limited by money and available resources, might not accommodate all the locations the script dictates, forcing you to consolidate existing locations. By combining several locations into one, you can simplify your production needs without necessarily compromising the requirements of the story.

Schedule MOS Days. If a sequence does not absolutely require location sound, you might be able to save valuable time by shooting without recording sound on the set. In the industry, this is called *MOS*. Not having to wait for planes to pass or annoying neighbors to quiet down will shave minutes from each take and allow the production company to schedule more scenes in a day.

Don't Be Afraid to Postpone the Shoot Date. You might sense that the preproduction period is being unnecessarily rushed. Perhaps you are having problems finding the right cast, crew, or locations as the shoot date approaches. Perhaps it is your first production, and you want everything to be right. By pushing the shoot date back, you might lose a specific location or actor, but what you will gain is a smoother shoot (and a little peace of mind).

Before you think about postponing the shoot date, however, make sure that you don't have any fixed dates that are necessary for your production, such as a parade (which obviously can't be rescheduled) or a special event that plays prominently in your story.

COMPUTERS AND PRODUCTION

Computer programs have been developed that facilitate the scheduling and budgeting process. Scriptwriting, script breakdown, scheduling, and budgeting have been combined into one piece of software (see the Bibliography). This allows you to see clearly how script changes affect the schedule and the budget. Most of the professional productions today use these programs. They have become an indispensable part of organizing a production.

DIRECTOR
Determining Coverage

The director might be very involved in the process of setting up a schedule, as described in the first half of this chapter. Just as the producer factors into the schedule actor availability, prerigging, and a desire to shoot out locations, so, too, he must consider the director's needs. The director discusses with the producer her intended pace and approach for the first day of shooting.

The director is integral to the scheduling process in that she must be the one to finally say, "I can shoot this script on this schedule." A director's main responsibility is to make the best film or video possible based on the script. Her secondary charge is to shoot the pages scheduled for each day. Making the pages means ending a day of production having reached the goal, set during preproduction, of that portion of the script.

The director sets the pace. If you are slow, then the shoot will be slow. Your energy impels the cast and crew. It is as if the energy of the director is translated through the cast and crew and onto the screen. Therefore, an understanding of the schedule involves an acknowledgment of one's capacities. Take care of your body with ample sleep and nutritious foods so that you will have the stamina necessary for the grueling pace of a shoot.

COVERAGE = TIME = SCHEDULE

The director determines how a sequence is to be staged and shot. Coverage is the number and types of shots used to record a sequence. Although the plan for shooting is determined during preproduction, on set, as the scene takes on a life of its own, the director may alter or enhance the planned coverage. She might base her plan on conversations with the screenwriter, art director, director of photography, storyboard artist, editor, or indeed anyone who has a good idea about an approach to a sequence. The final decisions, however, rest with the director.

Each shot is best communicated to the department heads through storyboards, though they often change once the cast and crew arrive on the set. Therefore, it behooves the director to indicate to the producer where she plans anything out of the ordinary, including crane shots, dolly moves, and extreme high angle shots.

A producer might assume that a dialogue sequence of five pages can be executed in a single day. However, if the director plans several complicated dolly moves to cover the scene, one day might not be adequate. Conversely, a seven-page dialogue scene can be shot in one day if the photography is kept simple or is planned as one or two long takcs. Remember, complicated dolly moves for every shot invite overtime.

The scene can be photographed or covered with a combination of master shot, minimasters, over-the-shoulder shots, and one or two closeups, or the director can light and rehearse one or two complicated dolly moves and shoot the entire scene toward the end of the day after exhaustive technical rehearsals.

If the scene is excessively storyboarded (too many shots per sequence), and especially if any one thing goes wrong (an actor arrives late, fuses are blown, etc.), then the potential to go over schedule increases. This is not to suggest that you compromise your shot list; instead, make certain that it reflects a practical schedule.

A scene that reads on paper like an easy sequence might take on an entirely different character when envisioned by the director. For example, one director might shoot a scene in which a woman is stabbed to death in a shower in one take. After the scene is lit, she might need only 10 minutes for that one shot. On the other hand, a director such as Alfred Hitchcock might design a more stylized scene that involves 88 setups and requires three days to shoot. (You'll find more on coverage in Chapter 12, "Camera.")

Each scene was numbered, as well as the shots within the scene. We then started putting the shots in the order of how we would shoot them. As it went along, there were constant little changes, based on things like the availability of the fire net or putting in a variable-speed motor and what day could we get these items for the cheapest rate. We made several

revisions on the schedule as we moved closer toward the shoot.

When most of our unknowns were resolved, we gave each shot a time value—how long we estimated the setup and execution of the shot would take—and we broke that down into 15-minute intervals. You could say something took two hours and 15 minutes, or 45 minutes, or a half an hour. So hopefully, we knew within 15 or 20 minutes where we should be each day. I was very, very concerned about keeping my promise to the parents that the filming be only between 8 a.m. and 6 p.m.

We were fairly tight on the time, so we tried to be honest with ourselves about how long each scene would take. Based on this kind of macro to micro approach of when events had to happen and when we wanted them to happen, we could finally print up a schedule about which we felt very, very confident.

Howard

THE FIRST DAY

The first day of principal photography is very important because it sets the tone for the entire shooting period. On the first day, the cast and crew are galvanized behind the director's leadership. A director who can instill confidence and make the first day's pages quickly earns the respect and cooperation of the crew. The director can approve a schedule with one of three approaches:

- *Day 1 is very light*. An easy first day gives the cast and crew time to build up a momentum and allows for the kind of first-day mistakes that are inevitable.
- *Day 1 is an average day*. Every day is important, so a day that has an average amount of pages to shoot is a fair day. This choice does not treat the first day as anything special.
- *Day 1 is heavy*. A deliberately heavy day in which the cast and crew have to hit the ground running is an opportunity to galvanize the company. Deadweight becomes obvious very quickly.

CONTINGENCY PLANS FOR OVERAGES

If the director falls behind on day 1, she will be playing catchup throughout the shoot. Going over sometimes means returning to a location, another company move, additional days of principal photography, and more money.

Although the director is shooting a movie and not a schedule, there is psychological strength in meeting the day's pages. Playing catchup is a drain on the director. Often, to get back on schedule, she will condense a scene or make judicious cuts in the script.

THINGS CHANGE

The schedule might constantly change during preproduction and production. The director needs to be flexible. She should memorize the schedule as well as the script so that she can make quick adjustments to her plan.

KEY POINTS

- The efficient use of time is directly related to production value.
- Memorize the schedule so that you can adjust easily to alterations.
- Settle on the priorities and coverage that will determine the basic approach to the schedule.
- If possible, shoot exteriors first because of weather variables.
- Shoot out interior locations if possible. It is not cost-efficient to have to come back to an interior location and relight it.

chapter five

Budget

In total I spent around $2,000 from start to finish. Of course, my shooting ratio was one to one.

Tatia

PRODUCER
Creating a Budget

Now that you have some idea of how long it will take to shoot your project and what elements will cost you money, creating a budget will be that much easier. If you have only so much money available or have set a limit on the amount of money you feel comfortable spending, put these figures aside for the moment and concentrate on creating a realistic budget for the script you want to produce. After the ink dries, see how your original figures compare to your financial limitations.

Even if you have all the money in the world, it doesn't make sense to spend it all on one picture. Throwing money at a project will teach you nothing about proper fiscal management, and it will leave you less money for your next endeavor. The goal is to get the most bang for your buck. Spend only what you need to spend.

The script and the budget are the two cornerstones of the production. The script is the creative bible, and the budget is the financial bible. The budget defines the parameters of what can and cannot be accomplished. It contains a complete and detailed breakdown of what it will cost to finish the entire project. This breakdown includes all projected expenses for preproduction, production, and postproduction. Each and every line item, whether it is photocopying scripts or securing a location, has a price and must be itemized, categorized, and ultimately accounted for.

Script and budget are inextricably tied to one another. Script decisions become budget decisions. For example, the director wants to add a car chase. Before the decision can be made as to whether to include the sequence, a budget must be prepared that itemizes all the expenses associated with the chase, such as the cost of the vehicles, stunt drivers, extra camera crews and cameras, water and fire trucks, police, standby physician and ambulance, traffic monitors, and, of course, feeding and possibly housing all these people for the days it will take to execute the sequence. The artistic value of the chase can then be weighed against its cost:

- Is the creative impact of the sequence worth the price?
- Can the present budget absorb the extra cost?
- If not, can the producer raise the additional money?

Money management performs an important role in picture-making and can play havoc with one's idea of "artistic freedom." Sooner or later, it dawns on every film- and videomaker that artistic freedom comes with a price: You must pay for every decision, every choice. This is an ironclad and immutable fact of life in the media arts. Even the lone videomaker shooting on the run with a camcorder has to eat and purchase tape stock.

The producer or production manager is responsible for drafting the budget. If you cannot afford to hire a production manager or an experienced producer, you will have to put together a budget yourself, even though the word *budget* may make you nervous.

> *I planned to spend about $6,500, and I came in at $6,000. This covered production.*
>
> Howard

However, accomplishing this seemingly onerous task will enable you truly to understand the nuts and bolts of how a production actually runs because, like it or not, it runs on money. Putting together the financial foundation of your project can be an exciting challenge. Through the mastery of learning what things cost and why comes the satisfaction of knowing that you have gotten the best deals without skimping on the needs of the script.

STUDENTS

Because this book is written for independents (who lack the resources of a film program) as well as film and video students, we approach the budget from a perspective that is valid for all short projects. Although as a student, you might not pay for labor or equipment (other than through your tuition), knowing their commercial worth fosters a healthy respect for these resources and prepares you for the realities of the professional world after school. If your school provides some of the line items for your project, such as stock and equipment, it is a good exercise to budget these items as deferred figures. That way, you will be aware of the full cost of a production.

THE BUDGET FORM

The standardized budget form simplifies working up a budget. This form demystifies the process somewhat by outlining all potential expenses. The short budget form is separated into two parts. The first part is the top sheet (Figure 5.1). The top sheet offers a financial overview or summary of all the major budget categories, which are also called *accounts*. The money for each category is placed in its own account, and each budget category is given its own account number for easy reference.

The second part of the short budget form, called a *detailed budget*, is a complete breakdown of each category (see our Web site). The detailed budget is completed first, and the total for each category is then entered under the appropriate budget column on the top sheet. For example, the total for the category "Equipment" on the top sheet reflects the cost of all the camera, sound, lighting, grip, and special equipment required for the production of the picture.

If you are creating a budget for the first time, you will need a thorough understanding of each department and how to evaluate its needs. Computing an accurate figure for each category requires an investigation into the process, as well as prices and resources available at the time and place of your shoot.

The top sheet, which serves as your complete "budget-at-a-glance," summarizes all costs related to manufacturing the picture. The following information can be gleaned from the top sheet:

- Subtotals of all categories
- Above-the-line and below-the-line costs
- Contingency
- Grand total

Film and video budgets are typically divided into two sections: above-the-line and below-the-line. This "line" separates two fundamentally different kinds of costs associated with a production. Above-the-line costs include fees negotiated for the producer, director, script, and actors. Below-the-line costs are all expenses related to the rest of the personnel and resources required to manufacture the picture.

Above-the-Line Costs

Consider above-the-line costs to be flat fees, or amounts that are negotiated for the run of the picture. For example, the director might receive $2,000 for her services, the writer will sell the script for $1,000, and an actor can be hired for the duration of the show for $3,000. These fees are normally paid out in installments rather than at a weekly or daily rate—for example, 25 percent of the negotiated salary on signing the contract, 25 percent on the first day of principal photography, 25 percent on the last day of principal photography, and the final installment of 25 percent on completion of the work.

001 Script and Rights

As mentioned in Chapter 2, securing rights means negotiating with an author, the author's agent, the author's estate, or the author's publisher for permission to use his or her material as the basis for your short work. It is imperative that you secure the story rights if your short film or video is based on a copyrighted work. There are only three exceptions to this rule:

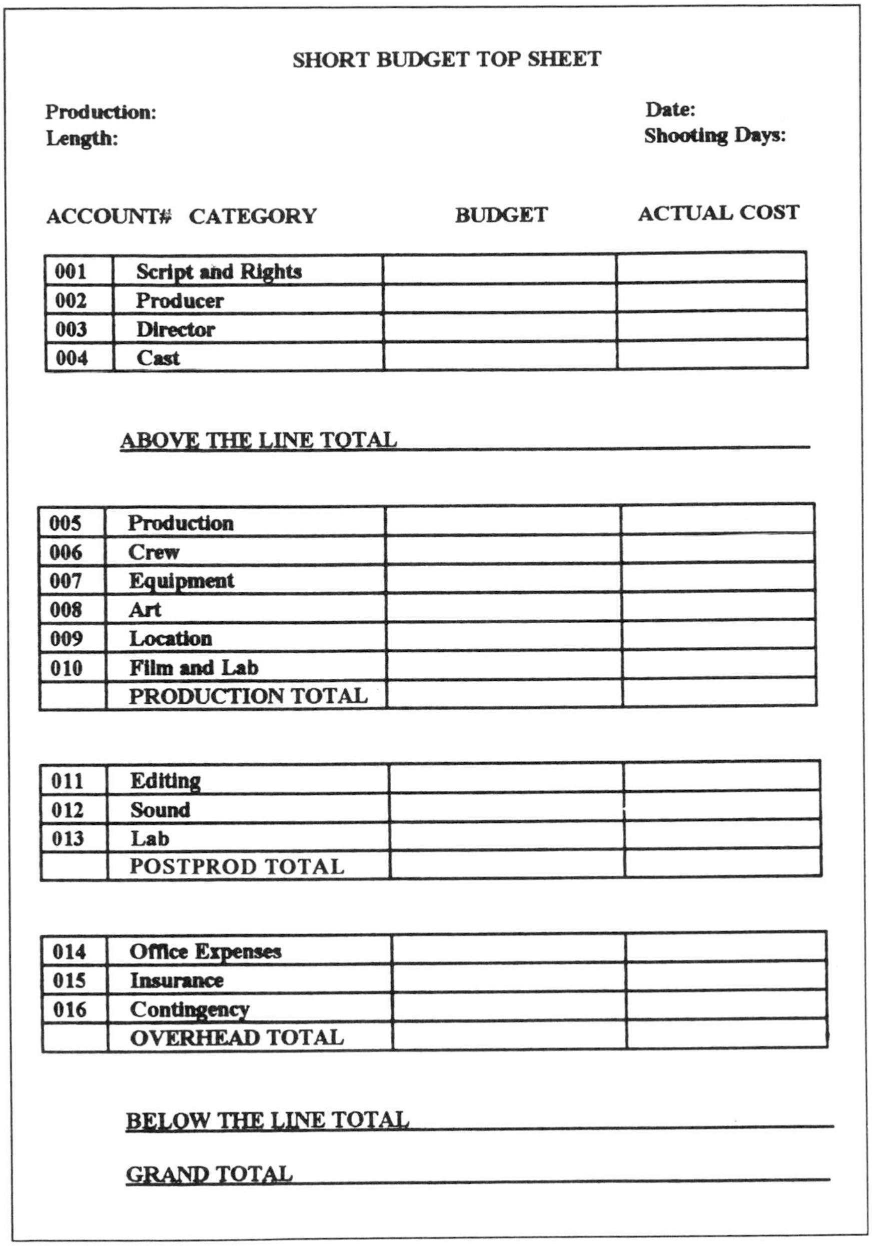

SHORT BUDGET TOP SHEET

Production: Date:
Length: Shooting Days:

ACCOUNT#	CATEGORY	BUDGET	ACTUAL COST
001	Script and Rights		
002	Producer		
003	Director		
004	Cast		

ABOVE THE LINE TOTAL _____

ACCOUNT#	CATEGORY	BUDGET	ACTUAL COST
005	Production		
006	Crew		
007	Equipment		
008	Art		
009	Location		
010	Film and Lab		
	PRODUCTION TOTAL		

ACCOUNT#	CATEGORY	BUDGET	ACTUAL COST
011	Editing		
012	Sound		
013	Lab		
	POSTPROD TOTAL		

ACCOUNT#	CATEGORY	BUDGET	ACTUAL COST
014	Office Expenses		
015	Insurance		
016	Contingency		
	OVERHEAD TOTAL		

BELOW THE LINE TOTAL _____

GRAND TOTAL _____

Figure 5.1 The top sheet of a short budget. Visit the companion Web site at www.focalpress.com/companions to download and print a copy of the "Short Budget Top Sheet."

You Are the Author of the Work. If you have written an original piece, you own the rights to it. To register your copyright, write to the Library of Congress (see the Bibliography) for a registration form. There is a fee.

You Do Not Intend to Market the Final Product. Legal action can be taken against you only if you use copyrighted material without securing the rights and the project is sold or money changes hands. A film or video made for a class or screened in a noncommercial venue does not violate existing copyright laws. Consider the marketing plans for your piece, and keep in mind that securing rights after you have completed the project might be difficult, expensive, or even impossible. Copyright laws apply to music as well. If you are making a television commercial and want to give the client an idea of how it might sound, you can use any music you like for the promotional reel. However, when the commercial is approved, before entering it into the marketplace, you must purchase the music or replace it with original music.

The Material Is in the Public Domain. An author's work sometimes becomes public property 50 years after his or her death. The Bible and the works of Shakespeare, Dickens, and Twain are all available at no cost. Be aware, however, that an author's heirs can extend the copyright of his or her work. An entertainment lawyer can perform a title search to check on the material's copyright status.

002 Producer/003 Director

If the producer or director is paid a salary, whether it is cash up front or a deferred sum, the amount should be entered in the budget. If no salary is involved, write in either "N/A" (not applicable) or "0.00."

004 Cast

This category refers to everyone who performs in your project, including principals, bits, and extras. Payment for these actors ranges from nothing to union wages and more. During casting, you might find that the actor best suited for an important part is a union member. In this case, you might decide to pay for the security of knowing that the role is well cast. Whether you pay for your cast or not, it is advisable to be familiar with the cost of union labor. You might not have to work with Screen Actors Guild (SAG) actors on this picture, but this union will no doubt play a large role in most of your future projects.

The Screen Actors Guild. When you use union talent, you must sign a contract with the union or guild. Becoming a signatory with the Screen Actors Guild—which also covers the American Guild of Variety Artists (AGVA), the American Federation of Television and Radio Actors (AFTRA), and Actor's Equity stage performers—is easy. Call SAG and speak to a representative. The guild will send the appropriate forms, and as long as you abide by the SAG Codified Agreement, you will be allowed to hire union talent.

Read the agreement carefully. The Screen Actors Guild rules governing rates, penalties, per diems, overtime, and so on are spelled out in detail. Play by the rules, or you might have to pay penalties later. On occasion, actors tell the producer that they are willing to "fudge" their time cards without informing the union, but then turn around and report the inequities.

Nonunion Talent. The only way around union rules is to hire nonunion talent. With nonunion talent, you can negotiate any deal you like with the actors. If you are working under a SAG agreement, you can only hire union talent. If you can obtain a waiver to hire nonunion actors, they will not be eligible to join the guild after working on your production if this is their first film job. The Taft–Hartley rule stipulates that after their second professional acting stint, they will be eligible to join the union.

There is a good reason why SAG is such a strong union. Its members are familiar with a difficult craft. They understand their duties and act like professionals. They are skilled in developing a character, listening to other actors, hitting marks, memorizing lines, and pacing themselves for long hours. Nonunion talent might not possess these skills.

STUDENTS

Some film schools have made special arrangements with the union for salary deferment. If your picture sells, you must compensate the actor before you repay yourself for the cost of making the film or video. For example, if you employ an actor for one day, you "owe" him or her one day of *scale* (minimum salary), which is approximately $700 ($2500 a week). If the film never sells, then you need not pay the actor anything. If you do sell the film, though, your SAG bill will be $700 for that one actor. Keep this in mind as you schedule talent, because there is no need to run up a big bill and have actors wait around the set if they are not needed. The Taft–Hartley rule, which allows an actor to join the guild after a second professional gig, does not apply to the student–SAG agreement.

Below-the-Line Costs

Whereas above-the-line personnel are usually paid a flat fee, below-the-line personnel are paid a weekly or daily rate. In a short film, there might very well be no fees, except possibly deferred fees, payable from profit. All other direct and deferred costs are reflected in the below-the-line section of the budget. Here is a formula for calculating the salary or rental cost for the picture:

Days at x rate + prep and wrap = fee

Basic Decisions

Before you can begin to put down numbers, you must make some basic decisions about the nature of your production. Every decision has a financial repercussion and will affect the hard costs of your project. Your decisions may change for a variety of reasons. For example, you might have to scale down your project to accommodate what you can raise, or you might find you have more money to spend than you had anticipated. Ultimately, your final budget will reflect what you can afford.

Will you shoot your picture on film or video? This fundamental decision will have an impact on cost, equipment, choice of crew, and the "look" of the final product. It costs more to shoot film than video. Traditional film postproduction had always been less expensive than linear video. Nonlinear computer systems have tipped the balance the other way. Shooting film, editing digital, and finishing in film are more expensive than traditional film post.

Video might allow greater shooting ease and flexibility, but the final product might have limited screening possibilities. Video can be screened on a monitor or projected by a video projection system. The image on video projection (unless with a high-end system) becomes progressively washed out the longer the throw, or distance, to the screen. It does not compare with the quality of film projection and has yet to reach a similar size. This will all change. *High-definition television* (HDTV) offers an image that is sharper and denser, making large projection of the video image more viable, and the shift toward *digital projection systems* is growing.

There is also the option of transferring the final product from video to film. This process is discussed in Chapter 18. These options should be thoroughly investigated beforehand.

How are you planning to edit your project? With the advent of digital nonlinear postproduction, the beginner is faced with many choices (see Part III). A good starting point is to decide what format you want to end up with, film or video. It was simpler when film to film and tape to tape were the only alternatives. These two options are easier to forecast and budget. However, if you are planning to shoot on film, edit digitally, and match back to film, there are many variables that, if not worked out in advance, can create unneeded complications and extra cost. For example, will you order "video dailies" (direct from the negative) from the lab, or transfer a film work print to video (more expensive)? Will you want the lab to *sync up* the dailies (more expensive), or will your editor do it? Filmmakers used to traditional negative matching should thoroughly research the costs in matching back to film from video.

If you are shooting a lot of footage (either in film or video), digitized video requires a great deal of memory. If you are planning to edit on a computer-based system, you will need a lot of hard drive space. If you plan to shoot video, traditional linear editing could makes sense if your project consists of long pieces of footage strung together with straight cuts (no effects).

By the time this edition comes out, there will be more choices and digital memory will continue to come down in price. Our advice: Do your homework. Decide what format you want to end up with and work backward. The goal is to end up with a game plan that supports your artistic vision and that is in line with the amount of money you have to spend.

Discover the format needs of the market you are interested in targeting: theatrical, nontheatrical, network, cable, festivals, Quicktime movie, streaming video, etc. (See Chapter 19, "Distribution," for more information.) What steps do you need to take *in advance* to be sure the movie is suitable for these outlets? Explore how the use of video might exclude you from some avenues of distribution. Consider shooting in video and transferring the final cut to film. This process is expensive, but it is an excellent avenue for the documentary, where shooting stock and processing can be limited by your budget.

If you choose to shoot on film, what format should you select? The two basic film formats are 16-mm and 35-mm. Some people still work in super-8-mm even though fewer labs process it and the equipment is harder to rent.

The cost of shooting in 35-mm is prohibitive for most beginners. It has a wonderful look, but to get 10 minutes of film, you have to shoot more than double the footage of 16-mm (1,000 feet of 35-mm equals approximately 400 feet of 16-mm), and 35-mm production equipment is expensive to rent.

For most beginners, 16-mm is the preferred film format. Over the past several years, Kodak and Fuji have come out with superb new 16-mm fine-grained film stocks with wide exposure latitudes, enabling them to be shot in low light.

If you need a 35-mm print for distribution but can't afford to shoot 35-mm, then super-16-mm is an option. It can be enlarged, or blown up, to 35-mm. Because there aren't many super-16 projectors, consider super-16 only if your goal is a 35-mm print without the expense of shooting a 35-mm camera negative. (Super-16 is discussed in Chapter 12, "Camera.")

Another decision that can have a financial impact on your budget is whether to shoot in color or black and white; 16-mm black-and-white raw stock is less expensive than color, but there are fewer labs that regularly process it. One lab known to excel in black-

and-white processing is Alpha Cine in Seattle. (See our Web site for additional black-and-white laboratories.)

If you decide to shoot on video, what format should you select? The video market is changing at such a rapid rate that whatever this book recommends could quickly become obsolete. However, digital video (DV) is now occupying a predominant position as the consumer video digital format. High-end DV systems such as Digital Betacam and DVCPRO offer superb video images, but it is the less expensive MiniDV cameras that are having an impact on student and low-budget production. These small, lightweight cameras achieve excellent quality, and their images can now be imported directly into the computer via IEEE-1394 (Firewire) for editing (more about this in Chapter 16).

Nevertheless, analog formats such as Betacam SP, Hi-8, Super VHS, and even VHS are still viable alternatives. Research the ever-expanding video market. Consider the aesthetic and the practical considerations of one format over another and the audio capabilities as well.

Do you want to mix formats? Nonlinear computer controlled editing systems have made it possible for film- and videomakers to mix DV, Hi-8, S-VHS, or Betacam SP with 16-mm, super-16-mm, or super-8 film. These multiple formats can be edited together and the finished project outputted to video and transferred to film if so desired.

Profit, Negative Cost, and Deferred Fees. *Profit* is defined as the money the production company receives after it recoups the negative cost. The negative cost is the cost of making a film or video project, from preproduction through a final print. If an individual is promised money for his or her services to be paid from the profit generated by the project, these fees are termed deferred. *Deferred* fees are not guaranteed. An individual or service company can work for no upfront money, opting to take their pay from the profits. If there are no profits, they will never see any money.

Film-developing laboratories often offer another option for payment. They sometimes agree to develop and process the negative film for no up-front money. If a laboratory has faith in your project, it might be willing to wait until you can generate enough funds to pay the bill. This type of deferment is simply a postponement of the bill.

005 Production Department

A good production manager and assistant director are worth their weight in gold, especially if the director is a novice. These people keep the production running smoothly and on budget. Experienced production and crew members can be hired for an up-front salary, a deferred salary, or a combination of the two. Inexperienced crew members might work for free merely to gain experience.

006 Crew

The size of your crew will determine a large part of your daily production costs—that is, how many people you need to pay, feed, transport, or house (if it is a distant location) while the picture is in production. It is therefore extremely important that you decide how many crew members are essential to support the demands of the script. (Refer to Chapter 6, "Crewing," for the 3–30 rule.)

The director might have certain specific requests regarding the size of the crew. She might prefer to work as light as possible, or perhaps she feels secure only with more bodies around her. Documentary crews are by nature small, but some fiction directors prefer this approach as well. There are several factors to consider when making this basic decision.

Elaborateness of the Production. In the next chapter, we list many of the important positions that are necessary for executing a well-run production. These positions represent the actual duties that must be performed on a set. Of course, not all productions are alike, but particular individuals are essential to ensure a smoothly run shoot, no matter how modest the scale.

It is logical that a two-character piece shot in a small apartment will make fewer technical demands than one shot during a high school basketball game. You can double and triple up on many positions, but don't think that you can get away with less than you need for something so "seemingly easy" as the two-character piece. The success of a single shot, whether in the apartment or at the high school basketball game, requires that many technical chores be performed perfectly on every take. *The Lunch Date* had a crew of five, *Truman* was shot with a crew of 10, *Crazy Glue* had a crew of one to eight, depending on art direction, and *Mirror Mirror* had a crew of two.

Stage versus Location. Some basic decisions will have an immediate impact on your crew requirements. The first is whether you will be shooting on a stage, in a practical location (an existing site), or both. Having to design, construct, and dress a set requires crew members whom you will not need if the entire production is shot in a practical location. (See Chapter 8, "Art Direction," for details.)

Union versus Nonunion Crew. If you can hire a union crew, you are usually guaranteed to get your money's worth. These are highly skilled and trained individuals prepared to perform under the stressful time constraints of large and small projects. Union minimum rates are available in *The Producer's Masterguide* or *Brook's Standard Rate Book* (see the Bibliography for details). It might surprise you how much even "scale" (minimum salary) is for most of the crew positions on a set. To keep this in perspective, Local 600 (camera guild) rates are as follows:

	Daily	Weekly
Director of photography	$653	$2,787
Camera operator	$509	$2,043
First assistant	$333	$1,348
Second AC	$262	$1,244
Film loader	$220	N/A

But keep in mind that although these are decent minimum rates, anyone on a production team might work only six months out of the year.

Learn about union work regulations. Such items as meal penalties, overtime, double overtime, and golden time can greatly inflate the budget. The union code of regulations and ethics should serve as a model for your production behavior, even if you do not use union labor. These regulations were developed to protect workers from exploitation and to guarantee extra payment if they are required to work additional hours.

Nonunion crew workers range in experience from recent film school graduates to the seasoned professional. The pay scale for nonunion labor is usually based on what the market will bear and on the crew member's experience. Everything is negotiable. Many directors of photography and production mixers work with their own equipment, so the price they quote includes labor and equipment (or, as it is sometimes called, their *kit*).

What you can expect is a flat rate per day, per week, or for the run of the show. The rate should be based on an agreed "day" of so many hours (usually 12). Because there are no nonunion regulations defining overtime pay, there should be some agreement about compensation for extra-long days. The 12-hour cap doesn't have to be strictly adhered to, but if abused, it can cause bad feelings that won't work to your advantage in the long run. Pushing the crew too hard without giving something back is considered exploitation. In addition, if the crew is too exhausted to work

effectively, you will reach the point of diminishing returns.

Credit and Experience in Lieu of Compensation (CELC). If you can find experienced crew members who want to make the jump from their current position to a more advanced position, such as a 2nd assistant director who wants to work as a 1st assistant director or a location manager who wants to try her hand as a production manager, you might obtain their services for free. The production benefits from their general experience, and they benefit by gaining specific experience in a new position.

Animation Crew. The first thing and most important thing a producer should know about animation is that it takes time—lots of time. Animation can add beautiful and compelling visuals to your piece, but it will require a different, more deliberate, way of working than live action.

Note that the time to experiment or make changes is during the boarding or animatic phase. After this point, hundreds of hours may go into the creation of even a relatively short scene. If you are paying the animators by the hour, changes after this point will be extremely expensive. If there is a flat fee on the job, multiple large changes to fully animated scenes will deteriorate a working relationship. On the other hand, an experienced animator will expect the storyboarding process to be rather fluid and subject to hours of discussion, so don't worry about expressing all of your concerns and ideas at that time.

Documentary Crew. Documentary crews are usually small and mobile. They require a director of photography and a production mixer who can move quickly and efficiently. Assistants can be employed to help set up lights and sound equipment and to control traffic.

> *I did sound on the shoots, and we always went out as a two-person crew, including on* Mirror Mirror. *We never had more than two people on location.*
> Jan

When Do You Need Them? The "Producer" section of Chapter 10 contains a detailed week-by-week preproduction schedule that indicates when particular crew members should begin work. There are no absolutes in this area, but this schedule can serve as a guide.

007 Equipment

Before approaching a rental house, you need to have some idea of the size of your equipment package. The following are some of the primary factors that will influence this decision:

Director's Visual Plan for the Picture. The director's ideas for the project might include the use of a dolly or some other elaborate equipment such as a Steadicam, jib arm, or crane. Eventually, you might discover that you cannot afford these items, but it is still wise to get an idea of their cost. It might be possible to negotiate a few days' rental of a dolly as part of a larger equipment package.

Size of Interiors that Must Be Lit. Your equipment package should accommodate all lighting requirements dictated by the script. You might need to scale down some of the lighting packages or else change the script to find a balance. Often, when the cost of a lighting package is examined, the all-important night scene easily can be shifted to an all-important day scene. In any case, it is a good idea to pad this area, because you don't want to get caught with too little money for grip and electric.

Special Equipment Requirements. Identify and budget the specialty rigs that the script demands, such as car mounts (if there are many driving scenes) and zoom lens motors. Now is the time to explore different equipment options and their cost. There are imaginative ways to shoot people talking in cars without elaborate rigs and slow motor zooms.

Ability to Work with Small Lighting Packages. The ability of the director of photography (DP) to work with small lighting packages can't be judged until you begin hiring, but it is good to know what you can afford so you can approach potential DPs with realistic expectations of the kind of equipment with which they will be working. If your DP is comfortable with the limitations of your budget and doesn't demand more lights, it is a good sign that you have hired the right person.

Deals You Will Be Able to Negotiate. Once you have determined the equipment required for the shoot, shop for a rental house. You can negotiate a deal at a special rate if you rent all your equipment from one source. Besides the big items like the camera, dolly, lights, and dolly track, you must allocate money for expendable items such as construction materials, bounce cards, gels, and diffusion material. (See the "Producer" section in Chapter 12, "Camera," for more about rental houses.)

It is best to price a number of equipment packages. Think of it as A, B, and C lists. The A list is the wish list, and the C list is the make-do list. The B list stands as a compromise between what you would like to have and what you can realistically afford.

008 Art Department

The art director supervises the team that is responsible for the total look of the picture. Props, wardrobe, set dressing, set construction, hair, and makeup all fall under the auspices of the art department. This catchall category also includes many items customized for your show, such as animals, special effects, and picture cars. A small-scale project might only need or be able to afford one to three people to handle this important area. Much depends on the requirements of the script and what you can make do with, given your limited budget.

A number of factors will affect how you approach the budget for this department. They include the following:

Script Requirements. The breakdown sheets provide you with a list of the props, wardrobe, and special hair and makeup required for the picture. From this starting point, you can begin pricing these items. The script of *The Lunch Date* called for the protagonist to wear a mink stole. This means renting or borrowing one, unless you are lucky enough to hire an actor who has one of her own and is willing to wear it for the show.

> *I said to the wardrobe designers, "Here's $1,200. You can take out of it what you want, and pay yourself what's left over." Basically that worked. They paid themselves $400, and used $800 for the costumes.*
>
> Howard

Sets that Must Be Built. Set construction—renting a stage, building sets, and dressing them—is a big-ticket item. Set construction is labor-intensive work and requires building supplies such as lumber, canvas, nails, and paint. There are ways to economize in this area, such as redressing already built sets, but there is no getting around the extra costs compared to working with practical locations. Because of the costs involved, the producer traditionally oversees set construction directly.

Amount of Set Dressing Required. How a location is to be dressed doesn't usually show up in the script. The writer might describe the general look or feel of a room without going into much detail. Set dressing comprises the objects that make up the world your characters inhabit. It is different from props, which are described in the script, but is no less important. Set dressing can come from many sources, including the actors themselves. A found location might already have personal items that are suitable for your picture, or it might have to be stripped down and dressed from scratch.

The Art Director. How experienced and frugal your art director is will have an impact on how much you get for your money. Inexpensive building materials and frequent trips to thrift shops can save money for the production.

Although this category is budgeted before the shoot, it should be well padded. Many unanticipated changes or necessities can arise, resulting in petty cash flowing like water from a leaky bucket. There is high risk of going over budget in the art department.

009 Location

The breakdown pages will furnish you with a list of all the location demands for the production. It's possible that one location can serve for many in your story. Perhaps one apartment can be dressed to feel like two. Although you might hope to secure most locations for free, it is best to budget as if you were going to pay for them (even if it's just $50). An exchange of money, however minimum, signifies a business transaction. It changes the relationship between you and the individual who is renting the location.

Near or Distant? Your script might indicate a location that is not available locally. Without having to scout different areas, the producer can contact local film bureaus, which have on file pictures or descriptions of available locations that suit the needs of the script. Shooting at a location more than 50 miles from your home base obliges you to transport, house, and feed the cast and crew for the duration of the shoot. This decision puts a strain on the budget, but might be unavoidable given the requirements of the script. For example, if the production base is in a city and the script is set in the woods, the company might have to travel to the countryside (the exception to this example occurs if a big city park can be manipulated to look like the woods).

This budget category can become inflated with little or no warning. Locations fall through or become more expensive on the day of the shoot. A neighbor can decide that he is disturbed and needs to be paid off to remain quiet. Vehicles break down, gas prices rise, it rains, there's an earthquake!

Transportation. The movement of people and supplies to and from the shooting location is an important part of a successful production. It requires proper vehicles and responsible drivers. This budget category also includes funds for gas, tolls, and parking. Rental companies often make good deals, so it pays to shop around.

Your transportation budget should reflect three basic items:

Size of Equipment Package. The size of the equipment package will define the kinds and numbers of cars, trucks, or vans you will need to rent. Several cargo vans might be sufficient to handle a small grip and electric package.

Size of Cast and Crew. If you are shooting at a convenient location in and around your home town, you will not need to transport cast and crew to the set. However, if you are moving the production unit to a distant location, you will need to rent enough passenger vans for the run of the show.

Requirements of Location. If you are shooting at an exterior location without an available green room nearby for the actors (see Chapter 7, "Location"), it might be necessary to rent a large van or recreational vehicle for the actors to dress, make up, and relax in when they are not required on the set. This is especially true for cold-weather shoots.

STUDENTS Vehicle rental is an area where students looking for a really cheap deal can get burned. If one business's price for a rental vehicle seems much lower than the competition's, be wary. While you are sitting on the road waiting for a tow truck, you will discover why it was so much cheaper.

Food. Cast and crew members run on their stomachs, and they like their food to be prepared well and tasty. You can estimate your food budget by using the following formula:

No. of days × no. of personnel
  × dollar amount per head = food budget

Caterers will quote how much they charge per person per meal. It might be $3.50 for lunch and $4.50 for dinner. Ask about specific menus for each meal, and have the caterer come to your office with samples.

You will usually be required to serve two meals a day: breakfast and lunch, or dinner and a late snack if shooting nights. For craft services, budget for a standing table of water, juices, sodas, fruit, and whatever snacks are convenient.

> **STUDENTS**
>
> Feeding a cast and crew can be expensive. If you wait until the last minute and have to send out for pizza or sandwiches, the price per head will be high. Plan out in advance each meal of each shooting day, decide who is going to make it, and determine how it will arrive on the set. Heating up a big pot of stew or cooking pasta for lunch can result in big savings. Keep a large coffeemaker on the set. This will be less expensive in the long run than sending out for individual cups of coffee. Finally, always try to buy what you can in bulk from discount warehouses.

> *I had a friend of my mother's cater, and I paid her $100 for the week and the rest went into food. You better be prepared to spend a great deal. It is important to keep your crew happy and make sure your meals are served on time and are good. A problem people often run into is they serve good meals but not on time. With kids, especially, you have to be very regular, otherwise they are going to get upset. No matter where we were in the day, we would stop at noon and have lunch. That time was for everybody to do what they wanted until we started again.*
>
> *Meals are very important. They should be adequate and nutritious. For that part of the budget, you have to plan how many paper plates you're going to buy, napkins, etc. Caterers take care of that for you, but it costs money.*
>
> Howard

Housing. Do not neglect the creature comforts. If you travel out of town, sleeping and traveling accommodations do not have to be first class (unless you are so obligated contractually), but if eight crew members sleeping in one hotel room means no sleep for anyone, then the next day's work will reflect their dissatisfaction and fatigue.

If you are offering to fill a number of rooms for a set period of time, hotels often make deals with production units. Remember, they're in business to rent their accommodations. They would rather have their rooms occupied than empty.

010 Film and Laboratory

Laboratories will make overall discount deals with filmmakers for processing and printing. You can calculate the lab bill based on the amount of stock you are planning to shoot. The price of stock, however, is a fixed figure. Film from Kodak or Fuji should be all from one batch—that is, the serial numbers for the film stock should be consecutive. Videotape should come from the same batch as well. This guarantees that the quality of the entire batch will be consistent from roll to roll.

Buying old stock or short ends (film leftovers from another production) can be risky, but is an excellent way to trim costs. With old stock and short ends, you need to weigh the savings against the risk that the stock might be outdated and therefore unusable. Video stock should always be new.

The laboratory's price for film developing the negative and making a work print is based on a price per foot. You can easily calculate this figure to place in the budget. Check this figure again as you get closer to production because laboratories change their prices often.

If you plan to shoot on film and edit digitally and wish to receive *video dailies* instead of a film work print, contact the lab and pick up a brochure. Learn about its recommendations for the proper technical steps of matching back to film and the potential cost. This will enable you, for example, to weigh the difference in price of having the lab or your editor sync up the dailies. Even with a brochure, we recommend that you visit the lab personally, especially if you are doing this for the first time.

> **STUDENTS**
>
> Many laboratories offer a student rate. Kodak offers a discount for raw stock to registered film students.

> *We underestimated slightly the amount of film stock we needed. During the production, the last day, we had to run out and get some more. I went through a film broker. I asked a DP who I knew for short ends, but he didn't have any 16-mm short ends, so he gave me 35-mm short ends instead. I traded those in for 16-mm black-and-white stock.*
>
> Adam

Amount of Stock to Order. You can determine the amount of stock you will need for your show once the director and the director of photography become involved. It is possible, however, to estimate how many rolls of raw film stock to order based on a projected shooting ratio (the ratio of film shot to film developed). If you are preparing a 10-minute film and anticipate a 4:1 shooting ratio, you need to buy 40 minutes of stock (four rolls of 16-mm at approximately 11 minutes per roll). This particular shooting ratio is considered lean even by professional standards and requires that the director be well prepared and economical with her shots. A more realistic shooting ratio for beginners would be somewhere between 6:1 and 10:1. It is best to budget for the larger figure, as it can always be pared down with input from the director when the budget is revised.

I budgeted myself 14 rolls of film, and that's exactly what I shot.

Howard

Video stock is inexpensive and rarely a budgetary consideration. This is an advantage if you are producing a documentary where the shooting ratio is usually very high. A box of a dozen 30-minute Beta tapes costs around $200.

Postproduction

Postproduction overwhelms many beginners. They focus so much energy on mastering the complexities of production planning that they neglect postproduction. You are sure to encounter hidden costs and unknowns that can't be clearly understood at this stage. How long a film or video will take to edit and complete depends on many variables. (See Chapters 16 through 18 for more details.)

The use of nonlinear editing systems has made the variables more complex. This applies particularly to those wishing to shoot film, edit digitally, and finish on film.

Strike a balance between allowing ample time to make the correct artistic choices and the amount of time that the budget can support. It is a reasonable estimate that your postproduction budget will equal your production budget. This equation is a good starting point when evaluating your numbers.

011 Editing

The main items in this category are the cost of the editor, the editing room, supplies, and the editing equipment. What format (film or video) one shoots and what system on which one plans to edit will define this budget category. This is a good time to research the cost of each route. For example, the weekly rental of nonlinear high-end editing system machines is expensive. Chapter 16 outlines the many choices that are now available to the film- and videomaker.

The final cost to complete your project will depend largely on how much time it will take to *lock picture* (complete editing). The length of your postproduction schedule depends on these factors:

Who Edits? A professional editor will speed the editing process along in both film and tape. It might take a beginner months to do a job that an experienced editor can do in several weeks (especially with nonlinear systems). If you are editing a short film or video for the first time, allow for a slow startup as the editor feels her way around the editing room. Beginners have been known to spend an inordinate amount of time working on a 15- to 30-minute short.

STUDENTS Nonlinear editing systems can accelerate the process, but editing is not always about speed. There are intangibles in fine-tuning your picture that only time will solve. Take your time to make the best film or video possible, especially since you are not paying the daily rate.

Access to Editing Room. This applies mostly to students and independents on a budget. Students with full-time class schedules or jobs might only be able to work for sporadic stretches at a time. It is difficult to sustain creative momentum with this limitation. Independents with limited budgets might have to rely on low-cost facilities from local media groups that don't allow full access to the equipment. Some expensive video facilities give customers a special price if they come in on a will-bump basis or during the graveyard shift.

Shooting Ratio. Even for professional editors, the more film or tape they must wade through and cut, the longer it will take to shape it into a final product. Documentaries traditionally use a very high shooting ratio, especially if they are using tape. It is only during the editing process that the true shape of the documentary emerges, so it is best to budget for a long postproduction period.

Rental or Purchase Deal. This is a good time for striking an excellent deal on postproduction equipment. Renting can be costly, but if a company's machine is not in use, one can make an offer based on the constrictions of the budget. Editing nights and weekends can save money. Most computers now have the drive space to accommodate nonlinear systems such as AVID Express and Final Cut Pro.

012 Postproduction Sound

The area of postproduction sound encompasses sound effects, Foley, automatic dialogue replacement (ADR), mixing, and the music track. There are a multitude of details related to these steps that involve the expenditure of money.

Postproduction houses may offer the student or beginner a set price for the sound design/editing/ADR and the mix based on a flat rate per minute. Bargains may be available if you are not in a rush and the post house can work on your project in the off hours.

The dimension and complexity of the job will ultimately define the final price. Projects requiring elaborate sound effects and a great deal of ADR will be more costly. Research this area well. Talk to several postproduction houses, and bring your script with you. However, don't confine your search to the larger sound houses. Because computers and digital technology have reduced the size and scope of the equipment needed to complete this kind of work, many sound designers have turned their houses/apartments into mini-sound studios.

STUDENTS Digital technology has made its way into film and video programs. For the current generation of computer-fluent beginners, integrating the learning experience with the new technology has not been difficult. Those wishing to work with a sound designer should look around the halls for ads.

Music. The music for your project, if needed, either will come from prerecorded sources or will have to be composed especially for the picture. One method is not inherently less expensive than the other. The rights to a few bars of a very popular song could cost far more than original music for the score of a short film or video. It happens that film composers in the early stages of their career will complete a score for very little for the chance to get valuable experience and expand their reel.

It is difficult to know at this stage what role music will play in your final product. Sometimes a piece of music indicated in the script has an important relationship to character, mood, or plot. If it is a popular song or recording, research the rights to the music now before it becomes a permanent fixture in the cut. Securing the rights to well-known songs can cost hundreds and even thousands of dollars, depending on when the song was released and the popularity of the recording artist. (See Appendix E for more information about music rights.)

Mix. During the film mix, the entire sound track for the project comes together. Call around to various mixing facilities, and ask for prices. Most offer student or night rates for independents on a budget. This usually means having a trainee mix your film or video. If you have finished your sound track on a digital audio workstation (DAW), you will still require a final mix, especially if you are matching back to film (see Chapter 17).

STUDENTS If your institution has an ADR, Foley, or mixing facility, it is best to work with it as much as you can. Mixing a 10- to 15-minute project professionally can add $2,000 to your budget. Make the first pass at your institution. Spend the time learning the intricacies of the mixing board without the financial pressure of the clock (at $150 to $250 an hour). If you are not happy with the result and decide to opt for a professional mixing stage, what you will have gained in experience and confidence will far make up for what you might have lost in time.

013 Laboratory Postproduction (Film)

Obtain a price list from the lab you plan to use. If you haven't decided on a lab yet, get a price list from any lab for a ballpark estimate. If your script is 15 pages long, figure that the film will be 12 minutes, or 425 feet. For postproduction lab expenses, such as the answer and release print, use the budget breakdown and simply multiply 425 times the price per foot. Make sure you include money for opticals, negative cutting, dirty dupe, reprints, tax, and so on. This budget category should be *padded*. You will encounter unanticipated expenses later on, so it's wise to have enough money in the budget to cover them.

If you're shooting on film, cutting on a nonlinear system, and matching back to film, make sure you spend time working through the details with the lab before beginning to budget. They are more complex than for traditional film. The *negative cutter* is a key player; make sure you contact her in advance as well.

Video Postproduction. Video is cut on nonlinear systems. We have included a postproduction budget for traditional linear film and nonlinear video post-production in our Web site.

Animation and Computer Graphics. In a live action film, integrating animated or computer graphics (CG) images needs to be coordinated from preproduction (storyboards) through production and married to the print in post. It is best to consider the work flow backward. The creation of a character model can take a great deal of time depending on the complexity, the amount of movement, and screen time. In a CG feature, the lead characters usually take from three to four months to model, texture, and rig. Rigging is the process of creating an internal skeleton for the model that helps the character bend, deform, and move in a believable manner. A background character may just take a few days. Preplanning is crucial with characters, because a good CG animator will only do what is necessary. For example, if the character is an extra and you decide to give it a speaking part, the animator may not have rigged the mouth to open or modeled any teeth.

As the costs have dropped dramatically, independent filmmakers have been drawn toward CG for relatively low budget films. For a CG effect to be effective in a live action film, it must be photorealistic with believable lighting, texture, proportions, and scale. A CG character must be equally convincing with lifelike movement and behavior to blend seamlessly with shot footage. Photoreal effects and animation require a great deal of skill, knowledge, planning, and hard long hours to achieve, so a filmmaker should use them only when necessary and with the proper resources.

014 Office Expenses

A good formula is to budget 5 percent of the below-the-line budget for your production office expenses.

015 Insurance

Do not neglect insurance. There are many companies that insure film and video shoots. Equipment and personal liability are the minimum insurance packages. You can purchase additional insurance for such items as stunt work, foreign or hazardous locations, and the negative; the last coverage protects the film once it reaches the laboratory. (See Appendix D for a complete breakdown of insurance options.)

016 Contingency

A contingency is a buffer between the budget and insolvency. The normal contingency figure is 10 percent of the below-the-line total. Although this number might seem high, contingency money is a key protection against cost overruns. Think of this as a slush fund for costs you cannot anticipate.

Petty Cash

One of the easiest ways to drain a budget and incur overages is to lose track of your petty cash. Petty cash is all the loose cash spent during production (not checks or prearranged expenses). During principal photography, money seems to fly out of the producer's pocket. Buy or make up petty cash envelopes. Then give each department head a fixed amount, say $100. He or she puts all receipts in the envelope and writes the expenses on the outside. When this allowance is spent, the department head turns the envelope over to the production secretary, who advances another $100. When possible, pay bills by check. Checks provide good record keeping for production expenses and for the government.

BEGINNING THE BUDGET

Armed with your shooting schedule and a set of basic assumptions, you can now enter some numbers. Remember that you have stripped out from the script the items that will cost money, so refer to your breakdown pages. They will tell you to which items you will need to assign a cost. Once you have decided on the size of the crew, estimating crew costs is just a matter of multiplying the number of people by the number of days you will be shooting, including prep and wrap time.

The Budget Process

Consider this first pass at the budget as one of many drafts. The budget will go through several incarnations as more production information is funneled into the process. Your estimates will become more realistic as you hammer out deals and set locations, cast, and crew.

Put the numbers in their appropriate categories, and add up the total. It is always good to overestimate at this point. If the numbers add up to less than you expected, you have room to pad specific areas. If the total is greater than you anticipated, look at the bigger budget items and begin to trim.

Information Is Power

The more choices you have, the better prepared you are to make the most sensible decisions. As you look around for the right deals, it is important to understand that the telephone is your weapon. Be ready to use it a lot. When seeking out the best deal for a van rental or production equipment, secure a local production guide (see the Bibliography) or a phone book and begin calling. Search engines on the Internet can find you companies and deals in a nanosecond. Here are several important tips for phone work:

Be Aggressive. Don't wait days for your call to be returned. If vendors don't call you back within a reasonable period of time, call them again. You are competing with others who want the vendor's attention. Keep plugging away until you get it. Remember that the squeaky wheel gets the grease.

Get the Name of the Person with Whom You Speak. Write down the complete name of whoever gives you information about a price or deal. Later, you can verify the figures by quoting the individual who gave them to you on the first call. Otherwise, another party can deny that anyone in the company ever gave you such a quote.

Take Notes of What You Are Quoted on the Phone. Get as much information as possible about what the vendor is offering and the price. Write it down neatly and carefully, and organize the notes in your production book so you can refer to the information. If, after you hang up, you realize you forgot to ask a specific question, call back.

Beware of the Really Cheap Deal. If you find a price that is suspiciously lower than everyone else's quote, be wary. Examine and test all goods. A *good* deal does not necessarily mean faulty equipment, but an incredible deal might spell disaster.

Meet the People with Whom You Will Be Working. This especially applies to film or video equipment rental houses, postproduction facilities, and film laboratories. You are creating a relationship not just for the duration of this particular project, but, it is hoped, for many to come. Vendors receive hundreds of phone calls a day, so be sure to help them connect your face with your voice. The personal connection will make an impression and might allow you to negotiate a better deal.

Don't Rush Through this Process. Take your time. Beat as many bushes as you can to find the best deals. Don't be satisfied until you have checked out every available rental company. Your legwork in preproduction might save enough money to enable you to purchase more stock or to rent the perfect location. The heat of production affords you little or no time to negotiate; production is not the time to strike deals.

Everything Is Negotiable. Don't be afraid to ask for what you want. Always start with your lowest bid for services, talent, and materials. All people can do is say "No." Enter a negotiation with a figure culled from the budget in mind, but try to get it for less. If you can secure a location or make a deal with a caterer for less, you can use the difference for a line item that costs more than you budgeted.

Get It on Paper. Get all agreements confirmed in a Letter of Commitment. Verbal agreements can be forgotten.

Above All, Be Friendly. Personal relationships are the foundation on which all business is conducted in the industry. This is a given. People generally want to work with individuals they know and with whom they are comfortable.

PRODUCTION VALUE

Production value is the quality of your production efforts in relation to the money you have spent. It is dictated by how many pages are to be shot per day on average, coupled with the amount of money allotted for each day: The budget (minus postproduction costs) divided by the total number of script pages equals the cost per shooting day.

You can get a feel for what kind of quality you're likely to end up with by comparing how much money you have to spend per day with your production demands. A high-budget picture burdened with expensive sets, many special effects, and high fees might have to be shot quickly for a large amount per day. Conversely, a low-budget show with few production needs might shoot over a longer period.

It's true that money can solve most production problems. However, money is often at a premium, especially in a low-budget arena, so ingenuity must take the place of unlimited funds. No matter how large or small your budget, its total is based on the production items needed to fulfill the script.

Many film and video producers get through the shooting stage by moving money from the postproduction categories to the production categories ("robbing Peter to pay Paul"), and ultimately, they cannot complete the picture because of lack of funds. When budgeting, err on the side of too much, because it is better to come in under the budget than over the budget.

Don't let money hinder your process. If you feel like you don't have enough, don't let that be a reason not to shoot your film. If you have enough to at least get started, I suggest doing it. And if you have a lot of money, I suggest being careful of how that money is being spent. Just because you have a lot of money doesn't necessarily mean you're going to come out with a good film.

Adam

Student Budgets

These are the key *production budget* items for a student film. They will be the bulk of the hard costs required to get a picture into the editing room. (See a sample student budget on our Web site.)

- Stock (film or video)
- Processing (film only)
- Food
- Location
- Art department (props, costumes, set design/ dressing)
- Transportation
- Expendables (gels, DAT tape, batteries, etc.)
- Petty cash

Students might also spend extra for special equipment that is not included in the equipment package they receive from their program, such as special lenses, dollies, and car mounts. If funds are tight, be sure that you will have enough money to get the film out of the lab (this is not an issue with video). You can use the time during postproduction to raise money to complete the project.

DIRECTOR
Shooting for the Moon

The director is not usually involved in calculating the budget. This is the domain of the producer. When asked, the director will most likely want to shoot for the moon and surround herself with as much time, equipment, and personnel as she can to achieve her goal.

However, a seasoned director can serve as a welcome consultant to the novice producer during the budgeting process by bringing her experience to play in several key areas, such as her shooting plan and her crew, equipment, and cast needs.

The budgeting process is a team effort. An experienced director can serve as a guide while the producer does the roadwork, making the calls and negotiating the deals. There can be a healthy dialogue between the two as the producer fleshes out the figures that represent the script's needs.

Garth was terrific. I couldn't have made the film without him. Basically, what happened was I had all the locations locked, and then as the film got closer, I started having to worry about how I would shoot it, so I loaded all the production concerns on him, and he was great.

Adam

The director can also advise the producer about her minimal needs to do the picture. There can be a "wish" version of the budget as well as a "bottom line" version of the budget. Ultimately, the director strives to make the best picture possible with the available resources, but it is also her duty to fight for her vision. If she feels that she needs additional time or equipment, she should request it. Her goal is to shoot for the moon while understanding the constraints of the budget.

I knew art direction in the fantasy sequences would play a big, big role. Much had to be done with the way they were dressed or the makeup effects, e.g., the arrows in the chest. It had to be lively and have a sense of fun about it . . . and I knew it was going to cost money. Nobody in film school can accomplish those effects. And you can't just wing it, or it won't have any weight to it.

Howard

LEARNING BY DOING

To gain an idea of what things cost, work on as many productions as possible in whatever capacity you can, ideally in some job that allows you access to the set. This entry-level job will most likely be as a production assistant, a catchall title for the person who does the grunt or "gofer" work (go for this, go for that) that isn't handled by any defined crew position. A production assistant might get coffee for the director, run errands for the producer, or help with traffic or crowd control, among other duties.

A set is a living laboratory. Soak in as much of the atmosphere as possible. Learn to identify everyone on the crew, what they do, and how they handle themselves. Get to know as many people as you can. You can't afford to be shy in these situations, although you should learn when it is acceptable to ask questions and when you should be silent. After a job is over, keep in contact with the key people you've met.

I got a job as a production assistant and just hung around with the grips for a while and started doing grip work. There was a shot with the fence swinging open in the wind, and I was there behind the tree with a fishing line pulling the thing back and forth.

Adam

The set is the ideal place to learn; however, working in the production office can also be educational. Aiding the production coordinator and production manager, even if it is by photocopying contact sheets, is an invaluable opportunity to experience the ebb and flow of daily production activity. Be enthusiastic about every job you are asked to do, no matter how menial it might seem. Prove yourself first on the basic tasks before bucking for the more demanding ones.

STUDENTS

Get as much experience as you can on "professional" shoots as well as your own student productions. Exposure to professional standards will invariably help your own work. You can never have too much experience. Each production has its own set of unique problems, and learning how others work through the process of solving them is an important part of your education. Through this process, you will surely learn valuable lessons that you can file away for use in similar situations on your own productions.

KEY POINTS

- Estimate the size of the production. Will you need a big cast, lots of crew, or many locations?
- Examine your resources and potential funding. Do not try to make an epic on a shoestring.
- Balancing the budget and the script is a constant struggle. If money becomes too tight, the script itself can be altered to reestablish a balance.
- Establish a system of petty cash vouchers to keep track of the cash flow. The art department can be an unexpected drain on the budget.

chapter six

Crewing

The most important rule of filmmaking is to always feed your crew well.

Howard

PRODUCER
Hiring the Crew

The *crew* is defined as all of the personnel, besides the actors, who are employed in the making of a film or video during principal photography. Just as important as finding the right actors to flesh out the story in front of the camera is the search for the right support group behind the camera. The crew represents the nuts and bolts of the production machine. The success of the project lies in their ability to collectively carry out the director's vision of the script. The sum of their energies and creative input is responsible for the project being produced.

The best-laid plans are only as good as the talented people who carry them out. The production hours are long and hard. Crew members who can be creative and inventive under pressure while maintaining a sense of humor are worth the search. These positions might not be romantic or showy, but they are all essential to the making of the film or video. If a production assistant doesn't control the flow of traffic, the director can't get the shot. If the assistant camera operator doesn't clean the film gate properly, a whole roll of film could be scratched. If the lens is not properly set or the lighting is inadequate, even the most brilliant performance will be out of focus or impossible to see.

WHO HIRES THE CREW?

The producer (in the role of production manager) is in charge of hiring the crew. His responsibility is to surround the director with the best creative team the project can afford. The director participates closely in this selection process, but it is the producer who negotiates with potential crew members, makes the deals, and, if necessary, does the firing. This is to ensure that the director's relationship with the crew is on a purely creative level and that any tension over business issues does not interfere with what should be a positive and supportive relationship.

WHEN DO YOU NEED A CREW?

Crew members not only need to be present for the duration of the shoot, but they also need time to prepare. This period is termed *prep time*. After the shoot, the crew requires a cleanup, or *wrap*, period to complete any work that has to be done after principal photography. The only exception to this is if a crew member is hired to perform a specialty job, such as prosthetic makeup, an explosion, or the operation of a second unit camera.

The amount of prep time needed depends on many factors. For short films and videos on tight budgets, it

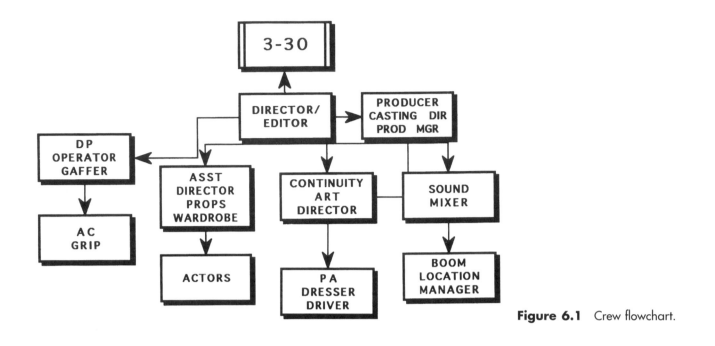

Figure 6.1 Crew flowchart.

depends on the availability of key people to give as much time as possible without being paid. (The "Producer" section of Chapter 10, "Rehearsals," outlines a sample preproduction schedule, which indicates when particular crew members should ideally come on board. Each project has its own set of requirements, but this schedule should serve as a model.)

> *The director of photography did have a meeting with the assistant camera, the grip, and the gaffers, his whole crew, for an hour or so the week before the shoot. They went over what he was trying to do, how he wanted to do it, and how he was going to run his department.*
>
> Howard

HOW BIG A CREW DO YOU NEED?

Only by recognizing the script's technical needs and understanding the director's design for translating the story into images can the producer adequately crew the project. If the director's shooting plan calls for several dolly moves, as did those of *Truman* and *The Lunch Date*, there will have to be someone on the set, at least on certain days, who can handle this technical responsibility. Tatia's crew for *Crazy Glue* fluctuated each day between one (herself on camera) and eight, depending on art direction requirements.

Documentary crews are small and compact by nature. They must be able to move quickly in and out of confined spaces. At the other end of the spectrum,

a full union crew will have a size and complexity that most beginning film- and videomakers do not need and cannot afford.

It is important for you to be familiar with the many positions that exist on a film or video crew and to understand the primary responsibility of each (Figure 6.1). Crew size is also a budget issue. They have to be fed, transported, and, if they are lucky, paid.

The 3–30 Rule

Short film and video projects employ a crew of from 3 to 30 members. Like so many aspects of the breakdown process, the script and the budget dictate the types of crew members required. Your challenge, should you have less than this number of crew members, is to determine how the positions will be filled by the number of personnel employed on your shoot. For example, if the script requires 30 crew positions but you can only afford a crew of 10, each person will have to perform an average of three jobs. Producers double as production managers, editors as script supervisors, and so on.

SELECTING THE CREW

It is not enough just to find hard-working and talented individuals. You also need to find crew members whose personalities complement one another. Crewing is similar to the casting process for actors. The chemistry of the group is important because these people will be working closely under the stress of production. It is also valuable to know the kinds of egos with which you will be working. Are these team players or prima donnas?

Talk to producers, directors, or anyone who has worked with these individuals in the past. Find out as much as you can before you decide to hire. If this is not possible, you must go with your intuition and instinct. There is no need to feel pressured to hire a supposedly "great" director of photography (DP) if you are uncomfortable with his attitude or arrogance. Beginners are bound to make mistakes in this area, but the more experience you acquire, the more astute a judge of character you will become.

If your choices prove to be wise ones, this project could signal the beginning of professional and creative relationships that last a long time. As a producer or director, you have to rely on dependable and talented crew members to execute your ideas. Finding people you can trust, who you enjoy working with, and who are good at what they do is a promising start of a solid creative network from which you can draw in the future. Remember that this business is built on relationships.

The worst and best choices you will make are your people choices—in other words, the crew and the actors. Everybody you choose to work on the project is going to influence the outcome, so you really have to be very careful about whom you're choosing: Are these people going to get along? Are they going to help me? Am I choosing this guy simply because I heard he was the best director of photography around? But if he has an ego problem, you're really going to regret that decision later.

You want people who like you, who like the project, and who want to be there, for obvious reasons, not somebody who's just doing you a favor. Students often throw people together just to get somebody there, and they get a person who doesn't want to be there or with whom they have a problem. The project gets made, but it becomes a very unpleasant experience, and people end up enemies. I've seen it many times.

Howard

Attracting the Right People

How you present your project to others will have an impact on the quality of the people who are interested in working with you. If you appear to be an organized and professional person, you will attract more of the same. Create a professional-looking flier to post at film programs, media organizations, and high schools or on Web sites (e.g., *Mandy.com*, *Shooting People.org* and *Craigslist.com*). Place advertisements in media journals, magazines, and newspapers. Nothing can replace the tried and true method of word of mouth, a very powerful agent.

STUDENTS You have the benefit of being able to draw personnel from your class and your program. Because a great deal of work is being done at film and video programs around the country, you'll find many young and old professionals alike eager to work on student projects. Professionals who agree to work on student projects know that there isn't much in it for them financially. They are attracted by the opportunity to work and, most important, by the material itself. A good script attracts good people, no matter what its source. Most people would rather invest their time and energy on a project with some inherent value, something they can be proud to put on their reel as a sample of their work.

INDEPENDENTS You can advertise in all the places students do. There are many eager students, hungry for experience, who are willing to put in long hours on a semiprofessional shoot. The good ones can be of great help in understanding the low-budget world because that's where they work and live.

Evaluating Credits

How do you know who did what? It can be risky hiring people that you either don't know, haven't worked with before, or both. Scrutinizing their reels and talking to producers, directors, and other crew members about them will definitely help. However, these solutions are not foolproof. Making a film or video is a collaborative endeavor. So many people can have an influence on the final product that it is often difficult to discover who really did what. Consider these examples:

The director of photography's reel might look great, yet he might have worked with a director with a good eye or he might have had an excellent gaffer who was responsible for much of the lighting.

A film or tape might be well edited, but the editor might have been slow, and you might not have the budget to accommodate her lack of speed.

You are on the right track if you find consistency from show to show. The fact that most of someone's work is mediocre except for one piece will tell you that someone else might have been responsible for that one piece's success. You hope to get honest answers from the people who worked on these films or videos, but this is not always the case. Who really did what might change depending on the person to whom you speak.

If you do your research well, you will reduce the risk of making a serious mistake. If things don't end up well, you always have the option to fire that individual and find another.

Negotiating the Deal

The producer negotiates a fee with each crew member. This is generally a flat daily or weekly rate, with some proviso for extra-long days. It is a good business practice to draw up a simple deal memo for each crew member. A *deal memo* is a letter of agreement between two parties that defines what services are to be rendered and the compensation for those services. The deal memo also either details the crew member's screen credit or contains a clause giving the producer the right to assign credits at his discretion.

If you negotiate a flat fee with the crew, the crew members will give you the hours you need as long as you do not abuse their time and energy. If crew members are on a daily or even an hourly rate, you need to pay special attention to their schedule. For example, if you need an extra hairdresser for a short period, make an effort to allow that crew member to perform her task and then leave the set, rather than linger and accrue additional compensation.

KEY CREW MEMBERS

The first step in assembling a crew is to choose the key people who will form the creative and technical nucleus of the production. Once you have chosen the key personnel, you can assemble the support crew based on their recommendations. These pivotal crew members work with their own smaller teams on a regular basis.

The following are the key people on a crew:

- Production manager
- Assistant director
- Director of photography
- Production sound mixer
- Art director
- Editor

The first five positions are discussed in this chapter. See Chapter 16, "Pix Postproduction," for information on the editor's responsibilities.

Production Manager

When the producer has a lot of money at his disposal, he hires an individual who is known in the industry as a *production manager*. This individual breaks down the script and creates a schedule and a budget. Once the budget is agreed to, the production manager (with the producer's approval) begins to organize the production. Unfortunately, a production manager is a luxury that most beginners can't afford. The producer usually assumes this important position on low-budget productions.

The following are the production manager's basic duties. As you can see, the position plays a pivotal role in the production process. The production manager performs these tasks:

- Coordinates, facilitates, and oversees all preproduction
- Prepares the script breakdown and preliminary shooting schedule
- Establishes and controls the budget
- Makes deals with the crew
- Makes deals for equipment
- Oversees daily cash flow
- Supervises the selection of locations
- Oversees day-to-day production decisions
- Facilitates schedule changes
- Manages all off-set logistics
- Arranges for housing and meals
- Sets up necessary insurance
- Ensures that permits are obtained
- Secures releases
- Keeps on top of all production activity to keep ahead of the director in production planning
- Completes a daily production report reflecting the status of the picture's cost

The production manager is the engine that drives the project. The importance of this position cannot be emphasized enough. It is also the least glamorous key position. It must be occupied by a well-organized person who wields power efficiently. The production manager answers to the producer.

> *The first person I chose after the director of photography was the production manager. Production managers take on such an enormous role, particularly on student films. I was fortunate that I had someone who was not only my friend and a good filmmaker but who really liked the idea. Not only did he fulfill the production manager role by lining up caterers and the like, but he was involved in the story process as well. He was one of the people who sat down with me, went over the story, and got excited by it. When people get excited, they put more of themselves into it at all levels.*
>
> Howard

The production manager hires the department heads, who, in turn, suggest personnel to make up the support teams for their departments.

> *I had a production manager, an assistant director, and a director of photography—they formed the core. Additionally, I had an assistant camera operator, a sound person, a boom person, and two grip/gaffers. Below that I had a runner/production assistant, a baby-sitter, and a costume person. If you want to go even farther down the line, I had the caterer. I don't know if you really call that a complete crew, but those were the people who were involved in the shooting of the movie.*
>
> Howard

Support Crew

The production manager's support crew consists of the following personnel:

Production Secretary. The production secretary is the liaison between the producer or production manager and the cast and crew. She is a key player at the hub of the production office. Some of her responsibilities are the following:

- Facilitates communication
- Disseminates information to cast and crew
- Coordinates transportation in the absence of a transportation coordinator
- Completes paperwork, cast and crew lists, call sheets, and so on

The production secretary should be a highly organized, efficient, and even-tempered individual who is accustomed to remaining calm in the middle of a storm. She is the producer's or production manager's right hand.

Location Manager. This crew member scouts and secures locations and serves as liaison between the production company and the location. His other duties include arranging for parking and catering and obtaining permits, location contracts, and certificates of insurance. He sets up each location so that the production unit can shoot properly, and then he arranges for the cleanup.

Caterer. All crew members and actors like to eat. Shooting a film burns up calories that must be replenished. Having someone manage the food affairs of the shoot can make for a smooth ride. The craft services people set up a table with food near the set for snacks throughout the day, and they arrange for midday meals in a comfortable setting.

Transportation Captain. If a project requires many vehicles, a key driver called the *transportation captain* is responsible for transporting the production from location to location. Being able to wrap out of a location and move to the next shot with efficiency saves time and money. It takes an ever-watchful eye to keep tanks filled with gasoline and maintain the vehicles. The captain hires a team of drivers to shuttle actors and equipment to and from the set, and she makes deals for picture vehicles. This position is often filled by a grip or a production assistant.

Assistant Director

The assistant director (AD) works closely with the producer or production manager to create a shooting schedule. He also has the responsibility on set of making sure that the production sticks to the schedule. He represents the production manager on the set as well as being the director's right hand.

The assistant director must communicate with all the actors and crew members because he is the company sergeant, the ship's pilot, the traffic cop. He has the onerous task of making sure that everyone is in the right place at the right time. He must constantly remind the cast and crew members of the schedule and must perform this task with grace and tact. The assistant director watches the clock while the director of photography sets up and fine-tunes the lights, the production sound mixer places microphones, the art director dresses the set, and the director rehearses the actors. Most of all, the assistant director must be totally in sync with the director.

> *I don't know, it was a miracle. We were never more than 25 minutes off our schedule. The AD did a great job. He was always looking at his watch, without making me nervous. He always knew where we should be and where we could make up time, which is the job of a good AD. Everything stayed fairly constant, it was like a vacuum-sealed environment— the same crew, the same people, the same location every day.*
>
> Howard

Support Crew

The assistant director's support crew (if hired; if not, the 1st AD will assume the following responsibilities) consists of the following personnel:

2nd Assistant Director. The 2nd assistant director's duties include preparing the call sheets, arranging call times, and coordinating all cast and crew arrivals to the set. The assistant director is also responsible for directing the background action. The 2nd AD is the off-set person responsible for having the actors prepared for their calls.

3rd Assistant Director. The 3rd AD telephones the actors in coordination with the production secretary to set up the next day's shoot. If traffic or crowd control is needed, all of the ADs are involved in securing the set.

Continuity (Script Supervisor). The script supervisor works closely with the director to determine what coverage has been shot and what shots remain. He marks the script with a description of each shot of each scene. He takes detailed notes after each take regarding action, dialogue, gestures, lens used, costumes, makeup, and so on to ensure continuity of all these elements from shot to shot and scene to scene. This script is then sent to the editing room so the editor has a written reference to the shoot. The script supervisor's other responsibilities include matching each actor's actions from take to take and from angle to angle. Neglecting this attention to detail can create major continuity problems in the editing room.

Director of Photography

The producer and director's concern is to hire the best director of photography (DP) they can afford. This is an important decision. The DP's job is to fulfill the director's visual design for the project and to participate in building the camera team. This means that before bringing on any of the camera crew, you must decide on a DP. On most small projects with a limited budget, the DP also operates the camera. So you are, in fact, looking for a DP and a camera operator in one.

The director of photography must be resourceful and able to make use of simple lighting situations or none, depending on the situation. He must be flexible and able to light and shoot on the run. If yours is a project like *Mirror Mirror*, the technical demands might be less rigorous. With only one setup in a studio situation, there was ample time to set up lights.

> *One of the great things about the cinematographer was that he was able to work very quickly and improvise as well. He could work under tough situations, with no light. That was important for me, having someone I could trust doing the camera. There were a few times when I didn't even look through the camera other than to maybe say, when we were first setting up the shot, "This is perfect," or "Maybe a little tighter."*
>
> Adam

STUDENTS On student productions, the DP might serve not only as the camera operator, but also as the gaffer and the grip! Try to avoid this.

Evaluating Potential Directors of Photography

When deciding among potential DPs, consider these criteria:

Previous Work. Look at the professional reel. However, you are not always looking for the quality of the work, but for the different kinds of lighting situations with which he has worked. A DP may be able to function with the flexibility of a set, but not be experienced or comfortable with limited lights in practical locations.

Is there something identifiable about his style that is compatible with your story? If his work is excellent but his lighting style(s) is very different from what you envisioned for your project, you may want to talk with him anyway. He may have been typecast to do a certain kind of work and may be eager to branch out and try something different.

What Formats, Cameras, and Stocks Has He Worked With? It might be an obvious point, but if you are looking for a DP to shoot video, he should be fluent with the specific format of video you wish to shoot. (You might lock into a specific video format because of a lucrative deal you have negotiated.) The DP must also know how to shoot and light for video. The lighting requirements for video differ from those for film.

If you're looking for a DP for film, ask about the experience candidates have had with different equipment and, more important, their experience with different film stocks in your chosen format. If a DP is shooting in 35-mm or 16-mm for the first time, it is appropriate to ask for tests with the equipment and stocks until you are confident that the DP is comfortable with the new format.

Speed. How long does it take the DP to set up the camera and lights? His sample material might look terrific, but if a candidate takes a long time to set up for each shot and you are working on a tight schedule, he might not be the best person for you. You want someone who can create stunning images, but you want it fast unless, of course, you have a luxuriously long schedule.

You can research a DP's speed by talking with the producers or directors who have worked with him in the past. Often, a DP will spend the morning lighting and breeze through the afternoon. If you want to sacrifice speed for a particular look, you can offset the longer setups by planning a smaller shooting ratio of 1:2 or 1:4. Use the extra setup time to rehearse the actors more thoroughly.

Does He Have His Own Equipment? Many DPs come with their own cameras and sometimes their own lights as well. The fee they quote includes their services and their equipment package. This can be an asset because not only does it simplify things, but if anything happens to the equipment, the DP is responsible. He might even have his own insurance policy. Don't assume that because a DP has his own equipment he is automatically good; the equipment is just a bonus.

Compatibility with Director. The director and the DP must get along and must share a mutual vision of the piece. There should be a tight creative bond between the two. It is the producer's job to support the director within the boundaries of the budget by providing her with a DP who satisfies her creative needs.

Schedule. Is the DP available and can he work on your scheduled dates? Is he booked so tightly that if your schedule fluctuates, he will not be able to accommodate you? Finally, can the DP work within your (probably tight) schedule?

The crew. There was my DP, whom I met at NYU sophomore year. He is an incredibly gifted cinematographer and director in his own right. He was my second brain. He didn't have to be there every day at all. He was with me during the second round of storyboards. He would set up every shot, angles, and lights, and then I would be there for a couple of days by myself animating it. So he was there every other day—every three days.

Tatia

Troubleshooting

The following warning signs could have an impact on your production planning and budget:

- An inexperienced DP asks for too much high-end equipment. Watch for these items in particular: HMI lights, expensive dolly, large equipment package, Steadicam, Luma crane, video tap, camera car. This might occur because the DP wants the opportunity to work with the fancy equipment or because he is not able to evaluate properly the technical needs of the show. Insecurity might lead the DP to order as much equipment as possible and then decide what he needs during the shoot. After doing a detailed location scout and discussing the director's visual ideas for the project, an experienced and resourceful DP should be able to give an accurate breakdown of the project's equipment needs for the entire show and know how to maximize the equipment package that you can afford. You might have room in the budget for some or all of these items, but you might not actually need them to fulfill the director's visual plan for the script. The money you save could be better spent on props, costumes, or an interesting location.

- You have hired a seasoned DP on a student or inexperienced crew, and the DP is trying to take over the creative aspects of the shoot. This can happen when an insecure crew doesn't stand up to someone who appears to know what he is doing. The DP might have strong ideas about how scenes should be photographed or staged that might not be in sync with the director's vision. If the DP's work is terrific, you don't want to antagonize him, but if he gets his way, the result won't be the piece that the director envisioned. This is a tough situation for beginners. As soon as this problem appears, it is best that the producer confront the DP. Remember that it is your film or video you are making, not his. However, if the director is insecure and doesn't provide leadership on the set, this will create a power vacuum, and it usually the DP who will fill it.

If you are working with an inexperienced or student DP, an experienced gaffer can be very helpful.

The next important search was to find a DP; I wanted someone to go over the storyboards; I wanted someone to be involved. I found an older student, and every week we'd have a story meeting where we'd talk about the story as well as the storyboards. In those sessions, other problems became apparent. We realized we'd need a 5.9, a very wide lens. We'd need to rent a variable-speed motor. But if you need a variable-speed motor, where are you going to rent it? The production manager was there and I'd say, "Ian, can you call a few equipment houses in Rochester and find out what their rates are for the day?" which then impinges on your budget. So when you start talking to each other, you realize how interconnected the process is.

Howard

Support Crew

Now that the DP is aboard, you can hire the support crew—camera, grip, and electric. The size of your particular crew will depend on the budget (what you can afford in the way of salary, transportation, lodging, and food), the demands of the script, the size and difficulty of lighting and filming the locations, and the director's visual plans for the material.

Does the director want a fairly static camera, long dolly moves, or both? Does she want high-key or low-key lighting? She might even be thinking of using a Steadicam for several scenes. After the director and DP finalize their overall visual plan, you will have a better idea of the crew needed to match the creative requirements of the production.

The DP will want to have around him people with whom he has worked before. In most cases, a DP's speed and effectiveness result from his support team. The support crew for this department consists of 10 positions with specific responsibilities for operating the camera, lighting for the camera, and moving the camera.

Operating the Camera

Camera Operator. Often, the director of photography is also the camera operator. If he decides to concentrate on the lighting, he has the option (budget permitting) to hire an operator whose job will be primarily to operate the camera.

Assistant Camera (AC). The AC's duties include changing lenses, following focus, and assisting in setting up the camera. He is the protector of camera equipment and very knowledgeable about all cameras—a very important position on student shoots!

2nd Assistant Camera. The 2nd AC, also called the *loader*, threads the film into the magazine. The 2nd AC slates each take and is therefore in communication with the script supervisor as to the numbering of the shots. The 2nd AC fills out the camera reports for the lab and for the editor.

Stills. A stills person takes photographs of key sequences on the set for publicity. He usually takes still photographs during rehearsals. A professional stills photographer can shoot the actual take, but only with a silent camera housing.

Lighting for the Camera

Gaffer. The gaffer serves as the DP's left hand. He is responsible for setting the lights and securing the power to illuminate them.

Best Boy/Electrician. The best boy is the gaffer's assistant. He runs cables to the set from generator or can "tie-in" (see Glossary) to an existing power source.

2nd Electrician. He rounds out the electrical team if the DP needs more than two assistants.

Moving the Camera

Key Grip. The key grip serves as the DP's right hand and supervises the physical movement of the camera. He coordinates the rigging of light stands, dolly, silks, and so on. He is the safety coordinator for the set and is capable of creating all kinds of rigging for the camera.

Dolly Grip. The dolly grip is the key grip's assistant and the person responsible for pushing the dolly.

Grip. Grips help set and take down the lights.

Swings. These are crew members who can do both grip and electric work.

Production Sound Mixer

Beginners usually find it easier to find a DP than a production sound mixer. Recording sound is not as glamorous as recording images. Beginners and students are usually more focused on getting the best DP they can than the best production sound mixer. This priority for camera is usually continued on the set as well. Time will be spent making sure the lighting is right, but many crews are hard pressed to repeat a take because of a sound problem. This attitude can result in acting that is beautifully seen but not properly heard.

This happens, in part, because it is technically possible to rerecord all the dialogue and add in other sounds in postproduction without going back to the original locations. It is far more expensive to have to reshoot a scene as a result of camera or lighting problems, because the entire cast and crew have to be reassembled at the original locations.

If possible, try to record clean dialogue, or *production sound*, on the set to capture the "magic" that can happen between actors during a scene. Dialogue can be rerecorded during the postproduction period, but this kind of sound work can be time consuming and expensive (see Chapter 17, "Sound Postproduction"). In addition, some actors, especially nonprofessionals, are not adept at recreating in a dark recording studio months after principal photography the dramatic chemistry they worked hard to convey on the set.

One of the inherent problems of evaluating a production sound mixer is not knowing if the dialogue in the final print was recorded on the set or in a recording studio. If it was recorded in a studio, was that because of unavoidable problems with the location that made it impossible to record clean production dialogue or because the production sound mixer did a poor job? These questions can only be answered by the producer, director, or editor of the project.

> *There was one guy doing sound. He was operating the Nagra and the boom, and then eventually he enlisted one of the homeless guys to help us, which turned into a disaster.*
>
> Adam

The director of photography may be able to recommend a sound mixer with whom he has worked with on other shoots. All hired crew can recommend other technicians for you to interview.

Evaluating Potential Production Sound Mixers

When selecting a production sound mixer, consider the following criteria:

Knowledge of Equipment. The production sound mixer should know the timecode DAT recorder, DVD Ram system, analogue Nagra, or whatever recording device you will be using. This might seem like an obvious point, but it is helpful for you to explore the candidate's technical sophistication. Most important, is the candidate experienced with a wide assortment of microphones, such as radio microphones and lavalieres?

Own Equipment? The production sound mixer who comes with his own recording equipment and microphones is very common in the industry. She is comfortable with her own rig and can rely on it. For the producer, it means that she can quote you a price that includes her services and her equipment. This figure is usually less than if you hired the production sound mixer and had to rent the equipment separately. However, do not hire a mixer just because she has her own rig. Always go for the best you can find. The rig should be a bonus.

Experience. Does the candidate have a wide range of experience working in challenging practical locations? It is less demanding to record *clean dialogue* (free of unnecessary sounds or noises) in a soundproof environment like a sound stage. You need to question how she has performed on locations that were not "sound friendly"—that is, those with distracting or loud ambient noises that interfered with the dialogue.

Temperament. The ideal production sound mixer is easy going but assertive on the set. She is adept at asserting herself if she feels that things are not right for sound. She might have to fight to be heard because the needs of the production sound mixer are many times subjugated to those of the camera. The production sound mixer must be sensitive to actors' needs and be able to discreetly but accurately tape a radio mike or lavaliere to an actor or to request volume adjustments. The production sound mixer can be a sea of calm in the midst of chaos.

Support Crew

The boom operator comprises the support crew for the sound department. The boom operator is an important position and should not be filled by just anybody. The best production sound mixer in the world can't record proper sound if the microphone is not pointed in the right direction. The production sound mixer you hire will most likely insist on a boom operator with whom he likes to work. The boom operator's duties include collaborating on the placement of the microphones and positioning the boom pole during takes to best record the dialogue or ambient sounds.

Art Director

This is a very important position and one that beginners often slight. The art director, also called the production designer, is responsible for fleshing out the director's vision of the script. It is her job to create, in tandem with the DP, the world that the characters of the script inhabit. You will most likely find promising candidates among those trained in designing for the stage. However, there are fundamental differences between designing for the stage and designing for film or video. The stage requires designing for an entire proscenium, whereas film or video requires designing only for what the camera will see. The camera might only see a wide shot of an entire room for several seconds and concentrate on a corner of the room for most of a scene.

Evaluating Potential Art Directors

Use the following criteria to select an art director:

Experience in Films and Videos. Your first choice should be an art director who has experience with cameras, not just theater, and who understands what the camera sees and how to control the visual environment. If your candidate is eager to get into motion pictures but has little experience, she should be prepared to spend time analyzing films and videos.

Ability to Work within a Low Budget. The art director must be inspired to use imagination instead of money. This might mean scrounging around thrift shops for bargains or creatively rearranging an existing environment.

Compatibility with the Director. The art director must share the director's creative vision of the story. A creative bond should develop between the two.

Support Crew

The art director is responsible for putting together her support team, which might consist of the following positions:

- Storyboard artist
- Construction coordinator
- Set dresser
- Property master
- Costume designer
- Dresser
- Makeup artist
- Hairstylist

Depending on your budget for the project, the art director might be asked to handle many of these responsibilities, including set dressing, props, and even wardrobe.

I knew art direction in the fantasy sequences would play a big, big role. I started calling older students, which is always a great idea when you've got production problems, and I found out who had made films with heavy costume designs or heavy makeup effects. I got names, and I started calling. That's how I met Jan Fennel, a costume designer in New York who does off-Broadway, commercials, and small production stuff. For costumes and salary, I had a total budget of $1,200.

Howard

Storyboard Artist. The storyboard artist translates the director's vision of each sequence of the script into drawings or panels that represent what each shot will contain.

Construction Coordinator. A construction coordinator plans, budgets, and oversees the work when a set, set piece, ceiling piece, or new floor must be constructed.

Set Dresser. The set dresser buys, rents, or makes set pieces and furnishings. During the shoot, the set dresser is on standby in case any of the set pieces must be adjusted or painted. The set dresser also works ahead of the company, if possible, to dress the set for the next day's photography.

Property Master. This crew member gathers all necessary hand and set props for the project and doles them out as needed. For example, if the actors are eating a meal on camera, it is the prop master's responsibility to keep the glasses filled and steam on the food from take to take and from angle to angle.

Costume Designer. Everything the actors wear in the show is prepared by the costume designer. This is done in conjunction with the art director's designs and the DP's contributions.

Dresser. On set, a dresser assists the actors in and out of their wardrobe. One dresser is employed for the men, and another for the women. If there are many actors and extras, additional dressers might be hired for big sequences.

Makeup Artist. The makeup artist designs and applies the actors' makeup and facial hairpieces. The makeup artist's responsibilities include the maintenance of continuity and script days.

Hairstylist. This crew member designs and styles the actors' hair and manages any wigs used in the production. The hairstylist also maintains the continuity of hairstyle. On a windy day, he stands by and recombs hair that has become mussed.

HIRING AN ANIMATOR

Animation takes time—lots of time. Animation can add beautiful and compelling visuals to your piece, but it will require a different, more deliberate, way of working than live action. The creation of a character model can take a great deal of time depending on the complexity, the amount of movement, and screen time. In a CG feature, the lead characters usually take from three to four months to model, texture, and rig.

About 10 years ago the software and hardware necessary to produce computer-generated images (CGI) was prohibitively expensive. It was therefore rare to find independent artists working as CGI animators. The cost of powerful computers and their components has dropped dramatically. The software has become more feature rich, inexpensive and user friendly, leading to the rise of many small one- and two-person shops. With that said, there is still a steep learning curve and price tag for a CGI studio. The most common professional animation software is @Alias, Maya. Many other excellent packages are available. 3D Studio Max, SoftImage XSI, Lightwave, and Cinema 4D all have their followings as well. Digital compositing and editing packages have also become more ubiquitous and inexpensive. The most popular are Apple's Shake, Adobe After Effects, the AVID line of composing products, Apple Final Cut Pro, and Combustion (and the higher end versions Flame and Inferno). The list goes on. You will find that each software package tends to have its own niche market and loyal following. For example, 3D Studio Max (or just Max as it is known in the trade) is favored by game artists because of its extensive modeling capabilities, plug-ins, and software development kit. Many broadcast designers will use Cinema 4D with After Effects because they are a straightforward on the Mac platform. Maya and Shake are favored by the makers of feature films because of the extensive features and node-based compositing. The popularity and capabilities change with each software upgrade. So the preceding combinations of tools will vary a bit from year to year.

When hiring a CG artist, it is a good idea to see the studio if you can. A professional should have more than one computer, a high-speed network, a high-speed Internet connection, backup drives, a means of video out (a DVD burner can suffice), as well as legal copies of the software. You won't be able to tell too much about what is under the hood of the computers, but if the primary workstation is over four years old, the artist may have trouble running the latest applications. Of course, the right hardware and software are not a substitute for talent, but they might indicate whether or not the person can get the job done without amateurish equipment problems. If the job is more than just a few frames, it is not unreasonable to ask for an equipment list.

Production Assistant

Production assistants (PAs) can be placed in any and all departments, depending on the needs of the company; the neediest department gets help first. If the company requires another driver, another camera assistant, a grip, or a dresser, the producer can place a PA in that position.

> *Students never plan for enough crew, and more importantly, they don't plan for enough PAs. You should have one or two PAs just to run around, pick up stuff, drop stuff off, and help the production manager. It's always the last person assembled in a student crew, and it's always a big mistake because then the energy starts draining away from the set; people are leaving to go buy extra quarter-inch tape, batteries, or whatever is missing at the moment. All of a sudden the crew is being cannibalized to become runners and PAs, and the set starts to fall apart. You lose a lot of time. Getting PAs for student films is always a difficult task. I was fortunate: My father was my PA. He took a week off work and ran around for me. Because he had no ego problems about doing that, it worked out really well.*
>
> Howard

Interns

Salaries on short films and videos often hover around nonexistent. The distinction between a PA and an intern is that the PA is assigned to perform a specific task or to assist a particular department. Interns often float between departments (so they can learn the ropes) and lend a hand where one is needed.

> *There were about 12 people that we found on Animation World Network who volunteered. They each gave us a day or two a week and that was the crew. They were there mainly for preproduction of the set. Most of them built the set with the art director, so anything from cutting wood to detailing, dusting, painting, building trees, building little models.*
>
> Tatia

Specialty Crew

There are many other crew members who cover specialty areas. These include special effects, choreography, standby painters, Steadicam operators, greens people, animal wranglers, tutors, and stunt coordinators.

Video Shoots

All the positions just discussed apply to video. In single-camera video shoots, there are some differ-

ences in the way jobs are performed. The most significant difference is that narrative video shoots require slightly different lighting plans.

Digital video is a constantly evolving technology. Larger video formats such as HDTV require special camera crews to service the camera on set to maintain consistent color and contrast. On a professional crew, for example, a producer is advised to hire a digital imaging technician (DIT). A designation of Local 600, IATSE, the cinematographer's guild, this crew member oversees and maintains advanced coloring (controller duties), setup, operation, troubleshooting, and maintenance of digital cameras (oversight of camera utilities), waveform monitors, downconverters (high-def to other formats), monitors, cables, digital recording devices, terminal equipment, driver software and other related equipment. He has a complete understanding of digital audio acquisition and timecode process and how they are integrated into digital acquisition format and post production environments. He is also responsible for in-camera recording. His is a supervisor responsibility for the technical acceptability of the image.

Documentarians work with a light crew so they can move freely in the field. Video cameras have microphones mounted on the camera; so technically, a video shoot can consist of one person.

> *In terms of roles, I wore many hats in* Mirror Mirror. *I was the production manager, I handled the budget, I decided on stocks and ordered fill, and I spent a lot of time trying to track down appropriate and affordable mannequins to use in the set.*
>
> Jan

Documentary Crews

What factors play an important role in hiring the crew for a documentary shoot?

> *Because* Mirror Mirror *wasn't shot on location, I did think about a third crew member as a production assistant. Ordinarily, I only work with one other person, as it keeps expenses down and minimizes our presence. In this case, I was wary about the crew outnumbering the subject, and I weighed the possible benefits of having a PA against the possible impact an additional person might have on the intimacy of the interviews. With just two of us, we were both involved in primary crew roles (camera and sound), whereas a PA would be there as an audience member. I decided against it.*
>
> Jan

Documentary crews are usually composed of the director/producer, DP, and production sound mixer. They need to be small and mobile. This has to do with budgetary concerns as well as aesthetic ones. Documentaries might be shot over long periods of time, and their budgets can't support a high overhead. Crews must keep a low profile and not get in the way of the people they are photographing. They should be able to move quickly and follow the action if necessary.

It is not unusual for the documentary film- or videomaker to serve as the producer, director, writer, and DP or production sound mixer. This person conceives, develops, finances, and creates the project. Producing a documentary can demand an intensive devotion over many months or possibly years of work.

This was now my sixth film in which I worked with a two-person crew—myself on sound and a cinematographer. What's important to me as both the director and the sound person is to get the best sound possible by wearing the headphones at all times so that I can monitor what is coming off the tape. In the case of Mirror Mirror, *it wasn't too hard because I set up a boom, so I didn't have to worry about handling the mike. Those women were in a static position—I knew they weren't going anywhere. For each interview, I would just set up the boom to an optimal position, check levels, and then I sat just to the left of the camera. The mike was far away from the camera, so we didn't have to worry about camera noise. I was just there with the Nagra, and I would ask my questions and be attentive to their responses while checking the modulometer periodically.*

Jan

DEVELOPING THE RIGHT CHEMISTRY

Preproduction is the time to shake out any potential crew problems before principal photography begins. If you hire key people early enough in the preproduction process, you will have time to get a sense of how well they will work with the director, producer, and other crew members. If you sense that potential problems are brewing, confront them immediately. Try not to wait until you are so close to production that replacing a key player would create a serious dilemma. If there is tension during preproduction, you can be sure it will only escalate during production.

If you discover you have a serious problem with a crew member, air it out reasonably. If the problem cannot be resolved amicably, it is time to look for a replacement. It is up to the producer to be the heavy and do the firing. Try to break off working relations as amicably as possible. Just because a crew member is not the right choice for your current project doesn't mean he or she won't work out another time. Don't burn your bridges with anyone if you can avoid it.

Always be prepared for the eventuality that someone you hire might not work out because of schedule conflicts, health problems, creative or personal differences, or for some other reason. You must be able to get on the phone and find a replacement immediately. This is only possible if you have a list of backups—that is, people you didn't choose for the position initially but who were good candidates. Backups are essential for the crew as well as for the cast and locations. An efficient producer will hold onto the names and phone numbers of the rejected candidates for all positions. Approaching people you have already rejected is usually not a problem as long as you were reasonable and fair the first time around. This is an established part of the business. If your backups have been working for a while, they should be used to it.

> **PRODUCTION**
>
> If you are in the heat of production and have to fire a key player, try not to fire that individual until you have found a replacement.

DIRECTOR
Hiring the Crew

For the sake of harmony on the shoot, the director must be intimately involved in choosing the key people around whom the crew will form. The director will be in charge of the set, and she must trust the key people to execute her vision for the script. She looks for creative partners as well as people with whom she can work and get along. The production hours are long and hard, and the director must feel confident that those around her will come through for her when needed.

During the process of choosing the crew, the producer and director have the opportunity to develop a complementary working relationship. They need to bond as a team and to develop a strategy for dealing with all sorts of production-related issues. It is difficult to make important decisions in a vacuum. The producer represents another set of eyes and ears as the director homes in on the right people for the project.

Together, the director and producer should develop a strategy for interviewing prospective crew members. After each interview, the director and producer can discuss how they felt about the candidate. Differences of opinion can be important not only in making the right choice, but also in learning about how each other views people. The ultimate choice must rest with the director (as far as the budget will allow), but by sharing impressions in an open forum, the director and producer develop a rapport and have a productive dialogue, the goal of which is to secure the best crew for the project.

Choices about the crew are only the first of many that will include decisions about the cast, locations, sets, props, costumes, hair, makeup, and so forth. The entire preproduction process involves a long string of decisions that will have a direct impact on the resulting film or video. As more of these decisions are made, the producer and director must develop into a tight-knit team, both moving to the beat of the same creative drum.

DIRECTOR'S DISEASE

There is a phenomenon in the business known as *director's disease*. It is a rash, a cold, or a headache that is directly related to the pressure under which the director puts herself.

> *I was by myself in the room and it was so beautiful and the film actually moved along, and I couldn't believe it. It was worth all the hard work. I had some tragic, tragic health hazards happening with* Crazy Glue. *I was so tense that I had a vein burst in my eye, so during a good portion of the shoot my eye was full of blood. And I inhaled a pin one day! Cause you use pins to move the eyeballs of the puppets. I inhaled it and had to exhale it somehow. The entire thing was very tiring and grueling. But when the dailies came back, the three weeks of torture were worth it.*
>
> Tatia

While shooting *Beauty and the Beast*, Jean Cocteau developed horrid boils that had to be lanced each evening. Miraculously, when the picture wrapped, the boils disappeared. Good health is a key factor in maintaining the rigorous pace of a shoot.

> *We started shooting on a Monday—it was the Martin Luther King holiday—and that weekend, out of nowhere, I suddenly came down with a 102° temperature. It was totally psychosomatic. I didn't even think I was going to make it to Monday. But then you just start working, and you go and you do it.*
>
> Adam

STUDENTS

We have identified several problems that are specific to student shoots. Understanding at an early stage what it means to be a professional takes time and experience. Let the crew members do their jobs.

The following guidelines should help a new director through those first projects:

Make It Clear Who Is in Charge. There must be a leader and a decision maker on the set. The director should know what she wants and be able to communicate her desires to others. The best way to insure this is to be prepared. *Do your homework* before you walk on the set.

Treat all Crew Members with Respect. In most cases, the crew (and cast) is working for little or no pay. Remember that they are all part of a team and that everyone on the team is important.

Know What Everyone Does. If you understand the value of every position, you can evaluate what you really need for a particular production. Know also what every piece of equipment does.

Clarify Job Requirements. If crew members hold more than one position apiece, be sure that job requirements don't conflict, and clearly establish who will do what. There shouldn't be any assumptions on the set; you don't want to hear, "I thought *he* was taking care of that." An effective crew should be able to accommodate any demands asked of it.

KEY POINTS

- The department heads are responsible for hiring their own crews.
- Make sure that the crew members you hire are people you want to be around for long days.

- If a certain crew member is not pulling his or her load, do not hesitate to terminate that person's employment. No one is irreplaceable.
- Crew members often have more than one job. Define all crew responsibilities.

- Maintain good health. The stamina needed for a shoot can be taxing.
- Qualified people are often interested in working on a short project to build their reel or to jump into another crew position for the experience.

chapter seven

Location

I got the stage free because it was part of the university where I taught.

Jan

PRODUCER

Securing Locations

In his task of securing locations for the shoot, the producer should communicate trust and confidence. People who might grant permission to use their home, restaurant, facility, loft, office, or building must feel that the production crew will take proper care of it. This means the crew should leave the location in as good a condition as when they found it (if not better). No matter how much or how little you pay for the location, this is proper professional behavior. The producer wants to establish a good reputation in the film and video community. It also might be necessary for the company to return to the location for reshoots.

Price, proximity, schedule—the producer sees all locations with these elements in mind. He negotiates for the location once members of the key creative team have made their choice.

If the director requests a particular location that is priced out of reach of the budget, the producer should suggest an alternate or backup location. Should the director insist on a particularly expensive location, the two will have to strike a compromise.

WHERE TO LOOK FOR LOCATIONS

When scouting for locations, seek the advice of professionals in the film and video business. Many cities

have a film commissioner at city hall, as well as a statewide film commission, to accommodate film and video shoots. Look in the paper for apartments for rent and inquire at local realtors. Sometimes, a house that is for sale can be rented for a short period of time. Ask friends, painters, and interior designers for leads. Put up fliers on community bulletin boards, at schools, and at local media organizations. Advertise in the local paper. These methods are especially useful for finding locations and housing when shooting at a distant location.

It's best to find locations as close to the production office as possible. When locations are 50 or more miles from the production office, the union rules governing professional actors and crew change. So, too, do the logistics, which will have an impact on the budget.

Take pictures of interesting locations with panoramic film or take enough shots to create a 360° montage of the area. A video camera also can be handy when scouting locations (see Figure 7.1).

> **STUDENTS**
>
> If you are filming in your hometown, avenues can open up because friends and family usually want to help young aspiring film- and videomakers. Expensive locations such as cafeterias and office space can often be secured for little or nothing.

- Are there toilet facilities for the cast and crew? Is there someplace they can go to relax?
- Is there a quiet area away from the set where you can leave food out all day for the company?
- On an exterior shoot, is there a place where the company can retreat from the elements if necessary (preferably someplace inside, such as a coffee shop)?
- Can a dressing room be rigged for the actors?
- Where will the actors apply their makeup?
- Is there an area off the set to store equipment?

Safety and Security

- How will you load equipment into the building? If shooting in an apartment building, check if there is a freight elevator. If not, ask whether the building superintendent will allow heavy equipment in the passenger elevator.
- Does the location require any security?
- Have you made arrangements to lock up any valuables?
- If the equipment is stored in a van and parked in a lot, is the lot bonded (insured)?
- Can the equipment be left in the location overnight?
- Do you need police from the city for traffic control?
- Are you performing any stunts or tricks that would require additional safety precautions?
- Do you have additional personnel to direct traffic or hold parking spaces?
- Do you have a fire sequence that requires a standby water truck?
- Are there stunts that require a standby nurse or ambulance?

SECURING THE LOCATION

You have now decided on the appropriate locations(s) for your project and need to contact the proper representatives. You must communicate clearly why you want the location and for how much time. (See our Web site for a sample location contract.) These are the next steps:

Location Contract

- Have you signed an agreement between the company and the location owner?

- Is the person signing the contract indeed the owner of the location?
- Have you been honest about the time you require (here it is best to overestimate)?
- Have you promised in writing to return the location to "as good if not better" condition?
- Have you offered the location owner a credit in the end crawl?
- Do you have permission to use the telephone and restrooms?
- Do you have the option to return for reshoots?

I had to find out if I could shoot in Grand Central Station. I found out that Grand Central is privately owned by Metro-North. I spoke to the public relations person there, and she said, "Yes, we love to help students." I asked about the cost, and she said it was free, as long as I didn't plug in any lights. Once I used their electricity, I would have had to pay some guy $15 an hour to sit there and watch the plug.

One of the stipulations for shooting in Grand Central was that I could only shoot between rush hours, 10 a.m. to 2 p.m. each day.

Then we ran into the usual hassles. Every morning when we got to Grand Central and started unloading the equipment, the stationmaster would come and kick us out. Because of the bureaucracy, the messages weren't coming through that we were allowed to shoot there. So we would run and find the woman in the publicity department—and get permission again!

Adam

Location Fee

- Have you negotiated a fair price for the use of the location?
- Does the fee include the use of power at the location?

> **STUDENTS**
> Even though someone may be willing to offer a location for free, some sort of compensation is recommended (however small). This elevates the exchange from a favor to a business relationship.

Permits

- Have the appropriate permits been obtained for the time and place of the shoot?
- Are the permits on the set, ready to be shown to authorities?

- Sometimes you need to secure additional permits. Do you have all the permits you need?

Insurance

- Have you obtained adequate insurance for the location?
- Does the insurance cover all the types of shooting that you are planning?
- Does the owner of the location require any special insurance?
- Have you allotted adequate time to process the insurance forms?

Communication

- Double-check all location arrangements. Have you alerted tenants of the production's impending arrival?
- Have a phone list of people to contact if there are problems. Who will let you in?
- Have you prepared maps and directions to the location for the cast and crew?
- Have the appropriate city officials been notified of your presence?
- Have you rented walkie-talkies for the crew if needed?

Transportation

Shooting sites, whether near or far, require that all departments, equipment, and actors be transported to and from the set. Transportation logistics must be planned in advance to maximize the time allotted for production. On feature films, a transportation captain is responsible for coordinating all this. On a short, the producer must assume this responsibility.

- Rent vans, trucks, and cars.
- Arrange for drivers.
- Coordinate company moves to and from each location.
- Calculate the time required for each move. Allow extra time for problems.
- Make travel plans for distant locations.
- Find and secure all on-camera picture vehicles.
- Make parking plans for all production vehicles.
- Rent the proper car mounts for moving vehicles. Hire an experienced grip to set the camera. You might need to secure special insurance and permits for towing picture cars.

- Create proper signage to direct the cast and crew to the location.
- Calculate all contingency plans, including weather, gasoline rationing, disaster, and personnel problems.

During the production period, drivers are constantly out in the field picking up actors, special equipment, and supplies. Pickup times are designated on the call sheet, and adequate time should be allowed for traffic and trips to the gas pump. Drivers are responsible for the vehicles to which they are assigned.

At the end of the day, during the *wrap*, the drivers return to the production office to drop off actors, run to the laboratory to drop off film, or take the principals to screen the dailies.

Catering

Like an army, a production cast and crew run on their stomachs. However, providing food need not cost a fortune. Planning ahead will always save money.

- Calculate a meal plan schedule for the entire shoot.
- Audition caterers by having them prepare a meal.
- Check with the cast and crew for any particular dietary needs.
- Have coffee and munchies available all day (craft services).
- Provide hot food for the midday meal if possible.
- Arrange a place where cast and crew can sit down for the midday meal and a short rest.
- Make provisions for a second dinner should the day's shooting run longer than anticipated.

Company Moves

If your project calls for several locations, it might be necessary to move the production unit during the production day. The time it takes to wrap out of one location, travel to another, and then unload and set up the equipment can monopolize a big chunk of a production day. This type of move should be avoided if possible. If it cannot be avoided, factor the time into your production schedule and remember the following:

- Create a detailed daily transportation plan.
- Assume that each move will take longer than anticipated.
- Do not leave equipment unattended in a vehicle.
- Keep the gas tanks full at all times.

- Travel time is time taken away from principal photography.

Parking

- Have arrangements been made ahead of time for parking?
- Have the appropriate permits been obtained and posted?
- Will the vehicles ever be in the way of a shot?
- Do you need parking spaces for picture vehicles?
- Will the equipment be safe in a parked car, van, or truck? Is the lot bonded?
- Does a street need to be blocked off the night before a shoot?

For Grand Central we got a permit to park near there, in a driveway, to unload. We went to the mayor's office and got a permit to park on the street.

Adam

Proximity

When deciding among several different locations, keep in mind that the crew will have to travel between them. Unless you are shooting your project a few days at a time, try to pick locations that are close in proximity to one another. This cuts down unnecessary travel time.

Backups

One final word about locations: It is highly advisable to secure a backup location in case the location you have chosen suddenly becomes unavailable. A standing set, one that is always at the ready, is called a "cover set." This is where you might run to on a rainy day.

DIRECTOR
Scouting Locations

As important as it is to choose the right actors for the piece, it is equally important to choose the right world, or at least the illusion of that world, for those actors to inhabit. The credibility of the story depends on it.

What does a particular environment do for the story? How can a specific locale enhance or detract from the script? Will the setting lend itself to an interesting visual background? Locations have symbolic meanings. The texture and feel of an environment can quickly and efficiently bring us into the province of a story as well as communicate exposition about the characters. It was crucial for the audience to feel that they were in a metropolitan train station for *The Lunch Date* and in a real gymnasium for *Truman*. The mannequins used as backdrops in *Mirror Mirror* served to visually represent society's ideal form. Every aspect of the sets in *Crazy Glue* made us feel we were in a real clay location.

By seeing where and how the characters live, we learn about who they are even before being introduced to them. This is subtle information that must be communicated. Your choices should not be arbitrary.

AESTHETIC CONCERNS VERSUS PRACTICAL LIMITATIONS

This should is an exciting and inspiring time for the director. The goal is to find places that represent the words on the page. You must find a balance between your aesthetic concerns and your practical limitations. The aesthetics of the location are based on the dictates of the script. A "dingy bar" does not mean the Oyster Bar at the Plaza Hotel, a "suburban house" does not mean an apartment building, and a "small park" does not mean a forest. The search for the appropriate location means ensuring that what the viewer sees on the screen is what was indicated on the page.

The practical considerations for choosing a specific site are based on what the budget can afford and the schedule will allow. A specific apartment might excite the director visually, but it might also involve inherent problems for one or more of the production departments. There may not be adequate power for the lights, it may be in a noisy neighborhood, or it may be too small or cramped. Balance is the key to a final decision about where to shoot a sequence.

The location became important to me early on. I saw getting a gym for a week for free and getting it near where these kids come from as a big problem. So I spent a great deal of time nailing down the gym. Then I could dream about it and mentally place my characters there. It wasn't just something I was hoping or wishing for. I knew it was there and that it was mine.

Howard

BE FLEXIBLE

Learn to be open and flexible. Don't look at locations (as with actors) with fixed ideas. Often a director will find a location that she never considered but that exceeds her expectations. Visually dramatic locations have been known to inspire directors. The director will then either alter the script or write a completely new scene to incorporate the location into the script. If you are in a real bind, you can always alter the script to accommodate locations that are available. This may sound like a compromise, but it could end up having a positive impact on the production.

THE POWER OF ILLUSION

As in so many aspects of production, you can employ tricks with the location to create illusions the script requires. For example, you can create movie magic by transforming a less than exciting site into a glamorous one described in the screenplay. The art department can work miracles to redress a location to look like the required setting. If the shots are specified, the redressing need only be done for the angles the camera will see. If you avoid shooting telephone wires and cars, your local park can look like a forest. By carefully choosing your camera angles, you can make a large loft space look like a tiny apartment.

In addition, you don't have to find your ideal location all in one place. A home can be pieced together out of many rooms in various houses that seem to fit together. Suppose, for example, that an actor walks out a door and the camera picks him up in the corridor. He walks to an elevator and gets in. We are inside the elevator with the actor. He alights into the building lobby and crosses to the front door. From outside, we see the actor come out onto the sidewalk. This could all be done at four different locations: a corridor, an elevator, a lobby, and a building exterior. The audience assumes the locations are all part of one building.

The cafeteria in *The Lunch Date* was not actually adjacent to Grand Central Station (it was several blocks away), but the audience connected the two because the filmmaker did. Adam Davidson did this with the sound. In both the station and in the cafeteria, we hear intermittently a train station announcer calling out track numbers and destinations over the public address system. Hearing the announcer in the station and in the restaurant binds the two locations together. What is amusing is that there is no public address system in Grand Central Station. The film-makers went to Penn Station to record the announcements! It is convenient to find everything in one place, but it is not essential.

> *I wanted to find a restaurant that would work. I knew there was nothing in Grand Central, but I wanted it to feel as if it could be a part of Grand Central. Because of that, it's really funny, what happens. There are no train announcements in Grand Central. I went to Penn Station and picked up train announcements there. So, of course, some people watch the film, and they say, "Wait a minute. This isn't right. There are no trains that go to New Jersey from Grand Central." Well, I never said it was Grand Central.*
>
> Adam

Many concerns about location are applicable to both narrative and documentary forms. With documentary subjects, however, you may not have any choice of where you film. Characters live and work where they live and work. The challenge is to work within the confines of each location and do it as unobtrusively as possible.

Each of the short films explored in this book is defined by the space in which it was shot. *The Lunch Date* employed New York's Grand Central Station; *Truman* was shot in a gymnasium; *Crazy Glue* had its two sets, an office and a living room; and *Mirror Mirror* was photographed on a soundstage (Figure 7.2).

What Does the Script Require?

The script might define specific kinds of locations, or it might describe locations so vaguely that it allows for leeway. "EXT. FIELD—DAY" gives little indication of what kind of field, how large, what kind of foliage, what time of year, and so on. "INT. OFFICE—DAY" leaves the kind of office open-ended. Is it a high-tech, ultramodern, antiseptic office or a wood-paneled, warm, cluttered room? The general nature of these descriptions can allow the director a great degree of flexibility and artistic license when it comes to picking a suitable location.

IDENTIFYING THE LOCATION

Each location is broken down into four categories for identification. These are the major factors

Figure 7.2 The gymnasium.

you must consider when scouting your shooting environments.

Interior or Exterior

The location you are identifying will either be interior (INT.) or exterior (EXT.): inside or outside. Both of these location settings carry with them a variety of factors to be weighed when determining a suitable background. Interiors are easier to control, but exteriors are less confining. Interiors can be blacked out, or tented, and shot at any time of the day, whereas the shooting schedules for exterior locations are dictated by the sun and the weather.

Day or Night

The script will indicate whether the scene is a day scene or a night scene (or dawn or dusk). Exterior day scenes mean that the source of light will be the sun. Remember that the sun has an arc, the sun may go in and out of the clouds, and daylight saving time reduces the number of daylight hours. Interior night sequences can be shot during the day if the windows are blacked out.

Stage or Practical Location

A scene will be shot either on a shooting soundstage or in a practical location. The stage is an ideal environment for controlling both light and sound, but the facility rental fee can be expensive. Practical locations look real but come with problems relating to space and control.

Stage

There are three main factors in determining whether you should use a stage:

Cost. Soundstages can be expensive. Check out prices. An unused stage might be rented to a film or video crew for a limited period at a reasonable rate to make a short. Empty warehouses and empty floors of buildings can be used as a stage.

Control. Soundstages exist for the sole purpose of providing the director with a soundproof, controlled environment in which to shoot. Stages provide a grid for hanging lights, which can be a major problem on a practical location. Stages come with unlimited power, heating and air conditioning, offices, dressing rooms, parking, telephones, bathrooms, and other conveniences that make the shooting process more convenient and comfortable than in a practical location.

A stage gives you the freedom to build any set and any backdrop. There is adequate room for the placement of lights, camera, and sound. This undisturbed freedom can translate into a focus on the job at hand that might not be available in a practical location. If the production team on location has to stop and start constantly due to noisy neighbors or cramped quarters, it drains the energy on the set (Figure 7.3).

Figure 7.3 A set built on a soundstage.

I knew from the outset that I was interested in shooting it in a studio. Although I have done only location shoots in the past, with Mirror Mirror, I wanted to use the studio sets to make a visual statement and thereby enhance the themes of the film. I felt that to have a woman talking about her body while seated in front of bookshelves in her living room or at her kitchen table would make a boring talking-head film.

Jan

Sets. If sets are required, they must be constructed. A stage is an empty shell that can be outfitted with walls, rooms, facades, and backdrops. The art department will rent or build walls, ceiling pieces, furniture, rugs, ashtrays, lamps—the works. Transforming an empty space to a lit set takes time. Constructing, furnishing, and striking the sets are additional costs that need to be factored into the stage rental.

Practical Location

Practical locations have two bright sides. The first is the cost. If your budget is tight, a soundstage will most likely be out of the question. Practical locations might be expensive, or they might be free. If the cost of a location is high, most likely the cost to reproduce the location on a soundstage will be higher. The second advantage of a practical location is "the look." A prac-

tical location will always appear real to the camera, whereas it is a challenge to make a set look like an actual location.

One of the main drawbacks to a practical location is the "boxed-in" feeling. Walls cannot be moved; ceilings cannot be raised. Lights must be set off camera in limited space. When the camera, lights, boom, actors, and crew are all assembled, the quarters are cramped, hot, and confining. Keep several fans on set for air circulation. In a cramped set, even the choice of lenses will be limited by the space allotted. An additional drawback is that often power is limited, which may require renting a generator.

Near or Distant

Your location, whether it is a practical location or a stage, day or night, interior or exterior, will either be near to the production office or distant from it. Having to transport cast and crew to and from the location is a major budgetary concern. If you employ union actors (SAG), the definitions of *near* and *distant* are very clear. On a map of the downtown area of your production, circle everything within a 50-mile radius. Any location within the circle is considered "near," and any location outside the circle is "distant." For a distant location, actors' travel time is factored into their hourly rate as if it were part of their workday. Also, a near location does not require the production company to transport the actor to and from the set.

Even if your company is a small unit with a van and several cars, traveling to and from the location uses up valuable time that might be better put into production. If a suitable location is found closer to the production office, precious time can be shaved off the production schedule.

> *It had to be something, first, that I could get for a week and, second, was located near the kids. I made* Truman *in Rochester, New York, where I grew up. This helped because I was able to draw from all of my connections. I got free scaffolding from a high school friend whose father was in the construction business.*
>
> Howard

If the location is so distant that plane or train tickets as well as hotel accommodations become necessary, your budget will need to reflect these costs. Employ a local contact person to smooth over rough edges with locals and to receive any goods or communiqués the company needs to send. There are some distinct advantages to working on a distant location. The cast and crew will bond quickly. The locals at most distant locations see a film or video shoot as a novelty. This may translate into *cooperation* and possibly free goods.

> *What jacked up the expense was shooting away from home. There are tremendous advantages to it—you have the crew at your disposal and they are there to focus only on your film and that's tremendous—but it makes for a more expensive shoot. Every location trip costs something. Getting people back and forth isn't cheap, and eating costs increase.*
>
> Howard

WALK-THROUGHS

Once you have secured the locations, it is advisable to call for a walk-through with the key personnel. During this floating production meeting, indicate how you will place the camera for the scenes in that particular location. The DP can sketch out a lighting plan so that on the day of the shoot, the gaffers will know where to place instruments and how to locate power. The production sound mixer can identify problems that might conflict with the track. All the department heads can ask questions during the walk-through. It is, in essence, a dry run of the production.

KEY POINTS

- Scout your locations with the full crew before the shoot.
- Try to centralize your locations.
- Arrange for locations with written contracts.
- Make sure you have backup locations.
- If possible, prerig an interior location by dressing it in advance and roughing in the lights.

chapter eight

Art Direction

I let the subjects know from the preinterview stage that if they were cast in the film, I would require them to wear a mask during the interview. Because it was a peculiar request, I didn't want to spring that on them when they arrived for the shoot.

Jan

PRODUCER
Assembling the Team

The producer has two major concerns with regard to the art department: hiring the best creative people for the project and creating a good look without having to pay top dollar. Production value is about balancing fiscal responsibility, and respect for the artistic mandates of the script. A good producer takes pride in stretching money as far as possible. The producer's role in terms of art direction involves these five steps:

- Hiring an art director
- Establishing a visual style
- Approving the budget and the schedule
- Hiring key support people
- Supervising the preproduction/construction schedule

THE ART DEPARTMENT

The art director, also known as the *production designer,* is the head of the art department. When working on small-budget projects, the art director sometimes has to handle all the duties of a full art team. (Refer to Chapter 6, "Crewing," for a description of a full art team.)

The art director is the person ultimately responsible for the overall look of the picture. She must be able to work in tandem with the director, the director of photography (DP), and the parameters of the budget. She creates the world of the picture, and the DP is responsible for lighting that world. She strives to fulfill the director's vision of the piece, but must do so economically. The art director scrutinizes the script carefully and, in conjunction with the director, arrives at a visual plan for the picture. Whatever the plan, the art director must come up with a comprehensive budget and a schedule to accomplish her task.

Most beginning film- and videomakers work with small budgets, forcing them to look for an art director who has experience working with limited resources. In hiring for this position, compare the candidates' flexibility, experience, and fee. Keep in mind that one art director might cost more than another but might be more inventive or a better negotiator and thus will actually save you money. (The topic of hiring the art director is discussed in more detail in Chapter 6, "Crewing.")

In many ways, money definitely makes the producer's job easier. With enough money, you can hire a comprehensive art department. If you can afford it, you can hire a hair and makeup person for the entire shoot, ensuring day-to-day consistency. An alternative is to rely on the actors to do their own hair and makeup. If you can afford standby painters, they can quickly take care of sets that need to be touched up or recolored. An alternative is to anticipate such changes and schedule around them.

No matter what the budget, someone has to make sure the crew is accountable for its work. The producer is the guardian of the budget and the schedule. He approves the budgets and production schedules devised by the key crew members and sees to it that everyone adheres to these figures and dates.

With all the weight we have placed on the art director's role in the creative evolution of a project, it happens that many student filmmakers treat art direction as an afterthought. It ends up becoming the collective job of everyone on the set. This occurs primarily because it is difficult to find other students interested in doing this important job.

IMAGES CAN TELL A STORY

The audience must believe that the actors are the film's characters, and they must believe that the rooms they live and work in, and the clothes they wear, are true to the world of your story. Nothing in any frame of your picture should disrupt the illusion you are striving to create.

Think about the seedy hotel room Travis Bickle inhabited in the film *Taxi Driver*, or the interior of the *Millennium Falcon*—the spaceship Han Solo pilots in the original *Star Wars* trilogy. Each of these decorated sets gives the audience a wealth of information about the identity and idiosyncrasies of the character. The producer's job is to spend as little as possible and still achieve these effects.

Adam Davidson secured Grand Central Station for free. Using this authentic location lent great credibility to the project, and getting it for free was probably the only way he could afford it. Howard McCain was able to shoot in a gymnasium for *Truman*, thus ensuring the realism of his script. Jan Krawitz surrounded her masked women with an array of mannequins. This imaginative set inexpensively symbolized and reinforced the theme of stereotypical female physical perfection.

RESPONSIBILITIES OF THE ART DEPARTMENT

Sets and Locations

During preproduction, you must decide whether to shoot your story on sets, in practical locations, or both. If you face this dilemma, compare the costs of constructing and dressing sets against the location fees. (In Chapter 7, "Location," you read about the pros and cons of working on a stage or in a practical location.)

In a practical location, the art director is confined to the space at hand. Her involvement in the search for locations, therefore, is crucial. She will have to transform these spaces into the world as defined by the director's vision of the script. She can alter and redress them, but only within the limits of the existing dimensions and only with the permission of the owner.

On a set, the world must be created from scratch. The primary benefit of shooting on a set is that it is a camera-friendly environment. A set can be designed for flexibility, ease of manipulation, and good camera angles, and it imposes none of the constraints of a "real" location. The process of creating a world from scratch follows specific steps:

- The art director analyzes the script.
- She engages in conceptual and practical discussions with the director, who has a vision for the piece as well as practical requests regarding the kind of coverage she plans.
- The art director furnishes the director with ideas through sketches of set renderings and pictures. These sketches might later be modified or altered.
- On approval of the basic design, a drafter executes blueprints. If necessary, a model of the set is constructed.
- The art director presents budget and building schedules to the producer. Design changes might be made to reduce costs. The department heads give final approval.
- The construction coordinator supervises the construction of the set according to the approved design.

The completion of a set must fit into the production schedule. If multiple sets have to be built, the construction schedule of each set must be timed so that the set is available when needed.

Probably the most important consideration when constructing a set is determining precisely what the camera will see. The art director must find a balance between (1) how the director envisions the scene and (2) the budget, allowing some leeway for adjustments. If the director only needs to see a bed in a corner of a room, the art director should not build a fully dressed four-walled room. Similarly, the director should not order a fully dressed four-walled room and then shoot only the bed in the corner. The entire art direction budget will be stretched during the shoot, so waste should be avoided.

However, a good art director will not build a set with just two walls and a bed. Standing by will be a third wall and maybe even a ceiling piece. If, as the director blocks the scene, she desires more room in which to shoot, additional set pieces can easily be provided if prepared in advance.

I was thinking about painting the floor in front of the mural. I knew I wanted it to be fairly monochromatic. I didn't want color in these sets, but I don't really know why. I suppose I wanted the women to stand out from the backgrounds and for the backgrounds not to be too assertive. I had a bunch of black-and-white linoleum tiles in my garage. You know, it is funny how ideas emerge. I was really wrestling with this floor dilemma, and suddenly I thought about those tiles and how I could make an interesting design with them. So I brought them into the studio and laid them out on the floor and thought that it looked pretty striking. Audiences commented on the floor—really noticed the black and white floor that the women are standing on.

Jan

It is important that there be a dialogue between the art director and the DP. For all the effort put into designing sets and dressing locations, the audience must be able to see them properly. For example, if the visual design called for a dimly lit room, the DP will then choose faster, more light-sensitive film stocks (not an issue with video). Also, everything is designed for the camera. Make sure the creative team spends its time on what the camera can see, and not on anything off-frame. If the director and DP are planning to photograph only part of an apartment, there is no need to dress the other half.

Set Dressing

The locations and their details set a tone for the film. They can help tell the story and convey a great deal of information about the characters themselves. Sometimes a key detail in the frame solidifies the credibility of a scene or moment.

Set dressing is everything that is placed on the set. This includes rugs, lamps, furniture, paintings, windows, chandeliers, and cabinets, as well as all of the extraneous details, such as plates in the cabinets and bulbs in the chandelier. Set dressing does not include smaller items, such as guns, canes, lighters, or rings that the actors use specifically. These are props.

The art department is responsible for "dressing" the location according to the director's wishes. Dress-

ing a location might be as simple as spreading a few leaves near a park bench to make it look like fall, or as complex as furnishing an entire set from scratch. If a director walks into a living room and decides it will work for the film, this might mean that the room can remain as it is, or it might mean that the room must be stripped down to the bare walls and everything, including the stains on the rug, must be "imported" from another location.

Duplicate Set Items

Each department is responsible for the manufacture or purchase of duplicates—that is, items that are to be destroyed, distressed, or consumed during the course of shooting a sequence. If a table is broken during a scene, it will need to be fixed or replaced for each take. It is also helpful to provide duplicates for items that are small or fragile, such as sunglasses, that could be either lost or accidentally damaged in the course of shooting.

Props

The property master is responsible for all the props identified in the script. A prop is a movable object, used by an actor, that is integral to the story. Props include jewelry, glasses, books, and weapons.

The beauty of film and video is that something doesn't have to be real to look real to the camera. Costume jewelry, for example, looks as real to the camera as do true gems. A person cannot deceive the camera, but a thing can.

The property master provides an assortment of props based on the needs of the script. He rents, buys, or makes the props. He might also use personal props provided by the actor. Like the costumer and the set dresser, the prop master should consult with the actors concerning their preferences. If there is little or no time for prior consultation, a good prop master will have several props available from which the actors can choose.

Most property masters own a kit or box of common props. This is called a *box rental*. Instead of shopping outside for some props, the producer can rent them directly from the prop master. Spend money on props that are dramatically important or used extensively. When disposable props are involved, have an idea of how many takes and retakes might be involved. Err on the side of having too many props rather than too few.

Figure 8.1 Weapons of any kind can be dangerous. Scene from *Truman.*

Weapons

All weapons fall into the prop category. It is the property master's duty to ensure safety with regard to these props (Figure 8.1). He must arrange with the local police for a permit to use firearms during the production, and the weapons' firing pins must be removed. The prop master usually gives a weapon to an actor just prior to the scene. Props, especially weapons, should not be handled except during a rehearsal or take.

The use and handling of weapons are delicate issues. Special permits and insurance must be obtained just to have a gun on the set. The prop master is responsible for the weapon before and after its use and must keep it in good shape. There is never a need to have live rounds on a set.

On an interior set, keep the prop secured until it is needed. On an exterior location, make sure everyone nearby, especially the police, is aware that a scene involving a weapon is about to be photographed. You never know when a passerby might misread the scene and return fire.

Food

If a scene requires that food be consumed, make sure it is purchased in advance and that someone can prepare it. Buy all food items in bulk if possible, and try to use wholesale clubs or discount warehouses to get the best buys.

Duplicate Props

Often props are eaten, damaged, or distressed during the shoot. The property master and director should discuss how many backups will be needed, and the property master should provide extras, just in case.

Wardrobe

The costumer, or wardrobe designer, works hand in glove with the art director. Together with the director, they develop the look for the show's wardrobe. The wardrobe department is charged with making the characters identifiable by the clothes they wear. They might decide to dress the lead actor in bright colors and the secondary characters in grays, or they might choose pastels, or specific materials—whatever they feel contributes to the overall statement of the story, the characters, and the style of the production.

The idea of the mask was there from the very beginning, although I don't remember what prompted it. I look back at my first proposal and see that it's in there. Two years before I shot the film, I was interested in homogenizing the faces so that the viewer's attention would be deflected away from the face toward the body. People look at bodies in this culture, but they are also judgmental about a woman's face. I wanted the audience to focus their attention on the bodies of the women and not have access to their faces.

Jan

What each actor wears provides worlds of information about the character he portrays. Even though we are taught that you cannot judge a book by its

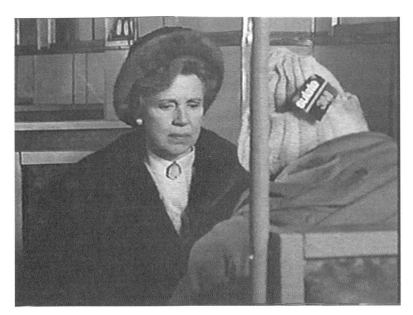

Figure 8.2 Scene from *The Lunch Date.*

cover, most people form a strong first impression based on how a person is dressed. In *The Lunch Date*, the contrast of wardrobe between the woman and the man having lunch together says a great deal about their stations in life (Figure 8.2). The woman is dressed in a fur coat and fur cap with elegant jewelry. The homeless man wears a hat with the manufacturer's tag still attached. This is a wonderful, subtle touch, which helps inform the audience of the type of character under the cap. Can you imagine the scene if the wardrobe were reversed, if the woman were dressed in rags and the homeless man were in a coat and tie?

Make sure the wardrobe doesn't look as though it just came off the rack (unless this is your intention). A garage mechanic should look like a garage mechanic, and the audience should believe he is a mechanic before he utters a line. The clothes should be aged, tattered, and stained with grease. The process of attaining this look is referred to as *distressing* the wardrobe.

Consulting the Actors

Who better understands the character than the actor who must portray him? Soliciting the actor's suggestions about style, color, and specific choices will increase his involvement in the show. If the costumer gives him an outfit that the actor feels is inappropriate, "creative differences" could result. It is best that the costumer consult with all actors or at least have several choices from which the actors and director can choose.

I went over the wardrobe with the actors. I had them bring down a few things, and my art director, Claudia, was there, and we discussed it together. This coat would be better than that. What was in the purse? The contents had to be identified.

Adam

Using an actor's own wardrobe is an inexpensive way to obtain clothes that fit. If your actors offer to supply their own clothes, ask them for a number of different items from which to choose. The company should see that the clothes are not damaged and that you pay for the cleaning of all wardrobe pieces that are worn.

Thrift shops are another source of some very interesting costumes at reasonable prices. Remember that clothes can be altered, dyed, and borrowed.

Specialty Garb

Period pieces, of course, require period clothes. Paying attention to history is critical. Each period of dress must be carefully researched and represented accurately. Certain genres, such as film noir or science fiction, require a special look that must remain consistent throughout the picture to maintain a specific style.

Duplicate Costumes

If a scene calls for damage to the costume, the costumer will need to have doubles and triples of the same clothes. Suppose, for example, that a character is supposed to be stabbed in the chest. A blood pack under the shirt is rigged to ooze red liquid, giving the illusion that the character has been wounded. When the director calls for the second take, the dresser replaces the stained shirt with a new one.

If an actor gets wet in a scene or spills ketchup on a costume, the wardrobe department will need to have another standing by for each additional take. Stunt people who double for an actor need to have a costume that is identical to the actor's. For some shoots, this might require three or more of the same suit.

Continuity and Script Time

The costumer is responsible for maintaining the continuity of the costumes. Using the stabbing example again, some scenes involving the bloodied victim might be shot before the actual stabbing scene itself is recorded. In this case, the costumer needs to distress one of the duplicate shirts to represent a stab wound as exactly as possible. This can get very complicated. Ideally, the assistant director will schedule the shoot with this problem in mind.

Script time is the logical progression of the days in the script. Wardrobe and script supervision are the departments most responsible for script time. If a story takes place over three days and there is a different wardrobe for each day (most people change clothes every day), the wardrobe department keeps a chart of what clothes are worn in each scene. Then if the script is shot out of continuity, the character will be wearing the correct clothes throughout the filming.

Consulting the Director of Photography

The costumer consults with the director of photography regarding colors and materials. Some DPs, for instance, are adamant about not allowing actors to wear bright white clothes. White can make lighting difficult because it reflects the light.

Makeup

The glamour of Hollywood is exemplified by the bright, clean, unblemished look of movie stars. In the old days, audiences did not seem to mind that their heroes on the screen could be kicked and beaten yet still look like a million bucks. Audiences today are more sophisticated and prefer greater realism.

Men wear less makeup than women. Sometimes, actors wear no makeup at all, or a director might demand that they wear none. Usually, though, they wear at least a base, a skin-toned makeup called *pancake,* which is spread evenly over the face and hands. With a base, the makeup artist can maintain a consistent skin tone throughout the picture. In addition to a base, women generally wear lipstick, eyeliner, mascara, and powder.

There is specialty makeup for creating cuts, wounds (fresh, oozing, and recently healed), moles, bruises, and so on. Anything more elaborate than these specialty items falls under the domain of the special effects makeup department.

Special Effects

The special effects makeup department might work in conjunction with the makeup artists or as a separate unit, depending on the nature of the project. These artists work on large-scale specialty makeup jobs, such as monsters, which require major prosthetics. They might also be called on to perform more subtle tasks, such as making an actor look older or younger. Special effects makeup techniques generally employ large latex pieces to reshape the actor's face or body. Special makeup sometimes requires camera tests. Hire a stylist to design makeup for each actor, and ask the actor to be responsible for sustaining it.

Hair

Hairdressers often use hairpieces, wigs, beards, and toupees. Many balding actors have maintained a full head of hair for years with the aid of a hairpiece. Some women prefer to wear a wig when performing because they don't have to sit in a chair for hours while the hairdresser creates an elaborate hairdo. They can slip the wig on and off without worrying about destroying the style. Another advantage to hairpieces of all types is that they can be maintained at a constant length and color. Actors need to have their own hair trimmed frequently to maintain continuity.

Men can use facial hair to achieve a different type of look. Beards and mustaches have to be made and fit well in advance of principal photography to ensure enough time for alterations. In addition, several pieces must be made as backups because facial hairpieces disintegrate after several wearings.

A typical production problem involves a character who has a "change of look" in the story. She goes from long hair to short hair. This can most easily be accomplished with a short haircut and a wig. If no wig is used, the schedule must reflect this choice: Any scenes that require long hair must be shot before the performer's hair is cut.

Actors might be required to change their hairstyle or hair color or even add facial hair for a role. Experiment before committing to a particular look.

ANIMATION

In traditional cel animation and with computer-generated images (CGI), the art direction is part and parcel of each frame drawn. In live action animation, as in claymation or any form of pixillation (see Glossary), the design of the characters and the settings is manufactured on a small scale (Figure 8.3). The principals are similar to any live action shoot, the technique is specific to the scale and materials of the animation project.

The class at NYU where I made the film is a yearlong class. The first six months I was very, very, very lax. I only did storyboards, one of the most important tools in the animated short. So I did that and recorded the voices. That was first semester. Then second semester hit and I went into a frenzy. My art director was in town. A woman I knew from childhood who was very talented and had a degree in industrial design. She knew how to use power tools. There is an expectation when you're a student animator that you can do all yourself. You will build a set yourself, you will do the puppets yourself, write the story yourself; the entire thing is usually a one-person effort. My biggest decision was to give the set design to someone else. I gave it to her and that decision probably made the film possible. First of all she came up with two beautiful sets for the office and for the apartment, and it freed me up to make the puppets and concentrate on that and the animation.

Tatia

THE PRODUCER'S ROLE

Question All Requests (within Reason). During the creative discussions between the director and her art director, the producer should, within reason, question every request. The creative process involves a series of discussions in which many ideas are bandied about. The solutions to a problem can run the gamut from very expensive to inexpensive. For example, should you wish to fly a character through the air, there are several ways to accomplish this stunt, including a wire-flying rig, blue-screen photography, and imaginative framing. The difference in cost among these three choices is enormous. The director considers each idea and, with deference to the budget, makes a suggestion that will be cinematographically satisfactory. When there is a choice, it behooves the producer to opt for the less expensive solution, of course (Figure 8.4).

I originally thought I would have the women wear different masks, and I spent a lot of money buying a variety of masks. After trying on the masks at home, I realized they were quite grotesque and not what I wanted. Finally, I found an inexpensive white kabuki-type mask in a costume store, and the minute I saw it, I knew this was the one. So I bought six of them, and I cut out the lips so the sound wouldn't be muffled.

Jan

Figure 8.3 *Crazy Glue* office sequence.

Figure 8.4 Each of the women in *Mirror Mirror* wears a mask.

Review Budgets Carefully. Always expect that the art department's needs will be more expensive than anticipated. Don't be afraid to play the heavy and challenge a production request. The director needs to be cozy with her creative team, but the producer doesn't. His job is to be cozy with the budget.

Keep Tabs on Weekly Spending. Money flows very quickly through the art department. Don't give the department the entire budget amount at once. Keep on top of the cash flow. Have each member of the department turn in receipts each week for everything bought or rented. (See "Petty Cash" in Chapter 5, "Budget.")

Keep an Eye on the Construction Schedule. If the construction personnel promise that a set will be completed by a particular date, follow their progress. When scheduling, it is prudent to allow extra time in the construction timetable. If the construction coordinator swears that the turnaround time for the next set is three days, schedule four.

DIRECTOR
Creating a Look

The "look" of any film or video project has its origins in the script. Its tone, the genre, and any specific elements described by the author will affect the final product. After the director and the director of photography plan how they will photograph the script, the art department details the elements within the frame and realizes them. Once the major location decisions have been made with the producer, such as construction, distant locations, or stages, the director works with the art director to shape the sets and locations.

The director must be familiar with the capabilities of all the production departments, especially her art direction team. Knowing how clever the team can be in stretching the budget is instrumental to her creative decisions. It is unfair to the production to request an item that might enhance the show but would overtax the art department's time, talents, and money.

The rental of the mannequins was too costly, so I had to be resourceful, and figure out how to get them for free. A friend of mine knew someone who worked in a large department store and he dressed the mannequins. He thought he might be able to loan me some damaged ones. So that's what I did. I went and borrowed five mannequins from this huge department store—unbeknownst to them, I think. He gave me a bunch of damaged mannequins from a back room and I was able to use them for the two-week shoot and then I returned them.

Jan

HOW TO DEFINE THE "LOOK"

It may be difficult to communicate what a "look" is. For example, each of us has our own sense of a particular lighting style; "mood lighting" may have a different connotation for different people. To bridge this gap, the director can gather concrete examples that represent what "mood lighting" means to her. Poring through magazines, tearing out images or *tear sheets*, and looking through photography books, the director searches for the images that represent the mood or look she wants. (The public library is an excellent source for classic photographs.) This can also be accomplished with scenes from films that best evoke the kind of "mood lighting" you want to imitate in your project.

ARCHITECT OF ILLUSION

The art director supervises a creative team that designs, builds, and dresses the sets and helps choose and dress the locations. Anything that communicates information to the audience involves a decision of some kind. Every piece of clothing, hairstyle, prop, or article within the frame tells us something about the character and the world of a story. Many aspects of art direction are also story points, such as the salad in *The Lunch Date,* the photo in *Crazy Glue,* or the rope in *Truman.*

The art director is responsible for interpreting the director's ideas and transforming them into a visual plan. Working from the script, photographs, paintings, and other films, these two department heads create a "look" for the film or video. The art director and her team are also responsible for overseeing the continuity and consistency from scene to scene.

The art director's duties vary from project to project. The script might require designing sets or simply altering existing locations. The screenwriter strives to craft a story in which every scene and character support the theme. The art director's job is to ensure that every article within the frame complements the story, illuminates the characters, supports the theme, and serves the director's vision.

The director chooses the actors who will portray the characters, the location or production manager secures the locations, and the cinematographer lights and frames the set. The art director is responsible for everything else. It is a key position and one that beginners frequently misunderstand, undervalue, and fail to appreciate. This is because the ability to create an illusion through art direction is like a magic trick: Everyone admires the end result, but no one realizes that it took hard work and special talent to achieve what is only an illusion.

For example, a cheap cardboard column is painted à la trompe l'oeil to look like marble, and voilà, the audience sees a stone pillar. A small off-screen wind machine blows small white polystyrene pellets at the actors, who pretend to struggle to stay afoot, and a "blizzard" is created.

Knowing how materials react to light and how they "read" on film and videotape helps the art director avoid buying unnecessarily expensive materials. A good art director knows that rayon chiffon looks exactly the same as silk chiffon on film.

Black and White versus Color

A good art director must have a comprehensive knowledge of color, color combinations, and the dramatic effect of color on an audience. She must also understand, if you plan to shoot with black-and-white film, as did Adam Davidson with *The Lunch Date,* the challenges of creating a world in shades of gray. Both color and black and white can subtly influence an audience's response to the visual story, but they do it in different ways. A red ball in a white room pops out in color film. In black and white, the ball reads simply as a gray object. The art director will consequently use different stylistic choices when she works with these two media to create the world of the story.

BREAKDOWNS—LISTEN TO THE SCRIPT

The look of the project has its origins in the script, and in the director's visual ideas for it. An in-depth analysis of the script affords the art director an understanding of the story, character, and theme evolving through the plot, all of which can and should be reflected by the art direction.

Consider an example:

INT. LUNCHEONETTE—AFTERNOON
    The woman walks into a station luncheonette. It is a simple place—a grill, some booths, and rows of refrigerated cabinets filled with salads and sandwiches. She reaches into a glass case and removes a salad.
    A COOK stands behind a white linoleum counter. He fiddles with his white paper hat and white apron.

Art department personnel breaks down this scene from *The Lunch Date* by creating lists of what they have to rent, buy, or make.

Location. The scene takes place in a luncheonette. The location needs to look as if it belongs in a train station. To find the appropriate location, the art director scouts for a real train station luncheonette. The location manager attempts to secure an actual luncheonette. If a real location cannot be found, the art director either builds a set on a soundstage or redresses an existing location to give the illusion of a working luncheonette. For this scene from *The Lunch Date*, the director decided to redress an abandoned lunch counter to look like a functioning establishment.

Dressing. Once the decision was made to use the defunct restaurant, the art department created a plan to bring the location to life. That meant cleaning, putting up signs and posters, and adding elements such as ashtrays, salt and pepper shakers, napkins, and extra salads.

Props. The key props for this scene included the salad, silverware, the woman's personal effects, her handbag, and change.

Wardrobe. The woman's wardrobe is the same throughout the piece. For this scene, the costumer needed to find a chef's hat and apron for the actor playing the cook.

Makeup and Hair. No special concerns.

Effects. No special effects.

DEFINING THE SPACE WITH STORYBOARDS

For adequate preparations, the director should give the art director the details of each shot, either with a storyboard or verbally (see Chapter 3, Figure 3.8, for sample storyboards). Storyboarding scenes in a film or video affords the director and art director common ground from which to create a frame. What should the character's habitat look like? How much of the space needs to be art "directed"? How much does the camera need to see?

Communication is the key to a successful shoot, and storyboards are a precise way to transmit information. If you have a set with no ceiling piece and in your storyboards you indicate a low-angle shot that will include the ceiling, the art director must make appropriate arrangements beforehand. If the director decides on the day of the shoot that she now wants a low-angle shot, the budget probably won't cover the cost of constructing a ceiling that quickly.

CAMERA TESTS

Depending on the nature and design of your project, it might be wise to shoot some tests with the actors in full makeup and wardrobe. This is an added expense, but it will clarify what you will be shooting during principal photography. Camera tests also inform the director and producer of the dynamics between the cast and crew in a work environment.

KEY POINTS

- Duplicates must be purchased, made, or rented for many items, such as food and wardrobe.
- Unless you shoot a scene only once, the art department will need to match each take with the previous one in terms of wardrobe, makeup, and hair.
- Much of art direction is an illusion. A piece of costume jewelry looks like the real thing to the camera.

chapter nine

Casting

I was affiliated with Blue Man Group doing some video work for them at the time and also working in the lobby. One of the Blue Men, Andrew Miller, had a beautiful, beautiful voice. We spoke one day and I realized that not only did he have a beautiful voice, there was something about his demeanor that was just right for the character of the husband in Crazy Glue. *So I asked him to do the voice and he said yes.*

Tatia

PRODUCER

Auditions

The credibility of the project rests on proper casting. It cannot be stressed enough how important it is to find the right actors for the project. The actors are the words with which you will tell your story. They allow the audience to enter the world of your drama by bringing to life the scripted characters. No matter how slick the camera work, it will be difficult for viewers to empathize with your story if they don't believe in your characters.

The young boy in *Truman* and the woman and homeless man in *The Lunch Date* seem to inhabit their roles effortlessly. As viewers, we experience the characters, not actors playing parts. This is also true with the anthropomorphic attributes of the clay-mation characters in *Crazy Glue*. This illusion is due partly to their performances and partly to their being physically right for the characters. Had the actors' physical and vocal types not suited the characters they were supposed to play, no degree of performance could have overcome this false impression.

I think the most important thing is to pick someone who you trust and whose work you respect. I don't think someone can create what you want if it's not their sensibility. I think the casting process is the most important one. You have to pick somebody you absolutely think is right and are profound and have subtext in their performances and then let them bring it out while giving them some direction in what it is you are looking for.

Tatia

No matter how many people participate in the casting process, the final decisions should rest with the director. Not only must the actors fit her vision for the project, but she must feel comfortable with their working relationship. The producer's job is to ensure that the director has the widest choices of talent to review. The producer also lends support by serving as a creative sounding board when the director requires an objective opinion.

The assistant director hires the background or extra players based on the number requested by the director. The producer must balance that number against the budget. Although it is always better to have a fully peopled scene, extras are paid a negotiated fee and must be fed and transported to and from the set.

THE CASTING DIRECTOR

An important addition to the creative team is the casting director. After gaining an understanding of the director's requirements, the casting director sifts through many of the submissions so the director sees only those actors who are genuine possibilities. The casting director looks at a script and, based on her experience in the field, establishes a viable list of actors for each part. The following are some of the elements a casting director brings to a production:

- Valuable creative input
- A solid resource bank (file of actors)
- Awareness of new talent
- Good working relationship with agents and managers
- Ability to make deals with actors (understanding of Screen Actors Guild [SAG] rules)

A good casting director does all the setup work so the director and producer need only make the decisions. If you can afford it, this is a valuable and worthwhile person to have on the production team. If you cannot afford to hire a casting director, the producer and director assume these duties.

To find a casting director, inquire of other producers and directors who work in the low-budget arena. Breakdown Service publishes a useful guide, the *Casting Director Directory for New York and Los Angeles*.

THE BASIC CASTING STEPS

Although the exact method used to cast a production varies from project to project, the following steps provide a useful overview of the basic process:

- Advertise specific roles
- Scout local theater companies
- Scout acting schools
- Organize submitted head shots and résumés
- Arrange casting calls
- Arrange callbacks

- Negotiate with selected actors
- Deal with rejected actors

Advertise Specific Roles

Use advertising to let the creative community—actors, agents, and managers—know about your project and the specific parts available. It is easiest to locate a variety of talented performers in major metropolitan areas. Actors are attracted to these areas because of the opportunities they offer for professional work. Here are some suggestions for advertising your project:

1. For a small fee, you can submit an advertisement in the appropriate trade publications, such as *Backstage* (New York City) or *Drama-Logue* (Los Angeles). (See our Web site.) The ad should be succinct yet clearly represent your casting requirements.

2. Create a professional-looking flier (desktop publishing programs are useful here) that clearly represents your project and available parts. Post it at acting schools, schools for the performing arts, community theaters, local college theater programs, high school drama societies, and community and acting guild bulletin boards.

I put a little survey out and said I'm a filmmaker. I didn't say I'm interested in meeting women who want to be in a film because I think that can be pretty threatening and off-putting. I just said I was doing research for a film about women and body image and I was interested in talking to as large a group of women as possible about their experiences with this. They had to fill in their name, height, weight, age, and phone number. I got about . . . 65 responses that way. I wrote them all a letter and thanked them for the responses and said I'd be back in touch with them.

Jan

3. Submit your project to Breakdown Services (see our Web site). This company is an excellent casting resource for producers. It distributes vital information about what films and videos are in the casting process and what roles are available throughout the United States. Agents and personal managers pay a weekly subscription fee for this information. You pay a small fee to

submit a synopsis of your project and descriptions of your principal parts. This information is submitted to all the agents and personal managers in your area who subscribe to this service. Represent the nature of your project accurately—that is, is it a non-SAG production? Does it include violence, nudity, or sex? Interviewing actors under false pretenses wastes everyone's time and will blemish your reputation as an ethical producer.

4. Locate a copy of the *Academy Players Directory*. This huge and expensive two-volume set is put out by the Academy of Motion Picture Arts and Sciences (see our Web site) and contains a photographic listing of practically every actor in the motion picture business, along with his or her agency representation and guild affiliation. You can usually find this directory in a library. You can also purchase it directly from the academy or at a media bookstore.

I started out with Backstage. *I put my ad in for $27 and got a whole stack of head shots. Next I wrote to Breakdown Services, which sent me people more in line for the gym teacher. Then I contacted talent agencies, which now is a very accepted thing, but it was not at that time in New York. I just said, "I'm doing this great film. It would be a wonderful reel piece . . . will pay expenses . . . Do you have anybody?" At the time, there was something called Manhattan Kids on Stage. I saw some performances and had a few more kids audition for me.*

Howard

Scout Local Theater Companies

If you live in a major metropolitan area that has small theater companies, such as New York City, Chicago, Los Angeles, Boston, or San Francisco, it can be useful for you and the director to scout out the currently running shows for new talent. These cities have many small and interesting theater groups, but don't discount the many community theaters all over the country. Don't ignore summer stock and dinner theaters either.

Check the cast lists for the specific types for which you are looking, and plan to see these actors in action. If you are impressed by an actor's performance and feel that he or she might be right for your project, go backstage after the show and introduce yourself. The actor will be flattered by the attention.

Scout Acting Schools

Many acting programs in metropolitan areas run their own theater groups, and these can be a good source of talent. Posting a flier may work, but contacting the teachers personally might be more effective. Ask them about the best ways to approach their students. They might allow you to sit in on a class.

Organize Submitted Head Shots and Résumés

When they hear that you are casting, interested actors or their representatives will submit a photograph, or glossy, with a résumé attached to the back. From the résumé, you can cull the following information: experience, height, weight, age, union affiliation, and the actor's contact number. A single advertisement in *Backstage* has been known to attract hundreds of 8 × 10 glossies. Organize and file the glossies according to the part.

From these head shots, look for actors you are interested in auditioning. This is a tough call because you will most likely be flooded with applicants. When choosing actors to audition, base your decision on their "look," their experience, and your gut instinct. However, be aware that a glossy may be an idealized version of what the actor really looks like.

Arrange Casting Calls

Find a space in which to hold the auditions. It should have some kind of waiting area where the actors can study the pages they will read for the audition. The audition space should be large enough to allow the director, producer, camera operator, and reader to sit comfortably and to allow the actors to move around with ease. The space you choose should also have adequate light for video.

Set up a working schedule for the day or days you plan to audition. Find out how many actors the director wants to see each day and for how long. Start with a plan for 15-minute intervals, and work from there. Call the actors or their agents to schedule appointments. If you can't reach an actor, leave a phone number where he or she can reach you or leave a message.

On the day of the audition, be sure to do the following:

• Have a production assistant log the actors in at the door.

- Be sure you have plenty of copies (at least one per actor) of the sides to be read.
- Arrange to have someone read opposite the actors. (The director should not read with the candidates because it will hinder her objectivity.)
- Have a pitcher of water and paper cups available for the actors.
- Keep the auditions as close to schedule as possible. It is impolite and unprofessional to keep actors waiting for long.

There's more information on holding auditions in the "Director" section of this chapter.

Arrange Callbacks

It is now that the casting process begins in earnest. The goal is not only to look for the best actors for the parts, but also to find the right chemistry or balance among the players. This is especially critical when casting a love story. Your two lovers must seem to be attracted to one another. To achieve the right chemistry, read actors opposite each other in different combinations. The best combinations can then be put on video. (See the "Director" section in this chapter.)

The Screen Actors Guild allows its members to attend three callbacks without a charge to the producer. After three callbacks, the producer must pay the actor to attend additional casting sessions.

Negotiate with Selected Actors

By the time you sit down with the actor you want to hire or with the actor's agent, everyone involved should already have an understanding about your budget constraints. Be honest and upfront at the beginning about how much money you have to spend.

If you have no budget for talent, your only hope to attract good actors is a well-written script with good parts that can showcase performers' talent. A video copy of the project might prove to be payment enough.

If you are working primarily with "struggling actors" who do not earn a living from their craft, you might have to work around their schedules. They usually have day jobs to pay the rent.

It is not uncommon for non-SAG talent to receive little or no compensation for work with beginning or student filmmakers. Generally, their entire compensation consists of the following:

- A screen credit
- A video copy of the completed film
- Transportation to and from the set
- Meals during the shoot
- Dry cleaning of the actor's personal wardrobe

If you are obligated to pay one of your principal actors, however, you should pay all of them (at least all the speaking parts) to avoid resentment on the set.

You can hire a nonunion player with a simple deal memo or letter of agreement that indicates the compensation (if any) and the performance dates (see our Web site). No contract is required.

If you hire SAG actors for your project, you must deal with a SAG contract, which involves minimum payments for daily or weekly rates, or what is called *scale*. What SAG actors receive even for scale can put undue financial stress on a small budget. If you hire a union player, you must become a signatory to the SAG contract and agree to all its provisions. When negotiating with a union member, remember that unions require payments to pension and welfare funds. In addition, if you have one SAG actor in a show, the union requires that all the actors be on a union contract. There are some exceptions to this ruling. Check with your local SAG representative.

STUDENTS

In some situations, scale payment for SAG talent is deferred. Some film and video programs in the United States have worked out an agreement with the Screen Actors Guild that enables the actors' salaries to be deferred until the film is distributed. Then, the first dollars from the distribution royalties (excluding film festival prizes) go directly to pay the actors' salaries. In effect, these salaries are tacked onto the negative cost of the picture at the end of the production process. This arrangement enables first-time directors to work with professional union actors without having to pay them if the project does not make money. Note, however, that if you use SAG, Equity (stage), AGVA (variety), or AFTRA (TV) actors under this waiver and book them for your shooting dates, they are under no obligation to stay with your project if they get a paying job. This often happens, so you are advised to have backup actors.

Deal with Rejected Actors

The producer should be the "heavy" when it comes to breaking the bad news to actors who have not been cast. It is emotionally difficult to call an actor who has come in for several callbacks to tell him that he has not been cast. The actor will appreciate a courteous phone call thanking him for his time and enthusiasm during the casting session. Always strive to build good relationships with good actors. What if you rudely reject the next Dustin Hoffman?

ADDED BENEFITS OF CASTING

The casting process offers many benefits besides finding the best talent for your project. Casting offers an excellent opportunity to audition the script as well as the actors. Hearing the lines spoken will give the director and writer a sense of what works and what doesn't. Scenes are often overwritten, and readings can expose fat that might be eliminated.

Through the casting process, the producer can get a sense of how the director works with actors. Is she comfortable? Does she put the actors at ease? The ability to find a rapport with her actors is a necessary part of the director's craft.

Finally, the casting process offers the producer and director an opportunity to meet and build relationships with talented performers. Once you have worked with an actor, if you feel that the results and relationship were successful, you might want to work with that actor again. The bond that results from the actor–director relationship is very special. It might last only for the duration of the shoot or for a lifetime.

From a selfish point of view, my documentary work has been a passport to experiences and people that otherwise would be completely off limits. For example, when I made Cotton Candy and Elephant Stuff, *I literally ran away with the circus for a month because I was making a film about them. Otherwise, I never would have lived with the circus for a month. And with* Little People, *I came to know a lot of dwarfs and midgets who are still in my life 12 years later.*

Jan

DIRECTOR
Auditions

As a director, your relationship to the actor is extremely important. The producer is involved in casting and is ultimately responsible for hiring the cast, but it is the director–actor dynamic that breathes life into the characters that propel the story.

The director, cinematographer, and art director exercise their craft behind the camera. It doesn't

matter how they look or how they feel when they work because they are not exposed to the camera's eye. The actor, though, is the very instrument through which the drama is played.

Actors must sometimes call on deep, personal feelings. Helping the actor discover the emotional life of a character is a trying, exciting, and sometimes painful process. When casting, you want to find the actors who have the craft to make truthful discoveries about the character and the talent to reveal these discoveries to others.

The life of an actor is not easy. Actors constantly audition for parts they don't get. Most work at acting intermittently. Many work at other jobs to pay their bills. When an actor auditions, he or she usually competes with dozens of other actors for a single part. To help you understand something of the actor's work process, consider attending acting classes. This will help you discover how to draw out the best in the performer.

I took acting classes while I was a student at Columbia University. We had a course in directing actors, but it wasn't enough, so I took some acting classes with Stella Adler. I learned you must respect actors and their process.

Adam

RESPECT FOR ACTORS

We want to suggest a simple but effective credo: Treat *all* actors with respect and courtesy. Make each experience pleasant and professional no matter how wrong for the part the actor may be. They have made the effort to come in and put themselves on the line. Respecting that effort, you create goodwill with that individual and show respect for the whole acting profession. You never know—they might be right for your next project. For those who are eventually cast, this first encounter represents a positive and congenial foundation on which to build.

CASTING

The audience attends a film or video to witness a story told through actors. If viewers do not care about the characters, then they will not care about the story. The case studies used in this book present characters in situations we care about. Will the woman in *The Lunch Date* stand up for herself and get the food she believes is hers? Will our couple reunite in *Crazy Glue*? Will Truman climb the rope? Will the women in *Mirror Mirror* tell the truth about their bodies?

Figure 9.1 Finding your lead actor is an exciting moment.

The important creative relationship between actor and director begins during the casting process. If the film- or videomaker makes an error at this juncture, it will affect the whole production. Choose wisely. Take your time. Be objective, and remember that the casting process is not perfect. Some actors, for example, audition better than others. This does not necessarily mean that the actors who audition well are the better actors.

Casting Children

Finding talented child actors can be particularly difficult. First, there are far fewer child actors than adult actors. Second, even trained child actors can be difficult to control. Many children are born performers. An untrained child can often give a more spontaneous and engaging performance than a professional child actor (Figure 9.1). When casting, assess a child's energy and attention span as well as his or her talent.

> *I had three casting sessions and didn't find anybody. Finding the little boy for Truman came out of sheer persistence. I told my acting teacher I was desperate and asked if he knew anyone (even his second cousin) who looked like the person I needed. He said, "Well, I met this playwright, and she had this kid with her, and he kind of looked like what you were talking about. I'll give you the number, and you can call and make your pitch." That's what I did. Once the kid walked through the door, I said, "That's Truman!"*
>
> Howard

Audition Guidelines

For a successful audition and to make the most of the search for the best actors, we recommend following the guidelines in the next sections.

Before the Audition

The audition can be held in any quiet room. A rented rehearsal hall is an ideal place to hold an audition. The space should contain at least three chairs: one for the actor, one for the director, and one for the person who will read opposite the actor. Some additional personnel might be present at the audition, including the producer, the casting director, and a camera operator if the audition is recorded on videotape.

Beginning the Audition

Introductions. The production assistant ushers each actor into the audition space. The director should attempt to relax the actor and put him at ease. If the director creates an atmosphere that encourages the actor to feel confident, the audition will go better. The actor will perform at his best, and the director will be able to make an informed decision.

The director should greet the actor, introduce the people in the room, and make small talk before beginning the audition. The actor will bring to the audition a recent photograph, called a *head shot* or *glossy*. Attached to the back of the photo will be the actor's résumé, which contains information about the parts the applicant has played. It also describes the actor's talents and interests and lists the teachers with whom he has studied.

This material can be used as a good place to begin small talk. For example, you might say, "I see you studied with Mira Rostova" or "Do you enjoy doing Mamet?" or "When you say here you speak French, are you fluent?"

Depending then on how much of the script the actor has read, you might briefly tell the story you plan to shoot. This will put the audition scene in context, which will be helpful to the actor. Only when the director feels the actor is ready should she begin the audition.

Types of Auditions

Sides. The most common method used to audition actors for a film or video project is to have them read a scene or part of a scene from the script. These pages are called *sides*. When the actor reads the sides for the first time at an audition, it is called a *cold reading.*

Auditions for the first call usually run at 5- to 15-minute intervals. The material you prepare for the actor to read should be short. This will allow you to make the most of the meeting.

The actor will need to act with a partner the production provides. This individual should not be the director, because she needs to observe and assess the performance. The reader can be the producer, a production assistant, or another actor.

The reader should make eye contact with the actor. This gives the actor someone to whom he can relate. Because the audition is for the actor, not the reader, the reader should not "act" nor read in a monotone, which would be equally distracting.

When the actor begins reading, allow him to read through the scene with no direction. This reveals the actor's interpretation of the role, which might bring a unique slant to the character, one you had not considered before.

If you like the actor, ask him to read the scene again for an emotional value different from that of the first reading. Ask him to find the humor in the scene, for instance, or the irony. This second reading is key because it gives you an idea of the actor's range and flexibility. During the audition process, it is more important to discover whether the actor can take direction than whether he already understands the character.

Take notes on your assessment of each actor. Your notes will help you decide at the end of the day which actors you would like to use or which you would like to call back.

Monologue. In addition to or instead of the cold reading, you can ask the actor to prepare a monologue for the audition or the callback. A monologue is a speech for one person from a play or film. It gives you the opportunity to witness a prepared performance. The combination of the cold reading and a prepared monologue offers that much more information on which to make casting decisions.

Improvisation. Another useful technique is to have the actor improvise a scene from the script—that is, to act like his character, spontaneously, in a situation you create. Improvisation is a specialized acting form. Some actors, especially comedians, are very adept at this type of performance. Other actors do not have this facility. It is, however, an acceptable request to make of an actor.

Evaluating the Audition

The primary goal of the audition process is to discover the actor's range of talent and his ability to take direction. If the actor reading for the part is absolutely perfect, indicate this in your notes, but never offer an actor a part during the audition. You never know who might come in later and cause you to change your mind. If the actor is not ideal but has interesting qualities, this, too, should be noted. After all, the ideal actor for the part might never audition. You will have to cast the role based on the talent available.

Keeping an Open Mind. The readings are an excellent opportunity to explore many different casting possibilities, and these possibilities are as varied as the actors who walk through the door. Remain flexible and open-minded as to the many ways a part can be cast.

Too often, directors have a set image of a character in mind during the audition. If an actor matching that image doesn't appear, the audition is merely an exercise. Casting against type often makes the script even more vital. Can the part be played by an African American, an Asian, or a physically disabled actor? It might be interesting to cast as the villain of your piece an actor who has the appearance of a nice guy. This will create a doubt in the viewer's mind and add a tension that wouldn't otherwise exist.

Use your imagination when casting. If a talented blond actor auditions but you see the character as a redhead, consider using a wig or asking the actor to dye his hair. The director must be aware of how the various departments can help shape an actor's look.

The audition process requires stamina and concentration. Reading actors all day with only a short lunch break can be exhausting. Be sure to give adequate consideration to the last few actors who audition. Among them could be the actor who is just right for the part. Remember, casting can make or break your project.

Notes. If you write pertinent observations on the actor's résumé or on a separate log sheet during the reading, you can later review the day's many auditions. It is also important to note the actor's schedule and availability.

> *Casting* Mirror Mirror *was an interesting process. I invited 60 women who had filled out questionnaires at a local film festival to attend one of several discussion group meetings that I had. My intent was to set up informal groups where the women would feel comfortable talking about issues related to body image and I could observe how articulate they were, what stories they had, and so on. The original questionnaire didn't ask for women willing to be in a film but only to participate in discussions as part of my information gathering. I gave them a choice of six different dates and some evenings. Two women might show up, and other nights, there would be a group of eight. None of the women knew each other or me. I decided not to prerecord at these sessions as I wanted the conversation to be as uninhibited as possible. However, after the session, I would make notes about what stories each of the women shared so I could use those as aids in casting the film. I made mental notes of what they each looked like.*
>
> Jan

Videotaping. Videotaping is an excellent way to review auditions and helps in making a casting decision. Recording the audition on video gives the creative team an opportunity to review the different combinations of actors at a later time. It also allows you to see how an actor relates to the camera. Certain actors have an affinity for the lens, and some don't. Some very talented people freeze under the scrutiny of the lights and the camera. Therefore, videotaping is best used for the second audition, or callback.

Using video during auditions is most effective with actors who have little or no exposure on film or tape. It is vital that you see them on tape before making any final decisions. A film test is ideal but is more expensive than shooting on video.

If you use a video camera during the audition, set up the equipment unobtrusively. For example, the camera might be placed in a corner, with a long lens at an angle, out of the actor's eye-line.

> **VIDEO OPERATORS** | Make sure there is enough light for the video camera. Shoot with lenses of several sizes. Start wide to see how the actor moves and communicates with his body. Then move in to a medium shot and finally a closeup to see the actor's face, particularly the eyes.

Callbacks

When the general auditions have been completed, the producer arranges for callbacks. A callback is another audition, but with actors who have already read for the director once and are being considered seriously for the part.

The callback can be conducted in the same fashion as the first audition, but with some modifications. The time periods are generally longer, say 15 to 30 minutes, which permits the director to work on specific details in the scene. Actors are asked to read opposite other actors who are being considered to determine whether there is the right kind of chemistry between them.

If the lead has been cast, you can ask that she read with all the candidates who might play opposite her in the film or video. This process, referred to as *mix and match*, is useful in casting family members.

If you can't find the actors you want, you might have to look beyond the normal casting arena. Leave no stone unturned.

> *At the end of these informational preinterviews, I asked them all if they might be interested in appearing in the film. Every single person I preinterviewed was interested in being in the film, although the initial call was just for information gathering and discussion. Not one person said no at the end of those sessions, which I found pretty extraordinary.*
>
> *There were a lot of great women among those initial 50, but there was a preponderance of women between the ages of 25 and 40, and they were mostly white. I knew from the outset that I wanted the film to be multicultural and, of course, to transcend any particular ethnic or racial delineation. So I had to cast the net a little farther, and I found out about a women's spirituality group at the Unitarian Church that was specifically for older women. I got permission from the organization to pitch the idea to them. From that group I was able to cast three women who wanted to be in the film.*
>
> Jan

Figure 9.2 Jerry Klein, who played the coach in *Truman*, was the Midas Muffler Man.

Things to Keep in Mind

Benefits of the Casting Session. The casting session is a learning process for the director. How lines are read, how a character is interpreted, and how a scene is performed all add to the director's excitement and enthusiasm during preproduction. Although the casting session is not foolproof, it is a time-tested process that generally provides successful results (Figure 9.2).

My experience was if someone's not busy and they're professional and they like you and they like your script, they'll do it. So I just started picking people out of the Academy Players Directory because there I could see their faces and head shots. And I hadn't really got anything I was satisfied with in Backstage. So I found this guy, Jerry Klein, and he came in, and he was terrific. He looked right. And even though the role is fairly one-dimensional, he brought something to it that made it kind of fun. . . . He's a professional actor—the Midas Muffler Man. He does all sorts of things.

Howard

The "Nonaudition." If you're interested in using an actor of some note, her body of work should be enough on which to base your decision. Actors like to work. They especially like to work on projects with good scripts.

I had advertised in Backstage and met a lot of people, but I didn't find anybody right. I went to a talent director, and she gave me Scotty's name, but she told me I couldn't audition her because she's doing it as a favor and she is beyond auditioning. All I could do was an interview. So I met her, we talked, and it was great.

Adam

KEY POINTS

- Leave no stone unturned in your search for actors. Once you have cast a part, there is no turning back.
- Watch for chemistry between actors who play opposite one another.
- Understand the life and process of the actor. This will enable you to get the most out of an audition.
- Be prepared to cast a backup actor in case your actor of choice must leave the production.

chapter ten

Rehearsals

This was a hard script to rehearse because it's basically all action with very, very little back-and-forth dialogue.

Howard

DIRECTOR
Working on Scenes

One of the director's primary responsibilities is to assist the actor in discovering and playing his role. The director accomplishes this through script, character analysis, and staging. Once casting has been completed, the character development process begins with rehearsals.

During the rehearsal period, the following takes place:

- The director gets to know the actor.
- The actors bond with each other.
- The director and the actor develop a mutual trust.
- A character research method is devised.
- Scenes are shaped, beats are discovered, and business is created.
- The director and actor evolve a shorthand for communicating on set.

If possible, do not wait until the cast is assembled on the set during principal photography to rehearse. This puts unnecessary pressure on the director, especially a beginner. Although the scene can be rehearsed on the set, time will not allow for long rehearsals with the entire crew standing by at full pay. The crew's presence can be distracting, and their salary is a drain on the budget. The set can be cleared for rehearsal, or you can move the cast to a separate space while the crew completes their preproduction work on the set. This might cause some delay in the day's schedule, but it is better than rushing a scene.

The first goal in rehearsal was getting Truman's confidence and trust.

Howard

BEFORE REHEARSALS

Getting to Know the Actor

Before rehearsals, the director can meet with the actor in a casual, nonwork setting. This is an opportunity to begin developing a rapport. There is little pressure in a meeting of two artists simply talking about their work. You might ask the actor questions like these:

- What are your work methods?
- How were you trained?
- How do you like to approach the development of a character?
- How do you see this character?
- How do you see this character in relation to the other characters and to the plot?

You might discuss the following with the actor:

- Your working method
- Your feeling about the material

- Your interpretation of the character
- Your plan for a shooting style
- Any difficulties you foresee in the production

In *The Master Director Discusses His Films* (interviews with Elia Kazan by Jeff Young, Newmarket Press, 1999), famed theatrical and film director Elia Kazan talks about his experience getting to know actors:

> *As a director, I do one good thing right at the outset. Before I start with anybody in any important role, I talk to them for a long time. I make it seem casual. The conversations have to do with their lives and before you know it, they are telling me about their wives, their mothers, their children. . . . You're storing it away. You're getting your material. By the time you start with an actor, you know everything about him, where to go, what to reach for, what to summon up, what associations to make for him. You have to find a river bend, a channel in their life that is like the central channel in the part. Without their knowing it you're edging them towards the part so that the part becomes them. The story of the part is the story of their lives or an incident in their lives. . . . You're in a position of trust, and the actors who trust you continue to tell you more. They work with you in an internal way.*
>
> Elia Kazan

DEVELOPING MUTUAL TRUST

Discussing the actor's character casually over coffee starts the process of discovery and trust in the director–actor relationship. Discovery is the process of finding things to help build the character, of seeing the character grow. Trust allows the director to be an integral part of that growth. Trust developed now will carry over through the rehearsal period and then onto the set. Without trust, unfortunately, there are usually friction and miscommunication.

> *The first aspect of rehearsal is actually no rehearsal at all. . . . I took Truman out for ice cream; we played video games and did "kid things." It was a way to gain his trust and make him feel comfortable.*
>
> Howard

RESEARCHING THE CHARACTER

An actor develops his own character under the director's guidance. If the actor is inexperienced, he might ask the director for her help. One way he can develop his character is by observing and studying similar characters. If his character is based on a real person, the actor can research material written about that individual and can seek out videotapes, radio broadcasts, and so forth. An essential resource for the actor is his character biography or *back story*: a full life story that supports the details in the script. It ensures that everything the actor does in the story is rooted in the patterns of the past. It furnishes depth and credibility to the performance and allows the actor to be able to justify everything his character does in the story. The rehearsal period is a good time for the director to meet alone with each actor to go over his ideas and to encourage, develop, or make adjustments.

An actor builds a life for his character based on the text. All the information that the actor and director need to develop a character should be found in the script. The author will have indicated important physical characteristics, emotional motivation, and pertinent surroundings. The story itself is the key to the arc of the character. For example, in *Moby Dick*, Captain Ahab begins as a rational and collected character. During his journey, as revenge comes near his grasp, he starts to lose his sanity. He will do anything to kill Moby Dick, no matter what the cost. The journey of that character, which spans the course of the novel, is referred to as the *arc* of the character. We say that a character has an arc when there is a discernible and significant change in that character.

The director and the actor should be in agreement throughout the shoot on the arc of the character. Film- and videomakers rarely record the scenes in screenplay order. If you must shoot the last scene first, it is imperative that you know how the characters arrive emotionally at that point in the story. Knowing the emotional arc of the piece allows you to shape each moment so that there is an appropriate dramatic build. If the final scene is played too low key, you will have nothing toward which to build. Conversely, if the final scene is played at a fever pitch, the actors might never be able to build truthfully to that pitch over the course of the shoot.

REHEARSALS

Benefit of Rehearsal

The rehearsal period may reveal problems with a particular actor, his working methods, or his chemistry with another actor. These kinds of problems can lead to a part having to be recast. Without a rehearsal period, they could surface on the set when it is too late. Unless you are able to shut down production, your only choice is to shoot around the actor until you get a replacement.

Rehearsal Schedule

As soon as the parts are cast, make a list of everyone's availability, and work out rehearsal times. Most people find it easier to work to a predetermined schedule, and it communicates an aura of professionalism. Make rehearsals brief and frequent rather than long, comprehensive, and potentially exhausting. You want to keep your cast fresh and lively; too long and there could be the issue of diminishing returns. Schedule the rehearsals in a quiet room or a setting similar to your location. There should be no crew, no equipment, and no time pressure—just the work.

Read-Through

The first step is to assemble the entire cast for a read-through of the script (before they have memorized their lines). This will give you an idea of how the whole piece flows and let everyone become familiar with the dramatic arc of the piece. It is an exciting experience and the first opportunity to address where potential problems may exist, such as in a particular scene, an actor, or even both. It is an opportunity to see how the actors interpret their roles and how they all work together.

We had a soundstage for a day. We read a few times. They were on books while reading it, so they didn't need to memorize it. I just had to find a good performance and to direct them a bit, and that was it. It was very easy and fast.

Tatia

Actors should be encouraged to use natural movement if they feel it is appropriate, although the primary purpose is to focus on the meaning of the words. Give little or no direction; you want to see what they spontaneously bring to their role and to the piece. Encourage the performers to work together. Although you have strong ideas about how the piece should be played, be receptive to your actors' input. This will send a message that you respect them as intelligent and creative people: that they are partners with you as you mutually explore the dramatic possibilities of the script.

The first read-through might reveal problems with the script itself. Is a scene too long? A scene or part of a scene that feels totally extraneous should be eliminated.

We rehearsed with the whole class. I wanted everybody to meet each other before starting. We had all the kids there Saturday afternoon, and we read the script out loud—this must have been the third time—now with their participation. Then we walked through it in the gym very quickly so it didn't get boring and I kind of said, "This happens and then this happens." This was more about making everybody feel comfortable with each other, feeling like they could be themselves. We did this quickly because I didn't want to lose the spontaneity.

Howard

Develop the Theme

The read-through is the appropriate time to discuss the theme of the story. You have carefully thought out what the piece is about and know what you want to communicate. Your task is to bring the cast along to your way of seeing the story, without imposing it on them. Ask your actors to discuss the purpose of the story. This might reveal a wide variety of opinions. Encourage all points of view, but impose none of your own at this time. Try to avoid lecturing; rather, adopt a way of directing their attention to the meaning of the piece with probing questions that can guide the cast to discover what you already know. The goal is to have everyone on the same page.

Keep Notes

It can be tough to remember all your impressions during the rehearsal period. Because you will need to always stay on top of what is going on, early impressions may be taken over by later ones. Avoid this by carrying a large scratch pad that you can occasionally write brief notes on.

Scene by Scene

After you have explored the arc of the story and its theme, you can now begin work on each individual scene. Try to rehearse the scenes in their order in the script; this will allow you to create some continuity. Don't worry about the memorization of lines (so you can avoid the actor getting locked into a specific reading). It is more important for the actors to understand the meaning of a scene than to know all its words. Work with defining conflict, character objectives, and, ultimately, the development of subtext.

Start off by not giving the actor too much instruction. Have a clear idea of what you want to achieve in a scene, but remember that the director should be flexible. An actor, following the flow and inclinations of the character, might discover a completely new approach to the material. Learn to guide actors in the direction you want to explore, but do not hinder their creativity.

The British director Ronald Neame (*The Odessa File*, *Hopscotch*) told this story during an interview with the American Film Institute:

> *I first learned this lesson from Alec Guinness of being completely fluid when I go on the set. . . . As a director the first film that I made with him was* The Promoter. *It was only the third film I had directed. I had got it all beautifully worked out. I had done my homework. We came on the set one morning and I said, "Alec, I thought that maybe you should do this, that, and the other thing."*
>
> *He said, "Well, Ronnie, I've been thinking. I'd rather like to play this scene lying on my back underneath the table."*
>
> *I said, "Lying on your back, underneath the table?"*
>
> *He said, "Yes."*
>
> *I said, "Well, you're out of your mind, Alec. What's that got to do with the scene?"*
>
> *He said, "Now wait a minute. Don't get impatient. Just bear with me a minute." Of course he suggested something in relation to the scene and it was absolutely marvelous played on his back underneath the table. That was the way that we shot it.*
>
> *If an actor can bring you something and wants to do it his way, provided that he is following the character accurately and he's not being absolutely stupid, then he should be encouraged to do it this way.*
>
> Ronald Neame

The goal of every actor is to have the camera capture every moment as if it were happening for the first time. There is no such a thing as rehearsing too much as long as you are exploring deeper layers of meaning within a scene. The director needs to be sensitive to her actors and should strive to find a balance that will allow the actors to be "fresh" during principal photography. If the actors perform for the camera as if they have been drilled, the performance will lack spontaneity; therefore, some directors do very little rehearsing. They want to save it for the camera. You will develop your own style, based on what you find works successfully for you.

Videotape the Rehearsals

Once the actors have memorized their lines and are moving freely around, it is useful to shoot the rehearsals with a video camera. This can be done with a continuous take or documentary approach so the flow of each scene won't be interrupted. The camera operator can move or zoom in for closer shots when appropriate. A few of the benefits of taping the rehearsals are as follows:

- It is an opportunity to judge the work on the screen from seeing what works on the screen.
- The cast becomes comfortable with a camera present.
- The director may catch subtle mannerisms in an actor that may need to be addressed.
- The director can begin to see where best to put the camera and from what angle.

These videotapes become part of the director's homework for shaping performances and for planning her visual approach for the project.

Shaping the Scene

Blocking Action

When *blocking* or choreographing a scene, don't "show and tell" the actors what to do. Instead, allow the scene to grow organically. Start the actors with no movement, perhaps seated. When it is indicated in the script or when the actors feel compelled to make a move, they should do so. Little by little, as the scene is repeated, various actions, known as *business*, will evolve, and the scene will begin to take shape. The idea of business is to integrate authentic behavior into an actor's performance. Examples of business are the lighting of a cigarette at a key moment in the scene or the jiggling of a set of keys to break a tense moment of silence.

It would be ideal to rehearse each scene in its "real" location, allowing the actor to interact specifically with his surroundings. If this is not possible, try to simulate the location. Use masking tape to mark out the floor plan of the location, including the walls, windows, and prominent set pieces. Then when the actors arrive on the set or location, they will already be familiar with it.

Discovering Beats

Just as the director breaks down the scene into shots and angles, she must also help the actor break down the action into dramatic beats. This enables the actor to develop the arc of his character moment to moment. Each scene has many small beats that together make up the major objective of the scene. As we established in the breakdown chapter, beats are influenced directly by character objectives. Each character has his objective for the whole story, each scene, and the beats within each scene.

The script gives the actor a situation. The actor explores with action and with dialogue how he might respond. With each change of the situation, a new beat begins. The director and the actor explore the beats of each scene together.

This is all apparent in the text and in how the director has broken it down into beats in preproduction. Occasionally, the director finds that what read well on paper does not play well in action. Often, action can replace dialogue or might render words unnecessary. The luncheonette scene in *The Lunch Date* is a good example of a scene in which a few lines of dialogue and a wealth of silent business and reactions create a full conversation. The rehearsal process is an excellent opportunity to trim any fat from the script or to revise the dialogue to accommodate blocking, props, or set pieces.

During the rehearsals, directors and actors often like to improvise a scene to help clarify the meaning of the scene, the subtext, or the dramatic beats. Improvisation is a spontaneous use of invention in which the actor keeps the character and the situation but is not tied to the text. For example, suppose a scene from the script is set at a park bench. A man is attempting to break off his relationship with a woman. The director can ask the performers to improvise the scene many ways, with each performance exploring different and subtle emotional nuances within that particular situation:

- The man can't go through with his speech.
- The park is empty.
- The park is crowded.

In the middle of the improvised scene, the director might add information to the situation—for example, it begins to rain, the woman begins to cry, or a nearby musician plays "their song." During the scene, the director might whisper a direction to the actor that will further adjust the direction of the scene. For example, she might tell him, "You suddenly realize you love her" or "Try to get the ring back." Each of these whispered directions will allow the actress to react without prior knowledge of what the director desires. An interesting discovery made during an improvisation can then be used in the scene.

The use of improvisation is an effective way to loosen the actor up. It can help the director discover new meaning in a scene as well as learn how well the actors play off of each other in unscripted situations. Improvs can also lead to discovering interesting staging ideas and novel bits of business.

Because there wasn't much dialogue for Truman's first rehearsal, we played some games. He pantomimed climbing up a rope with his eyes closed as well as various other little physical actions. Then I asked him to draw me some pictures—pictures of what he thought his character looked like and what he felt.

At the third session, we brought in the gym teacher so they could get comfortable with each other. They just talked and had a hamburger. From there, we actually did some minor improvs between the two of them. I had Jerry pretend to be his father. From that I could gauge how the little boy would react to him as a figure of authority.

Howard

Pace and Rhythm

Pace is defined as the rate of movement or progress. It is the amount of time required to bring the audience to the height of the emotions the scene requires. This is a primary responsibility of the director. During rehearsals, the director and actor determine the pace of each moment, each scene, and ultimately the entire show. The director can then instill the project with a pace, which can make or break it. If the actors peak emotionally too early or too late, the delicate fabric of the story can be torn. The director memorizes her feeling of the pace during rehearsal so she can be objective during the shooting period and remind the actor both of the pace itself and of how the pace fits into the arc of the story. Once the performances are recorded on film or tape, any further adjustments to the pace can only take place in the editing room.

Four key directorial phrases are often employed during rehearsals and when photographing a scene: louder, softer, faster, and slower. However, rather than imposing these words arbitrarily on a performer, encourage her to "use urgency" or "take your time" at a certain point of the scene, thereby allowing the pace to come out of the character.

An equally effective means of controlling pace is to give the actor a new objective or action. If a scene seems to be dragging, tell the actor, for example, that he has just learned that his friend's house is on fire and he needs to call the fire department. This action or directive will inject a more organic urgency to the scene.

Communicating on the Set

The director and the actors constantly refine a scene by honing beats, restructuring dialogue, and inventing business. With each adjustment, they come closer to developing a shorthand for communicating what they want to do. The director's notebook will include important details based on her observations during rehearsals and her private conversations with each actor. The director relies on these notes so she can say the right thing on the set to trigger the performance she seeks. The next time the director and the actors will work together is on the set, where time will be a critical factor. If they can work efficiently together, problems relating to script and performance can be solved quickly.

> We spent a long time going over the script, page by page, examining each thing that would happen—where Scotty would be, what was going through the character's head, etc.—which paid off in the end because I could do things on the set like say, "This is just after you lost your wallet, and this is going to happen next," and Scotty would know where she was, in terms of the character's emotions. We didn't actually rehearse until the day we arrived on the set.
>
> Adam

Special Situations

The director is often faced with a great diversity of acting styles from the talent she employs within a scene. Some actors are trained to improvise; others are trained in a Method school of acting. The director will need to use all her wiles to meld these acting styles and special situations together so that the scene looks like everyone on screen is part of a whole.

The Method

In the early part of this century, the Russian director Konstantin Stanislavsky developed a method of acting that became known as *the Method*. In this process, the actor digs deep into the well of her own experience and finds an emotional response similar to the one called for in the script. The actor tries to relate her own experience to the character's. This acting technique is also referred to as *emotional recall*.

It might take time, but by digging into her own emotional well, the actor brings a great deal of truth to the moment, and the results can be rewarding. As the actor's goal is to make each moment truthful, finding that truth within herself makes the result seem all the more genuine. The Method creates a very internal kind of performance; rather than acting, the actor seems to live the role.

Comedy

Comic acting is based on talent, skill, and timing. Many comedians excel at improvisation; spontaneity is an integral facet of the comic actor's skill. Because timing is so critical in comedy, it often takes considerable time to work out a routine or even a moment within a scene. Chaplin was famous for rehearsing on camera. He sometimes shot a sequence a hundred times, constantly refining the routine until the only business left was his exit through a revolving door.

Comedy is serious business. Just because the crew laughs doesn't mean that the scene will play in a screening room. The director is the only audience on the set who matters. If she thinks the scene is working, she can shoot it and then move on.

Understatement

Whether the scene is dramatic or comic, understatement will always work better than overstatement. It is easy for actors to play big, broad, and loud. For one thing, it feels good to use their instrument with full broad strokes. The line or moment that is understated, though, has twice the meaning. The camera picks up the most subtle details. The director needs to carefully watch actors who were trained for the stage. Their tendency is to play a scene to a large audience. In film, less is more.

Untrained Actors

Working with untrained actors can be both rewarding and frustrating. An untrained actor might be a natural for the part, but he will not be familiar or comfortable with the technical aspects of the actor's craft. Working to find a character, sustaining a performance, shooting out of continuity, and even hitting marks will be a mystery to him.

In this situation, the director must be especially patient. She should explain the process at each step, coaxing a performance out of the actor. With an untrained actor, it is permissible to give a line reading, which means asking the actor to repeat a line just as the director delivers it. Ask the performer to think the line before saying it. One of the things I did in terms of casting the film was I worked on food lines at Grand Central every night before filming, and I saw this guy Willie the night before. He had this harmonica and this great face, and I asked him to show up.

Adam

Interviews

Documentaries are based on spontaneity. The subject of a documentary is not an actor, so there is no rehearsing for a scene. Often, the director is in the field with a camera, capturing the subjects as they go about their lives. This doesn't mean the subject is totally "cold." A documentary director might inform the subject before the interview what topics and questions she might introduce. This gives the subject an opportunity to think about the shoot and how she might phrase her answers.

In *Mirror Mirror*, the director interviewed her subjects using a set of questions she felt would reveal interesting material on the topic of women's bodies. From the hours of responses to her questions, she pieced together a story that captures the spirit of her subjects.

I met these women a month before the shoot. I did not want to give them the questions in advance because I knew that if they thought too long about an answer, the responses would lose spontaneity. So when they arrived at the set, I said to them, "You're going to be seated there, and I will ask two questions. Then we'll move over here and do two more questions." I told them that any time they wanted to stop between the questions, they should let me know because I knew that the mask got hot. So I let them know that they were somewhat in control of the process.

Jan

Sometimes the director must probe for the kinds of answers she feels will best match the script she has previsualized. This approach might require asking provocative questions designed to stimulate the subject.

PRODUCER
Preparing Call Sheets

The preproduction period is one of planning, preparation, organization, communication, information gathering, checking, and double-checking. The producer or assistant director, those in charge of the preproduction period, gather and processes information from the department heads. They must consider and weigh this information when shaping the schedule and the budget.

The producer must keep the creative team focused on its goal: being totally prepared for the shoot. As each week of preproduction passes and as the cast, crew, and locations are locked into place, the producer adjusts the schedule to reflect their specific requirements. He and the other members of his department handle the multitude of elements that will affect the production. The production manager, the production coordinator, the location manager, and the office production assistants look at and take care of hundreds of details. (If you don't have these people working for you, then you must take on everything yourself.)

SAMPLE PREPRODUCTION SCHEDULE

To give you an idea of what the flow of activity looks like from week to week, this chapter includes a sample preproduction timeline for a 12-page script. It is difficult to predict how your project will fit into this model because each project has its own set of challenges. Your project might require devoting more effort to cast, location, or crew. The challenge of *Truman*, for example, was to find a 10-year-old boy to play the lead, children for the supporting characters, and a gym that was available for a whole week. *Crazy Glue* required months of building the puppets and sets. The producer of *The Lunch Date* needed to secure Grand Central Station and a luncheonette. Jan Krawitz had to find suitable women to interview for *Mirror Mirror* to bring the issue alive.

The sample schedule assumes six shooting days. At two pages a day, this is a reasonable schedule for a student or beginning film- or videomaker. Our formula for a beginner allows one week of preproduction for each day of principal photography. This gives you six weeks to prepare for the shoot. Depending on the experience of you and your crew and on the complexity of the script, the preproduction period might be longer or shorter. This prototype will at least give you an idea of what must happen before the cameras can roll. The order and the time during which each task occurs will vary from production to production.

The schedule below and on the next two pages assumes you have the following:

- A finished script
- A director
- Adequate financing
- A preliminary budget
- A shoot date

PREPRODUCTION PLANNING SUGGESTIONS

- If shooting at distant locations, have a production assistant on call at the base location to handle the dailies pickup at the airport. Film must be brought to the lab, and quarter-inch tapes must be brought to the sound transfer facility. The editor should arrange to pick up the dailies from the lab.
- If you are putting up the cast and crew at private homes, do not house more than two to a room. You want your cast and crew to be rested and comfortable during the shoot.
- Have one person at the lab act as your contact throughout the project. He or she should be able to verify over the phone that there are no problems with the dailies.
- If editing or screening facilities are not available at or near your location, have your dailies transferred to video and shipped to you.
- If your equipment vehicles must be driven to the location, allow enough time for a leisurely drive before the shoot.

PRODUCTION MEETING SUGGESTIONS

Production meetings are opportunities to brainstorm ideas and to solve problems. The key to running an effective production meeting is to be organized and to stick to the agenda. Maximize the time you spend with the crew. Respect all points of view, but don't linger too long on one issue with the whole crew present. Deal with a particularly thorny issue later with only the appropriate crew members. You might have to set up smaller meetings with individual department heads—art, camera, sound, wardrobe, props, hair, and makeup—to deal with specific issues in their respective areas.

Here are some additional suggestions:

- Hold the production meeting at the same time and place each week.
- Have refreshments available.
- Before the meeting, make sure everyone has a copy of the script.
- Moderate the meeting, keeping everyone focused on one topic at a time.
- Publish and hand out a written agenda if possible.
- Set a time limit for the meeting.
- Deal with one department at a time.
- At the end of the meeting, summarize the points of agreement.
- Assign tasks to appropriate crew members.
- Set an agenda for the next meeting.

Week 1

Producer	Director
Sets up office/furniture	Finalizes script
Buys supplies	Scouts locations
Sets up phone/answering machine	Discusses script with art director
Leases photocopier	
Buys or leases typewriter/computer	
Creates filing system to keep copies of all agreements	
Establishes company name (DBA, "doing business as")	
Buys cards/stationery	
Opens bank account	
Advertises for actors	
Advertises for crew	
Breaks down script	
Creates stripboard and schedule	
Submits script to insurance company for estimate	

Crew
Production manager
Location manager
Art director
Casting director
Production coordinator

Production Meeting 1—Key Points
- Introduce all crew members.
- Set up preproduction schedule.
- Set goals for next meeting.

Week 2

Producer	Director
Reviews budget	Scouts locations
Reviews shooting schedule	Art director presents
Collects, organizes head plans, ideas shots	Reviews head shots for actors

Signs SAG waiver or guild contract

Sets up auditions

Reviews proposed insurance package

Orders all necessary forms (location agreements, release forms, call sheets, petty cash envelopes, etc.)

Crew

Director of photography

Office production assistants

Production Meeting 2—Key Points

- Discuss art director's plans.
- Request art budget.
- Go over preliminary schedule and budget.

Breaks down script

Discusses script with director of photography (DP)

Makeup/hair

Transportation coordinator

Production Meeting 4—Key Points

- Discuss casting alternatives.
- Settle on final crew needs.
- Finalize transportation plan.

Week 3

Producer

Sets up auditions

Looks for postproduction facilities

Advertises for editor

Settles on insurance package

Negotiates with laboratory for overall package

Researches equipment houses, vendors

Crew

DP (starts lighting designs)

Wardrobe

Props

Special effects (if needed)

Production Meeting 3—Key Points

- Approve art department budget.
- Narrow down location choices.
- Approve construction schedule (if appropriate).

Director

Reviews location pictures

Visits locations with DP

Holds auditions

Week 4

Producer

Sets up more auditions

Finalizes locations

Forms crew

Reviews shooting schedule, budget

Sets up dailies, projection schedule

Negotiates agreement with caterer (meal plan)

Makes transportation plans

Rents vans, recreational vehicles

Sets up account with lab, sound transfers

Crew

Assistant director

Director

Holds callbacks

Finalizes locations

Creates floor plans, storyboards

Reviews wardrobe, props with art department

Reviews lighting plan with DP

Week 5

Producer

Finalizes cast

Negotiates cast contracts

Secures location contracts

Finalizes crew, crew deal memos

Publishes cast, crew contact sheet

Secures parking permits

Secures shooting permits

Makes security arrangements

Approves expendables request for all departments

Orders complete equipment package (camera, grip, electric, sound, dolly, generator, walkie-talkies, etc.)

Orders first-aid kit for set

Sets up tentative postproduction schedule

Crew

Key grip

Production sound mixer

2nd assistant director

Production Meeting 5—Key Points

- Discuss wardrobe, props, hair, and makeup issues.
- Discuss budget considerations.
- Have script timed.

Director

Begins rehearsals

Finalizes shot list

Reviews script

Reviews makeup, hair designs with art department

Finalizes lighting plan with DP

Week 6

Producer

Checks weather report

Finalizes budget

Distributes contact sheet

Finalizes schedule

Reconfirms locations

Confirms crew

Distributes one-liner schedule to cast, crew

Distributes call sheets for first-day cast, crew

Distributes maps of locations

Purchases film, tape stock

Orders expendables

Obtains certificates of insurance for locations, equipment, vehicles

Crew

Gaffer

Director

Holds rehearsals

Makes script changes

Visits set construction

Finalizes shooting script

Does final location scout

Walk-through with department heads

Boom
2nd assistant director
Production Meeting 6—Key Points
- Go over shooting schedule, day by day, with all department heads.
- Give general pep talk.

Week 7

Producer   Director
Picks up equipment, transportation

SHOOT DATE

KEY POINTS

- Plan your project on a week-to-week basis during preproduction.
- The goal of the rehearsal period is to work out the beats and the business. There will be little time to do this during production.
- The process of discovery is everything. Once you know how the piece should work, it will inform all aspects of principal photography.
- Use the rehearsals to develop a mutual trust with the actors and a shorthand for communicating with them.
- There is a fine line between rehearsing too much and rehearsing too little.

part two

Production

As the producer, you set the start date for production. During preproduction, this date inches closer and closer. If you are well prepared, the shooting period merely means shifting into a higher gear. If you are not prepared, you will experience problems that might be serious enough to force you to push back the start date.

The start of production is the moment when the ship has been constructed, the crew has been chosen, and the captain pulls up anchor and heads out to sea. The score has been written, the musicians are assembled, and the conductor raises the baton. The director will by this time know intuitively how to influence the creative drive of the production.

Production is also called principal photography. This is the industry term for the period during which the first, or principal, unit completes photography. (Professional shoots sometimes employ a second unit to shoot action sequences or scenes that do not involve principal players.)

During production, you can look back on the many hours of preparation, planning, and rehearsal and be thankful you took the time to refine the production schedule, look for that unique location, and develop a positive chemistry with the actors. Your hard work in preparing the picture should free the creative team to explore all the possibilities the script, cast, and crew have to offer.

Principal photography can be an intense and trying period. Working with the same people for long hours many days in a row tests the mettle of the strongest personalities. During the shoot, you will discover firsthand how important crew selection and casting can be. You will recognize almost immediately whom you can rely on and whom you can't. If you have a problem with a crew member or an actor on the first day, you must decide whether you want to give this person time to improve or replace him or her.

There is ample time during pre- and postproduction to solve problems. During principal photography, however, time is more precious. The production unit must be flexible but be prepared to make expeditious decisions. Even though compromise is inevitable during a shoot, there is no reason to sacrifice quality and integrity.

The best way to be flexible is to maintain the flow of communication among all parties, creating a Gestalt mentality. If, during preproduction, you anticipate all possible variables of what could go wrong on any given day, these problems can be addressed or a satisfactory compromise can be found with relative ease during the shoot.

To reach this level of communication, learn everything there is to know about the production process. This part of the book is organized to familiarize you with what happens during principal photography, when hard work and creative fervor transform the words on the page into the images and sounds that will become your final product.

A film or video is put together with some degree of magic and chance. Listen to the project as if it had a voice of its own. The finest films and videos are greater than the sum of their parts.

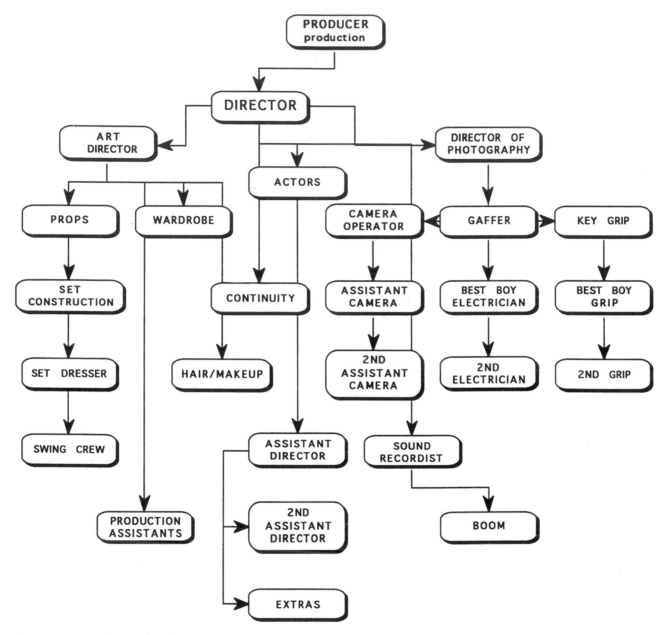

Figure II.1 Production flowchart.

BASIC PRINCIPLES

Clarify the Chain of Command to the Crew. Make sure everyone knows who's in charge. If there is a problem on the set, every crew member must know where to turn for an answer.

Avoid Duplication of Energies. It is not efficient to have two production assistants running around looking for the same prop.

Keep the Ball Rolling. Focus on where you are going and what you have to achieve. Don't let a problem with the cast, crew, or location slow down the momentum.

Keep Bad News from the Actors. Actors should always be in a positive frame of mind. If there is tension on the set, relax the actors while you deal with the problem.

Avoid Passing the Buck. If someone makes a mistake, don't waste time and energy placing blame. This is counterproductive. Put your energy into correcting the mistake. At one time or another, everyone will make a mistake, even professionals.

Do Not Assume Anything. Check and double-check all arrangements for cast, crew, transportation, meals, and locations.

Delegate Responsibility. Don't take on more than you can handle. Spreading yourself too thin usually means that nothing gets done properly.

Double the Time Allotted for Anything out of the Ordinary. Stunts, special effects, fire effects, car mounts, and even special effects lighting always take longer than you anticipate. The phrase "hurry up and wait" was created for the picture business.

Keep Murphy's Law in Mind. Be prepared for the worst, but accept the best. Don't keep waiting for the other shoe to drop because it just might not.

Stay Healthy. You are no good to anyone if you are sick, especially during the shoot when there is no downtime to rest.

Remember to Have Fun!

chapter eleven

Set Procedures

They told me, "Don't worry. Everything's fine. He's all set; he knows what he's doing." So the actors took their places, and we started, rolled sound, rolled camera. I called action, did the shot, called cut. It was great. Then, I suddenly notice there's a commotion going on next to me. I look over, and there's yards of magnetic tape spewing out of the Nagra, and the homeless guy, who was trying to help, now has his hands over his face. We quickly went back to the original way of the sound man operating the recorder by himself.

Adam

DIRECTOR
Control

RUNNING THE SET

The hierarchy of the crew is a pyramid, with the director on top. Her goal for production is to shoot the script within the schedule and to walk away with enough shots to tell the story adequately. Achieving this task depends on the director's ability to communicate her vision confidently to the cast and technical support personnel who will execute her ideas. A strong director creates a tone, attitude, and pace on the set that allows the team to respond to whatever problems and challenges arise. An insecure director, on the other hand, brings down morale and slows the natural pace of a well–oiled and capable crew.

On the set the director's word is law. Her talent, intelligence, and drive are applied to the script and the resources available to her. She is able to make choices and swift decisions because she's spent hours and hours formulating and interpreting the script in her mind. A director often seems to function by intuition.

Her decisions might be right or they might be wrong, but they are for her to make. She is free to consult whomever she chooses, and she can always change her plan for a scene. Ultimately, however, the vision of the piece is in her head. It is the director's job to impart that vision succinctly and successfully to the cast and crew through her words and performance.

STUDENTS

Chapter 6 presented the 3–30 rule for smaller shoots, which assists the director and producer with their staffing needs. Often in a short piece the director has raised all the funds with which to make the picture. This should by no means force the director to feel compelled to also "produce." The more the director can delegate authority to the producer, the more time she will have to actually direct the film or video. The producer, in turn, besides taking on the responsibility of assuring the funds are allocated in a professional and reasonable manner, often takes on the role of production manager to oversee the day–to–day operations. By coming to terms and agreeing on their roles prior to shooting, the director and producer will function as a better team.

A TYPICAL DAY

This is what happens on a typical day during production.

Cast and Crew Arrive on the Set. The director often arrives at the location before the cast or crew begins to arrive. It is a good idea to walk around the set to get a feel for the location. It might be the first time you have been on the fully dressed set.

The call time, indicated on the call sheet, tells each cast and crew member when to arrive. If a particular department needs lead time, the call times can be staggered. For example, if an actor has to undergo a lengthy makeup application, the location manager, makeup artist, and actor will be called before the rest of the crew. The assistant director makes these arrangements. Call times should be arranged so that when the actor is ready, the crew has arrived and he need not wait to begin rehearsal.

Shot Is Blocked for the Camera. As soon as the actors arrive, it is customary for the director to conduct a short run–through rehearsal of the first scene scheduled to film for the director of photography (DP), gaffer, and 1st assistant director (AD). The director and DP then make a plan for the day's photography, based on the storyboards or floor plans as well as information gleaned from the rehearsal.

As the director and DP talk over the shooting plan, they decide on the first setup and where the camera will be placed. On the basis of the rehearsal, the director might decide to shoot the scene differently than originally planned. Seeing the completed set or dressed location might inspire her to reveal the environment or characters in another way. This is the time to discuss any changes.

> *The scenes in the cafeteria I diagrammed from an overhead floor plan—the camera here, her walking this way and that. And the scenes in Grand Central I designed with storyboards. But you've got to get to the camera; you've got to look through the camera; you've got to see.*
>
> Adam

Marks Are Placed on the Floor for the Actors and Camera. If the blocking of the actors or camera is complicated, the key grip will put tape on the floor to mark the actors' and camera's positions. Any

camera move, such as a dolly, is rehearsed for smoothness.

> *The camera was on a dolly, so we could put tape on the floor to mark the exact position of the camera for both setups. The positions had to be precise from one interview to the next in order to ensure a jump-cut aesthetic. We were a little off on some of them. If you look closely, you can see the composition shift just a tad, but it's not something anyone really notices.*
>
> Jan

The Focus Marks Are Set. The assistant camera operator sets the focus for the actors' movements. Each time the camera or an actor moves, the operator adjusts the footage ring on the lens to maintain focus.

The Set Is Lit. The DP directs the gaffer to set the lights and the grip crew to set the camera. As the lights are being positioned, turned on, and aimed, the DP moves around with his light meter, checking light readings from each unit. Once the lights are in place, a stand-in sits or stands where the actor will eventually be placed so the camera team can reestablish focus, lens size, and lighting. During these technical rehearsals, the gaffer tries to keep the lighting instruments out of the shot and tries to block, or flag, any glare from hitting the camera lens.

The time it takes the camera team to light the set to the director's satisfaction is critical for meeting the daily schedule. The director's estimate of the number of scenes or shots for a day is based on the DP's projected setup time at each location. The DP bases his setup time on the location scouts and final walk-throughs. It is the assistant director's job to monitor the DP's schedule. If it appears that the lighting team will fall behind on its projected schedule, adjustments to the shot list might be required.

Rehearsal. While the set is being prepared, the director may feel it necessary to rehearse the scene further. She can then take the actors away from the set to another room.

Actors Are Dressed and Made Up. The actors are then sent to be made up and fitted in their wardrobe.

A Run-Through Is Held for the Actors and Camera. Once the technical aspects of the shot have been finalized, the actors are brought back to the set for a final dress rehearsal.

Adjustments Are Made for the Actors and Camera. Between the rehearsal and the lighting period, technical adjustments or new creative ideas might require altered or additional blocking for the actors and camera.

The Scene Is Shot. When the director determines that everything is ready, she shoots the scene. Each time the scene is shot from a particular angle with a specific lens, it is referred to as a take. The director shoots as many takes of each shot as she feels are necessary. Between takes, the DP walks into the shot and checks the light to see if the readings are correct.

> **STUDENTS** Don't act as though the production company can return to a location should the footage be incomplete. Get it right while you are there.

> *I didn't think I had everything by the end of the production. I thought, "Oh, my God, there are shots that I don't have." By the time I put the rough cut together, it occurred to me I could go back and get those shots, but the cost would have been too great.*
>
> Adam

The Director Might Request a Retake for any Number of Reasons. The director or an actor wants adjustments in the performance, technical problems occurred with the camera or lights, an actor flubbed or misread a line, an actor doesn't hit his or her focus mark, the dolly doesn't hit its mark, a microphone dips into the frame, the boom shadow enters the frame, a light bulb pops during a take, or an airplane or loud noise buries the sound.

Even if the director is satisfied with the first take, it is wise to take each shot at least twice, with one of the takes acting as a safety. Unforeseen mishaps often necessitate a safety shot being used in the editing room to get around a problem.

The Camera Is Moved for the Next Setup or Sequence. When the director is satisfied that all of the required takes from a particular camera angle have been shot, she requests that the camera be moved to the next camera position. In this way, the director works her way through the script.

> *Sometimes in shooting observational footage, I don't know exactly what I'm getting because I'm not actually behind the camera and there's little time to confer once a scene begins. There are always a lot of surprises—not big surprises because I'm on the shoot doing the sound, but I won't know exactly what the framing looks like.* Mirror Mirror *was different. We discussed each setup, and I looked through the camera beforehand because it was an entirely controlled shooting situation.*
>
> Jan

CAMERA MOVES

If the shot must be terminated because of a technical error from the cast or the crew, the script supervisor marks the shot as a false start. Out of 10 takes, there might be only 2 complete takes.

Every time you decide to use a moving camera, even for a small pan or tilt, you'll need time to rehearse the camera and the actors. Each member of the camera team has a particular function that must be performed properly. In a long dolly, crane, or Steadicam shot, the DP must light the entire area the actors and camera travel along and must make sure that everything is in focus. These moving shots often require that precision moves by the dolly grip or Steadicam operator be repeated exactly for each take. This increases the chance of something going wrong.

Static shots, where the camera does not move, are generally easier to set up and less risky to shoot than dolly or Steadicam shots. They also require less rehearsal time.

> **STUDENTS** Do attempt elaborate camera moves, but consider adopting an alternate plan if you face too many technical hurdles in getting a satisfactory shot. Don't give up unless it becomes obvious that time is being wasted. If the dolly shot you are attempting is taking too long, consider breaking the scene down into individual static shots (basic coverage). Your goal is to get into the editing room with something to cut.

VIDEO TAP

Many directors use a video assist (also called a video tap). The video tap diverts some light from the film camera to a small attached video camera that allows the director and others to watch the take as it happens on a monitor. The video tap can be recorded, enabling the take to be studied immediately afterward. This can be helpful for reviewing takes for framing and performance, for logging, or even editing footage before processing. It is especially useful for continuity when staging a complicated camera move. A video assist is crucial for Steadicam, crane, or car shots in which the camera operator cannot look through the viewfinder.

Video tap is also extremely helpful when the director is acting in the project. Being objective while acting is difficult. After the take, the director can watch the playback on the video monitor and judge for herself whether to move on or shoot another take.

There are, however, potential problems. Having the director or others look at each take can slow the production process down. The image quality is usually poor and can misrepresent what the film will eventually look like. And because you are not seeing the actual film, the tap can't inform you about other problems such as scratches or even a run-out.

Finally, those who are watching often become instant critics. As mentioned earlier, the only audience during principal photography should be the director.

I personally don't like video tap. It's a good way for producers to look at your dailies while you're on the set.

Adam

SLATES

In film, it is necessary to identify each sync sound take with a clapboard. This is also referred to a slate, clap sticks, or simply sticks. Written on the clapboard, or slate, is pertinent information about the take for the editing process (Figure 11.1). Information on the slate can include the name of the film, director, DP, scene and take numbers, sound take number (if any), camera and sound roll numbers, and date. A small gray card (see Glossary) may also be included to assist in color correcting the work print or video transfer.

When the sound and the developed film arrive in the editing room, the assistant editor matches the clap of the slate on the sound track to its corresponding film image. This is called syncing up the footage. This ensures that all the sound will be perfectly in sync with the picture. The editor must be able to read the material on the slate so she can relate her log books to the script supervisor's notes.

Slating Procedure

On the set, when the assistant director calls for the slate, the assistant camera operator holds the slate up

Figure 11.1 A slate contains information for the editor.

in front of the lens with the clapper open. The AD then calls for the sound person to "roll sound." The sound recordist turns on the Nagra or DAT, and when the tape is rolling at 15 inches per second (ips), he calls out loudly, "Speed!" The AD then calls out, "Roll camera!" at which point the camera operator turns on the camera. When the camera speed reaches 24 frames per second (fps), he calls out, "Rolling!"

At this cue, the assistant camera operator, or whoever is holding the slate, reads the information off the clapboard: "Scene 49 apple, take 2." ("Scene 49 apple" refers to scene 49A; using "apple" eliminates any confusion. "Baker" would then be used for B, "Charlie" for C, etc.) When the assistant camera operator has called out the slate information, he slaps down the upper bar onto the slate, which makes a sharp "clap" sound (Figure 11.2). The assistant camera operator hustles behind the camera position, crouches, and waits patiently and is very still until the take is completed.

When shooting the slate, the goal is to be able to read all the information clearly in the editing room. The slate must have ample light on it, be held steady when it claps, and be close enough to the camera to enable the editor to read the small print. In a low-light situation, the AC may shine a flashlight on the slate. A slate held far from a camera may require the operator to zoom in to shoot the slate and then zoom back out for the shot.

The person who holds the clapboard should be sensitive to the actors and not clap the slate in their faces.

Figure 11.2 Assistant director David Hamlin holds a slate to mark the beginning of a take on the set of *Truman.*

The "clap" sound doesn't have to be loud. If need be, use a tail slate. Also, if the camera misses the slate, and you have to do it another time, announce "Second sticks" to alert the editor.

> **STUDENTS**
>
> If you have a limited amount of film stock, you can conserve a few feet of film on each take by rolling sound first, having the information on the slate read, then having the AD call for the camera to roll. When camera is up to speed, the DP calls, "Mark it!" and the slate is "clapped" with the take information recorded on sound tape, not on the film. Those few feet of film saved on each take could add up to a considerable amount over the course of the shoot.

Slate Lights

Another slating device is called a slate light. This is a trigger connected to the recorder that, when pushed, flashes a small light and produces an audible beep. This system often is used in documentary filmmaking.

Smart Slates

Timecode offers many benefits for film production when editing will be completed on nonlinear or other video equipment. It can automate the syncing process as well as identify and locate audio material by timecode number (see Chapter 16 for more on the basics of timecode). It does this with the help of a timecode slate called a smart slate. With this system, a timecode generator feeds code to the audio recorder as well as

to the smart slate. This slate looks much like a standard clapboard with timecode display embedded on its face. Slates are handled in the usual way. When the clap sticks are lowered on the slate, the timecode at that instant is held for a few frames on display. Any sync sound camera can be used. After the film is processed, the sound is synced up either during the film to video transfer or after. The frame with the slate is stopped on the screen. The timecode is read visually and then entered into the computer. The system then locates the same timecode in the audio, and now the shot can be placed in sync with the sound.

When using timecode with film equipment, you have several options in terms of frame rates and timecode settings for camera and audio recorder. Before shooting, be sure to contact the laboratory or post facility that will be doing your transfer to find out its preferences. It is advisable to shoot a test before beginning a production to make sure all systems are working.

In-Camera Slates

There is a more sophisticated method of recording timecode using a camera with "in-camera" timecode capability. Timecode is recorded on the edges of the film while filming. With this system, both the camera and the audio deck are recording essentially identical timecode with their respective media. In postproduction, properly equipped telecines can read the film timecode and automatically sync it to the audio code. Auto syncing can also be done later on an editing machine.

Informal Slates

If you do not have a slate, you will still need some distinct event that can be clearly seen in the picture and heard on the track. You can make do by holding up fingers to indicate the take number, and then clap your hands together sharply. Another informal slate is called a mike slate. Hold the microphone up to the camera lens and tap it. The number of taps is the number of the take. This makes a sharp "bump" sound on the track by which the editor can sync up the material.

> I would start the Nagra, then slate the shot with a clapper, and then return to my seat and start the interview. Normally, when we're on location shooting observational footage, because there's not a third person, we use a bloop slate or a mike tap rather than a clapper.
>
> Jan

Tail Slates

When an opening slate would be impractical or inconvenient, a tail slate can be used. For example, the opening shot might have a very tight frame and then pull out to a wide one. In this case, slating the scene at the head of the take might prove difficult. It would be easier to start the scene without a slate, and when the director calls "Cut," keep the camera, Nagra, or DAT rolling and slate the take at the end, or tail, of the shot. Other appropriate uses for tail slates would be emotionally acted scenes or unstaged documentary filming, since they don't disrupt the beginning of a take. When tail slating, the clapboard is usually held upside down and the person announcing the slate calls "Tail slate" or "End sticks."

Video Slates

Slating is used in video for identification purposes only (unless a separate audio track is being recorded—the sound will then have to be synced up, just like film). There is no need to create a "clap," as the sound is recorded directly onto the tape stock. It is wise to log each shot into a notebook to keep track of what you have photographed. (Please refer to Chapter 13 for more information on recording sound for video.)

Action! Cut!

After the slate has been clapped and only when the director feels that everything is ready, she calls, "Action!" The scene plays as long as the director deems necessary, and then she calls, "Cut!" The director will ask for as many takes as needed or as time allows to get the best material in the can. The cast and crew make adjustments after each take. Hair, makeup, and continuity must be maintained from take to take.

CALLING THE SHOT

- *Quiet on the set!* This signifies the calm before the storm.
- *Roll sound!* The sound recorder is activated. Slate is called off.
- *Roll camera!* The camera is turned on and is recording.
- *Slate!* An electronic clapboard is placed in front of the lens to identify the shot. The clappers are snapped shut to mark the beginning of the scene and to create a digital timecode to match sound and picture.
- *Action!* The director signals for the actors to begin or for the camera to move.
- *Cut!* The director signals for the actors or camera to stop.
- *Check the gate!* This is to make sure the take was clean and that no dust or hairs were caught in the film camera pressure plate.
- *Back to one!* This signals a repeat of the shot
- *Camera moves!* When the shot is satisfactorily "in the can," the camera moves to the next position or "setup."
- *Martini shot!* The last shot of the day
- *That's a wrap!* Principal photography for the day ends.

SCRIPT SUPERVISION

The script supervisor keeps track of the slates, maintains the continuity within each scene and from scene to scene, and makes notes in her script about each shot. Besides taking notes about each shot, her duty is to ensure that the material delivered to the editing room can be cut together. The script supervisor bears the responsibility of making sure that the action is matched or duplicated from one shot to the next. For example, an actor crosses to a chair, sits down, and crosses his legs. Did he put the left leg over the right, or vice versa? In order not to confuse the audience,

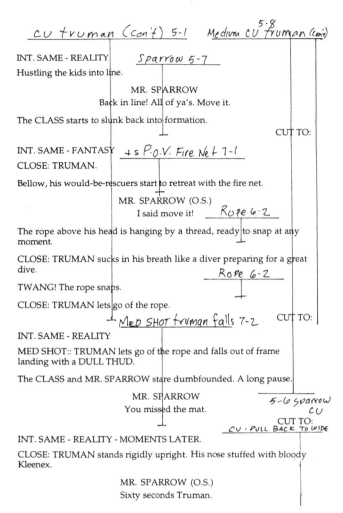

CU truman (con't) 5-1   Medium CU truman (con't) 5-8

INT. SAME - REALITY   *Sparrow 5-7*

Hustling the kids into line.

MR. SPARROW
Back in line! All of ya's. Move it.

The CLASS starts to slunk back into formation.

CUT TO:

INT. SAME - FANTASY   *+ s P.O.V. Fire Net 7-1*
CLOSE: TRUMAN.

Bellow, his would-be-rescuers start to retreat with the fire net.

MR. SPARROW (O.S.)
I said move it!   *Rope 6-2*

The rope above his head is hanging by a thread, ready to snap at any moment.

CLOSE: TRUMAN sucks in his breath like a diver preparing for a great dive.
        Rope 6-2

TWANG! The rope snaps.

CLOSE: TRUMAN lets go of the rope.

Med Shot truman falls 7-2   CUT TO:

INT. SAME - REALITY

MED SHOT:: TRUMAN lets go of the rope and falls out of frame landing with a DULL THUD.

The CLASS and MR. SPARROW stare dumbfounded. A long pause.

MR. SPARROW
You missed the mat.   *5-6 Sparrow CU*

CUT TO:
CU - Pull Back To Wide

INT. SAME - REALITY - MOMENTS LATER.

CLOSE: TRUMAN stands rigidly upright. His nose stuffed with bloody Kleenex.

MR. SPARROW (O.S.)
Sixty seconds Truman.

Figure 11.3 A lined script from *Truman*.

the same actions need to be repeated exactly from each camera angle.

The script supervisor's tools include an instant camera (to record continuity) and a stopwatch (to time the shots). The script supervisor's book contains shooting notes and a lined script for the show like the one in Figure 11.3. Her notes include the following:

- Brief description of what happened during the take
- At what point in a scene an actor does what
- Length of each shot (timed with a stopwatch)
- Lens used
- Director's comments
- DP's comments

After photography has been completed on a scene, the script supervisor transfers her notes onto a "lined"

or "continuity script." This copy of the shooting script has a series of vertical lines on it that indicate from which angle and in which take each part of the script was shot. If, at the end of production, a part of a scene does not have a line through it, it probably was not photographed. A precise record of what was shot is an important guide for the editor. Once in the editing room, the assistant editor can identify material to be used by first referencing the lined script. This saves time sifting through material on a flatbed or from the digitized (or undigitized) takes.

In working with a small crew, often the duties of the script supervisor fall to the entire crew. The director, actor, DP, or anyone who is a witness can identify continuity mistakes. But in the heat of shooting, some continuity issues can be missed. This is exacerbated by the fact that most scripts are filmed out of continuity. The pressure is usually so great on a director that she will opt to move on with the day's photography rather than spend time laboring over whether a shot may or may not match in the editing room. This happens to all directors, but as a director becomes seasoned, she begins to value the role of the script supervisor for the time it saves in the editing room solving shooting problems and for helping avoid expensive "pickup" or "reshoots."

When a director finally comes out the other end of the shooting period and settles down to edit, problems that arose or were neglected on set become glaringly difficult to fix. Even with a script supervisor, editorial problems can arise, which is why directors are encouraged to shoot cutaways and inserts, as these small pieces of film or tape can be used to good effect solving editing or continuity problems.

An actor sits down on a chair, takes a glass of water with his right hand, and crosses his left leg over his right leg. Later in the day, a tighter shot is done, but this time the actor uses his left hand to drink the water and crosses his legs right over left. To cut from a wide shot to a tight shot with two different leg crosses may look like a jump and could distract the audience from the flow of the story. Often an audience won't notice this continuity error. But, if the director has an insert shot of the hand reaching for the glass and lifting it out of frame, there is less chance the audience will notice the left hand/right hand, left leg/right leg continuity jumps.

If at any point in the film or video the audience takes a moment to ask themselves, "Did he pick up the glass with his right or left hand?" you have lost them for that moment and possibly for the duration of the show. A director's job is to create such a dynamic story that continuity errors will not break the suspension of belief, which is part of the contract between the audience and the screen. This is what editors mean when they say they try to achieve a "seamless picture."

There are occasions where continuity errors are acceptable. Sometimes it is more important to make a cut for performance, pace, or emotional kick than it is to attempt to correct a continuity error. The director and editor make the judgment call in the editing room as to the gravity of a continuity error. If a script supervisor can work with the director, DP, and actors during the shoot to guarantee seamlessness, then the effort to make a good cut will be less of a struggle.

Script supervision may seem like a luxury, but besides fulfilling her duties on set, which are numerous and take great skill of observation, there is one other aspect to the position that is of great help to the director and DP. At the beginning of the shooting day, after a run–through for blocking and lighting, the director will conference with the DP and script supervisor on the coverage they will shoot to record and develop the scene. The script supervisor not only makes notes and suggestions but may often assist in organizing the coverage to reflect editing style and schedule as well as continuity. It is the script supervisor to whom the director turns after every shot and asks, "What are we going to cut to, and what are we cutting from?"

Here are some examples of script supervision editing reminders:

Overlap the Action. When a character walks to a chair and sits down, always overlap the action. This means that in a wide shot, the character walks to the chair and sits. In the tighter shot of the character sitting, he must sit into the shot or, in other words, start with a clean frame and let the actor make an entrance and then sit down. Shooting the scene in this manner makes a very smooth cut.

Exit and Leave the Frame Empty. When an actor or action exits the frame, let the frame be empty for a few beats. This gives the editor options in making the next cut.

Inserts Should Be Lower and Slower. When shooting an insert, such as reaching for a glass on a table, shoot the insert at a slightly lower angle and ask that the actor reach slowly. This is because the action in the wider shot seems to take more time, so the low angle and slower motion make a better match on the insert of the hand reaching for and clutching the glass. Overlap the action by letting the hand enter the frame, and let the hand with the glass exit the frame before the director says "Cut."

Match Frame Size for Obligatory Reverse Shots. When shooting matching closeups, over-the-shoulder shots, reaction shots, or POV shots, be sure the frame size and composition are similar.

Video Tap. It is clear that one of the advantages of shooting video or using a video tap on a film camera is that the tape can be reviewed for continuity errors. However, the script supervisor is still an important asset for keeping an exact record of what was shot.

Editor. The editor may elect to act as script supervisor if the production cannot afford the position.

(See Chapter 12 for more on the 10 basic decisions about the shot.)

PRODUCER
Organize

The producer's responsibility is to ensure that from the beginning of the shoot, everyone has a precise idea of what they are supposed to be doing and when and where they are supposed to be doing it. This requires the following:

- Clear chain of command
- Realistic budget
- Day-out-of-day schedule
- Enough crew to carry out the director's visual plan
- Secure locations
- Call sheets
- Daily meal plans
- Transportation schedule

Unless the producer is also serving on the crew as the assistant director, there is no traditional position for him on the set. The director is in charge of production, and it is up to the assistant director to keep the production unit moving in accordance with the agreed-upon schedule. This allows the producer the freedom to deal with the problems that inevitably arise during the course of any shoot. (Murphy's Law applies to every aspect of the picture-making process.) The producer becomes involved with set operations only in special situations, such as these:

- The production unit starts to go over schedule.
- The producer is needed as a troubleshooter.

- He has to alleviate tension between the director and the DP.
- He has to reassure an actor.

During production, the producer keeps a daily watch on both the budget and the material that is shot. This requires that he oversee all aspects of the production. During the shoot, the producer does the following:

- Keeps on top of daily cash flow
- Finalizes location arrangements, transportation plans, and meal plans
- Deals with schedule changes
- Completes daily production reports

GUIDELINES

Each shoot presents unique challenges and obstacles. The producer must be ready to deal with each as it arises. The following guidelines should help the novice understand the producer's basic priorities, which can be applied to any production.

Keep Morale Up

As the producer, you are the head cheerleader and support person. You should remain positive and unflappable even under the most trying circumstances. Keep a "happy face," no matter what you are thinking or feeling.

Support the Director and the Creative Team

Support the director and the crew by creating a comfortable work environment that includes good food to eat. Production is stressful and physically demanding work. If the crew performs well, show your appreciation. Don't take the crew for granted; the success of your project rests on their shoulders. If you treat crew members well, they will be more likely to go that extra mile for you.

Watch the Budget

The budget dictates what the director can do. You must know from day to day if the production is on, over, or under budget. To do this, you must approve of and account for all expenditures and keep track of the daily cash flow—that is, the money being paid to vendors for food, supplies, or expendables. Keep a complete itemization of every expenditure and a thorough collection of receipts and bills.

Act as Coordinator

During principal photography, you must see to it that arrangements for locations, transportation, and food are confirmed and reconfirmed. (Never assume anything.) This includes establishing a regular system of getting the exposed film stock to the lab. (This is not an issue with video.) You must always keep ahead of the production unit to ensure that each day will go as planned. During this time, you should also be confirming the postproduction arrangements, such as editing space.

If exteriors are planned for the week, keep on top of the weather forecast. If the forecast is for rain, either have a cover set ready or assemble proper gear for shooting in the rain, such as umbrellas and parkas. The actors will need a dry and comfortable place close to the set.

Keep the Production Moving Ahead

Always keep the production unit focused on moving ahead. Don't let problems interfere with the momentum on the set or with the schedule. Keep problems away from the cast and crew if possible.

Be a Troubleshooter

You will need to find creative ways to solve problems if you don't have the money to do so. There is often a great deal of satisfaction in "saving the day" and allowing the creative team to complete photography by solving a difficult problem with your head rather than with cash. Some of the potential problem areas are the following:

Schedule. The key to making the daily schedule is to get the first shot by a specific time. The department heads agree to this time beforehand. If the crew does not complete the shot per this plan, it not only pushes them back for that day, it inevitably pushes them back for the entire shoot. They must either make up the lost time that day or squeeze it into another day. If the crew is pushed to make up the time, it infringes on proper turnaround, pushes the next day back, and so forth.

There are several ways to get the crew back on schedule so that one bad day doesn't throw off the whole shoot:

- Cut scenes or pages.
- Cut shots.
- Collapse several shots into one.

All these options must be considered and agreed to in a timely and calm manner.

It is the producer's job to serve as a stabilizing influence on what could be tough decisions for the director and DP. Compromise is an unfortunate but necessary part of the process. Having to make changes in the original plan doesn't necessarily mean that the original idea is compromised. Sometimes, the best ideas emerge from economic necessity.

On the basis of your experience with the crew's pace during the first few days, you might have to adjust the schedule. If the crew picks up speed along the way, so much the better.

Crew. During the first days, it will become clear whether you have hired the correct number of crew members. The effective people will stand out; the slackers will be revealed. It is good to cut the deadwood from the crew quickly so as not to slow down shooting. Finding replacements should not be too difficult if you kept a list of available crew people.

Department Heads. There needs to be a creative bond between all the department heads (camera, sound, art department) and the director. If there is tension, it can affect the entire crew. The director sets the tone and the pace of the production, and if she is unhappy, dissatisfied, or angry, it will have a ripple effect on everyone around her. Working on the set is difficult enough under the most ideal circumstances. Stress and tension between the key players can drain the energy and enthusiasm from the best of crews.

If there is a problem with the director's relationship with any of the department heads, the producer serves as the mediator (if the director and producer have words, they should take their discussions off-set). Some personality conflicts you must live with; others you must confront. For example, a strong, experienced DP might take over the set and override an inexperienced director's designs. If the DP is slow, you may need to replace him, even if the material looks terrific. If you have a suitable replacement, you might decide to fire the DP. Use your best judgment to resolve the situation quickly.

Location. Losing a location can throw a monkey wrench into the best-laid plans. If you are prepared with backups, the loss will be only momentarily disruptive.

Transportation. You must carefully monitor and coordinate key moves from set to set. Travel, even if across the street, eats some precious time from your shooting schedule. Company moves must be executed quickly and efficiently.

SAFETY ON THE SET

Safety and security are two of the producer's main concerns during principal photography. Equipment and personal items on the set are covered by the company's umbrella insurance policy, but these policies come with large deductibles. Follow these guidelines to reduce the risk of loss or injury:

- Do not leave equipment or valuables on the set or in a vehicle unattended.
- Do not place lighting instruments near pictures, drapes, or other items that are sensitive to heat.
- Lighting units must be secured and properly weighted down with sandbags.
- Keep electric cables away from sound cables and water.

PROPER WRAP-OUT

Make sure you leave each location in as good or better shape than when you arrived. One way to alleviate a major cleanup is to lay down plastic or butcher paper where the crew will be working. If objects, furniture, lights, pictures, or knickknacks have to be moved or put away before the crew can shoot, someone (usually a set dresser) should make careful notes of where these items were, arrange to have them stored properly, and then return them to the correct place when wrapping out of the location. It is helpful to record the original layout by taking Polaroids.

This is proper professional behavior. Keep in mind that you might need to come back to the location for additional work or reshoots. Even if you will never see the owners again, think of each location as if it were your home. Someone should be assigned to keep an eye on what is happening to the location during the shoot. Here are a few things to watch out for:

Placement of Gaffer's Tape. This tape has a tendency to peel paint off walls. Remove it carefully.

Garbage Disposal. A crew can generate a lot of garbage. Make sure it is packed up and disposed of regularly.

Major Cleanup. On leaving a location, arrange to have the area cleaned and, if need be, repainted.

DAILIES

Video dailies are instantly available for viewing and discussion. At wrap, the editor takes this material to the screening room. There she meets the producer, director, DP, and department heads, and they screen the footage. During the screening, important decisions can be made about the progress of the project. Should an actor's hair be changed? Does the lighting match? Should a costume be more distressed?

If you originate on film and are unsure whether the dailies are giving you accurate image information, the DP may request the lab to make a print of one section of the footage to ensure the intended quality is on the negative. Laboratories may take over a week to develop your film in which case the DP must rely on a lab report and view all the footage after principal photography.

During dailies screening, the director makes comments to the editor about the different shots. For example, she might instruct the editor to use the head of one take and the tail of another, to start it tight and reveal the master shot farther into the scene, or to use a specific take because of performance.

KEY POINTS

- The director has the final say on the set.
- Put safety first.
- Move the camera to the next setup position only after you are confident that you will not have to return to that position.
- Give the art department ample lead time to dress and strike the set.
- Wrap out carefully.

chapter twelve

Camera

It was very hot. The conditions were definitely not very pleasant because there were these lights . . . and it was summer in Texas!

Jan

DIRECTOR
Collaborate

All the planning, storyboarding, and previsualization that occur during preproduction are translated into a finished product during production by the camera. The camera is the tool through which the director realizes the script. The use of this tool is limited only by the imagination of the film- or videomaker.

Cinematography is an illusion—a magic trick. It is 24 still frames projected each second to create the illusion of a moving image (video is 29.97 frames per second [fps]). The illusions the director can create through cinema are boundless. Almost every aspect of film and video can employ a cinematic trick, perhaps a computer-generated optical effect, a miniature set, or the use of paste jewels in place of real gems.

The rise of digital recording over analog video recording has given the creative community a new technology to provide a higher quality video product. Some of the advantages of digital video recording include superior image quality, unlimited image reproduction, and the ability to edit layer upon layer of effects without quality loss. The small cassette size also greatly reduces the space needed for storage.

KEEPING UP WITH TECHNOLOGY

Technology moves quickly. It is an extremely complex area, and this is a book about the process. There is a tremendous amount of quality technical information located on the Web that does an excellent job reviewing and explaining the dense and complex digital video world of production and postproduction. For more detailed information about the current line of Panasonic and Sony equipment (the major suppliers of analog and digital cameras and equipment), log on to their Web sites at www.panasonic.com and www.sony.com. They furnish their complete line of products, their specs, reviews, and "white papers." For more independent evaluations of the current market, and, ultimately, what's best for you, there are Web sites put up by professionals and teachers. Two pertinent Web sites are www.videouniversity.com and www.creativecommunities.com. We have listed other such sites on the book's Web page.

STUDENTS Video versus film is all too often a decision based on budget and not aesthetics. The look of the project and intended distribution format should be the main consideration of film versus video.

STYLE

When choosing a style for a project or when developing a personal style of her own, the director should look first to the history of the medium. She needs to know what has come before so that she can help originate what will come after. The language of film is a relatively new vernacular (about a hundred years old), but it is rich in tradition and ripe for innovation.

155

A personal style comes only after acquiring knowledge of the craft and by much experience. By thoroughly understanding her craft, the director can respond to and meet each situation in production with confidence. Why a director makes a decision, alters a shot, or adjusts a performance is based as much on her intuition as on her knowledge. In the heat of principal photography, it is often an improvised moment, a jury-rigged set, or an accident that makes for exciting dramatic moments.

Personal identity with the form and the subject is what makes for a strong visual style. Jean Luc Godard said, "Style is just the outside of content, and content the inside of style, like the outside and inside of the human body—both go together, they can't be separated." This is excellent advice. When choosing an appropriate visual style for your project, work inside out, not the other way around. Don't shoehorn your idea into a style; discover the visual style that best suits your story. An inappropriate style will just call attention to itself and possibly throw your audience out of the story. If your idea is best represented by a static camera, resist the impulse to move it.

Documentary styles include interviews ("talking heads"), voiceovers with visuals to illustrate the text, or cinema verité. Some documentaries include elements of all three styles. One of the keys to a good documentary style is flexibility.

Collaboration with the Camera Department

The camera department consists of the director of photography (DP), camera operator, 1st assistant camera operator, loader/clapper, and stills photographer (keep in mind the 3–30 rule for student shoots). The gaffing department lights the scene. Under the direction of the director of photography, electricians move lighting instruments that will illuminate the set or location. The DP and the key grip are in charge of moving the camera. If the director calls for a complicated shot, they will find a way to maneuver the camera to best advantage. Given enough time, they will find a solution to almost any problem.

This section describes a few helpful ideas for collaborating with the camera department. Note that these suggestions should be carried out during preproduction.

Stock

Other than the director of photography, the choice of a film stock is the single most important decision for the look of the film. Black-and-white, color, or even a combination of the two is a creative choice that will have a substantial impact on the audience's appreciation of the story. It will influence not only how locations, props, and costumes are chosen, but the budget as well. There are not many different B&W film stocks, but there is a wide range of color stocks. Kodak has the widest selection and generally the most consistent in quality.

Most films are shot with negative film stock rather than reversal. (Reversal film is processed to a positive print. There is no "negative." It is the equivalent of shooting 35-mm slides.) Negative can handle a greater range of lighting conditions and is more forgiving of exposure errors. It is easier to make a good quality print with a good negative than in reversal. Labs offer more options and services; some don't handle reversal at all.

There are many kinds of color stocks; slower speed (less sensitive to light) stocks have traditionally had finer grain and sharper images, and faster speed film stocks (more sensitive to light) have had more noticeable grain. However, the newer stocks have managed to be fast, have terrific latitude, and offer the grain level of slower stocks.

Most of the stocks are balanced for indoor or tungsten light (3,200° Kelvin), but there are also those balanced for daylight (around 5,400° Kelvin). The questions most beginners struggle with have to do with mixing stocks with different speeds, as well as indoor and outdoor ones. They become concerned with the artistic consistency of style. Many of these decisions come down to price, availability, and flexibility. Your DP should be your guide in the selection of a stock.

The ascendancy of color in the film industry makes it difficult to find laboratories that do high-quality black-and-white work (see Alfa Cine in the Bibliography). Black and white, when used properly, can be beautiful. Good contrast is the key to this beauty. When the blacks turn muddy or there are no clear whites, the image looks dull. On the other hand, a print with too much contrast has a short tonal range and looks harsh. Films that mix black and white and color are printed on color film stock. Balancing color print stock to achieve a pleasing black-and-white look can be difficult.

Part of the aesthetic challenge is to render the world through the range of gray tones from black to white. In *The Lunch Date*, the black-and-white photography contributes a timeless feel to the film and a storybook quality. One of the film's greatest attributes is that the story can be appreciated the world over.

Figure 12.1 For *The Lunch Date,* studying the light at the location meant scheduling a shot for a particular time of day.

For the videomaker, videotape stock has no inherent visual qualities. It is the camera's pickup tube or its charge-coupled device (CCD) that determines the sensitivity to light and color.

> *I had thought a lot about shooting in black-and-white, but I wasn't sure. I started talking to the director of photography about the possibility of shooting in black-and-white. It turned out that it was going to be to our advantage to do it in black-and-white because without lights, black-and-white is a little more forgiving.*
>
> Adam

Consult with the Director of Photography

The camera crew executes the director's visual ideas for each scene. The individual responsible for translating those ideas into concrete decisions is the DP. The director is responsible for camera placement and for what the camera sees. The DP heads the camera team and is ultimately responsible for keeping the image in focus and illuminating and framing it properly. A good working relationship between the DP and the director is key to a successful shoot. The DP realizes the dreams of the director. Their relationship is like a marriage; there has to be a productive synergy between them.

The DP should be thoroughly versed with the storyboards and the floor plans developed during preproduction. These will help him translate the director's ideas efficiently into shots and enable him to create lighting designs for the floor plans and ultimately realize the director's vision for the script.

There are many ways to approach a scene visually, and ideas can come from anywhere. A good director taps the creative resources around her. As with all good teamwork, there must be a balance between the contributions of the individual members. The DP should be allowed to choose some, but not all, of the shots. He should be permitted to express his creativity on the set, but he must not be allowed to take over the show. This can occur if a director is tentative and indecisive. In this scenario, a creative vacuum can develop, and it is usually the DP who, by default, fills it.

On the other hand, a dominating director will reduce the DP to a mere technician. This might cause resentment and affect his overall performance on the picture. In practical terms, you want the best he has to offer. Any decisions, however, must ultimately reflect your overall vision for the show.

Until the film is processed, there is no sure way of knowing whether all the ideas created in preproduction and during the shoot were executed properly. This is one advantage of working with videotape, where, for better or for worse, you see the results immediately.

Do Your Homework

The success of principal photography depends on proper preparation before and during preproduction. The director brings weeks of work and preparation to the set. The director's "homework" gives her a thorough understanding of what she wants to see at each moment of the story, how she wants to manipulate the audience with sights and sounds, and how she plans to effect her vision.

During preproduction, the director creates a plan on paper in the form of storyboards and floor plans. She might videotape some scenes to evaluate their cinematic qualities. She balances her shot list with the planned schedule and determines at this point that, barring catastrophe, she will be able to realize her vision successfully.

The seriousness with which she has approached the project will not only prepare her for the shoot; it will rub off on the cast and the crew. Her vision and how she communicates it will evoke respect in the entire team. People will follow an organized visionary anywhere.

Shot List

The breakdowns prepared during preproduction distill the script into breakdown sheets, a schedule, a budget, storyboards, and finally a shot list. Although you will carry the script and all of these breakdowns with you onto the set, it's a good idea to write down the shots that you plan for each day on a three-by-five-inch index card, perhaps putting a bright-colored asterisk on those of highest priority. Keep these cards in your pocket, and as the shots are completed, tick them off one by one. At the end of the day, all of the shots listed on the card should have a check next to them (see the sample shot list in Chapter 3).

Introduce the Camera during Preproduction

It is highly recommended that you work with the camera during your preproduction rehearsals. The frame is as much a part of the scene as are the actors. What is included in the frame, what happens there, and how it moves are all part of visual storytelling.

With a film camera, the rehearsals are for framing and blocking only. Do not actually roll the camera. However, with video, you have the option to shoot the rehearsals for study purposes and to experiment with different ways to photograph each scene.

THE CAMERA AS STORYTELLER

The writer uses words and sentences to convey thoughts and ideas. Shots are the basic element of the director's visual vocabulary. She uses the camera to express ideas and to tell the story by combining shots. How the audience perceives these shots involves them in the story.

If every frame, every shot, and every scene have a visual dynamic, you will maximize their potential for impact on your audience. How you imbue each shot of a scene with energy and momentum is part of your plan. Consider the following when you compose a shot:

- Camera placement
- Composition of shot
- Use of color or B&W
- Type of shot
- Size of shot
- Camera movement
- Shot perspectives
- Coverage
- Continuity
- Specialty shots
- Lighting
- Editing

The camera is a storytelling device. No one on the set, from the DP to the set dresser, can begin to work until the director makes two decisions: first, where the camera will be placed, and second, how the actors will move in front of the camera. In placing the camera, the director or DP will ask, "Is the camera in the right place to tell the story properly? Are we seeing what we want to see?" All other camera decisions, including size and composition of the frame, derive from this basic judgment. To determine where the camera is placed, ask yourself, "From whose point of view is the scene experienced? Who is doing the seeing here?" Is it a main character's point of view, or that of an unknown bystander or the omniscient storyteller? The point of view can shift back and forth within a scene, but you should always know from whose vantage point the scene is unfolding.

You should determine whether the shot is objective or subjective. Distant shots tend to be objective and are well suited for the storyteller's point of view. The closer the shot, the more subjective it becomes. The dramatic tension within a scene can best be achieved by bouncing the camera between these two extremes. Characters speaking to one another with the camera directly over one character's shoulder creates an extremely subjective point of view. Techniques for playing a scene along this axis, or eye-line, are discussed later in this chapter (Figure 12.2).

The camera is normally placed at eye level. This is the position at which an audience sees the world.

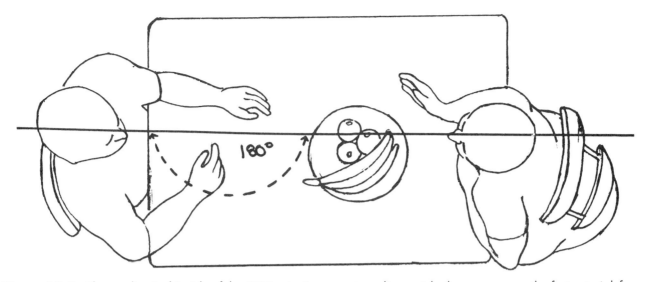

Figure 12.2 The eye-line is this side of the 180° axis. For correct eye-line match, the camera over the first actor's left shoulder should match the angle of the camera over the other actor's right shoulder.

Altering this perspective creates definite emotional responses from the audience. A camera placed high, looking down on a character, gives the audience a "god's eye view." A camera placed low, looking up to a character, makes that character seem powerful. If the camera is positioned to look down slightly on one character, it makes the other characters seem superior.

In the shot of Truman shown in Figure 12.3, even though he is eight feet off the ground, the camera has been placed at eye level, affording the audience the opportunity to share Truman's difficulty holding onto the rope.

In the final shot of *The Lunch Date* (Figure 12.4), like many closing shots, the director has chosen to put the camera on the ground to show the train speeding away from the station for dramatic effect. Directors often use low or high angle, or pull back shots, to signal the finale of a story.

Composition of Shot

Think of the frame as a picture frame surrounding a painting. Make the elements in that picture move, and then make the frame itself move. This is the magic of

Figure 12.3 Camera placed at eye level from *Truman.*

Figure 12.4 Low-angle final frame from *The Lunch Date.*

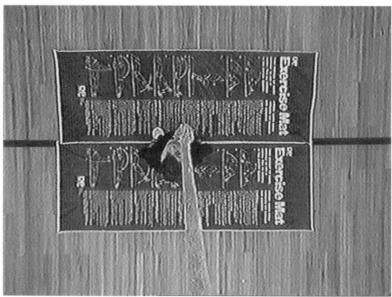

Figure 12.5 High-angle from *Truman.*

the camera, and the director orchestrates it. The director and the DP arrange the objects in the frame for dramatic, pictorial, and narrative considerations. Each frame may contribute to the telling of the story, reveal something about the relationship of the characters, and contribute to the tone and mood of the scene. The visual nature of a shot shouldn't be judged simply on whether it is pleasing to the eye; it should be a vital element in communication. Superior composition not only makes the subject accessible, it heightens the viewer's perceptions and stimulates the viewer's imaginative involvement.

Because each image will be juxtaposed with another, the director must also be conscious of how

each shot will cut with the next. For example, is there a stylistic consistency that is joining the different images within a scene and within the whole piece?

Composing a shot also takes into account the confinement of the set or location, the limitations of the equipment, the time allotted for setup of the shot, the outcome of the rehearsal, and the ability of the production team to solve problems successfully and quickly.

In this extreme high-angle shot of Truman studying his nemesis, the rope (Figure 12.5), the composition of the shot speaks volumes about the character. Here, he is small, in the dead center of the frame, looking up. The rope comes from the top of the frame,

Figure 12.6 ECU from *Truman*.

thick and ominous. The complementary rectangular mat further frames the rectangular floor. The omniscient view of the character demonstrates how insignificant Truman is in comparison to his challenge to climb the rope.

Frame

The frame can be empty, full, askew, off-balance, or in motion. Shots tilted sideways are called Dutch angle or canted and can be used to create tension to a static frame. The placement of characters and objects inside the frame can be balanced or unbalanced. A dramatic tension can be established, depending on how the director uses the frame, including foreground and background. Each frame is filled with information the director needs to tell her story. A frame from *Truman* (see Figure 12.6) filled with the second hands of a stopwatch informs the audience that time is ticking by for the main character.

Extending the Frame

The director can even design (and control) the space beyond the frame. Incorporating off-screen elements with sound through the audience's imagination is called extending the frame. For example, a beautifully composed landscape devoid of characters holds the audience's attention for several beats. A voice and a bell heard off screen pique the audience's interest. The voice and bell get closer and closer, and finally a man and a cow enter the frame.

Drawing the Viewer's Eye

The director places people in the frame. She places objects in the frame. She moves the frame. All this cinematic construction is not arbitrary. Composition within a frame, even a still one, has more or less dramatic tension depending on how the director juxtaposes all the elements.

The key is to draw the audience's eye to what you want them to see (see Figure 12.7). In motion pictures, sounds, as well as images, are used to direct the eye. A blacksmith hammering a horseshoe in the upper right background of the frame becomes more prominent if the only sound heard is the clanging of hammer on metal.

The director can further encourage the audience to focus on the blacksmith's work if a portion of the foreground frame is obscured by something, such as the hanging branch of a tree. The partially obscured frame forces viewers to look at the blacksmith.

In this shot from *Truman*, the director uses the kids and the coach as a frame within a frame, an effect that focuses our attention to the plight of Truman.

Depth

To create dramatic tension, the director can manipulate the foreground and the background. Although the frame is two-dimensional, the audience experiences the illusion that there is great depth within the frame. This is usually accomplished with a wide-angle lens. For example, in *The Lunch Date*, Adam

Figure 12.7 Four-shot from *Truman*.

Figure 12.8 A solitary figure in a wide frame of isolation from *The Lunch Date*.

Davidson placed a woman by herself in the distance of a huge train station platform, giving the audience a feeling of isolation (see Figure 12.8). When we see Truman in a closeup with his peers in the background sneering at him, a feeling of tension and compassion is created (see Figure 12.25).

Focus

With focus, the director both literally and figuratively informs the audience what it should be witnessing at any given moment. If a face in the foreground is out of focus and the background is in focus, the director wants us to look at the background. An excellent example of the use of sharp and soft focus is this shot from *The Lunch Date* (Figure 12.9). The director has chosen a camera position (close to the subjects) and lens (25-mm) that can be racked so that the main character is in focus while the homeless man who represents the confusing city life is soft. Focus is very effective in using film technique to force the audience's eye to just where the director wants them to look.

Figure 12.9 Focus creates depth in the frame from *The Lunch Date.*

Use of Color and Black and White

Color and black-and-white film stocks demand different aesthetic approaches. As was discussed in Chapter 8, "Art Direction," the sets, costumes, and locations read differently in black and white than in color. Visual ideas have to be geared to the palette you are working with. Imagine a wide shot of a playground on a gray day. A boy in the background bounces a ball. He is dressed in red and is the only element in the frame that is moving. The director is making sure that the viewer's eye is on the boy. If the same scene were filmed in black and white, the boy's red clothes would translate as a shade of gray, hardly an eye-popping item. To attract our eyes, he would have to be dressed in a white shirt.

Type of Shot

Staging for the Camera

Staging or blocking is at the center of the director's craft. It is the point of contact for acting, cinematography, and editing. The movement of the actors within the frame, coupled with the movement of the frame, shows how the director stages or choreographs a scene. It starts with this point. Everyone needs to know where the actors will be moving and then how they will be filmed. The director can block the camera, the actors, or both.

These are the ways in which the director organizes her staging ideas for the camera:

Master. Generally, the master is a wide establishing shot of the scene. (An establishing shot and a master shot can be the same.) Often, an entire scene is shot in one complete master. In this case, the actors can be staged to the camera (static master) as well as staging the camera to the actors (moving master). Shooting a master allows the actors to feel the organic flow of the scene from beginning to end, before the director breaks down the scene into individual shots. It also establishes everyone's spatial relationship and actions that have to be duplicated as the director shoots the scene from different angles (it's the job of the continuity person to keep track of this). By establishing the geography of the setting early on, the master shot also prevents the audience from possibly becoming confused (see Figure 12.30).

Minimaster. In a long scene, coverage can be broken up into several short, or minimaster, shots. Whereas a master shot for *Truman* (Figure 12.10) might take in the entire gymnasium, watching the action in that large setting would soon prove boring. Moving the camera to the action, but still keeping the angle wide, affords the director an opportunity to stage a good deal of the scene as a minimaster.

Four-Shot. Any scene with four actors in the frame at the same time is a four-shot.

Three-Shot. Any scene with three actors in the frame at the same time is a three-shot.

Figure 12.10 A minimaster from *Truman*.

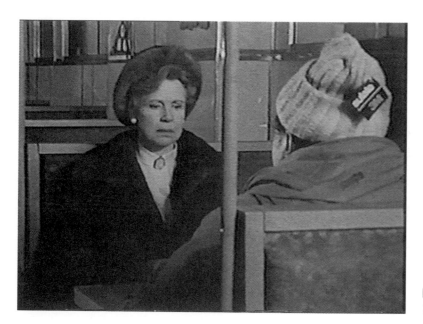

Figure 12.11 Over-the-shoulder shot from *The Lunch Date*.

Two-Shot. Any scene with two actors in the frame at the same time is a two-shot (see Figure 12.41).

It is worth noting in this example from Truman (Figure 12.12) that height becomes a factor when staging a two-shot. Having the coach squat down puts the two characters at a similar eye level, thus making the two-shot and over-the-shoulder shot easier to execute. Had the director kept the two characters standing, both the two-shot and the over-the-shoulder shot would have been awkward.

If the director chooses to have the two characters stand, the two-shot would have to be very wide to accommodate both characters' bodies. An over-the-shoulder shot would have required a tall ladder behind the coach and a low angle high-hat shot for the complementary angle behind Truman. Sometimes this is unavoidable. Even when it is unavoidable, it is permissible to cheat slightly the true distance between the characters' heads. An apple box could be used to bring Truman closer to the coach's size (see Figure 15.2).

Over-the-Shoulder Shot. A shot of one actor speaking to another when a portion of the second

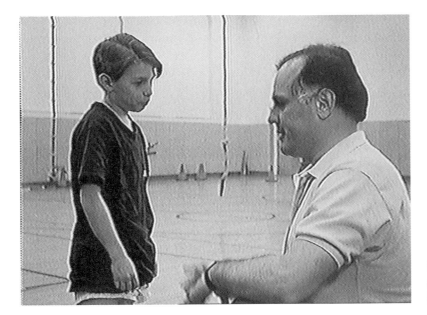

Figure 12.12 By staging the coach in a crouch, the director can get a tight two-shot from *Truman.*

Figure 12.13 Left to right from *The Lunch Date.*

Figure 12.14 Right to left from *The Lunch Date.*

actor's shoulder appears in the foreground of the frame is an over-the-shoulder shot (Figure 12.11). This shot allows the audience to get closer to each character while keeping the other one still in the frame.

Single. A single is a shot of one actor. This can be done as a close, medium, or wide shot. In shooting a scene with single shots, film the reverse single with a matching frame size and camera position. This will create a smooth editing pattern when you cut back and forth between the two-shots. Maintain the integrity of the 180° line so that eye-lines are correct

(Figure 12.2). In these two-shots of the main characters in *The Lunch Date*, the woman is looking left to right and the man right to left. (See Figures 12.13 and 12.14.)

Closeup. A tight shot of a portion of a frame, an object, or one actor's face and shoulders. In shooting a closeup of an actor, know that when the character is looking toward the camera (see Figures 12.28 and 12.33), we are placed in a closer relationship with that subject than if she were framed in profile. The profile shot places us in a more neutral relationship; the character is more distant.

Figure 12.17 Panning is a contrast reveal from *The Lunch Date*.

Figure 12.18

Figure 12.19

Figure 12.20 The camera reveals that there are no bags.

seamlessly integrated into the narrative. They are used to reveal exposition.

Movement can come from within the frame, the motion of the frame itself, or a combination of the two. The camera can be stationary, with the action in front of the lens choreographed, or staged, to its angle. Actors then move toward the camera into a closeup or away from the camera into a long shot.

To give her film an interesting pace, the director can use the camera to bring energy into a scene by moving the frame. A pan, tilt, dolly, zoom, or crane shot adds tremendous vitality to the images. For example, suppose that two characters are eating dinner in a restaurant. A waiter walks through the kitchen door and places their order on the table. You can use the waiter to motivate the pan or dolly through the restaurant to the table. In a dialogue

sequence that is photographed with a slow, constantly moving dolly, the movement is not motivated by any action but will add mystery and tension.

Camera moves can liven up a static dialogue scene. Allow the actors to explore the natural movement that either of the two characters might make (the rehearsal period is the time for this). The question you want to ask is: Do people in this situation actually stand in one place and talk to one another, or do they move in the space, sit down, open a window, and so on? If so, plan small but effective camera moves.

Television has effectively adapted the moving camera as a dramatic device. *NYPD Blue* used a roving camera to create anxiety, instability, and tension. *ER* uses a constantly moving camera to approximate the frantic pace and atmosphere of a real hospital.

Law and Order contrasts two different camera styles: When the first part of each show focuses on law, the camera is always moving, and when the second part focuses on order, the camera is static.

Here are some other motivations for moving the camera:

- To follow the movement of a character
- To allow a vehicle to motivate a camera move down a street
- To establish a landscape or scene geography
- To move in to a character to intensify our relationship with a character or object
- To move away from someone or something to see it more objectively
- To move to reveal important information
- To move to reframe or accommodate a rearrangement of characters
- To move the camera up or down for dramatic purposes

Moving the camera can energize a scene, but will take up time in the production day not only for executing the shot but for rehearsing it as well. The less experienced the crew, the more rehearsal is required.

Balance

Excessive camera movement may distract the audience from the flow of the story. The director must find a way to motivate the camera and to keep the movements subtle enough so that there is a balance between the storytelling and the energy from the camera. If the script calls for a bold camera action, such as a snap zoom or a fast dolly, the director should not hesitate to use all the facilities at her fingertips, within the confines of the budget and the schedule. A shot with a lot of energy that cuts to a static shot has a particular kind of effect, as does a high-energy shot, such as a fast-moving dolly, that cuts to another high-energy shot, like a moving crane.

One Long Take

Choreographing the camera, lights, and actors in a single shot is an ideal way to maintain the energy within a scene. It allows the actors to develop the beats within the scene organically. Using the dynamics of these elements of photography in one shot is the height of cinema aesthetics. However, staging a single-shot scene is time consuming. It requires a great deal of rehearsal for the actors and for the crew. If you find that the shot becomes too difficult to execute, you can resort to covering the scene in several different shots. Always have a backup plan.

A single-shot scene photographed in a single take is unusable unless it has the correct pace and rhythm. Therefore, when you design a sequence to be taken all in one shot, film some insert shots to give yourself an "out" in the editing room. Often, to save a single-take scene, the editor can use the beginning of a scene, cut to a matching insert or closeup, and then return to the single-take scene, using a different but better take.

Creating Camera Movement

There are several ways to move the camera:

- Pan
- Tilt
- Pan/tilt combination
- Zoom (cheap dolly)
- Dolly (with or without tracks)
- Trucking shot
- Handheld camera work
- Crane
- Steadicam
- Car, helicopter, boat (traveling shots)

These methods can be used in different combinations.

Pan/Tilt. A pan is when the camera moves horizontally to the left or right, and a tilt is when the camera points vertically up or down (see Figures 12.21 and 12.22). When drawing storyboards, one indicates pans or tilts by drawing several frames with arrows pointing from one frame to the next. This signifies camera movement. Pans work best when motivated by a subject moving through space. Panning with the moving object makes the rate and movement of panning natural. The most difficult pans are those across landscapes or still objects, because any unevenness in the movement becomes evident. They must be slow enough to avoid strobing unless you are planning a swish pan. Tilts are prone to the same issues. The pan/tilt combination is a useful tool.

Zoom. The camera has a lens that is able to optically change focal lengths without moving.

Dolly. The camera moves back and forth. The dolly moves on tracks or independently. The example in Figures 12.23 through 12.25 is a dolly back from *Truman*. Note how the main character's relationship to the frame stays the same.

Trucking Shot. The camera moves sideways with the action.

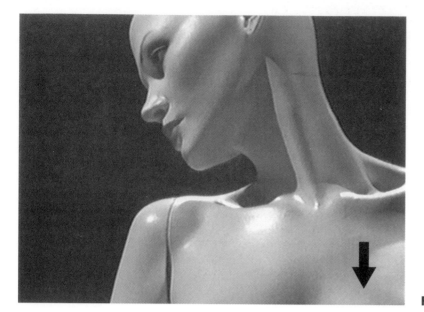

Figure 12.21

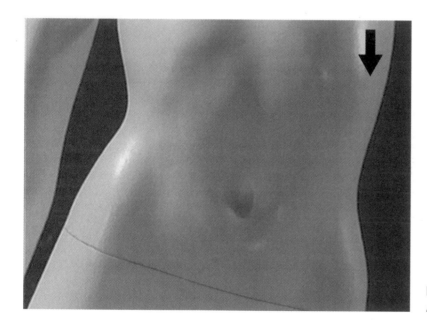

Figure 12.22 A tilt down from *Mirror Mirror.*

Handheld Camera Work. Handheld camera work brings a special dynamism to a scene. A slight movement in the camera, especially if the angle is from a character's point of view, adds both realism and tension to a shot. Be advised, however, that too much movement in a shot disorients viewers. Wide-angle lenses are more appropriate choices for hand-held work because they stabilize the image. Handheld camera work is most often used to give a documentary, "realistic," or cinema verité feeling to a shot. It can substitute for a dolly shot because, if you are pressed for time, shooting handheld saves considerable setup time.

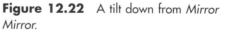

I saw Frederick Weisman's High School, *which was shot at a public high school in Philadelphia, and I was in a public high school in Philadelphia. I saw the film in Washington, D.C., because it wasn't allowed to be shown in Philadelphia. I saw it in 1969, and it really did blow me away because it was consonant with the reality of my life. It was a whole different style of documentary, cinema verité, which I hadn't been exposed to.*

Jan

Figure 12.23 Dolly back from *Truman*.

Figure 12.24

Figure 12.25

Crane. The camera is placed on a moving tripod that can be lifted up off the ground.

Steadicam and Traveling Shots (car, helicopter, and boat). These shots are discussed later in the chapter.

Coverage

A scene is photographed, or covered, from a variety of angles and points of view. When pieced together in the editing room, these angles should represent the director's visual plan.

When they were sitting at the table, I covered the scene in a standard way. I did a medium wide shot, both of them in frame, and then came in for closeups. Then I got insert coverage of the plates.

Adam

One of the director's main duties is to deliver proper coverage to the editing room. Coverage is the sum of all of the shots that go into the making of a sequence. There might be 20 shots that make up or cover a one-minute scene, or one shot that covers a five-minute scene.

Here are 10 shots from Truman's "hanging scene" that indicate roughly the coverage needed to tell a story:

1. First we see Truman looking up at his adversary.

2. Then his point of view of the humongous distance he has to make.

3. The third shot is his reaction to the task.

4. The next shot is him on the rope hanging on for dear life.

5. The wide pull back shows how high he is and who is egging him on.

6. A reaction shot from the other schoolchildren.

7. Another reaction shot from some other kids.

8. Truman looks up as the rope is pulling apart.

9. A closeup of the frayed rope ready to dump him.

10. Wide shot of the coach and kids experiencing rejection and failure.

A key to adequate coverage is to shoot the important elements of each scene from more than one angle. The scene with multiple shots—perhaps a combination of a master shot, two-shots, closeups, and dollies—is picked apart in the editing room, taking 10 frames from one angle, 20 feet from another, and so on, until the scene has the desired pace and rhythm.

> **STUDENTS**
>
> Many students plan too many shots. Experience will show you how to plan a day. A good rule is to aim for 5 well-executed shots rather than 10 sloppy ones. Be prepared to either cut or collapse several shots into one.

Making a student short film must be different from making a professional short film. Certainly, as a student, you are going to encounter a lot of problems with just getting the film made: getting equipment, getting a good crew—that's always difficult—dealing with a school's bureaucracy. And you're never going to have a perfect shoot. You're never going to have a perfect piece. Nothing is going to go as planned.

Adam

Second Unit/B-Roll

An inexpensive method of recording material that doesn't require sound (in film these are called MOS shots) is to use what has been traditionally called a second unit crew. In video, it is called B-roll. Second unit teams are small (usually exterior work), which means that they can move quickly and efficiently; they don't have to wait for a truck to pass by for good sound conditions. The second unit can be used to photograph establishing shots, transition shots, cut-aways, drive-bys—in fact, any action that doesn't require the principal actors. In film, they can use a small light-weight MOS camera, one that is not designed to shoot sync sound.

Continuity

Editors want to make a seamless picture, and this can only be accomplished with the proper coverage. The best way to guarantee a seamless cut is to maintain the continuity within a scene and to overlap action.

Continuity is the maintenance of the same action throughout a scene. If a character smokes a cigarette, it should get progressively shorter as the scene unfolds. If you shoot out of sequence, which is often the case, maintain the cigarette at a length that will match the real time of the scene.

Overlapping Action

Actors are required to match their actions from angle to angle. Cutting on an action produces a smooth transition from one shot to the next. Suppose a character sits down in a wide shot. The next camera position is a medium shot of the character in the chair. On "Action," the director should have the actor "sit into" the shot. Having the action of sitting from both angles will give the editor different choices to find a perfect place in the action to make the cut.

180° Rule

One of the more confusing areas of coverage has to do with the 180° rule. Although it is not inviolable (many directors have disregarded this rule), cutting from one character who is speaking to another character can look odd if the rule is not followed.

The eye-line, or where a character is looking, relates to screen direction. Viewers must be able to follow the eye-line from the character's eyes to what the character sees (see Figure 12.25). The camera operator needs to be sure of the match so that the cut will work in the editing room (Figure 12.27).

Refer back to Figure 12.2. If the director never crosses the 180° line, a character will always appear to be looking at the person to whom he is speaking. If the director crosses the line, it might appear as though the character is looking away from the person to whom he is speaking.

If character A looks at character B from screen left to screen right, character B must look at character A from screen right to screen left if the audience is to believe that they are speaking face-to-face. For an over-the-shoulder shot, the camera should be placed over character A's right shoulder. The complementary, or reverse, angle would have the camera placed over character B's left shoulder. With this setup, the characters will appear on screen to have eye contact with one another.

For a closeup of character A, the camera is placed where character B was sitting, or even a little closer, and the actor is asked to look to camera right. The off-camera actor can put his face right next to the lens. This gives the on-camera actor the correct eye-line. If the confines of the set do not allow the character B

actor to stand next to the camera, he must deliver his lines from elsewhere. To ensure correct eye-line, the camera operator can place a piece of white tape on the right side of the lens and ask the actor to speak to the tape.

When shooting a dialogue scene in which the camera swings around to shoot the reverse angle, the director and script supervisor can easily become confused as to which direction the character should look. Should he look screen left or screen right? Rather than take a chance, shoot it both ways. This gives the editor an opportunity to choose the correct position in the editing room.

Crossing the Line

You can cross the 180° line with a dolly move or an insert. By changing the audience's viewpoint, you establish a new 180° line. Make it clear to the audience where the scene is taking place. If, in a master shot, the director has clearly indicated where the characters are positioned and what the set pieces look like, it makes it easier to move the characters and the camera in this space to maintain clarity.

Keeping Score

The director risks losing the audience's attention if they are confused about technical points such as who is speaking to whom or where the characters are placed spatially in relation to one another. Both of these problems can easily occur, such as when a scene is shot exclusively in closeups. The audience needs reference points, such as a master shot that defines the space.

Screen Direction in Movement

Suppose that a character walks from screen right to screen left. If the next shot is a continuation of the walking shot, the character should maintain the same screen direction. If another character walks in the opposite direction and is intercut with the first character for parallel action, the audience will assume that they are walking toward each other and might eventually meet.

A moving vehicle traveling screen left to right should always maintain that direction unless the director wants to change the direction of the vehicle. She can execute this change by having the vehicle move directly toward or away from the camera. The director can then change the screen direction on the next shot (Figure 12.36).

Figure 12.26
Character's head indicates camera direction.

Figure 12.27
Point of view shot.

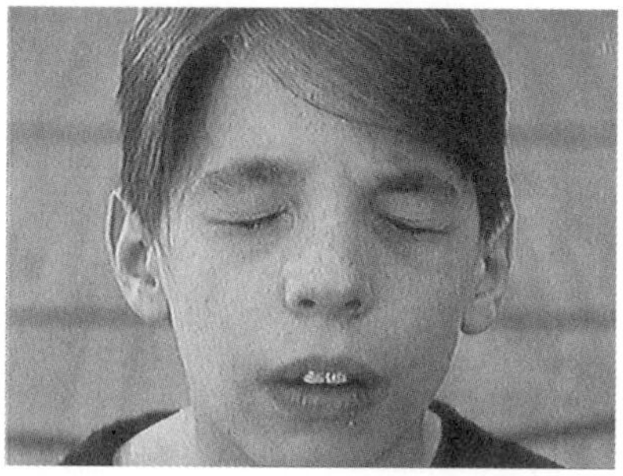

Figure 12.28
Closeup.

Figure 12.29
Single shot.

Figure 12.30
Wide shot.

Figure 12.31
Reaction shot direction.

Figure 12.32
Reaction shot.

Figure 12.33
Closeup.

Figure 12.34
Insert shot.

Figure 12.35
Wide-shot minimaster.

Figure 12.36 Vehicles should maintain a consistent direction. One way to change direction is to have the vehicle come toward the camera.

Specialty Shots

Confer with your DP to determine the best way to shoot special situations, such as variable speeds (slow motion, fast motion), manipulation of shutter speeds, shooting off the television, day for night, matte shots, miniatures, split screens, blue screens, and underwater photography.

To get this high angle of the woman from *The Lunch Date* (Figure 12.37) required a ladder and a steady hand.

Multiple Cameras. Some sequences (such as stunts or concerts) require that more than one camera be used at the same time.

Optical and Special Effects. See Chapter 18, "Laboratory/Online."

Lighting

The most significant addition to the composition of the frame is the use of light. Photographers have known this for years, which is why they describe their work as "painting with light." It should be the script that dictates the mood and amount of light. A chase sequence at night needs to be full of mystery: pools of light, areas of shadow. A comedy, on the other hand, is usually brightly lit.

Based on the script, the director and the DP determine a look for the staging, photographic, and lighting style for the project. This look can be either

Figure 12.37 High-angle shot from *The Lunch Date*.

naturalistic or stylized. Once a style has been determined, it should remain consistent throughout the shoot. The three case studies used in this book are good examples of a consistent look and style. *Truman*, a comedy, is evenly and brightly lit. *Mirror Mirror* has a glossy "studio" look. *The Lunch Date*, inspired by the black-and-white photography of Alfred Stieglitz, maintains a look that is consistent with that style (see Figure 12.1).

There are two basic artificial lights: hard light and soft light. Hard light has a single or point source, such as a candle, a bulb, or the sun, whereas soft light has a broad, diffused source. Hard lights include incandescent, quartz, ellipsoidal, and Fresnel instruments. The sun is considered to be a hard light. Soft lighting instruments include scoops, strips, and banks. Hard lights have a longer throw than soft lights and create more contrast. Hard lights create hard shadows; soft lights fill in soft shadows.

Classic three-point lighting uses three lights: key, fill, and back. Key light provides the main source of light on the set or subject. Fill light provides detail within the shadows and softens the impact of the source light. Back light outlines the subject, separating it from the background. From this basic setup, both naturalistic and stylized lighting designs can be produced, depending on the angle, distance, and intensity of the light from these three positions.

Lighting should generally be motivated (i.e., we should know the source of the light). Sunlight or moonlight shining through a window can be the source, or key, light. Other lights can fill in the rest of the set to reduce contrast. Contrast should not be so pronounced that the part of the actor's face in the key light is well exposed but the other side of the face is dark.

To develop a comprehensive and effective lighting plan, the director should consider the following questions:

- What is the source light?
- What is the time of day?
- What mood do you want to convey?
- Do you want high-key (Whistler, Degas) or low-key (Rembrandt, Caravaggio) lighting?
- Do you want high or low contrast?
- Is the scene intended to have natural or artificial light?
- Do the shadows have hard or soft edges?
- Is the key light at a high angle, at eye level, or at a low angle?
- Is the lighting setup frontal, broad, narrow, or backlit?
- What are the practicals (real lamps) in the scene?

- Must any practical lights be replaced?
- What is the intensity of the light?
- What is the direction of the light?
- What is the quality of the light?
- How can continuity of light quality be maintained from shot to shot?

The human eye is more sensitive than film. Use a contrast viewing filter to see what light really exists on the set.

Lighting for Exteriors

Shooting outdoors can be tricky if the production relies only on the sun for illumination. The sun's arc in the sky causes the direction of the light, the shadows, and even the intensity of the light to change constantly. In addition, the sun is often obscured. Should you wait for the sun to come out from behind the clouds? A good trick is to look at the sky in the reflection of your sunglasses. The sun will appear as a bright ball behind the clouds, and you can estimate when it might emerge from behind them.

There are several methods for overcoming the powerful influence of the sun. One is to erect large translucent squares called silks, which can act as a filter for the sun. With silks, a soft constant light can be maintained all day. If the sun goes behind clouds, electric lights can be pumped into the silk to maintain a consistent stop (see "Exposure" on page 186). Silks work only for medium and close shots. In a wide shot, they might appear in the frame. Try to grab the wide shot when the light on the set is appropriate for the scene.

Reflectors, or bounce cards, are commonly used in the field for fill light. When placed just off camera, these shiny or white surfaces reflect the sun's light (or any light source) onto the actors' faces. They produce additional light that separates the actor from the background.

When shooting outdoors, the company is at the mercy of the light and the weather. "Chasing the sun" is a common exterior location occupation. You cannot shoot until the sun has risen, and when it falls, the fading light will not be strong enough to light the scene.

Lighting for Interiors

Interior lighting comes with a different set of problems. Although day interiors can rely on the sun, it is easier to maintain a consistent look with artificial lights placed outside the windows. Study your location. From where does the light come? What are the practicals doing? In most cases, it is a matter of taking existing source light and enhancing it to obtain the desired f-stop.

The biggest hurdle to overcome with interior lighting is space. In a practical location, the combination of the lights, the set pieces, the crew, and the actors allows little room to maneuver. It is recommended that you use spreaders (see Glossary) to create a grid from which to hang the lights.

There were light problems: This gym was lit with fluorescent lights. I didn't have the time or money to gel all those fluorescent lights. There were over 120 of them, so we had to do all our lighting with the fluorescents, which meant we had to find an equipment house nearby that rented fluorescent fills.

Howard

Lighting for Documentaries

A documentary production company travels with little equipment. A few lighting instruments and a bounce card are usually sufficient to light a set for an interview. Outside, a sungun that runs off a battery belt will help fill in dark areas; there's no need to run the light to a power source. This gives the documentary crew freedom to be anywhere for filming. This is imperative when shooting cinema verité style.

As an aesthetic, I prefer exterior interviews. In documentaries I made about drive-in movie theaters and a traveling tent circus, it enabled me to use the exterior environment creatively in the interview setup. I like to avoid lights and usually just set up a flex-fill [bounce card] in an exterior location. I know that this is somewhat unorthodox because most documentarians put their subjects in offices or living rooms where they have complete control over the light. A major liability of exterior interviews is the sound. Documentary subjects always seem to live near a major airport!

Jan

Lighting for Video

In the past, heavy video cameras on pedestals in a three-camera setup required copious amounts of light. This is still true of any multiple-camera setup. To capture an image from several positions at the same time, there must be a flood of light on any set. As the look of video steadily began to approach that of film,

the lighting schemes also became similar.

Even today, the look of video is unlike that of film because the light sensitivities of film emulsion and videotape stock differ. This results in different depths of field and different contrast ratios.

Film has 10 f-stops or shades of gray plus pure white and pure black. Video has 4 f-stops of gray plus white and black. What this means is that film has much more subtle detail and information than high-definition television (HDTV) as an acquisition format.

Another issue is the sensitivity of film verse HDTV. The finest HDTV camera has an ISO rating of 300 without gain boost. Gain boost is a form of making the video format more sensitive to light, but when you use gain boost you add electronic noise that degrades the image. The fastest high-end quality film is 500 ISO, which amounts to almost 1 f-stop of light over HDTV. The net result is HDTV stumbles at night in low situations and you actually need more lighting work to get a quality image with HDTV versus film. Film can hold an average f-stop of 8 to 11 in a situation where the light goes from an f-stop of 22 to 2.8, but video cannot. The contrast ratio of video is approximately 40:1, equivalent to 5 stops. Film has a contrast ratio of 128:1, or approximately 10 stops. Film has a range of nine grays and video has only three.

The video image holds up well in closeups, but the image begins to break apart in very wide shots. This is significant because one of the primary distinctions between these two media is projection. Video projection is limited, so most of what we see is geared for the television screen. This frame size also is good for closeups, but it is difficult to hold wide shots, as the elements in the frame are less distinct.

When shooting video, avoid white backdrops and red costumes. The white tends to "blow out" the frame, and red may bleed. Never shoot into the sun. A film camera can be adjusted to shoot at the sun, but direct sunlight can damage sensitive components in a video camera. Video is also very sensitive to colored gels; use them less than with film.

Most video cameras are programmed with an automatic iris. This means that if the camera is recording a scene in a room and then pans toward a window, the light from the sun in the window will force the aperture to adjust quickly. The adjustment, which is visible, is a dead giveaway that the image was produced by a video camera. To avoid this problem, use the manual iris override.

Ultimately, video production is tied to broadcast standards. Using a waveform monitor while recording allows the videographer to determine how much light is needed to create a signal on the monitor that con-

Figure 12.38 *Medium reaction shot from The Lunch Date.*

forms to broadcast standards. In some cases, lighting that is meant to set a mood will prove unacceptable. The solution is more light.

To illustrate this point, consider video distribution. Suppose that a film with many night scenes is scheduled to be released on video. It is transferred from its 35-mm negative to a HDCAM master for editing. Because of HDTV contrast compression or narrow contrast latitude, the night scenes can be so dark and muddy that it is difficult for the viewer to see what is happening. As a result of this problem, many buyers for the video market, especially the foreign market, do not want films with too many dark, moody, or night sequences.

Editing

Think ahead to the editing room and consider editorial techniques when choreographing camera movements. Learn to think like an editor. Ask yourself these questions:

- What will the shot about to be taken cut from?
- What will the shot about to be taken cut to?

This will lead you to discover the transitions either between beats or between scenes. It will force you to think how you want to begin and end a shot. Will the scenes dissolve into one another, fade out and then fade in, or wipe? (See Glossary.) How would the story be affected if every scene ended or started with a closeup of the main characters?

Create a visual flow that disguises any editorial technique unless used for dramatic effect, such as a smash cut, a wipe, or a flip. (See Figures 12.38 and 12.39—reaction shot to insert shot.)

Some of the best directors have years of editing room experience. Editors quickly develop a sense of what works well cut together and what does not. All directors, DPs, and script supervisors should be aware of how a scene that is being shot will ultimately cut together.

Documentaries

For some documentaries, you might need cutaways and a reverse to the interviewer. These shots are usually mandatory so that the editor can keep the text flowing without a jump cut on the speaker. Besides learning from personal experience, the best way to learn coverage is to study great narrative and documentary film sequences. Count the number of shots and observe the variety of angles and how they cut together. On what line or movement is the edit made?

EQUIPMENT

As a director, you need not have a complete technical knowledge of the camera or other equipment, but you should be acquainted with its capabilities and uses. For example, if the director wants to move the camera, she should have an understanding of what her

Figure 12.39 Insert shot from *The Lunch Date.*

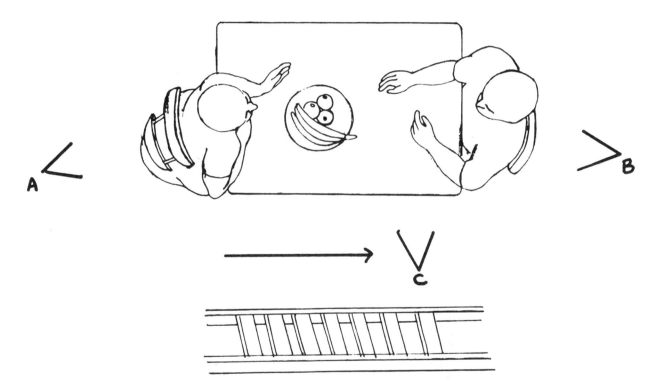

Figure 12.40 The camera angle on the left is a mirror of the angle on the right. A third position is added when camera angle C moves on the dolly from left to right. (Floor plan from *The Lunch Date.*)

choices are, what they accomplish, and how they can enhance the story. The lens is the tool the director must completely understand. Knowing how much of the world is revealed in each shot is integral to the ability to control how much information the audience sees at any given time. You should be completely familiar with the tools with which you will manipulate the content and ambience of the frame.

Film Camera

A motion picture camera is a lightproof mechanical device through which the unexposed film travels. A film camera contains the following components:

- The *lens* focuses light from the world onto the film.

Figure 12.41 Unique two-shot from *Crazy Glue*.

- The *lens mount* is an attachment to the camera body for lenses.
- The *viewfinder* allows the camera operator to see what image is being recorded on film.
- The *film chamber* is a lightproof compartment that holds the film before and after it is exposed to light. Many cameras use a detachable *magazine* to hold the film.
- The *motor* supplies the power to run the film through the gate.
- The *claw* pulls down each frame of film for exposure and holds it steady in the film gate during exposure.
- The *shutter* blocks light from the film as it moves between successive exposures.

Film Formats

Super-8

In 1932, 8-mm cameras were introduced that used 16-mm film slit down the middle. In 1965 Kodak brought out super-8 film that was 8-mm wide, but with smaller, repositioned sprocket holes, it could record an image 50 percent larger than regular 8-mm. 8-mm film is now almost obsolete.

Super-8 film cameras are inexpensive, portable, and easy to use. Film is inserted in pocket-sized cartridges. Many super-8 cameras can record sound in camera, but magnetic striped film stock capable of sound recording is hard to find. Super-8 was once the format of choice for home movies, but small video cameras eliminated them from this market.

Super-8 has recently undergone something of a revival because it is sometimes used in music videos, commercials, and even feature films (Oliver Stone and his DP Robert Richardson like to use it). It is being kept alive by companies such as Super8 Sound in Los Angeles (www.super8sound.com), which created the Pro8 Negative line of stocks by using a film-cutting machine to load super-8 cartridges with a wide range of color and black-and-white stocks. Rather than edit or distribute films in super-8, filmmakers are choosing to transfer the film to video or blow up (enlarge) to 16-mm or 35-mm.

Super-8 can offer much of the flexibility of a small-format video camera, but with a superior image. The filmmaker may be looking for a rough, grainy image for stylistic reasons or may want to duplicate the look of an old movie. Instead of trying to degrade a 16-mm or 35-mm image, the filmmaker can shoot one of the grainier or more contrasty super-8 stocks.

16-mm

Since it started out as an amateur format in the 1920s, 16-mm film has gone through enormous changes. The portability of 16-mm cameras made them the choice for news and documentaries. In the 1970s and 1980s, 16-mm cameras and stocks improved greatly, and 16-mm was used for TV documentaries, low-budget feature films, animation, and avant garde films. By the mid-1990s, many productions that had been shot in 16-mm were being done in video, and 16-mm as a distribution format had almost disappeared.

Despite this trend, there are now newer, fine-grained 16-mm (and super-16-mm) film stocks that are capable of capturing rich images that rival 35-mm, and 16-mm is still being used for higher budget documentaries, music videos, some TV shows, commercials, and many low-budget features.

Super-16-mm

In the 1970s, super-16 was created by extending the image into the side of the 16-mm film normally occupied by the sound track or the extra set of perforations on a double-perf film. Super-16 allows a 40 percent larger image to be recorded on each frame. It is not itself a release format, but was designed for blowing up or enlarging to 35-mm for theatrical distribution. Because super-16 records a larger and wider frame, less magnification and cropping are needed (than with regular 16-mm) to create the 35-mm widescreen image. Properly shot, super-16 films can look very good blown up to 35-mm (*Leaving Las Vegas* is an example). Super-16 is being used increasingly as an origination medium for programs that will be distributed in widescreen or high-definition TV formats.

Figure 12.42 35-mm film camera.

4:3 (1.33:1)
Academy Standard
Television, 35mm 16mm
and S-8mm film formats

(1.85:1)
American Widescreen
format

(2.25:1)
Vista Vision
format

(2.36:1)
70mm Full Aperture
format

Figure 12.43 Aspect ratio.

Some cameras (such as most Aatons) can be switched between 16-mm and super-16. To show a super-16 film, you have to transfer it to video, blow it up to 35-mm, or make a special 16-mm reduction print.

35-mm

The standard format of feature films, television commercials, and TV movies not shot on video is 35-mm. Traditional 35-mm cameras are heavy and expensive to rent. The newer generation of lighter 35-mm cameras can be handheld and with stabilization devices, such as the Steadicam, provide greater mobility and allow 16-mm techniques to be used in feature films. (See Figure 12.42.)

Aspect Ratio

A film's format refers to the width of the film material itself, as well as the size and shape of the image that is recorded on it. The 16-mm and super-16 formats use the same width of gauge (16-mm), but the size of their frames is different. *The aspect ratio* refers to the ratio of width to height of the image both on

film and on the screen. The standard for several formats (8-mm, super-8, and 16-mm, as well as the traditional video/TV) is an aspect ratio of four to three, or 1.33:1. It is spoken as "one three three to one" or just "one three three."

In 35-mm, the full frame for sound film has an aspect ratio of about 1.33:1 and is called Academy aperture, named for the Academy of Motion Picture Arts and Sciences that defined it. Though the Academy frame was once standard for theaters and is the traditional standard for television, it is considered too narrow for contemporary theater audiences.

Most movies viewed in American theaters are made to be shown at 1.85:1, which is a widescreen aspect ratio. European theatrical features are made for projection at 1.66:1, which, for the same height, is not as wide as the 1.85:1 image. Most widescreen systems work by cropping out the top and bottom of the Academy frame, making the image proportionally wider.

Camera Terms

Magazine

If the film stock comes on a very large roll (400 to 1,000 feet), it is placed in a magazine, which in turn is attached to the camera body for threading the film past the lens aperture. One side of the magazine is the supply reel. The film passes behind the lens for exposure and is spooled on the takeup side of the magazine.

Battery

Film cameras usually use separate rechargeable battery belts. Always check. Batteries put out much less power when they are cold.

Aperture

The plate between the lens and the film is the aperture plate. The aperture itself is a rectangle cut out of the plate through which light from the lens shines. The base of the film rests on the other half of the gate, which is called the pressure plate.

Shutter

Once the film claw has moved a frame through the film gate, the shutter opens to allow light to hit the film. The film comes to a complete halt before the shutter opens again for the next exposure.

Exposure

The amount of light that passes through the lens and the duration of time to create an image are called the exposure. Changes in the amount of light are measured in stops (f-stops and t-stops). On the lens is a ring that can open or close down the stops. Changes in exposure can also affect the depth of field. The film-maker has the following means of controlling exposure: film speed, the lens, shutter speed, and the amount of ambient light.

Lenses

Lenses are interchangeable. The lens placed on the front of a camera is determined by the needs of the shot. One shot might require a long lens (250-mm), whereas the next shot might call for a wide-angle lens (5.7-mm). "Super"-speed lenses (calibrated to be super-sensitive to light) can be helpful in low-light situations.

> *Because it wasn't a thesis, I wasn't allowed to use a lot of equipment at Columbia. I basically got the dregs. I knew there were a couple of things we had to rent. I rented high-speed lenses for the stuff in Grand Central, which economically worked out better than renting the many lights it would have taken to get exposure.*
>
> Adam

Although a wide variety of lenses are available in a camera package, most lenses fall into three basic categories for 16-mm:

Wide-angle Lenses. These lenses (5.9-mm to 12-mm) are used to capture a lot of information, or picture, in the frame. They take advantage of low-light situations, hold a large depth of field, absorb camera motion, and can be used to distort the image.

Normal Lenses. Normal lenses (16-mm to 75-mm) are used to gain a "normal" perspective on a scene or character. They hold a considerable depth of field.

Telephoto, or Long, Lenses. These lenses (75-mm to 250-mm) are used to shoot beyond unwanted foreground detail, to flatten and compress the perspective, or to create a dramatic visual statement.

Zoom Lens

A popular lens is the zoom, which allows the director of photography to change frame sizes quickly merely by "racking" through the rings of the zoom lens. Hard, or fixed, lenses, especially high-speed lenses, can expose film with less light than is needed for a zoom lens. Most video cameras use zoom lenses exclusively.

Filters

Filters, diopters, and gels can be placed directly in front of the lens to obtain a correct color balance or an interesting effect, to reduce light entering the camera, or as a polarizer (see Glossary).

Eyepiece

The camera eyepiece, which allows the director and the DP to see exactly what the lens sees, has a series of thin black frame lines that show what is inside the frame, on the edge of the frame, or outside the frame lines. This is especially helpful when determining how close the microphone can come to the actor without actually appearing in the frame.

These black lines also allow the camera operator to determine what will appear in the television frame if it differs from the aspect ratio chosen for the shoot. The television frame is smaller than the aspect ratio for film. If the action occurs within these lines, it is referred to as being in TV safe.

Light Meter

The exposure of an object on film or tape is related to the amount of light falling on the subject, which is known as incident light. An incident light meter measures the amount of light falling on the subject from all angles. The total amount of light on the subject can also be determined by measuring the light reflected off the subject. This reflected light is measured with a reflective light meter. Whereas the incident light meter is pointed from the subject toward the camera to read the light, the reflectance light meter is pointed at the subject. The meter reading tells the camera operator which stop to set the lens to in order to obtain the desired results.

Tests

Many elements (film or video stock, lens size, filters, lighting, and f-stop), combined with the director's aesthetic design for the shot, are calibrated to cause a specific result. If the result the director wants is complicated or out of the ordinary in any way, it is recommended that tests be made in preproduction to determine how the desired results can be achieved.

VIDEO

Video Camera

Like film cameras, the video camera uses a lens to capture an image, but instead of focusing that image on a strip of film, the video camera focuses the picture on a light-sensitive computer chip called a charge-coupled device (CCD). The flat surface of the CCD is divided into a very fine grid of spots or sites called pixels (picture elements). Each pixel acts like a tiny light meter that reads the brightness of light at that spot. When the pixel is struck by light, it creates and stores an electric charge. A given CCD chip may have thousands or even millions of pixels in a chip that is less than an inch across. The CCD measures the voltage of every pixel in the grid many times a second. It processes that information and sends it along as an electrical signal. The video signal can then be recorded or displayed on a monitor (TV screen).

Video cameras render color by separating the light coming into the camera lens into its red, green, and blue components. In single-chip color cameras, one method is to use tiny filters over the pixels that allow the CCD to measure the relative amounts of red, green, and blue light in a given area. In the generally superior three-chip color camera, a prism or mirror in the camera splits the light coming through the lens into separate red, green, and blue signals and then sends each signal to a separate CCD (much like the original 35-mm Technicolor film camera). The intensity of color in a video signal is called its *chrominance*.

Camcorder

The video camcorder combines a video camera and videotape recorder (VTR) into one unit. In studio settings, instead of camcorders, several independent cameras can be used with one or more separate VTRs. All camera/recorders share certain elements:

- The lens has controls for the focus of the image, the brightness of the image (using the iris diaphragm), and a zoom to change focal length.
- The CCD is the light-sensitive electronic chip that converts the light coming through the lens into an electronic signal.
- The camera processes the signal from the CCD before sending it on and adjusts the color of the image. It may also have the capability for adjusting the length of exposure using a shutter and changing the sensitivity of the CCD using the gain adjustment.
- The viewfinder is a small monitor that allows you to see the video signal.
- The VTR stores the signal on tape. It includes a tape transport, which moves the tape past the heads, which transmits the signal to the tape. The signal may be recorded in analog or digital form, depending on the VTR.
- Most camcorders have built-in or attached microphones. All have provisions to plug in external mikes.
- The camera can be run on rechargeable batteries or by plugging into an AC power supply.
- Most cameras have the capability of generating timecode, which is important for postproduction.

Many camcorders, especially consumer products, are highly automated, allowing the user to "point and shoot." Some of these cameras do not even allow you to make adjustments. Since the ability to control focus, exposure, and color is part of the creative process of shooting, it is not necessarily advantageous to have these features automated. Professional camcorders are generally not so automated, or at least offer manual override for most features.

Monitor

Many monitors use a cathode ray tube (CRT) to convert the electrical video signal back into its visible image. Inside the monitor, a cathode ray gun fires a stream of electrons at the back of the video screen (the opposite side from which you watch). The inside of the screen is coated with a phosphor surface that glows when it is excited by the ray of electrons. The ray "paints" the image on the screen, line by line. The higher the current of the ray, the more brightly the screen glows. The brightness of the video signal is called its *luminance.*

The video system processes the image by dividing the picture into a series of horizontal scan lines. This pattern of lines is called the raster. The camera scans the image starting at the top, from left to right. It reads the brightness levels all the way across a scan line, then returns to the left side and moves down slightly as it scans across again. This is much like the way your eye takes in a paragraph of written text. When it reaches the bottom of the screen, it returns to the top and starts over. The monitor's CRT makes the same scanning pattern, "painting" the image on as it goes. A sync signal makes sure the camera and monitor scan at the same time.

Many monitors now employ progressive scanning. What is most important is that on a video shoot the monitor be calibrated accurately. It becomes the DPs light meter.

Interlaced Scanning

In the United States and 29 other countries, traditional broadcast video systems use a standard established by the National Television Standards Committee (NTSC) in the United States in 1954. *NTSC* video runs at 29.97 fps and divides the picture into 525 horizontal lines (of which about 460 reach the home viewer), scanned in an *interlaced* pattern. In the United Kingdom, Western Europe, China, and Australia (59 countries in all), the video standard is called phase alternating line, or *PAL*. PAL was developed in Germany and the United Kingdom and first used in 1967. France, Eastern Europe, and Russia (23 countries in all) use the equential Couleûr à Mémoire (SECAM) standard. SECAM 625 was developed in France and first used in 1967. PAL and SECAM are also scanned in an interlaced pattern but run at 25 fps and divide the picture into 625 horizontal scan lines, creating a sharper image (more resolution) than NTSC.

Interlacing the image allows the capture, broadcast, and display of two half-resolution images in such a way that they looked like a single image on a TV set. Your brain doesn't notice that the images are half resolution as long as they are knit together accurately as a $\frac{1}{30}$th of a second full resolution image. In basic terms, video can be considered as being made up of numerous snapshots, called frames. The frame rate or the number of frames displayed each second is 29.97 in the United States and other NTSC-based countries. For sake of simplicity, we can round this number to 30 frames per second (fps).

Television, however, does not deal with video in terms of frames as we know from film. Instead, it displays video using half-frames called *fields*. Each frame contains exactly two fields. One field is made up of the odd horizontal lines in a frame. This is called the *odd field* or the *top field* because it contains the top line of the image. The other field is made up of the even horizontal lines in a frame. This is called the *even field* or *bottom field*.

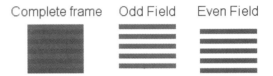

Television cameras actually shoot two separate exposures per frame, to capture the two video fields. The odd-numbered scan lines (lines 1, 3, 5, etc.) are shot first, than another field is shot to capture all the even-numbered scan lines (coming back to record lines 2, 4, 6, etc.). Thus, an image is captured in two separate passes. When the two fields are interlaced to fit together on TV, a frame is created from both fields to reproduce the full-resolution picture. Using the 480 line DVD standard as an example, the first 240 lines displayed are the odd-numbered lines (1, 3, and 5). The second 240 lines displayed are the even-numbered lines.

Since there are two fields in every frame, a television actually updates the display at 60 fields per second (or 50 fields per second for PAL/SECAM). Each field is displayed 1/60th of a second after the preceding field (or 1/50th of a second for PAL/SECAM video). Since two fields make up one complete frame, this results in video that runs at approximately 30 fps (1/60th + 1/60th = 2/60th = 1/30).

A major benefit of displaying and broadcasting in an interlaced format is that it acts as a form of compression, reducing the overall bandwidth required for delivering signals. The disadvantage is a loss of vertical resolution, known as the *interlace factor*. As a comparison, images on a computer are drawn progressively. It captures the whole image one frame at a time. Because of this, both fields that make up a video frame are shown simultaneously. This is called a *progressive scan display*. Progressive video formats preserve the progressive nature of film but require more bandwidth for broadcast than interlaced video.

Television signals are interlaced because of the nature of early television sets and the nature of human vision. When a series of frames are presented, the frame rate (the time interval between frames) has to be high enough to achieve *persistence of vision*, a continuous image without noticeable flicker. The United States uses a 60-Hz power cycle, but early television sets were only able to display at a 30-fps frame rate. Interlacing two 30-fps fields achieved an effective 60-fps frame rate, which solved the problem of low bandwidth and was high enough to provide persistence of vision at lower bandwidths than progressive scanning. The European standards PAL and SECAM use interlacing at 25 fps to achieve an effective 50-fps frame rate because Europe uses a 50-Hz power cycle.

Interlace Factor

If you are filming a stationary image, the interlaced images are excellent because both 1/60th of second images are identical. If there is motion, you may see the motion as jagged edged or blurred advancements. Motion *artifacts* and horizontal "line twitter" are the most notorious NTSC artifacts. Jagged edges occur because the object is in a different location every 1/60th of a second. The even lines show the object in one position, while the odd lines show the image in a different position. When you knit the odd and even scan lines together, you see ragged edges around moving objects. Furthermore, thin horizontal lines in the original image that are the width of a single scan line (or smaller) will flicker on and off as the image is panned vertically or if the object with horizontal lines moves vertically when the camera is not moving. The closer you sit to your TV set, the easier it will be to see NTSC artifacts in images.

Component versus Composite Video

We have established that video cameras generate separate red, green, and blue color signals. In *component* video systems, the red, green, and blue (RGB) signals, either in analog or digital format, are kept separate from one another. The individual color components are sent in separate channels (using separate cables) from one piece of equipment to another. Component video offers the sharpest and cleanest colors. The pictures look good and suffer little generation loss with each dub. It is expensive and requires special equipment that maintains the separateness of the colors.

In *composite* video systems, the color signals are mixed (encoded) with the luminance into one signal

that can travel on a single channel. It composites them. Composite video makes recording and broadcasting easier, but results in marked loss of image quality. The real problem, however, is the generation loss when the signal is rerecorded many times.

The method by which the RGB signal is compressed and encoded is based on government-approved standards (such as NTSC, PAL, or SECAM). Composite video is inexpensive and simple. Composite originated when color television was first invented and engineers had to find a way to cram the additional information into the existing black-and-white television signal.

There is a third option using two cables of video, one for the luminance (brightness) and one for the chrominance (RGB). This is called *Y/C or S-video* (separate video). It combines the colors into one chrominance signal but keeps them separate from the luminance. The image is not as good as component, but it is better than composite. An S-video cable has wires for Y and C. This format is used in high-end consumer video in the form of Hi-8 and S-VHS. These are the current digital formats and their relationship to component, composite, and S-video:

Component: D1 (19-mm digital), D5 (19-mm digital), Betacam SP ($\frac{1}{2}$-inch analog), MII ($\frac{1}{2}$-inch analog), Betacam ($\frac{1}{2}$-inch analog), Digital Betacam ($\frac{1}{2}$-inch digital), DCT (19-mm digital)

Composite: D2 (19-mm digital), D3 (19-mm digital), 1-inch type C (1-inch analog), $\frac{3}{4}$-inch Umatic ($\frac{3}{4}$-inch analog), $\frac{3}{4}$-inch SP ($\frac{3}{4}$-inch analog), 8-mm (8-mm analog), VHS ($\frac{1}{2}$-inch analog)

Y/C (or pseudo-component): S-VHS ($\frac{1}{2}$-inch analog), Hi-8 (8-mm analog)

Video Monitoring

Filmmakers have learned the value of a video tap on a film camera. It enables playback of footage shot on site, an invaluable tool. It is understood that the playback is just to roughly monitor framing, performance, and other factors and is not a true rendition of the film's contrast or saturation. This understanding must carry over to monitoring in video of video.

The true measurement of a composite video signal is done with two oscilloscopes, a *waveform monitor* and a *vectorscope*. Originally, these were separate devices; however, it is now quite common for the waveform monitor and vectorscope to be combined into single unit that can switch between the two functions. Some units even allow for the two functions to be superimposed. The combined device is simply called a "waveform monitor."

The *waveform monitor* graphically displays and monitors the brightness or *luminance* level of a video signal regardless of its format (e.g., NTSC or PAL). It can be used to display the overall brightness of a television picture, or it can zoom in to show one or two individual lines of the video signal. It can also be used to visualize and observe special signals in the vertical blanking interval of a video signal, as well as the colorburst between each line of video (see Figure 12.46).

Video measurements are made using Institute of Radio Engineers (IRE) units. Zero units represents absolute black, however, in NTSC video, blacks are clipped below 7.5, so the darkest part of a scene will read no lower than 7.5 units (between 0 and 7.5 is sometimes called blacker than black); 7.5 is also called the setup level. On the other end of the scale, 100 IRE units represent *peak white*, which is the maximum voltage the system can effectively handle. Any video that lies between the black and white levels corresponds to the different shades of gray in a monochrome picture. The 7.5 setup allows for a buffer zone between the black zones and the sync that was originally meant to prevent image information from entering into the synchronous pulses.

The waveform monitor is especially helpful in two phases of video production: shooting and online editing. Waveform monitors, together with light meters, are your primary tools for ensuring proper camera exposure and good video quality. If the average value of important information in the picture is more than 100 or less than 7.5 IEEE units, the exposure is off. This exposure can be adjusted by changing the camera's aperture or by adding more or less light to the scene. This is particularly important on multicamera shoots where many cameras are intercut together by a video switcher.

In an online edit session, the waveform monitor works the same way only this time it measures the values of images from videotape or other online devices like character generators or special effects generators. It can monitor and maintain video quality and scene-to-scene consistency. It is also a valuable tool to assist in telecine (film-to-tape transfer), color correction, and other video production activities.

The *vectorscope* displays and measures the color or *chrominance* of the video signal. It is a reliable instrument to judge the accuracy of color, as well as for setting up our equipment to accurately reproduce colors. In a television signal, color is encoded into the main signal with a subcarrier. The vectorscope measures the color information in this subcarrier using a circular display, or graticule (see Figure 12.46), for visualizing chrominance signals. The circle is overlaid with the color amplitude and phase relationship of the three primary colors (red, green, and blue). In the center of this circle graph is the luminance (black and white) value of the signal. Through this center point, three axes represent the primary colors.

The circle looks similar to the color wheel you may remember from art class. Instead of measuring brightness of color, it measures hue, the base color, and saturation (how pure the color is). Saturation can be thought of as the absence of white; the more saturated the color is, the less white it has in it. Since the center of the wheel is neutral, the closer a color is to the wheel's center, the less saturated (or closer to white) it is. The farther out a color is, the more saturated it is.

If you pointed your camera at a white card, the vectorscope would display a dot in the center. If this dot is off center, the white card would not be recorded as pure white, but with a tint of color. To record the white as white, the camera operator must use the camera's white balance control. The camera can also be adjusted internally with the red and blue gain control. On the vectorscope, this would be adjusted until the signal on the scope were dead center and not favoring red, blue, or green.

In the online edit session, the vectorscope determines the proper colors through the use of color bars. The standard procedure is for the camera operator to record 60 seconds of color bars at the beginning of every tape. This ensures that when edited, the colors will be the same from tape to tape and from any effect.

Since professional nonlinear editing systems (to be covered later) have both vectorscopes and waveform monitor screens that can be displayed, you can keep a constant eye on quality and make scene-to-scene adjustments as necessary. This is the only way that you will be able to consistently and unobtrusively cut a variety of scenes together during the editing phase.

Digital Impact

Originally, waveform monitors were entirely analog devices; the incoming (analog) video signal was filtered and amplified, and the resulting voltage was used to drive the vertical axis of a cathode ray tube. With the advent of digital television and digital signal processing, the waveform monitor acquired many new features and capabilities. Modern waveform monitors contain many additional modes of operation, including *picture mode* (where the video picture is simply presented on the screen, much like a television), various modes optimized for color gamut checking,

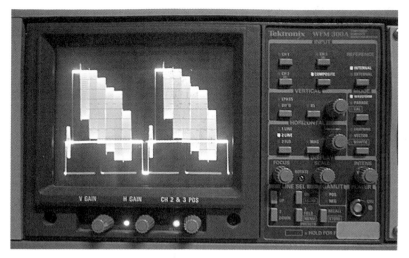

Figure 12.44 Image of a waveform monitor showing color bars (http://en.wikipedia.org/wiki/Image:Vectorscope_monitor.jpg).

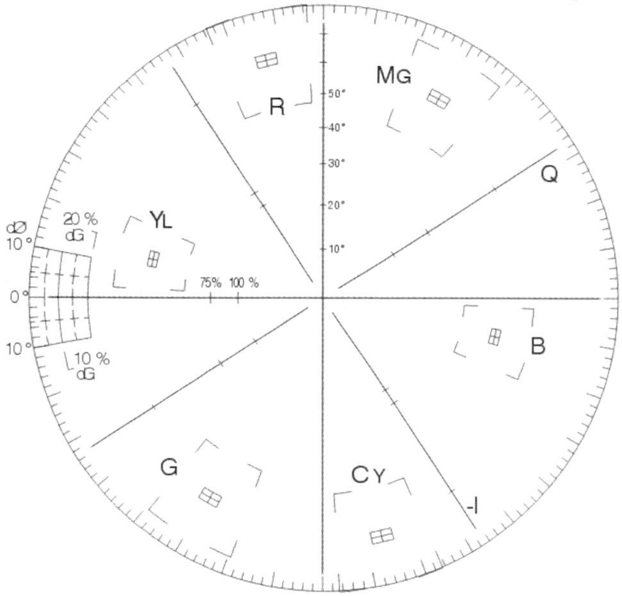

Figure 12.45 The graticule of an NTSC vectorscope (http://en.wikimedia.org.wiki/Image:Vectorscope_graticule.png).

support for the audio portion of a television program (either embedded with the video or on separate inputs), eye pattern and jitter displays for measuring the physical layer parameters of serial-digital television formats, modes for examining the serial digital protocol layer, support for ancillary data and television-related metadata such as timecode, closed captions, and the v-chip rating systems.

Modern waveform monitors have largely abandoned old-style CRT technology as well. All new waveform monitors are based on one of two display technologies: they either feature a flat-panel liquid crystal display (LCD) or else are sold without a display—the user is expected to connect a VGA monitor to the output. The latter type of device is commonly known as a *rasterizer*

LCD is short for *liquid crystal display*, a type of display used in digital watches and many portable computers. LCD displays utilize two sheets of polarizing material with a liquid crystal solution between them. An electric current passed through the liquid causes the crystals to align so that light cannot pass through them. Each crystal, therefore, is like a shutter, either allowing light to pass through or blocking the light. Although very expensive (check out the Sony LMD-9050 Portable HDTV LCD), as with all new technology the prices become competitive as the market for a product grows.

Setting up a Monitor

All of these quality measures have to be displayed accurately on a TV monitor in order to be verified, so it's important to be able to trust your video monitor. For the shooter, you might wonder why you couldn't just look at a standard video monitor to see if your picture looked all right. The problem is that the picture monitor is not a reliable guide to the picture you are recording or to how that picture will look in the finished videotape. A trip to a store that sells TVs will show how many different renditions of playback are possible for one signal

These are the eight steps involved in setting up a video monitor to display accurate color and contrast. To do this you need to have a SMPTE color bar feed, and a monitor with switches for the red, blue, and green signals, plus controls for chroma, hue, color/monochrome, brightness, and contrast. Professional color monitors should have all these controls.

- First, switch off the red and green colors. You should now see four vertical blue bars separated by three darker bars. At the bottom of each blue bar will be a small rectangular area.
- By adjusting the hue and chroma controls, you should be able to make each of the four vertical blue bars match the small area below it. (The hue control affects mainly the middle two bars, and the chroma affects mainly the two outside bars.) Keep working with these two controls until you get the best match possible.
- Switch the red, blue, and green colors back on.
- Note that below the red (sixth) bar on the screen there are three narrow vertical gray bars. If you don't see them, adjust the brightness control until you can clearly see these bars.
- Switch the color/monochrome switch to monochrome.
- Reduce the brightness control until center gray bar just disappears from the screen.
- Adjust the contrast control until the white reference square at the lower left of the screen is bright enough to appear white, but not so much that it causes adjacent areas to "glow." Since the brightness and contrast controls interact, you will probably have to play with both of these until you get the desired effect.
- Switch the color/monochrome back to color. The monitor is now set up and can be used to judge the chroma and luminance of displayed video.

Likewise is true with cutoff of frame. The eyepiece of a film camera will show framing in a much more exact way than a video viewfinder. The safest way to test cutoff is to frame something on the edge of the frame of the viewfinder and see if it is in the same place on the screen of another monitor. If another monitor is not available, one must allow for signal "cutoff." Because of the variances in screen edges of televisions, individual sets send more signal than necessary and then trim it. It is therefore unwise to assume that something on the edge of frame in a viewfinder will "make it home." It is always safer to allow a bit of room around the edges.

VIDEO FORMATS

Unlike comparatively faithful film formats, video formats are continually being invented, changed, and dropped as new and better ones arrive on the scene (there will undoubtedly be a new one by the time this book comes out). It is similar to buying a computer that could be outdated a few months after you bring

it home. The positive side of this change is that the systems are getting smaller, cheaper, and more powerful. The downside is that equipment becomes obsolete.

With film formats, there is a rough correlation between the size of the format and the quality it is capable of. You cannot make that assumption with videotape formats. A VTR running $\frac{1}{2}$-inch-wide tape may be much better quality than one running 1-inch tape.

Manufacturers generally identify the intended market for various pieces of equipment. The categories are not exact, but in descending order of quality there is broadcast, industrial, prosumer, and home/consumer.

Broadcasters have been traditionally exacting about the signal and image quality they will allow on the air, but small video cameras, especially, have clearly made substantial inroads.

Analog Formats

VHS

The video home system (VHS) is a composite, analog format using $\frac{1}{2}$-inch wide tape. For many, the idea of home video is synonymous with VHS. It is inexpensive and convenient, and there are millions of VHS machines in the world. In terms of image quality, it is (other than Fisher-Price Pixelvision) the worst format at 210 lines of resolution. The VHS quality also degrades significantly with recording at slower speeds.

The VHS hi-fi format is an upgraded version of the home consumer model, except the VTR circuitry is more advanced, so the picture quality and audio are reproduced with greater precision.

Super VHS

Super VHS (S-VHS) was first introduced by JVC in 1987 in an effort to match the performance levels of $\frac{3}{4}$-inch U-VCR systems. S-VHS is an S-video system, which is higher in quality than composite but not up to component. The resolution of S-VHS is 400 lines as opposed to 250 for standard VHS. S-VHS uses special $\frac{1}{2}$-inch videotape, made of specially formulated high-density ferric oxide, enclosed in a videocassette.

8-mm and Hi-8

The 8-mm video format is an improvement over standard VHS. The tape cassettes and camcorders tend to be smaller and the image quality is better. Hi-8 (highband 8-mm) is an improved version of 8-mm, and Hi-

8 camcorders and tape are more expensive. Like S-VHS, Hi-8 can output S-video and its resolution is about 400 lines. To get the most out of S-video, you need a monitor equipped with S-video inputs. Hi-8 is popular for home video use and became an effective news-gathering format where large cameras would be awkward, though digital video (DV) is now filling that role. Some Hi-8 systems have non-SMPTE timecode, and there are Hi-8 editing systems, but most often, 8-mm, Hi-8, and S-VHS are bumped up to larger formats for editing.

1 Inch, 2 Inch, and ³/₄ Inch

Introduced in the 1950s, the Quaddruplex VTR or quad is the original format of reel-to-reel VTRs using 2-inch wide magnetic video recording tape for broadcast. This system was replaced by improved 1-inch machines that became the standard throughout the 1980s and into the 1990s. As an analog, composite format, 1-inch was replaced by better-quality component and digital systems. Sony introduced the first U-Matic cassette recorder in 1971. Though inferior to 1-inch, ³/₄-inch systems were widely used for field recording, industrial, and broadcast applications. The ³/₄-inch decks are easy to use and the tape is rugged. At one time, ³/₄-inch was the chief offline editing format, though the image deteriorates with dubbing.

Betacam

Introduced in 1981, Sony's Betacam format was a response to the growing demand for smaller and lighter high-quality field equipment. Betacam was unique in that it created broadcast-quality images on a ¹/₂-inch videocassette using either a portable VCR or a camcorder unit that contained the camera and recorder in one lightweight package. Its high-quality recording is possible because it processes and records video in the component video format and provides outputs in both composite and component video. (Betacam, which is referred to as Beta, should not be confused with the little used consumer Betamax format, which also runs ¹/₂-inch tape, but at a slower speed and with lower image quality.)

Sony later introduced Betacam SP (Superior Performance) production VTRs, which are compatible with the current Betacam format and offer four channels of high-quality audio. In addition to the two longitudinal amplitude modulated (AM) audio channels, Sony added two frequency modulated (FM) audio channels, which are simultaneously recorded with the video information.

By the 1990s, analog Betacam camcorders had become the standard tool for a wide variety of broadcast and industrial production. Beta editing suites ushered in an era of affordable component editing.

Digital Videotape Formats

Digital videotape, once the domain of the high-end, high-budget production, has now become the mainstream with more than 15 formats or versions of formats currently available. There is no simple decision on which format is best. Price considerations must be taken into account. But price goes to more than the cost of purchasing or renting a given deck. Tape must be factored in as well as maintenance of any new equipment. Some formats may shine in postproduction but may be too big (in equipment weight or tape size) to make it reasonable for fieldwork.

D-1, introduced by Sony in 1986, was the first industry-accepted format by SMPTE. It has become the universal component digital standard with approximately 460 lines of resolution. The signal is recorded on a 19-mm oxide tape, offering the highest quality and the most flexible recording system. It is capable of recording compressed HDTV signals but does not compress standard signals. Although still considered a quality reference, D-1 is expensive to buy and use and has been mostly superseded by the more cost-effective later formats. It is still used for creating complex, layered graphics or as a mastering format for film-to-tape transfers and online video editing.

D-2, developed by Ampex around 1984, was the second SMPTE standardized digital system, but it is a composite system and thus doesn't provide the pristine video signal of component. The D-2 is accepted in many postproduction facilities because of its lower per-unit cost and because its composite video format is fully compatible with the existing composite analog equipment that the facilities already own. The video-cassette casings used by the D-2 format are identical to the D-1 cassettes; however, the videotape itself is a metal particle tape chosen for its high packing density, which results in a higher signal-to-noise ratio. Neither D-1 nor D-2 is practical for use in a camcorder because of the physical size of the tape transport system.

D-3 and D-5, both developed by Panasonic, are compatible systems, despite D-3 being designed as a composite system and D-5 as a component system. Neither system compresses the video signal, and both use 12.5-mm (¹/₂-inch) metal tape. While D-5 is still a studio format, D-3 camcorders are available from Panasonic. D-3 is used mainly in industrial and corporate communications, while D-5 is designed to record HDTV signals

D-4 doesn't exist, as number 4 is a major taboo in Asian cultures (pronounced the same as "death" in Japanese).

DCT (Digital Component Technology) is an Ampex format recording a compressed component signal on 19-mm metal tape. DCT technology is targeted almost exclusively for postproduction and film transfer applications.

Digital S format was developed by JVC. It uses a VHS tape and is intended for field production. This offers the benefits of digital recording in a relatively low-cost package. However, Digital S tapes are incompatible with analog VHS.

HD D5, a high-definition version of D-5, has been introduced by Panasonic. It uses standard D5 videotape cassettes to record HD material, using an intraframe compression with a 4:1 ratio. HD D5 supports the 1,080 and the 1,035 interlaced line standards at both 60 Hz and 59.94 Hz field rates, all 720 progressive line standards and the 1,080 progressive line standard at 24, 25, and 30 frame rates. Four uncompressed audio channels sampled at 40 kHz, 20 bits per sample, are also supported.

DV, DVCAM, and DVCPRO

DV (digital video) records an excellent digital component image on a very small tape cassette. Aimed at the prosumer market, the mini-DV camera brings digital recording to an affordable level. Within a few years of their introduction in the 1990s, mini-DV revolutionized independent and multimedia production the way Betacam once changed the broadcast world. For a few thousand dollars (probably lower by the time this book comes out), a videomaker can record video that rivals or surpasses that of an analog camcorder costing much more. DV has a resolution of 500 lines.

For industrial, broadcast, and dramatic use, Sony introduced the *DVCAM* and Panasonic makes the *DVCPRO*. Both are fully professional systems that record the same signal as mini-DV, but the tape formats are different. (DVCPRO machines can play mini-DV and DVCAM tapes with a cassette adapter. DVCAM machines cannot play DVCPRO cassettes.) The professional systems are more costly but offer more features and better quality camcorders than the mini-DV.

The *Digital Betacam* format (also called D-Beta or Digi-Beta) provides a very high quality component digital signal and is used for both production and postproduction. The cost and size of the D-Beta camcorder make it a tool for professionals only. The camera is easy to hand hold and is the same size as the analog version. D-Beta sets a very high standard for quality and versatility.

One of the innovations of DV is the use of FireWire (IEEE 1394, also called iLINK) technology (discussed in Chapter 16). A FireWire cable allows a direct digital two-way connection between DV devices, for example, between a camera and an editing system or VTR. Digital information can be recorded directly onto a hard drive, a Zip disk, or DVD (most commonly used now).

HDTV

HDTV (high-definition television, also called HD and hi-def) represents a substantial leap in resolution over traditional, analog systems and results in an image that rivals 35-mm film in clarity. It is a completely revised visual communication format for the production, postproduction, and transmission of television signals. HD provides the viewer with widescreen aspect ratio, vastly better image resolution, interference-free pictures, and CD-quality stereo sound.

Sometimes the term *digital television* (DTV) or *advanced television* (ATV) is used to refer to the new digital broadcast formats. Of these, there are several high-definition formats (HDTV) and standard-definition formats (SDTV). One HD system uses 1,080 scan lines (more than twice NTSC's 525-line raster) with an aspect ratio of 16:9 or 1.78:1. The result is an extremely sharp, widescreen digital picture that is only slightly less wide than the U.S. standard 1:85 widescreen theatrical films. Hard disk recorders now reach 4:4:4.

Brief History of HD

The coming of high-def has been a long journey. The earliest work in high definition began in Japan in 1964 when NHK, the Japanese broadcasting company, began producing prototypes. By 1984, it had developed an analog HD production chain that was developed enough to begin serious program production. By 1991, NHK was transmitting via satellite the 1,035-line high-definition "Hi-Vision" format to viewers in Japan. At about the same time in the United States, KCTS TV, a local public television station in Seattle, was experimenting with the format. Cameras and recorders were large and heavy and required lots of cable and power to operate. In spite of these limitations, that station managed to produce some impressive programs. The experiences of these early HD

Figure 12.46 Panasonic DVCPRO, courtesy of Panasonic Broadcast & Television Systems, Division of Matsushita Electric Corporation of America.

Figure 12.47 Panasonic Mini DV, courtesy of Panasonic Broadcast & Television Systems, Division of Matsushita Electric Corporation of America.

pioneers ultimately helped the technology mature and laid the groundwork for the digital revolution to follow.

As high-def was developing, the companion digital technology necessary for it to grow was in its infancy. The ability to transmit and store the large amounts of information that a digital HD format would require was cost prohibitive, if not technically impossible at the time. Also, early HD pioneers were restricted by the large size and complexity of the equipment used to acquire high-definition footage.

The breakthrough came in 1997 when Sony introduced the HDCAM videotape format and the first truly portable HD camcorder. It was compact, portable, and all digital. The clarity was incredible, and its price was dramatically less than all previous HDTV equipment. With the advent of the HDW-700 camcorder and a complete line of high-definition production equipment gear available, it was clear that HD had finally arrived.

The new format was introduced as a turnkey system, from camcorder to postproduction. Rental companies bought cameras and made them available. Panavision, Fujinon, and Canon created new zoom and prime lenses for the cameras. The first wave of business came from broadcasters; the "1080i" format was the best video anyone had seen. Television stations from around the country experimented with production and broadcasting in HD. NBC switched *The Tonight Show* to 1080i, and CBS switched their soap *The Young and the Restless* to HD as well. Unfortunately, sales didn't follow. The prices were too high, and the lack of programming prevented buyers from having any incentive to be pioneers. Unfortunately, most viewers never saw the few HD productions because without HD sets, they were only able to receive the standard definition analog broadcast.

It was clear that high-def production couldn't sustain itself without an outlet. Broadcasters needed HD viewers to offset the cost of producing programs in HD. Also, broadcasters didn't agree on a single HD resolution to transmit. Some went with the 1080i system where the image is 1,920 (H) × 1,080 (V) and is transmitted interlaced at about 30 frames (60 fields) per second. Others decided to go with a different HD format, "720P," which transmits a 1,280 (H) × 720 (V) image at 60 progressive frames per second. The evolution of HD almost came to a standstill until something happened that changed things forever.

George Lucas and 24p

George Lucas wanted to work with HD but had one problem—it looked too much like video. He along with others suggested to Sony that the company should explore an HD signal that was similar to film. Sony responded and developed a complete line of 24 frame capable HD gear. They dubbed their new line "CineAlta" which has become a world standard for 24p HD. Panavision worked with Sony to provide the HDWF-900 HD camera with lenses for Lucas and *Star Wars Episode II*. Lucas went off to Australia to shoot and was incredibly happy with the results.

The camera's format is 1080i (vertical) by 1,920 (horizontal) and is capable of shooting 24p, 25p, 30p, 29.97p, 23.98p, or interlace formats (60i, 59.94i). HDCAM, the tape format the camera records, is

Figure 12.48 Television aspect ratio 4:3 (http://en.wikipedia.org/wiki/Image: 4_3_example.jpg).

Figure 12.49 HD aspect ratio 16:9 (http://en.wikipedia.org/wiki/Image:16_9_example.jpg).

extremely versatile. The camera can deliver a signal that is ready for film transfer or down conversion to standard-definition (SDTV) in NTSC or PAL for broadcast. In addition, the camera is native 16:9, an aspect ration that networks are increasingly demanding new content to be composed in for content.

What Is 24p?

Lucas wanted a video camera to capture the cinematic feel of film. Film yields a slight blur in moving objects. This is known as *motion blur*, and it results in a distinct fluidity of movement—a prime contributor to the "film look." Motion blur is caused by film's relatively low frame rate of 24 frames per second. A telltale sign of video is its extreme sharpness and lack of motion blur.

NTSC video runs at 30 fps, so how can such a small difference account for the radical increase in sharpness? The reason is that there are two interlaced fields for every frame of video, so the effective rate is actually 60 images per second (30 fps × 2 fields). This virtually eliminates motion blur, creating an image that is a bit too sharp and devoid of fluidity.

The answer to this is a technical breakthrough called *progressive scanning*, where each frame is scanned once. In other words, the frame is scanned as a single field, with no interlacing. This process mimics a film camera's frame-by-frame image capture. The lower image rate reproduces motion blur comparable to film. These cameras generally use frame rates of 24 fps to 30 fps. The 24 frames progressive format, called *24p* (for progressive), simplifies combining video and film footage because there is a one-to-one frame relationship. The PAL version, *25p*, matches the European film speed of 25 fps. Many state-of-the-art cameras have switchable frame rates and resolutions.

Another benefit of progressive scanning is a dramatic increase in resolution. This occurs because progressive scanning eliminates interlace artifacts (combed edges in movement) and interline flicker (noise in fine patterns). It has been shown that that perceived resolution in progressive scanning is 50 percent greater than interlace scanning.

Panasonic Enters the Arena

Eventually, Panasonic entered the field with its own HD camera, the AJ-HDC27F, commonly known as the Varicam. This DVC-PRO HD format camera distinguished itself as being able to shoot variable frame rates (4 to 60 fps). The ability to undercrank or overcrank to create slow and fast motion was the next substantial step toward creating a video camera with the capability of a film camera. Before the Varicam, to achieve fast or slow motion effects on videotape the tape speed had to be altered in postproduction.

In addition to variable frame rates, the filmlike quality of the camera extends to its circuitry. The camera has two gamma files that closely mimic the tonal range (also known as the film's characteristic curve) of film as well as a gamma setting for video recording. The film settings extend the camera's ability to reproduce a wide array of colors in addition to gradations of light where other video cameras may not be capable.

HD and Postproduction

HD has been supported by nonlinear editing systems like Avid and Apple's Final Cut Pro, among others. In addition, there is a growing movement toward a workflow known as digital intermediate (DI). In a DI workflow, the picture is acquired on film and then scanned at high resolution HD (HDCAM or HD-D5) or data files at 2K or 4K or higher. Then the images are color corrected and manipulated before sending them back to film for projection. A reel of film at 24 fps can be shown anywhere in the world because the playback equipment is everywhere (more about this process in the post chapter).

24p Comes to DV

For a number of years, 24p was the sole domain of high-definition video. The next step was applying the 24p technology for standard definition TV and mini-DV. Panasonic was in the vanguard in this evolutionary leap with the AG-DVX100 (see Figure 12.50), a three 1/3-inch CCD mini-DV that can scan progressively or interlaced (24P, 24PA, 30P, 60i). It featured one of the widest lenses (10 × 4.5) and had 2 XLR inputs for sound recording with professional style microphones. The progressive formats are performed in-camera and 460 interlaced lines (traditional NTSC) is what is recorded on tape so there is no extra equipment needed to post. Canon followed soon after with its line of XL1s. Even those filmmakers who are not interested in transferring their video projects back to film may be transferring their shows to DVD, which is by nature a default 24p playback device.

HD + DV = The Future?

The next logical step was to create an affordable HD camera. That's where *HDV* comes in. It is a way of getting HD on DV tape. The term *HDV* is a combination of "HD" and the very popular "DV" format. It's done by using MPEG2 compression (see Glossary), which is the same compression used for DVDs. MPEG2 is a much more complex code (see Glossary) than DV, and this adds to the computer requirements. It allows a great amount of information to be compressed for recording and then decompressed for viewing. This is different than DV, which remains in its compressed state.

HDV is native 16:9 at a resolution of 1,280 pixels wide by 720 pixels tall. Supported frame rates are 60i (frames-per-second interlaced), 30p (progressive), 50i, and 25p. HDV is also an "open format," like DV, which means you do not have to stay with one brand

Figure 12.50 Panasonic AG-DVX100.

to use the format. The HDV standard was established in 2003 by four companies: Canon Inc., Sharp Corporation, Sony Corporation, and the Victor Company of Japan, Limited. Many companies, including most of the nonlinear software manufacturers, have expressed their support for the HDV standard. For the latest list of companies that support this format, visit www.hdv-info.org.

Why do so many companies support HDV? This is because it is a based on the global DV standard, and the same DV mechanisms can be used for HDV. Moreover, since it employs the broadcast standard for image compression, MPEG-2, it is possible to connect HDV devices with TVs and personal computers. HDV can also be downconverted to standard definition so that the hundreds of thousands of SD TV sets and DVD players can view it today. Downconverting the HDV footage can give you the best of all possible worlds.

As we see widespread adoption of HD broadcasting and HDTVs, many expect that the HDV standard will become the norm for a lot of video production. However, DV and its related formats are currently the mainstream as far as price and the popularity of cameras, decks, and editing systems are concerned. Nevertheless, there will soon be more models of HDV camcorders on the market, and when the prices come down, HDV will likely replace DV as the main standard.

The Cameras

JVC came out with the first HDV camera with the 2003 release of the single-chip GR-HD1 mini-DV and HD camcorder. In DV mode, the camera shoots at a standard 720 × 480 DV image at 30 fps of 60 inter-laced fields per second (60i) in a 4:3 aspect ratio. In SD mode, it shoots at the same vertical resolution (480 lines), but it shoots 60 progressive fps (60p) at a true 16:9 widescreen aspect ratio. Finally, the HD mode shoots 30p, 16:9 widescreen at 1,280 × 720. Unlike previous HD cameras, which were bulky, the camera was very small, about the same size as Sony's PD150.

JVC subsequently released a second-generation camera, the JY-HD10U, that added a color bar generator, XLR inputs, a higher resolution view screen, and the ability to see audio levels on the screen. Since the first camera, Sony and Canon have entered the market, and JVC continues to upgrade its line.

As of the writing of this edition, Sony is coming out with the HVR-Z1U, a 3-CCD professional camcorder that delivers high-quality 1080i but does not have the 24p capability. It does, however, provide a "cinelook" effect that simulates the 24p film look. JVC is introducing the GY-HD100U, a professional high-definition (ProHD) progressive camcorder with true 24p capture that records to DV tape and provides a removable bayonet mount lens and the BR-HD5OU ProHD recorder player.

ProHD is an HDV-compatible video system with professional specifications, including four-channel audio, timecode, true 24p HD, and dual media direct recording to HD cassettes and hard disks. JVC utilizes widely available nonproprietary technologies, such as MPEG-2 compression, DV recording media, and conventional hard disk drives to achieve an affordable HD solution. Finally, Panasonic is on the verge of introducing the AG-HVX2000 DVC PRO HD P2, which records in both 1080i and 720p formats and primarily to a memory card instead of videotape.

By the time the third edition is on the market, the future of HDV will be defined by how these cameras (and others) perform. Equally important will be how the format will be supported in postproduction. This issue will be covered in some depth in the postproduction chapter.

Tape Stock

Videotape, like audiotape, is composed of a Mylar backing and a thin magnetic layer that actually records the video signal. This magnetic layer was once made up of primarily ferric (iron) oxide. Now manufacturers make a variety of formulas for the magnetic layer, ranging from various oxides to higher quality metal tapes that have no oxide. A higher quality tape will have fewer defects and may allow you to record with less noise, clearer color, and better detail. But picking a tape stock is not like picking a film stock. Film stocks may vary in terms of basic color palette, contrast, and sensitivity to light. In video, the camera itself determines most of these things. The same video stock serves equally well for recording color or black and white, in daylight or indoors.

As video formats become smaller and attempt to record more information on narrower and shorter tapes, the quality of the tape stock becomes more important. Though tape stock is in theory reusable, each pass through the VTR adds to the likelihood of dropouts and other defects. Professionals usually use only fresh, virgin tapes for critical camera recording, as well as the best tape stock they can afford. Digital tape formats may have more leeway for reusing tapes. For editing purposes, used stock is fine for work tapes.

Finally, improperly stored videotape can deteriorate in various ways, including becoming brittle, stretching, or losing its magnetic charge. Keep tapes away from any magnetic fields. Store in places that are comfortable for humans (neither very dry nor very damp). No one knows how long newer tape formats will hold up over time. Since all tape formats eventually become obsolete, it's a good idea to transfer important masters to a new format every several years.

OTHER EQUIPMENT

Grip Package

The grip package brought to the set includes all the elements needed to move the camera, including tripods, heads, a dolly, and track. Heavy rigging equipment, such as rope and clamps, rides with the grips. The grips are also responsible for the apple boxes, which are used to raise the height of set pieces, actors, or camera operators.

Head

To keep its movement fluid, the camera is placed on a head, which allows for smooth pans and tilts. The head can be placed on a dolly or crane so that the pans and tilts can be accompanied by the physical movement of the camera.

Tripod

For static shots, tilts, and pans, the head is placed on a tripod, or sticks. For low-angle shots or if the sticks are too tall, the head is placed on a plywood base, on a high-hat, or even directly onto sandbags.

Dolly

A dolly is a moving tripod system, usually with attached chairs for the camera operator and the director. If the surface on which you wish to dolly is smooth, you might not need to lay track. Track must be laid on rough surfaces, however. The dolly is placed on the rails, and it glides smoothly along the track.

To extend the camera off the dolly, an additional piece of equipment, called a jib arm, is placed perpendicular to the post. The head is put on the end of the jib arm.

Crane

A crane is a dolly that has a movable extension arm. The camera is placed on this arm, which moves parallel to the ground and can lift the camera to great heights. Cranes are cumbersome, expensive, and unwieldy, but crane shots add a great deal of energy to a scene, especially one in which the director wants to move from a close shot to a very wide perspective, or vice versa.

Car, Helicopter, Boat

The ultimate in dynamic camera work is to shoot with your camera moving on a fast vehicle. Slow-moving cars are sometimes used as an alternative to a dolly. If you plan a shot from a car, it useful to let some air out of the tires. This adds smoothness to the shot. Shooting into a car or from a car, helicopter, or boat requires special mounts. You can also rent a camera car, which is a truck equipped with camera mounts in several places for specific kinds of shots.

Steadicam

The Steadicam is used today to provide a steady, interesting movement shot in films and videos. In this system, a gyro-balanced camera is placed on a rig that enables the operator to go where a dolly cannot go and obtain a smooth tracking shot. For example, a Steadicam operator can go up a stairway, through a crowd, or from a walking position to a seated position on a crane.

Lighting Package

The lighting package consists of all the instruments and globes the DP requires, plus lengths of cable for moving the lighting instruments some distance from the power source.

TRICKS

Over the course of your career in the film and video business, you will be forced to devise unique solutions to problems, and these solutions will become part of your personal bag of tricks. Some common camera tricks you might someday need to employ are described in the following sections.

Poor Man's Process

To shoot a scene with characters in a vehicle at night can be expensive and time consuming. At night, the rear window looks black. Shoot the vehicle in a stationary position, either inside or outside, and add these three elements:

- Have two crew members sit on the rear bumper and gently bounce the vehicle to simulate movement.
- Strafe the back window with a light at intermittent intervals. This simulates passing cars.
- In postproduction, add the sound of an engine.

Simple Mattes

Using a hard line in the frame, such as the horizon, black out the sky at the top of the frame and photograph the action in the bottom of the frame. Rewind the camera, black out the lower part of the frame, and reexpose the film with an image that will now be the "sky" part of the frame. This eliminates a costly painting and lab fee.

Night for Day

You will often run out of sunlight as you try to meet the day's schedule. For tight shots, HMI lights (see Glossary) simulate the color temperature of the sun. Therefore, even when the sun has set, you can still shoot as if it were day, and the material should match. Use this technique in emergencies only. Do not attempt to shoot all day and then all night just because you can get the exposure.

INTEGRATING ANIMATION

The addition of live action actors creates a unique set of issues to be addressed when shooting animation. The easiest solution would be to carefully plan the shot so that the actor or puppet and the digital elements or set pieces are not on the same part of the screen. The composite can be achieved with relatively simple masking away from the primary focus. With live actors and digital elements in the same location shot, a good visfx supervisor will usually request the same shot without any actors so his CG artists and compositors have a clean plate as the basis for the final composite. The clean shot will also be a great help to the CG lighters later in the process.

Professional studios will often use a process known as high-dynamic range imaging (HDR) that more accurately calculates how the environment affects the lighting on the digital object.

In the case of puppet animation, all elements can be filmed together at the same time frame by frame.

> *You have your sound track broken down to frames. You decide exactly how long each shot would be. I think when I came to shoot* Crazy Glue, *it was nearly edited in camera. I would just pick up the 16-mm Bolex, put it down, animate the shot, move it to the next cut, and shoot from there.*
>
> Tatia

Producer
Support

The producer's goal is to keep the operation running smoothly with minimum personal involvement. The director runs the show during production, and the producer should not interfere unless he is needed. He should feel confident in his choice of director and allow her to complete her task.

RESPONSIBILITIES OF THE PRODUCER

Laboratory

The producer should establish a contact person at the laboratory who will serve as a liaison through production and postproduction. During the shoot, the liaison at the lab should report daily to the DP about the quality of the footage.

Equipment

The producer must make sure that the equipment package is kept up-to-date. Any equipment that is not being used should be returned.

Rental House

It is the producer's job to negotiate with the film or video equipment rental house. This can be an intimidating experience, but it is possible, even for the beginner, to work out a reasonable deal and to turn the process into a learning experience.

Treat rental houses as more than just a place to pick up equipment. Go there with all your equipment questions before you decide what you want. This is the first step in being a more informed consumer.

Negotiate with an equipment house for the best values just as you would deal with a car or stereo salesperson. The rental house has expensive equipment on the shelves, and the company would rather rent it for a fraction of the full cost than let it sit there. This means you can shop around to different equipment rental houses looking for the best value and use one bidder against another to get the best price.

The producer and the DP need to determine what lights, camera, and grip equipment actually are required. Visit the equipment house and ask to be shown around. Establishing an in-person relationship will make it easier for you to negotiate. A tour will also give you the opportunity to see if the rental house is an impressive establishment or a two-bit operation.

The most expensive way to rent a piece of equipment is by the day. If you need the equipment for a week, you can get up to half off the aggregate daily price. Ask what kind of discount you can get for a set period of time. This is easier, of course, if you have done business with the company in the past and have established your credibility.

The following are other well-known ways to get discounts:

- Weekends count as one day. If you pick your equipment up on a Friday and bring it back on Monday morning, you pay for only one day.
- Travel days and holidays often are not charged.
- Use cash as an incentive. After you have negotiated a deal, offer to pay cash up front. This might get you an additional 10 to 15 percent off the one-day price.

Equipment houses make money charging for accessories that you thought were included in the package. Get a complete list of what you need, and make sure the price you are quoted covers everything.

The rental house will need to see proof of insurance. The company won't let its equipment out without it. If you are not covered by a policy through your film or video program or are an independent that cannot afford private insurance, you will have to pay the rental house's rate. Most houses offer some kind of in-house coverage, which might cost up to 10 percent of the rental fee for the equipment.

> **STUDENTS AND INDEPENDENTS**
>
> Being a student or an independent on a low-budget project is not necessarily a liability. Tell those who are dealing with you that you must try to get the best price you can because you simply don't have the cash. This predicament might get you sympathy and a better deal.

TECHNICAL CONSIDERATIONS

Power

If a shoot needs more power or a different power source than that provided at the location, it is necessary to supply a generator to power the lights. Generators can be noisy, so be prepared to run extra cable to move the generator as far away from the set as possible.

Be prepared to change fuses on location if you are using the power from wall sockets. If you know how much power each instrument draws and you know how much amperage is available from each socket, you can plug in all your instruments without blowing a fuse. Ideally, the director of photography or the gaffer should gather this information during a pre-production location scout.

Lights

Lighting instruments are placed on heavy-duty legs called light stands. These supports can be lowered or raised to position the instrument at a specific height.

Sandbags are placed on the base of the stands for security. Flags, cookies, or tree branches are often placed directly in front of a lamp to create effects or to prevent the light from falling directly onto the camera lens, creating a flare.

The stronger the light that illuminates the scene, the greater the detail that will be exposed onto the film. Less light, less detail. Areas of the scene that are lit will be exposed; unlit areas will "fall away."

When you're in the field, you've got to trust the cinematographer because you don't want to interrupt the interview. I see the scene in a wide shot because of where I sit as a sound person. If you film in someone's living room and position your subject on a couch, I'm not sure they feel very comfortable because all of a sudden, their living room has been transformed into a film set. There are lights and cables running everywhere. I prefer the naturalness of exterior interviews for that reason and have used them quite extensively in all of my films prior to Mirror Mirror.

Jan

Camera Noise

Although 16-mm sync cameras are designed to run quietly, often a camera leaks noise during a take. This is most noticeable when shooting interiors in a confined space. *Blimping*, or creating a soundproof housing for the camera, might reduce the noise that emanates from the lens mount, magazine, or body of the camera (this is the assistant camera operator's job). This muffling can be accomplished with a *blimp* or *barney*, which is a jacket that is specially designed for the camera. You can create your own blimp with anything that will deaden the camera noise, such as a changing bag, foam rubber, or a coat or jacket.

Fans

In a tight location, it quickly becomes warm under the lights. Be prepared to ventilate the room, and turn the lights on only when necessary.

It was very hot. The conditions were definitely not very pleasant because there were these lights, and the actors were wearing masks.

Jan

KEY POINTS

- Use camera language to shape the frame. This includes lights, camera positions, and lenses.
- What you shoot determines what can be edited, so shoot ample coverage.
- Plan your transitions from shot to shot and from scene to scene. Shoot overlaps.
- Blocking means that you can move the camera, the actors, or both.

chapter thirteen

Sound

There was a problem we weren't prepared for: the hum of the fluorescent lights.

Howard

DIRECTOR

Recording Clean Tracks

During the past 25 years, the processing and transmission of sound to film audiences have undergone a radical evolution. Today, projection sound systems such as THX, Dolby dts/sdds, and Surround Sound have heightened the aural dynamic of the film experience. Digital sound reproduction is drastically changing the way audiences hear sound tracks in theaters. However, with everything that can now be done in postproduction to process and deliver a complex and exciting sound track, the most important step in this chain is still the first one: the recording of good, clean sounds, especially dialogue, during principal photography.

Film- and videomakers have a wide range of options for recording audio. The Nagra analog tape recorder with $\frac{1}{4}$-inch tape was the industry standard for film shoots until the mid-1990s. These single-track recorders are still used, but only as backups to the newer generation of digital formats. Stereo DAT (digital audiotape), DVD Ram, and 8-track hard disk recorders have replaced them in the professional market.

When shooting video, sound is recorded right on the videotape in the camcorder. Different video formats have different audio capabilities. Some record digital audio, some analog, and some combine both technologies. Most professional video productions record sound double system sending the production mix to the camera for a guide track at picture editing.

Although the tools have changed, the process of recording sound has remained basically the same. These new recording devices can't perform magic. If the microphone is not placed properly in a dialogue scene, no recorder (analog or digital) will deliver a clear rendition of the actor's voice.

PRODUCTION SOUND

The sound recorded on the set, called *production sound*, is an extremely important aspect of your short film or video, and it should be examined, recorded, and mixed with the same care and enthusiasm given to the visuals. Production sound consists of dialogue, the natural sounds associated with each scene, and any other sounds that might be of value during the postproduction process. The person responsible for recording production sound is the *production sound mixer* because he controls, or *mixes*, the levels of the dialogue spoken on the set. Equally important is the *boom operator*, who positions the microphone for quality and purity of the sound.

Although all sounds, including dialogue, can be recreated during the postproduction process, it is economically and aesthetically best to record as much of the dialogue and natural ambience as possible at the location during principal photography.

Figure 13.1 It is important to pick up any wild sounds on location. Photo from the filming of *Truman.*

Dialogue can be replaced during postproduction with a process called *automatic dialogue replacement* (ADR), but ADR can be time consuming, costly, and problematic, especially for the beginner. It requires that the actors report to a studio months after the shoot to duplicate their original performances line by line. Even having to duplicate unique sounds from a particular location can be a problem. ADR using ProTools has become a flexible and economic way to postrecord unusable dialogue.

Aesthetically, the dialogue recorded on the set is usually the best representation of each scene. There might be interference, of course. Unavoidable noises from traffic or airplanes might make it impossible to record clean dialogue.

In the long run, the production sound mixer can save the production time and money by delivering an accurate rendition of the production dialogue. A little extra time setting up a microphone or stopping an annoying sound can save hundreds, even thousands, of dollars in postproduction.

In the final mixing down of the tracks, some extraneous sounds can be reduced, if not entirely eliminated. Air conditioning hums and low-pitched whines such as a refrigerator can be treated at low and high ends of the sound spectrum. Even camera noise, should the barney on a camera be insufficient or the camera placed in a confined location, can be treated in such a way as to diminish its effect on the track. Of course, the efficient plan is to shoot in a location where sound can be controlled, air conditioners turned off during takes, windows closed to reduce traffic sounds, and so on. This is why it is wise for the sound recordist to visit locations prior to the shoot

and offer his opinion on what the sound quality will most likely be (see Chapter 7, "Location").

This emphasis on location sound recording is all the more critical in 16-mm. The 35-mm format has better sound-reproduction capabilities. With 16-mm, any problems with sound quality on the set are compounded later in postproduction.

Along with a mastery of his craft, the production sound mixer should have a thorough understanding of the postproduction process—that is, what happens to the sounds after they are recorded in production. Being aware of what can be accomplished in postproduction gives the production sound mixer a proper context for judging the work he must do and for properly evaluating the sounds he must sometimes fight for in order to record clearly (Figure 13.1).

The production sound mixer must also have a clear understanding of all the crafts that interact with him, such as camera, lighting, and grip. He needs to find a way to achieve the best sound possible within the limitations of each lens choice, camera move, and lighting setup.

SOUND PREPARATION

Just as the director and the director of photography (DP) previsualize the picture, the director and the sound person "preaudiolize" the sounds. This requires reading and breaking down the script from the sound perspective: how much dialogue, how many characters, the nature of the locations, and any extra sounds that must be recorded. The script usually reveals many of the challenges for the production sound mixer.

Often, a bit of business or a joke relies on the presence of a sound, or at least the cue of a sound that will be added to the picture in postproduction, such as a gunshot, a doorbell, or the sound of screeching brakes.

> *We sat down and made a list of wild sound before the shoot, e.g., the sound of a squishing sole, a ball hitting the court, a hand on the rope. . . . We had a list of sounds that took about an hour to get once the shoot was over.*
>
> Howard

Location Scout

Having "preaudiolized" the project's sound requirements, the production sound mixer should visit the locations, preferably on the same day a scene is to be shot (live sound on a location is different on a Sunday morning than it is on a Friday night). Walking through the actual spaces in advance will reveal any inherent sound problems that the production sound mixer must deal with before the start of principal photography. The one location choice that has no inherent sound problems is a sound stage, which is a soundproof environment. The only noises you should hear there are the actors' voices.

When visiting a site, the production sound mixer needs to consider the following:

- How large is the space?
- What are the acoustics of the space? (Hard surfaces reflect sound.)
- Can a loud refrigerator or air conditioning system be shut down?
- Can neighbors be controlled?
- Are key windows right above traffic noise?
- If the location is near an airport, what are the air traffic patterns?
- Will sound blankets solve the noise problems?
- What time of day will the shooting occur, and how is the local traffic at that time?

Production teams often scout locations on weekends when it is quiet and peaceful. Then the crew shows up to shoot on a Monday, and the street activity makes the noise level inside impossible for sound recording. Therefore, it is highly advised that you scout the location on the day of the week and at the approximate time that you'll want to shoot.

The location manager can research any street maintenance scheduled to take place in and around your location during the time of the shoot. Many unfortunate crews have found their supposedly quiet neighborhood suddenly invaded by a team of construction workers and their equipment. Once they get started, there is nothing you can do about the noise.

Be sure to listen for planes. If a location is on a flight path, the production sound mixer will be hard pressed to record clean sound.

If recording clean dialogue in a particular location appears to be impossible, the production manager should be notified about the problem and asked if it's possible to look for another location that is more "sound-friendly." If the location is locked, the mixer will have to do the best he can.

> *We scouted the gym and listened for noise. There weren't any classes because the school was closed, but the bell was still working on a timer and scheduled to go off every 45 minutes. We had the janitor dismantle the bell so it wouldn't go off in the middle of the shot.*
>
> Howard

It's possible that the production sound mixer might walk onto the set for the first time on the first day of principal photography, whereas the director has visited it many times. In this case, the production sound mixer must play catchup.

RESPONSIBILITIES OF THE SOUND TEAM

The following are the basic responsibilities of the film sound team:

- Record "clean" dialogue.
- Match the sound perspective with the camera angle.
- Record sound effects to accompany the shot.
- Record room tone.
- Record additional sounds.
- Record the scene so it will cut smoothly (sound consistency).
- Keep accurate sound reports. (Voice slates with all the pertinent information camera/sound rolls, date/time, scene number, type of mike and coverage for each track recorded, time code, and sample/bit rates are the kinds of information that are invaluable to telecine and the assistant editor. Oftentimes on digital hard drive recorders like Diva, this information can be loaded directly to the sound file's metadata.)

Dialogue

The production sound mixer's primary responsibility is to record all the dialogue spoken on the set *clean*—that is, unencumbered by any other ambient sounds connected with the shot. Just as the DP is responsible for focus and proper exposure, the production sound mixer strives to record dialogue at consistent levels that can be replayed clearly. A great effort is expended to create magic on the set, and it should be recorded properly. You can't duplicate a magical performance in a postproduction sound studio.

If it is impossible to record the dialogue clean, the sound team records it *dirty*—that is, cluttered with the overbearing sounds of airplanes, cars, or ocean surf in the background. Although unusable as the final product, this recording is used as a reference, or guide track, in the editing room for both cutting and ADR work.

Perspective

The dialogue should be recorded at as close a perspective as the framing allows with as little reverberation on the master track as possible. Perspective is often added at the final mix stage. If the dialogue is recorded with perspective/reverberation/equalization (EQ) at the location, very little can be done at the mix to remove any inconsistencies. Ultimately dialogue should be consistent with the point of view of the camera and from the perspective of the lens used for the shot. If the camera sees the action from across a room, the sound should approximate that visual perspective and should sound somewhat distant. In a closeup, the sound should have an intimate, almost overbearing presence. Ideally, viewers should hear the sound from the same point of view from which they see the visuals. Of course, there are times when it's necessary to sacrifice perspective, especially if proper perspective means that viewers will not hear the dialogue.

There are times when the camera is so far away from the action that performers can only be recorded if their voices are transmitted to a receiver from microphones concealed in their clothing. An example of this is a scene shot with a long lens of a couple walking along a beach. The audience sees the couple from a distance but hears them as if they were right there. To help correct this "unnatural" perspective, sound effects of waves, seabirds, and wind can be added during postproduction.

Sound Effects

Footsteps, cloth rustling, and prop movement should be recorded on a Foley stage with no ambience added. The production mixer's job is to get as clean and discrete dialogue as possible. If any of the production effects are usable, then that is an added bonus for post. If there is time, and to avoid Foley work (it can be expensive), the production sound mixer can capture during production as many of the ambient sounds and live effects connected with the shot as possible. Examples are slamming doors, ball bounces, and windows opening. These extra or "wild" sounds should be properly slated and labeled for future reference. They will be mixed in separately during postproduction.

For example, in a bar scene, after the principal photography is completed or before the extras are dismissed, the production sound mixer should ask the assistant director for a short recording session in which the crowd chats, drinks, sings, and cheers as though it were in a real bar. Two minutes of this sound will furnish the sound effects editor with ample material to create a full bar atmosphere. Because the main dialogue is recorded while the crowd is silent, the editor will have the dialogue and the background sounds on two different tracks, giving him complete control over volume levels.

Room Tone

If you stand on a set and ask everyone to be still and quiet, the silence you will hear is *room tone*. The sound team should record 60 seconds of room tone from each set before leaving the location. It is important that the tone be recorded with the lights on and the *full cast and crew* on the set, with the same microphone that was used to record the dialogue and at the same levels. The assistant director will ask everyone to freeze in his or her place for one minute. These 60 seconds of tone can then be copied and used in postproduction to fill in holes and smooth out the dialogue tracks when preparing for the mix. If it is difficult to get the cast and crew to stand around at the end of a sequence, record the room tone before the first take of the day.

It is also suggested that you record the hum of a refrigerator, fluorescent lights, or other equipment separately. This gives the editor freedom to add that ambient sound during the editing process.

Additional Sounds

Supplementary sound effects should be recorded and delivered to the editing room. If the crew is shooting in an interesting location, especially if it is distant, the sound team should record any particular sound that is unique to that area. It saves time and money to record additional sounds during the shoot, rather than having to come back later. During the shoot, for example, if the production sound mixer knows that a school is near the location, he might go to the schoolyard and record children at play.

These sounds might be used for background ambience, or they might not. Regardless, they give the sound editor a variety of choices and might even stimulate other sound ideas during postproduction.

The production sound mixer tried to record everything, which I think was a smart move on her part.

Adam

Sound Reports

The production sound mixer should take clear and comprehensive notes of the dialogue recorded on the set and the "wild sounds" recorded on or off the set. He should confer with the script supervisor or assistant camera operator for the scene numbers and the director's comments. These notes, called a *sound report*, will later serve as a reference for the editor (Figure 13.2). "Wild sounds" are slated as 1,000 numbers.

Every night during a location shoot, as exhausted as I am, I will listen to all the sound recorded that day and do my sound log. It keeps me familiar with what I have, and it enforces that discipline of keeping my material organized and not assuming that I have something on tape and finding out that I don't.

Jan

For video shoots, someone may be assigned to keep logs of each take using a simple log form with columns indicating tape number, timecode start and stop, scene number or content, and any notes about whether the take was good or bad. There are electronic devices such as the *Shot Logger*, a handheld computer that allows information, including timecode start and stop, to be later uploaded to a nonlinear editing machine. The sound recordist should be in close communication with the script supervisor and share all log information for the script notes.

LOCATION SOUND CORP

10639 Riverside Dr.
North Hollywood , CA 91602
(818)980-9891

(Outside CA) (800)228-4429
FAX (818)980-9911
Internet   www.locationsound.com

Title: _____ Date: _____

Production No. _____ Roll No. _____

Mixer: _____ Sheet No. _____ Of _____

Boom: _____ Location: _____

☐ SYNC: _____ Hz   ☐ WILD   Time Code: _____ FR/S   ☐ Drop Frame

Head Tone _____ dBM   Sample Rate _____   Recorder _____

PRINT CIRCLED TAKES ONLY

Scene No.	Take	Roll	Notes	SMPTE Start
				: : :
				: : :
				: : :
				: : :
				: : :
				: : :
				: : :
				: : :
				: : :
				: : :
				: : :
				: : :
				: : :
				: : :
				: : :
				: : :
				: : :
				: : :
				: : :
				: : :
				: : :
				: : :
				: : :
				: : :
				: : :

IF LAST ROLL OF DAY—CHECK HERE ☐

Figure 13.2 Location sound report sheet. Courtesy of Professional Sound Services, New York, NY, www.prosound.com.

Consistency in Sound Recording

The production sound mixer's goal is record sound consistently from shot to shot. Audiences expect the sound quality of a motion picture or video to flow seamlessly and continuously. It does not matter to an audience that the final sound track was constructed out of numerous camera angles and takes, shot over a wide expanse of time. On screen, it becomes one continuous mise en scène. The realistic consistency or *continuity* of the final sound track is the goal of the entire production and postproduction sound team. It all starts with the production sound mixer. The production sound mixer must be concerned with the following:

- Consistency within the shot
- Consistency within shots within the scene
- Consistency between scenes

Within the shot, levels should remain relatively constant between actors and also between background ambience. Actors are not expected to match each other in terms of recording levels; variations are normal. But their levels should match themselves. As they speak, the actor's audio should appear somewhat constant. There should be no unwarranted sudden changes in volume, except when justified by dramatic intent.

In addition to the actors, the production sound mixer should be mindful of background noise. The side effect of continually adjusting the level of the mikes to balance the level of the actors may result in the background noise bouncing up and down. The problem can be avoided by taking advantage of the acoustic properties of the mikes to control the relative levels of the dialogue by positioning and angling the microphone rather than by electronically adjusting the gain (volume) at the recorder or mixing panel. This is why the boom operator is such an important player and why he should be provided with a good headphone. The recordist and boom operator should also be present during rehearsals before the first take to familiarize themselves with blocking, dialogue levels, and possible overlapped dialogue.

When the camera changes angle, the mixer must be especially attentive that the levels of the new shot match and be intercuttable with the previous angles. Minor changes in angle do not motivate drastic changes in audio. Panning or cutting from one closeup to another of two people standing and talking does not constitute a major perspective change. Levels and background are expected to remain constant.

However, when you move the microphone for a closeup, readjust the volume so that the actor's voice remains constant with the rest of the sequence. A character's audio should be somewhat constant throughout the course of the scene, even as the shot changes from wide shot to medium to closeup. If you close your eyes, the changes in audio from shot to shot should not sound unnatural or unexpected. To minimize this bump in volumes at the editing stage, mixers often use shotgun or lavaliere mikes that are more discrete in their sound collecting properties. Matching ambience between the cuts in exterior locations that change often, like background traffic, requires skillful dialogue editors to smooth the transitions between cuts.

Not only does sound need to be consistent within a shot and from shot to shot, but also since this footage will be integrated during editing, the sound must match up when scenes cut with other scenes. Throughout the duration of the production, try to establish and then maintain relative audio levels for all your characters. Of course, there are going to be some changes in the audio levels. The nature of production is such that we can't always control things as much as we like, such as mike placement and background ambience. The idea, though, is to try to keep the changes in levels minimal and as inconspicuous as we can when we record them and then to fix them during postproduction.

Playback/Music Video

When examining the script, the production sound mixer looks for any situation that might require unusual equipment such as radio microphones or a playback machine. The latter is necessary when actors must sing, dance, or otherwise respond on the set to previously recorded music. Because this music will be used later in the film or video, it must be recorded with reference *pilot tone* or *SMPTE time code* (SMPTE timecode is discussed in Chapter 16), so it can be later synchronized with the picture. Unless the sound person is familiar with handling playback duties, he may need to bring in a specialist on days when playback is required.

If you are planning to shoot a *music video*, the music will come to you on tape, CD, or other format. During the shooting of the "video," the band will lip-sync with the song. The production sound mixer is responsible for playing back the song. Shooting a music video with video cameras is fairly straightforward. As long as the playback is on a stable, speed-controlled format such as DAT, the singers' mouth movements captured on video should match up to the song in postproduction. Some video cameras may drift slightly in speed. A timecode or sync generator may be used to keep the audio playback and camera locked together. Even without it, if shots are kept short, they probably won't reveal noticeable sync drift.

Shooting with a film camera for release on NTSC video is slightly more complicated. If the camera is run at the usual 24 frames per second (fps), the picture will not hold sync with the song during editing. This is because the picture will be pulled down in speed by 0.1 percent during the film-to-video transfer because of the frame rate difference between film and video (24 fps versus 29.97 fps). Compared to the master recording of the song, the singers on video will be moving their lips 0.1 percent too slow. The most common solution to this problem is to shoot at standard 24 fps and pull up the music playback by 0.1 percent on the set. Several analog and digital recorders can be set to play exactly 0.1 percent faster. The lip-syncing is then done to the speeded-up song, but when the footage is transferred to video, it will drop down to the speed of the original song. You should always consult with the laboratory or whoever will be transferring your footage before your shoot. In video, if the camera and recorder/playback are set at the same timecode rate they will always stay in sync, even in double system mode. In film, the recorder or playback source should always be set at 30 fps 60 Hz. One second of sound is always equal to one second of film. If you are going to telecine, let the telecine house do the pull down to match the film/video transfer. Always note the sample rate, bit depth, and timecode rate on your sound logs.

SET PROCEDURE

On the day of the shoot, the first step for the production sound mixer is to decide where to place the recorder. It is best placed on the edge of the set, close enough for the production sound mixer to see and hear what is happening, but away from the traffic of lights and grip equipment. Careful attention must be paid to positioning the microphone cables. At no time should an electric cable and a microphone cable be parallel to one another. Electric AC current can induce hum into the signal in the microphone cable, making it impossible to record clean sound. A 60-Hz notch filter will remove most AC hum.

The next step is to decide how many microphones to use, what specific kinds to use, and where to place them. A production sound mixer is only as good as the

sound coming from his microphones. Choosing the type of microphone to use and where to place it are important parts of clean dialogue recording.

Much of sound recording involves "riding levels," which means leveling out the extremes of performance and balancing multiple characters. For example, the production sound mixer might have to handle dialogue between one actor who speaks softly and another who bellows.

Balancing these two performances is part of the art of mixing. It also requires maintaining consistent sound among the different takes of the same scene. If you have already shot the master of a scene and the background ambience is clean but a plane flies over when you shoot the closeup, you should redo the closeup to match the background of the long shot. The sound recordist should always alert the director to these problems after the take is shot and note them in his sound logs. Logs should also contain any lines obscured by prop noise and signal dropouts.

There are many variables in recording, and before making any decisions, the production sound mixer and the boom operator must watch a rehearsal of the scene (this is important for the sound and camera team). Knowing where actors will be positioned and how they will move allows the production sound team to make informed decisions. They must be able to see what the camera is seeing in order to keep mikes safely away from the frame line. This is accomplished by looking through the camera's viewfinder. Always be on the lookout for boom shadows.

Once the microphones are positioned, there should be a final rehearsal to enable the production sound mixer to adjust for proper recording levels. Actors should speak at the level they will be projecting during the actual take. The mixer should do a test that can be erased when you start recording for real. Now the production sound mixer is ready for the take. (See Chapter 11, "Set Procedures," for slating techniques.)

Basic Attitude on the Set

The production sound mixer's ability to record the best sound possible in any situation depends on his ability to communicate properly with the DP and the director. He must know when to fight for another take and when to let it go. The production sound mixer should be assertive regarding his needs. Set protocols require that these communications always be done with the director on a confidential basis.

In addition, the production sound mixer must be sensitive to the needs of the actors. He must use the utmost tact and grace when placing microphones on the performers. Working with actors who mumble or shout can also be problematic. If this is the case, the production sound mixer should request that the director ask the actor to speak more softly or loudly.

Communication with Boom Operator

Ultimately, the recording of quality production sound relies on successful teamwork between the production sound mixer and the boom operator. The mixer is not a magician; he can only record sound that is properly microphoned. Because they usually work at a distance from one another, they need to develop a shorthand communication that enables them to work quietly and efficiently. The sound team also needs to be able to communicate effectively and unobtrusively with the camera operator regarding the microphone's relationship with the *frame line*. To avoid having the mike accidentally appear in the frame during a shot, or cast a shadow, the sound and camera teams should rehearse each shot, especially if any camera move is planned.

> **STUDENTS**
>
> Hard as it can be to find a production sound mixer for a student shoot, it is equally difficult to find a boom operator. The boom operator is usually some PA who is not doing something else, or someone's best friend who is visiting the set. These are hardly the proper criteria for this important crew position. If a novice boom operator is recruited, it is recommended that the production sound mixer spend quality time before the shoot to rehearse proper boom techniques. Don't wait until the first real take!

APPROACHES TO RECORDING SOUND

The production sound mixer has four tools with which to record sound:

- Boom
- Plant
- Lavaliere
- Radio microphone

Boom

Using a boom is, in most cases, the best way to record dialogue. *Boom* is a generic term for any long pole with a microphone attached to the end of it that is used to record dialogue. It might be a complicated unit called a *Fisher boom*, which uses a pulley system to expand and contract, or a variable-length pole called a *fishpole*, with the microphone attached to a movable "shock mount" at the end. The latter is most common.

Fishpoles usually run from 12 to 18 feet in length and are rigid enough not to bend at full extension. (You don't want the microphone to dip into the shot.) The boom is used to position the microphone close to the scene to record dialogue between several actors simultaneously. The mount allows the boom operator to manipulate the microphone from one actor to another during the scene, depending on who is delivering lines. Because it is a mobile unit, the boom operator can follow moving action at a safe distance from the camera and still be close enough to pick up a clean signal from the actors.

The boom is usually held still and secure above the frame line and has a directional microphone (shotgun or hypercardioid) pointed down at the actors. (Microphones can be angled up toward the actor's mouth as well.) Boom movement should be practiced during rehearsals not only for sound quality, but also to avoid having the microphone interfere visually with the camera's frame line or to create unwanted shadows as it passes under lights.

During exterior shoots, a blimp-type windscreen is required to reduce the wind sounds the microphone picks up. Even when shooting interiors, always use a slip-on foam windscreen because some microphones (condenser-shotgun) are sensitive to even the most minute air movements.

The boom operator should use a set of headphones to monitor what is being recorded. The production sound mixer can give direction and speak to the boom operator through the headphones. This way, the production sound mixer doesn't have to shout to the boom operator.

A cable operator might be required if the shot calls for camera movement. This crew member keeps the microphone cables clear of the camera, grip, and electric equipment while the boom operator concentrates on following the action. The movement of the microphone cable might cause a rustling noise on the track, so it must be handled carefully.

Documentary sound crews usually do not have a separate boom operator. The production sound mixer acts as a self-contained sound recording unit. He does not have to be positioned far from the action and can easily handle the levels and position the microphone at the same time (Figure 13.3).

Figure 13.3 The production sound mixer needs to be quick in a real location. Photo from the filming of *The Lunch Date.*

The production sound mixer had done some documentary work, so he was used to both operating the Nagra and doing the boom at the same time. It was just luck. I don't remember thinking ahead, "Oh, we should get a guy from a documentary because I'm going to shoot this guerrilla style."

Adam

Plants/Stash

Plants or stash are microphones (usually omni or cardioids mikes with a wider pattern of sensitivity) that are not mobile; they are "planted or stashed" in a fixed location for the duration of the scene. For example, they might be used to pick up the voice of an actor who is too far away from the boom. They need to be hidden from the view of the camera. They can be taped or mounted in doorways, on bed headboards, behind pictures, under chairs, in flowerpots, and so on.

Lavaliere

This small, lightweight, omnidirectional microphone is pinned under an actor's clothing or taped to the body. It must be carefully placed so as not to pick up

the rustle of clothing as the actor moves, and it must be rechecked constantly in case it dislodges as a result of constant movement or moisture (if taped).

Lavalieres are effective microphones if the actor remains fairly stationary during a take, but if the actor is required to walk, dragging the microphone cable might be awkward. A radio microphone might be needed in this case. Lavalieres are often used when interviewing subjects for documentaries.

Radio Microphones

Radio microphones are used to cover hard-to-reach areas, such as a wide shot of a couple talking on a beach. If the actors are far from the reach of a boom, a plant, or a lavaliere, a radio microphone might be your only option. These microphones are attached to the body like a lavaliere, but they transmit the signal from a radio transmitter to a receiver. The basic problem with radio microphones is that they are apt to pick up other frequencies, such as police car or taxi transmissions, that interfere with your sound. They are expensive to rent and have the same inherent problems as lavalieres.

The only problem that we had—and one that wasn't immediately obvious—was the noise. Most people, if they see a highway outside their window, understand they're going to get car noise in the background or they choose another location. But in this case, it was an unseen thing that got us.

Near the school, about 400 yards away, was a high-powered radio station antenna that broadcast country music. Surprisingly, the boom pole was acting as a receiver, and country music was being picked up at certain times and transmitted into the Nagra and recorded onto the tape. We discovered that on the first day of shooting and were horrified. We realized very quickly that the microphone had to be placed precisely and not moved. If you moved the boom slightly, it came back into frequency. So only after we had the microphone set up—and it took several tries—we could shoot.

Howard

VARIABLES FOR PLACING MICROPHONES

The placement and use of the different microphones depend on the many variables of a particular scene. Evaluate the scene first, and then work with the following considerations:

The Director's Vision. Who and what does the director want to hear in the shot? Start with this as the basic premise of every decision.

Placement and Blocking of Actors. How much does an actor move in the shot? An actor pacing in the frame must be microphoned differently than one sitting still. A boom or two separate microphones might be necessary to record the sequence.

Placement of Camera. How far away is the camera from the action of the scene? This defines how close you can get with a microphone. If the most directional microphone is unrealistic, mikes are then "stashed" within the frame of the master shot closer to the action.

Size and Composition of Shot. What is the lens seeing? This affects a number of things. How close to the actor can the microphone on the boom be positioned without slipping into the frame line? The boom operator must be keenly aware of the frame line at all times. He should rehearse with the camera operator before the final rehearsal with the actors. Both the camera operator and the boom operator must be consistent in their moves. The size of the shot also affects the visibility of a lavaliere or radio microphone. A very tight shot of an actor will require that the microphone be more carefully disguised than in a long shot.

Lighting of Shot. The lighting plan can cause problems if the sound boom creates a shadow that can be seen in the frame. During the lighting setup, any boom shadows should be dealt with before the lights are fixed with the use of *flags* and *cutters* (see Glossary) on the lights. During the shoot, the elimination of boom shadows must be a coordinated effort between the boom and camera operators.

Movement of Shot. If a dolly is used for a shot, the boom operator must rehearse his actions around those of the dolly. A production assistant or cable operator might be needed to keep the microphone cable free from the path of the dolly and clear of the electric cables. The mixer also needs to avoid picking up the sound created by the dolly.

Acoustics at Location. The production sound mixer might need to position the microphone away from disruptive sounds to minimize their presence on the track. Common troublemakers are refrigerators, air conditioners, fluorescent lights, traffic noise from the windows, and natural echoes in the location. *Sound*

blankets might also be required to eliminate or at least lessen the problem.

Sound blankets can be used in a variety of ways to deaden the sound of "live" rooms by baffling the reflective sound echoes caused by hard floors, ceilings, walls, and windows. Sound blankets are heavy moving blankets, preferably with a white side and a dark gray or black side and grommets for hanging. They can be taped to walls, hung from C-stands and over windows, or even draped over refrigerators and air conditioning units to create a quieter environment.

> *We weren't prepared for the hum of the fluorescent lights. When you were standing in the gym, you didn't notice it, but it came out loud and clear on the sound track.*
>
> Howard

Camera Noise. Although 16-mm sync cameras are designed to run quietly, often a camera leaks noise during a take. This is most noticeable when shooting interiors in a confined space. *Blimping*, or creating a soundproof housing for the camera, might reduce the noise that emanates from the lens mount, magazine, or body of the camera. (This is the AC's job.) This muffling can be accomplished with a *blimp* or *barney*, which is a jacket that is specially designed for the camera. You can create your own blimp with anything that will deaden the camera noise, such as a changing bag, foam rubber, or a coat or jacket.

One way of cutting down on camera noise is to position the camera as far away from the microphone as possible during the take. A small amount of camera noise can usually be camouflaged by the other sounds or music that will inevitably be mixed in during postproduction. This is a good example of why the production sound mixer must understand what happens during postproduction to be able to effectively evaluate the sounds recorded on the set.

RECORDING CONCERNS

One of the differences between how sound and film images are recorded is that you can immediately hear a sound take played back on the set. Video has this advantage as well, but film must be sent to a lab to be processed. With the sound, if there is any question of quality, the director can listen to a take with the headphones on to decide whether he wants to do the shot over for sound or performance.

The director will ask whether a take is good for camera and whether it is good for sound. Camera will be first on the list. Asking for another take because of sound problems is a judgment call the director makes after listening to the track. Many sound problems can be addressed in postproduction, whereas picture problems must always be addressed on the set.

Pickups

If only a small section of a take is ruined because of extraneous sounds, it might not be necessary to do the complete take again. You might be able to "pick up" the section of the take that was spoiled. In a pinch, the sound can be also taken "wild" (audio recording only) and matched to the picture in postproduction.

If the day has been fraught with sound problems, holding a makeshift ADR session in a quiet room after the day's work can save a lot of money. If it is impossible to do it right after the scene is shot, have the actors come to the quiet area when they get out of makeup and costume. After the actors listen to their performance on headphones, they repeat the original dialogue for the production sound mixer. This material will most likely match well with the actors' lips in the editing room. If it does not, with some minor adjusting (stretching and shrinking), the new material can be made to fit. This method is most successful when used in wide shots when it is more difficult to see the actors' mouths.

Keeping It Clean

Be aware of actors who step on one another's lines. This is called *overlapping*. If two sounds are already blended on the track, they can never be controlled separately. They will be married forever. Record dialogue that can later be controlled in the editing room. In a single shot in which an off-camera actor has lines, he should make sure there is a pause between the on-camera actor's line and his own line. Recorded separately, or with a pause, lines can be manipulated in the editing room to create overlaps, but the editor will be able to control each voice.

If the director wants the lines overlapped for dramatic purpose, the off-camera dialogue should be microphoned as well. If the scene is a wide shot, overlapping lines may be an integral part of the drama.

Difficult Situations

The production sound mixer might not be able to achieve clean sound on a difficult set or location. Planes traveling overhead will destroy a sound take.

Some locations, such as Grand Central Station, are too busy to control. If the company is on a flight path where waiting for good sound translates to little or no photography, the director will have to bite the bullet and plan for ADR work. However, it is still important to record production dialogue. It can be used as a *guide track* for editing purposes and as a reference track for the actors when they perform the lines during the ADR session. Clean *ambience* (background sound) should also be taken to mix or blend with the lines that will inevitably be recorded later.

Crowd Scenes

To record clean sound in a crowded bar sequence, the assistant director instructs the background extras to mime speech and the clinking of glasses. This means that during the take, the background actors move their lips, but utter no sound. They raise their glasses, but do not let the glasses touch. They dance to a predetermined rhythm, but there is no music playing. These sounds are added later.

This allows the dialogue recorded on the set to be "clean." It will not have any dirty crowd noise to fight the dialogue. To maintain the illusion, the speaking actors must project their voices as if they were fighting the din of the crowd and the music. (To help the actors with this, it is good to rehearse the scene with the full-blown background noise.) This way, when the three sound tracks—dialogue, music, and background noise—are married in the mix, the volume of each track can be controlled separately. The scene will sound natural, and the dialogue will come through so that the audience can understand it.

VIDEO SOUND

Most amateur video sound recording is done *single system*, with the sound recorded right on the videotape (there are situations when audio is recorded separately). Most camcorders have microphones built into the camera. These are simple and convenient, but may result in inferior sound because the microphone is too far from the source for optimum recording. Different tape formats have different configurations of sound tracks, but most allow for *stereo recording* (two channels: left and right). Formats that allow you to record four separate tracks will give you flexibility in production, since you can assign different microphones to different channels. One of the virtues of video is that it is generally easy to transfer the project from one video format to another. One could shoot with a Hi-8 camera, *bump up* (transfer) the tape during editing to a four-channel format, and then release in six-channel DVD.

Professional-quality sound can only be achieved by using separate mikes that are placed closer to the subject. These may be fed to the camcorder or videotape recorder (VTR) through a cable or wireless transmitter. When a production sound mixer is on the crew, the mikes are often fed to a mixer, which allows easy monitoring of sound levels and blending of multiple mikes.

Most video productions record double system and send the production mix to the camera for a guide track at picture editing. There are several important reasons to separate sound and picture with video shoots:

- Sound editors/designers prefer a separate production track. Often when working in postproduction, sound technicians will ask for a clone of the production DAT. Depending on the sound editing software they are using they can use the production DAT to redigitize the sound and cut it in an environment that has a higher bit rate and better audio code. In addition, they can pull takes from the tape that the editor chose not to use or replace small sections of takes with other takes. This allows the sound person more freedom to create the best work possible and also reduce needed ADR.
- DV cameras can drift out of sync slightly when recording for long periods of time. It is a rare problem but it happens. Sony has tried to rectify this problem with the introduction of their DVCam technology. The DVCam tapes and recorders use the larger tape width (6.35-mm) to pack more audio information into the track. They call this feature *audio lock*. Friction increases between tape and recorder heads after repeated passes on the tape. DVCam tape has a significantly lower friction coefficient than DV. For the professional, this means greater recorded signal longevity, higher reliability, increased durability, and overall improved performance.
- For numerous reasons there have been digital audio glitches on the videotape. Most of the time it is because the record head was dirty or possibly someone used the wrong kind of tape in the

camera (depending on the camera it is sometimes better to use lubricated tapes as opposed to nonlubricated tape; this is especially important with the Panasonic DVX100/a). Once there is an audio glitch, that take is unusable. If you have a DAT recorder as well, the chance that you will run into this problem is slim. And in the event that you have to replace the take, you have the backup tape.
- It is always good to have a back up audiotape. The great thing about shooting with a video camera is that you can run a line-out from the DAT recorder directly to the video camera. That way you have sound on the videotape and a backup on the DAT.

Video sound crews vary according to the complexity of the production (how many characters have to be recorded in a sequence) and whether it is a location shoot or a studio shoot. A single-camera setup in the field might need only a one-person crew to operate the videotape recorder, mix the incoming microphone levels, and hold the boom. A scene with many characters requires a boom operator and a production sound mixer with a mixing unit that has anywhere from 2 to 12 inputs. A studio shoot with multiple cameras for one scene might use a mixing console of up to 18 tracks.

When shooting video, the choice of camcorder or VTR format is usually driven by picture needs, but these decisions will clearly have an impact on sound as well. In selecting a system, review these considerations:

- How many audio tracks do you need?
- Does the camcorder allow manual adjustments of audio levels?
- Can you use external mikes?
- Are there professional mike connectors (such as *XLR*), or will you need adapters?
- If you are working with a production sound mixer, will you need a mixing console so he can control levels?

These are important questions for those shooting on small video formats such as Hi-8, S-VHS, and MiniDV. Most professional camcorders give you a choice between manual and automatic control of audio levels. Many consumer models only have automatic control, which is convenient but may result in inferior recordings. Always choose a camcorder that offers the option of manual level control. Also, the consumer shotgun microphone that comes with the camera will usually sound fine, but plugging in a professional mike may result in a lot of buzz, hum, and lower audio levels because the built-in mike preamp is not matched to the XLR/phantom-powered output professional mike. (Always use a separate mike preamp mixer.) Make sure to plan and test your video sound recording system well in advance. You want the advantages that video can offer without having to compromise when it comes to the quality of the audio.

Documentary

Documentary crews are small and mobile. The production sound mixer and boom operator are usually the same person. He must be adept at booming, mixing (if additional microphones are used), and operating the recorder simultaneously. In unstaged documentary shooting for film, it is important that the production mixer be ready to roll at a moment's notice. If shooting is imminent, the recorder should be put on "standby" position and the recording level should be set. If the scene looks interesting, the mixer should not hesitate to roll sound. Tape is inexpensive. If the scene does not pan out, simply say, "No shot."

I always wear the headphones because I think you get in trouble if you simply trust the needle and assume that you are getting decent sound. I think the tradeoff of looking a little odd is incidental. It does remind your subjects that they're being recorded, but so does all the other equipment. What's important to me as both the director and the sound person is to get the best sound, and the only way to assure that is to be monitoring what's coming off the tape, not what I'm hearing in the environment.

Jan

PRODUCER
Controlling the Environment

Because one of the producer's major concerns is managing the budget, anything that contributes to saving time and money will get his attention. In the area of sound recording, hiring a skilled production sound mixer and boom operator is the first step. Be sure the production sound mixer knows that his main concern is recording clean production dialogue.

The following are additional areas the producer must focus on:

- Ensuring that the equipment needs of the production are fulfilled (recording devices, microphones, sound tape, etc.)

- Getting the best deals possible on the rental equipment
- Guaranteeing that all locations are "sound-friendly"
- Asking the production sound mixer to capture sufficient ambient and interesting sound effects from each location
- Ensuring proper care of the equipment

EQUIPMENT NEEDS FOR THE SHOOT

Once he understands the demands of the script and the locations, the production sound mixer can develop an accurate list of his equipment needs. These might include some of the following tools:

Film

DAT, DVD Ram and/or Nagra
Portable mixer
Assorted microphones
Headphones (two or three sets)
Microphone cables
Extra batteries
Tape stock
Shock mounts
Slip-on windscreen and blimp
Sound blankets
Blimp-type windscreen
Boom pole
Rechargeable batteries
Mounting clips

Video

Shotgun (hyper-cardioid) mike
Lavaliere mike, assorted clips
Wireless transmitter and receiver
Fishpole mike boom with shock mount
Zeppelin windscreen
Field mixer
Headphones
Cables for mike-to-mixer and camera-to-mixer connections
Sound blankets
Sound recorder

Digital recorders are the industry standard. They offer high quality in a small, light package and have had a huge impact on video and film production. There are many types of digital recorders used for field produc-

Figure 13.4 Tascam DA-P1. Portable DAT recording machine. Courtesy of TEAC, Inc.

tion. These include cassette tape formats such as DAT; open-reel tape recorders such as the Nagra D; disk recorders such as the Deva, which record on hard drives or computer tape data drives; chip-based systems such as the Nagra Ares C, which records on computer memory cards with no moving parts; and magneto-optical disc systems such as Sony's MiniDisk.

Compared to analog tape recorders, digital tape machines provide longer continuous recording on a smaller tape. (See Figure 13.4.) The DAT (digital audiotape) cassette is small enough to fit in a shirt pocket. Most DAT and other digital formats have very accurate speed control and can be used for film and video work with no additional modifications. Basic consumer DAT machines do not use timecode but, with a separate microphone preamp, may be used with a professional mike. Higher end recorders have built-in preamps and timecode capability. In this category, the Fostex PD-4 is one of the most commonly used timecode DAT machines currently in use.

DAT recorders employ a technology that duplicates a "clean" sound devoid of hiss or sound buildup. There is no generation loss with digital sound as long as it is duplicated onto other digital machines. (We discuss in more detail the basic differences between analog and digital technology in Chapter 16.)

Microphones

Microphones are delicate instruments that convert sound waves into electric signals. The production sound mixer must have a thorough knowledge of microphones and how they can be used effectively to capture sound under a wide variety of conditions. He must be able to identify the right microphone for each situation. Microphones (and speakers) are still

analog, so sound is captured and reproduced using the same equipment regardless of the recorder format. The sound signal comes from the mike and goes to an analog-to-digital (A/D) converter. To play back the tape, the digital signals are then sent to a digital-to-analog (D/A) converter, which transforms the binary numbers back to an analog signal that can be heard through speakers or headphones.

CARE OF EQUIPMENT

Proper care and maintenance of sound equipment are very important. Treat it with respect.

DAT

- Keep dust and dirt away from the tape; they can impair sound quality. Do not touch the tape.
- Keep the tape in its box, and protect it from temperature extremes.
- Keep the lid of the tape deck closed as much as possible.
- Do not smoke, drink, or eat around sound equipment—food and ashes have a way of winding up on the tape.
- Use alcohol-soaked cotton swabs regularly to clean the parts of the machine that touch the tape, including the heads, rollers, guides, and capstans.
- For a timecode-capable deck, check that the timecode can be properly recorded and played back.
- Rerecording over used tape is not recommended, as oxide tends to flake off and clog the very small recording heads.

Nagra Analog

- Clean the empty takeup reel each time it is used. Inspect it for warpage or rough edges. A damaged reel can tear or warp the edges of the tape and affect sound quality.
- Do not rewind the tape after recording or playback—leave it "tails out." Rewinding can cause a sound bleed-through.

KEY POINTS

- The production sound mixer should know what happens to sound in postproduction.

- Scout the location at the time of day or night for which the shoot is planned.
- During rehearsals, find the best places for the microphones and the boom. The boom operator should work out boom shadows and frame lines with the grips and the camera operator.

- Record room tone, wild sounds, and possibly even replacement dialogue at the end of the day.
- When shooting video, make sure that you plan your audio system well in advance. There are many video formats, and each has its own distinctive audio configuration.

chapter fourteen

Art

I think, as much as possible, it's important to visit your locations beforehand as many times as the budget and your schedule will allow.

Jan

DIRECTOR
Guide

In the process of creating a motion picture, the art director and the art department truly are magicians, often creating something out of nothing and making things appear from out of nowhere.

There is nothing like the feeling of walking on a dressed set for the first time: experiencing the culmination of weeks, maybe months, of preparation and planning by the director, the producer, the art department, and the director of photography (DP). A great deal of imagination and hard work have transformed the words on the page into the world of the characters through the choice of sets, dressing, costumes, props, and furniture.

SET PROCEDURES

The day starts early for the art department. Finishing touches are applied to the set to allow the electrical department time to set up the lights. Other members of the art department are already working on the next set in anticipation of the company's next move. During the shooting day, the art department is constantly on standby to adjust the set, dressings, and props for the camera.

Let's look at an excerpt from *The Lunch Date* as an example of how the art department approaches a scene.

INT. LUNCHEONETTE—AFTERNOON
The woman walks into a station luncheonette. It is a simple place—a grill, some booths, and rows of refrigerated cabinets filled with salads and sandwiches. She reaches into a glass case and removes a salad.
A COOK stands behind a white linoleum counter. He fiddles with his white paper hat and white apron.

                    WOMAN
          How much is this salad?
                    COOK
              Two dollars.
She puts the salad on the counter. She rustles through her pocketbook.
                    WOMAN
   Well, I'm not sure that I have that much.
The woman empties a dollar and some change on the counter.

                    WOMAN
          One dollar . . . here's some.
The cook fingers through the change.
                    COOK
A dollar fifty . . . two dollars. Here ya go lady.
She grabs the salad plate and her bundles.
                    WOMAN
                 Napkin.
The cook hands her a napkin. She walks toward the booths.

The duties of the art department for the scene are as follows:

Location. The location is secured during preproduction. If a location falls through, the art department must be part of the plan to move to an alternate location.

Set Dressing. Sometime before shooting the scene, the set dresser, cleanup crew, and painters "dress" the set to match the description in the script and any drawings, paintings, or photos given to the dresser. During the shooting, the set dresser readjusts any set pieces that have been moved for camera framing continuity. If the shoot is going well, the set dresser can leave the shoot and move to the next location to begin preparing it.

Props. The props are gathered prior to the shoot. When the set is ready, the property master places the food on the counter. He prepares the woman's handbag with the appropriate change. When the performer is called to the set, he hands her the handbag and her packages. He places some napkins nearby for the cook.

Wardrobe. When the actors arrive on the location, they are sent to change clothes after a brief rehearsal. The costumer dresses both actors in the costumes defined by the script. She asks the cook to keep the apron and paper hat neat and clean so they will match for each take. At wrap, the costumer helps the actors undress. She puts the costumes away neatly to be used another day. If they need washing, she takes them with her to be cleaned after the wrap.

Makeup and Hair. After the actors are dressed, they move on to the makeup and hair department. Here, their makeup is applied and their hair coifed to match a previous scene or the art director's design. When this job is completed, the makeup and hair people stand by off set to make adjustments between takes. At the end of the day, they assist the actors in removing their makeup and any hairpieces.

SET DRESSING

The set dresser decorates the set according to the art director's specific designs. This crew member is responsible for renting, buying, or making all the "dressing" that occupies the set—everything from the rugs on the floors to the magnets on the refrigerator. The set dresser should confer with the actor whose character "lives" in the location, and together they will create the character's environment.

The set dresser works in tandem with other departments, such as lighting. If the gaffer has lit the set brightly, a 100-watt bulb in a "practical" will not register on film or video stock. An electrician might need to replace the bulb with a special 500-watt lamp to balance light temperature correctly.

The set dresser is sometimes called on to assist other departments. The key grip might need help pulling up a rug during a take to get it out from under the dolly's wheels. Someone might be needed just off camera to jerk a curtain with monofilament wire (fishing line) to simulate the wind. These specialty positions often fall to the set dresser.

Not all set pieces are easy to find. If the director has a specific look in mind for a set piece, the art director and set dresser must make this item to the director's specifications if it cannot be found (Figure 14.1).

My dad put up the rope. He was my PA. We found a rope in another school and took it down. We built a special iron clamp because there wasn't one on the particular ceiling. My dad had a friend who was a metallurgist; he designed a specific clamp so that we could fasten the rope to the ceiling and support a person.

One very difficult prop—so difficult that we didn't find it until two days before the shoot—was the fireman's net. They haven't been used since the 1930s. They're very dangerous and very heavy. The reason they're not being used was that people would hit them and bounce out. They really didn't save many lives. The one we used we found in some guy's barn under a bale of hay. It was classic. The guy's father had been a fireman, and he let us take it out. It was very dirty and very, very heavy.

During the shot, the production manager was underneath the net, which weighed 400 pounds. The kids really couldn't lift it themselves, so he hid under it on his hands and knees, resting it on his back.

Howard

Continuity

The set is maintained by the set dresser to match the uninterrupted succession of the script's scenes. If there is a fight scene, for example, the set is each take, and all the broken set pieces are replaced. The duplicated set is matched each time to the script supervisor's snapshots of the original set.

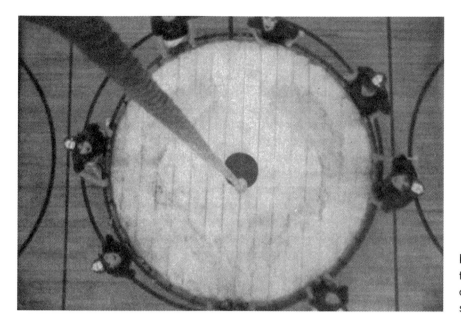

Figure 14.1 It's one thing to type the words *Fireman's Net* into the script and another to locate one for the shoot. Scene from *Truman*.

Duplicates

The set dresser should have duplicates of key items featured on the set in case they become damaged. Duplicates should also be provided for breakaway items. Breakaway chairs, for instance, are made of pieces of balsa wood that have been loosely glued together. A performer does not sit on this chair, but on the real chair. She is photographed as she stands up, and then the real chair is replaced with the breakaway chair. The character can then pick up the breakaway chair and heave it at another actor or stunt person. In the final product, this action will look real, but it is actually harmless. With the addition of sound effects, the audience viewing this footage will believe that the chair is hard.

PROPS

Because I had so few, I basically handled the props. It sounds kind of silly, but as a director you get very, very particular about certain props. I even went so far as to worry about what kind of kickball was used. It was important that it was one of those red, standard playground balls because that's what I grew up with. Gathering together those bows and arrows was also tough, as was getting permission to fire them in the gym.

Howard

Continuity

The prop department is responsible for maintaining continuity of props from shot to shot. If a scene requires the actor to eat a meal, for example, the level of the milk in the glass, the steam on the food, and the exact placement of the cutlery must be maintained. If it looks as though the production will run out of a food item, a production assistant is sent to the local store to purchase more.

Duplicates

If a scene calls for a watch to be smashed, the watch might have to be destroyed many times in the course of covering the scene. The prop master must have enough watches standing by to allow the director to shoot the scene to her satisfaction. If it is decided in preproduction that the character will wear a special watch, it might prove difficult to duplicate. The director should ask herself whether a more common watch, which can be easily and inexpensively duplicated, would compromise the story.

Food that will be consumed on the set must also be provided in duplicate. In a dining scene, the property master is responsible for all the food a character has to eat during the scene. If the script calls for the character to eat a salad, several complete salads should be standing by for each take.

Figure 14.2 Someone had to make the vomit. Photograph from the shooting of *Truman*.

> *The salad—we were not prepared for that: how much salad we would need for the whole day. If you're going to do the take over, the salad has to look the same all day.*
>
> Adam

Personal Effects

The property master might be responsible for safeguarding the actor's personal belongings during the shoot. He might accept her valuables when he gives her the character's personal props, trading them back at the end of the day.

Improvisation

What if the production has run out of milk and the stores are closed? What if the location is in the middle of nowhere? The director might take the scene over and over to capture the best performance, and the props must be there each time. Even if the director tells the property master in preproduction how many takes she thinks she will need, the crew must be prepared with extra props.

The art department might have to improvise with the milk, keeping in mind that the actor actually has to consume the substitute on camera. Perhaps some creamer substitute mixed with water will match the color of the milk from previous takes. Tricks of the prop master's trade include using iced tea to simulate

scotch, nontobacco cigarettes for nonsmokers, breakaway chairs for fights, sugar glass tumblers for breaking, and soup for vomit (Figure 14.2).

> *The makeup was another issue. We had to get a guy to make some fake vomit. When we were trying to get [Truman] to do the throw-up scene from on top of the scaffolding, he was really repulsed by the sight of the fake vomit and refused to get near the stuff. We wanted to put a little around his lips so after he had thrown up you could see the residue. Well, he refused to do it. At first, he laughed nervously, and then he actually started to cry. He went through a whole range of emotions. He just did not want to do this thing. I finally put some around my lips to show, "Hey, it's not bad. It's nothing but soup. Don't worry." That kind of calmed him down, and we made some jokes. About an hour and a half later— for something that was supposed to take only 15 minutes—we actually did it. That was the most difficult constraint, having to deal with the limitations of an eight-year-old boy. He did a great job. You have to remember, he was under a great deal of pressure, and I think he held up remarkably well.*
>
> Howard

WARDROBE

The company travels with all the costumes required for the show, including duplicate costumes for everyone and any sundry garb for the extras. It is important that the wardrobe be consistent with the setting.

In an exterior winter scene, for instance, everyone in the shot must wear a heavy coat to indicate the cold. This scene can be shot in hot weather, of course, because the audience knows the temperature only by what they see or hear.

Special Rigs

Special technical equipment is sometimes integrated into the costume, such as a radio microphone or a jerk harness. (When a character is shot with a big gun, he is jerked off the set by a wire attached to this harness.) The costumer works with the department responsible for the technical hardware to conceal it in the costume so that the audience will not be aware of the rigging device.

The costumer uses her bag of tricks during production. Quick changes and clothes that have to be removed during a take require special attachments. There is no question that the costumer's life became easier with the invention of Velcro.

MAKEUP

Continuity

After applying makeup to the cast, the makeup artist spends the remainder of the day on the set helping the actors maintain a consistent look. Under the hot lights, actors perspire and must be powdered or tissued down to avoid a shiny complexion. With prosthetics work, touchups might require applying entirely new latex pieces, which could be just as time consuming as the original application that morning.

Positive Reinforcement

The makeup artist is usually the last person to work with the actors before they begin a scene. Actors might be in the makeup trailer for some time, so the individual who works with them there helps the director by doing whatever she can to sustain the actors in an agreeable frame of mind. A makeup artist with a pleasant personality can help an actor maintain a positive mood.

Special Effects

Prosthetics work is very time consuming. It is not uncommon for an actor and the makeup artist to arrive on the set several hours before the crew call time to prepare and apply the makeup.

The art director helped me with the puppets. In Crazy Glue *the puppets were maybe ten inches tall, so the set was about six by six feet.*

Tatia

HAIR

The hairdresser works in tandem with the makeup artist. The look of hair and makeup must be coordinated, as must their application.

Continuity

The maintenance of hairstyle continuity is very important. The hairdresser takes instant photographs of each hairstyle. These photographs are kept on a large ring for easy reference, providing a convenient method for matching hair from scene to scene. This technique works well for all departments.

Hair gets mussed easily and therefore might not match a previous take, especially when shooting in a windy exterior location. Sustaining a consistent look can take a great deal of work. If an actress chooses not to have her hair touched up between takes because it disturbs her concentration, you might find in the editing room that the cuts do not match. The hairdresser has to be discreet in this situation. If the hair is passable, the hairdresser should not say a word, but if it will cause an obvious continuity error, the hairdresser should inform the script supervisor, the DP, or even the director to correct the match.

ADDITIONAL CREW

Depending on the nature of the shoot, the art department might also employ a standby painter, a special effects team, or a greens person (for on-set vegetation). In the production of a short film or video project, all these roles might be performed by only one or two talented people.

PRODUCER
Construction

The producer oversees any set construction. The location manager and the production manager can

chapter fifteen

Cast

She's a great actress, so I was very lucky.

Adam

DIRECTOR
Direct

Actors are the director's primary storytelling vehicles. A good actor can breathe life into a character and a script. Aiding and guiding the actors through the production are the director's jobs.

The relationship between a director and an actor is an important one. Many intangible elements must come together in front of the camera when the director calls, "Action." These elements include emotional tone, pace, projection, and the arc of the characters.

The director should know what the actor is capable of in any given situation. Casting and rehearsals will give the director a strong indication of the actor's talent and range, but the critical point comes when the cameras roll.

A primary goal for the director is to create an environment that is conducive to good work. The actors will be able to focus on their work if the atmosphere created by the director and her crew is relaxed and cooperative. If there are bickering and general chaos, it will be difficult for the actors to concentrate.

The well-known British director Joseph Losey (*The Servant, The Go-Between*) said this about directing actors:

Security is I think essential. If an actor doesn't feel secure, two things can happen. He starts to fail. Or else he sets up a psychological barrier to protect himself. Actors do their best for me when they feel free to make fools of themselves . . . when you have a good actor who knows what you want and is continually looking for things inside of himself, and knows that you are not going to make a fool of him either on the set or on the screen, then you can see extraordinary things happen.

THE PROCESS

There is a set order to the process of shooting a short film or video. The director needs to follow that order so that everyone on set knows what is happening at each moment. To this end, it is essential that the director know what she wants from the actor and how to get it.

Call Time

The actor arrives on the set at his appointed call time and checks in with the assistant director. The first

223

order of business is to conduct a brief run-through of the scene. Once the scene has been loosely blocked to the director's and director of photography's (DP) liking, the actor is sent to makeup. After makeup, the actor goes to wardrobe to put on his costume. After another stop at makeup and hair for touchups, he is ready for the camera.

If the assistant director has scheduled the actor's arrival correctly, he will have very little time to wait before he is called to the set for his scene. Do not call the actor to the set until the set is ready. On the other hand, make sure the actor doesn't keep the entire crew waiting.

Makeup and Hair

The director should be keenly aware of the personalities on the makeup and hair team. These crew members see the actor just prior to his arrival on the set. If they do not understand how to help the actor get into the right mood for a scene, they can destroy his concentration. Talented makeup and hair people who are friendly and supportive are priceless. They can ease the actor's tensions and put him in a positive mood.

Stand-ins

To free the actor from the set until his work begins, it is advisable to employ a stand-in. When preparing a scene, many time-consuming camera functions require that a live body be standing or moving in the actor's blocked positions. To flag and focus the lights and to practice camera movements, any body of roughly the same size will do as a stand-in for the actor.

On Call

An important consideration for the production unit is how the actor is treated while he is on call. Although this is primarily the responsibility of the assistant director, all principal parties must be aware of the actor's schedule and working environment.

For the actor, the emotional rhythm of a typical day is like a roller coaster ride. The actor might have to wait for long periods while the crew prepares and lights the sequence. Once the camera begins to roll, he must be able to find his peak energy level. To ensure that he has the opportunity to perform at his best, the production must provide food, a comfortable place to rest, and a call time that does not abuse his energies.

Consider the alternative: You are shooting in a freezing exterior location. The actor waits outdoors for the set to be dressed and lit. He is tired, hungry, and irritable. When you ask him to get in front of the camera, even the most disciplined actor might have difficulty "getting up" for his part. His poor performance will be reflected in the dailies and ultimately in the final product.

Final Staging

After the crew completes the time-consuming work of preparing for a scene, shooting or taping begins. The director will conduct a final staging rehearsal, during which last-minute technical adjustments are made. While performing on set, actors might discover moments or business that were not part of the rehearsal process. Props, set pieces, or a painting on the wall might inspire the actor and be just the thing to make a scene work better. If the technical adjustments are major (a total relighting of the set, for example), the actors should be excused and encouraged to return to the green room, makeup room, or rest area.

We knew if we didn't have all the kids in the shot, we could send the others off to the playroom. We made a playroom for the kids with a babysitter.

Howard

Gaffers and set decorators will make subtle adjustments, or "tweak" a set, until they are told to stop. As soon as the director feels that the set is ready, she should get to work shooting and covering the scene. The assistant director is helpful here in determining the preparedness of the set and being aware of the director's schedule.

The actors sometimes meet for the first time on the day their scene is to be shot. In this situation, the director should conduct off-set rehearsals and discussions to allow them to warm up. They will then require some time on the set to explore and get comfortable with the physical environment they will be performing in. Conduct the first run-through with more relaxed blocking.

I didn't have my two actors, Scotty and Clebert, together until the first day of shooting. In fact, the whole interaction with the salad, the orchestration of her sitting down and what she would say, him sitting at the table, getting up and getting the pepper, and putting that on the table—that took five minutes in between setting up the shots. I sat down with them, and we quickly figured out a little routine to do.

Adam

Technical Requirements

The technical requirements for the actor are a large part of film and video acting. The head must be tilted just the right way to catch the light. The eyes must be directed at what the character is supposed to see. The raised hand must be placed so as not to block an actor who is framed in the background. Stage and nonprofessional actors who are unfamiliar with technical aspects of film and video might cause the director problems. It might be exciting to find someone who is a "natural" for the part, but if he can't be "natural" and adhere to the technical requirements at the same time, the director's schedule might fly out the window.

Lenses

Generally, actors should be conscious of what lens is being used and how many cameras are rolling. The general rule is that the tighter the shot, the less the actor has to "perform" to create an emotion. Inform your actor if you plan a tight closeup, for example, so he will be aware of the frame size and won't exaggerate his movement or bob in and out of the frame. In a wider shot, if the actor shakes his head violently, he should be instructed to compromise the movement to match the lens size. Conversely, if the camera angle is very wide, the actor should know that subtle actions on his part will not be seen.

Eye-line is another technical area in which the actor must be concerned about his relationship to the lens. An actor might have to look just to the right or left of the lens to give the illusion that he is speaking to another character. If the actor to whom he is speaking cannot put his face in the correct position for the eye-line, the camera operator might put a piece of tape on the lens in the correct position, challenging the performer to act to a piece of tape.

The director should be aware of any obstacles in the way of the actor's eye-line. If in the distance, just off set, people are watching the shoot within the actor's line of vision, he might not be able to concentrate. In this case, have the assistant director clear the actor's eye-line (Figure 15.1).

Figure 15.1 Controlling the people in Grand Central Station was next to impossible. Scene from *The Lunch Date.*

When we were doing the shot where she loses her wallet, we covered it from a few angles. One of the angles I wanted was a dolly shot through Grand Central, right through the main hall. No tracks, but we had a dolly with wheels. It would cover Scotty after she looks at the boards and starts walking, and suddenly Bernard Johnson would enter the frame as she's walking, as we're dollying, bump into her, and then we'd cover it.

Because I wanted to leave it ambiguous as to where she actually lost the wallet, I had to have her lose the wallet somewhere in the shot without giving it away how she lost it. We start off in a tight shot, Scotty takes out the wallet, she looks up, we start dollying, she starts moving. As she was walking, she was going to drop the wallet so you wouldn't notice it.

People say New Yorkers don't care. Well, every time we did this shot, somebody inevitably would yell out, "Hey, lady, you dropped your wallet." And one woman even was so bold as to see the wallet being dropped, not pick it up, but turn and yell to Scotty that she had dropped her wallet, and when Scotty didn't respond, she ran over to her and hit her on the shoulder while the camera was rolling!

So that shot eventually was preceded by my assistant director yelling out, "This is a movie. This lady is going to drop her wallet. Please don't pick it up!"

Adam

In terms of position, that was the AD's job. He was just watching to make sure people hit the same marks, looked in the same way, that the screen directions were right. And he had no problem doing that because his basic function was just to make sure we were on schedule, that we were moving on to the next shot, that the kids were either there or not there as they should be, and that was it.

Howard

Apple Boxes

A common actor-to-lens adjustment is for height. An actor who is much shorter than his partner might need to be raised slightly in a two-shot or over-the-shoulder shot. Apple boxes, which are wooden boxes of various heights, enable the DP to put an actor at the required level so he can be in the same frame as the other performers (Figure 15.2).

Locations

An actor working on a complete set or in a location knows where he is and how his character would use the space. The art department works its miracles to make a set look the way the script says it should. However, the art department only takes care of the area that the camera will see.

Our last shooting day was in the restaurant. The first thing in the morning, we were setting up the equipment, and Scotty comes in. She looks around and sees the pushcarts and the things hanging from the ceiling. She sees the whole messy room. She comes over and says, "Adam, I have to talk to you." She has a very concerned look on her face. I say, "Scotty, what's wrong?" She says, "I've been trying, but I just don't see how my character would eat in a place like this!" I said, "Don't worry, you're only going to see the clean part in the shot."

Adam

But the most important point we can make about eyeline is that the camera must see the actor's eyes. This small part of the frame (bigger in XCU) is a shining star that attracts the audiences attention. Cheat if necessary to ensure the camera can see the actor's eyes. If an actor is standing under an overhead light, or if they have a deep eye socket under a protruding brow, shine light directly into the actor's eyes to make sure they are exposed.

Hitting Marks

It is often awkward for an actor to move in such a way as to play to the camera. Besides performing, the actor might be required to walk and stop at a particular point, called a *mark*. If the actor overshoots his mark, he might go out of the frame or out of focus. Grips sometimes place sandbags at the actor's final stopping position. This enables the actor to walk to his mark, feel the bag with his feet, and not have to look down.

The Director as Audience

In the theater, the rapport between the audience and the performer has a profound effect on the energy level and direction of the performance. In a film or video, the actor plays for the director. She alone knows how all the little bits and pieces will come together in the editing room, and she evaluates the performance. In this relationship, it is important to keep in mind that actors need feedback. The director's attention is always divided between cast and crew. Make sure that the actor feels that he is your priority.

Figure 15.2 Apple boxes have many uses, including adding height to actors.

DIRECTING ACTORS

Novice directors often give actors too much direction. You cannot request that the actor be angry, compassionate, and ironic at the same time. A good suggestion is to rehearse the scene first for anger, and then rehearse again, letting the actor add any other emotions that the scene requires. The beats of a scene are built like this: little by little, layer by layer.

If an actor is having difficulty creating a particular emotion, try speaking in terms of *what the actor wants* rather than how he is supposed to feel. Actors usually respond more effectively when given positive actions in a scene rather than results like "being angry" or "being sad." In the breakdown chapter (Chapter 3),

we broke down the scene from *The Lunch Date* into specific actions that created such responses as anger, frustration, and even sadness. The actions you come up with will create the circumstances for the feelings you would like to arise.

As she directs, the director must take into consideration the technical aspects of the performance. At a certain point in the scene, the actor must hit a specific place on the set where a particular light will illuminate his face. Again, build the sequence beat by beat. This allows the actor to memorize the specific beats, the camera requirements, and the order in which they come.

The Director's Tools

The director can use camera, lights, and editing to help shape a performance. The camera can magnify a performance in a closeup, or it can distance the audience with an extreme long shot. Unlike the theater, film and video acting requires little or no projection, and the camera is very unkind to overacting. If the director is dissatisfied with an actor's interpretation of his character, she might opt to shoot the actor from a distance and avoid closeups in difficult acting scenes, even if she had planned closeups in her storyboards.

Lighting can also be employed to disguise a weak performance. Imagine a scene where the actor is in a shadow. The audience's imagination will fill in a great deal of information that the actor does not provide. The director can control the performance even more by having the character to whom the actor is speaking well lit, so that the audience concentrates on that character's reaction to the dialogue.

Types of Characters

There are three types of script characters with which the director must be concerned: background, secondary, and primary characters.

Background Characters

Background characters, also referred to as *extras* or *atmosphere*, are the characters that fill out and populate the frame but have no direct relationship to the main players. Background characters "people" the sequence and represent the world of the story.

The presence or absence of background players contributes to the story. Imagine *The Lunch Date* without Grand Central Station teeming with people from all walks of life. What would the luncheonette scene in *The Lunch Date* be like with customers at every table?

Imagine, for example, that a scene takes place in a crowded bar:

INT. BAR—NIGHT
Joe enters the bar. He sees the love of his life, Amy, sitting at a table across the room. The bar is smoky and crowded. Joe winds his way through the crowd toward Amy's table.

It would be difficult to stage this scene as written without people to fill the barroom. If staged with only the main characters, this scene would say something very different from what the scriptwriter intended, and it would project a surreal quality.

The types of people in the background will tell the audience a lot about the bar. Is it in a large urban setting or in a small Midwestern town? Does it cater to an upscale, middle-class, or lower-class clientele? Are the patrons working people or retirees? These decisions are important.

The extras, who are traditionally directed by the assistant director, must create the illusion that they are chatting (or whatever) without making any noise. Nothing should interfere with the dialogue of the foreground action. Therefore, they must act in silence. The extras mime their noisy actions. They clap without clapping, clink glasses in a toast without allowing the glasses to touch, and throw their heads back in a laugh without making any noise. Later, in postproduction, the sound editor will add the sound of clapping, glasses clinking, and belly laughs.

If the scene requires the extras to dance, the sound recordist can play some appropriate music before the take and then shut it off before the director calls for action. This way, the extras share the same rhythm and appear to be dancing to the same beat.

Extras must maintain continuity within a scene. If, when Amy rises from her stool to greet Joe in the bar, a dancing couple stops to return to their table, they must do so in every take from every angle. The assistant director often calls, "Roll sound . . . roll camera . . . background action." Then when the director is ready, she calls, "Action." The assistant director and the script supervisor watch the extras closely to ensure that they perform consistently throughout the sequence.

Secondary Characters

Secondary characters are those characters who have several scenes, one scene, one line, or even only an interaction with the main characters. Unlike the back-ground players, who are usually instructed by the assistant director merely to stop and go on cue, the secondary players need specific instruction from the director.

INT. BAR—NIGHT
Joe enters the bar. He sees the love of his life, Amy, sitting at a table across the room. The bar is smoky and crowded. Joe winds his way through the crowd toward Amy's table. Joe passes by a coworker who shakes his hand and whispers something that makes Joe laugh. Another person at the table, Sam, pulls Joe aside.
                    SAM
Watch out for Amy. She's pretty angry.

In this scene, the coworker and Sam are not extras, but secondary characters. In the luncheonette scene in *The Lunch Date*, the cook is also a secondary character (Figure 15.3).

Primary Characters

The director's main job is to work with the primary characters who motivate and act out the plot. The audience should care about their lives. There are many different acting styles, and it behooves the director to blend them all into a convincing whole.

If the project is well cast, the director might expect the cast to perform with a minimum of direction. If working with less talented or less experienced actors, the director might have to rehearse the actors both off and on the set until the dramatic points of the scene are clear and solid. She might have to shoot many takes and work with the actors to improve each take before moving on to the next setup.

I could do things on the set, like say, "This is just after you lost your wallet, and this is going to happen." And Scotty would know where she was in terms of the character's emotions, but she'd also be able to divert from things and stay open. It was interesting. One time I was going over that shot where she is crying, after losing her wallet, and I said, "How did you find that? What were you going through?" And she said, "It was easy for me because the location gave me everything." She didn't have to draw something out of a bad childhood experience. She just was in the moment there. She's a great actress, so I was very lucky.

Adam

Figure 15.3 In this scene from *The Lunch Date,* the cook is a secondary character.

Continuity

An extremely important aspect of the shoot is maintaining continuity. Continuity is the uninterrupted succession of events. On the screen, a character appears to be moving from scene A to scene B to scene C, and so on. However, the norm is to shoot out of continuity: first B, then A, then C.

> *I tried to stick close to continuity, but where things like locations became important, we would go away from continuity. For example, as I mentioned before, we were only allowed to shoot on the platforms [at Grand Central Station] when the supervisor came down. So suddenly in the middle of the day, we would have to stop and do that.*
>
> Adam

In scene A, the actor has on a blue shirt. In scene B, she changes clothes and puts on a yellow dress. Scene C finds her in the same yellow dress. This is the progression in the script. The progression of the shoot requires you to shoot scene B first, with the actor in the yellow dress. If the next scene is A, to sustain script continuity, the actor must change to the blue shirt. The wardrobe designer or dresser maintains the continuity of the costumes the actors wear. This is accomplished with the aid of script notes, breakdown sheets, and snapshots of the actors in their various outfits.

> *Continuity was the AD's department. I felt the film was so well scheduled that the production manager, the AD, and the DP all understood what was supposed to happen each moment. It was fixed in our minds that each of us could have caught the other in a major continuity mistake. Thus, the AD, besides running the set, was handling the continuity. It would have been nice to have a continuity person, but it wasn't necessary. Except for the fantasy costumes, the kids were always in the same dumpy gym clothes, including the same socks with their names on them, so we knew they were getting the same costumes.*
>
> Howard

Here is another example of continuity: The shooting schedule calls for a shot in which the actor crosses his legs when he sits in a chair. Later that day, the director shoots a wide shot in which the actor walks into the room, sits down on the chair, and crosses his legs. Which leg did he cross in the previous shot? Will the two actions match in the editing room?

Script supervisors watch constantly for the matching of liquid in glasses, hand movements, lengths of cigarettes, eye-line, and any action. Actors need constant reminders of how to repeat the actions of a preceding take and at what point in the scene these actions happen. If there is no continuity person on the set, it becomes the duty of all parties to watch for this critical aspect of the shoot.

Figure 15.4 Working with children can be quite challenging. Child actor receiving direction during the filming of *Truman.*

Overlapping Action

When possible, the director should watch for places to overlap action. Action makes for a very smooth cut because the audience is concentrating on the character's movement in the frame. A cut from movement to movement is less obvious than a cut from a static frame to a static frame. For example, suppose that an actor sits down in a medium shot. When the director calls cut and moves the camera in for the closeup shot, she should have the actor "sit into" the shot in case she or her editor wants to make a cut on the action.

Special Situations

Children and Animals

If your script calls for a child or a pet or wild animal, you will face unique production problems (Figure 15.4). Children come with parents; animals come with trainers. There is a difference, however, between directing a child with little or no experience and directing a professional. There are children who have been acting since they were very young. They understand how to relate to the camera and can take direction. Even so, there are stricter time limits for how long they can work in a day, but the work they do will be professional.

Working with animals or with small children who are nonactors can be time consuming. Allow a grace period in your schedule for these tricky performers. Be prepared to simplify or cut. An uncooperative dog can be shot so that it is out of the frame. The actors' reaction and the sound of a barking, panting dog will give the illusion that the dog is in the scene.

Our single most difficult problem—besides the kids' stamina and interest—was the boy who played Truman. It wasn't an ego problem; it was an age and maturity problem. He was an eight-year-old boy, kind of hyperactive, who didn't want to be an actor. He got shanghaied into this because it sounded like fun. He looked right, and I convinced his parents.

He had never been away from home. His first night on location, he cried for an hour on the phone to his mom; he was frightened. He was also embarrassed to have to stand in front of all these people and pretend to be something he really wasn't. His natural reaction in dealing with pressure and insecurity was to giggle or to smile. Even though he had been to rehearsals, this was different. It was no longer just him and me, but a group of people with the camera rolling, everybody staring. He would smile or giggle or lose his composure halfway through the take. We were burning up so much film we had to buy extra.

Howard

Consider the child labor laws in the state in which you are working. The Screen Actors Guild can be helpful in determining proper work hours. Actors under 18 years of age may have to be tutored and depending on the age work fewer hours than adults. A baby, for instance, is only allowed to work 10 minutes at a time, which is why so many twin babies are cast, allowing a director to have the "same" baby for 20 minutes each hour.

Stunts and Nudity

Actors will do almost anything you ask of them with the exception of stunts and nudity. Although some

Figure 15.5 Actors are recorded prior to shooting in animation.

actors can perform their own stunts, it is imperative to employ a stunt double for dangerous sequences. If an actor is injured while performing a stunt, you might have to shut down production. Besides performing stunts, stunt people often can inform the DP about the best angles for recording the stunt.

Nudity is a delicate issue. If the story requires a nude scene, feel free to ask the actor to perform in it. If he agrees, understand that actors often balk just before the shot. Do not panic. This is why there are body doubles. Simply redesign your shots to use the actor as much as you can, and then use the body double for long, shadowy, or close shots in which the character's face is not visible.

Tips for Directing

- Novice directors sometimes feel uncomfortable working with actors for the first time. Their language and work methods can be intimidating. Be honest and upfront with your talent. Do not try to sound as if you know what you are doing if you do not. Keep your direction simple and to the point. The actors will most likely help you.
- Make all the actors feel they are important, no matter how small or large their part. Regardless of their screen time, each character is integral to the whole. After you call "Cut" at the end of a shot, do not ignore the actors or seem dissatisfied with their work.
- Resist the temptation to make each take perfect. A film is a series of moments. Part of one take may flow better with the part of another rather than using all the material from a single take. Watching each take either on set or on the video monitor tends to identify the take as a whole, rather than as a part.

- Shoot a scene as many times as you feel is necessary. If the scene is not working, shake things up: Shoot from another angle, change the blocking, shoot reactions, or break for lunch and come back to the scene later.
- Some actors need several takes to warm up, others get it on the first. Seek a take that allows all the actors in the scene to be at their best.
- Shoot the rehearsal. Often the best take is the first because it is fresh and spontaneous.
- Half your battle will be won if you cast well.

Interviewing for Documentaries

In a documentary, the performance comes from either the subject's actions in life or from her responses to the director's questions. Interviewing is an art form. Here are some suggestions for obtaining the best and most informative responses from the subject:

- Create a mood or setting that makes the subject feel at ease.
- Get the subject talking. The words will be edited at a later stage.
- Ask questions about the subject's personal experience, rather than questions of a general nature.
- Ask questions in an order that will lead the subject to reveal herself.
- Don't put words in the subject's mouth.
- Be patient.

If you have researched your subject thoroughly, you should be able to adjust your questions during the interview to ensure stimulating responses.

I let the women informally talk during the preliminary group meetings. I took notes after each session so that I could elicit those same responses again. You figure out the questions you need to ask to catalyze the stories and sentiments you may have heard in a preinterview. In Little People, *we met people a year before the shoot. In the interview, we could say, "When we were here last year, I remember you saying things about how you felt your parents felt guilty that you were born a dwarf. Could you talk about that?" And generally, they would discuss the same things we heard a year earlier. We all have our repertoire. It's reassuring to know that you can get a story again by asking the right question, but it's also important to be open to new and unheard responses.*

Jan

Interview Questions

Thirteen women were interviewed in *Mirror Mirror*. Filmmaker Jan Krawitz asked four questions of each woman, using a different camera setup for each question. Two sets were built in a single studio. In one set, each subject was seated in a row of theater chairs, surrounded by naked mannequins. Jan asked two questions in this location, one filmed in a medium closeup and the second filmed in a wider shot. The second set required the subject to stand in front of a mural that depicted the "Ideal Proportion, Female." Jan asked the following questions:

1. Seated mannequin set, wide shot: "At what point in your life did you first become aware of your 'body image'? Was this awareness catalyzed by a particular incident?"

2. Seated mannequin set, medium closeup: "How do you feel people respond to you or make assumptions about you based solely on your physicality?"

3. Standing mural set, wide shot: "Describe your body from head to toe, commenting on specific body parts—which parts please you and which displease you?"

4. Standing mural set, medium shot: "If you could redesign your body, what would it look like?"

Questions 1 and 2 resulted in distinct answers as predicted, so the responses to these questions were cut into two distinct sequences, using the jump cut aesthetic in which the composition and background remain constant while the subject changes in the foreground.

In the editing stage, Jan realized that there was often considerable overlap between the responses to questions 3 and 4. She ultimately constructed a single mural sequence in which the shots cut back and forth between the two compositions, dictated solely by the text of the interview.

It was different with Mirror Mirror *because here I had the four set questions, which is different from the way I usually interview. I generally allow the conversation to flow in directions that might not be preordained. I think it's important not to get too locked into your agenda. You want to remain open to a digression that could be fruitful for the project.*

You have to really listen to the person and gently guide the direction of the interview. You can't be sitting there worrying about your next question or how much film is running through the camera and how long they're taking to answer each question. You really have to listen because it's in those moments that you might hear something that causes you to ask something completely different from what you thought your next question would be.

Jan

PRODUCER
Accommodate

As long as the work is going well and the actors are comfortable, the producer is not involved in directing the actors. However, he does become involved as a mediator if a problem arises.

SOCIALIZING

The director and crew are busy all day long, but the producer has the opportunity to socialize with the cast and make them feel comfortable. He can lift their morale if they are feeling low and cue them on their lines. The time spent with the actors between scenes can be productive if their spirits are buoyed by the interaction.

CONTRACTS AND DEAL MEMOS

Even if the talent is working for free, a simple contract or deal memo between the production company and the artist is standard operating procedure. The following information should be included in this document:

- The amount or rate you will pay or any alternate compensation such as deferred money or a copy of the film or tape
- The "on or about" dates to lock the actor into your schedule
- Any unusual requests such as nudity or stunts

On or about is a legal term that allows the production company a grace period of two or three days on either side of the start date. If you are scheduled to start shooting on May 10 but for some reason do not start until May 13, the contract with the actor is still valid. If you postpone until June 15, though, the contact is void and will have to be renegotiated.

A release is required of everyone who performs in your project. The deal memo or letter acts as your release. It gives you permission to use the actor's picture and voice in your project. The release is a very important document. If not handled properly, it might adversely affect your ability to secure distribution for the picture. (See Chapter 19, "Distribution," for more information.)

The longest day you can employ an actor is 12 hours. Violating the 12-hour day or the 12-hour turn-around can result in penalties to your production. It is also common sense to make sure actors are not too tired to perform. Often the temptation for a director is to shoot until the scene is completed, no matter what the consequences. A responsible producer can help a director find a reasonable solution.

As long as you honor the terms outlined in the deal memo, the actor should be content. If you try to violate the conditions detailed in the memo or exploit the artist, you may incur problems. For example, if you ask an actor to play a scene in the nude without having discussed the scene with him or written the request into the deal memo, the actor has every right to balk.

Consider the following questions when preparing a deal memo:

- Are there any production dates that conflict with the actor's personal schedule?
- Should you ask the actor to provide her own wardrobe? Will you dry-clean the garments after production?
- If you will supply meals, does the actor have special dietary requirements?
- Are you obligated to provide the actor with a video copy on completion?

Wrap Out

Once a production has been completed, the producer ties up any loose ends with the talent. The SAG account must be closed, the actor's own wardrobe cleaned and returned, and time sheets handed in.

Firing Talent

After hiring and rehearsing the actors, it might seem strange to consider firing them, and, in fact, actors are rarely fired once shooting has begun. Everyone behind the camera can be replaced at a moment's notice, but to fire an actor means reshooting all the shots in which he appears. Firing someone has catastrophic implications on the budget and on morale. Still, if a casting mistake has been made, it is better to face it and replace the actor as soon as possible. Actors cannot be changed in the editing room.

KEY POINTS

- Respect the actors.
- Do not call them to the set until you are ready for them.
- If a scene or shot is not working, rehearse it until it is right.
- After each take, acknowledge the actors' efforts in a positive way.

part three

Postproduction

This part takes a traditional approach to the editing process. The book is predicated on the director–producer relationship. This part is no different. We have also introduced the editor to the mix. We will call this a professional model, one that mirrors the history of motion pictures. We will follow the more professional path, but we recognize that many of you will be doing it alone and acknowledge the pitfalls of doing so. In fact, the beginner/student reading this book may be functioning as the writer, director, producer, and editor.

Your film or video is now shot, or "in the can." The task of assembling and polishing the final product can now begin. During postproduction, the pictures and sounds that have been recorded are shaped to tell your story. It is time to create the "final draft" of the script, the draft that is pieced together with film or tape.

Director

During preproduction, the director translates the screenplay into storyboards and the storyboards into a shot list. During principal photography, she transforms the shot list into dailies. This material is now ready to be delivered to the editing room for assembly.

Postproduction is an exciting time. It is certainly a more relaxed phase than principal photography. Shaping the material one on one with an editor is an intense and exhilarating adventure for the director. She comes to the editing room filled with the enthusiasm and experiences of the shoot.

The final picture will only be as good as the dailies with which the editor works. A finished project can be made only from in-focus, well-exposed shots; it is not created from ideas, wishes, cut lines, or the big shot that got away (unless you are able to reshoot). Guided by the director's vision of the story, the editor's role is to make a seamless series of cuts so that the picture flows from one shot to the next. The goal is to produce the best picture possible.

If there is one rule of thumb for the director at this stage, it is to become ruthlessly objective with the footage as quickly as possible. It is natural to fall in love with what you've shot, making it difficult to cut anything out. However, to give the film or video a pace, the raw material must be shaped and trimmed. It is all right to hold onto footage for a while, but there comes a time when the editor must eliminate anything that does not propel the story forward.

Producer

Much of what an audience perceives on the screen is created during the postproduction process, when the raw material accumulated during the shoot is transformed into a product. This final phase involves thousands of details, a multitude of decisions, and many complex technical steps. Fortunately, it doesn't involve nearly as many people as production, so the overhead is manageable. However, it does demand a detailed plan and schedule.

The producer must always be aware of the big picture. He should understand the financial repercussions of every creative decision, keep track of all the expenses, and even be looking ahead for fund-raising opportunities. Time is still money, and though the daily rates are lower now, postproduction might seem to take forever. If the production phase is akin to a

235

sprint, postproduction is more like a marathon. Each project has many variables, so it is difficult to estimate how long a project will take to edit. The producer's goal is to surround the director with the right creative team to complete the project. This not only includes the right editor, but the entire postproduction crew: the sound effects team, and if appropriate, the composer.

The importance of sound and music to a picture should not be ignored. Having been brought up in a predominantly visual environment, novice film- or videomakers can distinguish a wonderful camera move or visual effect more readily than they can identify an effective sound or piece of music. Easily seduced by illusion, many novices do not spend enough time deconstructing all the elements of a film or video, and the contribution of aural elements eludes them. After the pictures and dialogue are cut, however, sound and music communicate a tremendous amount of information. Pictures can be only half the story; sound and music flesh out the experience.

IMPACT OF HOME SYSTEMS

Technology has compressed the process and condensed the systems that are able to perform the production tasks that used to take place in more organized spaces. Students and independents have access to technology to complete the picture and sound editing in a small apartment, especially picture editing. Avid Express Pro and Apple's Final Cut are both software-based systems that have taken the place of $100,000 systems only a few short years ago. The film editor Walter Murch *(The Godfather, Apocalypse Now)* cut *Cold Mountain* on Final Cut Pro and several off the shelf G-4's. He sifted through 600,000 feet of film to create a 2½-hour film on a system that any student can buy for less than $1,000.

From a producing standpoint, this gives the director/editor unlimited time (without cost of renting a facility) to experiment with the structure of the film or video. The downside is that beginners can get lost. Someone who writes, directs, and edits may quickly lose any objectivity to whether or not the piece works. Living with a film in your own home may seem convenient, but distant. One who spends hours in a small room staring at screens making sense out of hundreds or maybe thousands of images can only succeed by enlarging the scope of the process to include those who will view various cuts and versions of the material. It is the producer's responsibility to see that this happens.

THE POSTPRODUCTION PROCESS

All films go through certain basic postproduction steps. Video projects go through the same artistic process, but with some technical variations. The growth and development of computer-based nonlinear editing systems and the integration of digital technology have altered the way film and video are now being edited. There are filmmakers who never leave the film domain. They shoot, edit, and finish on film. In fact, one might argue that this age-old process is simpler. There are those who edit video in the traditional linear manner. However, nonlinear processes have mostly replaced that technology.

> Film editing, c. 1900
> Talking pictures arrive, 1928
> Analog audiotape editing, c. 1945
> Videotape editing, 1956
> Videotape editing with timecode, 1970
> Digital disk-based audio editing, 1985
> Digital disk-based picture editing, c. 1989

For almost 80 years, thousands of films were edited without the aid of a computer. It is important to acknowledge this fact. The technology that has now taken over the professional world has only been around for a relatively short time.

We are not going to argue about which is better. The fact is that the film and television industries have converted to the new technology. University film and television programs are now training their students with the nonlinear editing machines. Those who have worked primarily in video have easily adapted. It is those who come from a film background who have been challenged making the transition. It is for that reason that most of the computer-based nonlinear systems that have been developed were designed to be "film friendly" in their interface. Many of the terms were borrowed from film editing.

The merging of these two media has opened up a realm of possibilities for the beginning film- and videomaker. These are some of the options:

- Shoot film, edit film, finish on film (traditional film)
- Shoot video, edit video (linear), finish on video (traditional video)
- Shoot film, edit digital, finish on film
- Shoot film, edit digital, finish on video
- Shoot video, edit digital, finish on video
- Shoot video, edit video, finish on DVD
- Shoot video, edit digital, finish on film

- Shoot film/video, edit digital, finish digital (Internet/CD-ROM/New Media)

The merging of these two media through computer and digital technology has become more complicated. The choices seem overwhelming and confusing. The traditional "filmmaker" must not only adapt to a completely new editing machine, she must also have a basic understanding of video. Part of this is an understanding of the glue that holds film, sound, and video together: timecode. Timecode was developed in the 1970s to facilitate accurate video editing (this is mentioned in the following chapter). It is also the key ingredient that enables the filmmaker to shoot on film, edit digitally, and match back to film. This can be a complicated process because of the different frame rates of film and video (24 frames per second versus 29.97 frames per second).

The positive side is that there are now many more choices, and some are cost-effective for the beginner. The low cost of shooting video and the speed and flexibility of computer nonlinear systems are attractive. And if you still want the "look" of film, the line between film and video has narrowed. Cameras have filters that produce the "film look"; 24p video cameras can duplicate the frame rate of film; and NLE systems (see Glossary) have filters to simulate the film look as well. There are also tape-to-film transfers (the expensive part of this equation). The decision to follow a particular path has to do with aesthetics, money, availability, and time.

What haven't changed are the steps. Technology has aided the process, but certain creative and technical steps still must be adhered to. In previous editions, we have started this part with a comprehensive review of traditional postproduction steps for film and linear video editing. For some beginners, it may be important to have an understanding of the first two, because nonlinear digital editing is based on the foundation of traditional film and video editing. Interested readers will find this discussion on the companion Web site for this book at www.focalpress.com/companions.

Technology is a tool; it is not a magic wand. Students and beginners have to learn how to take advantage of its power and understand that some parts of the process will never change.

SHOOT FILM – EDIT DIGITAL – FINISH FILM

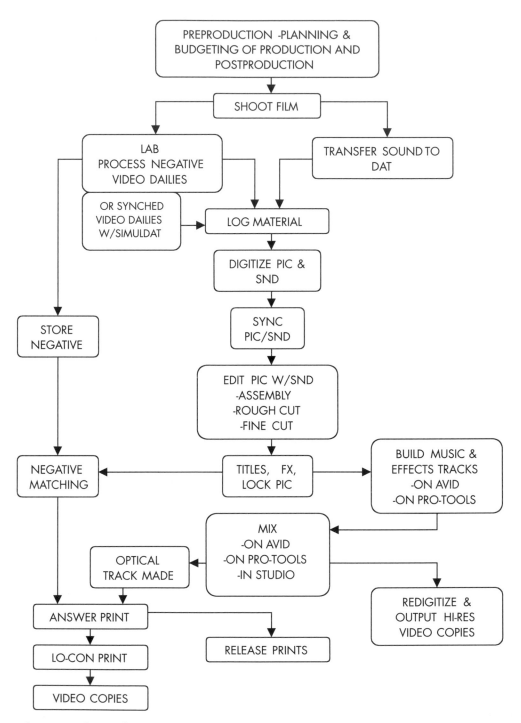

Figure III.1 Film postproduction flowchart.

chapter sixteen

Pix Postproduction

Don't force the film into preconceived notions. Let the film find itself. The same thing goes for narrative. Sometimes the script doesn't work.

Jan

DIRECTOR
Edit

Whether the director edits the film herself or collaborates with an editor, her vision for the material must now extend itself to the editing room. Much of the editing process is trial and error. Success is usually attributed to 10 percent inspiration and 90 percent perspiration. It is only through perseverance and patience that the project will come together.

There were two moments that I felt some satisfaction, which both had to do with the salad sequence. When I started shooting the salad sequence, and then when I started editing it together, I felt, "There's something here, I don't know what it is, but something is working here."

Adam

THE DIRECTOR AS EDITOR

Most beginning directors cut their own projects. They feel attached to the footage and want to shape the final product themselves. Physically joining the shots to tell a story can be very enlightening. The director can learn whether her coverage was adequate to tell the story. Does she have enough shots? Do these shots cut together? Proper coverage gives the editor choices in case he needs to strengthen a moment, enhance a performance, or telescope the story. By reflecting on how each scene is approached visually, the director can learn what worked, what didn't, and why. She can apply this awareness to her next project.

Equally valuable to the writer–director is how the structure of the script holds up as the first cut comes together. She might discover that certain moments were overstated and that others were not stated at all. Seeing ideas realized on film is an important part of learning dramatic and visual writing. Even if the director discovers she doesn't like editing, it is an important learning experience for her to edit at least one project herself.

However, the director as editor does present some inherent problems. Directors can exhibit a possessiveness that will hinder their ability to be objective about the raw material. This condition is exacerbated if they have written the piece. Being emotionally attached to the project can impair the director's ability to "see the forest for the trees" and make tough editing decisions.

The advantage to editing the film myself was that I was learning the process. The disadvantage was that I found myself losing myself, my perspective on the film, . . . because I started concentrating on each specific cut rather than on the whole picture. You start fiddling around with a frame here, a frame there, which becomes insignificant compared to whether the sequence is moving.

Adam

The director need not personally edit her own film or video to put her creative stamp on the material. Many first-time directors get bogged down by the mechanics of editing and organization. It inhibits their creative drive and may have a negative impact on the outcome of the project. An editor can bring objectivity to the process. The editor's skills and creative input free the director to concentrate on aesthetic concerns. The editor is the technical guide who implements the director's ideas. We discuss the value of having an editor on the project in the producer part of this chapter.

There are several other reasons for having someone else do the physical editing. First, the director is usually exhausted after the film is wrapped. The last thing she wants to do is run into an editing room to start logging the footage. There is no reason to slow things down while the director recuperates. Second, the director needs to step away from the material to gain some objectivity before she begins to edit. If the director does decide to edit, she should try to delay editing for several weeks while she winds down from production mode and is fully able to concentrate on the task at hand.

THE EDITOR

The editor is a craftsperson, technician, and artist who has the patience and facility to create order out of thousands of images. Beginning directors can learn much about the craft of editing and storytelling from an experienced editor. The editor's manipulation of sounds and images is often needed to realize the creative potential of the material. The script might be recorded on the set, but the film or video is built in the cutting room.

For many directors, the craft of editing has been an effective stepping stone. Robert Wise edited *Citizen Kane* before he went on to direct *The Set-Up, West Side Story,* and *The Sound of Music.* David Lean, director of *Lawrence of Arabia* and *Passage to India,* was one of England's premier editors before being hired to co-direct *In Which We Serve* with Noel Coward. Hal Ashby was one of Hollywood's better known editors before being given the chance to direct a small picture called *The Landlord.* He went on to direct *Harold and Maude, Coming Home,* and *Being There.* George Lucas, a talented director, preferred for many years to work solely in postproduction. These outstanding filmmakers spent years practicing the art and craft of storytelling while fixing the mistakes of the directors with whom they worked. They learned about rhythm and pacing and how to control it—all the tools a director must master.

THE EDITING PROCESS

The Creative Steps to Editing

One of the major differences between production and post is the lack of structure. The production period is structured by the script, the budget, and the shooting schedule. Money may also define the boundaries of how long you have to edit. In this case, you have as long as you can afford unless the producer can raise more money.

But there is no equivalent to the shooting schedule in postproduction. Certain things must happen but not always in a set order. The film is finished when you say it is. It may take a week, a month, or even a year in some cases.

For beginners who are editing on a system at home or at a film school, time or money may not be an issue. Either way, we want to offer an approach that developed over the years from traditional film and video editing. This is not a paint-by-numbers solution. Each film is tailor made and each has its own creative challenges. This is a road map with specific benchmarks and certain tried-and-true techniques that we hope will help you navigate your way through the postproduction process so you can make the best project possible from your footage.

What Is Editing?

There is an analogy to this process in scriptwriting. The axiom "Writing is rewriting" can be applied to editing as well. You are, in fact, writing your film with real images and sounds. Remember how many drafts were required before you created the final draft of your screenplay? Just as many if not more might be required before realizing your project. This time you are creating the final draft of the script, the draft that will be the film or video that audiences will see.

There are a few basic concepts that we believe can help this process along. Many believe that editing is just about cutting out the bad parts. This is a common misconception. Think of editing as fashioning a beautiful building out of the raw materials from the set. You are not just eliminating what is unnecessary; you are constructing a work of art.

It will involve letting go of the script, what happened on the set, what you should of, could of, but didn't get in the can. You will get the most out of what you shot by listening to what the images tell you. It can and should be an exciting journey of discovery.

Screening the Dailies (Working with an Editor)

At the end of the second day of principal photography, traditional film directors screen the first day's dailies to choose selected takes. It usually takes a day to process and print the film. More time might be required if the laboratory is far away or if it develops your type of stock only when there is ample material to justify filling a bath. (Film is developed by placing the negative in a bath of photographic chemicals.) Video dailies, on the other hand, can be screened immediately because they do not require chemical development.

The editor participates in screening the dailies. This initial session allows the director to offer immediate feedback about how she would like to approach the first cut of the film, which moments to use, and which to avoid. The director's notes will be the editor's guide, and he assembles the first cut of the film. Here are some suggestions that will ultimately help the editing process.

Take notes on all your first impressions. This is the only time you'll see the footage as the audience will ultimately see it. Record all the good moments of performance, camera moves, and shots. Also record how these moments made you feel. These moments and the emotions attached to them will become the ultimate building blocks of each scene. Beyond the script these moments will become your ultimate guide the structure of your story.

Take notes on any technical problems in the frame such as dirt, scratches, exposure, and focus problems. Let production know if they have to reshoot something before they tear down that set.

Finding the Story

The Loose Cut—The Assembly

First, the story is put together in the order indicated by the script. This loose cut sometimes includes only the master shots pieced together one after the other. It allows the editor, director, and producer to experience the flow of the story and gain a sense of the direction the film is taking. Some directors opt to skip this step and move right to a rough cut.

The Rough Cut

The rough cut is an attempt to view the picture as a whole with traditional editorial techniques. It includes shots to establish location, closeups to provide emphasis, insert shots to orchestrate the story, and dissolves to show the passage of time. This cut is a difficult one to view because it shows the story, yet lacks music, sound effects, and overlapping dialogue. In short, the entire sound design will not be present to assist the viewer in appreciating the full impact and flow of the film. The rough cut is strictly a visual cut with key dialogue.

The rough cut should follow the continuity of the script exactly. This is an important rule to follow. There should be no deviations, even though obvious changes might be required. One of the primary goals of this first cut is to evaluate whether the structure of the original script works. It isn't until you decide on the structure of your scenes that the true editing begins. The goal is to lock your structure in the quickest and most efficient way possible. Revelations that affect the rest of the editing process will come from viewing this cut.

I did a shot where I thought I needed to build up more to the character's anxiety about being in this unfamiliar world. So I shot a quick little scene where Scotty, the actress, goes into the women's bathroom at Grand Central. I don't know if you've ever seen what that's like, but it's horrible. I did a shot where she walks in and then backs out two seconds later. But by the time I got to putting together the film, the scene was unnecessary.

Adam

Guidelines for the Rough Cut

Speed in Editing. Editing a scene means using the images to create a rhythm that tells the story of the scene properly. Each scene forms a unit that, when joined with the other scenes, creates the rhythm of the entire film. The process of editing demands that the editor get into a rhythm of cutting. It is a visceral experience as much as an intellectual one. There is a direct relationship between the speed with which you cut and your ability to get in touch with and properly interpret the appropriate rhythm of any scene. You can't really know if a cut will work until you make it.

When in doubt, make the cut and move on. You can do it over if it doesn't work. There is no point agonizing over each cut—excessive thought about it is counterproductive; it only slows you down. Work quickly, and trust your judgment. The more quickly you make one cut, the sooner you can move on to the next one. This is especially important at this stage, when subtlety is secondary to seeing a first cut of the film.

It's hard to give it up, to know when you're done. I think the same thing probably happens in every process. Certainly with writing, you always feel like you can redo one scene, get a better line here, or whatever. Certainly, when you're shooting, there were more things you felt like you wanted to get. But with editing, you can tinker and tinker and tinker and tinker.

Adam

Rough Cut Editing Tips

- Take out any extraneous sounds on the track that will be distracting, such as the director saying "Action" or "Cut."
- Use straight edits when cutting dialogue. Do not begin to overlap dialogue yet. It is not necessary.
- Do not insert sound from other takes.
- Do not waste time fine-tuning scenes until they are seen in the context of the whole. You must have a sense of the rhythm and tempo of the complete piece before adjusting each scene.

Each stage is about discovering the story because you have what you think is the film on paper, in your script, and suddenly, as soon as you start casting it, as soon as you pick a location, suddenly what's on the paper gets more specific, so it starts changing. Then you start editing the film, and it starts changing once again. What I originally thought would be the film was nothing like what it turned out to be. Yet, I think you accept that. You don't accept necessarily the end result, but you accept the process. I think it's an interesting process. If you keep yourself open to it, you can make interesting discoveries.

Adam

STUDENTS

It is common for students or beginners who are editing their own projects to get bogged down with the editing process because with each shot, they are reliving the details (good and bad) of the shoot. Ridding oneself of the emotional baggage from the set is an important step to evaluating the footage in the context of the film. This is an experience an editor will not have. An editor is not involved with the shoot and doesn't care how long it took to execute a shot that may not be appropriate to tell the story properly. The director needs to think and act more like an editor and less like the director.

Analyzing the Rough Cut

You and the producer have just seen the rough cut, the first complete cut, of your film. Many feelings are evident in the room. You might feel depressed or exhilarated or something in between. You might even be in shock and ready to give up. Why? In this premier screening, you might make many discoveries:

- Do you have a story? Does it work?
- If you have a story, does the current structure work?
- If the story doesn't work, what can you do about it?
- Do you need to shoot more footage (if you can) to make the story work?
- Does the existing structure need to be severely edited?
- Do you need to come up with a new structure?

If the basic structure of the film works, you are off to the races. You can truly begin to edit the project. If not, you must focus on coming up with a new structure. Either way, you can put away the script. It has served its purpose. The film has now taken on a life of its own. Unless you can do more shooting, you must deal with the footage at hand.

I think I was ill when I saw my first cut. I thought it would never come together. I wondered how anybody could make a film out of all these bits and pieces of celluloid that didn't seem to add up to anything.

I remember thinking after the rough cut that it was not funny, that it was slow, and that it would never have any grace. It was really difficult to go in there the next day. I thought I had seen something that was unsavable and never going to work.

Howard

RESTRUCTURING THE PICTURE

An efficient way to preview what a different scene order might look like is to try it out on paper first. Reduce each scene to one line of description (similar to the one-liner in the scheduling process), and write down the order in which the scenes now appear in this version. You can also perform this paper cut with index cards taped to a wall. With this written overview, the creative team discusses possible variations before actually making another cut.

Paper edits can be used effectively any time you have a structural problem during the editing process. It is an efficient and time-saving device for previsualizing different structures without having to cut the film or tape.

> *I did a paper edit. I cut up the transcriptions and highlighted what I thought were the important phrases, so I had pages and pages with highlighted lines. Then I xeroxed it, so I had a master, and then I cut out the lines that looked good. I started doing a flowchart with them. I hung them on the wall and I would move them around, and I would read them out loud. If I cut from so and so saying, "I really hate my hips," to "My hips are the greatest thing since sliced bread," I could read them out loud and see what it would sound like before I actually made the cut.*
>
> Jan

SCREENING THE SECOND CUT

Screen a cut of the new structure. If the new version still doesn't work, the restructuring should have given you a clearer sense of what you need to try next. From this point, how long it will take to achieve a fine cut and picture lock will depend on a number of variables:

- How much productive time the editor can spend in the editing room
- Whether there are restrictions on money and the editor's availability
- How quickly the changes can be made after you've had a major screening and discussion

As in the first cut, prepare to be brutal with your cutting decisions. Avoid attachment to your footage. Don't worry about minor continuity problems. If you keep the story moving, no one will notice them. So what if there is a slight boom shadow? Only film professionals notice them, not the general audience—as long as they are engrossed in the story. Always cut for the performance.

Walter Murch is an editor, sound designer, and rerecording mixer of such films as *American Graffiti*, *The Godfather*, *Apocalypse Now*, and *The English Patient*. In his informative and inspiring book *In the Blink of an Eye*, he lays out his principles of what makes a good cut:

- Emotion
- Story

- Rhythm
- Eye-trace (concern with audience's focus of interest within the frame)
- Two-dimensional plane of screen
- Three-dimensional space of action
  He goes on to say:

> *For many years, particularly in the early years of sound film, you struggled to preserve continuity of three-dimensional space, and it was seen as a failure of rigor or skill to violate it. Jumping people around in space was just not done, except, perhaps, in extreme circumstances—fights or earthquakes—where there was a lot of violent action going on.*
>
> *I actually place this three-dimensional continuity at the bottom of a list of six criteria for what makes a good cut. At the top of the list is Emotion, the thing you come to last, if at all, at film school largely because it's the hardest thing to define and deal with. How do you want the audience to feel? If they are feeling what you want them to feel all the way through the film, you've done as much as you can ever do. What they finally remember is not the editing, not the camerawork, not the performances, not even the story—it's how they felt.*
>
> *An ideal cut (for me) is the one that satisfies all the six criteria at once. . . . Emotion, at the top of the list, is the thing you should preserve at all costs.*
>
> Walter Mulch

REFINING THE STORY

Editing Techniques

There are editing techniques you can use to smooth over rough spots, make transitions flow, and even perform miracles with a scene that refuses to work. These tricks range from standard editing techniques to less conventional solutions for editing problems. The film or video experience is an illusion. You might need to use a little smoke and mirrors once in a while to make the illusion complete.

In the end, all that matters is telling the story as best you can. Do not force the footage into what you would like it to be. Create the best from what you have, and build on that. The more you edit, the more confident you will become and the more you will trust your instincts. There can be great joy and satisfaction in solving a problem and in seeing your film or video come together, moment by moment and scene by scene, through hard work and perseverance.

At this point, logging notes made at the front end of the project can quickly become obsolete when the structure of the picture changes. With traditional film

Figure 16.1 Reaction shot from *The Lunch Date*.

and video methods, the editor is always scanning through material to look for a shot. Sometimes a shot that was cataloged for one context might now work for another. Keep all possibilities open when editing. You never know.

The following are some editing and transition principles to keep in mind and experiment with as you refine your story:

Dialogue Overlaps. A common device, when attempting to duplicate the normal speech patterns of people talking to one another, is to overlap dialogue and picture. This requires the use of the reaction shot—that is, showing the person whom the speaker is addressing, rather than the speaker. This way, we hear the dialogue while witnessing (and sharing) a reaction with the nonspeaking character.

Cutting on Movement. Cuts work well when they are made on a movement of some kind. For example, a cut made as a character sits down makes for a very smooth transition between shots. Even shots that have no logical connection with one another (and no continuity of space and time) can be cut smoothly with some movement in each shot to "mask" the cut—for example, the match cut of a cloud passing by the moon to a razor slicing a human eyeball.

Kinds of Cuts. A *cutaway* or *reaction* shot is a shot away from the action that can be used to cover discontinuities or to condense the action. An insert

shot serves the same purpose. Figures 16.1 and 16.2 are two examples from *The Lunch Date*.

Continuity. Do not be a slave to continuity. If you can't find the right reaction shot for a key dramatic moment in a sequence, look to another part of the scene for a shot you can "steal." It might be out of continuity, but as long as it works, why not use it? It might even be possible to steal a shot from an entirely different scene, as long as it was filmed in a similar location with matching light. If you are looking for a quiet reaction shot, try stealing a closeup of an actor the moment after the slate is pulled and the director calls "Action."

Dissolves. A *dissolve* is a cross-fading of two scenes to overlap images for dramatic or emotional effect. Dissolves can be short (8 to 16 frames) and called *soft cuts* or long (24, 32, 48, 64, or 96 frames) and called *lap dissolves*. Lap dissolves create the feeling of time passage.

FADES. A *fade* is a gradual picture transition from or to blackness. Fades can smooth out the transition from one scene to another and create the illusion that time has passed. It has the effect of closing "one chapter" and beginning another.

Sound Takes. For off-camera dialogue, look for the best line readings. It might be possible to combine parts of different readings of the same line as long as they are from the same aural perspective. That is,

Figure 16.2 Reaction shot from *The Lunch Date*.

the background sounds should be the same. Moving bits of sound around can solve many editing problems.

New Lines. The addition of a line or phrase often adds a piece of exposition that wasn't clear in the script. A line can be added to the beginning or end of a speech while the actor is either turned away from or completely off-camera. For example, suppose the character says, "In my life, I have made no mistakes." The director can add to the line, ". . . except when I fell in love with you." If this tag line is recorded by the same actor and added to a shot where his back is toward the camera, the director can significantly change the meaning of the scene.

Voiceovers. Any voiceover indicated in the script or created during the editing process should be recorded (even if it is a scratch track) and refined during picture editing to ensure proper timing before manufacturing the final sound track.

As you edit, keep these points in mind:

- Ask yourself, does this cut work? This is the only criterion for leaving a shot in the picture. It doesn't matter if it is a cheat (trick).
- Just make the cut! A cut won't happen by itself. You can't know if it will work or not until you try it.
- Cut as tight as you can. There is no reason to keep scenes loose. You can always put back what you've taken out. The sooner you see the potential of the piece, the better.

Editing can be very discouraging. You're by yourself, and that makes it very hard. If you can surround yourself with good people who will help you out, it will make the process easier, but you've got to stop falling in love with the film and just sit down and do it. Treat the editing process like work.

Howard

Cut with Sound in Mind

Work with or preview as many sounds as you can before locking the picture. If a particular sound effect will be used as an important tension-building device in a scene, transfer the sound and use it while you cut your picture. NLE systems have made this possible because one can hear eight or more (depending on the system) tracks at a given time.

A specific sound might change the way you look at a sequence. Perhaps the original scene was designed without a phone ringing. Now, in the editing room, you get the idea of adding this sound effect, even though the character does not answer or even acknowledge it. The sound effect might shift the meaning of the scene and even the entire story. The addition of the phone ring, if it works, would require the editor to lengthen the shot to allow viewers to ask themselves why the character doesn't answer the phone.

EVOLUTION OF THE EDIT

An actor slips on a line, stutters, or fumbles, but finally gets back on track with the dialogue. In the editing room, the director might decide that this human foible is perfect behavior to help the audience understand the character. After all, the actor was "in character," so it might very well have been a slip on the part of the character rather than the actor. Furthermore, the director might decide at dailies that the stutter should be maintained throughout the production to distinguish the character's actions.

A director must be open to all elements that come into play during production that might affect the project, including mistakes and accidents. Never forget that accidents (both good and bad) that happened during principal photography—tones, moods, emphases that shifted, and new ideas—all become part of this editorial phase.

In *The Lunch Date*, homeless people are integral to the story line. However, it was difficult to keep the real homeless people who congregate in Grand Central Station from looking into the lens, breaking the fourth wall, and therefore spoiling shots.

> *I worked on food lines at Grand Central every night before filming, and I asked some of the homeless men to show up when we were shooting. I saw Willie the night before, and he had this harmonica and a great face, so I asked him to show up too. I didn't even think he heard me. But we had a shooting*

> *schedule, so at about the time we needed to shoot this shot of Scotty reentering the station, we started looking around for Willie. We did a couple of takes with her just looking around for somebody. Then we did a couple of takes of her entering the station and being upset just by herself.*
>
> *Then I looked over, and I saw Willie! I approached him and said, "Willie, I want you to play the harmonica when I tell you." And he said, "Ah, okay, okay." I told Scotty that I didn't know what was going to happen, but just to go with it, to stick to her basic motivation, which was to be upset, and we'll see what happens. We rolled the camera, I cued Scotty, I cued Willie, and he entered. He did that number with the harmonica, looking almost straight at the camera, and then he walked off. I yelled "Cut," and my crew looked at me like I was crazy. I thought that it probably was a mistake. Willie walked off somewhere, so I couldn't get him back. I decided to go with a couple of different takes of Scotty by herself.*
>
> *But when I got into the editing room, there was something I liked about the shot. I knew it was a little dangerous because he looked in the camera, but it didn't bother me enough not to use it because there was something that was real about it that I liked.*
>
> Adam

The director chose to use several of these shots in the final cut of the film because they give viewers a documentary feeling, the sensation that they are there with the character at the station (Figure 16.3).

Figure 16.3 What seemed like a problem on the set turned into a bit of gold in the editing room.

Shifts in Tone

The main character in the script of *The Lunch Date* delivers the line, "Get a job," to a homeless person at the end of the script. This line was cut because the tone of the film had shifted between the writing of the screenplay and the editing process. The reaction of the woman to the man eating her salad was less hostile than originally envisioned, and this reaction to her mistake made for a lighter and happier tone than in the original script. For her to walk out into the station and deliver such a line, deliberately telling the audience that the character gained nothing from her encounter with her "lunch date," went against the grain of what the film had evolved into, and the line was therefore easily cut. The director was not aware of this shift until he arrived in the editing room.

Adam saw that to force the line into the film, just because it was in the script, would have been a mistake. The director must "listen" to the film. When screening various cuts of the film, the director must become as objective as the audience that views the film for the first time.

> *After the woman discovers that she sat at the wrong place, she goes and gets her bag and comes back into the station. I saw the film ending with her getting back on the train. I wanted to make a statement that people don't change. She certainly didn't change. When I shot it, I had a man begging for money. All my takes, I had her saying something to him. Basically, it was harsh—"Get a job," or "Get lost," or "Don't bother me"—because I thought this is true, this is what would happen. But while editing the film, I discovered that it was too harsh because something was working in the sequence with the salad. It just felt like a different movie, to have this sequence of her telling the guy to get a job. I like to believe that that was the film speaking to me.*
>
> Adam

When a shipbuilder puts a plan down on paper, like the script, it is not written in stone. As the ship is being built, as the film or video is being made, the work becomes three-dimensional. This growth is the creative process. It should be nurtured. This process can constantly change the shape and even the very nature of the work.

A good example of shifting tone is the approach the director takes with a documentary. The final script for a documentary is made during the editorial phase, not during preproduction. The director initially does her research and approaches her subject with an idea of what she would like to accomplish.

Along the way, however, the idea for the documentary might change. The chosen subject sometimes turns out to be less interesting than some other aspect of the narrative that begins to unfold to the director.

> *I think the editing is half of making the film in documentary. Much of the creation of structure and themes occurs at the editorial stage.*
>
> Jan

Adding Reshoots and Stock Footage

Once your film or video has found its proper structure, any new material, such as reshoots and stock footage, can be assembled and cut into the project. Before spending money (these items are expensive), wait until your film or video has found its proper structure so you can evaluate your needs. Changes in structure may happen during editing. Shots that you couldn't get during production may not be needed anymore for the revised structure

> *It is difficult to obtain footage from the Library of Congress because they're more there for research than for reprinting, but the National Archives is a completely separate building. It's in a different place. It's where Nixon's tapes are. They have a motion picture and record administration, and they have all the government footage that is public domain, and some protected material as well, such as NASA footage.*
>
> Jan

There are many companies that supply film- and videomakers with stock footage. This footage covers a wide variety of events taken over many years, including news, sports, nature, history, personalities, and distant locations. Images of almost any person, place, or thing can be found and used in your film or video. Most of the available footage was photographed in 16-mm or 35-mm film and is sold by the foot. *Mirror Mirror* incorporated stock footage very effectively from newsreels of a beauty contest during the 1920s and shots of women on antiquated exercise machines from the 1930s (Figure 16.4).

Figure 16.4 Stock footage can evoke the past.

> *My idea was to show how the tyranny of the ideal has existed over time and is still with us. In editing, the contemporary footage shot in gyms didn't work, so I had no problem throwing it out. You need to try things. You can't second guess completely what will work and what won't work. Ultimately, I went with stock footage only.*
>
> Jan

Many things change during the editing process. Other than inserting stock footage, editing might reveal the need for additional footage to tell the story properly. Putting in a single shot can sometimes make the difference between a scene working or not. "Connectors" that are often needed at this point include the following:

- Transitions between scenes
- An important closeup of a character to punctuate a moment
- An insert shot of an object to make a story point clear

Temporary Music

To ensure that the story has a flow and pace that will satisfy an audience, include a temporary music track, even in the rough-cut screenings. Always have tem-porary music added when screening important cuts in front of an audience. Even a seasoned filmmaker might have difficulty watching a silent sequence that normally requires music or sound. Previewing different kinds of "temp" music will shape the director's ideas about what she eventually will want for the sound track.

Temp music offers a wonderful opportunity to experiment with different kinds of themes and tempos for your picture. If you are going to be working with a composer, previewing a variety of pieces helps illustrate the kind of music you want. If you use preexisting music, be careful not to fall in love with a popular piece that might be out of your financial reach. If your goal is to distribute the project commercially, you must secure the rights to your music selections in advance. The rights to a small portion of a well-known tune might cost thousands of dollars. Even if you are only planning to screen your piece noncommercially at festivals and exhibitions, limited or "festival rights" must be secured.

Screen for Story

Preview different cuts of the film in a screening room or small theater as well as in the editing room. It is exciting to see your picture on a big screen once in a while. There is so much you miss when you see it on a small monitor. Invite a combination of those who are familiar with the project and those who have never seen it. It may also be valuable to invite key experienced people to serve as consultants. (If you are just learning, you will require assistance.) The fresh eyes may discover something that has eluded you. A key bit of exposition that you take for granted may be missing. A character's motivation may be unclear. You live with a project for months and what typically happens is that the more you look at it, the less you see, especially if you have been involved with the project from script stage.

Listen to what new viewers have to say, and take notes. Suggestions can come from anywhere. Their ideas might not be on the money, but their perspective should stimulate your thinking about the story.

For those projects that originate on film, cutting on a nonlinear system and matching back to film, it is equally important that you project various versions of your project. There is a marked difference on how the picture will "play" on a screen (a video projected screen in this case) than on the "box" you are cutting on. With traditional film editing, it is customary to screen the film with each new cut. In fact, even though most feature-length films are now cut on nonlinear editing systems, a film work print of each version is conformed for screening purposes to evaluate the project in the format (large screen) in which the audience will view it. Many low-budget productions can't afford this option. Neither can most students.

I had many screenings of the film, which were very helpful. However, the best screenings were the ones in which I had collective feedback; they turned out to be like the scriptwriting process. You turn out drafts of your script to a select group of people who care about you, care about the work, and are really into it. So I had similar sessions on the Steenbeck with half a dozen people at various stages. We'd go over a scene very carefully, talk about what worked and what didn't, and possible changes, and then I'd execute them. A week later, I'd show it again. So it was like the writing process, just writing in the cutting room.

Howard

Screen for Pacing

Screening your film in a large room will help you evaluate its true rhythm and pacing. There is a clear and distinct difference between how a film or video plays on the monitor of a NLE system and how it plays on the big screen. This is due to the difference in how we perceive images and how that change in perception impacts the flow of the story. Having worked with thousands of student filmmakers over the years, I have never failed to hear a student's reaction to the first time he or she sees the project projected on a big screen. The common reaction: "It drags."

The Impact of Nonlinear Editing Systems

Speed is great and NLE systems work as fast as the click of a mouse. Editing, however, is not just about speed. Sometimes it requires distance and perspective. There may come a time when you can't solve an editing problem, when you can't see the trees from the forest. In these instances, speed is not the answer. Films need to percolate. Finding the right balance of all the dramatic elements may require a different kind of energy that is the opposite of speed.

Although NLE systems can quickly and efficiently execute the ideas when you get them, they can't edit the project for you. The good news is that you have many options to play with and can save every single version. But for beginners, too many choices can be overwhelming.

LOCKING THE PICTURE

Finally, the picture is screened, cut, trimmed, and shaped to the liking of everyone on the creative team. The picture is now considered to be *locked*, and the product is known as the *fine cut*. Locking the picture means that the timing of each scene is fixed, and no more picture changes should be made. At this point, sound work can begin. Sound is either handled by the editor or farmed out to a specialist known as a *sound designer* or *sound effects editor*. A composer must now be selected if the choice hasn't already been made.

By the end of the film, you've forgotten what you originally intended.

Howard

TECHNICAL CONSIDERATIONS WHEN EDITING FILM ON VIDEO

For those who have shot on film, cut digitally, and want to finish on film, there are some issues to keep in mind while editing. Video and film are different creatures, and some things you might do in a video edit do not easily translate back to film.

When you are editing video, you can repeat a shot as many times as you want. In film, every shot is based on *one piece of negative,* which normally can only be put in one place in the movie. If you want to use the same shot twice, that footage will have to be *duped* or copied from the original negative.

At the head and tail of every shot, the negative cutter needs at least a half frame to cement splice the negative. If you take a shot and cut it into two pieces, you need to leave at least one cutting frame unused between the pieces. Some nonlinear systems have a feature like Avid's "dupe detection" that warns you if you have reused any part of a shot or left insufficient cutting frames between shots.

When making fades and dissolves, video editors can choose virtually any length effect. Film contact printing machines only offer a standard set of fade and dissolve lengths. Standards usually include 16, 24, 32, 48, 64, or 96, which at 24 fps translates to 0.67, 1, 1.33, 2, 2.67, or 4 seconds. Fades and dissolves may look different in film than they do in video.

DIGITAL BASICS

Key Terms

Before beginning this part, we present the basic terminology that is the foundation on which nonlinear digital computer-driven editing systems are based. This book can't get into all the dense, complex layers of technical information. We hope to give the beginner an overview. Many excellent technical books are available (some are listed in the Bibliography). Also, the Internet has become an excellent resource (we will give you the URLs of some key sites).

SMPTE Timecode

In the early 1970s, videotape editing adopted the use of timecode. This had a tremendous impact on video editing. Before timecode, there was no standardized way to repeat the edits of an editing session or to automatically reedit old work. In the United States and other parts of the world where NTSC (National Television Standards Committee) is standard, video runs at about 30 frames per second. The idea of timecode is to assign a number to every frame of picture or sound to easily identify those frames and work with them.

Timecode is a running 24-hour clock that counts hours, minutes, seconds, and frames (01:00:00:00) and that goes as high as 23:59:59:29. One frame later it returns to 00:00:00:00. Note that since there are 30

frames per second, the frame counter only goes up to: 29. This timecode system is called *SMPTE nondrop timecode* (pronounced "simpty").

The use of timecode sped up the editing process and was considerably more frame accurate than the earlier and cruder control track editing. Timecode is similar to the edge numbers found on film. It is an arbitrary number assigned to each frame of video, arbitrary because the important portion of the tape is not the number but the frame of picture that the code is electronically identifying.

Drop and Nondrop Frame Timecode

There are two kinds of timecode: *drop frame* and *nondrop frame. Drop frame timecode* (DF) is more time accurate, meaning that one hour of timecode is equal to one hour of videotape. *Nondrop frame timecode* (ND) is not time accurate. An hour of nondrop frame timecode is equal to one hour and 3.6 seconds of videotape.

The difference between the two types of timecode came about because the NTSC determined that color television signals would run at 29.97 frames per second rather than 30 fps (black-and-white TV signals ran at 30 fps). You can't see the difference, but this 0.1 percent reduction in speed affects the way timecode keeps time. Over one hour, the 0.03 frame per second discrepancy adds up to 3.6 seconds. This is because your videotape is actually playing more slowly. This is not a problem if your project is not meant for broadcast.

However, since broadcasters need to know the exact length of a program, *drop frame timecode* was developed. A system was devised to drop certain numbers from the counting. The numbers that are dropped are the :00 and :01 frames at every new minute, except at the 10-minute marks (10 minutes, 20 minutes, 30 minutes, etc.). This amounts to 108 dropped numbers or 3.6 seconds and allows drop frame timecode to keep accurate time. It also gave DF its name.

- One hour of real time is one hour
- One hour of drop frame timecode is one hour
- One hour of nondrop frame timecode is one hour and 3.6 seconds

With drop frame timecode, no actual frames of video are dropped, and the frame rate doesn't change. It is how the frames are counted that is affected. Switching a camera from ND to DF has no effect on the picture or on the number of frames that are recorded every second. The only thing that changes is the way the digits in the timecode counter advance over time.

Programs created for broadcast television are completed with DF timecode. Many editing systems work with either drop or nondrop, and shooting with nondrop doesn't prevent you from finishing with drop. Nondrop is often used for production. Mixing the two formats in the same project can, however, cause problems. DF is sometimes indicated with semicolons instead of colons between the numbers (01;13;26;15). (In Europe and other parts of the world where PAL is standard, video runs at exactly 25 fps. EBU (see Glossary) timecode uses a similar 24-hour clock, except the frame counter runs up to :24 instead of :29. EBU code keeps real time, so there is no need to drop frames.)

VITC and LTC

There are two ways you can record timecode on a piece of videotape: running lengthwise along the videotape as an audio type signal or vertically, in frame, as a video type signal. All of these originate with a timecode generator. The two types are longitudinal timecode (LTC) or vertical interval timecode (VITC). An audio type signal can be placed on one of the audio channels of the tape (running along the bottom of the tape) or in a special separate channel (running along the top). Because it runs longitudinally (lengthwise), this timecode is called *longitudinal timecode* (LTC). LTC might also be called *audio timecode* if it is recorded on one of the audio tracks or *address track timecode* if it recorded on a separate address track (see Glossary).

LTC is inexpensive to generate, record, and read because the encoders and decoders are affordable. However, it is prone to getting confused. A videotape machine can only read it when the tape is running within a narrow speed range. It is like an audio signal: When you slow it down, the words get more difficult to understand. It is likewise not perfect to edit with. It is not *frame accurate* at slo-mo or high-speed playback.

For a timecode to be really frame accurate, it must be readable while the tape is not in the play mode. *Vertical interval timecode* is a picture signal recorded in the vertical interval between the two fields of a video frame. This might seem confusing, because although the timecode is roughly vertical on the tape, it is horizontal on the monitor. The advantage of this type of timecode is that, unlike audio and address track timecode, it is readable even when the tape is not moving.

VITC (pronounced vit-see) must be recorded at the same time as the picture. Recording and decoding the code requires special equipment. In practice, VITC is usually used in conjunction with LTC. Being part of the video signal, VITC cannot be read accurately in fast shuttle or rewind speed, something LTC has no problem with at all. LTC can be added after material is recorded on tape.

Advantages of VITC

In addition to its ability to provide a readable display in freeze-frame and at a very slow tape speeds, VITC offers the following advantages over LTC:

- It requires no special amplification or signal processing equipment during playback or duplication.
- It provides field accurate access (as opposed to frame accurate access with LTC).
- It does not occupy an audio track, allowing for multitrack recording if desired.
- An error detection code (CRC) provides protection against errors.

Analog versus Digital

Until the 1980s, virtually all video and audio production was done using analog tape recorders. In the analog system, video and audio signals are represented by constantly changing electrical waves that correspond to picture or sound information. If you record someone with a microphone and a tape recorder, and the person speaks louder, the voltage of the signal sent from the mike to the recorder increases. The level of the electrical signal is *analogous* to the loudness of the sound.

There are many high-quality analog video and audio recording devices, but analog has a few key drawbacks. The electronics of any recording device and the tape stock on which you record are never perfect and may be susceptible to a certain amount of background noise. This may be noticeable as a low hiss during quiet passages on a sound recording. It may show up as grain or snow in a video image. When you make a copy or dub of an analog tape, noise builds up and other distortions are introduced into the signal. After several generations, this can be a serious problem.

The idea of digital recording is to measure the level of the electrical signal from moment to moment and record those measurements as discrete *numbers*. The original signal can be created later by referring to those numbers. Digital recording works by *sampling* the video or audio signal at regular intervals. Each sample is a measurement of the voltage at that moment in time. The rate at which the fixed intervals sample the original each second is called the *sampling rate*. That voltage measurement is then converted to a number that can be recorded on tape or on disk. In digital systems, the numbers are in a binary code, which uses a series of ones and zeros. Each digit in a binary code is a *bit* (101 is a three-bit number). Eight bits make a *byte*. Converting the original voltage into a number is called *quantization* or *quantizing*. The more bits you use per sample, the finer the gradations you can represent in color or brightness.

Sampling can be understood by thinking of a film camera that takes 24 still pictures per second. A sampling rate of $1/24$ second is perfectly adequate to record most visual activities. Although the camera door closes after each $1/24$ of a second and nothing is recorded, not enough information is lost to affect the perception of the event. For example, a running man does not run far enough in the split second the shutter is closed to alter the naturalness of the movement. If the sampling rates were slowed to 1 frame a second, the running rate would be quick and abrupt; if it were slowed to 1 frame per minute, the running would be hard to follow.

The entire process of converting a video or audio signal to digital form is called *digitizing* and is done by an *analog-to-digital (A/D) converter*. The converter may be a part of the camera, or it may be part of the audio or video recorder. To view or hear the signal, it can be reconstructed in its analog form using a *digital-to-analog (D/A) converter*.

Sampling Rate

How often a video or audio signal is sampled affects how accurately it can be recreated. It is the difference between sampling the rate of a turtle walking across a path and that of a hare.

In audio and video recording, the speed with which the signal changes is related to its frequency. The higher the frequency, the faster it is changing. Frequency is measured in *hertz* (see Glossary). To make high-quality recordings, high frequencies need to be captured. If a sound recording lacks high frequency, it may sound dull or muddy. If a video signal lacks high frequencies, fine detail in the image may be lost, making it not appear to be sharp. It was determined several years ago that the sampling rate has to be at least *twice* the maximum frequency that one wants to capture. Humans can hear sounds up to about 20,000

Hz (20 kHz), so a digital recorder needs to sample at least 40,000 times a second to capture the full range of sound. Generally, 44.100 equals CD quality and 48.000 equals digital video (DV) quality.

Digitizing video is a more complex process than for audio. Sound is measured in amplitude (loudness) and frequency (pitch) that change in time. A moving picture must be sampled in both time *and* space. Sampling in time is what a film camera does when it captures still images at 24 frames per second. Sampling in space is the process of capturing each single image. For film, the chemistry of the film emulsion responds uniquely to light. For video, it is a screen of dots. A digitized image looks a lot like a TV image. The picture must be broken down into tiny pieces, small enough that the viewer only sees the big picture and not the discrete pieces. The smallest piece of the video image is called a *pixel* (picture element). If you look closely at your TV, you can see them.

There are two kinds of information per pixel: *chrominance* and *luminance*. Chrominance refers to the color part of the signal relating to hue and saturation, and luminance is the brightness of the signal measure from black to white. The smaller the pixels, the sharper the image will look.

Advantages of Digital

For years, audiophiles and engineers have debated the merits of digital audio versus high-end analog systems, and to this day, there are audiophiles who swear by their analog systems. Digital audio has emerged as the winner by most accounts, but it's still useful to understand the advantages of digital versus analog audio, because many audio systems contain a mix of digital and analog components.

The advantages of digital audio can be summed up as follows: it has wider dynamic range and increased resistance to noise, it is easier to copy, and it offers film- and videomakers the ability to use error correction to compensate for wear and tear. Many types of digital media, such as CDs and mini-discs, are also more durable than common analog media, such as vinyl records and cassette tapes.

Digital audio can be copied from one digital device to another without any loss of information, unlike analog recording, where information is lost and noise introduced with every copy. Even the best analog systems lose about 3dB of signal-to-noise ratio when a copy is recorded. After several generations of analog copies, the sound quality will deteriorate noticeably. With digital audio, unlimited generations of perfect copies can be made. Perceptible noise will occur only if recordings are made with dirty heads.

Digital equipment will eventually be used for the entire video chain from shooting to recording, to editing, to broadcast, and finally for display. Until then, it will be used for various parts of the process. As of the writing of this book, digital images can be fed directly into a CPU via a *FireWire* (IEEE) without the need for a capture card or digitizing process.

FireWire, also known as IEEE (Institute of Electrical and Electronics Engineers) 1394, was developed by Apple Computer and is a standardized method for high-speed connections among a wide variety of professional and "prosumer" equipment. A project shot on a small DV camcorder with up to 500 lines of resolution can be inputted directly to a desktop computer. For consumer electronics, FireWire is very exciting because different consumer machines can be interconnected and controlled by a FireWire-capable computer.

Broadcast Quality

Broadcasters have numerous requirements referring to the aspects of the video signal. For years, the Society of Motion Picture and Television Engineers (SMPTE) set rules, adopted by the Federal Communications Commission, that defined what you could or could not broadcast. However, the relationship of image quality to broadcast quality is incidental. Although broadcasters were concerned with getting tapes with broadcast-quality video signals on them, the networks and stations were most concerned about the actual quality of the image. Each network came up with its own image quality criteria, but in time, limitations on image quality were dropped (hence the broadcast of favorite home movies). Therefore, the term "broadcast quality" comes from requirements for the *video signal,* not the way the image *looks.* This is important for the end user of a nonlinear system: "Broadcast-quality video" is an objective description of a video signal. As far as image quality goes, there is no such thing as required broadcast quality.

Resolution

Resolution refers to a system's ability to capture fine detail. It plays a part in how sharp the image can look. When fine detail is rendered clearly, an image will usually look sharp to the eye. There are, however, many factors that come into play in determining sharpness. These include the measurable fine detail of the image (resolution), the contrast of the picture, and the distance from which we view it. In general, high-resolution images look better, sharper than low-resolution images. Sometimes filmmakers deliberately soften a high-resolution image with filters for a particular look.

The term *resolution* also applies to the concept of how much *information* is stored in each film or video image or each second of an audio recording. There are various ways to measure how much information or data are used to capture and record an image or sound. With digital video recordings, we can count exactly how many digital bits of data are used for each frame. As a general rule of thumb, the *higher* the resolution, the finer the detail in the image and the more information or *storage space* is needed to record it. For example, 35-mm film is a higher resolution format than 16-mm, the 35-mm image being more than four times bigger. We will address the storage issue in the next section, for it is important when it comes to editing.

Digital Compression

Digital cameras and recording devices are being developed that are capable of capturing images and sound with greater clarity and fidelity. It takes a lot of information to record a full-resolution video image. (On the other hand, digital audio requires far less information and doesn't need to be digitally compressed for production work.) To make the cost-effective and efficient use of digital video recordings, ways have to be found to minimize the amount of storage, processing, and transmission equipment needed to deal with them. Some of the ways to do this are to make the picture smaller, to decrease the color quality and the frame rate (an unattractive alternative for editing), and to use some form of video compression.

Video compression takes the digitized information about an image and encodes it in such a way as to take up less space while maintaining the best possible picture and sound quality. Video and audio are compressed for storage and transmission and then decompressed in order to view and hear the signals. Compression schemes are sometimes called *codecs* (which stands for compression/decompression). The amount of compression to use is determined by the amount of storage capacity, the amount of source material, and its image complexity. After images and sound have been compressed, they take up less storage space on tape or computer disk. This allows us to use smaller and cheaper camcorders (production), load more footage into an editing system (postproduction), or fit a longer movie onto a disk for playback at home.

Compression is also useful because systems are often limited in how much data they can process per second. After a video signal has been compressed, it can be sent through a narrower pipeline or smaller *bus* of a computer. For example, images sent through the Internet may be compressed so they can be sent through telephone lines. Many homes still use old-style copper phone wires that pass much less data per second than a typical video cable, which is to say their *bandwidth* is less.

Types of Compression

Compression can be done in many different ways, and since technology is constantly changing, we will focus on some basic concepts and the two systems that have been used most widely. Compression involves compacting the digitized video information (a computer file) into a smaller space. For viewing, the data must be expanded or decompressed. *Lossless* compression means that after the file is decompressed, nothing is lost and it can be restored to its original condition. *Lossy* compression throws away information that can never be restored.

One approach to video compression is to delete information from individual frames, known as *intraframe* coding. Only one frame is compressed at a time, with no reference to other frames. This technique is used in several digital cameras. For example, Digital Betacam reduces the data by half (2:1 ratio), whereas the DV format compresses at 5:1. Compressing in the camcorder reduces the amount of information recorded per second, allowing for longer record times on a tape, and it produces a very clean low-noise signal. With intraframe coding, every frame of the original signal is stored on tape or disk, so we can easily isolate frames when needed to edit the material. This form of compression is called *JPEG* or *motion-JPEG* (pronounced jay-peg). It was created it in the late 1980s by the Joint Photographic Experts Group as a method of compressing still color images. Most nonlinear editing systems use JPEG.

Another method of compression, developed by the Moving Picture Experts Group in the early 1990s, is called *MPEG* (pronounced empeg) and was specifically tailored for moving pictures. MPEG doesn't just look at a single frame and compress it; it looks at adjacent frames to see which pixels are changing and which are mostly the same. This is called *interframe* encoding. For example, if your face is on the screen and you are just talking, probably the only part of the screen that is changing significantly is your mouth; the rest of you remains pretty much the same. By just concentrating on the interframe changes, MPEG greatly reduces digital video data, significantly more than JPEG. Another feature specific to MPEG is that it is designed to handle sync audio; the JPEG techniques only deal with pictures.

JPEG and MPEG are not products, only standardized techniques. Before they were standardized, companies developed their own way to compress video. With standardization, editing system and computer chip manufacturers utilize these methods in their designs. JPEG is considered the compression scheme of choice for applications that are concerned with still images, such as desktop publishing, electronic photo processing, digital scanners, and color laser printers. It is also an inexpensive and simple method; the same JPEG chips that compress can be used in reverse to decompress. This is called a *symmetrical* technique.

MPEG is an *asymmetrical* technique. Compression and decompression are handled differently, by different sets of chips (or software). This makes MPEG suited to different kinds of applications: playback of precompressed video from digital videodisks or CD-ROM, multimedia applications, and so on. It is designed for moving images and sync sound but has some trouble (presently) handling edits.

There are currently three versions of MPEG compression. MPEG-1 was designed for VHS-quality pictures (352×240 at 30 fps). MPEG-2 was designed for full-screen, higher quality images (however, MPEG-1 looks better than MPEG at certain compression rates). MPEG-2 offers resolutions of 720×480 and $1,280 \times 720$ at 60 fps, with full CD-quality audio. This is sufficient for all the major TV standards, including NTSC, and even HDTV. MPEG-2 is also used by DVD-ROMs.

MPEG-4 is a graphics and video compression algorithm standard based on MPEG-1, MPEG-2, and Apple QuickTime technology that was standardized in 1998. MPEG-4 files are smaller than JPEG or QuickTime files, so they are designed to transmit video and images over a narrower bandwidth and can mix video with text, graphics, and 2D and 3D animation layers.

When digitizing video or audio material into an editing system, you can usually select how much compression you want to do. The more you compress, the more footage you can store on the disks, and the lower the image quality. For example, Avid uses several AVR (Avid video resolution) levels to indicate different degrees of compression.

All the companies manufacturing nonlinear editing systems that utilize digitized source material must deal with all these parameters in designing their systems. The remaining factors—image size, resolution, color range, compression—must be dealt with in terms of the limitations of the system's memory storage and computer processing power. Ultimately, the question that always must be answered is, how good does an image have to be for offline editing? The answers seem to vary according to whom you ask, from D-1 quality to something better than recognizable.

WHAT IS NONLINEAR?

Film-Style Editing

Film-style editing is identical to nonlinear editing. It is a style of editing (video-style has meant linear editing). However, "film-style" is a term that has been applied to systems that softened the "cold" technological interface that videotape editors used for something more user friendly. Film-style systems adopted various kinds of fancy graphics and icons that are intended to make the computer easier for film editors to relate to. Film-style is a marketing term for *film-editor-friendly interface*.

These electronic editing systems were sometimes the first computers older film editors had ever seen. In the first years of electronic film editing, editors who had been editing television and movies on film for years were asked to adapt quickly to these new systems. It was critically important that film editors find them intuitive, easy to learn, and simple to use. They had to be a lot like editing on film.

Random Access

All editing is random access; that is the basis of editing. You access this scene, you go to that scene, then you pull a shot. What is generally meant by "random access" is quick or instant access to randomly selected frames of video or audio. The two terms *nonlinear* and *random access* are often used interchangeably. However, there is a fundamental difference between them. Nonlinear means that a series of shots can be rearranged quickly without the limitations of space. A random access editor is capable of seeking and then playing any footage instantly.

Traditional videotape editing is neither random access nor nonlinear. Traditional film editing has always been nonlinear. Shots can be changed at will without having to rebuild all the edits that follow. However, keeping track of thousands of feet of film and finding a few frames that were once at the head of an edit are tedious and time-consuming chores. Although film editing was (and still is) nonlinear, the record-keeping and filing system was labor intensive (the job of assistant editors), making it hardly "random access" as we are using the term.

Computers, with digital memory, are extremely random access. When your images and audio are digitized as a part of the computer memory, you have the ultimate in random access; RAM is virtually instantaneous. Therefore, nonlinear is a kind of editing, random access is a kind of cueing, and film-style is a kind of interface. These elements are combined in most modern nonlinear editing systems.

With the advantages that nonlinear and random access bring to the editing process, there may also be a drawback. Videotape and film editing both require editors to shuttle through the material to locate a shot or scene. Random access editing decreases the amount of shuttling that an editor must do. This may save time, but it reduces the familiarity an editor has with the raw material. The nonlinear editor may have logged the shots based on the original structure for the show. As editorial changes are made (as they invariably are), these shuttles could reveal a shot that, seen in a different context, could make the difference between a scene working or not.

Digital Nonlinear Editing

Traditional video editing as has been described is a *linear* process. You start at the beginning and lay down shots one at a time until a sequence is completed. Film editing is *nonlinear*. You can start whenever you want, move shots around, and change their length without having to produce generation after generation of dupes. To bring that flexibility to video editing, it was realized that if video and audio were converted to digital form, they could be loaded onto a computer's hard drive and manipulated much as a word processor handles text. Images and sound could be joined, deleted, and cut from one sequence and pasted to another. Actually, the nonlinear editing system went through several manifestations before computers were used. (Banks of videotape machines or laserdisc players were utilized to achieve the same goals.)

Videotape editors found this process extremely liberating. It gave them the freedom to experiment with changes and the ability to save multiple versions of the entire show. The editor became free to concentrate on cutting the project because all of the tedious tasks of editing became automated. Sound editing in traditional tape editing was particularly unwieldy.

Complex sound work was made easy with a nonlinear editing system. In nonlinear editing, the shots from the source tape are loaded into the computer. This process is called *digitizing* or *capturing*. It involves converting nondigital or digital video or audio material to digital form and then recording it on the computer's hard drive. The hard drive gives you instant, random access to any part of the footage. The idea of "editing" using a nonlinear system is creating a list of instructions that tell the computer's drives which sections of footage to put together in what order. In nonlinear terminology, the individual sections of video or audio are called *clips*. By selecting the length of each clip and the order in which it is played relative to the other clips, we are editing the project.

Nonlinear Offline

One problem with working with high-quality video (as we have stated in the section on compression) is that it requires a lot of storage space on the system's hard drives. Virtually all nonlinear systems use some sort of compression to reduce the amount of data in the video. This lowers the resolution and enables you to store more minutes of material on the drives. Generally, the more you compress the video, the more the picture quality diminishes.

Since the system may not have enough memory to allow you to digitize all the material at its highest quality, you will need to digitize your material at a lower resolution, which reduces the picture quality but allows you to edit the footage in an offline mode. The image may not be pretty, but it will allow you to take full advantage of the capabilities of the nonlinear system. After you've done editing, the system will generate an edit decision list, or EDL. You now have several options. You can take the EDL to a postproduction facility and do a traditional online session. If your system can accommodate it, you can redigitize at a higher resolution just the material in the edited version of your project. The final product is usually much shorter than all the raw footage and thus will be able to fit on the computer's drives. In the digital world, the same unit can be both an offline and online system. If you were editing material that originated on film and will be completed on film, the system can generate an EDL or film cut list as a guide for the negative cutter.

Basic Components of a Nonlinear Editing System

This is the basic simplified flowchart for creating a project in a nonlinear editing system:

- Shoot video (Mini DV, DVCAM, HDV, etc.) or transfer developed film to tape.
- Clone your original source material to end up with two tapes with identical timecode.
- Input (log and digitize) the source footage from clone to storage disk.
- Organize the footage. The editor organizes the footage in "bins."
- Edit the project (system of choice).
- Output the completed material to DV, Quicktime, DVD, and so on.

An important step that most students and beginners forget is to clone (copy) their original material. The original tapes should be cloned and stored away in a safe place. This is similar to what occurs with the original film negative, which is kept in the laboratory.

Basic Nonlinear Interface

A nonlinear editing system is basically software loaded in a computer with various devices attached or installed internally. The processing speed of the computer affects how quickly the system can create (render) video transitions and other effects.

Capture Card

One of the most sensitive functions of the computer is audio/video capture. The capture system is responsible for digitizing and compressing the audio and video as you bring them into the system. The capture process is done by a combination of hardware (the capture card) and software. Compression is done to reduce the amount of space needed to store the digitized video and audio material. Capture cards vary in their methods and sophistication, which can have an impact on picture quality.

Storage

Having enough storage makes all the difference with nonlinear editing. Digitized video and audio clips are stored on computer disks. Hard drives are generally used because they provide fast access time to quickly find material on the disk and they can move large amounts of data per second (high data transfer rate).

Sometimes drives are grouped together in sets to increase performance, such as redundant array of inexpensive disks (RAID). There are also removable disks. The storage capacity of computer drives is generally measured in megabytes (MB) or gigabytes (GB), commonly called "gigs"; one GB equals 1,000 MB. The buzzword, up to now, has been that *resolution costs money*, but hard drives continue to come down in price. Currently FireWire drives are affordable ways to handle the storage issue.

Monitors

The editing system's monitor allows you to view the picture and the graphical interface used to control the system. Most systems will include a source monitor to view the footage and a record monitor to play the sequence. It is important to have a TV monitor connected to the system. This is because the RGB computer monitor doesn't display the image the way it will look after it has been converted back to composite or component video.

Capturing and Organizing Clips

Before editing can begin, video and audio must be loaded into the system. Most systems allow you to digitize video and audio material at various quality levels or resolutions. The higher the resolution, the better the picture looks, and the more space the material will occupy on the hard drives. If you have sufficient storage capacity on your hard drives, then digitize at the highest resolution. If you have more footage than can be stored on disk at full resolution, you have these options:

- You can digitize at a lower resolution. This is using more compression to reduce the amount of data needed for each second of video and will reduce picture quality.
- You can digitize only enough material to work on a portion of the project at a time.
- You can start by digitizing the project in low-quality draft mode. When you're done with your rough cut, you can delete the unused material or outtakes and redigitize the movie.
- You can delete media files you no longer need.
- You can render only when necessary. If you render frequently, you end up rerendering effects multiple times, which consumes disk space. Any time you render an effect, the system creates a media file that takes up drive space.

You may want to look for the best balance between image quality and conservation of space. The compression you choose for your edit will be lower than the compression needed for the final product (if you're finishing on video).

Digitizing

When you digitize or capture a section of video or audio material into the system, it becomes a computer file (digital data) that is written (recorded) into the system's hard drives. This file is called a *media file* (or a source media file or source file). Say you digitized a shot of a man mowing the lawn and then digitized a shot of him relaxing in a hammock. Each shot would become a separate media file (actually, each shot would have one media file for the video portion and one for the audio).

When you edit your project and decide to put the mowing shot before the hammock, you are not moving the media files around. Instead, you move or arrange *clips*, which act as "pointers" that tell the computer to go to a certain media file and play a portion of it. For any media file you could have many different clips. For example, you could use a short clip of the man starting the mower at the beginning of the project and then use a longer clip showing him mowing the backyard later on. Different clips can reuse the same source media data as often as needed (unless this is a project that was shot and will be finished in film). Clips are stored on the computer's internal drive and don't take up much space. Media files require substantial storage space, and thus are stored on separate, large-capacity external hard disks.

Digitizing or capturing a continuous section of video onto the computer drives is referred to as *digitizing a clip*. The captured material becomes a media file. The clip that points to all the media files is the *master clip*. Any portions of the master clip used in the edited project may be called *subclips*.

The editing system allows you to give each clip a name and type in comments or other information about the clip. Clips may be digitized on the fly, which means that they are defined and labeled as they are loaded into the system. Some people prefer to preview the material before actually digitizing, when they can view the footage and log which clips they want and give them labels. This can be done using the editing system or, if the system is not available, using a VTR and a personal computer with a logging program such as *MediaLog*. To log the footage, go through the camera tapes, specifying by timecode address where clips are to start and stop, giving each clip a name and indicating which footage *not* to digitize. The log can be entered into the editing system, which then proceeds to batch digitize or batch capture, automatically recording the selected footage onto the computer drives while labeling the clips.

A large amount of work can be done on logging software, saving time (and money) on your editing system. You can even pick your preferred takes and their mark-ins and mark-outs, essentially creating a rough assembly before you even digitize. The more complete and detailed your logging is at this stage, the more smoothly the editing will go later.

Setting Color and Audio

When the video and audio material is loaded into the editing system, various settings need to be adjusted or checked. Just as in linear videotape editing, the playback source needs to be set up for proper color balancing by using the system's waveform monitor and vectorscope. Audio levels should also be set properly before and monitored during digitizing. Many editing systems give you the choice of sampling rate for digitizing audio: 44.1 kHz at 16 bits per sample is the equivalent of CD quality; 48 kHz is DAR quality, which is higher. If your audio is coming from a digital source, you want to use the same sampling rate as your source. If you are editing a project originally shot on film, audio material may need to be slowed down (pulled down) when it is digitized into the system because of the 24 fps/30 fps differential. Some audio decks and editing systems have an audio pulldown setting to accomplish this. Some systems run at exactly 24 fps. This permits you to bring audio recorded in sync with film (synced up at the lab) in and out of the system without changing speed.

It is important to note that digitizing takes place in *real time*: While the tape deck plays the source material, the nonlinear editing system digitizes the footage into the computer. A 20-minute tape takes 20 minutes to digitize (new DV and Betacam SX systems might soon increase this rate of transfer to four times real time). As the editor is doing the digitizing, she can use the time to get familiar with the footage. The time it takes to digitize will be more than saved when doing the first cut, which can be done in a fraction of the time it would have taken in a linear environment.

Finally, before digitizing, you will need to decide on the image quality of the digitized footage, which as we have stated is determined by the resolution, or the level of compression at which you digitize the source material.

Organizing Clips

Logging and organization are important when using any film or editing system. As clips are captured, they can be grouped for convenience. Just as film editors use various bins to hang pieces of film or sound, nonlinear editing systems have *folders* or *bins* in which certain clips or edited *sequences* can be kept separately from the rest of the material. Clips can be viewed in the form of a text and a single-image frame from the scene.

The list will have different fields of information about each clip, including the name of the clip, the starting and ending timecode, and the tape from which the clip came. Projects originating on film may need to keep track of keycode numbers, in camera or audio timecode, as well as camera roll, sound roll, and telecine reel numbers. Many editing systems have sophisticated database management programs that allow you to quickly sift through lists of clips.

Your editor may organize bins to make the clips easy to access and conform to her working methods. The time the editor spends organizing the footage at the front end will save you time and money during the edit by making it easy to locate needed footage.

EDITING SEQUENCES

Editing Interface and Time Line

Like word processing software, nonlinear editing systems differ in their particulars, but have certain fundamental concepts in common. The *editing interface* is the method by which you control the system; it is where the actual editing takes place. This is displayed on one or more computer screens divided into several areas or *windows* on the *desktop*. There are usually two windows that display video; one of them is the equivalent of a source monitor in linear tape editing. This is used to view unedited clips and mark the portions you want to use. The second window is the record or program monitor. This displays the edited sequence you are creating. There may be other open windows on the desktop such as titling or effects tools. The bin monitor displays the available clips in a bin.

Most systems also utilize a *time line* that graphically illustrates how the clips are edited together (see Figure 16.5). Colored rectangles are used to represent video and audio clips. Time lines move from left to right, with markings showing time (timecode) advancing as you move to the right. The length of a

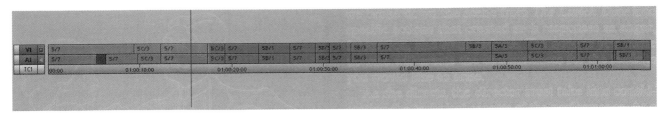

Figure 16.5 Timeline. Courtesy of Avid Technology, Inc.

clip on the time line generally corresponds to the length of time the clip will play on the screen.

Audio clips are represented by another set of tracks. These can be edited independently of the picture or locked together with the video to preserve the sync relationship. Most systems use a long vertical bar that crosses all the tracks and indicates the point at which the system is in *play mode* or in *edit mode.*

It's Only Virtual

It is important to realize that clips arranged on the time line are nothing more than pointers to the media files that are stored elsewhere on the hard drives. You are able to move, delete, change, or copy clips without affecting the original media they refer to. And like most word processing programs, they have *undo commands* in case you make a mistake.

However, as anyone who has used a computer knows, strange and mysterious things can happen. Files can be corrupted or lost, or your system can come crashing down unexpectedly. Make sure to *back up* your sequences and other files at least at the end of the day (and more often than that). Media files are usually not backed up because they are too big.

Marking and Assembling Clips

To begin editing, start by identifying the clips you want to use. On most systems, you simply move the mouse to a clip in the bin and double-click to play it in the source monitor. If you use only a portion of it, mark an IN point (start mark) and OUT point (end mark). You have just marked the clip. It is ready to be put in the film or video.

On some systems, you can place a clip on the time line simply by using the mouse to drag a clip from the source window to the time line (*drag and drop*). As in linear tape editing, most edits can be defined with three points, and you can string shots together without having to define the OUT points right away (open-ended). Most systems allow you to do a given task several different ways. You can use the mouse, the keyboard, or a combination of both. You will find the style that works best for you.

Adding Clips

As you edit, you build up a sequence of shots. When you want to add a new clip to an existing sequence, you indicate *where* on the time line to insert the new shot. In nonlinear editing, you have two options about how the new clip will affect the clips that are already in the sequence: *splicing* and *overwriting*. Splicing has the same function in nonlinear editing as splicing in film. When you splice, material you select in the source monitor is inserted into the sequence at a specified point. Any shots in the sequence after the edit point move down (or *ripple down*), lengthening the sequence.

Overwriting is the digital equivalent of a videotape insert edit. Using the Overwrite button, the editor replaces (writes over) existing sections of the sequence with new material. Overwriting does not change the sequence's length. You might use overwriting to add a cutaway over an existing interview in a documentary.

Removing Clips from a Sequence

Again, there are two options to removing a shot. You can extract a shot from a sequence, which removes material and closes the gap left by its removal. Extracting, like splicing, changes the duration of the sequence. It is comparable to removing frames from a film.

The second choice is to lift footage from a sequence, which removes material and leaves black or silence. It is like slugging a film work print with leader or fill, or the equivalent of recording black and silence over a portion of your tape master. Lifting, like overwriting, does not change the duration of the sequence.

Trimming Clips

After clips have been added to the time line, you need to be able to adjust their length. Trimming and editing in the time line might be the most powerful operations of the nonlinear editing system, the fundamental part of editing. Most systems have a *trim mode*.

In video terms, "trimming" means to adjust an edit point to either extend or shorten a shot. The trim editor may allow you to preview the edit with a *looping* feature, which plays the transition repeatedly while you preview it. There are many types of trimming methods, and different systems call them by different names, such as single roller trim, ripple edit, trim tail, dual roller trim, rolling edit, trim joint, and slim trim. Compared to film or linear videotape editing, trimming shots with a nonlinear system is a breeze.

Basic Sound Editing

Editing audio on a nonlinear system is fast: Sounds can be cut, pasted, copied, and manipulated at will. Some of the complicated operations of linear audio editing are unnecessary, such as adding new audio tracks and performing audio dissolves. The editor can now dissolve between the audio of two adjacent shots, on the same track. You no longer have to tie up two tracks to dissolve.

Most editing systems give you a choice of editing individual tracks independently or locking them to the video or audio tracks. When tracks are locked together, you can change them simultaneously with a single edit. When sound and picture are brought into the system in sync, as they are in digitizing a typical camera tape, many systems will tell you whether the audio and video tracks remain in sync. If during editing, you slip sync or move the audio relative to the video, a display will show you how many frames have displaced the audio.

Audio clips may appear on the time line as colored blocks. Many systems can also display *waveforms* that show a tracing of the actual audio signal. Waveforms make it easier to determine exactly where words or other sounds begin and end. An audio *scrubbing* feature helps you find individual sounds by playing only short bursts of audio or by slowing down the speed of the playback.

All systems allow you to set the volume level of each clip individually; some will allow what is called *rubberbanding*, a way of continuously altering sound levels throughout the clip. Depending on your system, you may have up to 24 audio tracks and be able to listen to 2, 4, 8, or more tracks at a time. If you want to monitor more tracks than you are allowed, some systems enable you to combine multiple tracks and

mix them down to a single track. You can then hear all your sound and still monitor new material on additional audio tracks. The mixdown is performed digitally and is of high quality. Even though the tracks are mixed down, they remain separate tracks.

SPECIAL DIGITAL VIDEO EFFECTS

Nonlinear editing systems differ in their effects capabilities. High-end systems can do complex effects in real time. With lower-end systems, the machine may need to first *render* (create) the effect before you can watch it with the rest of the project. Depending on your system, you might be able to create 2D effects, digital video effects (DVE), or 3D effects, each with variations in real-time capabilities and rendering times.

Types of Effects

Most systems offer a wide range of effects; some are applied to the segment (shot), and others are applied to the transitions between segments.

Transitions

Transition effects are used as a transition between two shots. They are similar to traditional video switcher effects. You can simply apply them to your sequence, or customize them by reversing them, repositioning them, adding a border, and so forth. Examples of transition effects are dissolves, wipes, spins, peels, and fades.

Segment Effects

Segment effects are applied to an entire shot or segment. Once an effect is applied, you can customize it, much like the transition effects. These are some examples. A *mask* masks out an area of the image and displays it over any background color. A *color effect* applies a color to the entire image. You can adjust parameters such as luminance, hue, saturation, contrast, and brightness. This effect can be used for color correction, as well as for special effects such as making an image black and white or sepia tone, solarizing, and even controlling the color grain. A *flop* reverses the camera angle, a *flip* places the image upside down, and a *resize* resizes the image and places it over the background color.

Figure 16.6 Title tool bar. Courtesy of Avid Technology, Inc.

Multilayer (Layered or Composited) Effects

Multilayering allows you to combine and play two or more video layers simultaneously. You can create pictures in picture (PIPs) in a fraction of the time possible with an online system. Two types are split screen and superimposition.

Keys

Keying is a way to superimpose two layers of video; one layer forms a sort of keyhole through which the other can be seen. In a *chroma key*, the keyhole is made up of every part of the image that is a certain color. A familiar example is a televised weather report, where the TV meteorologist performs in front of a blue wall. The chroma key "keys out" everything that is blue and replaces it with the weather map.

The *luma key* (for luminance key) carves out the keyhole based on brightness levels. Luminance keys are useful when the keyed graphic does not have a wide range of tones or brightness values. Examples include simple titles, graphic objects, and "spotlights" over an image.

The *matte key* applies a stencil to the sequence, creating a hole in the background shot that is filled with a foreground image. Matte keys are often used to create unusual blends between images and custom transitions.

Motion Effects

Motion effects allow you to create freeze frames, speed up or slow down a shot, or create a strobe motion effect. You can use motion effects to give your video a film look.

Creating Titles

Your editing system may have a Title tool that creates text and graphics that can be saved over a color background or keyed over video. (See Figure 16.6.) You may be able to control font size and style, kerning and leading, color and color blend, transparency, outlines, and shadows.

Performing Real-Time versus Rendered Effects

Real-time effects can be performed immediately after they are applied. Rendered effects need to be calculated ahead of time by the computer and stored on the hard disk as a separate media file. As a result, with rendered effects you need to be concerned with rendering time and disk storage. Two factors affect whether the effect is real time or rendered.

System Configuration. If your system has a board with real-time effects capability, it can play many effects in real time, without rendering them.

Nature of the Effect. Dissolves and superimpositions might be real-time effects, whereas *nested effects* (multiple effects added to a single segment of video) need to be rendered.

Working with Third-Party Graphics Applications

Software packages such as Adobe Photoshop and AfterEffects enable you to manipulate images in ways that previously were the exclusive domain of specialized graphic illustrators and designers. The software is relatively easy to learn and use, is (relatively) inexpensive, and can be run on just about any system.

There is an infinite number of ways you can take advantage of the integration of nonlinear editing systems and third-party graphics programs. Graphics software can be used to perform a range of functions, from fixing a problem, to enhancing an existing image, to creating a completely new graphic element.

Film Match Back Issues

However, if you have shot film and will be matching back for a final print, be careful with all the special video effects. Do your research, understand what the film lab or optical house is realistically able to duplicate, and, if so, how much it will cost.

Ending a Session

At the end of each session, you should back up the project file *twice* to a CD-ROM or even another FireWire disk. If your disk crashes, you will have lost media, which can be redigitized, but not the project file that contains all the logging data as well as your creative choices. Here are some terms to remember:

Project. In some systems, the project folder contains all files of your project (in Final Cut Pro, the project file just points to the media files on the disk). The project window is the place where your work is organized. It contains all the information about your current job, including a listing of all the bins and folders in the current project.

Bin. The "bin" is the storage container for the clips and sequences (edited programs) in your project. Depending on your system, you might also be able to store bins within folders, for one extra level of organization. It is the digital equivalent of the physical bin in which film is stored from retrieval during editing. Shots are logged and digitized into a bin and stored there for the editor.

Clip. A clip is a pointer (reference) to actual video or audio media. It does not contain the actual picture and sound data, just references to them. Think of the media file as your actual footage and the clip as an electronic pointer to the media file. When you play a clip, the system looks for media files that contain the video and audio.

Sequence. The sequence is your edited program, or "master tape." It is a "virtual master," easily created and modified. You create a sequence by editing clips together and storing them in a bin. When you play the sequence, the editing system accesses the clips.

Animation

Animation has become a very large and significant segment of filmmaking. With the advent of digital media, the definition of animation has expanded to include large portions of the visual effects and commercial production industries.

Computer-Generated Images (CGI)

CGI, or just CG, has become the most popular form of animation and visual effects in film and video production. Usually, the term CG refers to 3D computer animation and modeling. It is called "3D" because three-dimensional virtual models of all the characters and models are constructed within the computer. CGI has proven to be an effective method of producing almost anything a filmmaker can imagine. Hollywood films from *The Incredibles* to *The Matrix* trilogy have relied on CG to astound audiences with effects and believable animation that were not achievable without the computer. As the costs have dropped dramatically, independent filmmakers have been drawn toward CG for relatively low budget films. For a CG effect to be effective in a live action film, it must be photorealistic with believable lighting, texture, proportions, and scale. A CG character must be equally convincing with lifelike movement and behavior to blend seamlessly with shot footage. Photoreal effects and animation require a great deal of skill, knowledge, planning, and hard long hours to achieve, so a filmmaker should use them only when necessary and with the proper resources.

Digital Sets and Set Extensions

Perhaps the most cost-effective and straightforward use of CG would be the digital set or set extensions. The complexity of a digital set will vary depending on the length of the shot, the available assets, and, of course, the complexity of the set.

In its simplest form, CG can be used to enhance a still, or stock image. The CG artist must match the virtual camera lens, distance, and position to the actual camera and then build CG objects and buildings with matched lighting and perspective. The process is relatively simple technically because the artist can easily touch up the final with image editing software such as Photoshop to assure a seamless composite. If the shot is held for even a short while, it is always better to make it live by adding some looping animation. An animation loop is a bit of action that seamlessly repeats so the first frame can serve as the last. An animation loop can consist of smoke coming out of a chimney, a flickering light, rain, rippling water, waving leaves, or any other subtle motion that tells viewers they are not looking at a static image.

Adding digital set extensions to a live action shot with a moving camera becomes a more elaborate process. Depending on the complexity of the move, and especially if there are multiple shots of the same digital set, the CG artist will most probably opt to use match moving software. Match move software works by identifying certain points in an image and then determining the position of the camera at a given frame by calculating the difference of those points on screen over time. The software then generates a virtual camera that closely matches the movement of the original real camera. The accuracy of the match is greatly enhanced with the addition of real data such as lens type, as well as the height and position of certain objects.

If you are shooting with the intentions of adding CG elements, it is a good idea to have an experienced CG artist or visual effects (visfx) supervisor on set. To make match moving easier, a visfx supervisor will often place markers such as reflective squares or neon tape at even, measured intervals to give the match move software accurate reference points. The markers are then masked out later in the composite. Most visfx supervisors will ask for a separate shot of the set with a large white ball and then another with a large chrome ball. This is to help the CG artist with reference for shadow and reflection. Depending on the complexity and length of the shot and particulars of the set, it is sometimes easier to create an all-digital environment.

The addition of live action actors creates another set of issues to be addressed. The easiest solution would be to carefully plan the shot so that the actor and the digital elements are not on the same part of the screen. The composite can be achieved with relatively simple masking away from the primary focus. With live actors and digital elements in the same location shot, a good visfx supervisor will usually request the same shot without any actors so his CG artists and compositors have a clean plate as the basis for the final composite. The clean shot will also be a great help to the CG lighters later in the process. Professional studios will often use a process known as high dynamic range imaging (HDR) that more accurately calculates how the environment affects the lighting on the digital object.

Green Screen/Blue Screen

To effetely composite a live action actor with a digital environment, the actor must be shot against a uniform background that can easily be removed in the composite. These solid backgrounds are known as blue screens or the more popular green screens. The colors green and blue are used because they are at the other side of the color spectrum from most skin tones. The computer is then able to select a narrower color range to mask out the background and create a silhouette of the actor. Setting up a green screen shot is not a simple task. The screen itself must have bright uniform lighting. The actor should be at least 10 to 15 feet from the screen and should be lit with separate, warmer toned lighting. The distance is necessary to prevent color bleed from the background on the actor. The bright, evenly lit background is essential to reduce the range of color to be keyed out. Most film schools will have some kind of green screen setup. Professional productions will most likely use green screen studios designed for this purpose (see Figures 16.7 and 16.8). There are small green screen field kits that can be purchased for a few hundred dollars, but they will limit the shot to a small, locked-down area.

Motion Capture

Motion capture or "moco" is a method of digitally recording the movement and position of a live action performer to be used in an animation. There are a few competing technologies for doing this, but by far the most popular method is optical motion capture. Anywhere from 6 to 16 moco cameras are positioned in a large circle pointing inward. The studio should have at least 15 or 20 feet of space inside the circle for the performer to move. The performer wears a body suit with pickups on all of the joints and other key points along the body. The pickups are circular dots about $\frac{1}{4}$-inch wide made of reflective material. The pickups reflect infrared back to the specialized cameras. The multiple cameras are able to triangulate the points and determine the position of the dot within 3D space. This data are then applied to a CG character so it will move in roughly the same manner as the live action performer. Motion control setups are relatively complex and expensive. With prices around $70,000 for a minimal configuration, moco does require a specialized facility. Moco is used a great deal in the gaming industry for sport games and repeating animations. It has not been as successful for lead characters in film and video. A good animator will often work for weeks or months tweaking motion control data to add life back into the character. For short films and videos, it is often more cost-effective to simply film the performer and provide this as reference for the animator.

Keyframe

When most people think of computer animation they are most probably envisioning keyframe character animation. In this process, the animator sets the character in a series of poses over time. The computer software then interpolates the movement of the character

Figure 16.7 Green screen lighting control board.

Figure 16.8 Green screen studio and digital camera.

between each pose. The set poses are known as keyframes. Of course, it is a more complex process than just that. A technical director (or TD) can spend months preparing a model to be animated. Seemingly simple things like hair, clothing, eye movement, and even breathing need to be accounted for to create a convincing character. It is therefore cheaper and more advisable for a short film to use CG characters sparingly. If the character is on screen for a short time, or seen in the distance, or has limited movement, it will help speed up the process.

Rendering and Compositing
The final step in CG animation is rendering and compositing. When 3D software renders, it calculates the effect of light, shadow, color, reflectivity, transparency, diffusion, and hundreds of other properties on the surface of the CG geometry. A final render can take anywhere from a few seconds to days per frame. To quickly view the progress of the piece, a CG animator will create test renders and playblast. A playblast is a crude (usually low-resolution) render of the scene intended to show movement and timing. The playblast will show the models as they appear within the program without complex calculations of light and color. The test renders will be sample frames from different parts of the scene that will show the final look of the piece. Around one third of the resources of every major CG studio is dedicated to the task of rendering. There are usually more technical directors overseeing the lighting and rendering of a film than

character animators. So do not underestimate the importance of this phase of production.

Many studios render out the final frames in passes or plates. In a pass, the CG artist takes a portion of a scene, such as the foreground characters, shadows, or even highlights, and renders them out as a separate, silhouetted image. Unlike live action green screens, the elements are all generated in the computer. The masks are therefore perfectly registered and accurate to the pixel. The CG artist has a great deal more control when working with separate passes. For example, the shadow pass can be easily modified in a compositing program to have soft edges and darker areas toward the middle. If there is a change to one part of the scene, like a character's movement or a background color, the entire scene does not need to be rerendered.

Tools of the Trade

As recently as the mid-1990s, the software and hardware necessary to produce CGI was prohibitively expensive. It was therefore rare to find independent artists working as CGI animators. The cost of powerful computers and their components has dropped dramatically. The software has become more feature rich, inexpensive, and user friendly, leading to the rise of many small one- and two-person shops. With that said, there is still a steep learning curve and price tag for a CGI studio.

The most common professional animation software is @Alias, Maya. Many other excellent packages are available. For instance, 3D Studio Max, SoftImage XSI, Lightwave, and Cinema 4D all have their followings as well. Digital compositing and editing packages have also become more ubiquitous and inexpensive. The most popular are Apple's Shake, Adobe AfterEffects, the AVID line of composing products, Apple Final Cut Pro, and Combustion (and the higher end versions Flame and Inferno). The list goes on. You will find that each software package tends to have its own niche market and loyal following. For example, 3D Studio Max (or just Max as it is known in the trade) is favored by game artists because of its extensive modeling capabilities, plug-ins, and software development kit. Many broadcast designers will use Cinema 4D with AfterEffects because they are a straightforward on the Mac platform. Maya and Shake are favored by feature filmmakers because of the extensive features and node-based compositing. The popularity and capabilities change with each software upgrade. So the above combinations of tools will vary a bit from year to year.

THE HDV REVOLUTION (IN POST)

The HDV format is appealing to video producers, mainly because of its low-cost, high-definition production workflow. The goal is the ability to shoot and edit high-definition video using the same workflow as DV camcorders and editing systems. Even though a 1080i/60 HDV frame contains four times the pixels of its DV counterparts, its data take up the same bandwidth as regular DV (otherwise known as DV25) and use the same mini-DV tapes.

As of the writing of this edition, systems are being developed to create a true HDV post workflow keeping HDV in its native state through the editing process. Post systems will be able to cut it without down converting the signal. Final Cut Pro is currently one of those systems. By the time this edition comes out, we are sure there will be more.

FILM TO VIDEO

This sequence presents the most technical challenges. Filmmakers who want to shoot on film, cut digital, and match back to film must pay attention.

Telecine

The *telecine* is a device for converting film to video. It has a transport to move the film footage across a scanner that reads each frame and converts it to a video signal. Broadcast-quality telecine can handle a variety of film formats (35-mm, 16-mm, super-16, super-8). The telecine's precision film transport can accommodate either positive or negative film at several different speeds with no danger of scratching. One of the widely used telecines is the Cintel (formally the Rank Cintel) *flying spot scanner*. CCD scanners and film chains are also used to transfer film to tape. Commonly, the word *telecine* is used to mean any film-to-tape conversion. The telecine works with a color corrector and various audiotape decks for transferring production sound.

In Europe and countries where PAL or SECAM video is standard, transferring from film to video is fairly straightforward because film footage is shot at 25 fps and video runs at 25 fps. Each frame of film is transferred to one frame of video in a simple one-to-one (1:1) relationship. It become more complicated in North America and other places where NTSC video is standard and film speed is 24 fps. NTSC video

Four Film Frames

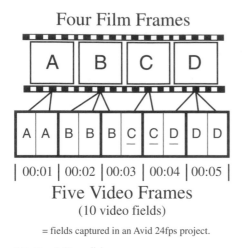

Five Video Frames
(10 video fields)

= fields captured in an Avid 24fps project.

Figure 16.9 3/2 pulldown.

runs faster at 30 fps (actually 29.97). If we simply transfer each frame of film to one frame of video, when we later play back the video, the action will run too fast. Something that took a minute on film will last only 48 seconds on video. Motion will look speeded up, and the sound track will quickly go out of sync. There needs to be a way to stretch out the film as it goes to video.

To keep the footage at the correct speed, some frames of film are transferred to more than one frame of video. A standard sequence called a *3/2 pulldown* (three two) or *2/3 pulldown* distributes every group of four film frames to five frames of video (see Figure 16.9). This creates six additional frames every second, bringing the total from 24 to 30 fps. The term *pulldown* in this sense refers to the idea of the intermittent film shutter mechanism that pulls down a frame.

Audio, on the other hand, does not have "frames" and thus does not move at 24 fps. It just keeps moving constantly all the time.

The 29.97 Complication

There is a complication that adds a wrinkle to this formula. As was mentioned before, NTSC actually runs at 29.97 fps (the color signal addition), which is 0.1 percent slower. The 3/2 pulldown creates a successful relationship between 24 fps film and 30 fps video. However, since the video is in fact running 0.1 percent slower, at 29.97 fps, we must also slow down the film in the telecine by 0.1 percent, to 23.976 fps. The eye cannot detect this slowdown, but it means that real time is disrupted. The importance of this wrinkle is that if you record sync sound while filming, *you must also slow the sound* by 0.1 percent during the transfer to keep it in sync with the picture.

The pulldown sequence can be one of the most confusing concepts in filmmaking. It doesn't concern someone originating in video, only when using non-linear or videotape editing systems to generate film cut lists or EDLs.

Video Dailies

For video dailies, the lab prepares the footage for the transfer and may need to check it over. The transfer technician must be instructed how they want the transfer done. This is a very critical part of the process. Your negative cutter is your guide in this matter.

Film/Video Dailies

The first decision to make is the format of your dailies. Film dailies allow you to view the film as *film*, projected, large, on screen. This is the only way to really see what you've got, and it is most advantageous to see your dailies this way. However, often your budget may not allow you to get both film and video dailies made. If you forego film dailies, you must remember that you are not really seeing all your material. You must keep in mind that the material you are cutting and viewing is video and will inherently look and feel quite different from your final film print. You will have to make decisions thinking ahead to what that might look like on projected film. Also, the smaller screen can also affect the level of detail you are seeing, and sometimes what may be a small, unnoticed detail on video can become a large and obvious mistake (grip stand, lights, actor looking into camera, etc.).

Synced Dailies

For an extra cost the lab can give you your video dailies synced. There is a great advantage in having one tape as your master, containing your synced audio and video with one timecode. If the lab is syncing your dailies, make sure that the slates are done correctly. You do not want the lab technician to take extra time trying to read them. The slates need to be clear, large in frame, in focus, in light, and so on. You will also want to give the lab clear camera and sound reports. You may consider using a "smart slate" in production. This, along with a recording on a timecode DAT recorder, should make the syncing process go smoothly. You can submit your sound on $\frac{1}{4}$-inch tape, which the lab will transfer to DAT for syncing. Also, remember to ask for a *simulDAT* from the lab. This will be a DAT copy of the sound, as it appears on the new synced Beta master, with the identical timecode as the Beta. This basically becomes your new audio master. If you choose to forego getting synced dailies, you will receive video-only dailies from the lab, and your sound will remain on DAT or ¼-inch tape. You will have to sync your material later on videotape or on a nonlinear system. You will have two distinct source tapes (video and sound) with two distinct timecodes.

Windowboxed Dailies

The video frame and the film frame are not the same aspect ratio. Because of this, it becomes necessary to have the lab "windowbox" your film frame within the video frame so you do not lose any information from the edges of the frame. The film frame is scaled down and fitted within black borders inside your video frame. If you do not do this, you will not see the image area around the edges of the film frame and could miss light stands, booms, and so on.

Burn-Ins—Visual Timecode (VTC)

Important information can be burned in (super-imposed) to your video image. The most common burn-ins are timecode and keycode. This gives you a visual connection to every frame's corresponding timecode and keycode. Other information can also be burned in, such as audio timecode and camera roll. You should check with your negative cutter and make sure you are giving her what she wants burned in.

Telecine Logs (Flex Files)

Telecine logs (also known as *flex files*) are files on disks that contain the relationship between your video dailies' timecode and your original film's keycode. They are given to you in a format that can be imported into your logs. By importing them, you have a reference in your logs back to your original film. Later, when you output a cut list for the negative cutter, all the cutting you did on the nonlinear system, which was timecode based, can then be converted back to keycode.

Color Correction

Generally, video dailies are made from the camera original. Color correction may be minimal ("one lite" transfer) or may be carefully done if no further transfer is planned. The colorist can adjust the image either for each scene or once for the entire roll (which is less expensive).

Video Format

Most transfer houses offer a variety of video recorder formats to choose from. For video dailies on projects that will be finished on film or when another transfer is planned after editing, you might use a low-cost format that is compatible with your editing system. If the audio will be synced up in the telecine, consider transforming to a format that has high-quality audio capabilities, such as Betacam or S-VHS.

Logging

Video dailies, either picture-only or synced, must now be logged. If your sound is on a separate source, to be synced later, this must also be logged. Logging used to be done with special software and then imported into the system you were going to use to cut your project. It is now possible to log through most NLE systems.

Bring in all your source tapes to the system. The station should be equipped with source decks (DV, Beta, DAT, etc.) and a monitor. You can now create your bins and log all your clips with as much detail as you want. If your dailies are not synced, remember that you will be logging both video and audio separately. As you control the deck with the interface, you log beginning and ending timecodes, duration, tracks selected, tape name, and any other comments that can help you identify the footage. When logging is completed, save the project to a disk.

PRODUCER
Advise

One of the producer's major responsibilities is to be one step ahead of what is happening. During preproduction, he assembles a well-run production unit, which allows the members of the creative team to function at their optimum ability. Once production is in full swing and, it is hoped, on schedule, the producer's next job is to prepare for postproduction. This is the time for the transition from producer as production manager to producer as postproduction supervisor.

Think of postproduction as a separate period with its own unique set of challenges and problems. Unfortunately, many novice film- and videomakers tend to resist beginning this part of the process. Much of their hesitation is due to their disappointment with the rushes. What was captured on film or tape might not have lived up to their expectations of the script. Each viewing during postproduction might revive some of the nightmare of production. This negativity must be replaced with the excitement and anticipation of being able to sit down and solve all the problems.

The producer can play an invaluable role in helping the director get over this psychological hurdle and get back on track. Even though editing can be downright frustrating, it should be an exciting experience. There might not be troublesome weather or temperamental actors to deal with, but there are still many creative challenges to face.

WHAT YOU WANT FROM A SYSTEM?

Nonlinear editing systems vary in their capabilities. Some systems are capable of very high picture quality, while others work at lower quality. Some have a lot of hard drive space, and some don't. Some have the software and hardware to do complex sound editing, and others have only basic sound capability. There is the question of what other kinds of software you want to interface with and the matter of graphics and effects capability.

As with other aspects of film and video, to be able to choose the right system for you and to work with the one you have, you will need to trace back from the end product. What level of video do you need? If the project is for broadcast, the standards for video are higher than if you are making a multimedia project for a Web site. If you are interested in distributing the project, contact the distributor. Do you require film match-back capability?

Then there is the question of storage. How much material will you be working with? Do you have 50 hours of camera tapes for a documentary, or only 30 minutes of animation? Storage is a huge issue (although it is getting more manageable by the day).

How complex are your sound needs? Do you need just one track of sync sound and a little narration, or will you need to be able to build a multilayered sound track with music and effects? Do you hope to do the sound work on one machine, or will you be outputting to a digital workstation?

Although it may seem that every editing system is unique, they all share certain commonalities that, once understood, need only be translated when switching from one system to another. Once you know one editing system, it becomes considerably easier to learn others. These are not a special set of features, but rather defining characteristics of professional nonlinear editing systems.

WHAT IS AVAILABLE?

There are hundreds of systems out there, and more come on the market all the time. These are just some of the better known ones:

Upper end systems: Avid, Final Cut Pro HD, Discreet Fire (online only), Vegas Video, and Sony

Software packages: Pinnacle DV300, Adobe Premiere, Movie FPC Express, Speed Razor, and MotoDV

EDITING ROOM

It is the producer's job to see that the editing room is properly equipped and that enough money is budgeted for supplies to last the entire postproduction period. Generally, the editor or assistant editor makes the order, and the producer negotiates the deal with the editing facility or vendor that supplies the editing suite or supplies.

POSTPRODUCTION SCHEDULE

With the mix date as your goal, create a schedule, relying on the steps outlined in this chapter. This schedule will undoubtedly go through changes. How long it takes to arrive at the fine cut of your project depends not only on the structural challenges of the picture, but also on how much time it takes to complete the changes for each cut. For students and independents, the availability of editing facilities will have an impact on postproduction progress. Fine-cutting a 10-minute project might take a professional several weeks, but for a beginner, it might take several months.

These various steps serve as benchmarks of your progress through the postproduction period. A convenient aid for staying on schedule is a large calendar board. This larger-than-life visual representation of your postproduction schedule will help the creative team stay focused on its goals as each level is achieved.

Finding an Editor

Good material is the most effective selling tool for attracting creative people. Make an interesting film or video, and people will want to be associated with it.

How much you have to pay for their services (if anything at all) depends on what you can negotiate. It is a given that you do not have much to spend. However, any compensation will create a business relationship and give you some leverage when asking for a 100 percent commitment.

INDEPENDENTS

Advertise through the local media organizations and the editor's guild. You might be able to find a professional assistant editor who works on features, documentaries, or industrials and is looking for projects to expand his reel and gain experience as an editor. It takes a while for an assistant editor to work his way up the union ladder to become a full editor. Short projects offer assistant editors an opportunity to express themselves creatively, and they provide valuable credits. Alternatively, you might find a commercial editor who is looking for narrative or documentary work or a video editor who is looking for film work.

STUDENTS

Ask around and advertise. Put together and post a professional-looking flier for your project. Search for talented students who are interested in pursuing editing as a career. They will be looking for projects like yours to gain valuable experience and expand their professional reels.

Evaluating Prospective Editors

Evaluating an editor's contribution to another film or video requires more than just judging the work. You will need to talk to the director and producer and anyone else involved in the editorial process to find out exactly what the editor's contribution was to the postproduction process. To what extent was the editor responsible for creating the rhythm and pace of the piece? How active a role did the director play in the editing process? Did she stand next to the editor and suggest cuts, or did she stay away from the editing room? Here are some other questions to ask: Was another editor involved? Did the director have to take over? Who was ultimately responsible for the final product?

Speed. How fast did the editor put together a first cut, and how closely did that first cut resemble the final product? How long did the editing process take, and how many assistants worked with the editor?

Footage. What kind of footage did the editor have to work with? Was the coverage terrific? Did it "cut like butter," or did the editor have to perform miracles in the editing room to salvage a piece that was not coming together easily?

Range of Talent. Can the editor serve as a sound editor as well? An editor with this flexibility can save you money and time.

Formats and Equipment. Does the editor have extensive experience in the format and gauge in which you are working (film: 35-mm, 16-mm; video: Beta, $^3/_4$-inch, $^1/_2$-inch, Hi-8, DV, HDV) or the different nonlinear editing systems?

Response to the Material. The director does not want to work with someone who sees the project as just a job. An editor should be inspired by the material and want to spend weeks or months shaping it into a final product.

Temperament. In the editing room, all the mistakes of production are played over again and again. The editor must be sensitive to the director's ego.

Support Crew. Budget permitting, it is helpful for the editor to have an assistant with whom to work. The editor will know an assistant to bring on board.

Compatibility with the Director. The editor–director relationship is important because the two of them will probably have to spend hours together in a small dark room, debating the progress of the project. If the director develops a good working relationship with an editor, she will probably want to continue working with him. They will develop a shorthand communication. The editor develops a feeling for how the director works, and vice versa.

STEPPING BACK AND LOOKING AHEAD

The person who is most responsible for spearheading the editorial process is the director. At this point in time, the producer steps aside and lets the director concentrate on shaping her vision of the film. The director might not want the producer anywhere near the editing room during this period. This gives the producer an objective point of view for the screening of the director's first cut.

While the editing is proceeding, the producer looks ahead and begins setting up the final leg of the postproduction process. An organized producer has already made a deal with a laboratory for all work on the film, from dailies through release prints. Now he must begin looking around for the best deals for the postproduction facilities and personnel who are going to be intricately involved with transforming the work print into a finished film. The postproduction personnel will be responsible for the following:

- Sound design
- ADR/Foley
- Music score
- Mix
- Optical track
- Titles/opticals
- Negative cutting (if matching back to film)
- Timing
- Answer print
- Online editing for video

Finding the right people and the right facilities for this last leg of the production involves research, phone calls, and bids. The more you know, the better prepared you will be to secure the best deals without jeopardizing the creative integrity of the project.

STUDENTS

Many schools have their own mixing, ADR, and Foley stages and transfer rooms. Major metropolitan areas such as New York, Los Angeles, Chicago, and San Francisco have postproduction houses that are willing to give excellent deals to students and independent filmmakers on tight budgets. In New York City, for example, postproduction facilities allow students to mix at night for reduced rates with mixers in training. However, students are advised to take advantage of whatever facility their program offers. It will save them money and enable them to take their time.

KEY POINTS

- Follow the steps described in this chapter in the proper order.
- Be ruthlessly objective in the editing room.
- Cut a film or a video together based only on the material in the editing room. The final product might be different from what you intended. Listen to the material.
- Don't think that technology is a substitute for hard work. Films and videos need time and patience.

chapter seventeen

Sound Postproduction

One takes the storyboards and makes a story real with the sound track. So you record both actors, animating later the sound track frame by frame, so you know exactly which syllable, which letter is sitting on which point in time, frame by frame.

Tatia

DIRECTOR
Building Tracks

Many motion pictures in the 1930s and 1940s relied on production sound—that is, all the dialogue and extra sounds recorded live on the set. Soundstages were quiet, controllable environments for recording not only "clean" dialogue, but also footsteps, door slams, or other sounds necessary for the scene. However, there were particular sounds that couldn't be created live. War movies, westerns, gangster films, horror, or boxing films required their share of gunshots, explosions, face punches, and thunderclaps to authenticate the visual experience.

To supply these films with these kinds of sounds and more, each Hollywood film studio developed its own sound library. For example, whenever it recorded sound for a western or a war movie for the first time, the studio would put a lot of creativity into it and then store these sounds for reuse. RKO's sound library was bolstered by the animal sounds recorded live for the landmark sound effects film *King Kong*. Warner Bros. recorded many kinds of exterior gunshots and bullet ricochets for its big battle movie, the 1936 *Charge of the Light Brigade*. The studio sound department used these same ricochets for decades. Two or three are familiar to modern audiences because they were used when the cartoon character, the *Road Runner*, zips away.

With the breakup of the studio system, and its sound departments, the use of sound in motion pic-

tures didn't progress creatively or technically until the mid-1970s. Filmmakers such as Lucas, Coppola, and Scorsese and sound designers like Walter Murch and Ben Burtt elevated the craft of sound design to an art.

Since then, the sounds that accompany the moving image have become increasingly sophisticated. Audiences now have greater expectations of what they will hear as well as see when experiencing a film or videotape.

For the beginner, the process of creating the final sound track can seem overwhelming. When the picture is cut, it feels finished. At this stage, however, the sound track usually contains only the dialogue recorded on the set. The recording levels are uneven, the quality of the sound ranges from good to unusable, and there are many dead spots, or *holes*, on the track. A few sound effects might have been recorded with the production dialogue, but these might have to be replaced by cleaner or more impressive effects.

In truth, your film or video is only halfway there. You and your team have yet to manufacture what will become the entire aural experience of the film or video.

Much work must still be done to create the sounds related to the world of your picture. Separate sound effects and music tracks must be organized, built, and eventually mixed together to form your sound track. Think of this stage as the final opportunity to polish and refine your picture by adding an exciting dimension of sound to complement and enhance the visual story.

SOUND IN THE DIGITAL AGE

The integration of digital technology into the manufacture and manipulation of sound for film and video has revolutionized how sound tracks are created. Before digital, sound for film would be recorded on the set and then proceed to go through, at least, seven generations before ending up on the screen. We have stated that the technical beauty (aesthetics aside) of digital sound is that it is unchangeable as long as it remains in the digital domain. It also helps that audio takes up nowhere near as much digital space as video and need not be compressed.

Nonlinear editing systems have altered how sound tracks are created. In the traditional film progression, it wasn't until picture was "locked" that the sound work truly began. In linear video, it usually wasn't until the tape was ready to be placed online that the sound was stripped and mixed or "sweetened" at a separate studio. By recording sound on computer hard drives, film- and videomakers can freely cut, paste, copy, and manipulate sounds the same way they can with pictures. The system will keep track of time-code for every piece (clip) of sound. This will enable you to easily determine if the sound is in sync with the picture, quickly and efficiently find material, and precisely locate sounds in your original video or audiotape that were recorded in the field.

Linking the editing of picture and sound allows for a more organic development of storytelling ideas. Film- and videomakers are now able to experiment with creative ways to manipulate how pictures and sound interact with each other. This is a sea change in the editing process.

The sound work completed on a nonlinear system can then be exported to a digital workstation for further sound work using the Open Media Framework Interchange, or *OMF*, format or straight to a mix.

The Digital Audio Workstation

The digital audio workstation, or DAW, has become an integral part of the audio postproduction process. Today, most feature film sound is done digitally on digital workstations. Using digital storage techniques, combined with computer hardware and software such as Pro Tools by digidesign, audio professionals have the capacity to perform most of the audio postproduction process right in the DAW system. For example, musicians can record directly onto the hard drive, create up to 48 virtual tracks, edit the tracks,

create music effects, and mix unlimited versions of the music piece, then output the finished piece at master quality.

The DAW is used to record the edited master audio track, instantly recall and precisely edit sound effects and music cues from libraries stored on hard drives, record and edit voice-overs and narration, and record and edit ADR and Foley effects—all without waiting for any tape to rewind—then mix the finished product in mono, stereo, or versions of both.

Digital audio workstations can provide instant access to all stored media, to design and texture original sounds, and to work with almost unlimited numbers of virtual tracks and interface with digital picture playback. It can be integrated with and networked to a collection of devices, such as other audio, video, and MIDI sources.

BASIC STEPS

Your sound editing work will depend on how the project was shot and what equipment you have available to you. Here are some possibilities.

Projects Shot on Video

Basic Nonlinear Edit. Sound editing is done on the nonlinear editing system. Audio is exported as a finished track, either with the video or separately (to be remarried to the picture after the online edit is done). This method is best for simple or low-budget projects. Some nonlinear editing systems have specialized audio editing software loaded into the system but may lack extensive audio editing power and not be set up for serious mixing.

Nonlinear Edit, Sweetening on DAW, Mix in Studio. Picture editing and basic sound work is done on the nonlinear editing system. After the picture is locked, audio tracks are exported to the DAW (there are several methods). Sound editing is done on the DAW. Mixing is done in a mix studio with good speakers and an optimum environment to judge the mix.

Projects Shot on Film

Traditional Film Edit, Film Mix. Production audio is transferred to 16-mm or 35-mm magnetic track for editing. Picture editing is done with one to three tracks. After picture lock, sound editing is done by splitting sound into many more mag tracks. Mag tracks are brought to the mix studio, where they are played on dubbers in sync with the picture while the sound is recorded onto a *master*, which is usually a *35-mm full coat*. The 35-mm full coat is transferred to an optical track or to whatever format is required for distribution.

The traditional process was the way sound was married to film for 60-plus years. It was a labor intensive method that is rarely done anymore. Digital technology has streamlined the process and given the filmmaker the creative freedom to develop the sound track while the film is being edited, a process that could not happen in the "traditional" manner.

Film-to-Tape Transfer, Edit Nonlinear. Film is transferred to tape for editing. Production audio is transferred with it (already synced up) or synced up on the system. Basic sound work can be done on the system. After the picture is locked, audio tracks are exported to a DAW. Mixing is done in a mix studio.

Traditional Film Edit, Film Mix. Production audio is transferred to 16-mm or 35-mm magnetic track for editing. Picture editing is done with one to three tracks. After picture lock, sound editing is done by splitting sound into many more mag tracks. Mag tracks are brought to the mix studio, where they are played on dubbers in sync with the picture while the sound is recorded onto a *master*, which is usually a *35-mm full coat*. The 35-mm full coat is transferred to an optical track or to whatever format is required for distribution.

These are just some of the options that exist. The technology you use affects the particulars of how you work and in some cases how much control you have. However, the fundamental principles of sound editing remain the same. Sound design is a craft and an art. These tools may help you to manipulate your aural ideas, but they won't do the work for you. ADR, Foley, sound effects, music, voice-over—these contribute to creating a sound track. Technology has changed, but the basic elements of what goes into a sound track have not.

RESPECT FOR SOUND

In every environment there exists a rich and densely varied world of sound. However, most of the information we derive from the world around us comes to us visually. We do not consciously hear. Thus, it might come as a surprise that there is really no such thing as silence. On a peaceful farm on a summer day, for example, you might hear several different kinds of birds, crickets, bees, a flowing stream, wind through the trees and fields, animal noises, a creaking barn, and so on.

If you wish to gain an appreciation for the inherent sounds of any space, try this simple but effective experiment. All you need is a blindfold and a partner you trust. Put on the blindfold, and have your partner lead you around the streets of your town or city. As your brain shifts from processing information from the eyes to processing information from the ears, you will begin to hear every sound around you. This exercise should be an aural awakening for you: You will realize how selective your hearing is. You will begin to see things because of what they sound like rather than what they look like. Cars will pass by, and you will be able to track their physical relationship to you solely from their sound perspective. A supposedly quiet afternoon will be transformed into a cacophony of sounds. If you try this experiment at home, you will discover the many subtle sounds that fill your apparently quiet room.

Your sound track need not include all the sounds that exist in a space at any given time. A sound track can easily become indistinguishable with too many simultaneous sounds. You should select sounds for inclusion on your track, basing your decisions on the criteria discussed in this chapter. Your choices will have a profound impact on the audience's response to the world your characters inhabit.

How We Perceive Sound versus Picture

Picture requires continual redirection of attention; we can only really "see" one shot at a time (even when the screen is split into pieces). We register sounds differently. Unlike the eye, the ear is sensitive to sounds reaching it from any direction, all at the same time. When a new sound comes within our audible range, it does not displace the others (as a shot would), but becomes part of the total sound we hear; it is omnipresent and layered.

Therefore, changes in the level and quality of sound are usually accomplished by dissolves and fades rather than by a simple cut. It requires a different approach than does picture cutting. However, sound design in relation to picture is not a contest of superiority. The sound–picture relationship is a symbiotic one.

Sound Equals Space

The sounds you choose will complete the film and video experience because they bring reality to the illusion of the image. We need to hear sounds that match the images on the screen: traffic on the street corner, birds chirping in a garden, or waves breaking on the shore. These natural elements bring us closer to the drama because they make us believe that what we are seeing is real. The bottom line is that we do not believe it unless we hear it. If we see an actor knocking on a door with no sound, it is not really a knock.

Sounds can indicate a world outside the frame—a world the audience need not see. Imagine, for example, that a couple is having a quiet dinner at home when a rock band begins to practice next door. We need only hear the band to believe that it is there. The rule of thumb for this approach is, *on-screen sound expands off-screen space.*

Sound can connect objects in space that have no inherent relationship to one another. Different shots of city streets can be unified with the addition of a bell tower chiming. If we hear the chimes while seeing the different city shots, we will believe that these streets are all part of the same town. The cafeteria in *The Lunch Date* seems to be a part of Grand Central Station, though shot blocks away, because of the simple train announcements in the background.

A sound can subtly affect how we respond to a scene emotionally. Imagine a scene with a couple in the woods at night, with the sound of crickets and an owl in the background. If, after a while, you add the sound of a howling wolf, it will give the scene a very different feeling. The wolf signals fear; the owl, comfort.

> *The whole element of sound—both music and sound effects—was a rediscovery for me of what the story was. My first idea behind making the film was to tell a story visually, silently. So in the beginning I cut the film together without sound. I wanted to see if it worked. By first doing the images, then doing the sound—suddenly I could think of the story as being a whole set of sounds as well: the train station, the track boards flipping, salad crunching.*
>
> Adam

Sound Equals Production Value

Building the sound track for your project not only is creative and exciting, but it can be cost-effective, too. A well-placed sound or noise brings much to a picture for relatively little expense. You do not have to shoot a rock band to include them in your project. The audience need only hear them. Police cars, fire trucks, or a parade can pass by your character's window without ever being seen.

THE DESIGN OF SOUND

The following is a partial list of the many people who are involved in creating a sound track:

- Sound designer
- Supervising sound editor
- Dialogue editor
- Foley artist
- Foley mixer/editor
- Effects editor
- Automatic dialogue replacement (ADR) supervisor
- ADR recordist
- Various assistants

For low-budget projects, one or two people handle the duties of many of these positions. If your editor will cut the sound on your project, she might also serve as the dialogue, effects, ADR, and Foley editor and might perform many of the Foleys herself. (See the discussion of Foley effects on page 286.)

Let's look at the responsibilities of each position in more detail.

Sound Designer. This term was first used as a professional craft designation in theatrical film in 1979, when an Academy Award for *sound design* was given to Walter Murch for *Apocalypse Now*. The sound designer is responsible for the development and design of all sound track materials. He oversees the entire production and might fulfill his duties by supervising the sound editor. This relatively new position arose out of the need for an overall style for many projects.

> *I owe a lot to the sound designer because one thing was that he got me to stop fiddling around with cutting the picture. The other was that we started discovering the story again. I basically became his assistant. I went to Grand Central again, getting more ambience, getting more sound. I went with a Nagra from school. I went to Penn Station and got train announcements. I did all the Foleys: the salad crunching and things like that. Then we started working on putting the tracks together, and it was a very interesting process.*
>
> Adam

Supervising Sound Editor. This person handles the creation of the dialogue and effects tracks, either working alone or supervising others.

Dialogue Editor. The dialogue editor is responsible for all technically good dialogue tracks. She prepares the tracks to be mixed properly and cuts in all ADR and voice-overs.

Foley Artist. The Foley artist creates sounds for a picture in a studio using his body and a variety of gadgets, hand props, and tools. These sounds must sync up precisely with the action on the screen.

Foley Mixer/Editor. This individual records all the studio-made sound effects. The Foley editor cues all the effects needed and supervises the Foley artist for correct sound of effect and sync.

Effects Editor. The effects editor provides all the required sounds for the picture—everything from birds chirping to cars screeching to doors slamming. These sounds come from sound effects libraries or live recordings on the set or are created by the effects editor. He is responsible for editing all sound effects and for their placement in the sound track in order to facilitate the final mix.

ADR Supervisor. This individual programs each line that must be replaced by ADR. He aids the director in determining the proper sync.

ADR Recordist. This sound person operates the ADR recording machine. He is responsible for microphone placement for perspective and matching of original dialogue.

Various Assistants. Among other things, assistant editors collect and log tracks, file trims, build reels, and keep the editing rooms organized and running efficiently.

The following are some of the tools for the digital sound designer:

- Digital audio workstation (DAW)
- Computer and hard disk
- ADR/Foley stage
- Mikes
- Cue sheets
- SFX library

If you stay entirely in a film environment, you will also employ these tools:

- Flatbed editing table
- Synchronizer
- Squawk box
- Splicer
- Trim bins

Do You Need a Sound Designer?

A short picture, 5 to 10 minutes in length, might end up with 5 to 10 tracks of dialogue, music, and effects. For a novice editor or director–editor, this is a manageable number. With more ambitious projects of 15 to 30 minutes, many beginners and students decide to work with a sound designer. Having just learned picture editing, they tend to be overwhelmed by the prospect of sound work. They know it is necessary, but are intimidated by this completely new technical challenge. If they can afford it, they bring in someone who will take them through the process, providing a valuable learning experience at the same time.

Working on a short film or video offers novice sound editors an opportunity to gain experience and build their sample reels. They might be drawn to your project because it offers a particular challenge or an opportunity to work with interesting material. If a salary is involved, it is probably below the norm for seasoned professionals.

Working with a sound designer has obvious benefits. Take advantage of the learning experience. Ask to be involved in all the sound design steps for your picture. Share your ideas, express your concept of sound, but give the sound designer the creative space to explore other interesting sound possibilities. A sound person who has been in the business for even a short time not only will have access to sound libraries, but will have built up his own "library." Give the sound editor accurate sound reports and continuity notes because he will need to get to the original DAT master.

The film came together because of the sound editor. He was the one who came in and said, "Listen, you've got to define this opening. Here's how we're going to use music and sound effects to do it, and what you're going to do is intersperse the titles," which really gave the opening a sense of focus. If you had the titles before the montage, it would seem very repetitive: titles, montage, and then Truman. By breaking up the montage with the titles, which was the sound editor's idea, and using the music the way we did, it gave an unexpected energy and a drive to that moment when we come down the rope and see Truman and the film officially starts.

Howard

PREPARING FOR THE MIX

All the work fleshing out the sound track is done to prepare for the mix, or, as it is called on the West Coast, the *dub*. The mix is the last opportunity you'll have to clarify your artistic goals for the piece. It is during this process that the picture is seamlessly married to the three basic sounds: dialogue, music, and effects.

To mix these elements together effectively, the tracks containing them are organized in such a way as to allow the mixer to set levels and equalization between sound cuts. The success of the mix relies as much on well-prepared tracks as it does on the skill of the individual who operates the board. To prepare properly for the mix, it is vital to understand what happens during the mix. Beginners should sit in on as many mixing sessions as possible and should talk to sound editors about what is required before the mix can take place.

Sound work should begin while the picture is still being cut. The sounds recorded on the set or researched through sound libraries should be collected, labeled, transferred, and logged. If you preview some sounds against the picture while you edit, by the time you are ready to build the tracks, you will have made some key decisions. For example, if sirens are to be heard during a scene, cut with those sounds already on the second track because they will affect the rhythm of how the scene is cut.

It might be necessary for the editor to go out to the field to record a specialized sound with a Nagra or DAT recording machine. If you are looking for the sound of a revving 1967 Volkswagen Beetle, you might have to find the car and record it yourself. Creating and previewing many of the sounds before locking the picture will ease the crunch during the final postproduction phase.

Once the picture is locked, the job of sound design begins in earnest. Only when the picture length has been finalized can the sound editor know the exact timing required for dialogue or effects tracks. If the picture is constantly changing, all the tracks and the mix cue sheets will have to be adjusted accordingly. All picture changes after the lock must be announced to the sound designer so that he can adjust the timing to keep the sound track frame-accurate.

SPOTTING

Once the picture has been locked, the director is ready to sit down with the sound team and decide what is needed to flesh out the sound track of her film or video. This process is called *spotting* the picture. The director, sound designer, and editor look at the picture in a precise and deliberate way, scene by scene, and indicate which sounds are appropriate at any given moment.

During the spotting session, they discuss the following:

On-Screen Sounds. These are sounds you can see being made in the frame, such as footsteps and door slams.

Ambient Sounds. These sounds are associated with the natural ambience of a space—for example, birds chirping, wind blowing, and traffic.

Off-Screen Sounds. Off-screen sounds occur outside the frame. Examples are neighbors arguing in the hallway and a television blaring in the next room.

Unusual Sounds. These sounds are not associated with the scene either on- or off-screen. If the director is planning a stylistic approach to sound, she might use surreal or manufactured sounds (the electronic buzz of the light sabers in *Star Wars*, for example) or ordinary sounds used out of context. An example is the climactic fight sequence of Martin Scorsese's *Raging Bull*, which features sounds that are not normally found in a boxing ring, such as wind blowing and animal growls.

Enhanced Sounds. For example, a lion roar could be used to emphasize the power of a wave.

Production Dialogue. The spotting session is an opportunity to review the quality of the production dialogue. The film editor should be able to point out the tracks that are good and those that might have to be replaced with new lines recorded with ADR. Hearing the production dialogue in a projection room with a good sound system will enable the editor to confirm any questionable tracks.

A general rule when spotting sounds is if you can see it, you should hear it. On the other hand, too many sounds might interfere with the dialogue, the mood of the scene, or the music the director is planning to use. The director should keep in mind how she plans to blend effects and music in a scene. (The use of music is discussed later in this chapter.) However, most effects editors approach each project as if there will be no music, and they give the director enough sounds to create a full and rich track without it because sound

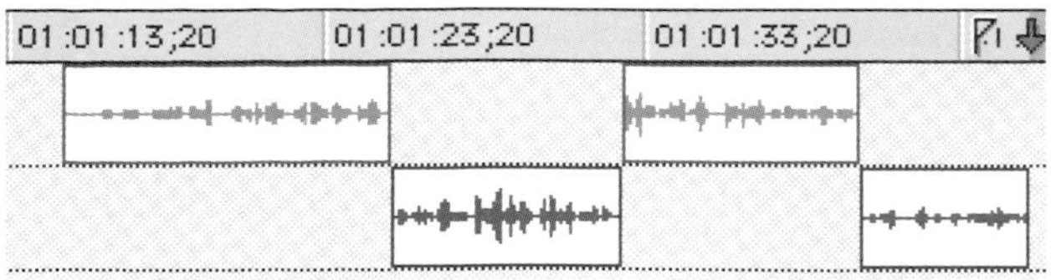

Figure 17.1 Split audio tracks.

effects often can stir audiences' emotions in a way similar to the impact of music.

DIALOGUE TRACKS

Unless the piece has no dialogue, your first responsibility is to make sure the audience can hear the dialogue. This includes words spoken by actors on-screen, off-screen, and in voice-overs. Analyze the production tracks and decide which ones are acceptable and which ones might have to be replaced. Replacements can be confirmed during the spotting session. The "clean" tracks and the "dirty" tracks should be obvious. Ask for advice with the questionable ones.

Much can be done in the mixing stage to clean up a line of dialogue. Inappropriate sounds such as camera noise or floor squeaks can be removed. The question is how much background noise can be tolerated. You don't want the audience to strain to hear the words. Background noise will become even more of an issue when the mixed track is transferred to the final digital master or optical track. Because some parts of the sound spectrum can be eliminated on the track, you might need to have a professional sound editor or a mixer analyze certain tracks. You might be forced to replace some or all of the "dirty" lines using ADR.

The editor now separates or splits the lines of dialogue onto enough tracks to enable the mixer to easily blend and equalize the dialogue (see Figure 17.1). Some situations require separate dialogue tracks.

Control Levels. A piece of dialogue must be separated if it requires its own sound level in the scene. It is difficult for a mixer to make radical adjustments between different lines of dialogue on the same track. If character A, meant to be played softly, is immediately followed by character B, whose delivery is meant to be loud, the mixer will not have time to set a new level for the incoming sound if it is on the same track. With separate tracks, the mixer can preset the appropriate levels.

Background Changes. Different camera setups sometimes involve different background ambiences. For example, a scene with two people talking on a street corner might have one background on the traffic side (loud traffic noises) and one on the sidewalk side (people walking). These two setups require two different levels.

Camera Perspectives. Different camera angles (wide, medium, and close) of the same scene have different sound perspectives. The lines for these camera angles might have to be put on different tracks to enable the mixer to set the appropriate levels. Sound perspectives ideally should match camera perspectives. Cutting between the different perspectives in the same scene will require separate sound adjustments so that the cutting seems more natural.

Overlapping Dialogue. If an on-camera character speaks and is interrupted by an off-camera character, the editor can overlap the two pieces of dialogue. Speech is overlapped in real life. Splitting tracks allows the editor to simulate this reality and allows the mixer to control properly the blending of the two voices on the final track.

Telephone Conversations. Tracks are also split to enable cutting between two characters who are having a phone conversation. The editor will cut between a clean sound and one with "futz" (the sound of a voice filtered through a phone line). Even though most of the conversation will be heard this way, it should be recorded clean on the set. Any sound that is to be deliberately distorted through bad speakers or behind doors should always be recorded clean on the set to give the dialogue editor and mixer complete freedom to control the nature of the sound.

Mixing Different Conversations. Imagine a character walking through a busy party. She hears snippets of different conversations as she passes from one group to another. Each conversation must be separated on a different track to enable the mixer to control the tone as well as the changing perspective of each voice as the main character approaches and moves farther away.

Cutting Dialogue

Much of dialogue editing consists of evening out the background ambience or room tone of each scene and replacing the holes, or empty spots, in the track. The editor blends together different shots with different backgrounds by creating what are called *dialogue extensions*. This requires adding extra room tone (preferably from the existing take) to the head of one dialogue track and the tail of another so the mixer can do a quick sound dissolve fade, or segue, between the two. The result is a softening of the "sound bump" that might be heard when cutting between two different sound backgrounds.

Automatic Dialogue Replacement (ADR)

What happens if the sound was not recorded well? What if there was a helicopter buzzing overhead during the take you want to use in the scene? What if you shot a scene by the ocean, and the rhythmic pounding of the surf does not match from cut to cut?

Mixers are miracle workers. They can sometimes dial out a low hum or even an airplane in the background, but dirty tracks are dirty tracks. The only way to fix a badly recorded track is to replace the dialogue. Looping a line with ADR does this. In this electronic process, the actor stands in a soundproof studio in front of a screen and wears headphones. The scene is projected on the screen. The actor sees and hears the way the line was spoken and practices matching its cadence. When ready for a take, the actor waits for a visual or aural cue and repeats the line into a microphone. He might get it right on the first try, or he might have to repeat the line a number of times before achieving proper sync and performance. In cases of lengthy lines or even speeches, he might have to pick the speech apart line by line or even word by word.

Some actors are adept at this process, and some are not. Some are intimidated by having to duplicate in a dark and sterile room what was created in the cozy environment of the set.

The editor then cuts the rerecorded line into a new dialogue track. If the actor has made a good match, the editor can simply drop in the new material. More often, the editor has to play with the line, cutting a frame here, adding a frame there, until the dialogue is in sync with the performance.

The ADR editor has many functions, including these:

- Programming ADR lines
- Selecting the exact footage and the exact line to be rerecorded

- Creating ADR cue sheets
- Helping actors with sync
- Cutting lines into the show

ADR is recorded onto an eight-track hard drive, so alternate takes can easily be saved. In fact, some directors use ADR not because of the quality of the sound, but because they want to improve or change the nature of a performance. Having the budget to accomplish this is a luxury for most beginners, who usually can't afford ADR at all.

Proper preparation for the ADR session plays an important role in its success. Paying for a studio and the engineer's labor is expensive. You do not want to waste any time in confusion over what needs to be recorded.

There are ways of creating effective ADR lines without going into a studio. You can create your own soundproof environment at home or in the editing room and perform many of these tasks there. With looping techniques and a portable cassette player, it is possible to have the actor listen to a line reading a number of times and repeat that line in a clean environment. It is not necessary to repeat long speeches. They can be broken up one line at a time.

> **DIRECTORS**
>
> If you are shooting a scene that will obviously need to be looped, take the actors and the production sound mixer off to a quiet room immediately upon completion of the scene. Have the actors listen to their lines on headphones and repeat them into a microphone and another tape recorder. This new dialogue might save you a trip to the ADR room. The actors are fresh from the scene and might be able to duplicate their tone and cadence perfectly. The lines might not be exactly in sync, but a good ADR editor should be able to shift them into place easily.

ADR Spotting

It is sometimes easier to replace an entire scene with ADR than to replace a few lines. It is certainly easier to redo a whole line rather than try to replace a word. Trying to match a line spoken on the set with one recorded in the soundproof environment of a studio is difficult. The sound editor must "dirty" the words with background ambience and other sounds. The mixer also has ways to help match the two. However, there always remains a perceptible difference between the tone and ambience of ADR and production dialogue, no matter what magic is performed to blend them together.

On the other hand, rerecording an entire scene allows the editor to create a consistent background ambience throughout the scene. Viewers accept the ADR and the background as natural because they are not comparing it to dialogue that was recorded on the set.

Adding and Altering Lines with ADR

During picture cutting, the director might realize that she needs to add off-camera lines that were not in the script. ADR offers an opportunity to add characters to a scene without visuals. They can exist outside the frame through sound as long as there is some logic behind their presence. In *The Lunch Date*, the audience could have heard the voices of a couple arguing in another booth. While the woman wandered through Grand Central Station, she could have heard bits and pieces of the conversations around her.

It is also possible to alter dialogue spoken on-screen. For example, if a character turns his head in the middle of a line and the director decides that she wants him to say something else, the new line can be dubbed in. The head turn distracts viewers from noticing that the mouth and the lines do not exactly match. It is possible to change a line without a physical distraction, although it is a little harder. The farther away the lips are from the camera, the easier it is to fudge the dialogue. Suppose the director wants the character to say, "I want to go to Miami" instead of the recorded line, "I need to get a new pair of shoes." Here are three ways to make this change:

- Dub the new line in as the character turns away.
- Match the new line to a reaction shot of the character to whom the line is addressed.
- Dub the new line in over a long shot in which the character's lips are not visible.

These simple manipulations can have a profound effect on the outcome of your story. The alteration of one line can change the dramatic content of an entire scene. The possibilities of postproduction ADR give the director other storytelling devices that can enhance and complement what she achieved on the set. These manipulations might seem like tricks, but remember that making a film or video involves illusion. It is best to make these decisions before locking the picture because these types of alterations affect picture as well as sound.

Walla

Walla is a specialized form of dialogue: the sound of generic voices that were not recorded on the set.

These sounds flesh out the background, providing verbal atmosphere for a busy bar or restaurant, a party, or any space with people talking or murmuring.

If the production sound mixer was unable to record wild atmosphere on the set, the sound effects editor can program a Walla recording session. Some experts in the industry have a special talent for looking at a scene and improvising general noise and whatever specific comments the scene requires.

The special voiceover groups or "Loop Groups" that perform Walla can also duplicate major characters who are not available for ADR postproduction work. If an actor is busy when you schedule the ADR sessions, rather than wait for her schedule to free up, you might employ a "voice alike" to impersonate her.

Voice-overs and Narration

A voice-over is a separate voice that is not in sync with the picture. It could represent, among other things, the main character commenting on or narrating the story. Some scripts start off with a voice-over built into the structure of the story. Even stories without this script device sometimes end up with some sort of voice-over in the final product. In the course of editing, the director might discover that she needs something to bind the audience more closely to the main character or narrative. Key exposition might be missing, the story might lack a focus, or it might not engage the audience sufficiently. Voice-over can help blend the images into a cohesive story.

There are three basic approaches to employing a narration:

- First person (the main character is telling the story, in his or her voice)
- Third person (a secondary character is telling the story)
- Omniscient (a voice of someone not in the film is telling the story)

If the story needs a unifying point of view, voice-over can do this very simply. It allows the audience to enter the world of the story through a particular perspective.

- It has the power to bind together shots or scenes that have no apparent logic to them.
- It can communicate important exposition that is not clear in the narrative.
- It can strengthen the main character's point of view and thus the audience's emotional

connection to that character by personalizing what viewers see.

Do not use voice-over to tell viewers what they are seeing. This would be redundant (unless you intend it to be for comic or ironic purposes). Think of voice-over as a device to broaden understanding of the story, the characters, or the conflict.

It is necessary to work with a temporary voice-over track while editing the picture in order to cut the picture to a specific length. A rough recording by the director or editor will do, just to get an idea. A polished recording with the actor will be made in a studio.

SOUND EFFECTS TRACKS

Sound effects add a whole new dimension to a picture. The most important consideration should be what you specifically want to hear in a scene. The first step is to isolate the sounds viewers can visually identify, such as footsteps or someone knocking on a door. The next step is to choose the sounds that are identified with a particular environment. In *The Lunch Date*, these are the sounds of Grand Central Station. From this point, the editor begins to assemble sounds that will enlarge the world of your project and add a level of information that doesn't exist in the picture.

Once the picture is spotted, the sound designer begins to accumulate the sounds needed to flesh out the director's ideas. These sounds come from many places:

- Wild sounds recorded on the set
- Sounds manufactured live on location
- Wild sounds recorded after principal photography
- Prerecorded effects from sound effects libraries
- Electronically manufactured sound effects
- Effects manufactured in a studio (Foley effects)

All these sounds must be dubbed from their original format to digital sound for video. Let's look at each of these sources in more detail.

Wild Sounds Recorded on the Set. *Wild sound* refers to any recorded sound that is not in sync with the picture. In addition to recording dialogue and room tone, during principal photography the production sound mixer should capture any wild sounds that might be used in the editing room. These include the pounding surf, frogs, wind in the trees, and any distinctive ambient sounds that are unique to a specific location.

Sounds Manufactured Live on Location. The production sound mixer sometimes records live sounds that accompany a shot—that is, sounds that happen within the frame, such as footsteps or door slams. The editor cuts these in later.

Wild Sounds Recorded after Principal Photography. The sound effects editor must sometimes record certain effects that are not available in a library and were not recorded on the set. This involves going out into the field with a Nagra or DAT recording device and picking up or creating unique sounds and aural effects. For example, the sound effects editor might need the sound of a broken lawnmower on a hot summer's day or the rumble of an old pickup truck.

Prerecorded Effects from Sound Effects Libraries. Many sound effects are available on CD. They offer a wide range of backgrounds and specific sounds such as birds, crickets, traffic, gunshots, tire squeals, or car noises.

Electronically Manufactured Sound Effects. Some sound effects can be manufactured on a synthesizer. Various live sounds can be recorded and then layered electronically one on top of another to create interesting and unique effects.

Online Sound Libraries. There are many Web sites dedicated to sound effects and music. Many offer royalty-free effects and music. Sounddogs.com is one of the largest online sound effects libraries on the Internet. Soundsonline.com is a source for professional copyright-cleared, royalty-free sounds in the industry offering more than 1,000 virtual instruments and sound libraries to choose from. Soundrangers.com was created to fulfill the sonic needs of a new technological generation. It specializes in generating state-of-the-art, royalty-free sound effects and music for such high-tech platforms as virtual user interfaces, games, online and CD-ROM entertainment, Web sites, and communication devices. SoundFX.com distributes the Sound Effects Libraries, Music Libraries, and Pro-Audio Software worldwide.

Effects Manufactured in a Studio (Foley Effects). Sounds that must sync up precisely with the picture can be created on a Foley stage. This includes all types of body movement, such as footsteps, or eating sounds. The specialists who perform these sounds are called Foley artists. The term comes from Jack Foley, the sound editor who pioneered this process.

> *I didn't go into the ADR studio at all. I didn't rerecord any of the dialogue. It was all there. The only material I had to add was some of the smaller sounds, which I Foleyed myself.*
>
> Adam

A Foley stage has many different kinds of floor surfaces that characters might walk on in the course of a scene, such as cement, hardwood, sand, and earth. It also includes an oddball selection of hand props and tools that can be used to create a wide range of noises. On a Foley stage, you might find wind machines, buzzers, door latches, all kinds of bells, drinking glasses, nuts and bolts, mallets, and so forth.

The key to this process is that the sounds themselves do not have to be created with the exact objects or movements seen on the screen. All that matters is that the sounds appear to match the visuals. A Foley artist chomping on an apple can imitate the effect of a branch breaking. When shaken, a belt buckle will sound like a horse's bridle.

Before starting sound work, the student or beginner is urged to visit a Foley stage and watch the process in action. Foley artists are talented mimics. They can watch a person on the screen walk down a hall once and, upon playback, can duplicate perfectly the rhythm and cadence of the actor's unique walk.

However, Foley rooms and Foley artists can be expensive. You can achieve excellent results from taping sessions at home while screening a video copy of the project. If the recording is not in perfect sync, some effort in the editing room moving the sounds back and forth should make the material effective.

> *We knew we were going to have to buy two hours of Foley time. We booked two hours, and that's all we used. We were very specific about what we were going to get. We didn't go after everything. We were going to go after footsteps and that was it, footsteps in the gym. The other Foley effects I did myself—the ones that didn't have to be in sync but could be slugged in. We could slug them into the track and get them into sync ourselves.*
>
> *A Foley artist, which student films don't normally use, did the actual Foley sounds. In the gym where we filmed, the sound of real footsteps was nonexistent. I wanted all the sneaker squeaks, how*

> *they resounded and how they echoed. We didn't hear them at all because of the way the floor was waxed. I thought the footsteps in the gym said something about this place, and I knew I had to recreate them, and a student really can't do that. You can't really cut several thousand footsteps into sync; you don't have time to do that. Those things had to be done by a Foley artist; they had to be put on 35 full coat and had to stay in sync.*
>
> *I also had some other ideas. I wanted Truman to have his own specific set of footsteps. I wanted them to have their own character and their own sound. So we got a very old pair of sneakers, put a sponge in them, and filled them with water. The Foley artists walked with wet sloppy sneakers on, and then we modified it so it had these squishy sounds. . . . All of his footsteps sounded like that.*
>
> *We spent the last two weeks of our five-week postproduction schedule putting effect sounds into place—adding the arrow sounds, adding the rope breaking (which was really the sound of a whip slowed way, way down), doing the Foley, bringing in my own Foley effects, taking sound effects off the CDs, and putting it all together.*
>
> Howard

Unique or Enhanced Sounds

For some reason, you might need to create an unusual sound for your picture. You might need to manufacture or invent something new. This is what sound designers are paid to do. If you are doing the sound on your own, look for ways to fabricate strange and interesting sounds from simple ideas. Natural sounds can be altered to resemble something completely different. The amplified and distorted sound of a person breathing can be terrifying, for example. Sounds can also be layered to create effects that are more interesting than any individual sound.

Cue Sheets

A convenient way of roughing out your sound ideas is to use mixing cue sheets as a visual guide (Figure 17.2). Each column on the sheet represents a single track; your short project might use anywhere from 5 to 20 tracks. Each track contains any number of specific sounds, which are laid out according to the exact number on the nonlinear timeline necessary to match the picture. Two large parts of sound editing are precision and accuracy. It is not only about what kind of sound to use, but also where it should be placed. In

MIXING CUE SHEET

DATE: _____

REEL: ___1 OF 2___

NAME: **J. SMITH**   SUBJECT: ___"TITLE"___   PAGE: ___1___

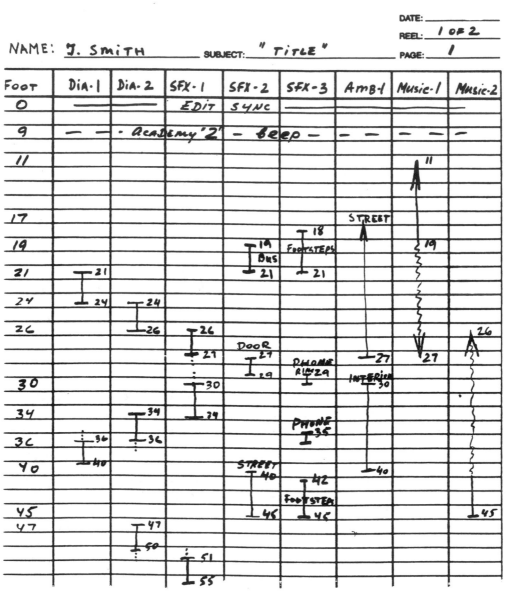

Figure 17.2 Sample cue sheet. This mix consists of two split dialogue tracks, three effects tracks, one ambience track, and two music tracks.

the developmental stage, however, you need only rough out sounds on the cue sheets to get an idea of the grand design for your picture. These rough ideas will serve as a preliminary chart of what will eventually become your sound track.

For the actual mix, the need for accuracy becomes apparent when you remember that the mixer sits in front of a console, facing a screen with a large digital footage counter at the base of it. This footage counter tells the mixer when to expect a sound cue to come

up. The counter and the cue sheets are the mixer's only references. They must be frame-accurate.

If you are bringing in a Pro-Tools session, it may not be necessary to supply a cut sheet to the mixer. It is best to ask the mixer in advance whether he or she wants a cue sheet or not and if so, what format is acceptable. The mixing facility may even have software specifically designed for cue sheets.

Two large parts of sound editing are precision and accuracy. It is not only about what kind of sound to use, but also where it should be placed. In the developmental stage, however, you need only rough out sounds on the cue sheets to get an idea of the grand design for your picture. These rough ideas will serve as a preliminary chart of what will eventually become your sound track.

As you break down and flesh out the sounds for each scene, deal with one sound at a time. One of the problems with sound editing on a flatbed editing machine is that you can't hear all the sounds together until you are in the mixing studio. You can only preview one or two sounds at a time (depending on the number of sound heads on your editing machine). For this reason, it's a good idea to have an interlock screening of the picture, with all the tracks running, before the final mix to see how well you are prepared.

As you accumulate and organize your sounds, you will fill up your cue sheets. They will resemble a checkerboard, with different sounds and bits of dialogue spread out over the tracks, allowing the mixer to set exact levels for each sound, dialogue, and music cue.

Laying in sound effects requires the time-consuming process of making sure each sound comes in and out in precisely the right relationship to the picture.

> **STUDENTS**
> Some schools offer the opportunity to cut on a flatbed for the "experience" of handling film and mag stock prior to entering the nonlinear editing environment. This philosophy affords the student a tactile understanding of the relationship between picture and sound. When building tracks on a flatbed, the sound is recorded onto magnetic tape and sections where there is no sound on a track is made up of "fill." This fill is discarded release print material that holds the place of the sound to match the cue sheets. Fill is not leader.

MUSIC TRACKS

The final major creative element attached to the picture is music. Music has been part of the motion picture experience since the days of silent films, when a piano, organ, or small instrumental group accompanied the actions on the screen. The reason for the music at first may have been pragmatic, to cover up the noise of the projector, but it was discovered that music added considerably to the emotional mood of the film. It also supplied an audible continuity that helped hold together the separate images on the screen.

In the early days of sound on film, music was only used sporadically or not at all because it had to be recorded as part of the scene or played offstage separately (which was why musicals became popular). It was not until 1932 that a sound mixing process was developed that permitted music to be recorded separately from the dialogue, thus allowing it to be edited and added at a later time.

The impact of music on your project cannot be underestimated. Music can ignite strong emotions very quickly. A well-chosen and well-placed melody can take your piece to a higher emotional level. On the other hand, inappropriate or excessive music can overwhelm the delicate fabric of your story.

What does music do?

- It binds a picture together, particularly cuts and sequences. It connects shots that might not have apparent connections.
- It triggers emotional responses from the audience.
- It can drive a sequence, instilling it with energy and purpose.
- It complements or underscores the drama on the screen, either by enhancement or counterpoint.
- It strengthens a character's presence through theme. If viewers can identify a character's theme, music can place the character in a scene without his presence.
- It has the ability to transport the audience to another time and place. A single instrument can be associated with an entire culture. When we hear bagpipes, we think of Scotland. The music of any time period has the power to carry us back in time immediately.
- It creates an expectation about the story. Wistful music denotes a sad or melancholy piece. A light and bubbly melody over the same footage sets the audience up for an entirely different story.

Music has the power to manipulate how we feel about what we are seeing in a way we take for granted. To get an understanding of this power, try this experiment. Screen a montage sequence from a well-known film or video that already has music on it. Then find a piece of music with a very different mood or feel. If the original piece of music is light and airy, choose a piece that is suspenseful or dark. Play the sequence again, substituting the new piece of music for the original sound track. You will discover that music has the power to alter completely how we perceive a series of images. Respect the power of music when choosing a selection for your short piece.

The music in a film or video can serve as either an underscore or a source. *Underscore* refers to music that plays under the action. There is no visible or implied source within the frame for this kind of music. On the other hand, *source* refers to music that emanates from a visible or implied source within the frame, such as a radio, a live band, or a tape player. The audience doesn't necessarily have to see the source of a piece of music to accept its presence. A radio might be turned on in another room, or a band might be playing in the next apartment.

Despite music's strong influence on the film and video experience, the composer is one of the last creative voices to become involved in a picture. It is very unusual for the composer to be called in at the script stage. I often go to see films that use really bombastic film music, and I'm completely distracted by it. I'm offended as a viewer when the music tells me what to feel. It usually indicates a failure of the footage to do its job. I frankly think fiction film is more guilty of this than documentary, although every once in a while you see it happening in a documentary, where music will underscore an interviewer's words. I'm much more into a minimalist approach.

Jan

The Music Team

A complete music team consists of the following individuals:

Composer. The composer is responsible for writing the original score. He might also arrange, orchestrate, and conduct the music.

Arranger/Orchestrator. The arranger adapts a piece of previously written music or the composer's basic musical ideas for the score and arranges it for the orchestrator, who creates parts and assigns them to various instruments.

Copyist. The copyist extracts the parts for the individual instruments from the score for use by the musicians and the conductor.

Music Supervisor/Producer. This person, a representative of the studio or production company, is responsible for overseeing the business, practical, and creative aspects of scoring the film or video.

Music Editor. The music editor handles all the details regarding synchronization of the score with the picture.

Music Contractor. The music contractor hires musicians, books the studio, and coordinates all business and financial activities for the recording sessions.

Musicians. Musicians perform their parts during the recording of the score. The number of players required depends on the nature of the arrangement.

Conductor. The conductor interprets the score and directs the orchestra to play on cue.

Mixing Engineer. The mixing engineer is responsible for mixing the various musical sounds into the recorded composite version.

The Original Score

Music for a picture can come from two sources. It might be either an original score written and orchestrated specifically for your project or prerecorded existing music.

Finding the right composer for your project is important. Your goal is to find someone who is sensitive to your story. Not all composers are right for all pictures. Some directors work with young composers who are interested in building their reels and gaining valuable experience. They need you as much as you need them. When working with a composer, you should provide him with a video copy of your fine cut (either shot or transferred off the editing table). The composer will use this to develop musical ideas.

Finding a Composer

It is much easier than you may imagine to find a composer for a short project. Composers who want to make the move into the film and video market are eager for experience and are willing to work either for free or for very little. As for all crew positions, you must advertise and ask around. If you see a short film or video with an impressive musical score, get in touch with the director and producer. Ask about his or her experience working with the composer. Then contact the composer and ask to hear more of his work.

You might want to let the composer hear the temp music you have cut to the picture. The risk of this method is that the composer might try to duplicate the temp music rather than come up with new musical ideas. The other method is to let the composer come up with his own ideas in response to the material. Give the composer the space to be inspired by the material.

There are several advantages in using a temp score when developing a relationship with a composer. It can give the composer insight into the director's musical ideas and serve as a point of departure from which they can discuss musical ideas for the film or video. The danger of a temp score is that the director might fall in love with music the composer cannot top and that is unavailable because it is too expensive.

Music Spotting

Once you have settled on a composer, you can begin spotting the picture in earnest. With the composer, review the entire picture, scene by scene, to discuss the *music cues*—that is, the moments that are appropriate for music. When working with film, spotting should be done on a flatbed editing table so that you can go slowly back and forth over the material.

Speaking the language of music can be frustrating if you aren't musically literate. In the absence of a temp track, you can give the composer an idea of what you are striving for by playing themes, instrumental pieces, and tempos you think are appropriate and talking about different genres of music.

The composer can help bridge this potential communication gap by bringing in selected music cues to play against the picture. This will help the composer get a clearer understanding of what the director wants. Music expresses emotion. It bypasses the brain and works directly on the heart. Yet what might be right for the composer might be wrong for the director or producer.

The addition of music will greatly enhance the film or video experience, but so will the sound effects. Do not let these two elements fight each other for dominance on the sound track. During the spotting session, if you know that you want a loud effect, have the composer keep the music gentle or use no music at all during that section of the film. One way to approach the spotting session is to let the composer go off with a video copy of your piece and spot it without your feedback. Allow the composer the freedom to respond to the material alone.

The Music Editor

After the director and composer agree on where music should be placed and on a musical style that is appropriate for the piece, the composer has two challenges: (1) to write music that enhances the visual imagery effectively and (2) to make the music fit precisely into exact music cues. It has traditionally been the music editor's role to break down each music cue into a series of beats by employing "click tracks." A *click track* is a synchronous metronome that is locked to the picture. It allows the composer to write a melody or musical riff that will stay in sync with the picture. The beats can be altered to satisfy any rhythmic changes, from slow and easy to fast and frantic. The important thing is for the composer to create a piece of music that can later be laid perfectly against the picture.

Computer programs calculate absolute times, allowing the composer to work at home. It is now customary for film and video composers to work with the Musical Instrument Digital Interface (MIDI) standard. With a MIDI-compatible synthesizer, contemporary composers can create an entire score in the privacy of their home or studio.

In the traditional method of composing for film, the composer writes the score, an orchestrator arranges the score for instruments, the copyist copies the different parts, and the composer–conductor scores the picture in a large scoring stage with the picture running.

This method is still sometimes used, but more and more composers prefer to work on a score in a layered fashion with synthesizers and a video copy of the picture. The video has SMPTE timecode burned in, showing the exact footage and times. When the composer works with a synthesizer, the director can preview the composer's work in progress in a more complete form than with the traditional method, in which the composer could only play themes on a piano.

Working with a Composer

A good working relationship with the composer is an important part of getting the best score for your project. It might be necessary to preview musical ideas from time to time to see whether the composer is on the right track. Do not let the composer complete an entire score without having heard at least his general approach. Scoring a picture can be an emotionally draining experience for both the director and the composer because so much is expected of music and so much depends on how it works. Allow the composer the time and space to work at his own pace.

Finding a language to communicate with the composer is imperative. Even musically inclined people must find some way of expressing their ideas about the score to the composer. Here are several methods to help you steer the composer in the right direction:

- Play existing music that appeals to you. The temp music you played with the picture for screening purposes will give the composer an idea of your musical designs.
- Explain to the composer the emotional values you are interested in expressing through the music. Is it a sad scene requiring sad music, or would you prefer the counterpoint of a calliope or banjo?
- Identify specific instruments and themes for characters. Listen to *Peter and the Wolf*, which was designed with a different instrument for each character. In many scores, the main character is identified by a theme played on a specific instrument.
- Study the work of the great film composers. Watch how they work their musical themes against the picture.
- When you spot the picture with the composer, make sure to point out any possible conflicts. If there is dialogue or a specific effect you want the audience to hear, don't let it fight with the score. The composer can request quiet music for these moments, but to rely on less volume in the final mix is a mistake.
- Look for places where music can also be an effect. If a glass falls and breaks on camera, do you want the sound of a breaking glass or perhaps a cymbal crash?

After the score has been completed and the music cues are ready to be cut into the film, there is a time of fine adjustment. A cue might have to be edited slightly or shifted to fit the exact requirements of the film. The only other change that can be made is to drop cues from the film during the mix. This is often done because directors usually ask in the spotting session for more music than required. The extra music allows some flexibility in the mix. It is better to have too much than too little. By the time you are involved in the mix, it is too late to ask for new music.

Preexisting Music

Preexisting music has some advantages. The audience knows the music or is familiar with it. Popular songs and music can make your piece accessible. To say that using preexisting music is less expensive than working with a composer is not always true. Of course, a piece of music that is in the public domain costs you nothing. However, don't fall in love with a Sinatra ballad or a Beatles tune, because the price tag for popular and current music is probably out of your price range. If you must use preexisting music, try to obtain music from a group that is not very well known and might relish the opportunity to have its work showcased in your project. (See Appendix E for more information on music rights.)

A special type of preexisting music is *canned music*, which is created to be sold and used in bits and pieces. This generic music can be purchased from a music stock house or from sound effects records. At a stock house, you buy a piece of music by dropping the needle onto the record (or beginning the tape or CD) and then lifting the needle when you have the amount of music you need. This is referred to as a *needle-drop* purchase.

Playback is another form of source music. This is prerecorded music, with or without lyrics, played back on the set during principal photography. The music is used to give dancers a tempo or for singers to lip-sync a song. The material is played back on the set on a Nagra, and recorded on a second Nagra as a scratch track. In the editing room, the original music is used, and the sequence is cut to that track.

> **STUDENTS**
> The temptation to flood the screen with music often stems from an insecurity with the material. Some stories require music from end to end ("wall to wall"), whereas others need none at all. You must have the courage to do the right thing for your project.

THE MIX

When the tracks have been lined up against the picture and the cue sheets have been filled out to reflect the exact position of the various sounds on the multiple tracks, it's time to take your picture to a mixing studio. There, you'll place it in the hands of the rerecording sound mixer, who is responsible for mixing the narration, dialogue, music, and effects. The sound mixer will work with the following tools:

- Mixing (dubbing) studio
- Multitrack recording hard drive
- Prepared cue sheets
- Prepared tracks

The producer should have arranged the mix date far in advance. The number of hours needed for the mix is determined by the length of the film and the number of tracks to be mixed.

It is during the mix that the total aural experience of your picture is created. The elements of dialogue, sound, and music are recorded and blended together to become a seamless unit. During the mixing procedure, the director and other members of the creative

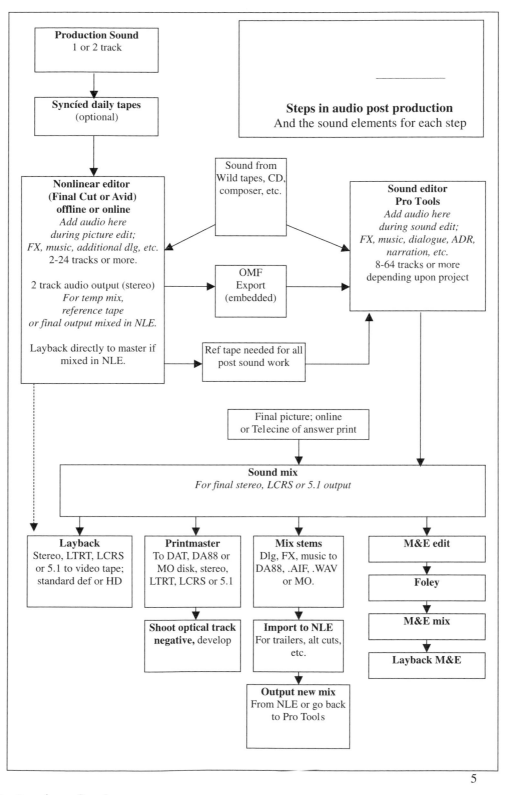

Figure 17.3 Sound post flowchart.

team can make significant artistic decisions about the relative balance between tracks, equalization, the amount of echo, the use of this track or the other, the amount of music to use, and so on.

The tracks are divided up into narration, dialogue, music, and effects. If any of these elements must be changed later, such as substituting a foreign language track for the English dialogue, it can be done without affecting the other tracks.

The success of the mix depends as much on the preparation of the tracks as on the ability of the mixer to blend them together into an organic whole. The prepared tracks represent your major creative decisions. You should have determined the specific sound effects, music, and dialogue you want to use before you walk into the mixing studio. These tracks should not only properly reflect your creative choices, but also meet the highest technical standards to maximize your time with the mixer.

Many mixing facilities provide written material that gives beginners a thorough explanation regarding how to prepare properly for the mix. This can save embarrassing, time-consuming, and costly delays in what is already an expensive part of the postproduction process.

The mixer watches the film on a digital projector. If the project stays in film, the work print is sent to the laboratory to make a *dirty dupe* or *slop print*—a direct, one-to-one black-and-white or color print of your work print. This is done for the mix, Foley, and ADR sessions to guarantee that the film will not break in the projector. These sessions involve a great deal of starting and stopping, which leads to wear and tear that your color work print might not stand up to, even if it has been double-spliced. It is not mandatory to strike a dirty dupe, but you should weigh the chances of breakage in the mix and the subsequent repair time against the dupe's cost.

The director's job during the mix is to inform the mixer about the levels at which the sounds should be recorded in relation to each other. Dialogue comes first, meaning that it is in the foreground. The audience should not have to strain to hear the dialogue. The balance between sound effects and music is an aesthetic choice the director should make in the editing room to avoid too much trial and error during the mix. Most mixers will offer advice about levels, based on their experience.

Rhythm of the Mix

Beginners should sit in on as many mixes as possible before their session to get a feel for the rhythm and pace. Mixing sessions involve a lot of waiting around. The mixer first runs through the entire show with all the tracks "full up" to get a sense of the material. You will, of course, be anxious to start because every minute costs money. However, you must give the mixer time to become familiar with both the picture and the tracks. Remember that you have spent months with your show and know it inside-out. The mixer sees it for the first time that day, unless she has already done an interlock or premix. She has only the cue sheets as a guide and must slowly feel her way through the film, scene by scene.

You might have specific ideas about how each scene should sound and how the entire piece should resonate. Communicate these ideas to the mixer, but also listen to her creative input. Don't relegate the mixer to the role of technician. You want to get her best work from her. Listen to what she has to say. At the same time, if you are not happy with what you hear, don't be afraid to ask her to do it again, even if you have to go over one moment many times.

Mixing is a methodical, time-consuming process. You can go back and forth over the same few feet time and again before it is right. It can be a delicate balancing act as you juggle all the sounds and music until they are just right.

The mix will sound great in a sound studio with professional speakers. Ask the mixer to play back the film through small speakers. When the film is transferred to video or onto optical or projected on a dubious projection facility such as a drive-in theater, the sound track will not sound as rich as when heard through professional speakers.

With a complete mix, the digital master can be laid off against the picture for a tape or DVD output. In film, the track is converted into an optical sound negative. This negative is later used with the picture negative to make a positive composite print.

Preparing for a Mix: Nonlinear

There are different ways to get the sound from one system to another when preparing tracks for a mix after cutting on a nonlinear editing system. Audio and video are stored on a media file on the system's hard drives. The file that contains the editing and control information for the audio clips you've used in the show is stored separately (this is called the *composition*). It is possible to export either the audio media files, the composition, or both using OMF and similar formats. The transfer is usually done on computer drives or disks.

The other way to export sound from the nonlinear system is to *lay off* to tape (print to tape). Here you are simply rerecording each track in videotape. Depending on the tape format, you can only do two to four tracks at a time. This method is cumbersome and makes it harder to manipulate the sound later.

DIGITAL MIX

Preparing for the final mix of your production is essentially the same in a nonlinear workstation environment as it is in a traditional mag-based linear environment. Tracks must be properly split to facilitate smooth transitions and consistent equalization. In a traditional film-mixing studio, tracks are assigned to faders and routed through various pieces of hardware to apply equalization, effects processing, and compression. In a nonlinear workstation environment, those pieces of hardware are replicated by software allowing the workstation mixer to apply the same processing to tracks as his or her counterpart in a traditional mixing studio. The workstation mixer has the added advantage of being able to literally draw in the processing through automation to allow precise control of each track.

It's important to note that a well-equipped digital audio workstation can do everything a regular mixing studio can do—but it also holds the potential to create conflict in terms of job assignments. Since the sound editor does not usually perform the task of the mixer, how much processing and volume control (essentially premixing) should be expected of the sound editor? The question of how extensively she should prepare the sound tracks prior to the mix should be discussed in advance with the sound mixer. Ultimately the decision whether to mix within a workstation or in a traditional film-mixing studio is most likely determined by budgetary concerns. Either way will probably achieve the desired effect with the skill and talent of the mixer being the main variable.

The producer's main criterion then should be to select a mixing studio that best represents the ideal screening environment for the final product. If it is slated for a home video or television release, then mixing in a small studio is fine. If, however, the production is to be theatrically released, then it is desirable to mix in a large studio to more closely represent what the production will sound like in a large theater.

DIFFERENT FORMATS

Today, most films and video are shown through more than one form of distribution. A project may be shown in theaters, on television, through home video, and possibly in different languages. Distribution technologies include videotape, DVD or CD disk, television (broadcast, satellite, or cable), or film prints. The various routes may call for different adjustments during the mix, or for different mixes altogether. Make sure you communicate clearly with the mixer in advance.

PRODUCER
Setting Up the Mix

The producer keeps on top of all expenses incurred during the postproduction period. He sees that everyone adheres to the budget and that all additional expenses can be covered with the money that is left. However, films and videos do go over budget, and what usually suffers is postproduction. Sometimes, all work on a project is suspended until further money is raised. This is not an uncommon situation for students and beginners. Projects go over budget for several reasons:

Unexpected Production Expenses. This is a common but unavoidable predicament, even for professional productions. Expenses that arise in the "heat" of principal photography must be covered if production is to be completed. You shoot more stock than anticipated or spend more on art direction, food, or transportation. With beginners especially, the original budget might not have been realistic. It is easy to say that you can "take it out of post" because postproduction seems to be a long way off when you are in a distant location and your van has broken down. With the entire cast and crew on payroll, spending the extra money to get a scene right seems justified.

Unexpected Reshoot Expenses. Additional filming might be needed if the production unit did not shoot all the planned coverage or if it becomes evident after extensive editing that there must be more shots to tell the story properly. This expense usually comes out of the budget contingency unless, along with other overages, the contingency has already been exhausted.

Hidden Postproduction Costs. Beware of the hidden costs that surface during postproduction. These costs often cannot be predicted because so much of postproduction is trial and error. For example, different pieces of music might be tested against the picture during cutting. The original music is transferred each time the director wants to preview the music or cut it to the picture. This requires labor hours and transfer time, which costs money.

Extended Postproduction Period. It is not uncommon for the student or beginner to run beyond the planned postproduction schedule. There is no way to know definitively how long it will take, and many variables can influence the creative process. (Some of these issues are discussed in Chapter 16, "Pix Postproduction.") Students might have limited access to their program's facilities, and independents on a limited budget might be able to edit only during the evenings because of job conflicts.

The following situations are equally difficult to predict:

- The editor needs to use the same shot twice during the film and thus has to make a new negative.
- The director decides she wants some unusual CGI effects.
- The mix goes over the schedule.
- The lab has problems printing an acceptable answer print of the film, and there are a number of passes before the lab gets it right.

These are just some of the situations that will cost money that might occur in the course of postproduction. However, all these extra expenses spring from the desire to make the best film or video possible.

Howard McCain designed the end of *Truman* around an optical effect called an *iris*. (See Figure 18.3.) As Truman is suspended over the class holding onto the rope, the image closes in on him, or *irises*, until all we see is Truman before fading completely to black. This effect isolates Truman at the end of the film. It is an effective use of the optical but was more expensive than a simple fade to black.

The following is a partial list of postproduction items to look out for (many are not very costly by themselves, but will add up over the long run):

- Screenings
- Scratch or temp mixes
- CGI effects
- Academy leader
- Elaborate title sequences
- Transfer time
- Reprints
- Transfer to video

All these additional expenses can hold up the postproduction process. Once the budget has been depleted, you might have to stop work at whatever stage you have reached. Perhaps you were ready to mix, cut negative, or online your show. You must now look for more financing to complete the picture. You have an advantage when raising money at this juncture that you lacked in the early fund-raising stage. You now have a picture. Having something concrete to show will help you attract potential investors who perhaps were not interested in your project at the idea stage.

You can now organize fund-raising screenings of the work in progress. Keep in mind that for these screenings, the film or video should sound as polished as possible. Most audiences are not used to hearing an incomplete sound track. You might need to add a few effects and music and make a temp, or scratch, mix. This rough mix does not reflect what the piece will eventually sound like, but at least it gives the picture a professional feel and covers up the obvious sound gaps. The goal is to have your project in the best possible condition for the screening.

You might find other opportunities for additional funds, such as postproduction grants or finishing funds, now that you have something tangible to show. Look into local, national, and university grants. Many film and television programs make funds available on a competitive basis for students with projects in the postproduction stage.

THE MORAL

When it is all over, make sure that you benefit from the lessons you've learned about the real costs of postproduction so you can be better prepared the next time. Your subsequent postproduction budgets should reflect the insight and experience of your previous project. Keep extensive records and receipts to document what happened on the entire shoot, and keep an accurate time log of the postproduction period so you will have a clearer idea of what has to happen, and when, the next time around.

KEY POINTS

- Sound design involves dialogue, effects, and music, with dialogue being the most important element.
- Effects can be in-sync, ambient, or "Foleyed."

- Once it is locked, spot the picture for effects and music cues. The footage marks for these cues should never change.
- Do not forget to record room tone when you are on the set. This material will be used extensively during the sound design process.

- Take the time to develop a communication link with the composer. Consider how you can best express your ideas to the composer.

chapter eighteen

Laboratory/Online

You've got to be very, very careful when cutting the negative; most students aren't that careful, not even with their own material. Everybody I know hired a negative cutter. To find a negative cutter, you call other students, see who they use, and find a good price. Prices do vary greatly, anywhere from $4 a cut to $1.50 a cut; it makes a big difference. There were 198 edits in Truman. That's a lot of cuts for a 10-minute film.

Howard

DIRECTOR

Time

The laboratory plays an important role throughout the filmmaking process. With digital video or high definition (HD), the laboratory is less involved; instead, the work is finished and fine-tuned in an online editing suite or on a nonlinear editing system, unless your plan is to make a film print. Strive to maintain a good relationship with the lab from the outset. The success of your film depends in part on the lab work. The lab is responsible for taking care of the negative and creating a final product that represents the best your film can be.

A laboratory representative should be assigned to your project from the beginning. During the production and postproduction process, direct any questions, problems, or concerns to this individual. It is proper and professional to meet the lab representative in person to become acquainted. Visit the lab, and ask to be taken around to see the facilities. Remember that representatives talk to hundreds of people a day on the phone. By being more than just another voice, you will be certain to get better results.

If you plan to shoot film, edit digitally, and match back to film, make sure that your material is prepared for the particular lab and negative cutter you are using. This is a complex process, and there are different approaches to executing the matchback. Some labs and negative cutters offer pamphlets with a list of recommended procedures. Northeast Negative Matchers, (800) 370-CUTS (www.nenm.com), are specialists in working with Avid Media Composers and offer their own proprietary "Video Matchback Checklist."

Treat the relationship you develop with the lab as the beginning of a long, fruitful partnership that will carry you through many films. If you are a student or beginner and plan to continue making films, the lab will hope to keep you as a customer, especially with so many filmmakers turning to digital video.

Since I shot Crazy Glue *pretty much on a one to one, editing was somewhat easy. Once I got the film out of the camera, I took it to Duart and got a one light work print. The lab was helpful every step of the process.*

Tatia

The laboratory is involved in the following steps in the filmmaking process:

- During principal photography, the laboratory develops and processes your film. The lab provides you with a digital video dailies, which is what the editor digitizes for cutting. The negative is kept for you in a vault at the laboratory.
- While the sound is being designed, the laboratory develops your titles and opticals.
- During the mixing of the sound, the laboratory can arrange for your negative to be cut (including the titles and opticals) and matched to your edit decision list (EDL).
- During the sound mix, the director, director of photography (DP), or both color-correct, or *time*, the film with the timer at the lab.
- Once the mix is completed, the mix is shot onto an optical track, and the laboratory marries the printed film to the sound track.
- During the printing of the A and B rolls of 16-mm negative, the laboratory can perform simple fades and dissolves if you request. The lab then strikes your first answer print.

OPTICALS

Opticals, which include everything from simple transitions such as fades and dissolves to elaborate CGI sequences, are created either at an effects house (in film or video) or on the computer in your edit suite. Computer-generated images can easily be married to your digital output if the final destination for is digital video projection or television. If you plan to output back to film, opticals and effects can be shot on film or generated by computer and then transferred to film. Digital video transfers are expensive and still do not match the quality of film. However, more labs are offering digital video-to-film transfer, and as such the cost will continue to go down and the quality rise.

The process of creating opticals for 16-mm is different than for 35-mm. All 35-mm optical effects must be designed and shot beforehand at a special effects house and developed at the lab. This involves making a new negative. The nature of 16-mm negative cutting allows the laboratory to create dissolves and fades during the printing process itself. (See the next section for information on A and B rolls.)

An important technical consideration is having enough film on either side of the dissolve so that the two shots can cross-fade with each other. Spend some time talking with the negative cutter before designing any film opticals.

Any opticals other than simple fades and dissolves must be shot by a company that specializes in visual optical effects. (The lab you are using might have its own optical division.) This is a time-consuming and costly process that sometimes requires trial and error. The optical house might not achieve the results you want the first time around. For example, the image that you want "blown up" is shot, and the new negative is sent to the lab to be developed and printed. You preview a work print of the new optical to be used in the film, but it doesn't work. It must then be shot and developed again, costing yet more money.

I wanted a crawl at the end and I wanted an iris effect, so I knew there was going to be an optical in both cases. To get those, you have to shop around, just like for a caterer or for anything else. Again, by looking at other students' work, you can tell which work you like and which work you don't.

Howard

The following are some of the opticals that require a wedge test and must be run separately from the final printing:

Superimposition. Superimposition is placing two or more images over one another.

Lap Dissolve. Especially long dissolves, usually more than 96 frames, are referred to as lap (as in overlap) dissolves.

Step Printing. The film can be slowed down or sped up by printing more or fewer frames than exist on the negative.

Blowup. An image can be enlarged to eliminate a boom pole or other unwanted element in the frame. Blowups are a last resort for solving an image problem, because when you reprint a shot, the grain on the film gets larger and thus creates a mismatch to the grain size of the shots before and after the blowup.

Titles. You might want to superimpose your main or end titles over images from the picture or create some special visual effect with your main title.

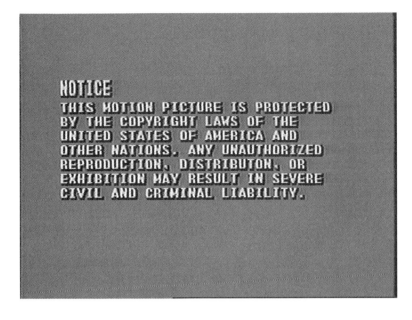

Figure 18.1 Disclaimer from *Truman*.

Figure 18.2 End credit from *The Lunch Date*.

End Credits. You might want the credits to scroll up or "crawl" continuously over black or over images for the end credits. (See Figure 18.2.) Often, preceding the head credits is an FBI disclaimer like the one put on *Truman* (Figure 18.1). Figure 18.2 is a title card for the tag to *The Lunch Date*. Note the fancy font that accents the timeless, storybook quality of the story.

Reprints. If you need to duplicate a scene several times in the picture but have only one take of it,

you will need a duplicate negative, or *dupe*, created from the original negative of the scene.

Special Visual Transitions. Wipes and irises are examples of special visual transitions (Figure 18.3). Optical work is expensive. If you have your heart set on a special visual effect, it is best to find out what it will cost before editing a sequence around it. This applies also to fancy title sequences. Laboratories execute opticals either on film or as computer effects to be transferred to film.

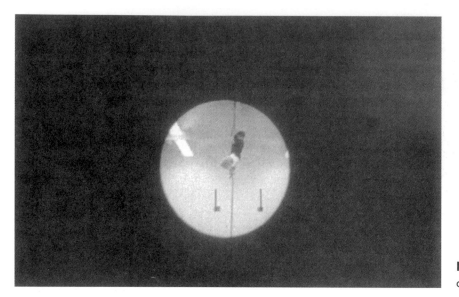

Figure 18.3 *Truman* ends with an optical: an iris-out.

ANIMATION AND CGI

Rendering and Compositing

The final step in CG animation is rendering and compositing. When 3D software renders, it calculates the effect of light, shadow, color, reflectivity, transparency, diffusion, and hundreds of other properties on the surface of the CG geometry. A final render can take anywhere from a few seconds to days per frame. To quickly view the progress of the piece, a CG animator will create test renders and playblast (see Figures 18.4 through 18.6). A playblast is a crude (usually low-resolution) render of the scene intended to show movement and timing. The playblast will show the models as they appear within the program without complex calculations of light and color. The test renders will be sample frames from different parts of the scene that will show the final look of the piece. Around one third of the resources of every major CG studio is dedicated to the task of rendering. There are usually more technical directors overseeing the lighting and rendering of a film than character animators, so do not underestimate the importance of this phase of production.

Many studios will render out the final frames in passes or plates. In a pass, the CG artist will take a portion of a scene, such as the foreground characters, or shadows, or even highlights and render them out as a separate, silhouetted image. Unlike live action green screens, the elements are all generated in the computer. The masks are therefore perfectly registered and accurate to the pixel. The CG artist has a great deal more control when working with separate passes. For example, the shadow pass can be easily modified in a compositing program to have soft edges and darker areas toward the middle. If there is a change to one part of the scene, like a character's movement or a background color, the entire scene does not need to be rerendered.

CUTTING THE NEGATIVE

During the mix, when the filmmaker is positive there will be no more changes in the picture, the editor sends an EDL to the negative cutter to have it cut, spliced, and prepared for printing. The director or editor can set up a clean room in which to cut the negative, but this is a somewhat tedious and critical part of the postproduction process. A mistake here could lead to disaster. A negative that is not cut or spliced properly could break apart in the printing process, permanently damaging part of your film.

If you plan to shoot film, edit digitally, and match back to film, it is important that you contact the negative cutter *before you start shooting*. The frame discrepancy between film and video needs to be addressed, as well as how the video dailies are pre-

Figure 18.4 Tree wire armiture.

Figure 18.5 Tree filled in.

pared. You need to be absolutely clear about your options.

The processes for cutting 16-mm and 35-mm negative are fundamentally different. Cutting the original negative in 16-mm and 35-mm requires that a part of the emulsion of one frame be scraped off and laid on top of the next frame. These are glued together and sealed with a heated splicer, creating a *hot splice*. The heat enables the splice to seal properly. Scraping off a frame of 16-mm film exposes part of the frame line, which will then print through as a white line. Because

of the density of 35-mm film, frame lines are not a problem.

To avoid having this visible splice, the original 16-mm negative is never cut with another piece of original negative. Instead, a shot is cut to a piece of black leader (the A roll), and the next shot is attached to a second roll (the B roll). The use of two separate rolls creates a checkerboard pattern called *A and B rolls*. This prevents one piece of original negative from being cut with another and makes it possible for the lab to print fades and dissolves (Figure 18.7).

FILM MATCHBACK

When you first transfer your film dailies to video, the telecine generates video timecode that gets recorded on the telecine tapes. The tapes are edited on either a traditional videotape editing system or a nonlinear editing system. You will generate an EDL that lists all your editing decisions according to video timecode. Through the process of *film matchback*, a negative cutter can take that EDL and create a *film cut list,* which tells her how to cut the film negative to match your video edit. The matchback process converts a 30 frames per second video edit to a 24 fps negative cut list.

This is how the process is done. Prior to the original telecine session, a punch mark is made on each roll of negative as a starting reference (more information on video dailies is given in Chapter 16). In the telecine session, the film key number and the video timecode at that reference punch are logged. After editing, to find any point on a roll, we relate it back to the reference punch.

To help automate this process, the keycode system was devised. Using keycode, a nonlinear editing

Figure 18.6 Cartoon sketch giant squatter tree.

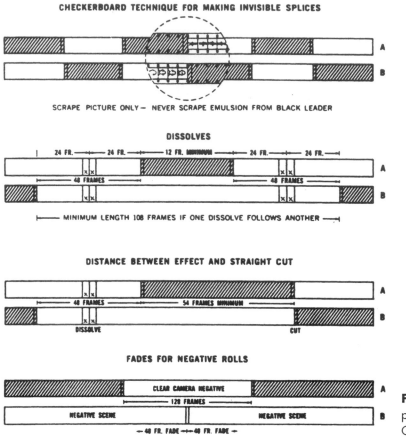

Figure 18.7 A and B rolls. Used with permission from the American Society of Cinematographers.

system can perform the matchback itself and generate a film cut list. Keycode is a machine-readable version of the key numbers that are exposed along the edge of the film negative. During the initial film-to-video transfer, the telecine machine reads the keycode and can burn the key numbers in on the screen so a human can read them during editing. The telecine can also create a database or log that correlates the key numbers to the video timecode that can be loaded into the nonlinear system. When you are done with your offline edit, the nonlinear editing system crunches these numbers and generates a film cut list, which saves the negative cutter from having to create her own list. Not all nonlinear systems can do matchback.

There are several types of film cut lists. A *pull list* tells the negative cutter which shots to take or pull from each camera roll. A *scene pull list* indicates all shots taken in their entirety from flash frame to flash frame. An *assemble list* shows all the shots in the movie in their final order. A dupe list shows which material needs to be duplicated. An *optical list* is a way to recreate on film those effects created and previewed on video. Many systems will locate effects in an edited sequence and generate a count sheet for an optical house to build the identical effect using film elements. This is a useful tool for translating the film.

24/30 Frame Issues

The 24/30 frame discrepancy between film and video is not an issue if you shoot on video, or if you shoot on film and are finishing on video and not matching back to film. It is an issue if you are shooting on 24p. If you are working on a 30 fps system and want to match back, be aware that during the matchback process (whether calculated by the nonlinear editing system or by the negative cutter), there will often be discrepancies between the video and the film. Most matchback programs are designed to drop or add a frame at the end of certain shots to keep the overall length and sync relationship between the film video and audio within a frame, plus or minus. Usually you won't notice the error.

To avoid these complications, films shot at 24 fps are often edited on a nonlinear system that runs at 24 fps, such as the Avid Film Composer. This offers a simple one-to-one relationship between the original film frames and the frames displayed on the nonlinear system. It allows you to edit at 24 fps and create frame-accurate film cut lists that correlate exactly to the original film negative, with none of the matchback discrepancies caused by converting from 30 fps to 24 fps.

TIMING

At the laboratory, a technician called a *timer* consults with the DP to create a visual continuity for the film. This means giving each scene a consistent color and tone as well as giving the whole film a specific look, whether it be cool (tending toward the blues), normal, or warm (tending toward the oranges).

It is not unusual for shots within a scene to be warmer or colder in color or lighter or darker in tone. They might have been shot at a different time of day or with a different batch of film stock. The timer tries to smooth out these inconsistencies in color film. She does this with a Hazeltine machine, which tells the printer how many points the valves should open on each light. There are 50 lights each representing 1/12th of an f-stop. To compliment the film color (cyan, magenta, and yellow), light bulbs—"lights" of green, red, or blue—are required in the final printing of each sequence. Color film is broken down into these three dyes. The balance of these three colors creates accurate skin tones. The timer sets the number of lights per color to make the flesh tones match the character.

The director and DP sit with the timer and make special requests if they want something other than "normal" printing. Suppose, for example, that a sequence was shot so that the dailies are bright and well saturated with color, but the director wants a dark and moody feel to the scene. The timer can instruct the printer to bleed some of the color from the scene and to make it less bright. If the timer has a lot of latitude, she can make some adjustments to the look of a scene. This requires that the negative be well exposed, or *dense*. There is not much a timer can do with a "thin" negative. The Hazeltine is not a magical instrument.

It is important to note that the timer cannot alter the color balance or flesh tones of only a part of the frame. Every adjustment, however minor, affects the entire image. The director can change the color scheme but must live with how it affects the characters' flesh tones.

Black-and-white film goes through a similar timing process, although the visual concerns are different. The timer works with a gray scale and black-and-white contrast ratios. She strives to smooth out the inconsistencies of lighting, to enrich the blacks, and to create a consistent tone for each scene and for the entire picture.

> *I went to get the answer print, and I called up the cinematographer, and we watched it together. I brought him there specifically to make sure they were printing it with enough richness and stuff. We went for a second printing and darkened it a little bit, just in some areas.*
>
> Adam

Color timing can be done when transferring film dailies to digital or tape for use in a nonlinear editing system.

TYPES OF PRINTS

The first print struck from the negative is a work print (or video, if you choose video dailies). The material is either timed scene by scene to correct for proper flesh tones or developed by one-light, which is an overall timing of one setting for the entire roll. When the negative is cut, you will begin to strike prints for screening purposes. The following sections describe the types of prints the laboratory can provide.

Mute Print

Before the mix is married to the optical track, the laboratory sometimes prepares a mute print. This is a picture-only print from the negative, which the director, editor, and DP can examine for color corrections or optical errors before an answer print is made.

> *The timer looked at the work print to get a sense of the film. It was really an odd film to time because the backgrounds had to look completely consistent, so the flesh tones become subordinate to the backgrounds. I'm sure if he had timed every shot according to flesh tones, he would have come up with quite a different timing. But you know, you can't have the gradation of the black-and-white floor changing or the mannequins' flesh tone jumping around from shot to shot.*
>
> Jan

First Trial

When the optical track is married to the print, the laboratory screens this print, called the *first trial,* for the production team to review for final corrections.

Answer Print

When all the corrections have been made, the next print the laboratory strikes is called the *answer print.* Once the answer print has been approved, additional prints can be struck.

Release Print

The next step depends on the number of prints you will eventually need (a distribution issue). The general rule is that the less you run your original negative (A and B rolls) through the printing process, the better. Too much wear and tear could damage the film or break the splices. Therefore, if you are planning to make more than a couple of release prints, it is best to strike an interpositive (IP) and then an internegative (IN). An *internegative* is a single strand of negative that can be run through the printer many times with no risk (it has no splices).

Video Copy

You will want video copies of your picture for cast and crew members, festivals, promotion, distributors, and so on. The print should be transferred to a master that will serve as your original, and dubs will be made from this. Today, Beta SP is the format of choice for the master. Make sure the sound used in the transfer is from the original mix. The sound quality is superior to the optical track on your print.

TRADITIONAL LINEAR VIDEO ONLINE

The online edit session is the time to rerecord the program at highest possible quality. Some houses still employ linear or tape-to-tape online suites. These houses like the quality of the larger tape formats and distribute exclusively to television.

After a show is built, the original materials are taken to an online edit room to be completed. Here, all picture and sound elements are conformed to the cut made on the offline master. A new online master is made, and it becomes the final product.

The goal of online is to complete the offline decisions with effects, color correction, titles, and audio sweetening. Online rooms, although expensive, provide the director with opportunities for elaborate and exciting opticals and titles.

The edit decision list (EDL), made from the offline edit, can be fed into the online computer to tell it where what images and what sounds should be placed on the master tape. Copies can be struck from the master tapes for distribution.

NONLINEAR ONLINE EDIT

The terms offline and online become blurred when it comes to the nonlinear editing system. The traditional offline edit meant using relatively inexpensive, lower quality equipment so you could afford the time to shape your project. The goal of offline was to produce an EDL and complete the project to broadcast specifications during the online session. Offline editing meant working on a product that was not finished, the finished piece being created later on another system.

With nonlinear editing systems, the idea of offline has shifted to mean working with "draft quality," whereas online means working toward a piece that is finished or "high quality." Both of these stages can now be completed on the same system. Images can be edited at a low resolution (draft quality) and, after the picture is locked, can then be redigitized and "onlined" at the highest resolution (high quality) the system has to offer.

These systems can also enable the film- and videomaker to execute complex *digital video effects (DVE), motion effects,* and hundreds of various *filter* effects. Titles and graphics can be created on the nonlinear system or imported from other software applications and *plug-ins* (added, standardized software). The use of such software as AfterEffects and Photoshop from Adobe Systems, Inc. (www.adobe.com), has brought about a convergence of TV and computer graphics. Higher end systems include Combustion, Flame, and Smoke. Complex two- and three-dimensional animation as well as multilayered (composited) images can be created and merged with video. Many types of file formats can be used to import graphics into the nonlinear system, including QuickTime, JPEG, TIFF, and BMP.

Ultimately, you will need to determine what level of video you require. This will be one of the defining issues for the system you chose in the first place. You may have a system that is not up to "broadcast quality" but may be polished enough for festival exhibition, a distributor, a corporate video, a multimedia project, a Web site, or even a QuickTime movie.

VIDEO-TO-FILM TRANSFER

Video-to-film transfers are used to make film negatives or prints from video material. The big-budget features use this technique to convert special effects created in computer graphics workstations back to film. The lower end of this market are the makers of independent or television movies who cannot afford to shoot film (or choose to originate in video for other reasons) but need to make film prints to show in festivals or for theatrical release. It can happen that projects originating in film and edited in video are transferred directly back to film (without returning to the negative) to save time and cost.

For video-to-film transfers, new technologies are developing, the quality is improving, and demand for these transfers is increasing, mostly for the longer projects but for shorts as well. At the same time, video projection is improving rapidly. It may not be necessary, in the near future, to put images on celluloid in order to view them in a theater. Film and video, however, have inherently different characteristics, and the simplest way to end up with a film is to shoot film.

Systems

There are several different systems for converting video to film, which range widely in complexity and cost. At the highest current level are film recorders. These systems use either a cathode ray tube or a laser to record very high resolution images onto 35-mm film. Film recorders are very slow, taking several seconds per frame. They are also very expensive: Each frame costs several dollars.

The *electron beam recorder* (ERB) uses an electron beam to transfer to three successive film frames, the red, green, and blue information from each video frame. The three film frames are then optically printed with colored filters to create a normal film negative. ERB tape-to-film transfers are done by Four Media Company (4MC) in Burbank, California. The Sony Pictures High Definition Center (SPHDC) uses ERBs with high-definition video technology. Standard-definition videotapes are upconverted to HDTV and put through a line doubler to increase resolution. ERB transfers cost from a few hundred dollars for the complete transfer up to several hundred dollars a minute.

The original video-to-film conversion method is the kinescope. This system uses a high-quality color monitor with a special film camera running at 23.976 fps (for NTSC) with a 144° shutter to create a flicker-free image from the video. A kinescope is the most economical transfer method and produces good results.

Most systems cannot transfer to both 16-mm and 35-mm. You may need to do a blowup or reduction to get the final format you want. A comprehensive list of places that transfer either from NTSC or PAL to film is given on our Web site. The DigiEffects Web page (digieffect.com/frames/main/html) offers excellent technical advice. There is a link to a comprehensive "white paper" written by Chris Athanas on "How to Transfer Video to Film." Newer systems coming online laser-write the tape to film.

Because of the variability in the lighting conditions under which your tape was shot and the format you used, it is impossible to predict what will be created from a video to film transfer. Tests are crucial to find out what works. Keep these considerations in mind:

- Get the framing right for your release medium. Are you going to 1:66, 1:78, 1:85, or some other aspect ratio? You need to know before you shoot.
- Know that pans and other camera moves may not look the same on film.
- Remember that visual effects that look smooth on a monitor at 29.97 fps may not look as good (or may look different) at 24 fps.
- Pay attention to audio specifications. It is best to record the audio apart from the video with a DAT recorder and then sync it up in postproduction.
- Be sure you know how much the services will cost and what you are paying for. Some facilities will not give you the negative for the quoted prices, only one print.

Post has changed immensely. It's desktop now, which is fantastic and easy. I think it's good if you're a short filmmaker to have some knowledge of computers and what you can do with them—to have more options.

Tatia

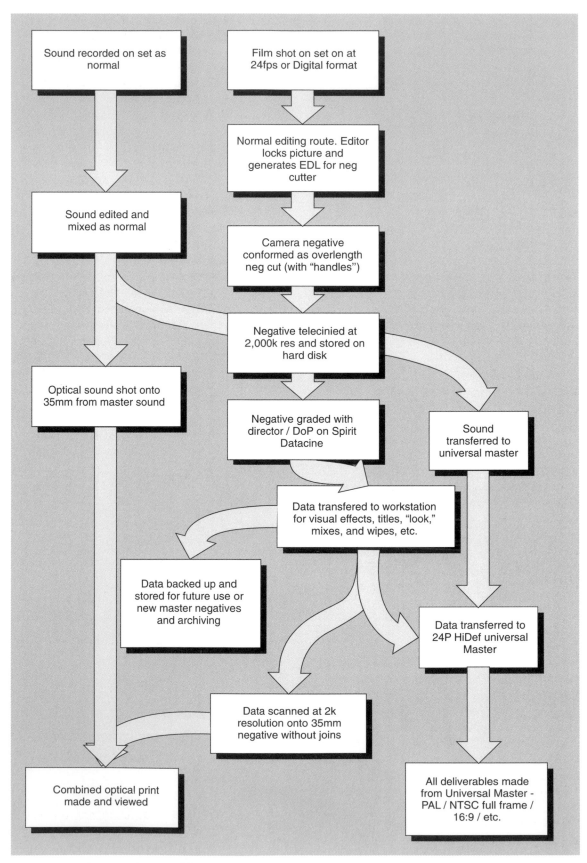

Figure 18.8 Digital intermediate workflow.

Digital Intermediate

The digital intermediate process is rapidly becoming the standard in the film industry and also an option for student productions wanting to finish on film (see Figure 18.8).

The film is transferred to video through telecine. A timecode file is made as well as a record of the corresponding keycode on the actual negative (flex file). The show is edited on a nonlinear system, and an EDL is generated.

At this point instead of going to an online session (if you were finishing on tape this is what you would do), the negative is scanned again at a high resolution (2k or 4k) on a machine such as a Spirit DataCine or a DaVinci. Only the footage that was used in the edit is scanned, usually with handles of 150 frames on either side of each cut.

The film is then reconstructed in a digital environment. All effects are recreated (fades, dissolves, wipes, titles) at a film resolution or in an HD environment. This is called the conform. The timer then color corrects the picture. At this point digital masters are output to tape and a high-resolution/uncompressed frame sequence is output to a hard drive. This is nicknamed the digital answer print.

The movie is then finally laser-recorded to a film print negative stock, with all the effects and color changes intact. It also has the same generational quality of the original camera negative (if not better). Some filmmakers chose to then optically time the film to make sure that the translation of the colors and levels are consistent from the HD environment to the film print. From this negative prints can be struck and optical or digital sound added. Although expensive, this method allows director's to create more effects and transitions without having to think about optical printing or generation loss.

PRODUCER
Making Prints

The producer plays a pivotal role during this final stretch of the postproduction process. He serves as creative partner, negotiator, deal maker, troubleshooter, independent eye, and promoter. The producer can do the following:

- Negotiate the overall deal with the lab. This should be done in preproduction. If possible, it is good to stay with one lab for the entire project because generally the lab's price for the entire

job might be a better deal than if you have only your dailies or your final printing done there.
- Negotiate a deal with an optical house if necessary.
- Review the bills for all postproduction expenses (lab, ADR, Foley, mix, offline, online, optical house) to check that they are consistent with the work done.
- Serve as an independent eye for the director throughout the timing process. Review color-corrected prints for quality control.
- Help organize the names and the design for the end credit sequence. Thanking the appropriate people and organizing the names in order of priority can be a big job.
- Troubleshoot if there are problems with the lab or the postproduction facilities. This process might go smoothly, or it might be a struggle. There might be sync problems with the optical track or color problems the lab says cannot be fixed. Remember that these jobs are done by humans who sometimes make mistakes. Unfortunately, they are not always willing to acknowledge them. It might be just a small project to the lab, but it is *your* film. Be prepared to fight for what you want.

LOOKING AHEAD

It is now time to begin planning what must be done once the film is finished. Here is a list of tasks the producer must handle as the physical process of creating the project winds down:

- Set up screenings for the cast, crew, and investors.
- Organize the press kit for festivals and distributors.
- Check the deadlines for key festivals.
- Decide how many video copies are required and who needs them.
- Prepare a list of potential distributors to contact.
- Write thank-you letters to vendors, volunteers, and the key people who helped to make it all happen. Thanking people for their hard work is easy to do and can go a long way in creating goodwill and support for your next project.

STUDENTS

Most information about laboratories is shared among students. Ninety-nine percent of the time this information is incorrect. See the laboratory representative directly.

KEY POINTS

- Wait as long as possible to cut the negative. Once the negative is cut, it cannot be reconfigured.

- The timer cannot change the negative, but she can alter the brightness and color.
- Consider the nature of your final output. Projecting on video in a large venue is less effective than projecting on film.

chapter nineteen

Distribution

I think the short is as healthy as ever. I think we are seeing a proliferation of film and video festivals that welcome the short form, whether fiction or documentary.

Jan

PRODUCER
Making a Deal

There is nothing like the feeling of having produced a creative work. What might have begun as a simple notion or image is now a completed film or video. You should congratulate yourself and all those who helped in the realization of this project.

The question now is, what are you going to do with it? Let's go back to the beginning for a moment to examine the reasons why you took on this project in the first place. It might have been to create something to advance your career as a producer or director. Perhaps you sought a learning experience, or maybe the picture is rooted in your fascination with the subject matter or your desire to say something profound with the visual medium. A sponsor motivated by the desire to serve a specific corporate or educational purpose of the organization might have financed the project. In any case, you have done your job and are ready for the next project.

Truman *got me some professional recognition, which is what I originally wanted. Besides being entertaining, I wanted* Truman *to be something I could put on a résumé reel. I wanted it to say, "I can make a movie, I can direct, I can put the camera in the right place, and I can do something fun." It did well for me. I got a manager and an agent out of the blue, so I was thrilled. In terms of its goal and its aspirations, I think* Truman *more than fulfilled them. It also got distributed. It put me on a professional path. It's making a little money now, and all of this for 10 minutes.*

Howard

You might have thought that there was a predetermined audience, or market, for your project that would eventually lead to financial remuneration. This might not have been the sole reason for your effort, but you probably want people to see your work, and it would be nice if they paid for the privilege. A project that an audience never sees is like a tree that falls in the woods: Does it make a sound?

Looking for financial gain does not taint or undermine your serious or "artistic" intentions. If people pay to see your project, it is a tribute to its power. In addition, it will make it easier for you to raise money to make more projects. Remember that there are now investors with whom you have a business relationship. They might not have expected a return from your first project, but repayment of the debt will foster goodwill and perhaps lead to future investments.

All film- and videomakers want their vision and ideas to be experienced by as many people as possible. All artists want their work to be displayed, but there is a different relationship between the work and the audience in film and video. Most art is experienced on a one-to-one basis. Our relationship to a book, poem, or painting is a private one. Although many viewers might have similar reactions to a painting and appreciate its artistic merit, they do so as a result of an individual, not a group, experience.

A unique aspect of film and video is that much of their power stems from the dynamic of being experienced by a group. The impact of a piece resonates with an audience. A film or video viewed by a large audience offers a group catharsis. This is most evident while watching a comedy. Laughter is contagious. The consensus of the group grants the audience permission to express not only laughter, but also the myriad emotions that play throughout the piece.

305

The exhibition of motion pictures and videos in front of an audience is a vital component of their existence. If your goal is to expose the piece to the audience it deserves, you will need a calculated way to reach that audience—in other words, a coordinated marketing and distribution plan.

START EARLY

If you are interested in exploring distribution options for your short project, we recommend starting your research in preproduction. *Talk to as many distributors as possible* (a partial listing is given on our Web site). Contacting distributors early in the project's life will, to begin with, make the task of finding a distributor that much easier. It may also give you a realistic sense of the market potential for your proposed project. For example, if you are planning to do a documentary on deforestation in the Northwest, distributors can tell you if the market is saturated with this kind of project, and if it is, whether your project offers a fresh viewpoint that hasn't been explored before.

Make sure you have someone taking professional-looking stills (B&W and color) from the actual scenes during production. If this can't be done for the entire shoot, choose one important scene with all the principals. They will be superior in quality to blowups from the final print and can be used for promotion, your press kit, news stories, to post on the Internet, or for your videotape jacket.

Set aside money for distribution in your budget. If you decide not to pursue the distribution route, these funds can be used to prepare for the festival circuit, especially for making extra prints or dubs of your project for festivals (students are usually surprised to discover how much it costs to enter festivals).

Think about promoting your project in the local press. There may be something newsworthy or controversial about your subject matter; a documentary about pollution in the local river could garner some press attention. Many of our students who come from small towns have been able to exploit themselves as human-interest stories: "Local media heroes take first steps toward Hollywood." These articles will form the foundation of your press kit (talked about later in the chapter). Preproduction can also be the time to prepare a brief synopsis of the story, biographies of the cast and crew, and background information about the project. Some sort of graphic image to identify your project would be helpful, but not absolutely necessary.

Start selling before you begin to shoot. The preparation work done in preproduction will jumpstart your efforts to find an audience for your project. Whether or not you decide to go this route, these efforts will help you promote your film to festivals.

THE MARKETS

There are six basic markets:

- Theatrical
- Nontheatrical
- Exhibition
- Television (cable and network)
- Video (home video, DVD, consumer market)
- Internet

The first part of this chapter is devoted only to the United States and Canada, which is known as the *domestic market*. Foreign distribution is discussed briefly later in this chapter.

Theatrical Markets

There are few possibilities for short films to be released in theaters. At one time, a short film, an animated cartoon, and newsreels in addition to previews for coming attractions preceded feature films. Commercials and previews now dominate this period.

Some people have tried to distribute a collection of short films in the form of a feature. This has been successful when combining award-winning animated short subjects into longer programs (Tour de Animation), but it hasn't been as successful when it comes to combining narrative shorts. There have also been several occasions when feature-length films have been deliberately constructed from three or four short pieces (*New York Stories, Akira Kurosawa's Dreams, ARIA*); these are referred to as *anthology films*.

Nontheatrical Markets

The most substantial domestic market and potentially the most lucrative one available to the short film or video is nontheatrical. Nontheatrical customers are institutional buyers who integrate video into their training and educational programs. For example, a ninth-grade biology teacher will buy videos to supplement her classroom lecture. Nontheatrical distributors supply fictional and nonfictional films and videos: narrative, documentary, animated, and experimental. The basic criterion for a successful film in this market is subject matter that can serve some kind of educational or instructional need.

This covers a broad spectrum of interests. The best way to discover whether your project fits into this market is to submit it for consideration to one or all of the nontheatrical distributors that interest you (see the Bibliography). Educate yourself about what products have traditionally performed well in these markets. Keep in mind that documentaries form a large part of the nontheatrical market. They have obvious educational appeal because they are factual explorations of real events; they serve as both historical and behavioral models.

Fiction work, whether narrative, animated, or experimental, doesn't fall automatically into any educational niche. There must be something in the subject matter that can be used in an educational context. The story must provoke a moral or ethical discussion. Narrative stories, whether they are live action or animated, can offer strong metaphors for human behavior. If your story explores the nature of human relationships in a poignant way that could serve as an educational model, it might have a continued life in the nontheatrical marketplace.

The nontheatrical market is truly content driven. If you want your film to be distributed, you must have something a library or school would want to buy, because they are the major purchasers of short films in this country. The short film market is about education. Can you sell your project to a library or school? If your film is a wonderful art film, in all likelihood it just isn't going to be distributed. There are distributors who will pick it up, but it will probably sit there. Sometimes, the overseas market is a little different because the short film life is longer, they have a wider appreciation for it, and they can sell the film to foreign television.

> *Now I'm making money off of* Truman. *Someday, I might make all the money back—maybe 20 years down the road. But I'm starting to see $500 here, $500 there, which is great. I did not expect it. Schools and libraries have limited budgets. If they can go out and buy* The Wizard of Oz, *with Judy Garland, at $19 a copy, what would possibly motivate them to pay $75 for a 10-minute copy of* Truman? *That's what the educational market is running into; there are very limited resources, and Hollywood is dumping tremendous amounts of videotape on the market at very, very cheap prices.*
>
> Howard

Within the nontheatrical family, there are four basic markets: education, institutional, corporate training, and health care. The education market can itself be subdivided into a number of categories: kindergarten through 12th grade (K–12) and colleges, universities, and graduate schools (higher education).

Education

K–12. The K–12 market represents a potential audience of more than 100,000 schools and approximately 55 million students. Teachers use videos to supplement lectures and lesson plans and have specific criteria about program format and content. Video is widely used in the classroom; in fact, more than 90 percent of the country's classrooms contain at least one VCR. Teachers, librarians, media buyers, or principals make buying decisions. When producing or adapting a film or video for this market, consider the following.

The Curriculum. The project must directly support the teacher's classroom activities and ideally support the curriculum. Many states publish curriculum guidelines. You can get copies by calling the state departments of education. (Much of this information is now on the states' Web pages. Also, try an Internet search with the word "curriculum.")

Funding for Education. Each year the federal government appropriates funding to youth education and assistance programs. These funds support a variety of programs, some of which involve media acquisitions. There has been, in the past, an emphasis on substance abuse prevention, AIDS education, violence intervention, self-esteem, and multiculturalism. For more information, you can contact the U.S. Department of Education.

Length of the Program. The standard class period is 45 to 50 minutes, so the ideal project should run 15 to 20 minutes, but no more than 30 minutes.

Appropriateness. Schools are very conservative. It is important that projects used in the classroom reflect cultural and ethnic diversity and gender equity. Media material must not have excessive profanity, nudity, sexually suggestive situations, or violence, or promote negative ethnic stereotypes. It is also suggested that you present a balanced political perspective.

Teacher's Guides. A teacher's guide must accompany every project for the school market.

Discussion or activity guides help teachers integrate the project into their teaching plans. It can be a brief overview of the project and also feature a list of suggested activities and discussion topics for the classroom. Your distributor will assist you in putting together this kind of guide.

Marketing to schools is largely the domain of 15 to 20 educational distributors who reach buyers through a combination of direct mail, telemarketing, print advertising, sales representatives, exhibits at conferences, and now also with a substantial presence on the Internet. The major trade journals for this market include *School Library Journal*, *Media and Methods*, *Curriculum Administrator*, *T.H.E. Journal*, and *Science Books & Films*. These journals all have their own Web sites on the Internet.

Higher Education. This market of more than 7,000 institutions, most of which are two- and four-year colleges and universities, doesn't offer the same potential as the school market. As with schools, funding cuts have hurt colleges and universities. The college market is more decentralized than the school market. Professors and department chairs have more discretion than grade school teachers about how they will teach a subject and are the primary decision makers about the purchase of textbooks and other media. In general, videos are used to supplement a lecture rather than to teach a core concept.

Videos that have potential in the high school market often have crossover potential in the higher education market and vice versa. This market is reached in much the same way as the school market.

Institutional Market

Libraries. There are approximately 16,000 public libraries in this country. About three quarters of these have video collections. Their buying decisions reflect consumer interest because they buy on behalf of their patrons. State and local budget cutting has hurt libraries. Without a mandate to build video collections, many have stopped buying videos. Most traditional nontheatrical distributors no longer find direct marketing to libraries cost-effective and instead rely on wholesalers such as Baker & Taylor and Ingram (both located on the Internet).

The Head Librarian Makes the Purchase Decisions. Most library collections represent a mix of feature films and how-to titles, with a small selection of higher quality documentaries and educational programs. The key to library sales is favorable reviews in a handful of trade journals: *Library Journal*, *Video Librarian*, and the *Video Rating Guide for Libraries* (all available on the Internet).

Community and Religious Groups. Community and religious groups such as churches and local PTA chapters also buy videos for Sunday schools, after-school activities, guidance and counseling programs, and discussion groups. These groups buy general-interest programs, with a special emphasis on guidance subjects such as substance abuse and personal ethics. Some distributors market to religious and community groups through direct mail and telemarketing. However, most of the purchasing takes place through retail outlets and wholesalers.

Prisons. Prisons buy videos as well. Many inmates work toward high school and college equivalency degrees through correspondence courses. Videos are also used in counseling and therapy sessions.

The Corporate Training Market. Corporations spend billions of dollars on staff training and development and close to $2 billion on off-the-shelf materials such as books, videos, computer courseware, and other prepackaged training products. Video has been the most popular information delivery system. Companies use videos to motivate staff and to improve skills. In contrast to the school market, tough financial times have not hurt businesses. In the corporate arena, a well-trained and informed work force is a valuable commodity, and video and other forms of media are cost-effective.

In a larger company, the people responsible for staff development (human resources or training departments) make purchasing decisions. In the smaller companies, it is often the president or a high-level manager who makes these decisions. Companies buy directly from distributors and from wholesalers such as Baker & Taylor. Some of the leading distributors in this field are CRM Learning, Blanchard Training and Development, and Video Arts. The two best sources of information on the corporate arena are the American Society for Training and Development (www.astd.org) and *Training Magazine*.

The Health Care Market. Hospitals, health care centers, and emergency service providers such as emergency medical services and police forces are considered part of the larger corporate training market, but they require very specialized kinds of programming. The ever-changing health care landscape calls for a continuing stream of up-to-date information for patients, staff training in OSHA regulations, health care procedures, and issues. Heath care information is one of the growth areas in the nontheatrical market.

There are more than 6,500 hospitals and 500 HMOs in this country purchasing off-the-shelf material for training. Psychiatric and mental health care facilities also purchase videos. Health care video distributors can de divided into two general categories. Distributors such as the *American Journal of Nursing* and Medcom-Trainex market products that are highly technical. Distributors such as AIMS Media, Pyramid, and Fanlight market a broader array of products that range from technical to general-interest treatments of health care issues (autism, disabilities, physical challenges, psychological issues, etc.). These companies also distribute to the educational and institutional markets.

Exhibition

Exhibition is a broad term that represents the many opportunities film- and videomakers have to screen their work in front of an audience. These are some of the venues that fit under this category:

* National festivals (domestic and foreign)
* Museum showings
* Cultural societies
* Film school festivals
* School and community groups

Exhibition opportunities serve a number of purposes. They give the film- or videomaker an audience response to the picture, public acknowledgment for excellent work, the potential for financial reward, and valuable exposure.

National Festivals

Festivals are a wonderful opportunity to share your work with an audience. It gives the general public an opportunity to see new films and videos. For distributors, it is an opportunity to look for new product. For the film- and videomaker, it can provide valuable contacts and the experience of reaching a broader and more critical audience than friends and family. There can be much to learn (and grow from as a creative person) from a variety of opinions and public

responses to your work. Different venues will lead to different reactions. That is why it is important to enter more than one festival.

There are hundreds of festivals. The Bibliography lists important and historically well-attended festivals. Also included are recommended readings and a book listing all the current festivals and their vital information. The Association of Independent Video and Filmmakers in New York City (AIVF) publishes monthly festival listings in its magazine, *The Independent*. The Film Arts Foundation in San Francisco has a similar magazine called *Release Print*.

> *I think film festivals are springing up all over the place. We have a new one in San Jose. I recently went to the Rocky Mountain Women's Film Festival in Colorado Springs, which was in its fifth year. I'm going to Louisville in a couple of months to judge their festival. I think there's a lot of people with initiative who are starting film festivals in small communities and providing a forum for this work to be shown, and I think that will continue.*
>
> Jan

Many festivals are competitive or have competitive sections in which prizes or cash are awarded. The valuable exposure you receive after winning awards at various festivals can elevate your status in the industry, not only for the purpose of finding work as a producer or director, but also for building an impressive portfolio. (It is also very useful if you are interested in attracting a distributor.) This portfolio will come in handy when you are raising money or applying for grants for future productions.

It seems as though new festivals sprout up every year. The larger festivals are Sundance Film Festival, Telluride Indiefest, New York Film Festival, San Francisco International Film Festival, Montreal World Film Festival, Toronto International Film Festival, Berlin International Film Festival, Cannes International Film Festival, and Oberhausen International Short Film Festival.

Other noteworthy ones are The Hamptons International Film Festival, Nantucket Film Festival, Clermont-Ferrand (France), The Los Angeles Independent Film Festival, Slamdance, and Shorts International Film Festival. For documentaries, the Hot Springs Documentary Film Festival, The Margaret Mead Film and Video Festival, and the Yamagata International Documentary Film Festival (Japan) are just a few of the well-known ones. The Independent Documentary Association (IDA), an excellent organization that supports the documentary field, holds its own Documentary Awards Competition and the David L. Wolper Student Award Competition.

Specialty Festivals

If your project falls into a specific category or genre, there may be one or several festivals that are more appropriate. You will find festivals that focus on particular areas of interest such as Latino, Native American, gay and lesbian, Jewish, Asian American, underground/experimental, and digital art, to name just a few. The San Francisco International Lesbian & Gay Film Festival, the Jewish Film Festival, and the Native American Film and Video Festival are just three of many examples of festivals that are targeted to a specific subject matter or theme.

Applications

Most of these festivals are located on the Internet. Some applications can be printed right off the Web. Most have entrance fees between $20 and $50. Ultimately, you need to compare the benefits of a particular festival to the costs of submitting your work. The entrance fees, although not expensive individually, can add up. Other usual requirements are an advance video copy, a composite print (if a film), a synopsis of your project, a cast and crew list, a time framework for completion (for example, must have been completed no later than . . .), and a time limit (short films can be as long as 40 minutes). Some festivals will even require a press kit.

The "festival game" is expensive. You've got to be selective, and the way to be selective is to look in the magazine, The Independent, *which lists all festivals throughout the world and what kinds of films these festivals are looking for, what they're interested in.*

Howard

Museum Screenings

Museums regularly screen the work of emerging film and video artists. This type of screening is highly prestigious and an excellent opportunity to have your work seen by a potential distributor or buyer.

Cultural Societies

If your film or video deals with ethnic issues or concerns, research organizations that are seeking a visual device as a springboard for discussions.

Film School Festivals

All film and video programs hold an annual screening of their students' work. These festivals provide an opportunity to be recognized by your institution and to be seen by the industry. If your film or television program is located in a major urban area, it is likely that distributors, agents, and industry professionals will attend to become familiar with the new talent.

In Israel the Sam Speigle School was turning out amazing, amazing short work. I would go to year-end screenings, and there would be five fabulous pieces. All the graduating films were absolutely amazing. So there were many years in Israel where short films was where you could see the talent of filmmakers because there was no money in the industry so the features were not as good. But whatever was done in film school was remarkable.

Tatia

School and Community Groups

This category includes church groups, union organizations, local institutes, corporations, and youth programs.

What's most satisfying out of all the things that have happened with The Lunch Date *is the requests I get from schools and other instructional institutions and groups like the Girl Scouts, asking for the film because they're using it to discuss race relations. That, for me, is what I had set out to say with the picture. So that's been very rewarding for me: that the film is being used for instructional purposes.*

Adam

Television

Television might seem to be a natural conduit for the short subject, but this market is in transition. In the past, local access channels and cable networks such as HBO, Showtime, A&E, Bravo, and MTV offered the short film airtime. A&E has since dropped its "Short Subjects" programming, but there are other opportunities. Nickelodeon developed an animation department that offers young and innovative animators a chance to develop unique styles and story lines. Recently, the Independent Film Channel and the Sci-Fi Channel have introduced a shorts program. The Sci-Fi Channel has even included profiles of the film- and videomakers whose short films it is showcasing.

The medium is constantly evolving. The development of fiber optics is revolutionizing the industry. The blossoming of the cable industry with an anticipated 500 channels offers unlimited possibilities. There will no doubt be a real need for original programming. However, there is no way to predict what role short films or videos will play in this evolving scenario.

> *The other myth is, "I'll sell my film to cable television. There's a lot of money in cable television." Well, it's become increasingly harder to sell films to HBO, Showtime, or A&E. They've all dropped their short tapes programs. If they do buy, they pay very, very little. There is no market for a short film in television—what are you going to do with a 10-minute piece? It's not long enough to program any commercials around; it doesn't draw any names. It's not worth anything in terms of advertising time, so stations will basically use it as fill. The market has definitely decreased all the way around for short films.*
>
> Howard

Video

It is rare to be able to find short films on video or DVD at your neighborhood video rental outlet. You will have more luck in the larger cities at the more eclectic video stores. These videos are usually self-distributed (discussed later). The film- or videomakers pay for the tapes, transfers, artwork, and promotion themselves and literally peddle the tapes from store to store.

> *Once you have a video master, you can make dubs very cheaply. If you have a distributor, you'll get a nice cover for your video box, but be forewarned— the dubs and artwork will be charged back against the profits you make.*
>
> Howard

The Internet

The Internet is clearly becoming the "next mass medium," but with economic models vastly different from those of other mass media such as television or radio. On the one hand, the Internet's ability to narrowcast (see Glossary) and reach niche audiences has opened up tremendous opportunities for individuals and organizations to spread their messages or content. However, the noise of millions of Web sites trying to attract an audience means that it is not clear how these sites will find a large enough audience to justify the cost involved in producing and "webcasting" content, especially video.

It is also evident that by 2010 TVs and PCs may converge into one device. This convergence will affect programming greatly, as there will be an unlimited number of "channels" that will no longer be linear in nature. One will be able to get what one wants, when one wants it.

To a degree this is true today. The Internet is currently capable of sending audio and video, and it is available at the click of a mouse, or in other words, "on demand." However, quality problems exist, as good-quality video cannot be transmitted over a normal phone line. With faster connections, which are growing in use, decent video is available.

Even with a high-bandwidth connection, the problem remains today that most users are accessing the Internet via a personal computer. This is not an ideal environment to watch a longer video program because one tends to be in an active mode in front of the PC as opposed to the more passive mode of sitting on a couch watching television.

So what will an Internet user watch today? To overcome the hurdles mentioned, the content needs to be unique (unavailable in any other medium) and short. Short films and animation ("shorts") fit this category perfectly and are indeed growing in popularity on the Internet via sites such as AtomFilms.com, Hollywood.com, Warnerbros.com, and reelshort.com. In addition to their technical and sociological (the active environment of the PC mentioned earlier) advantages of being short, they have traditionally been too "niche" to be broadcast or played in movie theaters, but have a strong consumer following. The economics of Internet webcasting are still forming, but it is clear that there is room for innovative programming, and shorts fit this perfectly.

At this juncture it is difficult to generate profit from the Internet. It behooves the film- and videomaker to be aware that selling Internet rights may negate sales to other venues. The Internet has the potential to overexpose work, so a traditional short film outlet, such as the educational or television market, would prefer a product that has retained Internet rights. Putting your film or video on the Internet may prohibit you from selling your film to a distributor.

In most cases, the Internet is not really a market as there is no payment involved. The Internet is a place to showcase your work. If you have a short that plays at a number of festivals, Web sites may contact you to allow them to stream your work on their site. Getting your work online may be a great way to promote yourself to get attention for future work (see the Bibliography for Web distributors).

Consider also making your own Web site to display your work.

Foreign Markets

The short film is considered more of an art form in Europe and around the world than it is in the United States. For films made in the United States or Canada to have an appeal in the foreign or European market, the film's basic narrative must come through in the visuals. It must be driven by image, not dialogue. Comedies do not necessarily travel well because humor sometimes reflects national sensibilities.

What is clear about foreign markets is that they are generally much more creative from a programming perspective. The BBC programs short dramatic pieces in the afternoon so that a school class can turn them on and watch. After the piece is finished, the class uses the short film as a tool to deal with language skills, social studies, group dynamics, or whatever the strength of the piece is. The BBC puts together study guides to go along with the short pieces so they can be used within a proper educational context. This approach has been so successful that the BBC has programmed these short films during the evening primetime slot as well.

Foreign distribution plans must also consider issues related to subtitles. Some distributors arrange for subtitles to be shot locally. Others put into your contract a requirement that you must deliver a print with subtitles already burned in. In either case, the producer is required to supply a complete transcript of the project. You may also need to clear rights for foreign distribution and pay for the PAL conversion.

The market is currently growing as new regional cable and satellite stations are coming on the scene in the Middle East, Asia, and Latin America as well as in Europe. Talk to as many foreign distributors as you can.

DISTRIBUTION OPTIONS

Self-Distribution

One option is to distribute the film or video yourself. The primary advantage is that no one is going to care about your film or video as much as you do. Self-distribution is, however, a full-time job. It requires a realistic evaluation of the film or video's market, money, a professional approach, strategic thinking, busywork, and, most important, a sincere commitment to the process. It also requires a great deal of self-promotion and the ability to "think outside the box." In many ways, it is a natural outgrowth of production work. Distribution completes the circle.

One of its rewarding aspects is the opportunity to interact with the groups and individuals who you hoped would see your work when you decided to start this project.

If you are successful at it, you will save yourself the considerable distribution fee. Distributors often retain as much as 75 percent of net sales to cover their costs and profit, and pay the producers the remaining 25 percent. The figures of a distributor's percentage of sales are:

Television Market = 20%–30% of gross
Education Market = 60%–70% of Gross
Home Video Market = 70%–80% of net

> *I approached SAG because the film was going to be commercial, and you have to do this. I paid the actors their wages. Then I purchased the music rights, and so I own it now. I distribute the film myself. I like knowing where it's going. I like to give the film away free to hear feedback because I get a lot of requests from institutions. There wasn't a distributor that really interested me.*
>
> Adam

Self-distribution can be an excellent way to raise your profile and build networks with the people who are interested in seeing and promotion independent media. These are the basic steps of self-distributing your projects:

EVALUATION

- Evaluate the market for your production
- Evaluate your costs
- Get quotable reviews
- Do well in festivals

PRODUCTION

- Get photographs
- Make a video master and strike 50 copies
- Create a cover for the videocassette
- Set a realistic price for your work

MARKETING

- Obtain suitable mailing lists
- Have a brochure made up

- Have a system in place to receive and place orders
- Be professional!

Distributor

On the other hand, you can place the project with a distributor. Most film- and videomakers would rather spend their time producing and let the distributor, who is presumably more expert at marketing, do this important job.

Because Mirror Mirror *focused on women's issues, I contacted Women Make Movies as a possible distributor. I sent them a tape, and they were very interested, as was a second distributor. I decided to go with Women Make Movies because I felt that the subject matter fit their catalog and that it might find a larger audience through their mailing list.*

I negotiated for a one-sheet flier for Mirror Mirror *that they would send out as a special mailing at their expense. I signed with them in the fall of 1990 and gave them nontheatrical rights. In the winter of 1992, I placed the film with Jane Balfour Films in London for international nontheatrical and foreign TV.*

Since I retained domestic television rights, I entered Mirror Mirror *in the PBS series POV, which showcases independent documentaries. It was accepted and was broadcast in the summer of 1991. It was clustered with four other short films into a 90-minute program. The license agreement with POV was the standard PBS exclusive: four broadcasts in three years. Unfortunately, after the initial broadcast, it will not be aired again, but I am prevented from marketing it further until the license agreement expires later this year.*

I think it has done well in nontheatrical distribution. I'm not ready to retire off of the royalties, but they have probably sold about 80 video copies in three years, and the rentals are four times that amount. It has an active rental life in both film and video, which I like.

Jan

APPROACHING A DISTRIBUTOR

Many distributors specialize in the short form in both the domestic and foreign markets. Ask for catalogs from the distributors that interest you, and study them thoroughly before approaching anyone.

Rather than run out and find a distributor first thing, I did what I always do, which is to show it at a couple of festivals and see how people respond. It's easier to get a distributor if you have a product that other people have conferred recognition on. It becomes more marketable.

Jan

One way to find out whether a particular distributor is right for you is to set up a meeting and ask the following questions:

General Distribution

1. What kinds of markets does your company target?
   - Nontheatrical
   - Theatrical
   - Video
   - Television
   - Foreign or domestic

2. With which markets have you had the most success?

3. How has current technology affected the marketplace?

4. What are some examples of successful shorts from your catalog?

5. Do you work with a publicist? Do producers have approval or input over marketing and distribution plans?

6. What kind of subject matter is easiest to market and sell? Is there any type of picture you are specifically looking for now?
   - Narrative
   - Documentary
   - Animation
   - How-to
   - Sports
   - Fine arts
   - Business and industry
   - Health sciences
   - General interest

7. What lengths or running times have been most successful for you? Is there a relationship between the length of a project and its success in the marketplace? Is there an ideal length for any particular market?

8. What rights do you handle (i.e., nontheatrical, television, etc.)?

9. Is there much potential revenue in the television market?

10. Do you use film festivals to promote your new products? Which festivals in particular do you feel are the most important?

11. How do you use preview copies?

12. Do filmmakers ever approach you with an idea for a new project? How do you respond? Do you offer advice about the chances of that particular idea for distribution?

13. What do you offer to a film- or videomaker that your competitors do not?

14. Do you cover the costs of duplication?

15. Do you use a tiered royalty scale based on the market of a film? Is this a gross or net point? Is it based on the cost of the film rental and sales?

16. Do you give advances?

17. What is the average contract length and is it automatically renewable?

18. Does it matter if a product is on film or video? Which formats do you prefer?

19. What materials do you require from a film- or videomaker?

Foreign Distribution

1. Do you handle foreign rights for any of your films or videos?

2. How familiar are you with the foreign markets: theatrical, nontheatrical, television, video?

3. On which markets do you focus?

4. Which film festivals are most important overseas?

5. Which film markets do you attend (Cannes, Berlin, Claremont-Ferrand or Oberhausen?)?

6. Does your company use sales agents or subdistributors abroad?

7. What are the strongest foreign markets for the short today?

The responses to these questions will help you decide which distributor to employ. When all is said and done, most distribution contracts are similar. Your decision will most likely be based on the people who run the company, their track record with works of a similar nature, and your gut response.

Show the contract the distributor offers you to an entertainment attorney. You will need to understand the difference between gross and net points, deferments, and the various positions for recoupment. A lawyer can help you understand the difference between a profit and a nonprofit company. The Bibliography at the end of this book lists several books to assist you with contracts.

Contracts

To own the copyright, the filmmaker must have releases or contracts for everything related to the picture. This list may include the following:

- Actors and extras
- Music rights (see rights sections)
- Locations: any private or public property
- Décor: any and everything on the walls or furniture or exteriors of buildings and other people's copyrighted material (posters, book covers, paintings, etc.)

MARKETING YOUR SHORT FILM OR VIDEO

It is up to your distributor to sell your film or video project, so ask prospective distributors about how they would market it. *Marketing* means promoting what is best about your work, giving buyers a reason to want to own or rent it. Any ideas you have about how and what to promote will help the distributor devise a successful marketing campaign. You'll need a good marketing plan to make your venture into the marketplace a fruitful one.

Deliverables

Distributors of short films will require most of the same items required by a feature film distributor at your own expense:

Figure 19.1 Publicity still from *Truman*.

- One BETA SP (Stereo) videotape master of the picture in NTSC format (PAL if requested for foreign sales)
- Five VHS NTSC videotape copies
- Five DVD copies
- One dub from the digital video master
- Current list of festivals and awards
- Stills (usually color) in JPEG format
- Postproduction script (lined script)
- Key artwork
- Music cue sheet
- Copyright registration for the film and other chain of title and insurance information
- Release print(s) in available format if requested for theatrical rental
- An authorization to the laboratories and suppliers of preprint materials and foreign tracks
- Copies of all release forms and contracts

The Press Kit

You can promote yourself and your product by creating a press kit. A press kit presents your project to the public and to prospective distributors and entices them to screen it (see Figure 19.1). The kit should contain at least the following:

Cover
- Title
- Length and type of film or video (comedy, drama)

- Your name
- Contact number and address

Inside
- Black-and-white production still
- Still from the show
- Your résumé and telephone number
- Details about the production
- Reviews and clippings
- Credit list
- Transcript for foreign markets

DIRECTOR
Publicity

There is no better person than the director to publicize the short picture or to build an audience for it. The best sales tool is the picture itself. Favorable word of mouth, festival prizes, and ultimately distribution are based on the quality and salability of the final product.

> *Students put a lot of time and energy into production values, and the film may look like a million bucks but have no center. I think that's why* The Lunch Date *did so well. It's a simple film. Technically, it doesn't have a lot of bells and whistles, but it's got a great story, and the story is really well told in a filmic way.*
>
> Jan

We end this chapter with the extraordinary festival and distribution stories of *Truman, Mirror Mirror, Crazy Glue*, and *The Lunch Date*, as told by the filmmakers themselves.

TRUMAN

Truman did well in the festivals, but the "festival game" is expensive. It's $25 to $50 a shot, and you have to put out for the tapes, which you don't think of. This is one of the nice things about distribution: Once a distributor makes you a one-inch video master, and they have it, they can make dubs for you very cheaply, and they just charge it back to whatever profits you make. So it's a nice way to get dubs and a nice cover for your video copies.

The magazine The Independent *lists all festivals throughout the world and what kinds of films these festivals are looking for, what they're interested in. You have to be careful, but even if you're careful, you can still pick 25 festivals for the year. The festivals I submitted to were recommended to me by my distributor, Direct Cinema, and they said it would help enhance the market for the film in terms of the educational market. The film won the Princess Grace Fellowship, a Warner Bros. Film Fellowship, was a Regional Finalist—Student Academy Awards; it screened at the Sundance Film Festival, was voted one of the top 10 best children's films of 1992 [American Library Association], and is one of the highest-grossing children's films of 1992.*

It was really a learning process, going through this negotiation process for a short film, because a short film is not like another kind of contract. The whole means of supply and return is different; the market is different. The first thing that came as quite a shock is that when you get your film distributed, they have to make it an interpositive so they're not striking prints from your original negative. Well, guess who pays for the interpositive? You do, because it's yours; you own it. This is a huge expense, even for a 10-minute film. It was around $3,000 for the interpositive. So whatever money you make for the first year or so goes into paying off this interpositive you bought and/or whatever video, whatever dubs, you get struck for yourself.

It's been several years now, and I've only started to make money, even though the film has drawn astronomically well for [the distributor]. For a 10-minute film, it has done very well. In fact, a year ago, I think it was one of the top 10 children's films in the USA—short films. But, again, now I'm just starting to see money. I never expect to make all my money back. . . . The only film market that really exists for short films is the educational market. Now, I never imagined my film would be considered educational, but [middle schools] often buy it as a way to entertain kids on a rainy day, which is always how I imagined it, so it's turned out well.

It's only 10 minutes long, so it's really a diversion for kids at school, and because it's what's called an evergreen film, that's part of what's attractive about it. Evergreen means that it is always in season. There is nothing about this film that will date it. It is what it is: kids in a gym with sneakers. I mean, the themes in it, what it's about, will never get old. So it's attractive to schools even though it's not directly educational. If they have this film in their library, they can always pull it out for another 20 years to show the students, and it will always be of interest. That's really what a film distributor looks for because the short film market is about education. Can I sell this to a library or school?

I heard a story about my film that tickled me a little bit and surprised me because I didn't know what had happened. Apparently, when the film was done and it did well at the NYU screenings, it began to circulate. Copies get out that even you don't know about. People make dubs of dubs, and they start circulating the picture. I met this friend two years later who had another friend who was a West Coast junior agent for a while. He was talking to his friend, and his friend said, "There's this film that's the hot thing in Hollywood right now. Everybody's trying to get it, and there are very few copies available. Everybody wants to see this film, and I can't get a copy of it. I think it's an NYU student. Have you heard about it? It's about this kid climbing this rope."

This all went on unbeknownst to me. All of a sudden, without my knowing it, my film was a hot thing in Hollywood, and everybody wanted to get their hands on it, and there weren't enough copies to go around. That was two years ago, and I found out about it a year later. So if your film finds a certain niche, people will start talking about it, people will hear about it, and it will get around. Which is how I guess my agent found me. He must have been one of those people who had seen the tape, and he just called me out of the blue.

Howard

MIRROR MIRROR

The first real public screening of Mirror Mirror *was at the Margaret Mead Film Festival, which I had entered the previous spring with a videotape because the film wasn't completed at the time I entered it. People liked the film at Margaret Mead, and they started asking questions about this statement versus cross-cultural perceptions of body type. The kinds of questions you get at festivals are like that, which was fine. And then the film started doing very well. The next good thing that happened was it won the best documentary at the New York Film Expo. It won the director's choice at Black Maria Film Festival, and a Jury Award at the Big Muddy Film Festival. It won best documentary at the Humbolt International Festival and was the Judge's Choice winner at the Louisville Film and Video Festival. It was shown in London at the London International Film Festival. It didn't get into Sundance, although the director wrote me a note and said it came very close. So it wasn't a total flat-out rejection.*

For distribution, I contacted Women Make Movies. I sent them a tape, and they were very interested. I felt comfortable about putting the film with them because if people don't know about this film but they're teaching a "Media and Women" course at Podunk U. and trying to find a film, it seemed to me that they would look up the Women Make Movies catalog first. If they called around and asked if there is a distributor who distributes films about women, that's where they would end up.

I did negotiate for them to do a one-sheet flier just on this film, which to me meant a lot because it meant they would target this film—and direct it to a mailing list that was appropriate and so on—at their expense. So I signed with them in the fall of 1990. I only gave them nontheatrical; I retained domestic TV rights for myself, and I retained international, which eventually went to Jane Balfour Films in the winter of '92.

In terms of domestic TV, because I had retained it for myself, I entered it in POV, *and it got in. It was broadcast in the summer of '91. I received all the revenue since I was the one who had made the deal. Now they have an exclusive. I can't do anything with it, cable or PBS, for three years. That's their deal. Because it is a PBS contract, it has been on two other PBS series. First was the* Territory *series that comes out of Houston, so it's been shown down on Texas public television independently of* POV, *on this other series in Houston, Corpus Christi, and Austin. So I got some more money for that. And then it's also been on the* Through the Lens *series, which I think is on WYBE. It's a public station in Philadelphia. They put together a program of independents, unbeknownst to me—they actually went through Women Make Movies to get it—so it was on there. And now actually it's showing this month in the "What's Happening" series at MOMA.*
I think it's done well. I'm not getting rich off it, but

when I look at the statements—I don't know how it's done compared to the distributor's other films—but I think it's really getting out there.

Jan

CRAZY GLUE

I was just hoping to make a good film that would take care of itself and that's what happened. One festival brought another festival and I got some purchase requests from various television stations. It was distributed by Atom Films for a while. It was never a money-making venture, but it did get some awards and some additional sales. Since it's so short—short films are sold by the minute—it was never a huge amount, but it was nice. The market definitely paid back the $2,000 it cost me to make the film.

Tatia

THE LUNCH DATE

The first three festivals I sent The Lunch Date *to didn't accept the film. I found this very discouraging. I think the first festival to accept it was San Francisco, and then suddenly every festival I applied to, it got into. I believe the film took on a life of its own. Once you're done with a film, it's out of your hands. There's nothing you can do. It has its own life, and who knows what that's going to be. I got very lucky: first in Atlanta and Houston—it won prizes there—and then AFI, which was noncompetitive. The only one I went to out of all of those was the AFI because it was an excuse to go home. For all those who I'm sure are wondering how the hell it got into Cannes, I can tell you it was just a fluke of luck.*

Adam

Cannes

Around the time I finished the film, I screened it for my professor, Vojtech Jasny. After showing it to him, he told me two things. One was that I should submit the film to Cannes, which I thought was completely crazy. He said, "Submit it; the festival is coming soon." I didn't act on that right away. I delayed. Eventually, I sent the film to Cannes.

The other thing Vojtech told me was that he had a friend who was a casting director, Diane Crittenden, who was in New York casting a film, and she was looking for an intern, an unpaid intern, to run a video camera during the casting of her next movie, and would I be interested? And I said, "Sure." I always like to work, and casting was part of the process I had not gotten to see. I was working part-time doing the same kind of thing at a commercial house, but I was interested to see how different it was for a movie. So I spoke to Diane, and she said she had heard from Vojtech that my movie was good, and would I send her a tape? She was going to Los Angeles, but she would call when she got back.

I sent her the tape, and a few weeks went by. We eventually got in touch again, and she said that she didn't need anybody anymore, but that she had seen my film and she liked it. We had a little talk on the phone, and she suggested I come down to meet with her, just to talk. We set up a date.

I ran all the way over from Fifth Avenue to Eleventh Avenue where her office was, and for some reason it didn't connect with me what she might be doing. I went up in the office, and there were all these signs for Green Card, *and I thought that was her casting company or something. I got upstairs and saw it was a film production, and I realized, "Oh, this is* Green Card, *Peter Weir's film." So I went into the office, and I asked someone if they could show me to Diane Crittenden, my name is Adam Davidson. The receptionist said, "Oh, you're the person who made that short film, the one that takes place in Grand Central?" And I said, "Yeah, yeah." Then she said, "Diane's been showing everyone that film, and we all love it." I said, "Really?!"*

I went down into her office and met Diane, and she said yes, she had been showing it to everyone. In fact, she had shown it to Peter Weir, who loved it and had taken the tape home to show Gerard Depardieu. Then she said, "Do you mind that I gave the tape out?" I was flabbergasted.

Then I got a call at work which I thought was a joke: "Hi, my name's Andy. I'm Peter Weir's assistant. I just wanted to tell you that Gerard Depardieu has recommended your film to Cannes, and he has given me this number that he wants you to call to contact Cannes." And I thought, "What! This is unbelievable." I called this number, and it was a French film office in New York. They said, "We got a call from Gerard Depardieu, and we would like to see your film." And I said, "Well, I submitted it about three months ago on my own. You have it. It's in France." "We have it?" "Yes, yes." "OK, we'll get back to you."

About a week later, the French woman from the Cannes office called, saying, "Your film has just been accepted at Cannes." It was amazing,

absolutely amazing. I went over to Cannes. It was interesting.

First of all, I went there with these very naive film-school fantasies of what Cannes would be like. I figured, it's the oldest film festival, it's France, the last bastion of where film is considered an art. I could walk down the street and see Akira Kurosawa and say, "Hey, Akira, let's go get a cup of coffee and talk about film and talk about cinema." Of course, it's nothing like that. It's a market. Now there's the festival there, and there's also the Cannes film market. There are these beautiful châteaus there, and these beautiful hotels, covered with giant Schwarzenegger posters and giant Stallone posters. It's a zoo, and I hated getting in a tux.

It was incredible because when I was going there, they were showing the new films of my heroes. Kurosawa was there with Dreams. *Godard was there with* Nouveau Vague. *Fellini was there with his film* La Volce de la Luna. *So I was happy to have a chance to see these movies.*

Supposedly, I could get into any film, but I had to report to this one office every day. It was always the same story. I'd go in, and I'd have this list, and I'd say, "I'd like to see this at this time, and this at this time." I tried to only see the films during the day because going at night meant getting in a tux. There was only one way to enter the theater. You have to enter down the red carpet where people have gathered the whole day to get a glimpse of whoever was in the movie. So there I would be—alone— walking down, just feeling like the biggest loser in the world. I tried to go during the day when the press was going.

But every time when I went to get tickets, it was always the same answer. "Non, monsieur, c'est complet. Je suis désolée. I'm very sorry, but we're all filled." And then I'd sit there. I don't know why it is, it seems with the French, their first answer is no. Because then you sit there and ask, "Don't you have one, just any ticket?" And they say, "Oh, let me check." Then she'd open the door beside her, and she'd say, "Oh, I do have one." So I'd get my one ticket. So the screening of films came about.

There are all *these shorts. In Cannes, the short category can be anything as long as it's short—under 15 minutes. So there were, in my category, a few animated films and something that resembled a documentary. Most of them were 35-mm. Most of them were color. After seeing that screening, I was convinced that I didn't have a chance. It didn't matter. I was glad to just be there.*

I was convinced the film wasn't going to win, and the day of the awards . . . I hadn't received anything about if I should go, where I should go. And I went down to the office to speak to the same woman and said, "What am I supposed to do?" And she said,

"You're supposed to get a ticket." "Well, do you have one?" "Non, monsieur, je suis désolée. C'est complet." I said, "Are you sure?" She opens up the drawer, and there is one.

So I go to the awards thing, and they seat me. It was in the front row! And I'm sitting between two guys who are in the short film category. One guy turns to me and says, "Is my hair okay?" And I say, "Yeah, it looks fine." And he says, "Good. This is my third time here." I said, "Great. Congratulations."

The show starts, and it's strange. It's like a mixture of The Dating Game *and something else. It goes by very fast. It's not like the Academy Awards, where they stop to do numbers and things like that. The host came out, the back door opened up, and—like* The Dating Game*—the eight jurors come out on this sliding platform, sitting on stools. Bernardo Bertolucci was the head of the jury that year. They're going through the different categories, and with my French, I'm picking up some of it. And then they get to the short film. They announce the award for the short film, and the two guys sitting next to me both get up at the same time and go up. And I thought, "Whoa, what a relief. It's over. The anxiety is over. I don't have to worry anymore." And these guys go off. Then Bertolucci starts speaking again because he gives the award as the head of the jury. He starts talking about short film again. And he says, the Palme d'Or, which is the grand prize in Cannes . . . goes to Adam Davidson. I went up on stage. He handed me what looked like a diploma thing, and I didn't know what the hell to do.*

The next thing I know, I'm standing before this microphone, and I just wanted to make sure that I had thanked people. Well, as I'm speaking—and I was very nervous—I hear the emcee, who is a Johnny Carson type guy, start speaking too. And I was convinced (because I wasn't really listening) that this guy was saying, "What the hell is the stupid American doing? We don't want to hear it. It's just a short film. Get on with it." What I didn't know was that he was trying to translate. I just looked over at him and just kind of said, "That's it."

The whole thing with Cannes was a fluke. If it wasn't for the chance that Depardieu had seen it accidentally, I don't think it would have gotten in, even though I had sent it out there.

The Academy Awards

The Academy Award is the highest honor a film artist can achieve. It is a massive career jolt, often a box office boost, and most definitely an emotional high. The award is a ticket to an elite club that, once given, can never be taken away. What one makes of the opportunity is, of course, always up to the winner.

Some are stymied by the attention; others brush it off as merely a career milestone. But whatever the reaction, receiving an Academy Award is a good thing.

The Academy Award is focused on feature-length films, but both short narrative and short documentary films (less than 30 minutes) have received Academy Awards over the years, and their impact on the filmmaker and the film community is no less profound.

But there is trouble in paradise. The Academy has been shaking the awards tree of late, hoping to shed excess fruit. As anyone who watches the Academy Awards show knows, it is long. Between the dance numbers, the singing of all the Academy-nominated songs, and the passionate speeches where leaving someone off a thank-you list might prove politically devastating, the television producers are always looking for ways to trim the length of the show. In 1996 and in 1998, the short format came under fire and would have been excluded save for the efforts of all the filmmakers who value the nature of the format and the learning curve associated with short work.

The Academy's argument is simple. The Academy Award is for theatrical motion picture work. Whereas in the past shorts had a life on the big screen, this is no longer the case. For a film to qualify for Academy consideration, it must play for at least one week before January 1 on at least one screen in Los Angeles. Since most short narrative and documentary films are not destined for big screens, the filmmakers must negotiate with theatre owners for screen time around Christmas to be eligible for the award.

So, in 1996, the Academy said that short narrative films do not screen theatrically, and so the category should be eliminated. The same statement was made two years later referring to short documentary work. The outcry from the creative film community was overwhelming. Many filmmakers got their start experimenting with the short form before graduating to longer work. Letters and protests caused the Academy to back off and allow these two categories to remain—for now.

I submitted the film on my own to the Student Academy Awards. It won in the category there. I was informed that since my film won there, it qualified for submission to the Academy Awards. I'd had enough of awards and things, so I said, "No thanks." After the urgings of a few people, family, and agents and at the insistence of Rich Miller, the head of the Student Academy Awards, I said I would submit it. It was nominated. So I went to Los Angeles for the awards ceremony.

I decided to bring Scotty [the lead actress in the film] as my guest, but she doesn't fly, so like her character, she took a train all the way out to Los Angeles. She telephoned me the day of the ceremony and said, "What time is the limo coming by to pick us up?" I said, "Well, the Volkswagen will be by at such and such a time." We went together. We were seated in the middle of the row. You know how a mind works: I figured, "Obviously, this whole show is rigged, and they seat the people who they know are going to win by the aisles so they can get out easily. So at least I don't have to worry about that."

And then I saw my mother, and she came and sat down behind me. It was pretty quiet in that theater, in that space, and she leans over and not too quietly says, "Adam, do you have enough room so you can get out?" And everybody—all the other nominees—just turns to look at me scornfully.

The category came up, and the film was announced. It didn't hit me. The name was said, and I heard this primal yell. It was my father, who was touching the roof of the theater. I got up—and I was just hoping I wouldn't trip—and got up on stage. It's pretty terrifying. You suddenly face 6,000 people, and the cameras are on, and they have this huge television monitor that they wheel in front of you, which basically flashes "30, 29, 28, 27 . . ."—how long you're allowed to speak. I think I thanked everybody. It was funny. I had gotten a seat for Garth Stein, my friend and the film's co-producer, and he was seated up in the balcony. When I thanked Garth, I said something like, "I'd also like to thank Garth Stein." And I looked up and said, "Who's somewhere up there." I think a lot of people imagined Garth had passed away or something.

The moral of this story about the film is that it does take on a life of its own. I would say to any student out there: Don't be discouraged if you don't get into your first couple of festivals. It is important to try to give the film a chance.

Adam

Genres

EXPERIMENTAL OR ALTERNATIVE

The short film or video has been an ideal form for experimentation. Filmmakers have been experimenting with the possibilities of what film can do since George Méliès's time. Many major European directors who became famous in the 1930s and 1940s began their careers in the 1920s with short films: Jean Renoir, René Clair, Luis Buñuel, and Julien Duvivier are among them. The artists Man Ray and Marcel Duchamp both explored the possibilities of film's pure visual form. Many early experimental pieces relied on seemingly random images, with no apparent story or narrative expectations to engage the audience. These filmmakers played visual tricks with the medium, dealing with surrealistic film fantasies. They later incorporated into their features many of the filmic ideas explored in these short experimental films.

The independent avant-garde, or underground, movement in the United States began as a protest against Hollywood's conventions and standard narrative expectations. Many of the early short films in the 1920s focused on pure images and had little form or content. It was Maya Deren in the early 1940s who realized that noncommercial, personal short films could do more than just photograph a series of shapes and forms. She created a series of surreal films that played with the perception of space and time as well as the line between dream and reality. Her films greatly influenced the underground movement in the United States in the 1950s and 1960s. Aided by the increased availability of 16-mm and 8-mm film equipment, new filmmakers such as Stan Brakhage, Robert Breer, Shirley Clarke, Bruce Conner, Kenneth Anger, Bruce Baille, George Kuchar, Jonas Mekas, Ed Emshwiller, and Andy Warhol emerged as explorers in "personal filmmaking."

The availability of portable video in the 1970s and 1980s allowed a new generation of artists to emerge aided by the technological ease with which images could be created and the endless possibilities for electronic manipulation. No longer were images relegated to one screen. Installations became an intricate part of experimental presentations, embodied in what are referred to as *video walls*.

Multimedia, which mixes live performances with video installations, became an effective tool for musicians and dancers such as Meredith Monk, Joan Jonas, and Bob Flanaean to use in expanding the reach of their art. Media organizations and artist support groups have sprouted up across the country to support new generations of visual artists who are expressing themselves in radical new ways. In the 1990s, the lines between film and video blurred with the impact of digital technology. Compact digital cameras and home desktop editing systems are empowering those who wish to express themselves in alternative ways. Visual artists are looking to the Internet as a viable distribution outlet for their short works.

CORPORATE

Businesses and other types of organizations (including educational and nonprofit institutions and government agencies) use short films and videos (usually 10 minutes or less in length) for a variety of purposes: to help launch new products or services, to explain new ideas or strategies, and to educate and train employees. Such media are known collectively as *corporate* or *sponsored* media.

With the rise of the Web, video has become a communication commodity—ubiquitous, but not as hot as it was in the 1980s and early 1990s. Often, video (and sometimes film) pieces are incorporated into other formats, particularly Web sites and CDs, as well as trade show presentations and mixed media installations in museums or other exhibits. Currently, the lack of Internet bandwidth and slow connection speeds put severe limits on the length of Web-based motion segments.

321

The objective of most corporate media is to communicate messages and information to specific, targeted audiences in such a way as to move them to some desired action or change their attitudes about an issue. Most corporate work is produced in video, rather than film, and uses a variety of creative approaches, including computer graphics, animation, documentary, and dramatic narrative.

Despite the general decline of the influence of video, high-quality pieces are still produced when an important message needs to be delivered and distributed widely and requires a running time of several minutes. The best corporate work can transcend its business objectives and achieve the status of art. *Powers of Ten* (1978), by Charles and Ray Eames, was sponsored by IBM to help audiences understand the scale and power of large computers. *Knowledge Navigator* (1987) was produced by Apple Computer to provoke audiences into thinking about the future of interactive computing; it was aired on network television, shown at conferences, and analyzed in major publications such as *Scientific American* and *Fortune*.

In today's constantly changing, culturally and geographically diverse organizations, these media have become important means of communication. Many businesses maintain extensive production facilities for both traditional and new media; others contract with agencies, producers, and design firms that specialize in corporate work. Many writers, producers, directors, shooters, designers, programmers, and others find corporate work interesting, creatively demanding, and financially rewarding—but not the best way to fulfill personal artistic ambitions.

COMMERCIALS

A commercial is a short. It has a beginning, a middle, and an end. It sets up conflict at the beginning and tries to persuade us that the only way to resolve that conflict is to buy a particular product—and it does this in as few as 15 seconds. Commercials are small, succinct stories that carry a great deal of weight. For many young people, the television commercial is their only opportunity to experience an idea expressed in less than a half-hour.

The one thing that can be said about any commercial, whether "good" or "bad," is that it has tremendous power. Commercials disrupt our regular viewing, creating a hostile relationship, but then are able to sway us emotionally and sell us something. The power of a television commercial is in its manipulation of the medium for one purpose. There are differ-ent kinds of commercials, including political commercials, which are designed to sell a candidate, and public service announcements (PSAs), which are designed to communicate an important issue. Whether they are designed to tell us whom to vote for, about the dangers of AIDS, or what detergent to use, commercials are about the power to persuade.

Since television commercials were first introduced in the early 1950s (when they were broadcast live), they have managed to manipulate contemporary technology and current social and economic trends to successfully sell their wares. They exploit popular icons and ideology in an effort to access our personal psyches—all this to promote toothpaste or beer. Millions of dollars are spent on 30 seconds of screen time. During the 1960s, there was a renaissance in commercial activity, and commercials were almost considered the best thing on television. This soon stopped. People were so entertained by the commercial that the product went almost unnoticed.

In the 1990s, there was a return to more entertaining commercials with dazzling displays of technological wizardry. Advertising agencies with huge expense accounts utilize high-end computer-driven systems to create sophisticated 3D graphics. Some campaigns have steered away from the old-fashioned "hard sell" to subtler, almost abstract approaches aimed at the modern consumer. Comedy has even resurfaced as a selling tool.

MUSIC VIDEOS

Although they are called music "videos," these short pieces have been traditionally shot on film. They emerged in the 1980s as vehicles to revive the music industry. The idea of showcasing musical talent and songs was born, however, many years before. There is a long tradition of performing songs on film and television; musicals were a Hollywood staple from the introduction of sound up until the 1960s. Many of these were based on Broadway revues, themselves vehicles to showcase songs and talented performers with a bare thread of a plot to tie them together.

First radio and then television used the variety show format to showcase popular music and its performers. The *Ed Sullivan Show* was one of the earliest and certainly one of the most popular in television. It featured singers or groups such as Elvis Presley, the Beatles, and the Rolling Stones. Later, popular recording stars such as Sonny and Cher and the Smothers Brothers would have their own variety shows. The 1960s spawned music/dance shows such as *American Bandstand* (1957–1989), *Shindig*, and

Hullabaloo (1964–1966), and in the 1970s, *Soul Train*. Groups such as the Beatles, the Beach Boys, the Righteous Brothers, Chuck Berry, Sam Cooke, Neil Sedaka, and the Everly Brothers appeared on these shows, giving audiences a chance to see their favorite groups performing their hit songs (although they were usually lip-syncing). Music documentaries such as *Don't Look Back*, *Monterey Pop*, and *Woodstock* made an indelible mark with young audiences by featuring live performances in concert.

The music video liberated the performers from the context of a show or concert and gave each song and performer its own self-contained presentation. Earlier music videos tried to adhere to some narrative that was loosely based on the lyrics of the song, but this format has largely disappeared. Narrative expecta-tions have vanished. Many display random images and visual nonsequiturs strung together by the persona of the artist, hip visual effects, and, of course, a song. From the record company perspective, their primary purpose is to create an image for the group rather than to sell a particular song.

The music video owes its stylistic debt to the Beatles' first feature, *A Hard Day's Night* (1968). Directed by Richard Lester, this highly successful film dazzled audiences with its frantic pace, zany antics, jump cuts, and, of course, the endearing personalities of the Fab Four. Music videos have been a successful training ground for many directors and a wonderful opportunity for beginning film- and videomakers to get valuable experience and create a body of work.

appendix B

Screening List

The following is a partial list of recommended short films and videos. You will find their distributors on our Web site. Many of these are also available at public and school libraries. Shorts are now distributed on the Internet. Some of these sites are also listed in the bibliography.

SHORT FILMS AND VIDEOS

The Lunch Date. Directed by Adam Davidson, 12 minutes, B&W, Academy Award—Best Live Action Film, 1990, USA.
The Lantz Office
200 West 57th Street
Suite 503
New York, NY 10019
Tel: (212) 586-0200

A chance encounter between a wealthy suburban woman and a homeless man at a lunch counter in Grand Central Station.

Truman. Directed by Howard McCain, 12 minutes, color, 1992, USA.
Direct Cinema
P.O. Box 10003
Santa Monica, CA 90410
Tel: (310) 636-8200/(800) 525-0000
Fax: (310) 636-8228

An 11-year old boy confronts his imaginary fears about climbing a rope in gym class.

Crazy Glue. Directed by Tatia Rosenthal, 5 minutes, color, 1997, USA
Tatia Rosenthal
Tel: (917) 6132-667
rosenthal@yahoo.com
An animated clay puppet short adapted from a story by Israeli author Etgar Keret. This claymation

(see Glossary) film tells the story of one innovative attempt to patch up a disintegrating marriage—through the use of Crazy Glue!

Mirror Mirror. Directed by Jan Krawitz, 17 minutes, color, 1990, USA.
Women Make Movies
462 Broadway
Suite 500
New York, NY 10013
Tel: (212) 925-0606
Fax: (212) 925-2052

A documentary exploring women's feelings about their bodies; 13 masked women speak about their bodies, intercut with historical footage.

Akira Kurosawa's Dreams. Directed by Akira Kurosawa. 119 minutes, color, 1990, Japan/USA. (Home Warner Video) A collection of tales based on the actual dreams of Akira Kurosawa. Very personal short films with breathtaking imagery.

All the Boys Are Called Patrick. Directed by Jean-Luc Godard, 21 minutes, B&W, 1957, France. (Biograph Entertainment, Kit Parker Films) Two roommates both meet boys named Patrick; they begin to suspect and later realize that their two Patricks are actually the same boy.

Amblin. Directed by Steven Spielberg, color, 24 minutes, 1968, USA. Two wanderers meet and hitchhike together, but when they reach their destination, the beach, the girl discovers that the boy is not what he seemed to be.

An American Time Capsule. Written and directed by Charles Braverman, 3 minutes, color, 1968, USA. (Pyramid Film/Video, Biograph Entertainment) Two centuries of American history condensed into 3 minutes. It uses 1,300 still images flashed before the eyes.

Bambi Meets Godzilla. Directed by Marv Newland, 2 minutes, animated, B&W, 1969, USA. (Chicago Filmmakers, Biograph Entertainment) Movie credit titles run over the animated image of Bambi, until Godzilla comes into view to squash Bambi.

The Battle of San Pietro. Directed by John Huston, 32 minutes, B&W, war documentary, 1945, USA. (Biograph Entertainment) A documentary about the Battle of San Pietro, in which more than 1,100 U.S. soldiers were killed while trying to take this small Italian village from the Germans.

Betty for President. Directed by Max Fleischer, 7 minutes, color, 1932, Betty Boop cartoon, USA. (Biograph Entertainment) Betty Boop's campaign against Mr. Nobody tries to appeal to everyone. It is a parody of real candidates, and the House of Representatives is portrayed by elephants and asses.

Big Business. Directed by James Wesley Horne, 20 minutes, B&W, music track, 1929, USA. Cast members: Stan Laurel, Oliver Hardy. (MOMA, Biograph Entertainment) Laurel and Hardy are in the business of selling Christmas trees.

The Big Shave. Directed by Martin Scorsese, 6 minutes, color, 1968, USA. (Available on laser disc, *Three by Scorsese*; also on VHS: Home Vision Cinema) As he shaves, a young man cuts himself until he is covered in blood. A statement on the Vietnam war.

A Chairy Tale. Directed by Norman McLaren, 10 minutes, B&W, 1957, USA. (Biograph Entertainment) Pixelation is used to tell the story of a young man and a chair that refuses to be sat upon.

Un Chien Andalou. Directed by Luis Buñuel, 20 minutes, B&W, silent, 18 fps, 1928, France. (Chicago Filmmakers) The classic surrealist film made up of abstract and bizarre images.

City of Gold. Directed by Wolf Koenig, Colin Low, 21 minutes, B&W, produced by the Canadian Film Board, 1956, Toronto, Canada. (National Film Board of Canada) This film tells the fascinating history of Dawson City during the Klondike Gold Rush.

The Critic. Written and directed by Ernest Pintoff, color, 1963, USA. (Biograph Entertainment) A comedy that pokes fun at the meaningless symbolism of avant-garde cinema, employing ever-changing abstract patterns.

The Cure. Directed by Charlie Chaplin, 19 minutes, B&W, music track, 1917, USA. (Biograph Entertainment) Charlie Chaplin wreaks havoc at a health spa.

A Day in the Country (Une Partie de Campagne). Directed by Jean Renoir, B&W, 37 minutes, 1949, France. (MOMA) A Parisian shop-owner's family spends a day in the country, where the daughter falls in love with a man at the inn.

The Dove (De Duva). Directed by George Coe and Tony Lover, 15 minutes, B&W, 1968, USA. (Biograph Entertainment) A hilarious satire on Bergman films.

Dr. Ded Bug. Directed by Ethan Cohen-Sitt, 10 minutes, B&W, 1989, USA. (Chicago Filmmakers) A comedy about a mad chef who goes insane trying to kill a cockroach in a restaurant kitchen.

Dream of the Wild Horses. Directed by Denys Colomb de Daunant, 9 minutes, color, 1960, France. (Biograph Entertainment) A breathtaking slow-motion film of wild horses in the Camargue region of France.

Entr'Acte. Directed by René Clair, 20 minutes, B&W, silent, 18 fps, 1924, France. Infused with the Dada spirit of mockery, a surrealist classic in which inanimate objects have a will of their own; "delightfully preposterous."

The Fat and the Lean. Written and directed by Roman Polanski and Jean-Pierre Rousseau, 15 minutes, B&W, 1961, France. (Flower Films, Biograph Entertainment) An allegory about the tyrant-slave relationship, employing a combination of mime and surrealism.

Fetch. Directed by Lynn-Maree Danzey, 7 minutes, color, Best Short Comedy—Just For Laughs Comedy Festival, Montreal, 1998, Australia. (Direct) A man arrives at a woman's apartment to take her out on a first date, but events conspire against him. An amusing and dark look at the bad luck that can plague even the most innocent circumstances.

Frank Film. Directed by Frank Mouris, 9 minutes, color, Academy Award—Best Animated Short, 1973, USA. (Direct Cinema, Biograph Entertainment) A continuous flow of thousands of overlapping images/incredible collages recounts the events of Mouris's life.

A Game of Catch. Directed by Steven John Ross, adapted from short story by Richard Wilber, 15 minutes, color, 1990, USA. (Pyramid Film & Video) A 12-year-old boy tries unsuccessfully to play catch with two other boys with almost disastrous results.

The film conveys the heartrending feeling of being an outsider and explores the tension between imagination and reality.

A Girl's Own Story. Directed by Jane Campion, 27 minutes, B&W, Best Direction—Australian Film Awards, 1986, Australia. (Women Make Movies) A look at three teenage girls in the Beatles era.

The Great Train Robbery. Directed by Edwin S. Porter, 10 minutes, tinted, music track at silent speed, 1903, USA. (MOMA, Biograph Entertainment) The first American film with a complete story line; pioneered parallel editing and double exposure, among a number of other early innovations.

Hardware Wars. Directed by Ernie Fosselius and Michael Wiese, 13 minutes, color, 1978, USA. (Biograph Entertainment, Chicago Filmmakers) A parody of *Star Wars;* special effects are made using household appliances found in any hardware store.

La Jetée. Written and directed by Chris Marker, 29 minutes, B&W, 1962, France. (Biograph Entertainment, Kit Parker Films) Utilizing a series of still images, this futuristic film explores apocalyptic post-World War III Earth, in which survivors live underground and perform experiments in time travel.

Leon's Case. Directed by Daniel Attias, 25 minutes, color, 1982, USA. (Chicago Filmmakers) The story of a 1960s activist who has been living as a fugitive for 12 years and decides to surrender.

The Life and Death of 9413, A Hollywood Extra. Directed by Salavko Vorkapich and Robert Florey, 12 minutes, B&W, experimental, 1928, USA. (Biograph Entertainment) The story of the Extra and a successful movie star named Mr. Blank was the first American experimental film influenced by German Expressionism. Greg Toland (*Citizen Kane*) shot it.

L'toile de Mer. Directed by Man Ray, 15 minutes, silent, 18 fps, B&W, 1928, France. (Biograph Entertainment) An attempt to visually create the mood and images of the surrealist poem by Robert Desnos.

The Man Who Planted Trees (L'Homme qui Plantait des Arbres). Directed by Frederic Back, 30 minutes, color, animated, Academy Award—Best Animated Short, 1987, Canada. (Direct Cinema) The story of a shepherd who repairs the ruined ecosystem of a secluded valley by single-handedly cultivating a forest over a 30-year period.

Meshes of the Afternoon. Directed by Maya Deren, 20 minutes, B&W, 1943, USA. (Chicago Filmmakers, MOMA, Biograph Entertainment) One of the major American experimental films of all time. Deren plays a woman driven to suicide by her obsessions and hallucinations.

Minors. Directed by Alan Kingsberg, 36 minutes, color, USA. Winner Student Academy Award, 1st Prize FOCUS Awards, 1984. (ADK Films, 212-529-2440) The story of a teenage girl who needs a subject for her science project and a minor league pitcher struggling to make it to the majors.

Les Mistons. Directed by François Truffaut, 18 minutes, B&W, in French with English subtitles, 1957, France. (Biograph Entertainment, Kit Parker Films) Truffaut's first film is about a group of boys who fall in love with a charming girl and how they come closer to understanding their own feelings.

Moods of the Sea. Directed by Slavko Vorkapich and John Hoffman, 10 minutes, B&W, 1942, USA. (Biograph Entertainment) A visual experience of light and motion that juxtaposes images of breaking waves with music.

Moonbird. Directed by John and Faith Hubley, 10 minutes, color, Academy Award—Best Animated Short, 1960, USA. (Biograph Entertainment) A delightful adventure of two small boys who go out one night to catch a "moonbird"; captures the wonder and mystery of childhood.

Night and Fog (Nuit et Brouillard). Directed by Alain Renais, 30 minutes, color, subtitled documentary, 1955, France. (Biograph Entertainment, Home Vision Cinema) Filmed at the postwar site of Auschwitz, this film is one of the most vivid depictions of the horrors of Nazi concentration camps. It tells the story of the Holocaust and of the horror of man's brutal inhumanity.

No Lies. Directed by Mitchell Block, color, 16 minutes, 1972, USA. (Direct Cinema) In conversation, an interviewer's questions strip away a young woman's defenses, revealing the trauma of sexual assault. *No Lies* is not a documentary, but the film is produced in the style of "direct cinema," creating a provocative tension between fact and fiction.

Number Our Days. Directed by Lynne Littman, 29 minutes, color, Academy Award—Best

Documentary Short, 1976, USA. (Direct Cinema) A documentary about a group of elderly Jews in Venice, California.

NY, NY. Directed by Francis Thomson, 16 minutes, color, Academy Award—Best Short Film, 1957, USA. (Pyramid Film/Video, Biograph Entertainment) New York City is bent, stretched, fractured, and shattered; a classic experimental film creates a beautiful variation on the reality of a great city.

An Occurrence at Owl Creek Bridge. Directed by Robert Enrico, 27 minutes, B&W, 1962, France. (Biograph Entertainment) A Civil War soldier is about to be executed by hanging, but escapes to find his way home, with an ironic ending. Film utilizes compelling distortions of time and sound.

One Week. Directed by Buster Keaton and Eddie Cline, 20 minutes, B&W, 1920, USA. (Biograph Entertainment) A newlywed couple receives a build-it-yourself house kit and a plot of land—but the numbers on the boxes have all been altered, and Keaton builds a completely crazy house.

Pas de Deux. Directed by Norman McLaren, 14 minutes, B&W, experiment with dance, 1969, Canada. (Biograph Entertainment) Blending sound and motion into visual poetry, McLaren has fragmented, overprinted, and utilized frame repetition to create an innovative classic.

Passionless Moments. Directed by Jane Campion, 13 minutes, B&W, Best Short Film—Sidney Film Festival, 1988, Australia. (Women Make Movies) A film about everyday moments in the lives of 10 characters, each with an uneasy familiarity.

Peege. Directed by Randal Kleiser, 28 minutes, color, 1974, USA. (Biograph Entertainment) The story of a family's Christmas visit to their grandmother (a patient at a nursing home), seen through the eyes of her eldest grandson. Flashbacks of her life are a vivid contrast to the present.

Peel. Directed by Jane Campion, 9 minutes, color, winner of the Palme d'Or at Cannes Film Festival, 1982, Australia. (Women Make Movies) A father, his son, and the father's sister on a drive back home. The boy continuously throws orange peels out the window, and the situation soon gets a little intense.

La Poulet (The Chicken). Written and directed by Claude Berri, 15 minutes, B&W, subtitled, Academy Award—Best Short Film, 1963, France. (Biograph Entertainment) A young boy becomes so fond of a rooster bought by his parents for Sunday dinner

that he decides to trick them into thinking it's a hen to keep it alive. His ploy works until the rooster one day wakes them up with its crow.

A Propos de Nice. Directed by Jean Vigo, 23 minutes, B&W, silent, 1929, France. (Biograph Entertainment, Kit Parker Films) A landmark film in cinema history, this silent documentary is an ironic satire on the French Riviera.

Rain. Directed by Joris Ivens and Mannus Franken, 12 minutes, B&W, documentary with music track, 1929, Holland. (Biograph Entertainment) Impressionistic study of a rain shower in Amsterdam, using no titles or narration.

The Red Balloon. Written and directed by Albert La-morisse, 34 minutes, color, nonverbal, 1956, France. (Biograph Entertainment) A parable about a lonely boy who rescues a red balloon that then follows him. A charming and witty film.

The Rink. Written and directed by Charles Chaplin, 19 minutes, B&W, music track, 1916, USA. (Biograph Entertainment) The girl of his dreams invites Chaplin to the roller skating rink. He starts a riot, the cops show up, and then he escapes by hooking his cane onto an automobile and skating away.

Screen Test. Directed by Frank and Caroline Mouris, 20 minutes, color, 1975, USA. (Biograph Entertainment) Nine of Mouris's friends dress up and ad lib every situation imaginable; bizarre, funny, campy, sad, and unpredictable.

A Shocking Accident. Directed by James Scott, 25 minutes, color, Academy Award—Best Short Film, 1982. (Direct Cinema) Adapted from a Graham Greene story. An English schoolboy learns from his boarding school headmaster that his father has been killed in a bizarre accident. The death haunts him for years until a girl he meets helps him shake the terrible memory.

Sticky My Fingers, Fleet My Feet. Directed by John Hancock, 23 minutes, color, 1973, USA. (Biograph Entertainment) Norman and his friends are a group of huffing, puffing middle-aged men addicted to Sunday touch football in the park. When they patronizingly let a boy join their game, his performance leaves them dazed.

String Bean (Le Haricot). Directed by Edmond Sechan, 17 minutes, color, 1964, France. (Biograph Entertainment) A simple and beautiful tale of an old lady who cultivates a potted plant with tender devotion.

Sundae in New York. Directed by Jimmy Picker, 4 minutes, clay animation, Academy Award—Best Animated Short, 1983, USA. (Direct Cinema) In this clay-animated film, a character resembling Ed Koch (onetime mayor of NYC) sings a variation on "New York, New York."

Sweet Sal. Directed by Tony Buba, 25 minutes, B&W, documentary, 1979, USA. (Chicago Filmmakers) A documentary about a small-time hustler in a dying steel town, the depth of insight and range of emotion he conveys make this a standout portrait.

THX 1138. Directed by George Lucas, color, 1969, USA. (Swank) A future where love is the ultimate crime.

A Trip to the Moon. Directed by Georges Méliès, 10 minutes, B&W, 1902, France. (Biograph Entertainment) This science fiction film contains a great number of the earliest special effects and is the most popular of Méliès's films.

Two Men and a Wardrobe. Directed by Roman Polanski, 15 minutes, B&W, 1957, Poland. (Biograph Entertainment) Two men emerge from the sea carrying a large wardrobe; an allegory on isolationism and man's tendency to shun strangers, the film considers the costs of private lives in the modern world.

What's a Nice Girl Doing in a Place Like This? Directed by Martin Scorsese, 9 minutes, B&W, 1962, USA. A writer becomes obsessed with a picture of a boat on a lake. He attempts to regain a normal life, but eventually succumbs to his strange anxiety. An experimental satire by one of today's most influential directors.

appendix C

Case Study Scripts

Included in this appendix are a synopsis and a screenplay or transcript for each of the four productions used as case studies in this book.

THE LUNCH DATE

Written and directed by Adam Davidson, 12 minutes, black-and-white film (1991).

Pitch

A well-to-do woman's unusual encounter with a homeless man while waiting at a train station to return to the suburbs.

Synopsis

A well-attired and seemingly elegant older woman arrives at Grand Central Station after shopping in New York City. While she is waiting to return to her home in the suburbs, her purse is knocked out of her arms, spilling her possessions all over the floor. She quickly picks up her personal effects and runs to her track, only to just miss the train. She checks her purse and finds that her wallet is missing. She seems lost and close to tears.

With time before her next train, she buys a salad with her remaining small change at a nearby cafeteria. She places the salad and her packages at a booth and goes back to the counter for a fork. She returns to discover a homeless man eating her salad. Indignant, the woman plants herself in the booth and grabs for her salad, but the man refuses to let go. She spears a piece of lettuce with her fork. She keeps picking at it, but the man doesn't protest. In fact, he eventually gets up and brings the two of them coffee. This is their "lunch date."

The woman hears her train being called and gets up to leave. On her way to the platform, she realizes that she has forgotten her packages and rushes back, only to find the homeless man and her packages gone. Pacing back and forth, the woman finally sees that her untouched salad and packages were at the next booth the whole time. Realizing what's happened, she grabs the packages and heads for the train. This time she makes it.

The Lunch Date

FADE IN:

INT. GRAND CENTRAL STATION—DAY

A middle-aged "Waspish" WOMAN walks across the station. Her appearance is refined but subdued—a dark winter coat with a mink stole, a lace-collared blouse.

She carries several shopping bags from Bloomingdales and others.

The woman stops to check the schedule board on the wall. She rustles through her pocketbook and removes her ticket.

The woman hurries by a homeless man begging in the station.

In her rush she collides with a BLACK MAN. An explosion of pill bottles, lipstick, and knickknacks from her purse sprinkles to the floor.

> **WOMAN**
> Oh, oh my Lord!

She kneels down to collect her stuff.

The black man kneels beside her. His appearance is professional but rough enough for New York commuting—a silk tie and mirrored sunglasses.

> **BLACK MAN**
> I'm sorry. Let me get you that.

He begins picking up the loose items.

> **WOMAN**
> No. No.

> **BLACK MAN**
> Let me give you a hand.

She rushes to claim her belongings.

> **WOMAN**
> No, don't, you're making me miss my train.

The woman grabs her stuff and runs toward the platforms.

CUT TO:

INT. GRAND CENTRAL TRAIN PLATFORM—DAY

A train rolls down the tracks as the woman arrives. She is left alone on the platform.

Out of breath and slightly disheveled, the woman reaches for her bags.

Her wallet is gone. She collects her bags and walks back toward the station.

INT. GRAND CENTRAL STATION—DAY

The woman returns to the station floor where she looks up to the schedule board as the times change. Light tears appear in her eyes, which she quickly dries with a white handkerchief. She stares ahead, lost in thought.

A black MUMBLING MAN walks by playing a harmonica. He stares into an imaginary audience. He is homeless. He rambles as he passes the woman.

> **MUMBLING MAN**
> Lord have mercy! Ha! Ha! Ha!
> He know it, he know it! How you doing!?
> You know who it is this morning! I know who are...
> Hot dog!
> You know who you are!
> Happy New Year's. God bless ya!

The woman walks away.

> CUT TO:

INT. LUNCHEONETTE—DAY

The woman walks into a station luncheonette. It is a simple place—a grill, some booths, and rows of refrigerated cabinets filled with salads and sandwiches. She reaches into a glass case and removes a salad.

A COOK stands behind a white linoleum counter. He fiddles with his white paper hat and white apron.

> **WOMAN**
> How much is this salad?

> **COOK**
> Two dollars.

She puts the salad on the counter. She rustles through her pocketbook.

> **WOMAN**
> Well, I'm not sure that I have that much.

The woman empties a dollar and same change on the counter.

> **WOMAN**
> One dollar...here's some.

The cook fingers through the change.

                         COOK
          A dollar-fifty . . . two dollars.

Here ya go, lady.

She grabs the salad plate and her bundles.

                         WOMAN
                    Napkin.

The cook hands her a napkin. She walks toward the
booths.

INT. LUNCHEONETTE BOOTH—DAY

The woman walks down the aisle looking for a
suitable booth. She places her salad plate down and
pushes her bags into a booth.

She sits but does not settle. She stands, carrying
only her napkin.

INT. LUNCHEONETTE—DAY

The woman walks to the front of the luncheonette.
She reaches into a steel bin and takes a fork. She
examines the fork, wiping it with a napkin.

Fork in hand she searches for her booth and
suddenly stops in her tracks.

                                        CUT TO:

INT. LUNCHEONETTE BOOTH—DAY

A HOMELESS BLACK MAN sits opposite the woman eating
a salad. He is dressed in a thick wool coat and a
flannel shirt. On his head, a winter hat still has
the tag attached. He looks up to her.

The woman sits across from him in the booth.

                         WOMAN
                    That's my salad.

                  HOMELESS BLACK MAN
                   Get out of here.

                         WOMAN
                    That's my salad.

She reaches for the plate. He pulls it back.

                  HOMELESS BLACK MAN
                     Hey!

The woman watches him chomping away at the bits of
lettuce. He ignores her.

Moments pass.

She reaches over with her fork and swipes a piece of food off the plate. The woman quickly chews while keeping her composure. He goes on eating.

She takes another bite. Then another. And another.

The man does not respond. Suddenly he stands and walks down the aisle. She continues munching away at what remains.

He returns with two cups of coffee with saucers. He places the cups on the table and sits.

He offers her sugar.

WOMAN
No, thank you.

He offers her a packet of Sweet & Low from his coat. She accepts.

WOMAN
Thank you.

Checking her watch she stands with her purse and leaves. He watches her exit, somewhat disappointed.

CUT TO:

INT. GRAND CENTRAL—DAY

The woman walks quickly through the station and then stops. She left her bags in the luncheonette! She runs back toward the luncheonette.

CUT TO:

INT. LUNCHEONETTE BOOTH—DAY

She arrives at the booth and the bags are gone. Only two empty cups of coffee and a plate remain. She begins to pace the floor nervously.

She paces back and forth. In the next booth we see her shopping bags and her salad uneaten. The woman discovers her bags and the salad. She sits down and laughs to herself. Realizing the time, she grabs her bags and runs out of the luncheonette laughing.

CUT TO:

```
INT. GRAND CENTRAL—AFTERNOON

The woman runs quickly through the crowds to her
platform. She passes a BEGGAR on crutches.

                        BEGGAR
     Spare some change. Please, please ma'am. I'm
                       starving.

She ignores him and continues through the crowd.

INT. GRAND CENTRAL—AFTERNOON

The woman runs down the platform to the train.

INT. TRAIN—AFTERNOON

The train rolls down the tracks into darkness.

FADE OUT

THE END
```

TRUMAN

Written and directed by Howard McCain, 12 minutes, color (1991).

Pitch

An eleven-year-old boy confronts his imaginary fears while attempting to climb a rope during gym class.

Synopsis

Truman, a timid 11-year-old boy, feigns a stomachache to get out of climbing the rope during gym class. The coach doesn't buy it and threatens to make the whole class run a mile if Truman doesn't climb. Suddenly feeling much better, Truman starts to climb but then imagines that the rope turns into a noose, the coach into an officer of the Civil War, and the students into his prisoners.

Truman keeps climbing and he imagines the rope starting to unravel and the students bringing out an old fireman's safety net. His imagines the rope snapping, the net being pulled away at the last moment, and Truman falls to the ground, missing the gym mat and bloodying his nose.

The coach then gives Truman a final ultimatum: He must hang onto the rope for one minute only, and if he does not, the whole class will have to run a mile. Truman is determined to give it his best, and the whole class pulls for him. He climbs, and as the seconds wind down, he imagines that the coach is the Sheriff of Nottingham, one student is Robin Hood, and the class is Robin's Merry Men. They shoot their longbows, and as the sheriff falls, so does Truman, one second away from victory.

As the class leaves to run the mile, the coach empathizes with Truman's dilemma. The coach asks Truman to clean up and leaves. Alone in the gym, Truman regards the rope with determination. He runs and attacks the rope with a vengeance. Meanwhile, the class and the coach return in time to see Truman reach the ceiling. A proud Truman looks around and smiles. An amazed coach yells at Truman who, looking down for the first time, gets queasy. Realizing how high up he is, Truman throws up all over the coach. The class goes wild, the coach is dazed, and we leave Truman hanging on for dear life.

Truman

FADE IN:

THE SCREEN is BLACK. We HEAR a military drum MARCH. Then the CREDITS. The last TITLE CARD comes up, the MARCH abruptly stops, as we CUT sharply to:

INT. JUNIOR HIGH SCHOOL GYMNASIUM—DAY

WIDE: A dull, suburban gym. A SWISHING SOUND . . . and a long rope swings into FRAME. The SOUND of WHISTLE.

CUT TO:

MONTAGE

CLOSE UP: A man, 43, with hairy eyebrows and red face blows hard on a WHISTLE. He is obviously a GYM TEACHER.

TAYLOR, about 12, dressed in a maroon reversible and gold gym shorts—standard issue—runs forward. A brief second and another child steps up to replace him. WE can see a line of kids stretching out behind him.

CLOSE UP: TAYLOR grabs the rope and starts to climb.

WE HEAR the SHOUTS of the GYM TEACHER, an occasional CRY of encouragement from a fellow gymster, and, as always, the WHISTLE.

CLOSE UP: TAYLOR touches the cross beam.

CLOSE UP: GYM TEACHER BLOWS his whistle.

CLOSE UP: TAYLOR'S feet touch the gym floor. The next KID in line rushes forward.

CLOSE UP: KID jumps on rope.

CLOSE UP: GYM TEACHER BLOWS his whistle.

CLOSE UP: The next KID is up.

CLOSE UP: GYM TEACHER BLOWS his WHISTLE.

TAYLOR steps up into line again. Everyone has gone.

OFF SCREEN: The urgent CALL of the WHISTLE.

TAYLOR just stands there. WE HEAR the WHISTLE a second time. Still . . . no one moves. A final WHISTLE BLAST and the

CAMERA PANS DOWN to reveal a scrawny boy, 11, at the front of the line. This is TRUMAN, and his eyes tell it all—he's terrified.

CUT TO:

INT. GYM—DAY

The climbing rope stretches up into the distance. The CAMERA begins to TILT DOWN, TRACKING BACKWARDS as it does so. The CAMERA continues down to the bottom of the rope to find it knotted in a hangman's noose.

WE linger on it only a second, and then the CAMERA RACK-FOCUSES through the noose to find TRUMAN standing on the other side, paralyzed. He clenches his eyes shut.

The SOUND of the WHISTLE OFF SCREEN, as a figure moves into FRAME. TRUMAN remains still.

CUT TO:

CLOSE: The GYM TEACHER spits the whistle from his mouth and storms forward, calling.

GYM TEACHER
All right! What's going on, Truman?

The CLASS immediately straightens up. He pulls TRUMAN from the line.

GYM TEACHER
Well?

TRUMAN slowly opens his eyes and looks up at the intimidating figure before him. This is MR. SPARROW, and he is the wrong man for the job. He has all the mannerisms of a football coach, although he's not. He carries a small playground ball in one hand.

TRUMAN
(weakly)
I feel sick.

The CLASS, obviously a little frightened by this man, does its best to remain stone-faced, but a few giggles slip out. TRUMAN bows his head, and for an instant MR. SPARROW can't decide whether he is really dealing with a sick kid or not.

But the CLASS's mockery makes it all seem to be a joke at his expense.

MR. SPARROW
All right, back of the line, Truman.

TRUMAN looks at him for a moment. He is not sure whether he is being punished or forgiven. MR. SPARROW eyes him coldly, and TRUMAN, now feeling the former, heads for the back of the line.

The CAMERA TRACKS with TRUMAN down the line. He does his best not to look anyone in the eye.

MR. SPARROW
Next. TAYLOR is next.

TAYLOR
But I already went, Mr. Sparrow.

TRUMAN slides into the back of the line, chagrined.

MR. SPARROW
That's right. Everyone's going again . . .
(pausing for effect)

The CLASS groans.

MR. SPARROW
. . . until Truman decides it's his turn.

Silence. He has just dropped the bomb. MR. SPARROW smiles coldly back, waiting and watching Truman's face, as if it might crumble at any moment.

The CAMERA TRACKS BACKWARDS from MR. SPARROW, revealing the rest of the line. Some KIDS groan, while others look back at TRUMAN. As the CAMERA reaches the end of the line, it PANS back to face TRUMAN, head-on.

No one moves. TRUMAN looks at the class and then back to MR. SPARROW, and he knows that if he ever wants to survive gym class, he has got to go.

TRUMAN summoning his courage, steps from line.

TRUMAN
(barely)
I'm feeling better.

His CLASSMATES look suspiciously at him, not being sure if he is serious or if this is just another weak answer.

TRUMAN
(defensively)
I am!

He is a little surprised by his own forwardness, but his confidence quickly fades with one look at MR. SPARROW, who seems utterly pleased by the whole situation.

MR. SPARROW
Well, then, let's get a move on.

TRUMAN starts to walk forward. THE CAMERA TRACKS with him as he walks down the line of kids, who are all now looking noticeably more compassionate toward their suffering comrade. The MARCH MUSIC from the opening CREDITS is heard.

TRUMAN fixes his gaze forward.

ANGLE FROM ABOVE: TRUMAN comes to a stop at the base of the rope and pivots about to face the class. The MARCH ceases.

The CLASS stares expectantly back.

LONG SHOT: TRUMAN, the CLASS, and MR. SPARROW—all waiting to see who's gonna make the first move.

CLOSE: TRUMAN looks ever so cautiously up.

HANDHELD P.O.V.: The rope dangles above him, beckoning. The gym is silent.

> **MR. SPARROW (O.S.)**
> Are you ready?

CLOSE: TRUMAN closes his eyes and nods. The instant he nods, the SOUND of DRUM ROLL commences.

CUT TO:

INT. SAME—FANTASY

CLOSE: TRUMAN gags. His eyes fly open like window shades. THE CAMERA TRACKS quickly back, as a noose is stretched over his neck.

The CAMERA is on MR. SPARROW, who is now a CIVIL WAR ARMY OFFICER, presiding over TRUMAN'S execution. He draws his sword from its sheath and raises it into the air.

The CLASS, shackled together at the wrists and ankles, is a beaten horde of Confederate prisoners. The CAMERA TRACKS quickly down the line of hollow faces.

CLOSE: MR. SPARROW nods and clicks his heels. The CLASS tenses up.

MR. SPARROW drops his sword with a WHOOSH. The CAMERA RUSHES in on TRUMAN'S face as the SOUND culminates in a loud SNAP. TRUMAN drops out of FRAME and the rope TWANGS tight.

CUT TO:

INT. SAME—REALITY—A SPLIT SECOND LATER

THE SAME SHOT: A beat. The rope creaks and twists, as if a small boy might indeed be hanging on the other end. Then, a hand suddenly swings into the FRAME and grabs a tight hold on the rope.

THE CAMERA begins to DOLLY back as TRUMAN climbs into FRAME. The noose is gone, and as we PULL further back, we find the CLASS still in line and MR. SPARROW circling close. All traces of TRUMAN'S fantasy are gone, and only brutal reality remains.

From the way TRUMAN struggles, it is obvious that this is not easy for him, further hindered by the fact that his eyes are still clenched shut.

CLOSE: TRUMAN misses the rope with one hand.

> **MR. SPARROW**
> Hey Truman! Open your eyes. You can't go up like that.

TRUMAN continues blindly on.

> **MR. SPARROW**
> Hey Truman! Hey! I said open your eyes.

ANGLE FROM ABOVE: MR. SPARROW circles the rope. He has begun to wave his arms a bit out of frustration, trying to jump up and tug on TRUMAN'S leg.

TRUMAN, apparently unable to hear, continues upward.

> **MR. SPARROW**
> Open 'um . . .

TAYLOR, seeing a keen opportunity, starts jumping and waving his arms, in mock imitation of MR. SPARROW. He steps from the line and begins to circle TRUMAN.

The CLASS follows TAYLOR'S initiative, start to wave their arms and break formation.

MR. SPARROW
Now!

MR. SPARROW has managed to gain a hold of TRUMAN'S leg and he shakes it once. MR. SPARROW catches sight of the class. Caught in mid-flap, they freeze, their expressions quickly melting.

CLOSE: TRUMAN's eyes fly open and look up. HIS P.O.V.: The rope above unraveling. TRUMAN looks down.

INT. SAME—FANTASY

TRUMAN'S P.O.V.: His feet now dangle 30 feet from the ground. The SOUND of SNAPPING twine. His CLASSMATES jostle into position with a large fire net, ready to catch stranded TRUMAN.

INT. SAME—REALITY

Hustling the kids into line.

MR. SPARROW
Back in line! All of ya's. Move it.

The CLASS starts to slink back into formation.

INT. SAME—FANTASY

CLOSE: TRUMAN.

Below, his would-be rescuers start to retreat with the fire net.

MR. SPARROW (O.S.)
I said move it!

The rope above his head is hanging by a thread, ready to snap at any moment. CLOSE: TRUMAN sucks in his breath like a diver preparing for a great dive. TWANG! The rope snaps. CLOSE: TRUMAN lets go of the rope.

INT. SAME—REALITY

MED SHOT: TRUMAN lets go of the rope and falls out of frame, landing with a DULL THUD. The CLASS and MR. SPARROW stare dumbfounded. A long pause.

MR. SPARROW
You missed the mat.

INT. SAME—REALITY—MOMENTS LATER

CLOSE: TRUMAN stands rigidly upright. His nose stuffed with bloody Kleenex.

MR. SPARROW (O.S.)
Sixty seconds, Truman.

The CAMERA DOLLIES back to reveal MR. SPARROW moving into FRAME as he reaches over and pulls the Kleenex from TRUMAN'S nose.

MR. SPARROW
You couldn't cut it going up, so all you gotta do is hang on.
Hang on for a minute, and you pass.

The CAMERA continues back. The CLASS circles around.

MR. SPARROW
But if you don't pass . . .
(pausing for effect)
everyone has to run a mile!

The CAMERA stops DOLLYING. The CLASS instantly erupts into cries of protest. "A whole mile!?"

MR. SPARROW
Five thousand, eight hundred and eighty-two feet . . . outside!

The CLASS gives MR. SPARROW the COLD snake eye. Their hatred of him and what he is putting TRUMAN through is obvious.

MR. SPARROW feels those stares drill right into him, but he is shaken for only a moment and quickly turns to TRUMAN and hoists him up, off the ground, by the shoulders.

MR. SPARROW
Are you ready?

MR. SPARROW and TRUMAN are now head to head. For the first time, TRUMAN stares MR. SPARROW directly in the eye. The room is silent. A beat. Then . . .

MR. SPARROW
Go!

He drops TRUMAN onto the rope. TRUMAN gets an instant grip. He hangs there, three feet off the ground, twisting. MR. SPARROW starts to circle TRUMAN again, bouncing his playground ball.

MR. SPARROW
(reading from his watch)
Ten.

TRUMAN'S eyes are clenched shut. He's holding on with all his might. The CLASS watches MR. SPARROW with utter contempt.

MR. SPARROW
Twenty.

CLOSE: TRUMAN'S grip is slipping. TRUMAN'S feet are about a foot off the ground. Sensing the danger, he opens his eyes, looks down, and bends his legs back, giving himself another foot or so.

MR. SPARROW
Thirty.

HANDHELD: TRUMAN looks out at the CLASS.

MR. SPARROW
Forty.

MR. SPARROW gets down on one knee. TRUMAN'S feet are barely above the pine.

MR. SPARROW
Ten . . .

Truman slips a bit more, clenching his eyes shut. The CLASS winces.

MR. SPARROW
Nine . . .

The CAMERA begins to DOLLY in on TRUMAN'S grimacing face.

MR. SPARROW
Eight . . . seven . . . six . . . five . . .

The CAMERA moves in TIGHT, and suddenly we hear the SOUND of

TRUMPETS calling. TRUMAN'S eyes fling open.

INT. SAME—FANTASY

CLOSE: TAYLOR rises into frame, dressed like a ROBIN HOOD ARCHER, with a long bow, arrows, and a look of death.

MED: He steps forward and lets fly an arrow.

THUNK! The arrow sinks into MR. SPARROW'S back. He spins around, gasping, his eyes popping from his head, to meet . . .

The WHOLE CLASS, rising in formation, with bows drawn and aimed. They fire . . .

LOW ANGLE: MR. SPARROW stumbles back, a DOZEN arrows now stuck in his chest. He falls out of FRAME in a bloody death.

THUD.

INT. SAME—REALITY

ANGLE FROM ABOVE: TRUMAN'S knees fall into frame and hit the gym floor. The CAMERA pans up to reveal TRUMAN'S face. He opens his eyes. The gym is silent. Slowly he looks down.

MR. SPARROW (O.S.)
(satisfied)
All right, everyone up. Pick up your gear and pack it in. Let's go! Let's go!

The CAMERA DOLLIES BACK to reveal the CLASS and MR. SPARROW. It is obvious that TRUMAN has failed. The CLASS, now on the ground, rolls over and groans. The CAMERA STOPS DOLLYING.

MR. SPARROW starts to collect the rubber balls and put them into a movable bucket. TRUMAN pulls himself from the floor.

The CLASS begins to walk toward the gym door. TRUMAN hangs back, waiting for some final confirmation on his failure. Not getting any, he starts to exit with the rest of the CLASS. He gets about 20 feet.

MR. SPARROW
Hey Truman.

TRUMAN stops cold. Here it comes. MR. SPARROW pushes the rolling bucket up to TRUMAN. (The CLASS looks on.) MR. SPARROW looks directly down on TRUMAN.

MR. SPARROW
(incredulous)
You still feel sick?

TRUMAN
No.

MR. SPARROW
Good.

Without waiting to hear more, TRUMAN turns and starts to leave. He only gets two steps.

MR. SPARROW (O.S.)
Not so fast . . .

TRUMAN stops. MR. SPARROW wheels up the bucket of balls.

MR. SPARROW
(tone of familiarity)

. . . You know, Truman, today it was only the rope, but someday . . . when it's your big turn in life . . .

A beat. Suddenly, the SOUND of the SCHOOL BELL. The moment has been broken. The CLASS automatically turns and starts for the door.

MR. SPARROW
HOLD IT! Where do you think you're going? You owe me a mile.

The CLASS really groans this time.

MR. SPARROW

What'd you think? I'd forget? Four times around the field. Let's go!

MR. SPARROW starts to wheel the bucket out the door along with the CLASS, leaving TRUMAN behind. The look on his face is a mixture of anger and hurt. The CLASS and MR. SPARROW exit.

MED: The expression on his face slowly melts. He takes one step forward, when the gym door opens again. It's MR. SPARROW. He leans halfway in.

MR. SPARROW
Don't bother running with the others.

A beat. MR. SPARROW retreats. The DOOR SLAMS shut.

LONG: TRUMAN stands alone in the gym.

CLOSE: His face burns. There is nothing he can say and no one to say it to.

LONG: TRUMAN stands alone again.

CLOSE: He bites his lip and starts to take a small step forward and then, in midstep, stops. Another pause, shorter than the last, as if he is about to step in front of a speeding train. Then he wheels quickly around and is off like a shot, running for the rope.

The CAMERA DOLLIES with him as he speeds across the gym.

HIS P.O.V.: He rushes headlong at the rope.

THE CAMERA DOLLIES back with him as he leaps up and grabs hold of the rope. He swings back and forth once and then begins to climb upward.

CLOSE: TRUMAN struggles upward.

HIGH ANGLE: TRUMAN is nothing but an ant at the bottom.

INT. SAME—MOMENTS LATER The gymnasium door opens, and in steps TAYLOR. He picks up a sweat shirt, left lying near the door, and then looks up. A smile breaks over his face.

INT. SAME—SECONDS LATER HIGH ANGLE: TRUMAN struggles upwards.

INT. SAME—MOMENTS LATER

The CAMERA TRACKS down the faces of the entire gym class. They stand huddled near the door, staring silently upwards.

LONG: TRUMAN nearing the top.

CLOSE: He pulls himself up into FRAME, and suddenly the tremendous NOISE of CHEERING fills the air.

The CLASS is going wild. From down the hall comes sound of MR. SPARROW approaching, barking angrily.

The CLASS instantly quiets as he bursts through the door, totally unaware. Then he sees TRUMAN. His face goes blank with surprise.

TRUMAN, a foot or two away from success.

MR. SPARROW steps through the crowd and stops. His face still expressionless.

TRUMAN reaches out his hand and hits pay dirt: the cross beam. His journey over, TRUMAN is very still, breathing, smiling, his eyes still closed, as if the air, the wonderful air, was indeed different up here after all.

CLOSE: The CLASS is in silent awe.

CLOSE: TRUMAN just breathes in the air.

CLOSE: MR. SPARROW breaks into a wide grin and heads forward.

MED: MR. SPARROW positions himself at the bottom of the rope.

> **MR. SPARROW**
> Hey Truman!

TRUMAN, shocked to hear MR. SPARROW'S voice, opens his eyes.

> **MR. SPARROW (O.S.)**
> Truman!

Suddenly, the feet fall away beneath TRUMAN; for the first time he sees how high up he really is. Total vertigo.

> **MR. SPARROW**
> Hey . . .

CLOSE: TRUMAN. A shudder of fear. Then something begins to rumble deep inside him. A rushing he can't hold back.

> **MR. SPARROW**
> . . . I didn't think you had it in you.

TRUMAN vomits. MR. SPARROW, exactly 20 feet below, his eyes popping from their sockets. WE don't see it, but WE HEAR it—SPLAT! (The CLASS)

CLOSE: Vomit splatters over MR. SPARROW'S sneakers. TRUMAN is horrified. MR. SPARROW is stunned.

> **TAYLOR**
> Nasty!

MR. SPARROW lets drop from his hand the small playground ball. TRUMAN, still in shock, wipes his mouth on his shoulder. The playground ball rolls across the gym floor, toward the CLASS, where TAYLOR suddenly breaks rank and gives it a good swift kick. It sails across the room and . . .

School's out! With wild cries, the class surges forward, scattering in all directions. A gym class riot.

Half-blinded, MR. SPARROW spins about, lost in the onrushing mob.

CLOSE: The bucket of balls is overturned, sending them to be kicked, thrown, and bounced in all directions.

LONG: High above hangs TRUMAN, while below the melee erupts.

LONG: TRUMAN'S face slowly starts to register what is going on.

LONG: The crowd CHEERS and SCREAMS in wild abandon.

CLOSE: A funny look starts to break over TRUMAN'S face.

A flying playground ball beans MR. SPARROW on the back of the head.

MR. SPARROW
Who threw that ball! Who threw that ball!

But he is quickly drowned out in the rising cries of freedom.

CLOSE: OUR HERO. And the funny look on his face starts to grow into a wide smile. You could say it blossoms, like a time-lapse picture, only more perfect.

TRUMAN just hangs there, twisting slowly, giving the world below the greatest smile of his career.

We linger on this for a moment, and then the PICTURE starts to fade and the CHEERING grows dim, as we slowly lose TRUMAN to the darkness.

THE END

CRAZY GLUE

Written and directed by Tatia Rosenthal, 5 minutes, color (1997).

Pitch

An animated clay puppet short adapted from a story by Israeli author Etgar Keret.

Synopsis

This claymation (see Glossary) film tells the story of one innovative attempt to patch up a disintegrating marriage—through the use of Crazy Glue!

Crazy Glue

INT. LIVING ROOM—DAY

A husband and wife sit separately in their living room. Husband is having his coffee, the wife is doodling inside of a cookbook titled "Cooking for Two." The husband picks up something from the counter. It's a Crazy Glue tube with a picture of a guy glued to the ceiling by his legs.

BESSA
Don't touch it.

MEMOUCHO
What is it?

BESSA
It's glue. Crazy Glue.

MEMOUCHO:
What did you buy it for?

BESSA
I've got tons of stuff to glue?

MEMOUCHO
I don't understand why you buy all this junk.

BESSA
For the same reason you married me. To kill time.

MEMOUCHO
No glue can hold someone like that. They put the
chandelier on the floor and shot it up
side down. (his beeper goes off) I got to run.
I'm going to be late tonight.

BESSA
I know, overtime.

Cut to:

INT. OFFICE—DAY

Fax machine is spitting out papers.

MEMOUCHO
Sell sell buy, sell buy, buy that now. No wait until
it goes up and then buy, buy it all. What else?

Memoucho pushes a button on his phone.

Cut to:

INT. LIVING ROOM—DAY

Bessa is watching TV.

Cut to:

INT. OFFICE—DAY

MEMOUCHO
Dina listen I've got Chester on line two and I'd
like to get him off. I have nothing more to say
to him, and hold all the rest of my calls for today.
I'm very busy in here and can't be disturbed.
Thank you.

Cut to:

INT. LIVING ROOM—DAY

Bessa turns the TV off and gets out of her seat.

Cut to:

INT. OFFICE—DAY

Memoucho dials another number.

> **MEMOUCHO**
> Hey, it's me. I can't make it tonight. I think she
> Knows. Don't—don't, listen someone just got . . .
> I have to go. We'll talk tomorrow. Promise.

Cut to:

INT. LIVING ROOM—DAY

Bessa is standing in front of a dresser. She examines their wedding photo, and her face in the mirror. She pours Crazy Glue onto the wedding photo's frame.

Cut to:

INT. OFFICE—SUNSET

Memoucho sits in his office at sundown brooding with his back to camera.

Fade to Black:

OS sound of a phone ringing.

INT. LIVING ROOM—NIGHT

Memoucho opens the door to their apartment. The phone is ringing. He walks over to pick it up but can't—the receiver is stuck to the phone. He uses so much force he spins around and kicks a small stool—the stool is stuck to the floor. He looks down to the dresser and sees the wedding photo face down. He tries to pick it up and can't—it too is glued.

OS sound of Bessa laughing.

Memoucho looks up to see her stuck upside down to the ceiling.

> **MEMOUCHO**
> Are you out of your mind?

He piles up some books on the ground and climbs them.

> **MEMOUCHO**
> Hold on. I'll get you down.

He tries to pull her down in vain.

> **MEMOUCHO**
> This might hurt a bit.

Still no movement.

> **MEMOUCHO**
> I'll get help.

He climbs down.

BESSA
I'm not going anywhere.

He turns to look at her. Something passes between them. He goes back up on the pile of books and kisses her. The books fall down, and he stays in the air glued to her lips.

End

MIRROR MIRROR

Produced and directed by Jan Krawitz, 17 minutes, color (1991).

Pitch

A documentary featuring women speaking about how they and others perceive their own bodies, intercut with historical footage of how the media emphasize women's bodies.

Synopsis

Thirteen women wearing white masks and leotards are interviewed on a stage in front of unclothed store mannequins and a poster of the "ideal proportion female." Because the women are faceless, the audience's attention is focused on their bodies. Each woman talks about how she feels about her body in relation to what she and society expect of it. Each woman eventually removes her mask and reveals her face.

The interviews are intercut with shots of the mannequins and archival footage and voiceovers from:

- A beauty contest from the forties, "the girl with the most beautiful gams"
- Shots from old magazines about the ideal form, "the gal who wins is the chick who is thin"
- Shots of women on antiquated exercise machines

The theme is women's dissatisfaction with their bodies, as influenced by the narrow range of beauty standards in society. Some of the specific issues addressed are:

- The awkwardness of a developing body
- Sense of self as forged by one's perception of her body
- Comparison of one's body to others'
- Feelings about constant judgment of body appearance
- Positive and negative feelings about specific body parts and wishes that some could be different

Mirror Mirror

DISSOLVE from BLACK to:

Nude female mannequin. Pan down over breasts, stomach, to waist.

CUT TO: Shot of head of mannequin and bare breasts of another mannequin in profile.

WOMAN (off-screen, as shot dissolves several times to more shots of heads of mannequins): There are lots of ideal bodies that I think about. I guess the striking thing is that they're not mine.

CUT TO:

WOMAN 1 (standing in front of "Ideal Proportion Female" poster): As a woman I'm always supposed to be aware of how I look. In any situation, in any environment, doing whatever, anything I'm doing, I'm supposed to be aware of how my body looks. How am I standing, you know, is my stomach in, are my—is my bust such and such, is my . . . And somehow I feel like if I had that kind of figure I would have to accept that, to go along with it, which is a funny thought.

CUT TO:

Newsreel "The Legs Have It"

NEWSREEL ANNOUNCER (off-screen, as women parade their legs and are examined): Beauty from the ground up parades for the title awarded, "The Girl with the Most Beautiful Gams." The girls are masked and air vents lift the skirts automatically, and oooh, let's look at the view. The contest at Palisades Park, New Jersey, unveils well-lined sights. And there are some modest girls who take no chances, you can bet. And now for the thrilling moment as 50 well-turned calves line up for the final judging. The judges are beauties of the nineties who once won contests of their own. They pounce on this pair as the shapeliest of them all.

CUT TO:

(Following are wide shots of each woman seated alone with nude mannequins in background.)

WOMAN 2: I think the first time I thought about how I look was in the seventh grade, in gym class. It was the first time I had to go somewhere in a big room and undress in front of other girls. And there was one girl who was in the class who had developed earlier than the other classmates. And she was actually quite pretty, and I envied her.

WOMAN 3: I came home one day from school. I was in junior high, and I was crying because kids were teasing me because I didn't have any breasts. And it seems that like the next year they just grew tremendously. So it was like one year I was crying because I didn't have any, and the next year I was complaining because I had too much.

WOMAN 4: There was something about being not noticed, being a sort of flat-chested, gawky girl—nobody really notices you, but once you start to sprout a chest, then people notice you. And there was a part of me, that despite the side of me that really was excited about getting a bra, this other side of me wanted to wear really baggy clothes all the time.

WOMAN 5: Well, my mother is very voluptuous. I always thought that that was real pretty, and then my sister came along, and she came out real voluptuous too, so I assumed that that was what I was going to look like, and when I didn't, this wasn't the best thing. I was pretty upset about it for a while. But that was about ten, eleven. Thirteen is when it really set in that I was never going to have breasts like my mother or my sister.

WOMAN 1: I think from very early adolescence, feelings of not quite knowing how to do it right, you know, not being this enough or that enough, and there were—and all the things you had to wear in order to be a woman, garter belts and stockings and brassieres and makeup and . . . I think most of my life I've had a feeling that I don't quite know how to do these things right, you know, the way other women do.

WOMAN 6: It seems like most of my awareness of myself as being different from other people was always called to my attention by a man pointing it out to me, like you know, look at, you know, Carol over there, she's really thin and real attractive—and not really saying, you're so overweight, you really ought to do something about that. At least maybe not at first. And I think that was, you know, those were the situations in which I became most aware that I was different than other people—that I was taller than they were, you know, not as thin as they were, or just generally I guess not as attractive.

Newsreel "Novel Method Used to Judge Beauty Winners"

NEWSREEL ANNOUNCER (off-screen, with shots of women waiting in line, being measured and judged): The form divine is well displayed by these modern Venuses at Steeplechase Park, Coney Island, New York. And they well know how to strut their stuff. It's a tough job with so much (unintelligible word) around to select a winner, but you can always pick a champion. They say a straight line, is oh well, with so much curvaceous beauty around, why bother with straight lines? Hey, anybody got a ladder? No matter how pretty they come, there's always a winner. And the laurels go to Evelyn Peterson of Long Island, a mighty fetching modern Venus.

CUT TO:

(Following shots are all of women, each seated alone with nude mannequins in background; tighter shot than before, showing only head and shoulders of each.)

WOMAN 4: I don't look over at someone and say, "Oh what a nice body. Isn't it nice that this person has a nice body?" I can't just let them have a nice body not being relative to me. I have to look at their body and say, "What a nice body. Why isn't it mine? Why doesn't mine look like that?"

WOMAN 3: I think I'm pretty lucky in the sense that I have what people have termed a pretty face, so, and my height, and so it kind of, that initial impression is a good one, even though I am overweight, or my size is larger than I want to be.

WOMAN 1: In a funny way, I almost feel like I have more presence being big and that I don't look like a kid, and I don't look like a little girl.

WOMAN 7: People approach me as a sweet little Oriental woman. First of all, I'm not little. Physically, I'm pretty big for a Japanese, and often, I'm not sweet.

WOMAN 8: I'm not viewed with as much credibility as people who are an average height, and I think that, compounded with my blond hair, is kind of a double negative.

WOMAN 9: People will look and see gray hair and think, old lady, and they don't go any further.

WOMAN 10: I think that because I am tall and that because that, combined with the fact that I am middle-aged and that I'm frankly middle-aged—I don't dye my hair, I haven't had a face lift or eye tucks or anything of these things—that this is fairly intimidating.

WOMAN 8: When I had blond hair, everyone thought I had an easy life, that it meant I was probably a cheerleader and had a real storybook life. When I dyed my hair brown, people were more accepting of my opinions. They thought I was more of an interesting person.

WOMAN 11: I am more aware of what other women will think of me and the way I appear than any consideration of appealing to men.

WOMAN 4: Like I feel badly that I look over at women who have a little bit fatter stomach, or, you know, their legs are a little bit heavy, and then I get some enjoyment out of seeing women whose bodies look less appealing than mine.

WOMAN 1: A friend and I had an experience. We went down to Port Oranges for the weekend, and we walked at about ten o'clock at night down to the beach, which was only a couple of blocks from where we were staying, and had the experience of having young men in pickup trucks yelling at us, yelling names at us: fat broads. It was a real shocker. I think partially because we neither of us expected to draw any attention whatsoever from that age group, particularly both of us forty-year-old ladies. But that whole thing, that we were committing some kind of crimes in their minds by being in the universe.

CUT TO:

Magazine cover of thin woman in bathing suit standing in front of heavy woman in bathing suit. Pan from legs to faces. (Song begins: "Now girls, a word of warning, I hereby do impart, now don't let an oversized physique, upset your apple cart . . .")

CUT TO:

Two semicircular B&W photos: woman in dress on left, woman in bathing suit on right. (Song continues without break: "Because ladies, we love you all . . .")

CUT TO:

Close-up of old B&W photo of woman in bra. (Song continues without break: "Big, fat, thin, and tall . . .")

CUT TO:

Magazine pages with photos of woman in bathing suit wearing sash. (Song continues: "But the gal that wins is the chick that's thin . . .")

CUT TO:

Old print ad with photos of women and headline: "You Can Improve." (Song continues: "Please listen to my call . . .")

CUT TO:

Old print ad with bathing beauty and headline: "It's Easy to Put on Lovely Curves Now." (Song continues: "Now she was neat and sweet and twenty-two, a solid sender . . .")

CUT TO:

Succession of B&W film clips of women exercising with machines. (Song continues: "Through and through, but her time is gone forever more, big and fat and forty-four, ain't no use in frettin', wastin' time and sighs, 'cause she keeps on gettin' heavier from diet and exercise . . .")

CUT TO:

Quick succession of print ads: "Reducing and how!" "What Type Overweight Person Are You?" "Girls with Naturally Skinny Figures," etc. (Song continues: "Now she's big and fat, and she can't get thin. She's gotta wrinkled neck and a double chin. She ain't like she was before. She's big and fat and forty-four. . . . You know, my gal, boys she's a mess. Takes a circus tent to make her a dress. Feet so big she wears a ten. Her waistline is about to bust her skin. She goes to sleep and starts to spread . . .")

CUT TO:

Succession of film clips of women on exercise machines. (Song continues: "Darn near takes up all the bed. Still, at that, she means no harm. She might be fat, but she sure is warm.")

CUT TO:

Poster of "Ideal Proportion Female" (Music fades out)

DISSOLVE TO:

(Following shots are all of women, each standing alone in front of "Ideal Proportion" poster.)

WOMAN 12: You know, I'll see someone that's not necessarily real skinny, that I think is real attractive, or someone who is tall and kind of chunky and I think is real attractive, so I don't really have an ideal body that I think is attractive, but I don't feel like mine's it.

WOMAN 9: I look at pictures of myself when I was young, and I think, I was really quite slender and had a nice-looking figure, but I was never satisfied with it or happy with it.

WOMAN 10: I no longer am wistful about having perfect thighs or perfect breasts or a smaller waist or whatever it seems to be the ideal of the time.

WOMAN 13: I'm pretty content with the size of my body, that is, the proportion of my body.

WOMAN 4: I sometimes think it would be really neat to be petite, that I think of myself as too tall.

WOMAN 1: I think in some ways I'd like to be a big strong woman, but big more in the sense of muscular, large than fat.

WOMAN 7: I'd like to be much thinner.

WOMAN 3: As a matter of fact I'm trying to lose about 40 more pounds.

WOMAN 6: I like my hair. My hair is OK now because I have it colored, because there's a white streak that comes right here that I don't particularly care for.

WOMAN 4: Sometimes I think the gray makes me look sophisticated and trendy, and sometimes I'm really self-conscious about the fact that it's showing my age.

WOMAN 1: I like my hair, but it's too fine and thin.

WOMAN 8: I think my neck is OK. I feel pretty good about my neck.

WOMAN 2: My neck, I wish there was more to it, lengthwise.

WOMAN 9: I like my shoulders and my upper chest.

WOMAN 12: I like my shoulders, that, that's really the only part of my body that I think is totally acceptable.

WOMAN 8: My arms are probably what I like best about my body because they look toned.

WOMAN 6: Sometimes I think my arms are a little long. You know, you get the gorilla look.

WOMAN 4: I like the fact that my arms are the skinniest part of my body.

WOMAN 9: I don't like the way it's changed here.

WOMAN 5: I hate that when it gets flabby back here.

WOMAN 11: There is a bit of extra flesh down here.

WOMAN 3: My breasts are too large.

WOMAN 9: I'd just as soon they would be smaller.

WOMAN 5: I like my breasts right before my period because they're bigger and they're rounder.

WOMAN 6: It'd be nice if they were the classic up, just a little firmer.

WOMAN 4: I'm high waisted. I think my waist is too high.

WOMAN 9: I never have had a waist.

WOMAN 2: My waist, I wish there was much less of it.

WOMAN 3: My hips seem small because my stomach is large.

WOMAN 7: My hips always were a little bit too big.

WOMAN 12: My hips have always been too small.

WOMAN 8: I have a full bottom.

WOMAN 7: I always thought my bottom was real low.

WOMAN 3: My legs are pretty decent sized. I got those from my mother.

WOMAN 13: I would give myself nice long legs.

WOMAN 7: My legs are short.

WOMAN 11: My legs, I ignore them.

WOMAN 8: Probably what I don't like is this part right here.

WOMAN 4: I probably think my thighs are bigger than they should be.

WOMAN 6: Thighs are too large for my taste, too loose.

WOMAN 10: I always had good calves, good ankles.

WOMAN 4: A lot of exercise, so good calves.

WOMAN 9: I think I really have beautiful feet.

CUT TO:

Nude mannequin in front of mirror. Pan up to waist, breasts.

DISSOLVE TO:

Face of one mannequin partially obscured behind arm of another.

VOICEOVER (unidentified woman; continues while women remove masks): I remember when I wanted to be smaller, more fragile, because then I thought that's what was attractive.

(Following shots are of each woman, seated alone in front of nude mannequins.)

WOMAN 8 removes mask.

WOMAN 9 removes mask.

WOMAN 7 removes mask.

WOMAN 3 removes mask.

DISSOLVE TO:

Breasts of nude mannequin and pans over other mannequin's VOICEOVER (unidentified woman begins to talk as

WOMAN 3 is removing mask; continues after dissolve to mannequins):

I think if it was up to me, it really wouldn't matter what size I was. But because society feels size is important, I think that has caused me to be very aware of my size.

DISSOLVE TO:

WOMAN 2 removes mask.

VOICE-OVER (unidentified woman): I don't think I'd like major changes. I'm OK the way I am.

WOMAN 10 removes mask.

WOMAN 13 removes mask.

WOMAN 12 removes mask.

WOMAN 5 removes mask.

WOMAN 11 removes mask.

WOMAN 6 removes mask.

WOMAN 1 removes mask.

VOICEOVER (unidentified woman): I don't think anymore in my life I would even want to be a glamour girl.

WOMAN 4 removes mask. VOICEOVER (unidentified woman): It's just that I want to be different from who I am.

DISSOLVE TO:

Faces of mannequins

FADE TO BLACK

Credits

Insurance and Legal Matters

INSURANCE

Insurance plays an important role in motion picture and video production. Having insurance is as essential as having film stock or the right camera. In the course of normal life, calamities can happen and life goes on. In the course of a production, a car accident, sickness, a robbery, or a fire can bring the production to a screeching halt.

A budget, even with a contingency of 10 percent, is not flexible enough to cover keeping a crew standing for days, even weeks, while the lead actor recovers from an accident. This is why you need some type of protection for the unexpected occurrences that could happen in the course of the finely orchestrated movement of material, equipment, and people. Think of it as insurance for the possibility that Murphy's Law will prevail and everything will go wrong.

Some insurance companies specialize in entertainment insurance packages. They will evaluate the needs of the production and provide a price for appropriate coverage. You might not be able to afford everything they recommend, but it is highly recommended that you carry at least equipment and comprehensive liability coverage. You don't want to be personally responsible for property damage or injury on the set. Equipment houses will not rent to you without equipment insurance. Some offer their own insurance, but many don't.

What follows is a brief description of the many types of coverage available to film and video producers. The most common types of insurance are covered here. There are also special types of coverage that reflect unique demands.

Comprehensive Liability

Comprehensive liability coverage protects the production company against claims for bodily injury or property damage liability that arise from filming the picture. Coverage includes use of all nonowned vehicles (both on and off camera). This coverage is required before filming on any city or state roadways or at any location site.

Comprehensive liability policies do not cover accidents arising from the use of aircraft or watercraft. This coverage must be purchased separately.

Miscellaneous Equipment

This policy covers you against risk of direct physical loss, damage, or destruction to cameras, camera equipment, and sound, lighting, and grip equipment owned or rented by the production company. Coverage can be extended to cover mobile equipment vans, studio location units, and similar units upon payment of an additional premium.

Third-Party Property Damage Liability

This coverage pays for the damage or destruction of the property of others (including loss of use of property) while the property is in the care, custody, or control of the production company and is used or is to be used in an insured production.

This coverage does not apply to the following: liability for destruction of property caused by operation of any motor vehicle, aircraft, or watercraft, including damage to the foregoing; liability for damage to any property rented or leased that may be covered under props, sets, or wardrobe, or miscellaneous equipment insurance (although loss of use of any such equipment is covered).

This protection is not included under the comprehensive liability policy. Property damage coverage written as part of the comprehensive general liability policy excludes damage to any property in the production company's care, custody, or control.

Errors and Omissions

Distributors usually require this coverage before the release of any production. It covers legal liability and defense against lawsuits alleging copyright infringement; unauthorized use of titles format, ideas, characters, or plots; plagiarism; unfair competition; and invasion of privacy. It also protects against alleged libel, slander, defamation of character, and invasion of privacy suits.

Cast Insurance

Cast insurance reimburses the production company for any extra expense necessary to complete principal photography due to the death, injury, or sickness of any insured performer or director. Insured performers or directors must take a physical examination before they can be covered. Coverage usually begins three weeks before the beginning of principal photography.

Negative Film and Videotape

This is coverage against all risks of direct physical loss, damage, or destruction of raw film or tape stock, exposed film (developed or undeveloped), recorded videotape, sound tracks, and tapes, up to the amount of insured production cost.

This coverage does not include loss caused by fogging; faulty camera or sound equipment; faulty developing, editing, processing, or manipulation by the camera operator; exposure to light, dampness, or temperature changes; errors in judgment in exposure, lighting, or sound recording; or from the incorrect use of raw film stock or tape.

Faulty Stock, Camera, and Processing

This policy covers loss, damage, or destruction of raw film or tape stock, exposed film (developed or undeveloped), recorded videotape, sound tracks, and tapes caused by or resulting from fogging or the use of faulty equipment (including cameras and videotape recorders); faulty sound equipment; faulty developing, editing, and processing; and accidental erasure of videotape recording.

Props, Sets, and Wardrobe

This insurance provides coverage for props, sets, scenery, costumes, wardrobe, miscellaneous rented equipment, and office contents against all risk of direct physical loss, damage, or destruction during the production.

Extra Expense

Extra expense coverage reimburses the production company for any extra expense necessary to complete principal photography due to damage or destruction of property or facilities (props, sets, or equipment) used in connection with the production. It protects against loss that delays production.

Workers' Compensation

State laws mandate that this coverage be carried. It applies to all temporary or permanent cast or production crew members. Coverage provides medical, disability, or death benefits to any cast or crew members who become injured in the course of their employment. Coverage applies on a 24-hour basis whenever employees are on location away from their homes. Individuals who call themselves *independent contractors* are usually held to be employees as far as workers' compensation is concerned. The failure to carry this insurance can result in having to pay any benefits required under the law plus penalty awards.

Hired, Loaned, or Donated Auto Liability

This insurance covers all company-owned, hired, or leased vehicles used in connection with the production. Only vehicles that are being rented under the company's name and are issued certificates of insurance are covered under this policy.

Hired, Loaned, or Donated Auto Physical Damage

This coverage insures company-owned, hired, or leased vehicles against the risks of loss, theft, or damage (including collision) for all vehicles used in company-related activities. It covers vehicles rented from crew or staff members when the production company has assumed responsibility for the vehicles.

Guild/Union Travel Accident

This coverage provides Motion Picture/Television Guild or union contract requirements for aircraft accidental death insurance to all production company cast or crew members. Coverage is blanket, and the limit of liability meets all signatory requirements.

Office Contents

This is "all-risk" coverage (subject to policy exclusions) on office contents, subject to a low deductible.

Animal Mortality

When animals are used in the production, consideration should be given to this special coverage. This policy insures against the death or destruction of any animal covered. A veterinarian's certificate is usually required for this coverage. If the animal is a principal character, the cost to be paid to finish principal photography might be covered under cast insurance.

LEGAL

Music Rights

All music is subject to copyright protection unless it is in the public domain (see the next section). It is very important that before deciding on using a particular piece of music or a song in your film or video, you secure its clearance.

Clearance means determining who owns the copyright to a piece of music and negotiating a license to use that material for exhibition and distribution in specific territories and media in exchange for the payment of a fee to the copyright owner. If the clearance process is begun ahead of time, the producer can determine if the budget can accommodate the price of a particular song or musical selection.

If you want to use a preexisting recording, you will need to obtain permission to use the musical *composition*, as well as permission to use the particular *recording* of it. Generally, songwriters assign or sell the copyright to their work to a publisher, who pays the writer a share of the royalties if the song is used in a film or video. The record company that paid for the recording session or that had the recording artist under contract usually owns the recordings.

To secure rights to a composition, start by approaching the author; the author's estate, lawyer, publisher, or agent; or the organization that repre-

sents the publisher and licenses those rights on its behalf. One example of the last is the Harry Fox Agency (offices in New York and Los Angeles and online at www.harryfox.com). It represents thousands of publishing companies. If this agency doesn't handle the composition you want, contact one of the performing rights societies: American Society of Composers and Publishers (ASCAP), Broadcast Music, Inc. (BMI), or Society of European Stage Authors (SESAC). All have offices in New York; BMI and ASAP are also located in Los Angeles and all have Web sites.

To include a musical composition in your project, you need *synchronization* or *sync rights*, so named because the music is synchronized to the picture. To perform the music in public, you need public performance rights. In the United States, public performance rights are generally included in the deal you make for sync rights; you don't have to pay for them separately. For projects that are broadcast on TV, the broadcaster usually pays for the performance rights.

If you want to use a preexisting *recording* of the song, contact the owner of the recording, usually the record company (look on the sleeve of the CD for the address). You will need a *master use license* to use the actual recording (performance) in your project. So for the classic situation of trying to clear a recording by an artist you like, you will be requesting two licenses: a sync license with public performance from the publisher and a master use license from the record company.

If you use a song that has not been cleared, you carry the risk of being caught. Failure to clear the music might result in an injunction and large legal fees. You may have to pay an out-of-court settlement or have to make extensive changes to your show to remove the musical selection. Some public broadcasting entities, such as PBS, have blanket agreements and compulsory licenses that may allow you to use music without clearing it with rights holders. This only applies to television broadcast. You may still need other rights if the project is shown elsewhere.

Festival rights might not require any payment at all; however, festival rights are negotiated in the same manner as if you were seeking commercial rights.

Public Domain

Music created after January 1, 1978, is protected by copyright for 50 years after the death of the last surviving writer. Works that were made for hire, such as an original film score, are protected for 75 years from publication or 100 years from creation, whichever is less.

You might have heard that you can use a few bars from a song for free. This is false. "Fair use" is another questionable area. This is an exception to the exclusive rights of copyright owners. Fair use permits limited use of a copyrighted material in a number of circumstances. In theory, the public interest is served when the material is used for purposes of criticism, comment, news reporting, scholarship, teaching, and so on. Parodies using the material for humor or social commentary are also allowed, but this area of law is constantly changing and should be reviewed carefully.

For help in this area, get some legal assistance. If you cannot afford an entertainment attorney, you'll find free legal aid groups in major metropolitan areas that can answer many of your basic questions. One example is Volunteer Lawyers for the Arts. You may also check an excellent Web site at www.pdinfo.com (for Public Domain Information).

Film Schools

The latter part of the 20th century has seen the emergence and proliferation of film and television schools. Whereas in the middle part of the century it was the goal of many young artists to express themselves by writing "the great American novel," it is now their goal to make "the great American film."

> *Everyone who received their acceptance letter and came to the first day of class thought that the guy next to them was the next Scorsese. After a few days you realize everyone is in about the same boat. That was a big relief to me.*
>
> Howard

And no wonder. Film and television are the two potent communication tools in the world today. More than 500 universities in the United States and Canada now have programs involving communications or media arts studies or film, television, or radio production. The magnetism, influence, and responsibility of the film and video communications artist are not to be taken lightly.

> *I'm a supporter of film schools because I think it's a quick and dirty way to get a lot of experience under your belt. If the school is run right, it teaches you to work under the kinds of constraints that will exist in the outside world, in terms of budget, deadlines, and peer review.*
>
> Jan

Film and television programs offer the fledgling communications artist many educational opportunities not afforded in the past. At the core of the experience is a chance to experiment, to fail, to work out ideas, and to make contacts and liaisons that could last a lifetime.

The film and television industry is a tough nut to crack. We believe that a film school education can qualify a student not only for a career in film or television, but it also can provide skills in communications, writing, and interpersonal conflict management that are useful for any of a number of fields in the communication and media arts: politics, advertising, education, radio, social work, and so on.

PROGRAMS

Film and television programs offer a variety of graduate and undergraduate degrees that concentrate on the study or writing and production of film, television, and radio. Also, many programs offer degrees in such areas as mass communications, telecommunications, media arts, broadcast journalism, communications arts, and other specialties.

> *I decided to go to film school because I realized after going to high school and seeing that my hobbies were painting, photography, and acting that film would be the one discipline in which I can combine all my hobbies. I think also through the years films has been my favorite pastime along with reading. I went to film school expecting that I will adapt books by Israeli writers eventually as my career into films and bring them to more international audience. Surprisingly, it sort of went in that direction. I wound up adapting short stories by my favorite Israeli writer who became my partner in quite a few projects. Film school was in itself wonderful. I don't think I had in mind how fragmented an experience it could be as far as the different crafts. You can learn each of the crafts, but you're still not a filmmaker. That was something I had to struggle with—how to combine every tool I got in film school into voice. By the end of it I felt very, very happy and satisfied.*
>
> Tatia

The undergraduate degrees offered are bachelor of arts, bachelor of science, and bachelor of fine arts. B.A. and B.S. degrees usually involve only two years of production or media study, whereas B.F.A. programs involve four years of training or study in a major. There also are junior colleges that offer film, television, and communications-related programs.

Graduate programs offer master of arts, master of fine arts, and doctorates. The highest degree for programs concentrating on production is an M.F.A. Generally, a Ph.D. is offered for cinema studies and mass communications studies, among others.

Among this list are art schools, where the emphasis is on film, graphic arts, photography, or video. Certain programs focus on different disciplines within their curriculum such as documentary, experimental, narrative, or animation. Video production has taken the place of film in many programs; students wishing to make "films" should check out schools carefully.

> *I did have a professor that I liked very much at Columbia, Vojtech Jasney. I had shown him the script. He was the one who encouraged me to go and make it.*
>
> Adam

Pick a program that is in line with your overall goals. There are obvious advantages to schools located in major urban areas like New York, Los Angeles, Chicago, or Boston, but there are plenty of excellent programs in smaller communities around the country. Look at the size of the program as well. Big is not always better when it comes to the kind of individual nurturing and guidance needed for film and video courses. (A complete list or prominent schools here and abroad follows.)

> *Film schools can really choose, as I see it, between two things. One is to be a stepping stone into the industry. Now that the apprentice system isn't really in place anymore in Hollywood, there isn't any building up of one's craft. Film schools can say, "We're out here to be your stepping stone into the film industry. Come here, we'll make films that Hollywood will like. We'll teach you how to make them, and we'll show them off to Hollywood." Or it says the opposite, "We don't care what Hollywood is doing. We want you to come here to learn things and to try things and to fail. You're safe here."*

> *I think that if a school chooses to do the latter, they will eventually get Hollywood's attention. Because Hollywood is always looking for material, and if there's a school where suddenly things are coming out of it that are interesting and different, and some of it's bad, but some of it's really wonderful. Hollywood will take notice.*
>
> Adam

REFERENCES

Individuals interested in applying to a film and television program can begin by reviewing the first two reference guides. The *AFI Guide* has been out for several years, but the Pintoff guide is new to the market. Don't assume, however, that all the information in these guides is up-to-date. Check it out for yourself.

Laskin, Emily, Editor/Director. *The American Film Institute Guide to College Courses in Film and Television*, 8th ed. Englewood Cliffs, NJ: Prentice-Hall, 1990.

Pintoff, Ernest. *Complete Guide to American Film Schools and Cinema and Television Courses*. New York: Penguin, 1994.

A list of some of the film programs in the United States and abroad follows.

UNITED STATES AND CANADA

American Film Institute
Center for Advanced Film and Television Study
2021 N. Western Avenue
Los Angeles, CA 90027-1657
(310) 856-7600
Degree offered: M.F.A.

California Institute of the Arts
School of Film and Video
24700 McBean Parkway
Valencia, CA 91355-2397
(661) 255-1050
Degrees offered: B.F.A., M.F.A.

Canadian Film Centre
Windfields
2849 Bayview Avenue
Toronto, Ontario
Canada, M2L1A8
(416) 445-9481

Columbia College Chicago
School of Media Arts
600 S. Michigan Avenue
Chicago, IL 60605
(312) 663-1600
Degrees offered: B.A., M.F.A.

Columbia University
School of the Arts, Film Division,
513 Dodge Hall
2960 Broadway
New York, NY 10027
(212) 854-2815
Degree offered: M.F.A

Emerson College
Department of Visual Media Arts
120 Boylston Street
Boston, MA 02116
(617) 824-8500
Degrees offered: B.F.A, B.A., B.S., M.A. (video only)

Florida State University Film School
Undergraduate Film Program
University Center 3100A
Tallahassee, FL 32306-2350
(850) 644-7728
Degree offered: B.F.A.

Florida State University Film School
Graduate Film Program
University Center 3100A
Tallahassee, FL 32306-2350
(850) 644-7728
Degree offered: M.F.A.

Ithaca College
Roy Park School of Communications
350 Park Hall
Ithaca, NY 14850
(607) 274-3242
Degrees offered: B.S., B.F.A.

Loyola Marymount University
School of Film & Television
One LMU Drive
MC8320
Los Angeles, CA 90045-8347
(310) 338-3033
Degrees offered: B.A., M.A.

New York University
Tisch School of the Arts
Department of Film and Television
Undergraduate Division
721 Broadway, 11th Floor
New York, NY 10003
(212) 998-1700
Degree offered: B.F.A.

New York University
Tisch School of the Arts
Department of Film and Television
Graduate Division
721 Broadway, 10th Floor
New York, NY 10003
(212) 998-1780
Degree offered: M.F.A.

Northwestern University
Radio/TV/Film
1920 Campus Drive
Evanston, IL 60208
(847) 491-7315
Degrees offered: B.S., M.A., Ph.D., M.F.A.

Ohio University
School of Film
Lindley Hall 378
Athens, OH 45701
(740) 593-1323
Degrees offered: B.F.A., M.F.A., M.A.

San Francisco Art Institute
Filmmaking Department
800 Chestnut Street
San Francisco, CA 94133
(415) 771-7020
Degrees offered: B.A., M.A.

Stanford University
Documentary Film and Video Program
Department of Art and History
450 Serra Mall
Stanford, CA 94305-2050
(650) 723-1941
Degrees offered: B.A., M.F,A., Ph.D.

Sundance Institute
19 Exchange Place
Salt Lake City, UT 84111
(801) 521-9330
Certificate Program

Temple University
Department of Film and Media Arts
School of Communications and Theater
Annenberg Hall
Philadelphia, PA 19122
B.A. Program: (215) 204-3859
Degrees offered: B.A., M.F.A., Ph.D.

UCLA
School of Theater, Film, and Television
102 East Melnitz Hall
Box 951622
Los Angeles, CA 90095-1602
(310) 825-5761
Degrees offered: B.A., M.F.A.

University of North Texas
Division of Radio/Television/Film
P.O. Box 310589
Denton, TX 76203-0589
(940) 565-2537
Degrees offered: B.A., M.A.

University of Southern California
School of Cinema/Television
Office of Admissions & Student Affairs
University Park, CTV-G130
Los Angeles, CA 90089-2211
Phone: (213) 740-8358
Degrees offered: B.A., B.F.A., M.A., M.F.A.

University of Texas-Austin
Radio-Television-Film
1 University Station A0800
Austin, TX 78712-0108
(512) 471-4071
Degrees offered: B.S., M.F.A., M.A., Ph.D.

York University
Department of Film
224 Centre for Film and Theater
Toronto, Ontario,
Canada, M3J 1P3
(416) 736-5149
Degrees offered: B.F.A, B.A., M.F.A., M.A.

INTERNATIONAL

Australian Film and Television School
Box 126, North Ryde
N.S.W. 2113
Australia

Deutsche Film- und Fernsehakademie Berlin GmbH
Pommernalle 1
1 Berlin 19
Germany

Dramatiska Intitutet (The Swedish Media School)
Filmhuset
Borgvagen
Box 27090, S-102
51 Stockholm
Sweden

Film and Television Institute of Tamil Nadu
Department of Information and Public Relations
Government of Tamil Nadu, Madras
Adya, Madras 600 020
India

Film and Television School of India
Law College Road
Poona 411 004
India

Hochschule für Fernsehen und Film
Ohmstrasse 11
8000 München 40
Germany

L'Institut des Hautes Études Cinématographiques (IDHEC)
4 Avenue de L'Europe
94360 Bry-sur-Marne
France

London International Film School
24 Shelton Street
London WC2H 9HP
England
Tel.: 01-240-0168

National Film and Television School
Beaconsfield Film Studios
Station Road
Beaconsfield, Bucks HP9 1LG
England
Tel.: 04946 71234

Panswowa Wyzsza Szkola Filmowa, Telwizyjna i
Teatraina im Leona Schillera, U1
Targowa 61/63
90 323 Lodz
Poland

Vsesoyuzni Gosudarstvenni Institut
Kinematografi Ulitsa Vilgelma Pika 3
Moscow 129226
Russia

appendix F

A Short History of the Short Film

The short film played an important part in the development of the modern cinema. From Thomas Edison to George Lucas, filmmakers have depended on the short format to exhibit new technology, advance artistic ideals, or simply catch the eye of the ever-important audience.

It was the audience that first motivated Thomas Alva Edison to commission his assistant, William K. L. Dickson, to begin research in 1889 on a device that would enhance his earlier invention, the phonograph. Photography had become increasingly popular since its inception in the 1860s, and with the invention of rolled celluloid film by George Eastman, the time was right. In 1891, Dickson projected the first motion picture images for his boss. Edison was granted a patent in 1893 for his Kinetoscope, an odd cabinet with a peephole viewer, and cinema was born.

Edison's first films were necessarily short. The Kinetoscope's compact design limited the length of the first films to 50 feet. The limitation was a commercial one. Edison knew that to make motion pictures financially viable, he needed to distribute not only films, but also miniature theaters.

These early Edison films were simple: one shot of a simple action. The photographic record of a sneeze, gloriously titled *Fred Ott's Sneeze*, is thought to be the oldest remaining motion picture film. The Kinetograph, Edison's camera, was a clunky contraption that could not be moved beyond the walls of its dark studio, the Black Maria. This was not a problem for Edison. His films were novelties, short glimpses of a new technology for a price.

The creative constraints of Edison's distribution and production were soon resolved by two brothers on the other side of the Atlantic. Auguste M. L. N. and Louis Jean Lumière developed a motion picture camera that could also develop and project film. The Cinématographe was portable and depended on a hand crank, rather than electricity, for power. In 1895, the brothers produced their first film, *Workers Leaving the Lumière Factory*, a short static exterior shot of workers leaving their factory. The Lumière brothers opened their first public theater on December 28, 1895, in the basement of the Grand Café. At the showing of *L'Arrivée d'un Train en Gare*, the audience screamed and ran from the theater as a train barreled toward them on the screen.

Early filmmakers continued to use the convenient and economical short film format. Improvements in cinematography and a growing sophistication of content led to multishot narratives. An excellent example is George Méliès's *A Trip to the Moon* (1902), which involved several static shots at different locations edited together. Edwin S. Porter's short film, *The Great Train Robbery* (1903), innovated continuity editing to build the narrative.

Motion pictures were by this time big business. Edison's company and others, including American Mutoscope and Biograph, began to compete for a piece of it. Nickelodeons, large store theaters, began spreading across the country after the first opened in Pittsburgh in 1905. The nickelodeons created an additional demand for films and kept the short film alive until great directors such as D. W. Griffith insisted on creating feature-length films. By 1914, the feature film (four or more reels) had become the dominant form, and the studios began to relegate the shorts to the role of filler in a feature program. There were few exceptions.

The demand for product was a catalyst for the creation of serials. These short episodic films were centered around a few key characters, and they were exhibited in installments. In 1912, Edison's Kinetoscope Company began the first serial, *What Happened to Mary*. With a unique publicity campaign involving *The Ladies Home Journal*, which printed the new story each week, the format became highly successful. The clichés of the cliff-hanger soon appeared. Studios such as Selig Polyscope Company and later Metro-Goldwyn-Mayer capitalized on the format to become major contenders in the business.

A young director named Mack Sennett, unable to produce comic films under Edison or Biograph, formed the independent film company Keystone Pictures. The Sennett shorts were characterized by their sight gags and slapstick humor. In 1913, British actor Charlie Chaplin joined Sennett. Chaplin later created several great shorts, including *One A.M.* (1916), *The Tramp* (1915), *Easy Street* (1917), and *A Dog's Life* (1918). The Chaplin comedy shorts were unique in that they presented social commentary under the guise of silliness. Later, the short film became a vehicle for other comic giants, including Buster Keaton (*The Goat*, 1922) and Laurel and Hardy (*Putting Pants on Philip*, 1927).

All was not comical in the early years of the 20th century, however. Artistic movements triggered by World War I and the Russian Revolution influenced all media, including film. Directors became proponents of German Expressionism (Erich von Stroheim, Ernst Lubitsch, and Fritz Lang) or Soviet Montage (Sergei Eisenstein and Vsevlod I. Pudovkin). The short film became an experimental form for these new cinematic ideas.

Documentary, which had been reduced to travelogues and novelty films, gained momentum as a genre with Robert Flaherty's *Nanook of the North* (1921). Flaherty's work gave legitimacy to the documentary form and began an important artistic tradition.

Sound was the next major technical hurdle. There had been several attempts to synchronize sound and film during the early years of motion pictures. By 1919, a workable system had been devised. Lee de Forest, inventor of the vacuum tube used for amplification, began showing the first sound films, which he called *Phonofilms*. These were short demonstrations by famous personalities speaking or singing on screen. Vitaphone (the first commercial sound film company) and later William Fox's Movietone both began to distribute short sound films.

An example of one of these early sound shorts is Movietone's *Shaw Talks for Movietone* (1927). In 1927, Fox-Movietone premiered the first newsreels.

At the end of the 1920s Disney introduced its first *Silly Symphony*, titled *Skeleton Dance*. These animated shorts coupled recent advances in film sound with Disney's unique artistic vision to create fantastic musical revues.

While Disney was busy with his favorite mouse in *Steamboat Willy* (1928), the avant-garde movement was awakening, led by such filmmakers as Jean Renoir, Man Ray, and Luis Buñuel. Classic short films such as *Ballet Mecanique* (Fernard Leger, 1924), *Un Chien Andalou* (Luis Buñuel and Salvador Dali, 1928), and *Entr'Acte* (René Clair, 1924) revealed the strong intellectual influence on film from painting, psychology, and other areas.

Television changed films in general, but especially short films. With the inception of television, the 30-minute and 60-minute format became popular. In 1951, Columbia formed Screen Gems to produce product for television, marking a new area for studio dominance.

During the 1950s, several independent animators experimented with techniques such as pixillation and drawing on film. With his experimental shorts *A Chairy Tale*, *Neighbors*, and *Pas de Deux*, Canadian director Norman MacLaren is the best known of this group. Animation techniques further influenced directors such as Albert Lamorisse (*The Red Balloon*, 1956).

In the wake of World War II, a new wave of filmmakers emerged in France. A strong documentary tradition pushed these new filmmakers toward fresh artistic expression in documentary shorts. The stylistic devices of the documentary—location shooting, direct sound, and handheld camera work—further influenced their narrative work. Leaders in this movement included Alain Resnais (*Night and Fog*, 1955), Chris Marker (*La Jetée*, 1962), Jean-Luc Godard (*All the Boys Are Called Patrick*, 1957), and François Truffaut (*Antoine and Colette*, 1962).

The 1960s, a time of social and cultural change, saw the growth of the underground independent short filmmaker. Many classic short films were produced during this era, including Roman Polanski and Jean-Pierre Rensseau's *The Fat and the Lean* (1961) and Robert Enrico's *An Occurrence at Owl Creek Bridge* (1962). The introduction of the 8-mm and 16-mm formats made film more accessible and affordable to more people. Andy Warhol, the famed pop artist, was one of those who crossed over into film as an alternative medium.

The accessibility of film to the public allowed younger and younger people to dabble in filmmaking. Film schools began to appear throughout the United States and the world. George Lucas's student film, *THX 1138*, inspired his later science-fiction feature with Robert Duvall. Francis Ford Coppola, Steven Spielberg, Oliver Stone, and others began as student short filmmakers in the late 1960s and early 1970s.

Today, the short narrative and documentary film survives in film schools and festivals throughout the United States and in the booming European film community. Other forms, including music videos and television/film commercials, have given new filmmakers applications for their cinematic ideas. With the continued growth of film schools and the proliferation of video technology, the short format probably will continue into the future.

Glossary

A and B cutting A method of assembling original 16-mm film material in two separate rolls, allowing optical effects to be made by double printing (A and B printing).

A/B editing (video) An editing system that can control more than one playback machine and perform dissolves.

A- and B-wind When a roll of 16-mm film, perforated along one edge, is held so that the outside end of the film leaves the roll at the top and toward the right, A-wind has perforations on the edge of the film toward the observer, and B-wind has perforations on the edge away from the observer. In both cases, the base surface faces outward on the roll.

above-the-line The part of a production budget earmarked for the creative aspects of production, including the salaries of the producer, director, writer, and talent.

abrasion mark A scratch on film caused by grit, dust, improper handling, emulsion buildup, and certain types of film damage such as broken perforations.

Academy leader A film leader, placed at the head end of a projection reel, that contains identification and timing countdown information for the projectionist and is designed to meet the specifications of the American Academy of Motion Picture Arts and Sciences.

acetate A commonly used base for film stock, which is coated with light-sensitive emulsion.

AD See **assistant director**.

A/D (analog to digital) Electronic circuitry for converting analog audio or video signals to digital.

address A precise frame location on a videotape identified by timecode number; also, the location of specific data in a computer memory.

ADR See **automatic dialogue replacement**.

aerial shot Shot taken from the air.

AES/EBU American Engineering Society/European Broadcasting Union.

AGC See **automatic gain control**.

agent/talent agent An individual or company licensed by the state to represent a particular talent in the entertainment field and to seek employment and negotiate contracts in his or her behalf. The standard fee is 10 percent of the client's salary. Agents can represent above-the-line talent (actors, writers, directors, producers) or below-the-line talent (art directors, directors of photography, editors).

aliasing Erroneous frequencies occurring in digital recordings when frequencies greater than half the sampling frequency are sampled.

ambient noise (1) Background noise. (2) Sounds that occur naturally in a location or in a studio, without dialogue or other production-created sound.

amplitude The scientific measure of the comparative intensity of a signal. Most commonly used to measure the loudness of sound.

analog A recording system that creates modulations analogous to the modulations of sound or video waves.

anamorphic A term used to denote a difference in magnification along mutually perpendicular meridians. Anamorphic systems are basically image-distorting systems. A wide formatted image will be compressed horizontally creating a "squished" looking picture to fit into a narrow medium (film or video). For proper viewing, the image must be expanded back to its original wide format.

angle With reference to the subject, the direction from which a picture is taken—that is, the camera–subject relationship.

animation The act of making inanimate objects appear to move. This can be done by exposing one or two frames of film, moving the objects slightly, exposing one or two more frames, and so on.

answer print The first print of a completed film project in composite form (audio is married to the print), which the laboratory offers for approval. It is usually

365

studied carefully by the director, producer, and DP to determine whether changes in color or density are required before the lab makes any additional prints.

aperture (1) In a lens, the orifice, usually an adjustable iris, that limits the amount of light passing through a lens. The width of a lens aperture is expressed in f-stops. (2) In a motion picture camera, the mask opening that defines the area of each frame exposed. (3) In a motion picture projector, the mask opening that defines the area of each frame projected.

aperture plate A metal plate, containing an aperture, that is inserted into a projector or camera.

Arriflex Brand name of a high-quality 16-mm and 35-mm film camera.

ASA The exposure index, or speed rating, that denotes the film's sensitivity to light, as defined by the American National Standards Institution. (It is actually defined only for black-and-white films, but it is also used in the trade for color films.) The stock used in videotape does not determine the light levels required for image recording. It is the camera's pickup tube or its charge coupled device (CCD) that determines the sensitivity to light.

ASC American Society of Cinematographers, www.theasc.com.

ASCII American Standard Code for Information Interchange; the standard that governs the sequence of binary digits on a computerized timecode or video editing system.

aspect ratio Screen size as expressed by the ratio of the width to height, such as 1.33:1 (16-mm), 1.85:1 (35-mm), or 2.35:1 (70-mm).

assemble edit In film, the assemble edit includes all the shots with their slates, assembled in proper viewing order. In video, the assemble edit is the product of an offline editing session.

assistant director (AD) In video production, the person who relays the director's commands from the control booth to the studio floor and who keeps an accurate account of time. In film production, the person who helps the production manager break down the script during preproduction and keeps the director on schedule during production. The AD also hires, controls, and directs background action, including extras and camera vehicles.

asymmetric compression Compression techniques that require a greater amount of processing power to compress a signal than is required to decompress a signal.

atmospheric effect An environmental special effect such as fog, mist, rain, or wind.

attack (sound) The beginning segment of an audio cue.

audio sweetening Enhancing the sound of a recording with equalization and various other signal-processing techniques during the postproduction process.

automatic dialogue replacement (ADR) A process during postproduction in which an actor replaces any of her lines in the film or video because of disruptive sounds on the set or the need of the director to change the performance. Also called **looping**, it is accomplished by replaying the scene over and over in the studio while the player lip-syncs to the picture.

automatic gain control (AGC) A device that maintains a constant audio or video signal level on a videotape or audiotape recorder.

B roll In film, the incoming shot of an A/B roll. In video, it is the copy of an original tape (a dub) or background or extra material shot for cutaways.

baby legs A small, miniature tripod for low-angle shots.

back lighting Lighting from behind the subject.

back story The events stated or implied to have happened before the period covered in the film or video.

bandwidth This refers to the number of bits per second of material. The computer is tasked with processing a number of bits per second when digitizing; that number becomes a limiting factor. The computer can process only a certain number of frames and a certain amount of information for each frame every second.

barn door A frame with adjustable flaps that is attached to a lighting instrument to control unwanted spill light or the spread of the beam of light.

barney A lightweight padded covering that reduces the sound emanating from within the camera, such as noisy gears or takeup reels. Heated barneys are sometimes used to facilitate shooting under extremely cold outdoor conditions.

bars Standard color bars that are generated in video systems, usually by the camera.

base makeup Makeup that hides blemishes and creates a consistent overall texture and color on the performer's face, arms, and hands.

battery belt A belt containing a rechargeable camera battery.

battery pack A battery power source for a camera or other location equipment.

baud Unit for measuring the rate of digital data transmission. Usually one baud equals one bit per second.

beat (1) The point in a scene where a character's tempo, meaning, or intention shifts. (2) A musical tempo used for timing motion picture action.

below-the-line The part of a production budget allocated to the technical aspects of production, including the salaries of the crew and equipment and material costs.

binary code A series of ons and offs (or ones and zeros) that digitally represent a wide range of values in coded form.

bins In film editing, the large metal storage tubs with thin metal hooks used to hang trims. In nonlinear editing systems, the "bin" is the storage container for the clips and sequences (edited programs) in your project.

blanking Portion of the composite video signal between the active picture segments for making the horizontal and vertical retrace scan lines invisible.

blimp A soundproof enclosure that completely covers a camera to prevent camera-operating noise from being recorded on the sound track. A blimp is similar to a barney but is made from a solid material.

blocking How the director positions the actors and the camera on the stage or set.

blow up To enlarge a portion of the original image to full frame size in the copy by means of an optical printer. Running the entire film through an optical printer can enlarge 16-mm film to 35-mm size.

blue screen An effect (in film) in which a character or object is photographed in front of a blue backing or screen. Later, in an optical printer, that object or character is combined with a background image by eliminating the blue area of the foreground. The process in video is electronically controlled and called a *chroma key effect*.

boom A support pole, held by a boom operator, used to hang the microphone close to the performers but just out of the shot.

bounce light Light that is reflected off white cards, ceilings, or walls to illuminate a subject indirectly.

breakdown sheet A list made from a script that includes all elements needed to produce a sequence.

breakup Disturbance in the picture or sound signal caused by loss of sync or by videotape damage.

broad light A soft, floodlight-type lamp that cannot be focused.

business Activity invented by actors to identify their characters' behavior. Business is a physical action that arises from dialogue, silences or pauses, or audio cues (such as a doorbell or ringing phone). It might involve movement from one part of the set to another (crosses) or the use of props and set dressing. Examples: lighting a cigarette at a key moment in a scene or jiggling a set of keys to break a tense silence.

byte Computer term for a group of binary digits operated upon as a single unit. In most editing system computers, one byte equals eight bits.

cable television A means of distributing television signals to receivers via a coaxial cable.

call back To ask actors to audition for a second or third time.

call sheet A daily production schedule indicating where and when the production takes place and who is to be where and at what time.

camera axis A hypothetical line running through the optic center of the camera lens.

camera car A specially equipped truck that can tow a picture vehicle and offers several shooting positions from the truck. This enables the actors to act and not drive.

camera operator The person who operates the camera. This person might also be the director of photography.

canted angle See **Dutch angle**.

cardioid microphone A microphone whose responsiveness to sound forms can be described by a heart-shaped pickup pattern.

catharsis (1) A purifying or figurative cleansing of the emotions, especially pity and fear, described by Aristotle as an effect of tragic drama on its audience. (2) A release of emotional tension, such as after an overwhelming experience, that restores or refreshes the spirit.

cathode ray tube The electronic device, a type of vacuum tube, that creates the picture in a television set by sending a directed stream of electrons at a phosphorus material that covers the inner viewing surface of the tube. Cathode ray tubes are also the picture-making elements found in computer monitors, vectorscopes, and oscilloscopes.

CCD (charge coupled device) An electronic chip that converts light into electrical impulses used by most modern video cameras.

CD-ROM Compact disc, read-only memory.

CG See **character generator**.

CGI Computer-generated images.

changing bag A black light-tight cloth or plastic bag used to load and unload camera magazines with film stock.

character (1) A person portrayed in an artistic piece, such as a drama or novel. (2) Single letter, number, or symbol used to represent information in a computer or video program.

character generator (CG) An electronic device that creates letters on a television screen for titles and other purposes.

chroma Pure color in video, without gray or black.

chroma key A method of electronically inserting an image from one video source into the picture from another video source by selectively replacing the "key color" with another image.

chrominance Saturation and hue characteristics of the color television signal: the portion of the TV signal that contains color information.

cinema verité A documentary film technique in which the camera is subservient to real events.

clapsticks Two boards hinged at one end that are slapped together to indicate the start of a filming session (take). Editors use clapsticks in conjunction with a slate, which provides the corresponding visual cue, to synchronize sound and image.

claymation See **pixillation**.

clear To obtain written permission from the proper individual or entity to use a certain item, music as an example, in your film.

clicktrack An audio track with rhythmic clicks used as cues for music or rerecording sessions.

clone Digital video process of duping in which there is no generational loss.

closeup (CU) A tight shot of an object or an actor's face and shoulders.

C-mount A screw mount for 16-mm film and video lenses.

coding Edge numbers that are placed on the film and mag stock so that a number of picture and sound rolls will have the same sequence. This gives the editor a visual reference to maintain accurate sync.

color bars The standard video test signal, which involves a series of vertical bars of fully saturated color: white, yellow, cyan, green, magenta, red, blue, and black.

color correction The process of altering the color of a scene or scenes. In video, it is done either with a time base corrector or color corrector. In film, color correction is called timing. It is performed in the laboratory where *the timer* determined the best density printing values of each color and the overall balance of the entire film.

color internegative A negative-image color duplicate made from a positive color original. It is typically used for making release prints.

color negative A negative (opposite) image. The colors in the negative are the opposite of the colors in the scene: Light areas are dark, and dark areas are light.

color reversal film Like photographic slides, reversal film uses a different development process from negative and yields a positive image that can be directly projected without the need of a print.

color saturation The degree of absence of white in a color. The more saturated a color (the less white), the more intense the color appears.

color temperature The color quality of the light source, expressed in degrees Kelvin (K). The higher the color temperature, the bluer the light; the lower the color temperature, the redder the light.

colorist An individual who understands color. Interfaces between a production's need for color treatment of images and the equipment necessary to accomplish that treatment. Colorists have traditionally worked with telecine film output and now also work in tape-to-tape applications in SD and HD.

component video A video signal in which the luminance (the black-and-white levels) is recorded separately from the chrominance (color information).

composite print A film print that contains both picture and optical sound track.

composite video A video signal that transmits or records luminance and chrominance as a combined signal.

composition (1) The arrangement of artistic parts to form a unified whole. (2) The balance and general relationship of objects and light in the frame.

compound lens See **lens**.

compression (audio) In analog, audio term for the process of reducing the dynamic range of the audio signal.

compression (video) In analog, video term for the lack of detail in either the black or the white areas of the video picture, due to improper separation of the signal level. In digital, term for leaving out amounts of video information in order to store more video data on a storage device.

computer enhanced graphics Images (drawings, photos, graphs, graphics) that are photographed by a camera, then manipulated by a computer and an operator.

concept A general idea derived or inferred from specific instances or occurrences in a film. This idea drives the story.

conflict Opposition between characters or forces in a work of drama or fiction, especially opposition that motivates or shapes the action of the plot.

conforming In film, it is the matching of original material to an edited work print. In video, an online editing session at which camera original footage is conformed to an offline work print.

contingency fund A sum of money, approximately 10 percent of the budget, which is added to the overall production budget in case of cost overruns and production problems.

continuity The smooth flow of action or events from one shot or sequence to the next.

continuity script A script made for postproduction by the script supervisor. A continuity script contains a shot-by-shot account of the contents of the film.

contrast A comparison of the brightest portion of the picture to the darkest. Film has a higher contrast ratio than video.

control track Portion of the video recording used to control the longitudinal motion of the tape during playback.

cookie A thin panel with regular or irregular shapes cut out, permitting light directed through it to form a particular arrangement on a part of the set. Also known as a *kukaloris*.

costume designer The person who designs and supervises the making of garments for the actors.

cover set A predressed location available in case inclement weather forces the company to move indoors.

coverage The different angles from which a particular scene is shot.

craft services The person or persons responsible for feeding the crew.

crane A boom that supports the camera and can be raised or lowered during the shot.

crawl Graphic information moving either vertically or horizontally through the picture.

cross fade A transition in which one sound source is faded out while another is faded in over it.

crystal sync A synchronization system in which separate crystal oscillators in the film camera and in the synchronous sound recorder drive the camera and the sound recorder extremely accurately, enabling double-system synchronous sound to be obtained without a cable connection.

CS Close shot. See also **closeup**.

C-stand (century stand) A tripod-based stand for holding lighting instruments, flags, gobos, and sound blankets.

CU See **closeup**.

cue To instruct the computerized editing system to shuttle a videotape reel to a predetermined location.

cutaway A shot of an object or a view that takes viewers away from the main action.

cuts only An offline or work print editing system that does not have a switcher installed in the system. Without a switcher, the only transition that can be made is a cut.

D-1 A component digital videotape format, 19-mm wide, that records its information using three separate encoded signals rather than one, which makes for more precise reproduction of the original signal. It is preferred for effects and graphic work.

D-2 A composite digital videotape format, 19-mm wide, that stores its color information in one encoded signal. D-2 is the preferred editing and show format and is fully compatible with other standard video editing house equipment.

D-3 A component digital videotape format (half-inch wide) that was developed by Panasonic as a cost-effective alternative to D-1 and D-2, and possibly one-inch.

D-5 A component digital tape format (half-inch wide) employs 10 bits per pixel sampling. As a result, D-5 provides superior performance to D-1, especially with regard to keying operations for multilayering.

D/A (digital–to-analog) Electronic circuitry for converting digital audio or video signals to analog signals.

dailies Picture and sound work prints of a day's shooting; usually, an untimed one-light print, made without regard to color balance.

DAT See **digital audio tape**.

data transfer rate The amount of information a computer storage drive can write and read in a given amount of time.

DAW Digital audio workstation. The DAW, such as Pro Tools by digidesign®, is the audio equivalent of the nonlinear editor, an electronic device that uses digital audio rather than audiotape to combine sound sources.

day out of days A detailed schedule of the days the actors will work on a film or video production.

D-Cinema Digital Cinema. Digital distribution and projection of cinematic material. Advances in digital video technology, digital video projectors, and new methods of duplication and distribution are coming together to offer a new distribution model that doesn't involve film prints.

deal memo A letter between two parties that defines the basic payment and responsibility clauses and the spirit of what will later become a contract.

decay The gradual diminishing of a concluding sound.

decibel (dB) A unit of sound measurement.

degauss   To erase recorded material on videotape or audiotape.

depth of field   The range of object-to-camera distance within which objects are in sufficiently sharp focus.

deus ex machina   An improbable event imported into a story to make it turn out right.

dialogue   The portion of the sound track that is spoken by the actors.

diffuse light   See **soft light**.

digital   An electrical signal encoding audio, video, or both into a series of assigned numbers or binary code rather than analog voltage.

digital audio tape (DAT)   A superior recording system achieved through the conversion of sound into a binary stream of ones and zeros that are computer-stored for later signal conversion and amplification without the risk of distortion. See also **binary code**.

digital Betacam   The digital Betacam format (also called D-Beta or Digi-Beta) provides a very high-quality component digital signal and is used for both production and postproduction. The cost and size of the D-Beta camcorder make it a tool for professionals only. The camera is easily to hand hold and is the same size as the analog version. D-Beta sets a very high standard for quality and versatility.

digital intermediate (DI)   A digital intermediate is the result of the process of shooting in high definition, or shooting on film followed by scanning to film quality data files, editing the project in high definition, and applying the creative process of color correction and color treatment to the completed master. This digital intermediate then becomes the master for video, DVD, or for theatrical output by transferring this data master back to film. The big advantage over the conventional method is in the creative process. Once you have scanned your feature to a data master, you have the same creative ability and freedom that is available when mastering a television movie or high-end television commercial. Creative decisions on effects like speed ramps, freeze frames, dissolves, dips to color, wipes, multilayers, and reuse of material are all very simple. Most "optical" effects are part of the automatic conforming process in online editing. Trailers can be cut from actual film footage because the original film now exists in an HD digital format.

digital S   JVC has the digital S format, which uses a VHS tape and is intended for field production. This offers the benefits of digital recording in a relatively low-cost package. Digital S tapes are incompatible with analog VHS.

digital video   A video signal encoded in electronic units of ones and zeros. Rather than representing a video signal through continuously varying voltages (analog), digital processes divide a signal into extremely minute units of time, measure the signal strength within each time unit, and then represent that strength in numeric code.

digital video effects (DVE)   A generic word that indicates the manipulation of the information composing a frame of video through the use of a special electronic processor. Also a generic term for the electronic devices that that perform digital video effects.

digitize   The process of measuring the video waveforms at regular intervals and converting the voltage information into a binary code.

directional microphone   A microphone that picks up sound only from the direction in which it points. A commonly used directional mike is a *shotgun microphone*.

director   The person who interprets the written book or script and oversees all aspects of a film or video production.

director of photography (DP)   In production, the person who directs the cinematography (the lighting and camera setup and framing).

dirty dupe   A splice-free print of the work print, also called a *slop print*. Used in the mix to avoid breaking splices. Using the dupe frees the work print to be sent to the negative cutter.

disc   Generally refers to devices containing video or audio information, such as video discs, lasers discs, or compact discs.

disk   Generally refers to devices containing computer data, such as floppy disk, hard disk, or magneto-optical disk.

dissolve   An optical or camera effect in which one scene gradually fades out as a second scene fades in. There is an apparent double exposure in the middle of a dissolve sequence where the two scenes overlap.

distributor   A company that sells, leases, and rents films.

DIT   A digital imaging technician. A designation of Local 600, IATSE, the cinematographer's guild. Advanced coloring (controller duties); setup, operation, troubleshooting, and maintenance of digital cameras (oversight of camera utilities), waveform monitors, downconverters (high definition to other formats), monitors, cables, digital recording devices, terminal equipment, driver software, and other related equipment. Complete understanding of digital audio acquisition and timecode process and how they are integrated into digital acquisition format and postproduction environments. Also responsible for in-camera recording. Supervisory responsibility for technical acceptability of the image.

Dolby™ A trademarked audio noise reduction system, developed by one of the original inventors of videotape, Ray Dolby. The concept behind the Dolby system is to push the audio levels higher during recording and then to lower them during playback plus notch a portion of the high spectrum where tape hiss is found.

dolly (1) A truck built to carry a camera and camera operator to facilitate movement of the camera during the shooting of scenes. (2) To move the camera toward or away from the subject while shooting a scene.

double (multiple) exposure The photographic recording of two or more images on a single strip of film.

double printing Optically slowing down film action by printing each frame a multiple of times.

downconversion The process of converting high-resolution video to lower resolution video.

DP See **director of photography**.

dress rehearsal The final rehearsal or technical drill for a production before actual filming. A dress rehearsal involves costumes, props, and dressed sets.

drop frame timecode SMPTE timecode format that skips (drops) two frames per minute except on the tenth minute, so the timecode stays coincident with real time. Compare to **nondrop frame timecode.**

dropout An area on videotape that is missing oxide and thus can have no picture or audio information recorded there. Dropouts may be the simple result of defects in tape stock or produced by mishandling or malfunctioning equipment.

dub To copy from one electronic medium to another. Both sound and video picture can be dubbed.

dubber A long vertical machine with supply and takeup reel, that is capable of reading the audio on the film mag. A dubber is used in the audio mixing (dubbing) process of film postproduction.

dubbing The process of melding several sound components into a single recording.

dump To copy stored computer information onto an external medium, such as hard copy, paper, paper tape, or floppy disk.

dupe/dupe negative A duplicate negative, which is made from a master positive by printing and development or from an original negative by printing followed by reversal development.

Dutch angle A shot made with the camera deliberately tilted. Also known as a *canted angle*.

DV Digital video.

DVC Digital videocassette.

DVCAM Component digital video format introduced by Sony.

DVCPRO Component digital video format made by Panasonic.

DVD Digital versatile disk, disk of the size of a CD, but with a storage capacity of up to 17 Gbyte. The single layer one side DVD stores up to 4.7 Gbyte, more than eight times as much as on a CD. It is an ideal media for video and multichannel audio applications. The term DVD has become synonymous with DVD-Video, which holds MPEG-2 compressed video, multichannel audio, subtitles, menus, and other features onto a DVD disk for playback in industry standard players.

EBU European Broadcast Union.

edge numbers Numbers on the edges of film that identify the film. They are used to help match original film and sound to the edited work prints. Latent-image edge numbers are put on by the manufacturer and appear during development. Also known as *key numbers*.

edit controller An electronic device used to switch among various video inputs to record on a videotape recorder. It controls the edit by preroll cueing, edit auditioning, and performing the edit by punching in and punching out.

edit decision list (EDL) A list of edits performed during offline editing in video. The EDL is stored in hard copy, floppy disk, or punch-tape form and is used to direct the final online editing assembly or negative cut.

edited master The final edited version of a tape program.

editing The process of selecting the shots and sequences that will be included in the final product, their length, and the order in which they will appear.

editor The person who decides which scenes and takes are to be used, how, where, in what sequence, and at what length they will appear.

EDL See **edit decision list**.

effects track An audio track with sound effects only, without music or dialogue.

electrician A technical crew member who moves and places lights and electrical connections. The electrician works under the direction of the gaffer.

emulsion The chemically active portion of film that preserves the photographic image. The emulsion side of the film is the dull side, the shiny side is the base or celluloid backing.

encoding   Adding technical information such as a timecode, cues, or closed caption information to a video recording.

end crawl   The names of the cast and crew who worked on a production that rolls up or "crawls" vertically at the end of a film or video.

equalization (EQ)   Altering the frequency/amplitude response of a sound source or system to improve the sound quality. Treble and bass are adjusted, as is the relationship of various frequencies.

establishing shot   A shot that establishes a scene's geographical and human contents.

exposure   The amount of light that acts on a photographic material. Exposure is the product of illumination intensity (controlled by the lens opening) and duration (controlled by the shutter opening and the frame rate).

exposure index   A number assigned to a film stock indicating that film's sensitivity to light.

exposure latitude   The range between the lowest and highest exposures that will ensure a readable image on the screen.

exposure meter, incident   A meter calibrated to read and integrate all the light aimed at and falling on a subject within a large area. The scale might be calibrated in footcandles or in photographic exposure settings.

exposure meter, reflectance   A meter calibrated to read the amount of light, within a restricted area, reflecting from the surface of a subject or an overall scene. The scale might be calibrated in footcandles or in photographic exposure settings.

eye-line   The line from an actor's eye to the direction in which the actor is looking. If the actor looks at coperformers and behind them is an audience, the actor might become distracted. It is important to keep crew members out of an actor's eye-line during auditions and principal photography.

f-stop   The ratio of the focal length of a lens to the diameter of the lens opening and, thus, a unit of measure for the lens opening, or aperture. This formula allows one to know exactly how much light is falling onto the film or photosensitive mechanism. Each successive f-stop is a doubling or halving of the amount of light admitted to the film through the aperture. The 10 standard f-stops are f1, f1.4, f2, f2.8, f4, f5.6, f8, f11, f16, and f22.

fade-in   A gradual visual transition from black to picture.

fade-out   A gradual visual transition from image to black.

fast lens   A lens that admits large amounts of light to pass through it. Also called *super-speed lens*.

feed   The part of a recording device that supplies tape or film.

fiber optics   A small cable through which information, carried by light, travels through a telephone line. Also used for lighting.

field   One-half of a television frame consisting of every other scanline of video information (in NTSC video, 262.5 horizontal lines at 59.94 Hz; in PAL, 312.5 horizontal lines at 50 Hz). Two fields make a frame.

fill   Old, unneeded film used to temporarily replace audio tracks to maintain sync with picture in areas where sound track is missing.

fill light   Light used to fill in shadows, either on a set or on a face.

film chain   See **telecine system**.

film cut list   The film counterpart of an edit decision list, important for matchback purposes.

film gate   The components that make up the pressure and aperture plates in a camera, printer, or projector.

film perforation   Holes punched at regular intervals in the entire length of film. The perforation is engaged by pins, pegs, and sprockets as the film is transported through the camera, projector, or other equipment.

film rights   A film industry term for a collection of different rights. Those rights include the right to make a film for initial exhibition in theaters or in television. The right to make sequels and remakes of that film, the right to distribute the film on videocassettes and other media, even those that are not invented yet.

film speed   The sensitivity of a film's emulsion to light.

film-to-video transfer   The process of copying a film on videotape through a telecine or flying spot scanner.

final cut   The last editing of a work print before conforming is done and before sound work prints are mixed.

Final Cut Pro   Apple's Final Cut Pro (www.apple.com/finalcutpro) editing software.

fine grain   Emulsion in which the silver particles are very small.

FireWire   FireWire, also known as IEEE (Institute of Electrical and Electronics Engineers) 1394, was developed by Apple Computer and is a standardized method for high-speed connections among a wide variety of professional and "prosumer" equipment. A project shot on a small DV camcorder with up to 500 lines of resolution can be inputted directing to a desktop computer.

fishpole   A handheld microphone boom.

flag   An opaque sheet that is separate from a lighting instrument but is used to shape the light and prevent light from falling on certain areas.

flare   A streak of light that is recorded on the film or video stock when the light of the sun or an artificial instrument shines directly into the camera lens.

flashing   A technique for lowering contrast by giving a slight uniform exposure to the film before processing.

flats   Relatively lightweight, flat, rectangular boards that can be lashed together to create a temporary wall in a studio.

flip   A revolving effect. In film, the optical printer is used to squeeze one image into the center of the frame and then reveal a new scene. In video, this process is accomplished through the use of a digital video effects device.

floodlight   A lighting instrument without a lens that uses reflectors and diffusers to spread and soften the light it emits.

floor plan   A scale drawing of a location that is used to plan lighting, camera, and actor blocking.

floppy disk   Flat, flexible magnetic medium used to store data in computer-readable form. In video editing, floppy disks are used to store edit decisions lists (EDL).

flying spot scanner   System for transferring film to videotape in which the electron beam inside a cathode ray tube continuously scans the moving film.

f-number   A symbol that expresses the relative aperture of the lens. For example, a lens with a relative aperture of 1.7 would be marked f1.7. The smaller the f-number, the more light the lens transmits. Also known as f-stop.

focal distance   The length between a camera's lens and the point of focus of the subject.

focus   To adjust a lens so that it produces the sharpest visual image on a screen, on a camera film plane, and so on.

Foley   Named for sound effects editor George Foley, who created the process. The producing of sound effects in a studio in synchronization to the picture.

footage   (1) The length of a scene measured in feet. (2) All the visual production material of an individual program or scene.

footcandle (fc)   A unit of light intensity that equals the power of one standard candle at a distance of one foot. Footcandles are measured with incident light meters.

forced development   A use of increased time or temperature in the development process of film to adjust for underexposure of the original film during production. Also called *pushing* the film.

foreground   The part of the scene in front of the camera that is occupied by the object nearest the camera.

format   The size or aspect ratio of a motion picture frame.

fps   Frames per second.

frame rate   The number of frames per second that are being displayed. The standard frame rate of film sound is 24 frames per second, NTSC video is 30 fps (actually 29.97), and PAL video is 25 fps.

freeze frame   An optical printing effect in which a single frame image is repeated so as to appear stationary when projected.

full coat   A film stock used for audio recording whose width is completely coated with oxide. Full coat is usually delivered at the end of a dubbing session. On the full coat would be four mixed tracks: music, narration, dialogue, and effects.

gaffer   The head lighting technician for a film or television program. The gaffer is responsible for carrying out the plans of the director of photography.

gain   Amplitude (strength) of the video or audio signal.

gate   The aperture assembly through which the film is exposed in a camera, printer, or projector.

gel (gelatin)   Translucent material in a variety of colors that is placed in front of lighting instruments to alter the color of the light. Gels are held in place by barn doors.

generation   The number of duplications away from the camera original. First generation would be one copy away from the original camera image.

genre   A category of film categorized by a particular style, form, or content, such as horror, sitcom, western, and domestic drama.

glitch   Any short interruption of a video signal that can be caused by bad tape stock, a poor edit, or a broadcast transmission problem.

gobo   A panel of opaque material on a footed stand with an adjustable arm. Gobos are used to confine the area that a light illuminates or to keep light from shining directly into the camera lens.

golden time   A rate of pay equal to triple the base hourly wage.

grain   Fine photosensitive crystals of silver halides suspended in the gelatin of a film emulsion that become exposed to light and developed into an image.

gray card   A commercially prepared card that reflects 18 percent of the light hitting it. Visually, it appears as a neutral, or middle, gray halfway between black and white.

green room   A comfortable holding area for the actors.

grid   A system of ceiling pipes for hanging lighting instruments over a stage. See also **spreaders**.

grip   A crew member responsible for moving camera support equipment, such as the tripod, dolly, and any other items, in and around the camera.

guide track   (1) A temporary audio track for the purpose of presentation. (2) An audio track recorded during production used for lip syncing (ADR) in postproduction.

guillotine splicer   A device used for butt-splicing film with splicing tape.

hard disk   Rigid disks, coated with magnetic oxide, for storage and fast retrieval of computer data; these are available as fixed, removable, or disk packs.

hard light   Illumination made up of directional rays of light that create strong, hard, well-defined shadows. Also known as *specular light*.

hardware   Mechanical, electrical, or magnetic equipment used in video recording or editing.

Hazeltine   Manufacturer's name for a film electronic timing device and color analyzer. The Hazeltine analyzes the film negative and sets the timing lights.

HDTV   See **high-definition television**.

head   Magnetic pickup device in a VTR used to record, erase, or reproduce video or audio signals.

headroom   Compositional space in a shot above the actor's head.

hertz (Hz)   The number of vibrations or successive waves of sound that pass a specific point each second.

Hi-8™ (High Band 8-mm)   A Sony Corporation trademarked name for its 8-mm-wide video format that is an improved version of 8-mm. Like S-VHS, Hi-8 can output S-video and its resolution is about 400 lines.

high-definition television (HDTV)   High-resolution (approximately 1,000 lines) television signals, which can produce wide-screen images that are roughly comparable to film images in terms of overall sharpness and detail (lines of resolution).

high-hat   A tripod head mounted onto a flat board. This allows the camera operator to place the camera on the ground or on a table for a low-angle shot.

high-key   A lighting style that produces an overall and even brightness with few shadows. The low contrast is created by a low lighting ratio of key to fill light.

highlights   The brightest areas of a subject. In a negative image, highlights are the areas of greatest density; in a positive image, they are the areas of least density.

HMI light   The high-intensity, daylight-balanced light produced by energy-efficient, portable, lightweight HMI lamps.

hook   A dramatic device that grabs viewers' attention and secures their involvement in a story.

hue   The sensation of a color itself, measured by the color's dominant wavelength.

Hz   See **hertz**.

image lag   An afterimage left on a video monitor, usually resulting from bright objects.

IN   See **internegative**.

in-camera timecode   Timecode data exposed onto the film negative between perforations.

in-point   Starting point of an edit.

insert   A close shot of detail.

insert edit   Electronic edit in which the control track is not replaced during the editing process. A new segment is inserted into program material already recorded on the videotape.

intensity (light)   The total visible radiation produced by a light source. The term refers to the power (strength) of the light source.

interface   Device used to connect two pieces of equipment.

interframe coding   A method for compression in which certain film or video frames are dependent on previous or successive frames. Used with MPEG compression.

interlace scanning   NTSC scanning process in which two fields of video are interlaced to create one full frame of video. This is done by first scanning the odd-numbered lines, then the even-numbered lines. The two scans, each a field, constitute a single video frame.

interlock   A system that electronically links a projector with a sound recorder and is used during postproduction to review the edited film with the sound track to check timing, pacing, synchronization, and so on.

internegative   (dupe negative) A negative film created from the interpositive (IP). Internegatives are used for making positive prints for distribution.

interpositive (IP)   A positive film created from the original camera negative. The IP is used as protection for the cut negative or as an intermediate step in the process of making a print for protection. The IP produces a timed internegative.

iris (1) An adjustable opening that controls the amount of light passing through a lens. (2) An optical effect that starts with a small dot of an image and "irises out" with an expanding circle to fill the entire frame with the next shot. This iris effect can also be used in reverse.

jam sync Process of locking a timecode generator to a videotape, then recording that generator's code back onto that original tape or onto another tape.

jib arm A miniature unmanned camera crane that is remotely or manually operated. A video tap is often used because of the difficulty in seeing through the eyepiece while a jib arm is in use.

jogging Process of moving the videotape forward or backward one frame at a time.

JPEG (Joint Photographic Experts Group) A group set up to standardize techniques for digitally storing still images.

jump cut The seeming jump of aspects of a picture when two similar angles are cut together.

key Electronic method of inserting graphics over a scene (luminance key) or of placing one video image into another (chroma key).

KeyKode™ Eastman Kodak's machine readable bar code, created to enable computerized identification and tracking of film segments.

key light The main illumination of the subject.

key numbers See **edge numbers**.

key-to-fill ratio See **lighting ratio**.

kicker A separation light placed directly opposite the key light to create side and back light.

kinescoping A film image made by photographing a television monitor.

kukaloris See **cookie**.

laboratory A facility that processes and prints film and sometimes offers additional services, such as coding, negative cutting, editing, and film storage.

lavaliere microphone Small lightweight, usually omnidirectional microphones that are pinned under an actor's clothing or taped to the body.

layback Transferring the finished audio track back to the edited videotape master.

leader Blank film, either black or white, used to maintain sync in A/B editing or to slug small amounts of the program where the trim (footage) is missing, or placed at the front or tail of a reel.

lens (1) A ground or molded piece of glass, plastic, or other transparent material with opposite surfaces, either or both of which are curved, by means of which light rays are refracted so that they converge or diverge to form an image. (2) A combination of two or more such pieces, sometimes with other optical devices such as prisms, used to form an image for viewing or photographing. Also called *compound lens*.

letterboxing Film transfers that preserve the aspect ratio of the film as originally shot.

lighting director In video production, the person who designs and supervises the lighting setup.

lighting ratio The ratio of the intensity of key and fill lights to fill light alone.

light meter An electrical exposure meter for measuring light intensity.

limiter Electronic circuitry used for preventing the audio signal from exceeding a preset limit.

linear A term used to describe editing systems that are locked into a straightforward, or "linear," approach to putting scenes together, as in traditional video editing systems.

lined script A script marked by the script supervisor to show the editor which take number was used to record each part of all scenes.

line item A budget entry.

lip-sync The simultaneous, precise recording of image and sound so that the sound appears to be superimposed accurately on the image, especially if a person is speaking toward the camera.

liquid gate A printing system in which the original is immersed in a suitable liquid at the moment of exposure to reduce the effect of surface scratches and abrasions.

list management On computer editing systems, a feature that allows the editor to change, trim, or shift editing decisions stored in the editing computer's memory.

load To transfer data to or from a storage device.

locked picture A picture whose editing is finished.

longitudinal timecode (LTC) Type of SMPTE timecode that is recorded on the audio track of a videotape. It is a digitally encoded audio signal and can only be read when the tape is in motion.

long shot (LS) The photographing of a scene or action from a distance or with a wide angle of view so that a large area of the setting appears on the film and the scene or objects appear quite small.

looping The process of lip-sync dubbing. See also **ADR**.

lossless compression The process of compressing information without irretrievably losing any of the data that represents that information. To be lossless, a great deal of analyzing must be done.

lossy compression The process of compressing information that results in a loss of some portion of the data in the original message.

low-key   A lighting style that uses intermittent pools of light and darkness with few highlights and many shadows. The contrast is created by a high ratio of key light alone to key and fill lights.

LS   See **long shot**.

luminance   The amount of pure white in a video image.

MII™   Panasonic's half-inch broadcast video format whose major competitor is Sony's half-inch Betacam format.

magazine   A removable container that holds fresh or exposed film.

magic hour   The time between sundown and darkness when the quality of light has an especially "magic" or warm quality—twilight.

magnetic film (mag)   Audiotape with sprocket holes and the same size as production film. It is used in the editing process to cut audio.

magnetic sound   Sound derived from an electrical audio signal recorded on a magnetic oxide stripe or on full-coated magnetic tape.

master license   License to use a specific recording. This name refers to the fact that you are licensing the master recording of a song.

master shot   Usually a long shot in which all action in a scene takes place. Action is repeated for the medium shot and closeup, which may be cut into the same scene.

master tape   The tape to which other material will be added during videotape editing.

match cut   A cut made between two different angles of the same action using the subject's movement as the transition.

matte   An opaque outline that limits the exposed area of a picture, either as a cutout object in front of the camera or as a silhouette on another strip of film. In video, it is a form of key.

meal penalties   A fine levied against the production to pay additional money to actors who were not allowed to eat at the prescribed break time.

medium shot   A scene that is photographed from a medium distance so that the full figure of the subject fills an entire frame.

MIDI   Musical instrument digital interface; the interface responsible for the translation of musical information into digital terms.

mise-en-scène   The totality of lighting, blocking, camera use, and composition that produces the dramatic image on film.

mix   To combine the various sound tracks—dialogue, music, and sound effects—into a single track.

mix cue sheet   A list of all dialogue, effects, and music cues for a sound mix. Mix cue sheets are organized sequentially for each sound track.

mixer   (1) Circuitry capable of mixing two or more sound inputs to one output. (2) The audio console at which mixing is done. (3) The person who does the mixing.

moire   In video, a beating pattern produced by harmonic distortion of the FM signal.

MOS   Short for "Mit out sound," which is what German directors in Hollywood called for when they intended to shoot silent.

motion control   A computer-assisted camera and rig with multiple moving axes, enabling high precision, repeatable camera moves.

MPEG (Moving Picture Experts Group)   A group set up to standardize compression techniques for digitally storing moving images, digital audio, and audio/video synchronization. It is a lossy compression method.

multitrack   An audiotape with multiple tracks or an audiotape recorder/player capable of accessing multiple audio tracks.

Murphy's Law   The observation that "anything that can go wrong will go wrong."

music clearance   Obtaining the permissions necessary to use specific preexisting pieces of music in a film.

music cue sheet   A list of all music cues and timings for the picture to be used for royalties and publishing.

music publisher   An entity that manages a song and collects money for the writer from the royalties derived from its exploitation.

Mylar™   A polyester film used as the base for magnetic tape. Mylar is the base of magnetic film (mag), quarter-inch audiotape, and videotape.

Nagra   Brand name of a quarter-inch audiotape recorder/player used in film production audio recording.

narration   The off-screen commentary for a film. Also known as *voice-over (VO)*.

narrowcast   To transmit data to selected individuals.

needle-drop fees   One means by which royalty payments for music library selections are made. A fixed fee is charged each time a phonographic needle is dropped on a particular recording—that is, each time it is played.

negative cost   The amount of money required to complete the film or video.

negative cutting   The process of conforming camera original negative to the editor's fine-cut work print.

neutral-density filter   A filter that is gray in color and affects all colors equally. It is used to reduce the amount of light passing through the lens without affecting color.

NLE Non-linear editing.

noise Distortions in a signal, such as "snow" in video and "hiss" in audio, which are created by multiple-generation duplication.

nondrop frame timecode SMPTE timecode format that continuously counts a full 30 frames per second. Since video runs at 29.97 fps, nondrop frame is not coincident with real time.

nonlinear A term used to describe editing systems that are capable of working out of sequence or in a random manner, as in film editing.

NTSC (National Television Standards Committee) The American color television standard system, which defines video as having 525 interlaced scan lines per frame, a frame rate of approximately 30 frames per second (30 fps at nondrop frame and 29.97 at drop-frame), and a 60 Hz transmission standard.

offline edit Preliminary postproduction session, used to establish editing points and to prepare an edit decision list. Compare to online edit.

OMF (Open Media Framework) It is a format for file compatibility to fully describe all relationships between source material and effects.

omnidirectional Responsive to sound from all directions.

180°-axis-of-action rule A means of camera placement that ensures continuity and consistency in the placement and movement of objects from shot to shot.

online edit Final editing session, the stage of postproduction in which a edited master tape is assembled from the original production footage, usually under the direction of the edit decision list. Compare **offline edit**.

on-screen sound A sound emanating from a source that is visible within the frame.

optical Any visual device, such as a fade, dissolve, wipe, iris wipe, ripple dissolve, matte, or superimposition, prepared with an optical printer in a laboratory or online for video.

optical printer A printer that is used when the image size of the print film is different from the image size of the preprint film or when effects such as skip frames, blowups, zooms, and mattes are included.

optical sound A system in which the photographic (optical) sound track on a film is scanned by a horizontal slit beam of light that modulates a photoelectric cell. The voltages generated by the cell produce audio signals that are amplified to operate screen speakers.

optical track Sound track in which the sound recorded takes the form of density variations (variable-density track) or width variations (variable-area track) in a photographic image.

option The exclusive right to purchase something in the future, on fixed terms and conditions.

original negative The film negative that was exposed in the camera. Also called camera original.

out-point End point of an edit.

outtake A take of a scene that is not used for printing or final assembly in editing.

overexposure The result of a purposeful or accidental allowance of excess light onto each frame of film giving the image a pale, washed-out look.

over-the-shoulder shot A shot in which a camera is placed behind and to the side of an actor, so that the actor's shoulder appears in the foreground and the face or body of another appears in the background. This type of shot tends to establish a specific subject's physical point of view on the action.

overtime Additional salary that is paid if someone is asked to work longer than his or her contracted hours.

oxide Metallic coating on videotape that is magnetized during the recording process.

PA See **production assistant**.

pace A subjective impression of the speed of the sounds or visuals.

painting Adjusting the color controls on a video camera or a telecine system.

PAL (phase alternating line) A color TV standard used in many countries consisting of 625 lines scanned at a rate of 25 frames per second. Compare to NTSC color video standard.

pan A camera move in which the camera on a fluid head appears to move horizontally or vertically, usually to follow the action or to scan a scene. In animation, the effect is achieved by moving the artwork under the camera.

paper edit Preparing a rough edit decision list made by screening original material, but without actually performing cuts.

performing rights society (BMI and ASCAP) An organization that monitors the performance of music and collects royalties due the songwriter from performance on film, radio and television, in restaurants, lounges, bars, hotels, and so on.

perspective The technique of representing three-dimensional objects and depth relationships on a two-dimensional surface.

pistol grip A handheld camera mount.

pixel   The smallest unit of a reproduced image. Short for picture element.

pixillation   The frame by frame movement of an object in a live action setting.

playback   Previously recorded music or vocals to be used on the set for the actors to perform to or mime. Playback is used when filming songs (music videos), instrumental performances, or dance.

playback head   A magnetic device that is capable of transforming magnetic changes on a prerecorded tape into electrical signals.

plot   (1) The plan of events or the main story in a narrative or drama. (2) The arrangement of incidents and logic of causality in a story. The plot should act as a vehicle for the thematic intention of the piece.

point-of-view (POV) shot   A shot in which the camera is placed in the approximate position of a specific character. It is often preceded by a shot of a character looking in a particular direction and is followed by a shot of the character's reaction to what he or she has seen. The last shot is sometimes called a **reaction shot**.

pot   A dial that can be rotated to increase or decrease the sound level. The term is short for potentiometer.

POV shot   See **point-of-view shot**.

practical light   A source lighting instrument on the set, such as a floor or table lamp, that appears in the frame.

prerig   To set up the lighting instruments based on a lighting plan devised by the director of photography a day or two before the shoot date. Prerigging can be done by a "swing crew" the night before the shoot.

preroll   Process of rewinding videotapes to a predetermined cue point, so the tapes are stabilized and up to speed when they reach the edit point.

presence   A recorded sound track from the location used to fill sound gaps in editing.

prime lens   A fixed focal length lens, as opposed to a zoom lens, which has a variable focal length.

production assistant   An inexperienced crew member who floats from department to department, depending on which area needs help the most. Duties can range from running for coffee or holding parking spaces to setting up lights and slating.

production supervisor   An assistant to the producer. The production supervisor is in charge of routine administrative duties.

prosthetic makeup   Makeup and latex pieces designed to transform the appearance of a performer's face or body. Examples include a long nose for Cyrano or stitches and a big head for Frankenstein's creature.

protection copy   Duplicate of the edited master reel, kept as a backup in case the master is damaged.

proximity effect   A poor-quality audio transmission caused by having the microphone too close to the sound source.

public domain   Literally, "owned by the public." A property to which no individual or corporation owns the copyright.

pull-down claw   The metallic finger that advances the film one frame between exposure cycles.

punch tape   A paper punch record of videotape edit decisions for a computer or for printing commands in film printing.

quantization   In digital recording, the amplitude value of the analog signal at the instant of sampling, rated in binary bits per sample. For example: 8 bits/sample = 28 = 256 increments of measurements per sample period.

QuickTime™   A set of operating extensions to the Macintosh Computer platform that allows Macintosh computers to display time-dependent media such as video, audio, and animation and to combine these media with time-independent media such as text and graphics.

rack focus   A focus that shifts between foreground and background during a shot to prompt or accommodate an attention shift (a figure enters a door at the back of the room, for instance).

random access memory (RAM)   Computer memory system that allows users to store and retrieve information rapidly.

raster   Area of the TV picture tube that is scanned by the electron beam. Also, the visual display present on a TV picture screen.

raw stock   Unexposed and unprocessed motion picture film, including camera original, laboratory intermediate, duplicating, and release-print stocks.

reaction shot   A closeup of a character's reaction to events.

reference white   A white card or large white object in the frame that can be used for white balance or the proper color adjustment in video.

reflected light   Light that has been bounced or reflected from objects, as opposed to direct or incident light.

reflected reading   A light meter reading of the intensity of light reflected by the subject or background.

reflector   Any surface that reflects light.

registration   The steadiness of the film image in the gate or aperture.

release   A statement giving permission to use an actor's face or likeness. It also releases a producer from future legal action, such as for slander or libel. It is signed by people appearing in a video program or film who are not professional performers.

release print   In a motion picture processing laboratory, any of numerous duplicate prints of a subject made for distribution.

rendering   When an effect is desired that cannot be accomplished in real time, the entire effect, or a portion of it, must be recorded to disk or RAM in order to see the effect play in real time.

research   (1) To study something thoroughly so as to present it in a detailed, accurate manner. (2) The process of uncovering sources of information about a prospective video or film topic or audience.

residuals   A payment made to a performer, writer, or director for each repeat showing of a recorded television show or commercial.

resolution   The amount and degree of detail in a film or video image.

reticle   A grid or pattern placed in the camera viewfinder used to establish scale or position. See **TV safe**.

reversal film   Film that is processed to a positive image after exposure in a camera or in a printer to produce another positive film. See also **color reversal film**.

RGB   The primary colors: red, green, and blue.

room tone   The natural acoustical ambience of the area around which the scene is shot. Room tone can later be mixed with the dialogue to smooth cuts and create a more realistic presence of a space.

rough cut   A preliminary stage in film editing in which shots, scenes, and sequences are laid out in the correct approximate order, without detailed attention to the individual cutting points.

royalty fees   Money paid to composers, authors, performers, and so on for the use of copyrighted materials.

rushes   Unedited raw footage as it appears after shooting. Also called **dailies**.

S-video   The S-video signal is one in which the luminance channel is separated from the chrominance signals, but unlike component analog, the chrominance signals are not separate.

SAG   The acronym for the Screen Actors Guild. The SAG contract also covers members of Equity (stage actors), AGVA (Variety members), and AFTRA (television actors).

sampling frequency   In digital recording, the number of times per second that an analog signal is examined. For example: 13.5 MHz = 13.5 million times per second.

saturation   Amount of color in the television picture.

scale   The base union wage.

scanning   The process by which a video signal is converted into an image that is displayed on the inner surface of a cathode ray gun. A stream of electrons emitted by an electron gun within a tube precisely traces this inner surface in a pattern of horizontal lines, illuminating phosphors coating the inner surface and creating the image.

score   Music composed for a specific film or videotape.

scratch mix   A preliminary or trial mixing of sounds against picture.

scrim   A translucent material that reduces, like a screen, the intensity of the light without changing its character.

script supervisor   The person who maintains the continuity in performer actions and prop placements from shot to shot and who ensures that every scene in the script has been recorded.

SCSI   Small computer systems interface. Common hardware and software method for connecting computers and peripheral devices. (Pronounced "scuzzy.")

SDTV   Standard definition television.

SECAM (Sequential Couleur à Mémoire)   A TV standard developed by the French and used primarily in France, Russia, and Eastern Europe. Like PAL, SECAM has a normal playback of 25 fps with a similar scan rate.

setup   The combination of lens, camera placement, and composition to produce a particular shot.

SFX   See **sound effects**.

shading   Adjusting the brightness level, light sensitivity, and color of a video camera.

shock-mounted microphone   A microphone that is designed to minimize all vibrations and noise except those inherent in sound waves.

shooting ratio   The ratio of the material recorded during production to that which is actually used in the final edited version.

shooting script   The approved final version of the script with scene numbers, camera setups, and other instructions by the director.

shot   An unbroken filmed segment; the basic component of a scene.

shotgun microphone   See **ultracardioid microphone**.

shutter   An opaque device in a film camera that rapidly opens and closes to expose the film to light.

sides   Part of a scene given to actors to read during an audition.

signal-to-noise ratio   The ratio of desired to undesired sound, the latter of which usually comes from equipment or tape noise.

silhouette   An outline that appears dark against a light background.

slating   The process of placing, at the beginning or end of a shot, a common reference point for separate but synchronous film images and sounds as well as an identification of the recorded material. See also **tail slate**.

slaved timecode   Timecode that is taken from a source videotape and fed into a timecode generator, which replaces the source code.

slop print   See **dirty dupe**.

slow motion   The process of photographing a subject at a faster frame rate than used in projection to expand the time element.

smart slate   An electronic slate used in film production that displays an LED readout of the sound reel timecode. This allows the film to be quickly synchronized with the sound reel during the telecine transfer.

SMPTE   Society of Motion Picture and Television Engineers, the organization responsible for defining standards and specifications for the motion picture and broadcast industry including SMPTE timecode, NTSC, HDTV, and so on; www.smpte.org.

SMPTE timecode   A binary timecode denoting hours, minutes, seconds, and frames that was standardized by the Society of Motion Picture and Television Engineers.

snip book   A notebook used to store trims without identifiable edge code numbers.

soft cut   A very short dissolve.

soft light   Light made up of soft, scattered rays resulting in soft, less clearly defined shadows. Also known as *diffuse light*.

sound effects (SFX)   Any sound from any source other than the tracks bearing synchronized dialogue, narration, or music. The sound effects track is commonly introduced into a master track during rerecording, usually with the idea of enhancing the illusion of reality in the finished presentation.

sound gain   An adjustment to control the sound recording level.

sound speed   The reference to running film or tape at standard speed for any format: film is run at 24 fps, NTSC at approximately 30 fps (29.97), PAL at 25 fps.

specular light   See **hard light**.

split diopter   A special filter placed on a camera lens that allows portions of the frame to remain in focus, even though they are beyond the lens's depth of field.

splits   A shooting period that consists of half a day and half a night of principal photography.

spotlight   A lighting unit, usually with a lens and a shiny metal reflector, that is capable of being focused and produces hard light.

spot reading   A light-meter reading of the intensity of the light reflected by the subject in a very narrow area, as determined by the angle of acceptance of the spot meter.

spotting   The process of viewing a film or video in order to accurately locate the start and stop points for music, sound effects, ADR, and narration.

spreaders   A bracket system for placing pipe or two-by-four lumber to act as a lighting instrument grid.

sprocket   A toothed wheel used to move the perforated motion picture film.

spun glass   A flexible light diffuser made out of fiberglass.

staging   The process of planning how the action of a scene will take place.

stand-in   Someone who takes the place of an actor during setup or for shots that involve special skills, such as horse riding or fight scenes.

Steadicam®   A registered trademark for a servostabilizer camera mount attached to the operator's body to minimize camera vibrations when the operator moves with the camera.

Steinbeck™   Brand name of a flatbed film editing machine.

sting   A musical accent to heighten a dramatic moment.

stock   The physical recording medium on which an image or sound is recorded.

storyboard   Semidetailed drawings of what each shot will look like; similar to a multipanel cartoon.

streaming   A technique for transferring data (audio and video) such that it can be processed as a steady and continuous "stream."

stripboard   A scheduling device. Each shot is represented by a strip of cardboard on which is encoded all the pertinent breakdown information. The strips are put in the desired order of shooting and are affixed to a multipanel stripboard. This board can then be carried to the set in the event that adjustments need to be made in the schedule.

subjective point of view   A story told from the perspective of a specific character or participant in the action.

subjective shot   A presentation of images supposedly dreamed, imagined, recollected, or perceived in an abnormal state of mind by a character or participant in a videotape or film.

subtext   The underlying personality of a dramatic character as implied or indicated by a script or text and as interpreted by an actor in performance.

sun gun   A high-intensity, portable, battery-powered light. It is usually used for news or documentary work.

supercardioid microphone   A microphone with a highly directional pickup pattern.

superimposition   Two images occupying the entire frame at the same time. Normally, one image is dominant and the other subordinate during a superimposition to avoid visual confusion. The more detailed the images, the less clear and visually pleasing the superimposition is likely to be.

super objective   The overarching thematic purpose of the director's dramatic interpretation.

S-VHS   A technical improvement over VHS home video format. An S-video half-inch format that is comparable with Hi-8.

sweetening process   Process of mixing sound effects, music, and narration with the edited master's audio track. Also called audio postproduction for video.

swing crew   A team of gaffers or grips that sets the stage, lights, or both for a big or complicated sequence before the main production unit arrives.

swish pan   A rapid turning of the camera on the tripod axis, causing blurring of the image. A swish pan can be used as a transition device between scenes.

switcher   A video editing device that controls which picture and sound sources are transmitted or recorded. It can be used during multiple-camera production or during postproduction.

symmetrical compression   A compression technique that requires an equal amount of processing power to compress and decompress an image. This is important because, in applications designed for editing, the compression of a frame must occur in real time. Decompression of that same frame must also occur in real time.

sync   Maintaining the corresponding relationship between sound track and picture. In video, the coordination of the vertical and horizontal blanking pulses with the electron beam of a television or camera so that the picture remains stable both horizontally and vertically.

synch rights   The rights to record music to be heard as a part of a film.

synchronizer   A film editing device that maintains several picture and sound tracks in sync during the editing process.

T-grain™   A trademarked film and development process of the Eastman Kodak company. The T-grain is a grain of silver halide that is rectangular rather than globular, presenting a wider, flatter surface that provides thinner emulsion and more sensitivity.

t-stop   A calibrating system for determining how much light a lens transmits to a film. Unlike f-stop calibration, which measures transmitted light only as a factor of the lens aperture, the t-stop system uses both aperture dimensions and factors of lens absorption and reflection to determine the actual amount of light that will fall on the film. T-stops offer a more accurate number.

tail slate   A sync mark used when a scene begins in action or from an extreme closeup, making it difficult to slate from the beginning. After the director has called "Cut," the slate is clapped, upside down, to give the editor a sync mark.

take   A photographic record of each repetition of a scene. A particular scene might be photographed more than once in an effort to get a perfect recording of some special action.

TBC   See **time-base corrector**.

telecine system   An optical/electronic system for transferring film to videotape. Also known as a *film chain*.

telephoto lens   A long-focal-length lens that foreshortens the apparent distance between foreground and background objects.

telescope story   A script or editing device used to make a leap in time.

tent   (1) A tent of heavy black velour drapery that can be rigged around a window to allow a sequence shot during the day to simulate night. (2) A box built outside a window that is draped but allows enough room to place a light outside the window, permitting a constant light source to appear through the window.

theme   (1) A central concept, idea, or symbolic meaning in a story. (2) A repeated melody in a symphony or long musical composition.

three- or four-point lighting   A basic lighting technique that helps create an illusion of three-dimensionality by separating the subject from the background, using key, fill, and separation lights.

three stripe   The magnetic 35-mm film on which the sound is mixed together. This full-coat mag has three tracks: one for dialogue, one for sound effects, and one for music. Should a track need to be replaced—

to make a foreign dub, for example—the remaining two tracks will be undisturbed.

3:2 pull-down (2:3) Telecine method of converting 24-fps film to 30 fps video by transferring each film frame at an alternating rate of two video fields, then three video fields.

tilt The process of swiveling the camera in a vertical arc, such as tilting it up and down to show the height of a flagpole.

time-base corrector (TBC) Electronic device used to correct signal instability during the playback of videotape material.

timecode A frame monitoring system that provides an exact numerical reference for each frame of film or videotape. Timecode is divided into hours, minutes, seconds, and frames.

timing A laboratory process that involves balancing the color of a film to achieve consistency from scene to scene.

title search A legal process whereby it is determined whether a show title is available for use.

tracking Speed and angle at which the tape passes the video heads.

trims The unused pieces of film cut out of a scene. They are labeled and stored throughout postproduction until the final prints are struck. In video, trimming means subtracting or adding frames from an edit point.

trompe l'oeil A style of painting, sometimes used in interior decorating, in which objects are depicted with photographically realistic detail.

turnaround The time between ending one day's work and beginning the next day's.

turret A pivoted plate that allows a choice of lenses to be swung rapidly into position.

TV safe The innermost frame outline in the viewfinder is called *TV safe*, or the area that will be seen when screened on a television monitor. Elements outside this frame line may be missed. See **reticle**.

Tyler mount A helicopter or airplane camera mount that reduces vibrations.

ultracardioid microphone A microphone with the most directional (narrowest) pickup pattern available. Also known as a *shotgun microphone*.

underlying rights The foundational rights that you must control to have the right to make and distribute a film based on a script that is based on an underlying property (such as a novel, short story, play, or true story).

upconversion The process of converting lower resolution video to higher resolution video.

variable-speed motor An electric drive motor for a film camera whose speed can be varied and controlled.

VCR (videocassette recorder) Usually referring to a tape machine that only accepts cassettes. An open reel machine is often referred to as a VTR.

vectorscope A special oscilloscope used to monitor hue and color saturation in video signals.

vertical interval timecode (VITC) Timecode that is inserted in the vertical blanking interval of a video signal. The vertical blanking interval is the period during which the TV picture goes blank as the electron beam returns (retraces) from scanning one field of video to begin scanning the next.

video assist A video camera attached to a film camera for instant dailies, allowing the shot to be immediately judged on playback. Also known as *video tap*.

video gain An adjustment to control the picture recording level.

video tap See **video assist**.

video-to-film transfer Copying a videotape on film. Also known as **kinescoping**.

viewfinder An eyepiece or screen through which a camera operator sees the image being recorded. See also **reticle**.

visualization The creative process of transforming a script into a sequence of visual images and sounds.

visual timeline Computer display of the edit decision list as a series of stacked bars representing video and separate audio channels running horizontally across the screen.

VO Voice-over. See **narration**.

VT Videotape. Oxide-coated, plastic-based magnetic tape used for recording video and audio signals.

VTC Visual timecode burned into the lower part of the frame for a visual frame accurate reference.

VTR Videotape recorder.

VU meter A device that measures audio levels.

waveform monitor A type of test equipment used to display and analyze video signal information.

wedge test When making an optical, a test is done in which the elements of the optical (lap dissolves, superimposition, mattes) are photographed with one frame of each f-stop. When the test film is developed, the laboratory can identify the exact exposure reading that will produce the best effect.

whip pan A very fast panning movement. Also called a **swish pan**.

white balance Electronic adjustments to render a white object as white on screen.

wide-angle lens   A lens with a wide angle of acceptance. Its effect is to increase the apparent distance between foreground and background objects.

wild   (1) Picture shot without a synchronous relationship to sound. (2) Sound shot without a synchronous relationship to picture.

wild sound   Sound that does not have a synchronous picture or recordings of sound effects that are available on the location and may be hard to either obtain or create at a later time.

windowdupe   Copy of an original master recording that features character-generated timecode numbers inserted in the picture.

windscreen   A porous cover that protects a microphone's diaphragm from air currents.

wipe   Special effect transition in which a margin or border moves across the screen, wiping out the image of one scene and replacing it with another.

wireless/radio microphone   A cordless microphone that transmits its output to a recorder via a receiver.

work print   A print derived from the original negative to be used in the editing process to establish, through a series of trial cuttings, the finished version of the film. The negative is later conformed to the work print when a final cut is achieved.

wrangler   An animal trainer and supervisor.

wrap   The period at the end of a day of shooting during which the crew must store the equipment.

Y/C (or pseudo-component)   Symbol for luminance separated from chroma (color) information; a type of recording used in S-VHS and Hi-8. Also called **S-video**.

zoetrope   An optical toy with a series of pictures on the inner surface of a cylinder. When the pictures are rotated and viewed through a slit, the toy gives the impression that the pictures are moving. This device, a precursor to film projection, was a popular form of entertainment in the 19th century.

zoom lens   A lens whose focal length varies between wide and telephoto.

Bibliography/Software/Internet

ACTING

Hagan, Uta, with Haskel Frankel. *Respect for Acting.* New York: Macmillan, 1973.

Meisner, Sandford, and Dennis Longwell. *Sandford Meisner on Acting.* New York: Vantage Books, 1987.

Moore, Sonia. *The Stanislauski System.* New York: Viking Press, 1965.

Podovkin, V. *Film Technique and Film Acting.* New York: Grove Press, 1982.

Stanislauski, Constantin. *An Actor Prepares.* New York: Theater Arts, 1948.

Stanislauski, Constantin. *Building a Character.* New York: Theater Arts, 1981.

Young, Jeff. *The Master Director Discusses His Films* (Interviews with Elia Kazan by Jeff Young). New York: Newmarket Press, 1999.

ANIMATION

Blair, Preston. *Animation and How to Animate Film Cartoons.* New York: Walter Foster, 1989.

Canemaker, John. *Felix: The Twisted Tale of the World's Most Famous Cat.* New York: Abbeville Press, 1987.

Canemaker, John. *Paper Dreams: The Art & Artists of Disney Storyboards.* New York: Hyperion, 1999.

Layborne, Kit. *The Animation Book.* New York: Three Rivers Press, 1998.

Solomon, Charles. *The Complete Kodak Animation Book.* Rochester, NY: Eastman Kodak Co., 1983.

White, Tony. *The Animator's Workbook.* New York: Phaidow Press, 1986.

CAMERA

Almendros, Nestor. *Man with a Camera.* New York: Simon & Schuster, 1985.

Carlson, Verne, and Sylvia Carlson. *Professional Lighting Handbook.* Boston: Focal Press, 1985.

Clarke, Charles G., ed. *American Cinematographer's Handbook.* Hollywood: American Society of Cinematographers, 1993.

Elkins, David. *The Camera Assistant's Manual*, 3rd ed. Boston: Focal Press, 2000.

Fielding, Ray. *The Technique of Special Effects Cinematography*, 4th ed. New York: Hastings House, 1985.

Malkiewicz, Kris J. *Cinematography: A Guide for Filmmakers and Film Teachers*, 2nd ed. New York: Prentice-Hall, 1989.

Millerson, Gerald. *The Technique of Lighting for Television and Motion Pictures*, 2nd ed. Boston: Focal Press, 1982.

Samuelson, David. *Motion Picture Camera Data.* London: Focal Press, 1979.

Schaffer, D., and A. Ritsko. *Masters of Light.* Berkeley and Los Angeles: University of California Press, 1984.

CRAFTS

Baker, Patsy. *Wigs and Make-up for Theatre, TV and Film.* Boston: Focal Press, 1992.

Dunn, Linwood G. *The ASC Treasury of Visual Effects.* Hollywood: American Society of Cinematographers, 1983.

Kehoe, Vincent J-R. *Special Make-up Effects.* Boston: Focal Press, 1991.

LoBrutto, Vincent. *By Design.* Westport, CT: Praeger, 1992.

Maier, Robert. *Location Scouting and Management Handbook: Television, Film, and Still Photography.* Boston: Focal Press, 1994.

Miller, Pat P. *Script Supervision and Film Continuity*, 2nd ed. Boston: Focal Press, 1990.

Olson, Robert. *Art Direction for Film and Television.* London: Focal Press, 1993.

Preston, Ward. *What an Art Director Does*. Silman James Press, 1994.

DIRECTING

Bare, Richard L. *The Film Director*. New York: Collier, 1971.

Buñuel, Luis. *My Last Breath*. London: Flamingo Press, 1986.

Caine, Michael. *Acting in Film: An Actor's Take on Moviemaking*. (Videocassette) New York: Applause Theater Book Publishers, 1990.

Clurman, Harold. *On Directing*. New York: Macmillan, 1974.

Katz, Steven D. *Film Directing: Shot by Shot*. Studio City, CA: Michael Wiese Productions, 1991.

Kurosawa, Akira. *Something Like an Autobiography*. New York: Vintage Books, 1983.

Lumet, Sidney. *Making Movies*. New York: Alfred E. Knopf, 1995.

Mamet, David. *On Directing*. New York: Viking Press, 1991.

Nilsen, Vladimir. *The Cinema as Graphic Art*. New York: Hill & Wang, 1985. Foreword by S. M. Eisenstein.

Rabiger, Michael. *Directing, Film Techniques and Aesthetics*, 2nd ed. Boston: Focal Press, 1997.

Travis, Mark W. *The Director's Journey*. Michael Wiese Productions, 1997.

Truffaut, François. *Hitchcock*. New York: Simon & Schuster, 1967.

Weston, Judith. *Crafting Memorable Performances for Film and Television*. Studio City, CA: Michael Wiese Productions, 2001.

DISTRIBUTION

Bowser, Kathryn. *The AIVF Guide to International Film and Video Festivals*, 3rd ed. New York: Foundation for Independent Video and Film, 1992.

Council on International Nontheatrical Events. *The Worldwide Directory of Film and Video Festivals and Events*, 4th ed. New York: Council on International Nontheatrical Events, 1993–1994.

Franco, Debra. *Alternative Visions: Distributing Independent Media in a Home Video World*. Los Angeles, Washington, DC, and New York: American Institute Press, 1990.

Gagney, Alan E. *Gagney's Guide to 1800 International Contests*. Glendale, CA: Festival Publications, 1993.

Reichert, Julia. *Doing It Yourself: A Handbook on Independent Film Distribution*. New York: Association of Independent Video and Filmmakers, 1977.

Warshawski, Morrie, ed. *The Next Step: Distributing Independent Films and Videos*. New York: Foundation for Independent Video and Film, 1995.

Wiese, Michael. *Film and Video Marketing*. Studio City, CA: Michael Wiese Productions, 1989.

DOCUMENTARIES

Baddeley, W. Hugh. *The Technique of Documentary Film Production*, 4th ed. New York: Hastings House, 1975.

Ivens, Joris. *The Camera and I*. Cambridge, MA: MIT Press, 1969.

Rabiger, Michael. *Directing the Documentary*. Boston: Focal Press, 1987.

Rosenthal, Alan. *Writing, Directing, and Producing Documentary Films*. Carbondale and Edwardsville: Southern Illinois University Press, 1990.

EDITING

Dmytryk, Edward. *On Film Editing*. Boston: Focal Press, 1984.

Hollyn, Norman. *The Film Editing Room Handbook*, 2nd ed. Los Angeles: Lone Eagle, 1990.

LoBrutto, Vincent. *Selected Takes. Film Editors on Editing*. New York: Praeger, 1991.

Maitland, Ian. *Film Editing Glossary*. Dubuque, IA: Kendal/Hunt, 1990.

Murch, Walter. *In the Blink of an Eye*. Los Angeles: Silman James Press, 1995.

Ohanian, Thomas A. *Digital Nonlinear Editing*. Boston: Focal Press, 1992.

Oldam, Gabriella. *First Cut: Conversations with Film Editors*. Los Angeles: University of California Press, 1995

Reisz, Karel, and Gavin Millar. *The Technique of Film Editing*. Boston: Focal Press, 1968.

Rosenblum, R., and Robert Karen. *When the Shooting Stops . . . the Cutting Begins*. New York: Da Capo Press, 1979.

Rubin, Michael. *Nonlinear: A Guide to Electronic Film and Video Editing*, 2nd ed. Gainesville, FL: Triad, 1991.

Solomons, Tony. *The Avid Digital Editing Room Handbook*, 2nd ed. Los Angeles: Silman James Press, 1999.

FILM AND VIDEO BASICS

Adams, William B. *The Handbook of Motion Picture Production*. New York: John Wiley & Sons, 1977.

Pincus, Edward, and Steven Ascher. *The Filmmaker's Handbook*, revised ed. New York: New American Library, Plume, 1999.

Wiese, Michael. *The Independent Film and Videomaker's Guide*, revised ed. Boston: Focal Press, 1990.

Wilson, Anton. *Cinema Workshop: The Basics of Film and Video from the American Cinematographer*, revised ed. Hollywood: ASC Holding Corp., 1983.

GRANTS

The Foundation Center (site for Grants), fdcenter.org.

Gibbs, Lissa, ed. *National Alliance for Media Arts and Culture Member Directory*. Beverly Hills: NAMAC, 1992.

Niemeyer, Suzanne. *Money for Film and Video Artists*. New York: American Council for the Arts/Allworth Press, 1991.

Renz, Loren, ed. *The Foundation Directory*, 11th ed. New York: Foundation Center, 1987.

Warshawski, Morrie. *Shaking the Money Tree: How to Get Grants and Donations for Film and Video*. Hollywood: Michael Wiese Productions, 1994.

THE INDUSTRY

Behlmer, Rudy, ed. *Memo from David O. Selznick*. New York: The Viking Press, 1972.

Capra, Frank. *The Name Above the Title*. New York: The Macmillan Company, 1971.

Eaker, Sherry, ed. *The Back Stage Handbook for Performing Artists*, revised and enlarged ed. New York: Watson-Guptill, Back Stage Books, 1991.

Kindem, Gorham, ed. *The American Movie Industry: The Business of Motion Pictures*. Carbondale and Edwardsville: Southern Illinois University Press, 1982.

Litwak, Mark. *Reel Power*. New York: William Morrow, 1986.

Mayer, Michael F. *The Film Industries: Practical Business/Legal Problems in Production, Distribution and Exhibition*. New York: Hastings House, 1978.

Squires, Jason. *The Movie Business Book*. New York: Simon & Schuster, Touchstone, 1983.

Vogel, Harold L. *Entertainment Industry Economics*. New York: Cambridge University Press, 1986.

PRODUCTION

Baumgarten, Paul, Donald Farber, and Mark Fleisher. *Producing, Financing and Distributing Film*, revised and updated ed. New York: Limelight, 1992.

Behlmer, Rudy, ed. *Memo from David O. Selznick*. New York: Viking Press, 1972.

Chamness, Danford. *The Hollywood Guide to Film Budgeting and Script Breakdown for Low Budget Features*, 5th ed. Hollywood: Stanley J. Brooks, 1988.

Curran, Trisha. *Financing Your Film: A Guide for Independent Film Producers*. Westport, CT: Praeger, 1985.

Davies, Sally. *The Independent Producer: Film and Television*. London: Hourcourt, Howlett, Davies, Moskovic, Faber & Faber, 1986.

Goodell, Gregory. *Independent Feature Film Production: A Complete Guide from Concept through Distribution*. New York: St. Martin's, 1982.

Gregory, Mollie. *Making Films Your Business*. New York: Schocken Books, 1979.

Singleton, Ralph S. *Film Scheduling: Or, How Long Will It Take to Shoot Your Movie?* 2nd ed. Los Angeles: Lone Eagle, 1991.

Singleton, Ralph S. *The Film Scheduling/Film Budgeting Workbook*. Los Angeles: Lone Eagle, 1984.

Wiese, Michael. *Film and Video Budgets*, 2nd ed. Boston: Michael Wiese Productions/Focal Press, 1995.

Wiese, Michael. *Film and Video Financing*. Boston: Michael Wiese Productions/Focal Press, 1991.

REFERENCES

Brook's Standard Rate Book. Los Angeles: Stanley J. Brooks, 1994. [Union rates and rules.] (310) 470–2849.

Capogrosso, Eric, ed. *The 1994/95 Industry Labor Guide*. Los Angeles: Industry Labor Guide Publishing Co., 1993.

Detmers, Fred, ed. *American Cinematographer Manual*. Hollywood: ASC Press, 1986.

Donaldson, Michael C. *Clearance & Copyright, Everything the Independent Filmmaker Needs to Know*. Los Angeles: Silman-James Press, 1996.

Gore, Chris. *The Ultimate Film Festival Survival Guide*, 3rd ed. Los Angeles: Lone Eagle Publishing, 1999.

Konigsberg, Ira. *The Complete Film Dictionary*, 2nd ed. London: Meridian, 1997.

The New York Production Manual. New York: Producer's Masterguide, 1994.

Production Boards and Strips: For Features and Television. Los Angeles: Stanley J. Brooks, 1991.

Singleton, Ralph. *Filmmaker's Dictionary.* Los Angeles: Lone Eagle, 1986.

SOUND

Alten, Stanley R. *Audio in Media*, 3rd ed. Belmont, CA: Wadsworth, 1981.

Anderson, Craig. *MIDI for Musicians.* New York: Amsco Publications, 1986.

Bell, David. *Getting the Best Score for Your Film.* Silman James Press, 1994.

Carlin, Dan, Sr. *Music in Film and Video Production.* Boston: Focal Press, 1991.

Karlin, Fred, and Rayburn Wright. *On the Track: A Guide to Contemporary Film Scoring.* New York: Schirmer Books, 1990.

Kerner, Marvin M. *The Art of the Sound Effects Editor.* Boston: Focal Press, 1989.

LoBrutto, Vincent. *Sound-on-Film. Interviews with Creators of Film Sound.* Praeger, 1994.

Mott, Robert L. *Sound Effects: Radio, TV and Film.* Boston: Focal Press, 1990.

Nisbett, Alec. *The Technique of the Sound Studio*, 4th ed. Boston: Focal Press, 1979.

Nisbett, Alec. *The Use of Microphones*, 3rd ed. Boston: Focal Press, 1990.

Pendergast, Roy M. *Film Music: A Neglected Art*, 2nd ed. New York: W.W. Norton, 1992.

Sonnenschein, David. *The Expressive Power of Music, Voice and Sound Effects in Cinema.* Boston: Michael Wiese Productions, 2001.

Thomas, Tony. *Music for the Movies.* South Brunswick, NJ: A.S. Barnes, 1973.

Weis, Elisabeth, and John Belton, eds. *Film Sound: Theory and Practice.* New York: Columbia University Press, 1985.

Yewdall, David Lewis. *Practical Art of Motion Picture Sound.* Boston: Focal Press, 1999.

Online Sound Libraries

Many Web sites are dedicated to sound effects and music. Many offer royalty-free effects and music.

Sounddogs.com is one of the largest online sound effects libraries on the Internet.

SoundFX.com distributes the Sound Effects Libraries, Music Libraries, and Pro-Audio Software worldwide.

Soundrangers.com was created to fulfill the sonic needs of a new technological generation. It specialize in generating state-of-the-art, royalty-free sound effects and music for such high-tech platforms as virtual user interfaces, games, online and CD-ROM entertainment, Web sites, and communication devices.

Soundsonline.com is a source for professional, copyright-cleared, royalty-free sounds in the industry offering more than 1,000 virtual instruments and sound libraries to choose from.

VIDEO

Beacham, Frank. *American Cinematographer Video Manual.* Hollywood: American Society of Cinematographers Press, 1994.

Huber, David Miles. *Audio Production Techniques for Video.* White Plains, NY: Knowledge Industry Publishing, 1987.

Mathias, Harry, and Richard Patterson. *Electronic Cinematography: Achieving Photographic Control over the Video Image.* Belmont, CA: Wadsworth, 1985.

Millerson, Gerald. *Video Production Handbook*, 2nd ed. Boston: Focal Press, 1992.

Ratcliff, John. *Timecode, A User's Guide*, 3rd ed. Oxford: Focal Press, 1999.

Verna, Tony. *Global Television: How to Create Effective Television for the 1990s.* Boston: Focal Press, 1993.

Watkinson, John. *The Art of Digital Video*, 2nd ed. Boston: Focal Press, 1994.

Wiese, Michael. *Home Video: Producing for the Home Market.* Westport, CT: Michael Wiese Film/Video, 1986.

WRITING

Armer, Alan. *Writing the Screenplay for Film and Television.* Belmont, CA: Wadsworth, 1985.

Cowgill, Linda J. *Writing Short Films.* Los Angeles: Lone Eagle, 1997.

Eisenstein, S. M. *The Short Fiction Scenario.* Methuen: Calcutta, Seagull Books, 1988.

Field, Syd. *The Foundations of Screenwriting.* New York: Dell, 1982.

Goldman, William. *Adventures in the Screen Trade.* New York: Warner Books, 1984.

Howard, David, and Edward Mabley. *The Tools of Screenwriting.* New York: St. Martins Press, 1995.

McKee, Robert. *Story: Substance, Structure, Style and the Principals of Screenwriting.* New York: HarperCollins, 1997.

Phillips, William H. *Writing Short Scripts.* Syracuse: Syracuse University Press, 1991.

Seger, Linda. *Making a Good Script Great.* Hollywood: Samuel French, 1987.

PERIODICALS/NEWSLETTERS

American Cinematographer. ASC Holdings Corp., 1782 N. Orange Drive, Hollywood, CA 90028: (800) 448-0145 or (213) 969-4333.

Backstage. 1515 Broadway, 14th Floor, New York, NY 10036: (212) 764-7300; or 5055 Wilshire Boulevard, Los Angeles, CA 90036.

Cinéfantastique. 7240 W. Roosevelt Road, Forest Park, IL 60130: (708) 366-5566.

Film Comment. Film Society of Lincoln Center, 70 Lincoln Center Plaza, New York, NY 10023-6595: (800) 783-4903.

The Independent. Foundation for Independent Video and Film (FIVF), 625 Broadway, New York, NY 10012: (212) 473-3400.

Millimeter. Penton Publishing, Subscription Lock Box, P.O. Box 96732, Chicago, IL 60693: (312) 477-4700 or (312) 960-4050.

Premiere. P.O. Box 55387, Boulder, CO 80323-5387.

Variety (daily or weekly). 5700 Wilshire Boulevard, Suite 120, Los Angeles, CA 90036: (213) 857-6600; or 249 W. 17th Street, 4th Floor, New York, NY 10011: (212) 645-0067.

Videomaker. Subscription Information, P.O. Box 3780, Chico, CA 95927-9840: (800) 284-3226; www.video-maker.com.

Video Magazine. 460 W. 34th St. New York, 10001: (212) 947-6500.

SCREENWRITING SOFTWARE

Final Draft
(800) 231-4055
(818) 995-8995
Fax: (818) 995-4422
info@finaldraft.com

HollyWord®
SidebySide®
Simon Skill Systems
P.O. Box 2048
Rancho Santa Fe, CA 92067
hw@simon1.com

Movie Magic Screenwriter 2000
Screenplay Systems
(800) 84-story
www.screenplay.com

Scriptware
Cinovation, Inc.
1750 30th Street, Suite 360
Boulder, CO 80301-1005
(303) 786-7899
Fax: (303) 786-9292
Orders and info only: (800) 788-7090
http://scriptware.com

Script Wizard™
Stefani Warren & Associates
Voicemail: (818) 236-2092
Fax: (818) 500-7283
E-mail: sales@warrenassoc.com
www.warrenassoc.com

The Writers Store™
2040 Westwood Blvd.
Los Angeles, CA 90025
(800) 272-8927 (U.S. or Canada)
Fax: (800) 486-4006 (U.S. or Canada)
International callers: Please use our local numbers
(310) 441-5151
Fax: (310) 441-0944
E-mail: sales@writersstore.com

Companion Software

Dramatica Pro
Movie Magic Budgeting
Movie Magic Contracts
Movie Magic Labor Rates
Movie Magic Scheduler

INTERNET
Databases

African-American Video Media Resource Center:
www.lib.berkeley.edu/MRC/AfricanAmVid.html

Index

Also available from Focal Press

Directing
Film Techniques and Aesthetics

Michael Rabiger

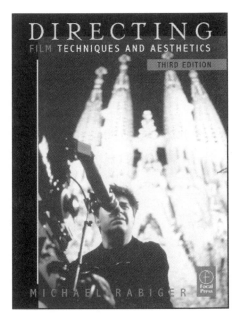

Comprehensive: Dissolves the barriers between the aesthetic, conceptual, and technical

Updated: Reflects the revolutionary shift to digital filmmaking

Practical: Exercises throughout help you to follow along

Also available from Focal Press

Film Directing Fundamentals
See Your Film Before Shooting

Nicholas Proferes

New edition includes:

- **Unique, focused approach to film directing that shows how to use the screenplay as a blueprint**

- **Clear-cut methodology for translating a script to the screen**

- **Case studies featuring famous films**

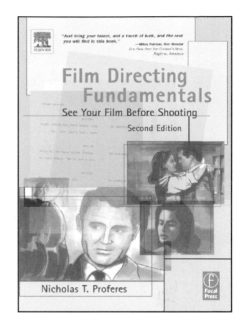

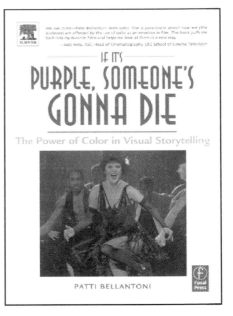